CIMA

STUDY TEXT

MANAGEMENT

PAPER E2

PROJECT AND RELATIONSHIP MANAGEMENT

Our text is designed to help you study **effectively** and **efficiently.**

In this edition we:

- **Highlight** the **most important elements** in the syllabus and the **key skills** you will need
- Use the same **case study** throughout to help **build understanding in a practical and engaging way**
- **Signpost** how each chapter links to the syllabus and the learning outcomes
- Use **overview and summary diagrams** to develop understanding of interrelations between topics
- **Provide** lots of **exam alerts** explaining how what you're learning may be tested
- **Include examples** and **questions** to help you apply what you've learnt
- **Emphasise key points** in **section summaries**
- **Test your knowledge** of what you've studied in **quick quizzes**
- **Examine your understanding** in our **practice question bank**

SUITABLE FOR EXAMS IN 2017

PUBLISHED NOVEMBER 2016

Third edition 2016

ISBN 9781509706815
e-ISBN 9781509707256

British Library Cataloguing-in-Publication Data
A catalogue record for this book
is available from the British Library

Published by

BPP Learning Media Ltd
BPP House, Aldine Place
London W12 8AA

www.bpp.com/learningmedia

Printed in the United Kingdom by

Wheatons Exeter Ltd
Hennock Road
Marsh Barton
Exeter
EX2 8RP

Your learning materials, published by BPP Learning Media Ltd, are printed on paper sourced from sustainable, managed forests.

We are grateful to the Chartered Institute of Management Accountants for permission to reproduce past examination questions. The suggested solutions in the exam answer bank have been prepared by BPP Learning Media Ltd.

Contents

Page

Introduction

How our Study Text can help you pass iv
Features in our Study Text v
Streamlined studying vi
Syllabus and learning outcomes vii
Studying E2 xii
Assessment xvi
Case Study xvii

Part A Introduction to strategic management and assessing the global environment

1A Introduction to strategy – Part A 3
1B Introduction to strategy – Part B 25
2 General environment 57
3 Competitive environment 97

Part B The human aspects of the organisation

4 Key concepts in management 155
5 Culture 213

Part C Managing relationships

6 Communication, negotiation and conflict 237
7 Control and the finance function 267

Part D Managing change through projects

8 Change management 317
9A Project management – Part A 341
9B Project management – Part B 369
10 The project team 409

Practice question bank 441

Practice answer bank 455

Index 483

Review form

How our Study Text can help you pass

Streamlined studying	• We show you the best ways to study efficiently • Our Text has been designed to ensure you can easily and quickly navigate through it • The different features in our Text emphasise important knowledge and techniques
Exam expertise	• **Studying E2** on page xii introduces the key themes of the syllabus and summarises how to pass • We highlight throughout our Text how topics may be tested and what you'll have to do in the exam • We help you see the complete picture of the syllabus, so that you can answer questions that range across the whole syllabus • Our Text covers the syllabus content – no more, no less
Regular review	• We frequently summarise the key knowledge you need • We test what you've learnt by providing questions and quizzes throughout our Text

Our other products

BPP Learning Media also offers these products for the Objective Test exams and the integrated case study (ICS) exams:

i-Pass	Providing computer-based testing in a variety of formats, ideal for self-assessment
Exam Practice Kit	Providing helpful guidance on how to pass the objective test and more question practice
Passcards	Summarising what you should know in visual, easy to remember, form
ICS Workbook	Providing help with exam skills and question practice for the integrated case study exam

You can purchase these products by visiting www.bpp.com/cimamaterials

Online Learning with BPP

BPP's online learning study modes provide flexibility and convenience, allowing you to study effectively, at a pace that suits you, where and when you choose.

Online Classroom Live	Through live interactive online sessions it provides you with the traditional structure and support of classroom learning, but with the convenience of attending classes wherever you are
Online Classroom	Through pre-recorded online lectures it provides you with the classroom experience via the web with the tutor guidance & support you'd expect from a face to face classroom

You can find out more by visiting www.bpp.com/cima

Features in our Study Text

Chapter Overview Diagrams illustrate the connections between the topic areas you are about to cover

Section Introductions explain how the section fits into the chapter

Key Terms are the core vocabulary you need to learn

Key Points are points that you have to know, ideas or calculations that will be the foundations of your answers

Exam Alerts show you how subjects are likely to be tested

Exam Skills are the key skills you will need to demonstrate in the exam, linked to question requirements

Formulae To Learn are formulae you must remember in the exam

Exam Formulae are formulae you will be given in the exam

Examples show how theory is put into practice

Questions give you the practice you need to test your understanding of what you've learnt

Case Studies link what you've learnt with the real-world business environment

Links show how the syllabus overlaps with other parts of the qualification, including Knowledge Brought Forward that you need to remember from previous exams

Website References link to material that will enhance your understanding of what you're studying

Further Reading will give you a wider perspective on the subjects you're covering

Section Summary Diagrams allow you to review each section

Streamlined studying

What you should do	In order to
Read the Chapter and Section Introductions and look at the Chapter Overview Diagram	See why topics need to be studied and map your way through the chapter
Go quickly through the explanations	Gain the depth of knowledge and understanding that you'll need
Highlight the Key Points and Key Terms to Learn	Make sure you know the basics that you can't do without in the exam
Focus on the Exam Skills and Exam Alerts	Know how you'll be tested and what you'll have to do
Work through the Examples and Case Studies	See how what you've learnt applies in practice
Prepare Answers to the Questions	See if you can apply what you've learnt in practice
Review the Chapter Summary Diagrams	Remind you of, and reinforce, what you've learnt
Answer the Quick Quiz	Find out if there are any gaps in your knowledge
Answer the Question(s) in the Practice Question Bank	Practice what you've learnt in depth

Should I take notes?

Brief notes may help you remember what you're learning. You should use the notes format that's most helpful to you (lists, diagrams, mind maps).

Further help

BPP Learning Media's *Learning to Learn Accountancy* provides lots more helpful guidance on studying. It is designed to be used both at the outset of your CIMA studies and throughout the process of learning accountancy. It can help you **focus your studies on the subject and exam**, enabling you to **acquire knowledge, practise and revise efficiently and effectively**.

Single Case Study Company

The single case study is a teaching tool used in the E2 BPP CIMA Study Text.

Using an example organisation throughout the text provides a logical structure which will help you to understand how the ideas and concepts you are learning will apply to a real company. This helps you both to grasp the concept initially, and remember and apply it.

Employability: In addition to passing the exams, this approach helps you to understand how the theory that you are learning in the classroom can be applied in the workplace, improving your employability.

Integration: Using this same case study throughout the Study Text will help you to understand how the different topic areas within the syllabus fit together in the real world. This will increase your awareness of how different teams and departments work, reducing the silo approach to studying as well as providing a stronger framework for understanding and retention of knowledge.

The background to the single case study company is on page xvii.

Syllabus and learning outcomes

Paper E2 Project and Relationship Management

The syllabus comprises:

Topic and Study Weighting

		%
A	Introduction to strategic management and assessing the global environment	30
B	The human aspects of the organisation	20
C	Managing relationships	20
D	Managing change through projects	30

Learning Outcomes		
Lead	**Component**	**Syllabus content**
A Introduction to strategic management and assessing the global environment		
1 Discuss developments in strategic management	(a) Discuss the concept of strategy and the rational/formal approach to strategy development	(i) Defining strategy and strategic management (ii) Core areas of strategic management (iii) Levels of strategy within organisations (iv) Stages in the rational approach to strategy developments
	(b) Compare and contrast alternative approaches to strategy development	(i) Intended, emergent, logical incrementalism, and political approaches. (ii) Resource-based view – resources and competencies, internal value and dynamic capabilities (iii) Strategy development in different contexts, eg SME's, public sector, not-for-profit (iv) Strategy and structure
	(c) Explain the approaches to achieving sustainable competitive advantage	(i) The concept of competitive advantage (ii) Generic competitive strategies (iii) Value, rarity, inimitability, non-sustainability as bases of competitive advantage (iv) Achieving sustainable competitive advantage

Learning Outcomes		
Lead	**Component**	**Syllabus content**
2 Analyse the relationship between different aspects of the global business environment	(a) Distinguish between different aspects of the global environment, including the competitive environment	(i) The macro and micro environments (ii) LoNGPEST analysis and its derivatives (iii) Globalisation (iv) Country and political risk factors (v) Emerging markets (vi) Porter's Diamond and its use for assessing the competitive advantage of nations (vii) Porter's Five Forces model and its use for analysing the external environment
	(b) Discuss the approaches to competitor analysis including the collection and interpretation of trend data	(i) Key concepts in competitor analysis (ii) The role of competitor analysis (iii) Approaches to collecting competitor information (iv) Sources, types and quality of competitor data (v) Analysing and interpreting competitor data (vi) The application of Big Data to competitor analysis
B The human aspects of the organisation		
1 Discuss the concepts associated with managing through people	(a) Discuss the concepts of leadership and management	(i) Fundamental and contemporary concepts in management (ii) The concepts of power, authority, delegation and empowerment (iii) Different approaches to leadership, including personality/traits, style, contingency/situation, transactional/transformational, distributive (iv) Leadership in different contexts
	(b) Discuss HRM approaches for managing and controlling individual's performance	(i) HR policies and procedures (ii) Different approaches to employee performance appraisals (iii) The contribution of coaching and mentoring in enhancing individual and organisational performance (iv) Equality and diversity practices (v) Disciplinary and grievance procedures in resolving poor performance (vi) Dismissal and redundancy (vii) Employer and employee responsibilities in managing the work environment (eg health and safety)

Learning Outcomes		
Lead	**Component**	**Syllabus content**
2 Discuss the hard and soft aspects of people and organisational performance	(a) Discuss behavioural aspects of management control	(i) Theories of behavioural aspects of control (ii) Performance management and measurement frameworks eg – Target setting – Management by objectives – The balanced scorecard (iii) Trust and control
	(b) Explain the importance of organisational culture	(i) Explaining the concept and importance of culture (ii) Levels of culture (iii) Influences on culture (iv) Analysing organisational culture – the cultural web framework (v) Models for categorising culture (vi) National cultures and managing in different cultures
C Managing relationships		
1 Discuss the effectiveness of organisational relationships	(a) Evaluate the issues associated with building, leading and managing effective teams	(i) Building effective and high-performing teams (ii) Leading and managing teams (iii) Factors associated with effective team work (iv) Motivating team members (v) Resolving problems and conflict in teams
	(b) Discuss the effectiveness of handling, relationships between the finance function and other parts of the organisation and the supply chain	(i) Management of relationships between the finance function and other parts of the organisation (internal) (ii) The concept of the Chartered Management Accountant as a business partner in creating value (iii) Transaction cost theory in the context of shared service centres and outsourcing, including contractual relationships, SLAs (service level agreements), bounded rationality and co-creation with customers
	(c) Discuss the effectiveness of handling relationships between the finance function and external experts and stakeholders	(i) Management of relationships with professional advisors (external) eg accounting, tax and legal auditors and financial stakeholders such as shareholders and other investors to meet organisational objectives and governance responsibilities

Learning Outcomes		
Lead	**Component**	**Syllabus content**
2 Discuss management tools and techniques in managing organisational relationships	(a) Discuss the roles of communication, negotiation, influence and persuasion in the management process	(i) The communication process, types of communication tools and their use, ways of managing communication problems (ii) The importance of effective communication skills for the Chartered Management Accountant (iii) The importance of non-verbal communication and feedback (iv) Developing effective strategies for influence/persuasion/negotiation (v) The process of negotiation (vi) Negotiation skills
	(b) Discuss approaches to managing conflict	(i) The sources and causes of conflict in organisations (ii) The different forms and types of conflict (iii) Strategies for managing conflict to ensure working relationships are productive and effective
D Managing change through projects		
1 Advise on important elements in the change process	(a) Discuss the concept of organisational change	(i) Types of change (ii) External and internal triggers for change (iii) Stage model of change management (iv) Principles of change management
	(b) Recommend techniques to manage resistance to change	(i) Problem identification as a precursor to change (ii) Reasons for resistance to change (iii) Approaches to managing resistance to change
2 Discuss the concepts involved in managing projects	(a) Discuss the characteristics of the different phases of a project	(i) Definition of project attributes (ii) Time, cost and quality project objectives (iii) The purpose and activities associated with the key stages in the project lifecycle (iv) Examples of the role of project management methodologies in project control (eg PRINCE2, PMI)

Learning Outcomes		
Lead	**Component**	**Syllabus content**
	(b) Apply tools and techniques for project managers	(i) Key tools for project management, including work breakdown schedule (WBS), Gantt Charts, and Network analysis (ii) Managing project risk (iii) PERT charts (iv) Scenario planning and buffering (v) The contribution of project management software
	(c) Discuss management and leadership issues associated with projects, including the roles of key players in projects	(i) Project structures, including matrix structure and their impact on project achievement (ii) The role and attributes of an effective project manager (iii) The role of the Chartered Management Accountant in projects (iv) The role of other key players in a projects (v) Managing key project stakeholders (vi) The lifecycle of project teams (vii) Leading and motivating project teams

Studying E2

1 What E2's about

1.1 Strategic management

Strategic management is a particularly important syllabus area that you need to be comfortable with as a number of the topics covered at E2 are assumed knowledge at the Strategic level of your CIMA studies.

In this Text we introduce the main issues which drive and shape the strategy an organisation may pursue. We place a strong emphasis on the important role that the rational model plays in helping senior management to understand the internal and external challenges facing the organisation. At this stage consideration is also given to the need for management to conduct regular competitor analysis.

A significant number of theoretical models and frameworks are covered in the opening chapters of the Text. You need to ensure that you spend sufficient time committing these to memory as there is a high likelihood that questions in your E2 exam will require you to draw on this knowledge.

1.2 Human aspects

The key concepts of management and organisational culture are bound up together. In this section of the Text we examine a number of different approaches to managing people in the workplace. Although, some of the concepts explored may today appear a little out of touch with modern management thinking it is important that you appreciate how such thinking may be employed. We also explore the key differences between the role of the leader and manager. We also consider the important role that culture plays in all organisations.

1.3 Managing relationships

We then move on to consider the need for effective management of organisational relationships. Particular attention is devoted to the need for effective communication and negotiation skills. Both of these skills will be crucial for modern managers in managing organisational conflict. We also explore the increasing role that the finance function is now being expected to play. It is important to note that there has been a shift in the way the finance function is viewed, with many organisations now choosing to treat finance as a business partner, which operates not only to produce financial statements but to provide timely business advice to other departments.

1.4 Managing change through projects

In the final section of the Text we consider an important part of the E2 syllabus, the role of project management in modern business. We explore the key differences between 'business as usual work' and the distinct characteristics associated with project work. Consideration is given to the role of key project stakeholders, most notably that of the project manager and project team.

2 What's required

2.1 Strategy, management and projects

Applying your strategy, management and project knowledge may require you to:

(a) Identify/analyse key issues featured in question scenarios

(b) Explain different approaches that management can employ to help the entity deliver its strategy or project successfully

You should read the question requirements carefully as these will drive how you are expected to respond.

In the integrated case study you may be required to make recommendations based on the findings of your work. It is important any recommendations or advice that you give is **specific and realistic**. It will not be enough just to say for example, that management should adopt a new strategy. Instead you should specify what strategic **options are available to the organisation featured, what are the merits of pursuing one strategy over another,** equally consideration should be given to how the organisation's existing strategy could be **enhanced. This skill is likely to be critical when attempting the integrated case study, as it is your opportunity to show the marker that you can** apply your knowledge to a scenario and that you have the ability to draw realistic conclusions.

3 How to pass

3.1 Study the whole syllabus

You need to be comfortable with **all areas of the syllabus**, as questions in the objective test exam will cover all syllabus areas. **Wider reading** will help you understand general business issues, which will be particularly useful in the integrated case study exam.

3.2 Lots of question practice

You can **develop application skills** by attempting questions in the Practice Question Bank. While these might not be in the format that you will experience in your exam, doing the full question will enable you to answer the exam questions. Similarly, in the integrated case study exam you will have to answer questions that combine the E2 syllabus areas with P2 and F2. By answering questions on E2 you will develop the technical knowledge and skills in order to answer those questions.

However, you should practise OT exam standard questions, which you will find in the BPP Exam Practice Kit.

4 Brought forward knowledge

The examiner may test knowledge or techniques you've learnt at lower levels. As E2 is part of the Enterprise pillar, the content of E1 'Organisational Management' will be significant.

However material from other papers is relevant as well, including:

- Risks and risk management
- Management accounting techniques, for example the balanced scorecard
- Information systems
- Human resources
- Organisational structure
- Corporate governance
- Ethics

5 The Integrated Case Study and links with F2 and P2

The integrated case study exam is based on the expectation that students are developing a pool of knowledge. When faced with a problem students can appropriately apply their knowledge from any area of the syllabus. Students will avoid a historical problem of partitioning their knowledge and accessing, for example, their knowledge of IFRS only when faced with a set of financial statements.

The integrated case study may require you to draw on knowledge from all the pillars. It is quite possible that a question may require you to analyse the financial performance of a competing entity. Such a question may require you to calculate key ratios or identify movements in key performance indicators and compare these against the main organisation featured in the pre-seen information. This analysis is likely to be needed when forming a recommendation on the chosen strategy of the entity featured. It is critical that you are able to draw an insight from such data, this is a key skill. Being confident in interpreting and drawing conclusions on the numbers you calculate is particularly important.

6 What the examiner means

The table below has been prepared by CIMA to help you interpret the syllabus and learning outcomes and the meaning of questions.

You will see that there are 5 levels of Learning objective, ranging from Knowledge to Evaluation, reflecting the level of skill you will be expected to demonstrate. CIMA Certificate subjects only use levels 1 to 3, but in CIMA's Professional qualification the entire hierarchy will be used.

At the start of each chapter in your Study Text is a topic list relating the coverage in the chapter to the level of skill you may be called on to demonstrate in the exam.

Learning objectives	Verbs used	Definition
1 Knowledge What are you expected to know	• List • State • Define	• Make a list of • Express, fully or clearly, the details of/facts of • Give the exact meaning of
2 Comprehension What you are expected to understand	• Describe • Distinguish • Explain • Identify • Illustrate	• Communicate the key features of • Highlight the differences between • Make clear or intelligible/state the meaning or purpose of • Recognise, establish or select after consideration • Use an example to describe or explain something
3 Application How you are expected to apply your knowledge	• Apply • Calculate/compute • Demonstrate • Prepare • Reconcile • Solve • Tabulate	• Put to practical use • Ascertain or reckon mathematically • Prove with certainty or to exhibit by practical means • Make or get ready for use • Make or prove consistent/compatible • Find an answer to • Arrange in a table
4 Analysis How you are expected to analyse the detail of what you have learned	• Analyse • Categorise • Compare and contrast • Construct • Discuss • Interpret • Prioritise • Produce	• Examine in detail the structure of • Place into a defined class or division • Show the similarities and/or differences between • Build up or compile • Examine in detail by argument • Translate into intelligible or familiar terms • Place in order of priority or sequence for action • Create or bring into existence

Learning objectives	Verbs used	Definition
5 Evaluation		
How you are expected to use your learning to evaluate, make decisions or recommendations	• Advise • Evaluate • Recommend	• Counsel, inform or notify • Appraise or assess the value of • Propose a course of action

Competency Framework

CIMA has developed a competency framework detailing the skills, abilities and competencies that finance professionals need. The CIMA syllabus has been developed to match the competency mix as it develops over the three levels of the professional qualification. The importance of the various competencies at the management level is shown below.

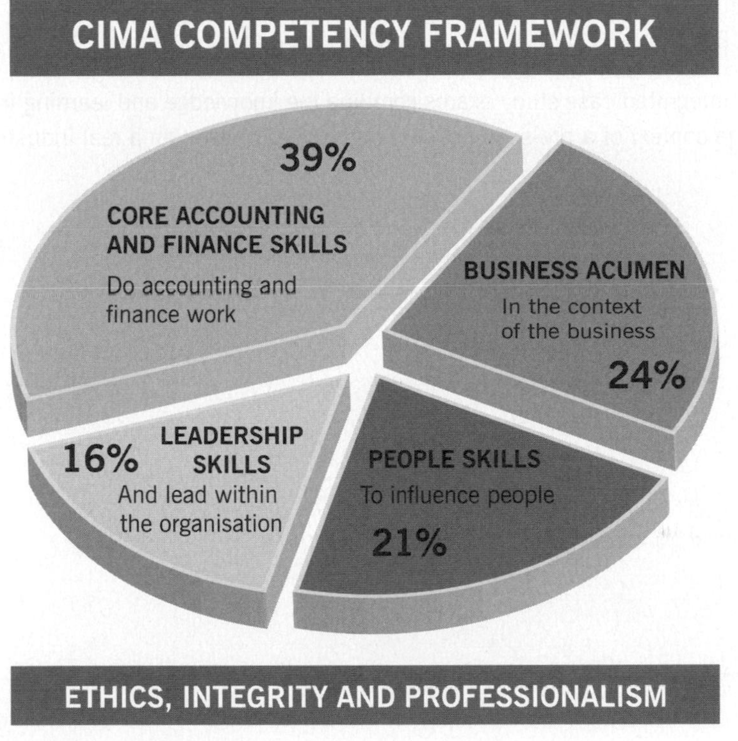

Assessment

The CIMA assessment is a two-tier structure with objective tests for each subject and an integrated case study at each level.

Objective test

The objective tests are computer based and can be taken on demand. The student exam preparation on the CIMA website (www.cimaglobal.com) has additional information and tools to help you become familiar with the test style. Make sure you check back regularly as more information may be added.

Integrated case study

Candidates must pass or receive exemptions from the three objective tests at each level, before attempting the integrated case study exam for that level.

The integrated case studies are available four times a year.

The integrated case study exams combine the knowledge and learning from all the pillars. They will be set in the context of a pre-seen fictional organisation based on a real industry.

Single Case Study – Farmers

Farmers Supermarkets

Market overview

Industry sales for supermarkets tend to be non-cyclical. Competition for customers can be intense, which helps to explain the unimpressive profit margins. Consumers typically have a variety of options to choose from when deciding where to purchase items. Not only do they often have a choice between competing neighbourhood supermarkets, but they can also shop at alternative retailers, such as large national discount chains and warehouse stores.

The range of products offered has also changed over the last few years and shops are now meeting customer demand for a larger range of international foods and ready meals using better quality products by using premium ingredients. While shops are able to command a higher average price for their products by using quality and place (particularly location and opening times) as differentiators, price is a sensitive factor when comparing like with like on generic products.

In addition to the supplier branded products, there are a large number of own brand products in the most lucrative product areas.

Supermarkets have expanded the range of products that they offer to include household goods, clothes, books, toys and even financial services such as insurance, credit cards and loans.

From an operating perspective, supermarkets are a homogenous group. Factors that may cause results to vary, aside from a company's ability to execute its business plan, include geography and store formats. Generally, though, investors can use common analytical benchmarks to evaluate the performance of these retailers.

Farmers' personnel

The career histories of Farmers' Directors and key employees are shown in **Appendix 1**.

The first Farmers shop

Nick Farmer, the founder of Farmers, founded the first shop when he realised that the produce from his parents farm was being retailed at many times the price paid to his parents. He decided that if he could retail direct to the consumers he could increase the profits from the farm. His original plan was to have over five shops opened within five years and he wanted the cash generated from each shop to finance the opening costs for the next shop. He had put together a business plan to get a personal loan, which was secured on both his own property and his parents' farm. This loan, together with his savings, was used to acquire £300,000 of equity in Farmers.

Farmers was formed over one hundred years ago with 2 million authorised shares of £1 each, of which 300,000 shares were allocated to Nick Farmer and these shares were fully paid up at par value. At the time these shares were issued, £1 per share at par value was considered a fair value.

Nick Farmer opened the first Farmers shop over one hundred years ago in London, in rented premises.

The growth of Farmers

Twenty years after first opening, Farmers had opened a further five shops in London, in rented premises to reduce the initial set-up costs

After the success of the London sites Farmers decided to expand into other towns and cities and now has shops in every town and city in the UK, and is one of the main brands in the supermarket sector in the UK.

The Farmers business has a high turnover. However, profitability was still lower than some of its competitors, for several reasons as follows:

- High rental costs;
- High staff costs, as good customer service remains a high priority for Farmers;
- Lower than average gross margins on some products due to the higher than average procurement cost of the quality ingredients that Farmers has selected;
- Lower margins on some products as Farmers has a policy of buying locally where it can, with local managers being responsible for sourcing milk, meat and seasonal, UK produce.

Staffing issues and performance related bonuses

Most management responsibilities were devolved to the shop managers, who are responsible for local procurement of food supplies, staff recruitment and day-to-day staff management.

The descendants of Nick Farmer are still very involved in the business. Heather Farmer is the Procurement Director, Helena Farmer is the Finance Director and Steve Farmer is the HR Director.

Quarterly performance related bonuses for all employees are based on the sales revenue and the net margin for each shop. The bonus is paid quarterly to recognise the previous quarter's results and to motivate staff to stay with Farmers.

Fair Trade produce

Nick Farmer, coming from a farming family, felt that farms were being treated badly by existing retailers and set a policy that Farmers should pay fair prices to the farms that it buys from. The relationships with farms set up many decades ago are still in existence, and Farmers sources much more of its produce from the UK than other supermarkets.

More recently, Farmers has become involved in the Fair Trade movement. Fair Trade benefits hundreds of thousands of farms worldwide selling a wide variety of products. Farms are organised into small co-operatives, whereby products are procured at an agreed minimum price, which is above the price that some small independent farmers would be able to achieve for their crops on the open market. Fair Trade produce is successfully breaking the cycle of poverty for farmers in many countries and the coffee industry is one where Fair Trade has been very successful. Heather Farmer feels strongly that in today's world where consumers are demanding more humane and more environmentally sensitive products, the use of Fair Trade coffee in Farmers shops is a responsible and sensible choice of supply.

Farmers was bought by a conglomerate recently. At the moment the conglomerate, Cherry Picker Holdings (CPH), has been content to let Farmers carry on the business without any interference.

The statement of financial position, statement of profit or loss and statement of changes in equity for Farmers for the last two financial years are shown in **Appendix 2**.

Shareholdings at December 20X4

CPH owns 100% of the shares of Farmers. CPH is a public listed company.

The Farmers Board comprises the Directors of the company, plus a director nominated by CPH.

Farmers' expansion plans

The current five-year plan was approved by CPH, and subsequently the Farmers Board, in December 20X4. This plan includes the expansion of Farmers by 70 shops by the end of 20X9. An extract from this current five-year plan is shown in **Appendix 3**.

Much of the expansion planned is due to be financed by cash generated by operations, as well as additional loan finance from CPH. The amount of loan finance will be determined by whether the new openings will be in rented premises or whether the company will be required to purchase the site. Much will depend on the location selected and the alternatives available in each town or city targeted for expansion.

The criteria for the selection of new sites for future Farmers shops include:

(1) **Competition** – the strength of the competition in the proposed market place and whether the competition will stimulate growth, but not be too strong so as to restrict profits.

(2) **Resources.** Whether there are adequate resources, staff and supply links to set up a new shop.

(3) **Consumer demand.** Is there sufficient demand for a Farmers shop and what is the current level of demand and how is it being met? A further issue is whether the area has the income to create profitable demand for Farmers.

Some relevant factors in the Farmers expansion plan are the population size and the population density. When population becomes concentrated it often tends to take on a different character. Urbanisation produces the need for a higher level of products and services. Farmers uses a number of easy measures such as the presence, or absence, of well-known chains of clothes retailers, to determine the potential for a new shop location.

Other recent developments in the Farmers business

In April 20X3, Farmers introduced its first delivery service from three of its central London shops. This delivery service to local customers works by customers placing orders on-line to their local Farmers shop. Despite a few initial problems, the delivery service is working well, although sales are still very low.

Farmers wants to continue to be innovative and to be ahead of its competitors in terms of the types of foods offered. Farmers are in contact with a number of food manufacturers to explore offering a wider range of foods. They need to ensure that any new food ranges fit in with Farmers' current pricing and food quality levels.

Proposed expansion of Farmers overseas

The current five-year plan, is based on operating an additional 45 shops in the UK by 20X9 and 25 shops in major cities in Europe.

There are a number of reasons why Farmers are considering expanding abroad and these include:

- Saturated home market where competition is so intense that it can no longer gain any significant market share improvement.
- Competition may be less intense in a different market.
- Comparative advantage in product against local competition, particularly in areas dominated by British people living and holidaying abroad, which is becoming increasingly popular in some areas of Europe, especially Spain.

Appendix 1

Farmers' personnel

Adrian Williams: Chairman and Managing Director – Adrian Williams has worked in Farmers since leaving school.

Jane Li: Marketing Director – Jane Li had previously worked in marketing for a mobile phone company and more recently for a leading high street fast food chain.

Heather Farmer: Procurement Director – Heather Farmer has worked for Farmers since leaving university. A direct descendent of Nick Farmer, she is passionate about the values of the company. She has worked in the procurement division for many years, and has many contacts in the farming sector in the UK.

Steve Farmer : Human Resources Director – Steve Farmer has a degree in Human Resource management and has worked in human resources (HR) for a chain of department stores before joining Farmers.

Helena Farmer: Finance Director – Helena worked for a leading audit group for over ten years before she moved into management consultancy. Since joining Farmers, Helena's team handles all accounting and finance matters in-house.

Ross Halep: Investment Director, Cherry Picker Holdings (CPH) – Ross Halep is the liaison manager at CPH who is responsible for Farmers. The companies that CPH has acquired vary greatly and are operating in a wide range of industries.

Appendix 2

Farmers' statement of financial position, statement of profit or loss and statement of changes in equity

Note. All data in this appendix is presented in international financial reporting format.

Statement of financial position

	As at 31 December 20X4		As at 31 December 20X3	
	£'m	£'m	£'m	£'m
Non-current assets (net)		7,025		2,958
Current assets				
Inventory	420		395	
Trade receivables and rent prepayments	209		124	
Cash and short term investments	391		85	
		1,020		604
Total assets		8,045		3,562
Equity and liabilities				
Equity				
Paid in share capital	1,000		600	
Share premium reserve	2,630		630	
Retained profits	1,751		854	
		5,381		2,084
Non-current liabilities				
Loans				
Bank loan at 12% (repayable in 20X5)	300		300	
Bank loan at 12% (repayable in 20X6)	200		200	
Bank loan at 12% (repayable in 20X7)	100		100	
KPE loan at 10% (repayable in 20X8)	300		–	
		900		600
Current liabilities				
Trade payables	1,367		689	
Tax	283		160	
Accruals	114		29	
		1,764		878
Total equity and liabilities		8,045		3,562

Note. Paid in share capital represents shares of £1.00 each at 31 December 20X4.

Statement of profit or loss

Year ended 31 December

	20X4	*20X3*
	£'m	£'m
Revenue	13,918	7,962
Total operating costs	12,651	7,225
Operating profit	1,267	737
Finance costs	(87)	(69)
Tax expense (effective tax rate is 24%)	(283)	(160)
Profit for the period	897	508

Statement of changes in equity

	Share capital	*Share premium*	*Retained earnings*	*Total*
	£'m	£'m	£'m	£'m
Balance at 31 December 20X3	600	630	854	2,084
New shares issued during 20X4	400	2,000	–	2,400
Profit for the period	–	–	897	897
Dividends paid	–	–	–	–
Balance at 31 December 20X4	1,000	2,630	1,751	5,381

Note. For the purpose of the case, it should be assumed that the accounts for the year ended 31 December 20X4 are final and have been audited.

Appendix 3

Extracts from Farmers 5-year plan

	Actual			*Plan*		
	20X4	*20X5*	*20X6*	*20X7*	*20X8*	*20X9*
Number of shops:						
Start of the year	410	418	426	436	448	460
New openings	8	8	10	12	12	20
End of the year	**418**	**426**	**436**	**448**	**460**	**480**
Analysis of new shop openings:						
UK	8	8	9	5	5	10
Overseas	–	–	1	7	7	10
	£'m	£'m	£'m	£'m	£'m	£'m
Shops revenue	13,498	22,176	37,072	57,378	82,553	110,751
Revenue from new product launches in each year	420	1,560	2,200	2,900	3,800	4,800
Total revenue	**13,918**	**23,736**	**39,272**	**60,278**	**86,353**	**115,551**
Pre-tax operating profit	**1,267**	**2,160**	**3,613**	**5,606**	**8,203**	**10,977**
Capital expenditure	**4,800**	**2,700**	**3,400**	**3,800**	**4,100**	**5,000**

Note. The extracts from the 5-year plan shown above were approved by CPH and the Farmers Board in December 20X4.

INTRODUCTION TO STRATEGIC MANAGEMENT AND ASSESSING THE GLOBAL ENVIRONMENT

Part A

INTRODUCTION TO STRATEGY – PART A

'Introduction to strategic management and assessing the global environment' is Part A of your syllabus. Chapters 1A to 3 are very important, as 30% of the E2 syllabus is focused on the role of strategy in modern organisations.

Chapter 1A sets the scene for strategic management by exploring a range of key concepts and theories that you will need to learn before attempting your E2 examination. Reading through these early chapters should help to put into context how the topics covered later in the Study Text (which focus on the role of manager, relationships and project management) are ultimately driven by those decisions made at the very top of an organisation.

Strategy deals with **how an organisation achieves its objectives**. We look at contrasting ways in which different researchers consider that strategy **should be** made and how strategy **is** made.

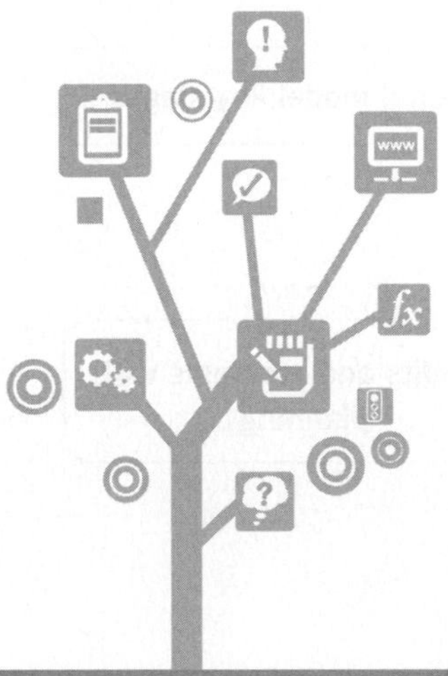

- In the **rational model** (Section 2), decisions are made by logical analysis of the environment and the organisation. This is followed by the generation of alternative strategies, which are then evaluated objectively on their merits. The aim might be to secure a 'fit' with the environment, or a **positioning** approach.
- The emergent **strategies** model (Section 3) argues that strategy can be generated from the 'bottom up' as well as from the 'top down'. Strategic management can mean 'crafting strategies as they emerge'.
- The **muddling through or adaptive approach** (Section 4) suggests that strategies in many organisations are small-scale adjustments, which react to events.
- The **bounded rationality** and **logical incrementalist** (Section 4) models seek a middle ground between these two extremes.
- **Chandler** identified the evolution of structure as organisations mature and their strategies change. This is covered in Section 5.

Topic list	Learning outcomes	Syllabus references	Ability required
1 What is strategy? Background	A1a	A1(i), (ii)	Analysis
2 Planned strategies – the rational model	A1a	A1(iv)	Analysis
3 Crafting emergent strategies	A1b	A1(i)	Analysis
4 Other approaches to strategy	A1b	A1(i), (iii)	Analysis
5 Strategy and structure	A1b	A1(iv)	Analysis

Chapter Overview

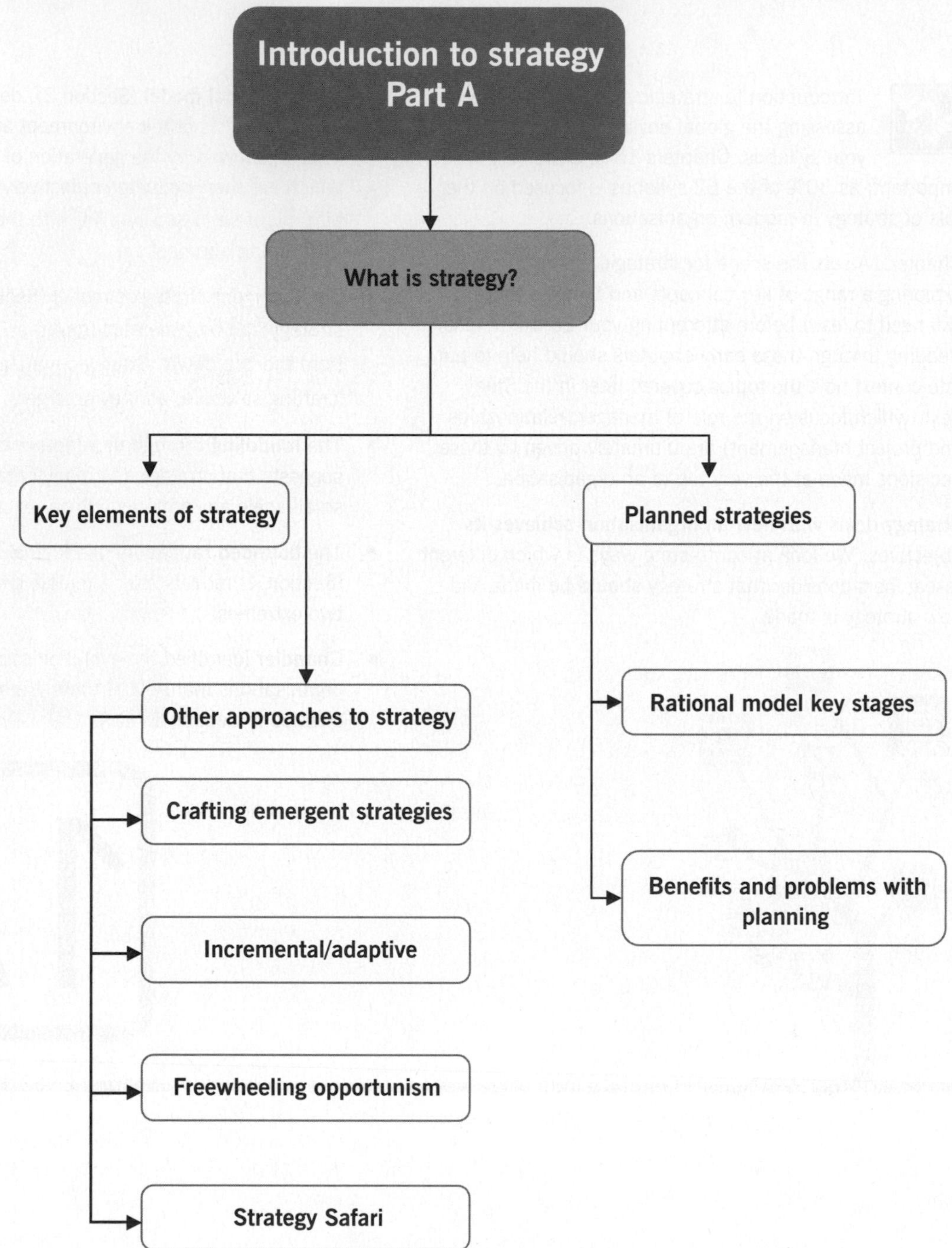
Introduction to strategy Part A
What is strategy?
Key elements of strategy
Planned strategies
Rational model key stages
Benefits and problems with planning
Other approaches to strategy
Crafting emergent strategies
Incremental/adaptive
Freewheeling opportunism
Strategy Safari

1 What is strategy? Background

KEY TERMS

STRATEGY. A course of action, including the specification of resources required, to achieve a specific objective.

STRATEGIC PLAN. Statement of long-term goals along with a definition of the strategies and policies that will ensure achievement of these goals.

POLICY. Undated, long-lasting and often unquantified statement of guidance regarding the way in which an organisation will seek to behave in relation to its stakeholders.

(CIMA Official Terminology)

Introduction

Strategy can be quite a difficult idea to grasp. Make sure you understand the definitions here, and how strategic decisions differ from others.

Strategy is about the higher direction of an enterprise. In organisations it is the concern of top management. In less exalted contexts it might be a simple technique.

An organisation's objective is the desired outcome of the organisation's activities. The strategy specifies in broad terms how this should be achieved. (**Tactics** are the 'most efficient deployment of resources in an agreed strategy'.) This can be summarised in a diagram.

Current state ⟶ [Strategy tells you how] ⟶ Desired objective

An overall **objective** of a government's road safety policy might be to reduce deaths and injuries. There might be several **strategies** to achieve this objective: more stringent law enforcement, advertising, speed limits and so on.

CIMA's *Official Terminology* suggests the following example for a company. If the primary objective is 25% return on capital, and the secondary objective is to increase market share, a **strategy** would be to 'sell on the basis that a 20% increase in sales and production capacity will reduce unit costs by 25%. Use £10m capital'.

1.1 Strategic decisions

What distinguishes strategy from other types of organisation decision? Johnson and Scholes have summarised the characteristics of **strategic decisions** for an organisation.

(a) **Scope**. Strategic decisions will be concerned with the **overall, long-term direction** of activities.

(b) **Environment**. Strategy involves the matching of an organisation's **activities** to the **environment** in which it operates.

(c) Strategy also involves the matching of an organisation's activities to its **resource capability**. Strategic decisions include the allocation or reallocation of resources.

(d) Strategic decisions will **affect operational decisions**, because they will set off a chain of lesser decisions and operational activities, involving the use of resources.

(e) Strategic decisions will be affected by the **values and expectations of the people in power** within an organisation.

(f) Strategic decisions have implications for **change** throughout an organisation, and so are likely to be **complex** in nature.

It is possible to think of strategy under three headings.

(a) **Financial strategy** is about raising capital and satisfying the requirements of providers of capital for income and capital appreciation. It encompasses capital structure, dividend policy, investor relations, risk management and hedging.

(b) **Investment and resource strategy** uses capital to provide resources of strategic value, such as premises, and new products and brands, and to finance growth by acquisition.

(c) **Competitive strategy** is about how the business makes its market offering and seeks to outperform its commercial rivals. Competitive strategy generates the earnings needed by financial strategy. There is thus a flow of value linking the three elements together.

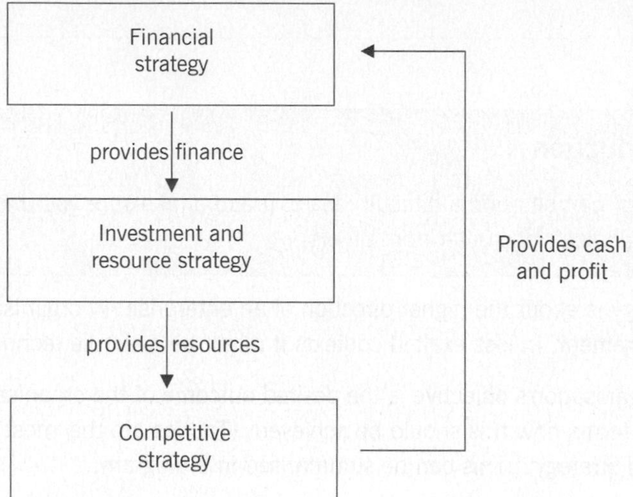

1.1.1 Mintzberg's 5 Ps

Strategy can play a number of roles within an organisation. Henry Mintzberg suggested five such roles, known as the 5 Ps of strategy.

(a) **Plan**. Strategy can provide a course of direction for an organisation.

(b) **Pattern**. Strategy, whether intended or not, will be evident as a consistent pattern of behaviour over the long term.

(c) **Ploy**. Strategy can be used as a tactic to deter or confuse competition.

(d) **Position**. An organisation's strategy can provide an indication as to where that organisation places itself within a particular market or environment.

(e) **Perspective**. Strategy indicates more than just a chosen position; it represents the unique way in which an organisation perceives the environment in which it operates and how it interprets the information from it. Two organisations with an identical strategic perspective may still respond to the same environmental stimulus in completely different ways, perhaps due to different organisation cultures. Mintzberg uses this to suggest similarities between the strategy of an organisation and the personality of an individual.

1.2 Competitive advantage

So far, we have discussed organisations in general terms. Business organisations differ from other types of organisation in that their fundamental objective is **financial**. Smaller, owner-managed businesses may be content to proceed without making too much effort or achieving significant success but, for most businesses, the aim of strategy will be to achieve a **competitive advantage** that leads to **superior profitability and return on investment**. In economic terms, they are seeking **supernormal profit**, a phrase you may recall if you have studied economics previously.

This is only possible where conditions of **perfect competition** do not apply: that is to say, supernormal profit would normally be associated with firms operating under monopoly, oligopoly or monopolistic competition, any of which should give them some degree of **market power**. All these market forms are based on the idea of making it difficult for potential competitors to erode that market power through effective competition. You should keep this idea in mind when we come to discuss the means by which firms typically seek to achieve competitive advantage.

Section summary

Strategic decisions affect the scope of an organisation's activities, the environment, resource capability and allocation, and the organisation's long-term direction.

2 Planned strategies – the rational model

KEY TERM

RATIONAL MODEL. Rational models can be set up to solve most problems. In the context of management, 'rational model' usually means a comprehensive and systematic system of strategic planning. The rational approach is also often termed the **formal** approach.

Introduction

The rational model is likely to be the model that comes to mind when you think about strategy. It is a planned and methodical way of looking at strategy in the organisation. It has three main steps: **analysis, choice and implementation**. According to the model, strategies are made at the top of the organisation and flow down to the operational level. At each level, supporting strategies are devised that cover activities at those levels. So for instance, the Marketing Director would have a strategy for each market and there would be operational strategies for issues such as pricing and personnel.

Exam alert

You will need to watch out for the use of the term 'formal' in addition to (or instead of) 'rational' in exam questions.

2.1 Plans

A plan is a consciously intended course of action. Many early books on business strategy supposed that strategy making was necessarily a planning process. Often, this involved delegating the task of strategic planning to a separate department.

Drucker defines strategic planning as having three aspects.

(a) 'The continuous process of **making present risk-taking decisions** systematically and with greatest knowledge of their futurity' (ie their future effect)

(b) '**Organising systematically** the efforts needed to carry out these decisions'

(c) '**Measuring the results** of these decisions ... through organised, systematic feedback'

2.2 The need for planning

KEY POINT

Characteristics of strategic plans:

(a) They are written down.
(b) They are circulated to interested parties in the organisation.
(c) They specify the outcomes (eg where the business wishes to be in five years' time).
(d) They specify how these are going to be achieved.
(e) They trigger the production of operational plans lower down the hierarchy.

Advantages of having a plan

(a) It helps the organisation to take a long view and avoid short-termism, while at the same time providing a sensible approach to the uncertainty of the future.

(b) It guides the allocation of resources.

(c) It co-ordinates the activities of the various parts of the organisation, ensuring the integration of operational management decisions into the higher strategy, the wider organisational context and longer-term goals.

(d) It sets a standard by which the actual performance of the organisation is measured and controlled.

(e) It comforts providers of finance in particular, and encourages suppliers and employees to think in terms of a long-term relationship.

(f) The process of forming strategy requires wide and complex input, so it can have a beneficial effect on managers' personal development and awareness, and can assist with management succession planning.

2.3 The rational model

The rational model represents the **planned approach** to strategy development. Through a sequence of logical steps it will allow the development, appraisal, choice, implementation and control of strategies that allow for both **internal** and **external factors**.

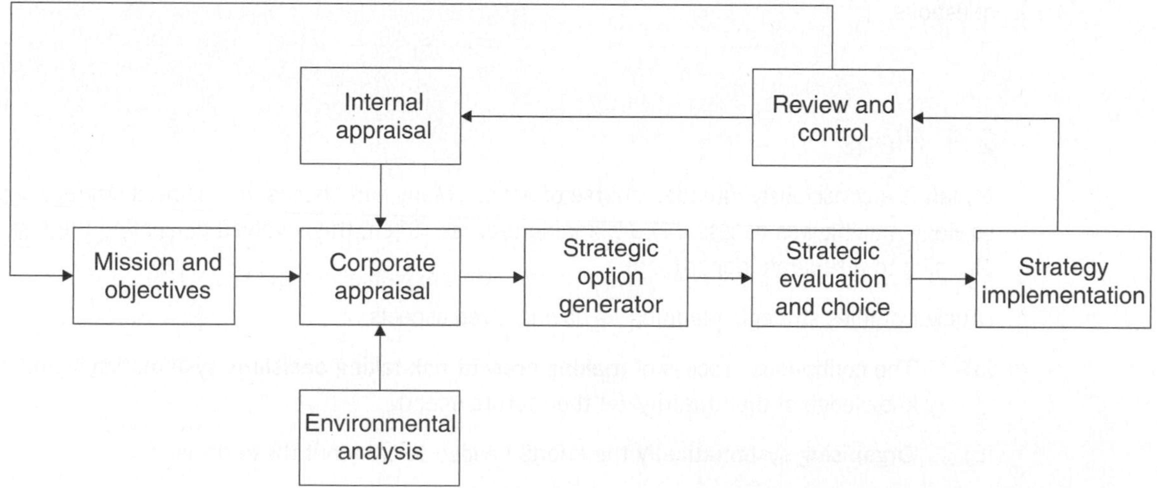

2.3.1 Strategic analysis

Strategic analysis is concerned with understanding the strategic position of the organisation in the widest terms.

(a) The organisation operates within its **environment**. This has political/legal, economic, social and technological aspects. The environment contains both **threats** and **opportunities**.

(b) The **resources** of the organisation (its **strengths** and **weaknesses**), how it adds value and its **distinctive competences** (what it does best or uniquely) must be matched to opportunities.

(c) **Mission and objectives**. The firm sets goals. The expectations of **stakeholder groups** must be considered. For example, if the organisation is financed by venture capitalists, a strategy might require sufficient growth generation to allow them to recover their investment.

(d) **Corporate appraisal** assesses the overall importance of strengths, weaknesses, opportunities and threats in the light of the organisation's mission and objectives. We revisit corporate appraisal in Chapter 3, when we consider how the organisation appraises its internal strengths and weaknesses, and external environment.

2.3.2 Strategic choice

Strategy development has three phases.

(a) **Strategic options generation**. A variety of options can be set up for consideration. The aim is to build on the firm's capabilities to exploit market opportunities.

(b) **Strategic options evaluation**. Each option is then examined on its merits.

(i) Is it **feasible**?
(ii) Is it **suitable**, considering the firm's existing position?
(iii) Is it **acceptable** to stakeholders?

A variety of techniques is used to assess and value strategies. Some will be assessed on financial criteria such as net present value. Where this is not possible, or where the uncertainty in the environment is great, other models are used. For instance, **scenario building** postulates a number of possible futures based on different assumptions about such things as worldwide economic growth, interest rates and competitors.

(c) **Strategy selection**. A strategy is chosen, according to the evaluation above. This process is strongly influenced by the **values** of the managers concerned.

2.3.3 Implementation of strategy

The chosen strategy is embodied in a corporate plan. From this, plans for operations are developed. The diagram below relates the corporate strategy to the activities of the sales force.

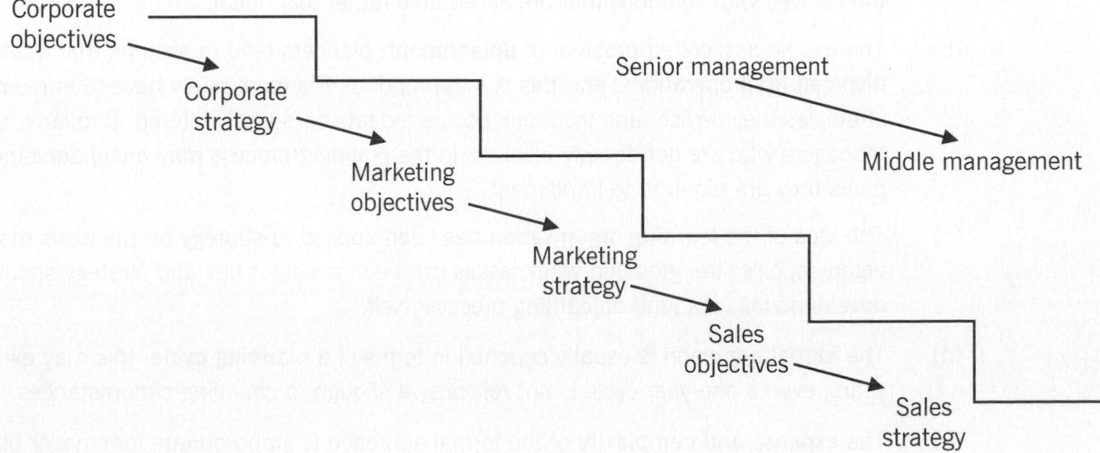

KEY POINT

In this case, what is defined as 'strategic' is in part determined by where you are, and your own relation to the plan. Similar cascades will relate corporate strategy to the plans of other departments, such as production and human resources management.

2.3.4 Benefits of formal planning

The advantages of a formal system of strategic planning are explained in the table below.

Advantages	Comments
Identifies risks	Strategic planning helps identify and manage risks.
Forces managers to think	Strategic planning can encourage creativity and initiative by tapping the ideas of the management team.
Forces decision making	Companies cannot remain static – they have to cope with changes in the environment. A strategic plan draws attention to the need to change and adapt, not to just 'stand still' and survive.
Better control	Management control can be better exercised if targets are explicit.
Enforces consistency at all levels	Long-term, medium-term and short-term objectives, plans and controls can be made consistent with one another. Otherwise, strategies can be rendered ineffective by budgeting systems and performance measures that have no strategic content.
Theory of the business	The management writer, Peter Drucker, has argued that an entrepreneur who builds a long-lasting business has 'a theory of the business' that informs their business decisions. In large organisations, that theory of the business has to become public knowledge, as decisions cannot be taken only by one person.

2.4 Problems with planning

The concept of formal processes for strategy generation and their limited success in practice has led to criticisms of both the rational model and the very idea of strategic planning as a separate business activity.

(a) The formal approach encourages a sense of **omniscience and control** among planners: this is dangerous because of the **inherent unpredictability of the business environment**. In practice, strategic thinking tends to be iterative and even muddled, with the various processes and stages being undertaken on an *ad hoc* basis. Moreover, as we shall see later, many developments of strategic significance, or information about them, occur at **operational** level. Environmental uncertainty also tends to lead managers to adopt an approach of **bounded rationality**, satisfying themselves with solutions that are acceptable rather than ideal.

(b) There is an associated problem of **detachment**: planners tend to assume that strategy can be divorced from operations, and this is inappropriate. Planners rarely have to implement the strategies they devise, and feedback occurs too late or is badly filtered. Similarly, more junior managers who are not directly involved in the planning process may misunderstand or resist the plans they are required to implement.

(c) The idea of the **learning organisation** has been applied to strategy on the basis that an organisation's strengths and weaknesses can be in constant flux and strategy should reflect current developments as a kind of learning process itself.

(d) The formal approach is usually couched in terms of a **planning cycle**: this may extend for up to five years; even a one-year cycle is not responsive enough to changing circumstances.

(e) The **expense and complexity** of the formal approach is inappropriate for smaller businesses.

(f) There has been much comment on the place of **strategic objectives**. A sociological perspective, such as that of Cyert and March, views the emergence of strategic objectives as the result of a **political** or **bargaining process** involving a variety of priorities and interest groups. Today, the capitalist, free market philosophy seems more strongly established than ever and most Western business organisations acknowledge the creation of shareholder value as their primary objective.

(g) There is a view that great strategies should not really be rational at all, but should emerge from **inspiration and entrepreneurial talent**. Brunsson argues for the selection of a reasonable course of action from among a small number of choices, while Ohmae finds that good strategy is made by practical people who 'have an intuitive grasp of the basic elements of strategy'.

The criticisms are directed less at planning in principle, than at the assumption that **planning can create strategies** as opposed to supporting strategic decisions, co-ordinating them and mobilising resources.

2.5 A strategic planning system

The rational model of strategy making, or any other formal system, has distinct **organisational implications**. Indeed, it is really only where strategy develops over time (as is often the case in smaller businesses) that there is no requirement for systems to support the strategy process. Even then, it seems likely that such an approach to strategy would be more effective if some of the features outlined below were incorporated.

(a) A **system to collect strategic information** should be established. This would have dedicated human resources (which might be as little as a few hours per week for one or more individuals) and information systems to support them. Information about the environment and internal matters could be accumulated on a routine basis via, for example, data service subscriptions and management accounting reports. These could be **supplemented by specific investigations**, perhaps using consultants to do the work.

(b) A **strategic planning committee** or team formed at the strategic apex should be established, but with staff support and advice from subordinate managers. Such a team should meet regularly to direct information gathering, consider reports and liaise with consultants. It would also have the task of debating and agreeing future strategy: even where strategic decisions are taken by a single person, they are likely to be improved by such a process of consideration.

(c) A **system to implement and control the chosen strategy** might include a written summary plan; live or video presentations to stakeholders; detailed plans and budgets developed to support the overall plan; and the establishment of financial and non-financial targets for managers and staff. Suitable reports should be made and control action taken.

It would also be necessary to renew existing strategy regularly as a kind of **double loop control**, checking that current objectives, methods and plans were still relevant.

Section summary

Strategic plans are formal statements of direction. The planning process suggests a sequence of strategic analysis (of the environment and the organisation), strategy generation and evaluation (several options are weighed up and compared) and strategic choice of the best alternative.

3 Crafting emergent strategies

Introduction

Johnson, Scholes and Whittington describe **emergent strategies** as those that develop out of the day to day and routine activities of the organisation. These strategies are not drawn up as a separate activity, unlike the rational strategies we have just read about.

Mintzberg refers to 'crafting' strategies. Even though strategies are emergent, they are guided and moulded by managers.

3.1 Types of strategy

KEY TERM

EMERGENT STRATEGIES arise from *ad hoc* or even uncontrolled responses to circumstances. If they work and have potential, the quick solutions may be developed into strategies.

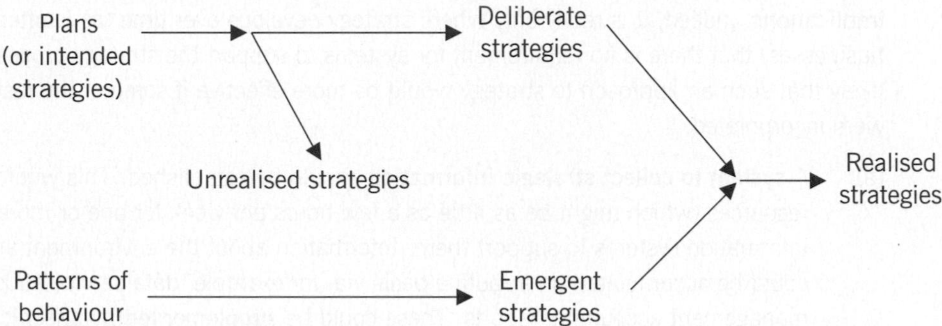

Intended strategies are plans. Those plans or aspects of plans that are actually realised are called **deliberate strategies.**

Emergent strategies are those that develop out of patterns of behaviour. 'Because big strategies can grow from little ideas ... almost anyone in an organisation can prove to be a strategist.' A salesperson may sell to some new customers, with the result that the company enters a whole new market.

Question 1A.1 Deliberate strategy

Learning outcome A1b

'Deliberate strategies are always based upon earlier planning.' True or false?

The task of strategic management is to control these emergent strategies in the light of a broader insight into the business's capabilities.

3.2 Crafting strategy

There will come a point when even an emergent strategy will need some conscious direction, perhaps to change its course. Alternatively, senior managers, when faced with an emergent strategy, might favour some aspects of it over others. For example, a company might pride itself on the high quality of its products, even though this involves expensive labour costs. If the quality strategy is favoured, management might try to develop practices that reduce the cost of this given quality.

Mintzberg uses the phrase **crafting strategy** to help understand this idea. The planning approach encountered already implies rational control and systematic analysis of competitors and markets, and of company strengths and weaknesses. However, the idea of strategy as a **craft** evokes an idea of 'skill,

dedication, perfection, through mastery of detail'. More importantly, forming a strategy and implementing it are 'fluid processes of **learning** through which creative strategies evolve'.

Mintzberg uses the image of a potter's wheel. The clay is thrown and, through shaping the clay on the wheel, the potter gives shape to the lump of clay through a gradual process. Mintzberg believes this is a good analogy for how strategies are actually developed and managed.

(a) The potter can introduce innovations during the process of shaping. The potter is both the producer and consumer of the vase. The gap between thinking and doing is short.

(b) A sales representative who discovers a new way of providing customer satisfaction may have to convince large numbers of people within the organisation of the idea's merits. The gap between insight and execution is a long one.

The trouble with the long **feedback** loop is that there is a separation between 'thinking' and 'doing' when it comes to strategy. This has the following results.

(a) A **purely deliberate strategy prevents learning** (once the formulators have stopped formulating). For example, it is hard with deliberate strategies to learn from mistakes, or stumble by accident into strategic growth.

(b) A **purely emergent strategy defies control**. It may in fact be a bad strategy, dysfunctional for the organisation's future health.

Deliberate strategies can introduce strategic change as a sort of quantum leap in some organisations. In this case, a firm has only a few strategic changes in a short period but these are very dramatic.

3.2.1 How to craft strategy

Mintzberg mentions a number of essential activities in strategic management.

(a) **Managing stability**. Most of the time, managers should be effectively implementing the strategies, not planning them: formal planning is the detailed working out of the agreed strategy. Obsessions with change are dysfunctional: **knowing when to change** is more important.

(b) **Detecting discontinuity**. Environments do not change regularly, nor are they always turbulent. Strategists should realise that some small environmental changes are much more significant than others, though guessing which these are is a problem.

   (i) **Technological developments** are hard to assess. Drucker quotes the example of Hoffmann-LaRoche, a Swiss-based pharmaceutical company, which began as a small firm making dyes. It acquired the patents to vitamins when no one else wanted them, and invested and borrowed all it could into producing and selling them. It is now an industry leader. Other technologies, combined with cheap production processes, can revolutionise certain industries (eg the motor car revolutionised transportation).

   (ii) International developments are frequent causes of uncertainty. Spotting international trends that are important to the organisation (which markets are likely to grow and so forth) must be supplemented by assessments of commercial and political risks.

(c) **Knowing the business**. Strategic management involves an intimate feel for the business. This has to include an **awareness and understanding of operations**.

(d) **Managing patterns**. 'A key to managing strategy is the ability to detect emerging patterns and to help them take shape.' Some emergent strategies must be uprooted, others nurtured.

(e) **Reconciling change and continuity**. 'Crafting strategy ... requires a natural synthesis of the future, present and past.' Obsessions with change and/or continuity can both be counterproductive.

Question 1A.2 Plan or vision

Learning outcome A1b

Britannia Hospital has just appointed a new director, Florian Vole, imported from the private sector, where he had run Hanky House, a niche retail operation specialising in handkerchiefs and fashion accessories. The recession put the business into receivership, but Mr Vole was sought out to inject his private sector expertise in running a public sector institution. He calls a meeting of the hospital's senior managerial, medical and nursing staffs, at which he states: 'What the public sector has been missing too long is vision, and when you're eyeball to eyeball with change, it's vision you need, not planning documents and statistics. We need to be nimble and quick to adapt to our customers' ever-changing needs. That is our strategy!'.

Required

What do you think of Florian Vole's approach?

Section summary

Emergent strategies are those that develop out of patterns of behaviour, which are not consciously thought out, but which eventually have a long-term, 'strategic' effect. Emergent strategies need to be crafted by managers and shaped to the organisation's advantage.

4 Other approaches to strategy

Introduction

Incrementalism is taking **small steps** or 'muddling through'. This is the opposite of rational planning and its **long-term approach** to making strategy. There is a middle way, of course, and **logical incrementalism** refers to managers taking small steps and testing strategies as they go along.

4.1 Incremental/adaptive strategy

Rationalism and **incrementalism** are the two models that are generally represented as occupying opposite ends of the spectrum of approaches to strategy making.

When an organisation appears to be '**muddling through**', then it is likely to be adopting the **incrementalism** approach involving developing the business through a series of **small logical steps**. Management's role will be to provide information, overcome change and plan future developments while building support and awareness for those.

Lindblom argued that comprehensive rational planning was impossible, and likely to result in disaster if actively pursued. Strategy making involving small-scale extensions of past practices was more likely to be successful: it would avoid major errors, and was more likely to be acceptable, because consultation, compromise and accommodation were built into the process. This **incrementalist** approach was referred to by Mintzberg as the **adaptive** mode of strategy making.

Critics argued that such muddling through was not a good prescriptive model.

(a) **Muddling through** does not work where radical new approaches are needed, and it has a built-in conservative bias. Lindblom denied the accusation of conservative bias, and suggested that it was possible to achieve a radical shift in policy over a period as a result of a series of incremental shifts. But he partially conceded the case for some forward planning in later versions of his model.

(b) Even as a descriptive model of the **public sector**, it does not always fit. Some changes do not seem incremental, but involve dramatic shifts. Examples include the reorganisation of the UK National Health Service.

4.2 A middle way? Logical incrementalism

KEY TERM

LOGICAL INCREMENTALISM was identified by James Brian Quinn. Logical incrementalism is not just muddling through: 'it is a purposeful, effective, proactive management technique for integrating both the analytical and behavioural aspects of strategy formation'.

(a) **Strategy is best described as a learning process**, by which managers have to deal with major internal or external events. One of the problems is that it is impossible to predict the long-term consequences of decisions made in those situations of crisis or change. For example, the ramifications of a radical new technology may not be foreseen.

(b) **Managers have some notion as to where the organisation should be.** They 'may be able to predict the broad direction but not the precise nature of the strategy that will result'.

(c) **Managers deliberately keep their decisions small-scale**, so that they can be **tested** in small steps, as there is so much uncertainty. However, unlike muddling through, which appears simply reactive, the logical incremental model suggests a **conscious** process of decision making.

The implications of the rational model and incrementalism can be expressed in diagrammatic form.

(a) **Rational planning model**

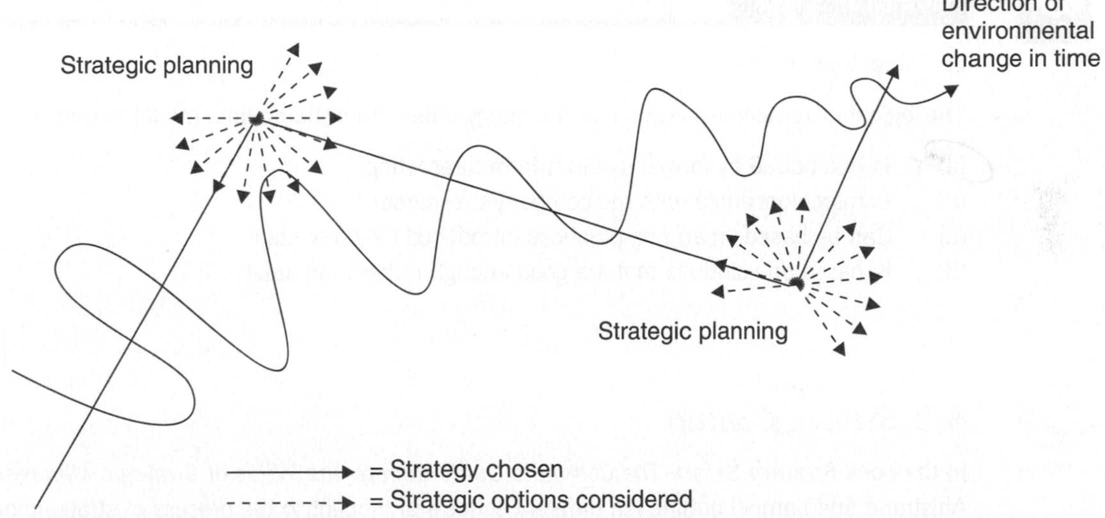

The dangers of the rational model are that the environment may change too quickly for the planning processes to react. All directions are considered, however.

(b) **Incremental model**

As we can see, the advantage of incrementalism is that it can map the environment closely. However, incremental change may not be enough, as the number of strategic options considered may be insufficiently radical in terms of their ability to cope with environmental shift.

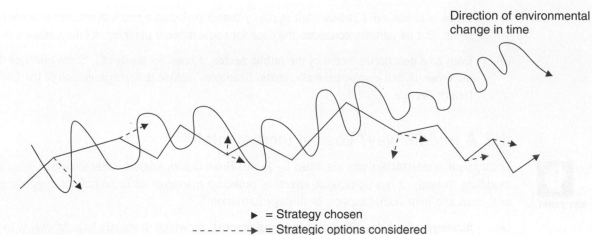

Direction of environmental change in time

► = Strategy chosen

- - - - -► = Strategic options considered

The two models are not mutually exclusive.

(a) The **rational model** may be appropriate where the change in the environment is significant or where incrementalism is not enough.

(b) **Incrementalism** may be appropriate where there is significant uncertainty, so that the organisation follows, rather than pre-empts, changes in the environment.

Both the rational model and logical incrementalism contrast with the idea of emergent strategies, in that they hold that strategy is made by managers, whereas in the emergent strategy model it can grow from the lower levels of the organisation.

Question 1A.3 Incrementalism

Learning outcome A1b

The logical incrementalist approach to strategy differs from the rational model in that it:

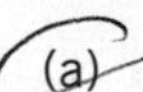

(a) Is less bound by formal medium-term forecasting
(b) Is more concerned with the company's resources
(c) Can be based on *ad hoc* practices introduced by junior staff
(d) Is based on solutions that are good enough rather than ideal

4.3 Strategy Safari

In the book *Strategy Safari: The Complete Guide through the Wilds of Strategic Management* Mintzberg, Ahlstrand and Lampel outline ten different schools of thought to the process of strategic development.

The design, planning and positioning schools of strategy development are prescriptive in their approach and are closely aligned to the rational model. The remaining schools offer alternative, descriptive approaches to strategy formulation.

The design school (conception). An organisation's strategy is developed through a two-stage approach. Firstly, consideration is given to the organisation's internal strengths and weaknesses and its external possibilities represented by opportunities and threats. Secondly, this analysis is used to determine the 'fit' between the organisation's internal capabilities and external possibilities.

The planning school (formal). Strategic development involves following a rigorous formal planning methodology which involves the setting of organisational objectives, followed by an external audit of the business environment and an internal audit of the organisation's capabilities. There is little focus on the role of creativity in the development of strategy.

The positioning school (analytical). Strategy is developed by considering where the organisation sits within its industry. The focus thereafter involves improving the organisation's strategic positioning in the industry by making both defensive and offensive moves. The use of theoretical models including Porter's five forces and value chain frameworks and the Boston Consulting Group matrix are common features of the positioning school (we explore these models later in the Study Text).

The entrepreneurial school (visionary). Strategy is developed as a result of the vision, wisdom and experience of a charismatic leader.

The cognitive school (mental). Strategy is developed by considering how the human mind perceives patterns and processes information. Strategies in the cognitive school emerge as concepts, maps and frames of reality. There is a strong focus on the creative aspects of strategic development.

The learning school (emergent). Strategic development involves management identifying those strategies that have worked well in the past and those which did not work as originally intended. The lessons learned are then factored into future strategic planning. The learning school draws parallels with the emergent approach to strategic development.

The power school (negotiation). Strategy is developed as a result of negotiations between senior figures within the organisation and powerful external stakeholders.

The cultural school (collective). Strategy is developed through co-operation with different groups throughout the organisation. This approach emphasises the importance that shared values and beliefs have on the process of strategic formulation.

The environmental school (reactive). Strategy develops in response to the challenges presented by the external business environment.

The configuration school (transformation). Strategy is the process of changing or transforming the organisation from one form of decision-making structure to another.

Mintzberg, Ahlstrand and Lampel do not claim that one particular approach to strategy development is best. Their work simply offers a range of different ways in which organisations may approach the process of strategic development.

4.4 No strategic planning – 'freewheeling opportunism'

The **freewheeling opportunism approach** suggests firms should not bother with strategic plans and should exploit opportunities as they arise.

The opportunist approach means that an organisation can **seize opportunities** quickly as they arise (rather than getting slowed down by formal planning processes), but the lack of planning may also mean the organisation **fails to identify possible opportunities** that might be available.

Advantages

(a) Good opportunities are not lost through spending time completing formal planning processes.

(b) A freewheeling opportunistic approach would **adapt to change** more quickly (for example, if there were a very steep rise in the price of a key material input, the opportunist firm would look to find any alternative material as quickly as possible).

(c) It might encourage a more **flexible, creative attitude**.

Disadvantages

(a) **No co-ordinating framework** for the organisation, so that some potentially valuable opportunities get missed.

(b) It emphasises the **profit motive** to the exclusion of all other considerations.

(c) The firm ends up **reacting** all the time rather than acting purposively.

4.4.1 Management accounting and freewheeling opportunism

A **freewheeling opportunism** approach abandons the careful routine of planning, and instead seizes such opportunities that arise. Not all 'opportunities' will work out, and there may be problems sustaining this policy.

The management accountant's role will be **investigative**.

(a) What are the financial characteristics of the proposed strategy? For example, in an acquisition, what is the effect on **cash flow**?

(b) How does the proposed strategy affect the firm's **risk profile**?

(c) What **new markets** will the firm be entering by pursuing this strategy? If so, what is the likely response of competitors?

4.5 Strategic issues of small businesses

Small organisations have specific strategic problems.

(a) **Lack of economies of scale**. A small business will not qualify for the best purchasing terms from suppliers; will probably have to pay a higher rate of interest on its bank borrowings; and will not be able to afford to employ specialist staff, instead having to buy in their services at very high hourly rates.

(b) **External factors**. It is a constant complaint from businesses in the UK that there is an ever-increasing **burden of regulation and compliance** on them. To the extent that this is true, this burden is likely to weigh most heavily on the small, owner-managed business, with its very limited administrative capacity.

(c) Overreliance on a few key individuals can produce catastrophe if one of them leaves or is sick for a prolonged period.

(d) **Small market areas or a restricted range of products** mean that small businesses are particularly vulnerable to environmental changes. They tend to have all their eggs in one basket.

(e) **Cannot raise money**. Many small businesses complain that they are unable to raise finance and rely heavily on bank loans. (Many proprietors, however, are unwilling to sacrifice control in order to raise bank finance.)

4.6 Strategic issues of start-ups

In addition to the problems that can affect small businesses generally, the **start-up** business has its own particular weaknesses.

(a) **Lack of profit**. A new venture is unlikely to turn an accounting profit for two to three years because significant investment has to be made in such things as premises, stocks, recruitment and business development before turnover starts to build up. It is essential, therefore, that start-ups have the financial resources to run at a loss for several years.

(b) **Poor cash flow**. Managing cash flow is a demanding job: many owner managers do not possess the necessary skills. The problem is exacerbated when the business is undercapitalised, which is often the case with start-ups. A further problem is that large firms often fail to pay their small business suppliers on time.

(c) New owner managers are often **deficient in other skills** besides financial ones. New businesses are often founded by a person, or group of people, with expertise in only one or two business disciplines. Typically, these will be selling and/or technological expertise. Knowledge of procurement, logistics, personnel management, production engineering, marketing techniques and the essential detail of administration will often be missing. As a result, the aspiring sole trader or

partnership is likely to find that unforeseen problems arise and consume an inordinate amount of time, hampering the deployment of the skills the managers do possess.

(d) **Marketing expertise** is a particularly crucial requirement for the new business. Where the business is founded to exploit a new technical development, there is a long journey from the initial idea to market success. A fertile target market must be discovered by market research or created by promotional techniques; distribution systems must be set up and, perhaps most important of all, a suitable price must be set. Where distribution is to be through agents or wholesalers, as will often be the case, important discounts must be conceded without undermining either immediate cash flow or ultimate profitability.

(e) Another important area of skill that is frequently lacking in new businesses is **personnel management**. Information technology applications have reduced the requirement for staff in terms of overall numbers but have increased the requirement for staff with a high level of specialised skills. Whether staff are engaged in large or small numbers, they must be managed carefully if they are to be motivated to support the firm's efforts. All too frequently, staff are taken for granted, poorly organised and even abused.

(f) The effect of the **business cycle** should not be overlooked. A business starting up at the peak of the cycle is likely to have only three or four years in which to establish itself and secure its position before the economic trend starts to decline. When times are hard, it will be difficult for most businesses even to maintain turnover, and expansion will be a remote dream. Larger customers are likely to be merciless in their exploitation of small businesses' unwillingness to press them for payment, while suppliers will be equally merciless in demanding payment. During the trough of the cycle, larger businesses will cut costs by reducing their headcounts. The option of self-employment is likely to be quite attractive to some of those made redundant, but their prospects are not good: they will be starting up in a sluggish market and in the face of increased competition (including competition from each other).

Section summary

Logical incrementalism makes strategy in a series of incremental changes rather than big leaps. It suggests practical limits to the rational model. People make strategic decisions on the basis of precedent, accepting satisfactory rather than ideal solutions.

In the book ***Strategy Safari: The Complete Guide through the Wilds of Strategic Management*** Mintzberg, Ahlstrand and Lampel outline ten different schools of thought to the process of strategic development.

The **freewheeling opportunism approach** suggests firms should not bother with strategic plans and should exploit opportunities as they arise.

5 Strategy and structure

Introduction

The debate around whether the strategy an entity pursues is determined by its organisational structure or whether the structure should be built around the chosen strategy is not new. In this section we explore some of the factors which influence an organisation's structure before looking at the work of Chandler.

Chandler's study of US corporations revealed that they developed their structures to accommodate the strategies they pursued. The large corporations he looked at had all ended up with a decentralised structure. Chandler believed this was a structure designed to cope with the problems of growth and control brought about by the strategic choices of these corporations.

Structure is an important aspect of the implementation of strategy and must be optimised to support it, although the relationship may not be straightforward.

5.1 Factors influencing structure

There are a range of factors which may influence an organisation's structure; some of these are considered below:

(a) **The external business environment**. Dynamic environments are often characterised by constant changes in consumer tastes and the need for innovation in the products and services offered. Such environments require organisations to adopt a structure which is fairly flexible to facilitate the need to constantly move with the times.

(b) **The strategy being pursued**. A company which is trying to achieve high growth may initially adopt an organisational structure with few levels of hierarchy as the focus is on achieving growth in market share and not on managing the structure.

(c) **Life cycle**. The organisation's position in the industry life cycle will impact on its structure. For example, mature organisations may change their structure through a programme of management de-layering in order to improve profitability and efficiency in response to new competitors entering the market.

(d) **Size**. Small organisations may have a very small structure; this reflects the fact that there are fewer workers undertaking a limited range of activities. By contrast, larger organisations are likely to have a formalised structure, with many managers and supervisors monitoring the work of employees.

(e) **Technology**. The degree of technology used in an organisation's operations will impact on its structure. The increased use of information systems has resulted in new approaches to working and has most notably resulted in closer collaboration between organisations.

5.2 Chandler

Alfred Chandler conducted a detailed historical study of the development of four major US corporations: Du Pont, General Motors, Standard Oil Company of New Jersey and Sears Roebuck. He found that all four had evolved a decentralised structure based on operating divisions, though by different routes. In order to reach this final stage, the businesses typically grew through four structural stages.

(a) Entrepreneurial structure
(b) Functional structure
(c) Holding company structure
(d) Divisionalised structure

This would seem to be a normal evolutionary process for a business organisation to experience as it expands.

Chandler suggested that during the period 1850 to 1920 (which he describes as the formative years of modern capitalism), the development of high-volume production to serve mass markets forced the replacement of entrepreneurial, owner management by innovative professional managers. Ultimately, these managers created the modern, multi-unit corporation as the best response to the administrative problems associated with growth. The **divisionalised organisation** is thus a response to strategy in its broadest sense.

Chandler discerned two main types of strategy, positive and negative. **Positive strategy** is aggressive, seeks new markets and leads to growth by product diversification. **Negative strategy** seeks to defend a current position and leads to growth by vertical integration based on mergers and acquisitions. In both cases, the initial structural response is likely to be centralised control based on functional departments. Both Du Pont and Sears Roebuck went through this stage.

Unfortunately, this approach has important disadvantages, especially where there is geographical dispersion. Du Pont therefore created an innovative decentralised structure of largely autonomous product-based business units co-ordinated rather than controlled by the corporate headquarters. General

Motors copied the idea to overcome a lack of overall control in its loose federation of operating units. Standard Oil Company of New Jersey followed suit after a series of *ad hoc* responses to crises of control; its particular problem was the need to allocate and co-ordinate resources. Sears Roebuck went through essentially the same process as Du Pont.

The creation of the **multi-unit structure** was thus a logical managerial response to the problems associated with strategies that create very large organisations.

Chandler described different levels of management activity typical of this structure.

(a) The **general office** is the headquarters, responsible for overall performance. It allocates resources to the divisions, and controls their performance by setting targets. Divisions are responsible for a product line or sales region.

(b) The **divisional central office** is responsible to the general office. Divisions are organised internally on a functional basis.

(c) Each function, such as production or sales, has a **departmental headquarters**, which manages **field units** such as manufacturing plants or a sales team. Only at field unit level do managers carry out day to day operational work.

It has been argued that an established and well-functioning structure can influence strategy as, for instance, when two retail organisations merge because the geographical pattern of their branches is complementary. Similarly, **value chain analysis** and **activity-based management** will tend to take existing structures as given factors, though they may lead to structural improvements. However, these are really aspects of organisational strengths and weaknesses analysis. Structure should, if necessary, be adjusted to suit the chosen strategy.

5.3 Organisational consistency

It is often difficult to identify a single best solution to the problem of organisation structure, particularly when the considerations point in different directions. For example, departmentation by geography or by function is often a difficult decision to take and usually produces a range of possible solutions. Child has shown that when the contingency approach seems to allow several different outcomes, it is important to ensure **internal consistency** in the measures adopted. For example, if a decentralised solution is chosen, leadership and control mechanisms based on centralisation will be inappropriate. Intangible aspects, such as culture and management philosophy, must also be considered.

Section summary

Strategy and structure must be in harmony and it will normally be appropriate to regard organisation structure as an aspect of strategic implementation. **Chandler** believed that structure should follow strategy and charted the development of structures from **entrepreneurial** through **functional** to **divisional**.

Exam alert

Remember, the rational model is not necessarily suited to all organisations, and emergent or incremental strategies may be better in certain cases. If faced with a question of this type, read the scenario carefully and give plenty of thought to which you believe is best suited to the specific organisation with which you are presented.

Chapter Summary

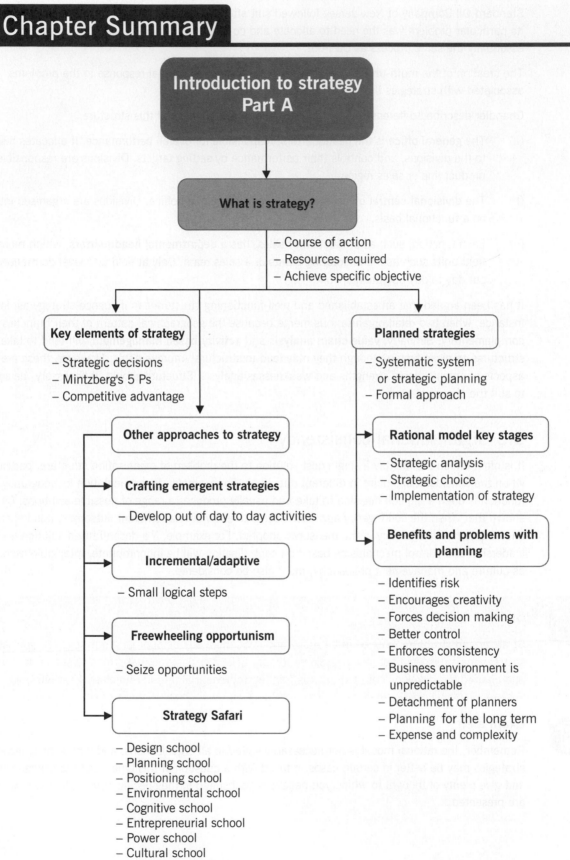

Introduction to strategy Part A

What is strategy?
- Course of action
- Resources required
- Achieve specific objective

Key elements of strategy
- Strategic decisions
- Mintzberg's 5 Ps
- Competitive advantage

Other approaches to strategy

Crafting emergent strategies
- Develop out of day to day activities

Incremental/adaptive
- Small logical steps

Freewheeling opportunism
- Seize opportunities

Strategy Safari
- Design school
- Planning school
- Positioning school
- Environmental school
- Cognitive school
- Entrepreneurial school
- Power school
- Cultural school
- Learning school
- Configuration school

Planned strategies
- Systematic system or strategic planning
- Formal approach

Rational model key stages
- Strategic analysis
- Strategic choice
- Implementation of strategy

Benefits and problems with planning
- Identifies risk
- Encourages creativity
- Forces decision making
- Better control
- Enforces consistency
- Business environment is unpredictable
- Detachment of planners
- Planning for the long term
- Expense and complexity

Quick Quiz

1 Define business strategy in fewer than 20 words.

2 Strategic decisions affect operational decisions because:

A Operational level managers will always participate in the making of strategy
B Strategy is concerned with short-term concerns
C Operational decisions relate to the environment
D Operational decisions are based on assumptions that flow from prior strategic decisions

3 Complete the statement below using one of the phrases in the list in brackets.

'In the rational model, mission and objectives; environmental analysis; and internal appraisal lead directly to ....'

(strategic options generation; corporate appraisal; strategy selection; stakeholder expectations)

4 Is the statement below true or false?

'Corporate strategy differs from business strategy in that the former relates to a given market, while the latter is about what kind of business the company should be in.'

5 Which of the following statements is not true of the emergent strategy approach?

A It prevents learning
B It defies control
C It requires an awareness and understanding of operations
D It requires no detailed planning

Answers to Quick Quiz

1 A course of action, including the specification of resources required, to achieve a specific objective

2 D A and B are untrue. C is irrelevant.

3 Corporate appraisal

4 False. The opposite is true.

5 A It depends on learning.

Answers to Questions

1A.1 Deliberate strategy

The statement is true and is really a point of definition.

1A.2 Plan or vision

Mr Vole hasn't quite made the transition from the fashion industry, where desire for silk handkerchiefs is relatively fickle, to an institution like Britannia Hospital. Here planning **is** necessary. Resources must be obtained to cope with future needs. 'Customer needs' are likely to be fairly basic (ie security, comfort, medical attention, stimulation). However, in the actual delivery of care and services, Florian Vole has a point: experimentation with new care techniques might improve the hospital's service to its patients. In this case, pursuing his 'vision' rather than simply following old procedures might be a good approach.

1A.3 Incrementalism

A B is untrue, C is true of emergent strategy, and D is a description of bounded rationality.

Now try these questions from the Practice Question Bank

Question	Level
1A.1 – 1A.5	Practice
Four Star Products	Practice

INTRODUCTION TO STRATEGY – PART B

We have just looked at different ways of making strategies. Now we turn to the ways in which strategies relate at different levels in the organisation. In the last chapter we looked at this briefly when we studied the **rational model**.

This chapter also considers ideas in established and emergent thinking in strategic management. By this we mean views such as transaction costs, resource-based view and the ecological perspective.

- **Transaction costs** consider how organisations arrange production on either a market or hierarchy basis.
- The **resource-based** approach argues that, rather than fitting strategy to the external environment (positioning), an organisation should seek to exploit its distinctive internal competences and resources.
- The **ecology model** suggests that, as an organisation's environment changes, it will only survive if it **adapts** and **evolves**.

We conclude the chapter by briefly running through **vision, mission, goals and objectives**. We look at how the organisation's **strategic intent or vision** becomes reality throughout the organisation.

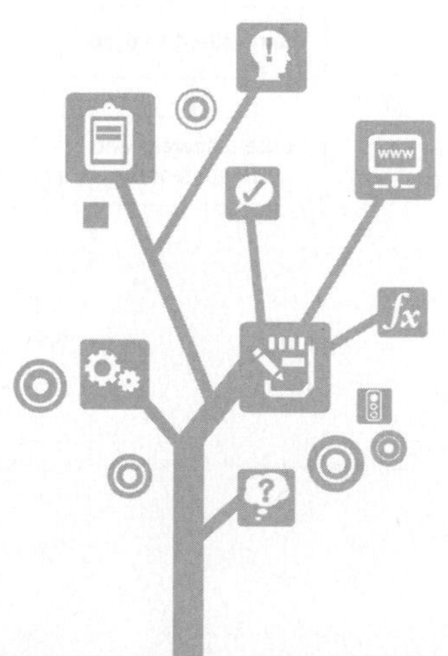

Topic list	Learning outcomes	Syllabus references	Ability required
1 Levels of strategy	A1a	A1(iii)	Analysis
2 Concepts in established and emergent thinking in strategic management	A1b, c	A1(ii), (iii)	Analysis/ comprehension
3 The transaction cost approach	C1b	C1(iii)	Analysis
4 Mission	A1a	A1(ii)	Analysis
5 Goals, aims and objectives	A1a, b	A1(ii), (iii)	Analysis
6 Implementation	A1a	A1(ii), (iii)	Analysis

Chapter Overview

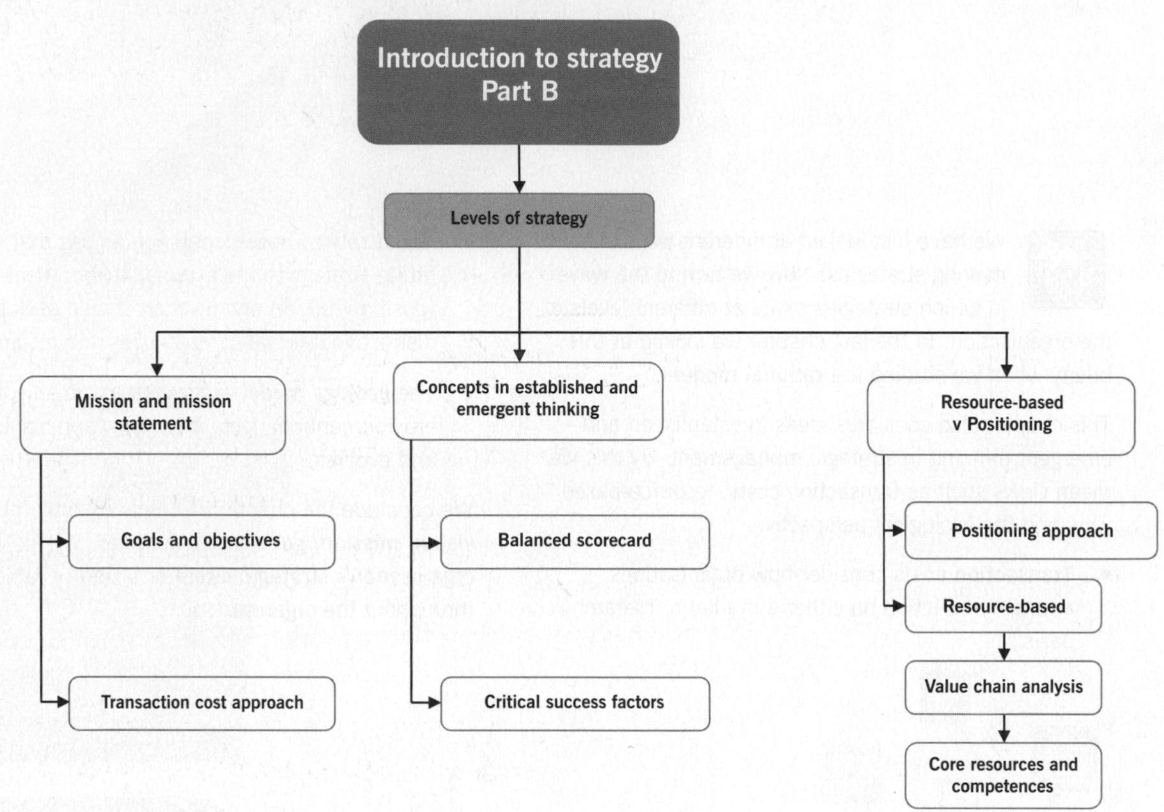
Introduction to strategy
Part B
Levels of strategy
Mission and mission statement
Goals and objectives
Transaction cost approach
Concepts in established and emergent thinking
Balanced scorecard
Critical success factors
Resource-based v Positioning
Positioning approach
Resource-based
Value chain analysis
Core resources and competences

1 Levels of strategy

Introduction

In the previous chapter, we looked at the implementation of strategy throughout the organisation by cascading strategies down the organisation. Hofer and Schendel take this further and make the following distinction.

(a) **Corporate strategy** is the most general level of strategy in an organisation. In the words of Johnson and Scholes, corporate strategy is 'concerned with what types of business the company as a whole should be in and is therefore concerned with decisions of **scope**'. An example would be choosing between diversifying and limiting the activities of the business.

(b) **Business strategy** defines how an organisation approaches a particular **market**, or the activity of a particular **business unit**. For example, this can involve decisions as to whether, in principle, a company should segment the market and specialise in particularly profitable areas or compete by offering a wider range of products.

(c) **Operational and functional strategies** involve decisions of strategic importance, but which are made or determined at operational levels. These decisions include product pricing, investment in plant, and personnel policy. The contributions of these different functions determine the success of the strategy as, effectively, a strategy is only implemented at this level.

Many large firms are organised into **strategic business units** (SBUs).

KEY TERM

A **STRATEGIC BUSINESS UNIT (SBU)** is a 'section, usually a division, within a larger business organisation, that has a significant degree of autonomy, typically being responsible for developing and marketing its own products or services'. (*CIMA Official Terminology*)

A typical SBU is a division of the organisation where managers have control over their own resources, and discretion over the deployment of resources.

Question 1B.1 Levels of strategy

Learning outcome A1a

Ganymede Co is a company selling widgets. The Finance Director says: 'We plan to issue more shares to raise money for new plant capacity – we don't want loan finance – which will enable us to compete better in the vital and growing widget markets of Latin America. After all, we've promised the shareholders 5% profit growth this year, and trading is tough'.

Required

Identify the corporate, business and functional strategies in the above quotation.

Section summary

Strategy can exist at three levels within an organisation; corporate level, business level and the operational level.

2 Concepts in established and emergent thinking in strategic management

Introduction

This section is quite theoretical, but keep in mind that certain organisations work flexibly and **evolve**. They inspire creativity and initiative. Others are more rigid and the **rational model** we studied previously suits their management style better.

We also look at **resource-based strategy** where organisations get ahead by exploiting their individual competences and resources. This approach contrasts the **positioning approach** which fits into the **rational model**, whereby an organisation seeks to position itself by aligning its strategy with the external environment.

There is an argument that modern organisations need to be flexible to adapt their strategies and a positioning approach is too difficult to sustain.

2.1 Ecology, adaptation and individualisation

Some writers have applied the ideas of **evolution and natural selection** to organisations. This **ecology model** suggests that as an organisation's environment changes, it will only survive if it **adapts** and **evolves**. Business history is littered with the corpses of once-powerful companies that failed to adapt. In this theory, an organisation survives if it finds a niche that provides both demand for its outputs and resources for it to use. Change plays an important role in determining whether or not an organisation finds a viable niche.

KEY POINT

You should compare this idea with the various approaches to making corporate strategy discussed earlier. Much strategic theory makes an implicit assumption that success depends on achieving a close correspondence between what the organisation does and what its environment needs or can accept.

The rational model is, of course, an example of a strategic method that is based on careful study of the strategic environment. However, it is also, almost inevitably, a **rather bureaucratic method** and suffers from the common weaknesses of bureaucracy, including inflexibility of method, complexity of process, poor communication, ponderousness and a tendency to play safe.

Some large commercial organisations, such as General Electric, 3M, Unipart and Asea Brown Boveri, seem to have achieved a more responsive and agile approach to strategic management. The methods employed by these companies are described by Ghoshal and Bartlett in their book *The Individualized Corporation.*

In a dynamic global environment in which competition is increasingly service based and knowledge intensive, they recognised that human creativity and individual initiative were far more important as sources of competitive advantage than homogeneity and conformity.

Ghoshal and Bartlett suggest that these companies have three distinguishing characteristics.

(a) They are able to inspire **individual creativity** and **initiative** in their people, based on a fundamental faith in them.

(b) They build on pockets of entrepreneurial activity and expertise by building an integrated process of **organisational learning**.

(c) They continuously **renew** themselves.

Developing the ability to operate in this way requires a new approach to human behaviour and organisational management (at least insofar as it affects middle and senior managers: this is not a recipe

for lower-level supervisors). The organisation's **behavioural context** must be changed from one of **repression** to one of **renewal**. Each type of context has four important characteristics.

2.1.1 The repressive context

Compliance with central policy ensures that the direction set by top management is followed by all. However, it also results in inflexible procedures and intolerance of dissent, the latter leading to the perpetuation of the former even when they become obsolete.

Control of divisionalised companies, intended to enhance accountability through sophisticated budgeting systems, can lead to defensiveness and risk aversion.

Contract is the basis of some adversarial relationships that grow up as a result of massive restructuring programmes with their attendant downsizing; people distance themselves emotionally from the organisation and see their relationship with it as legalistic and financially based.

Constraint prevents the inefficient use of resources by clearly defining the boundaries of corporate strategy and delegated responsibility.

2.1.2 The context for renewal

Discipline becomes 'an embedded norm that makes people live by their promises and commitments'.

Support replaces control: the role of managers becomes one of coaching, helping and guiding both subordinates and colleagues.

Trust is built by transparency, openness and fairness. It allows people to rely on each other's judgements and make reciprocal commitments to one another.

Stretch liberates and energises by lifting individuals' aspirations and expectations of themselves.

2.2 Resource-based strategy

2.2.1 The positioning approach vs the resource-based approach

We have seen that a rational approach to strategy involves analysis of the environment of the organisation to identify (internal) strengths and weaknesses, and (external) opportunities and threats to the competitive position of the organisation. However, there are two approaches to dealing with this information.

(a) The **positioning approach** suggests that the main source of competitive advantage lies in how the organisation fits its strategy to its external environment. Strategic objectives are set by reference to product/market opportunities and threats – and organisational resources are developed and deployed to exploit those conditions and get the organisation to where it wants to be. (This is the basis of strategic planning: environmental analysis, corporate appraisal and the selection of best-fit strategies.)

(b) The **resource-based approach** suggests that the main source of competitive advantage lies in how the organisation exploits its distinctive (unique, hard to imitate, competitively value-adding) internal competences and resources. Strategic objectives are set by reference to what the organisation is best able to do (or able to do better than competitors).

2.2.2 Criticisms of the positioning approach

Various writers have argued that sustainable competitive advantage can no longer be assured using a positioning approach.

(a) The **rate of environmental change is too great** for effective positioning strategies to be developed. The rate of economic and social change brought about by globalisation, rapid technological innovation and changing consumer taste make a measured response out of date before it can take effect.

(b) **Positioning advantages cannot be sustained in the long term**. Advantageous product-market positions are too easy to copy to last long, and more rapid product life cycles erode initial advantage.

(c) It is **more difficult to adapt the organisation than to adopt a new environment**. The positioning approach may require significant change within the firm, which is difficult to achieve. It may be easier to move to a market environment that suits existing arrangements, skills, culture and capabilities.

2.2.3 Core resources and competences

Resources can be classified in one of two ways:

KEY TERMS

BASIC RESOURCES (THRESHOLD RESOURCES) are those resources needed to meet the customer's minimum requirements.

UNIQUE RESOURCES are those resources that underpin competitive advantage and are difficult for competitors to replicate.

Unique resources may be obvious things such as favoured access to a particular **raw material** or a piece of legally protected **intellectual property**; they may also take less tangible forms, such as a well-known **brand**. Some theorists argue that the possession of unique resources enables organisations to generate greater profits than those achieved by competing firms.

Barney (1991) proposed the following four-point criteria when evaluating the value of an organisation's unique resources:

(1) **Valuable**. The resource must enable the organisation to take advantage of opportunities and help reduce its own internal weaknesses.

(2) **Rare**. To be a unique resource it is important that competitors do not possess the same resources.

(3) **Imperfectly imitable**. Means that competitors are unable to obtain the unique resource possessed by an organisation.

(4) **Substitutability**. If a unique resource can be substituted by a similar resource then this reduces the competitive advantage that it generates an organisation.

Competences can be classified into two types:

KEY TERM

THRESHOLD COMPETENCES are those activities and processes needed to meet the customer's minimum requirements.

CORE COMPETENCES are those activities that underpin competitive advantage and are difficult for competitors to replicate.

Core competences can be very specialised indeed or may be transferable between markets. For example, Enron, in its early days, established a core competence in price risk management that was equally applicable to the oil and gas industries. It is important to realise that it is possible to acquire or develop new competences, but this takes time. The possession of a particular advantage thus constitutes a competitive advantage, but its validity may decline if other firms develop equivalent capabilities. Competences must therefore be developed and kept up to date on a continuing basis.

Johnson, Scholes and Whittington (2008) define **CORE COMPETENCES** as 'the skills and abilities by which resources are deployed through an organisation's activities and processes such as to achieve competitive advantage in ways that others cannot imitate or obtain'.

The concept of core competences is key to the modern trend for **outsourcing**: organisations focus their activity on core competences, and contract non-core activities to other organisations that have distinctive resources and capabilities to add more value than the outsourcing organisation could do in-house.

2.2.4 Distinctive capabilities

Resource-based theorists have attempted to identify where internal competitive advantage comes from.

Kay (1997) suggests that competitive advantage comes from a combination of the following:

(a) **Competitive architecture** refers to the relationships that make up the organisation. These break down into:

  (i) Internal architecture (relationships with employees)
  (ii) External architecture (relationships with suppliers and customers)
  (iii) Network architecture (relationships between a group of collaborating firms)

(b) **Reputation** refers to the standing that the organisation has created among key stakeholders including customers, suppliers and investors. Building a positive reputation among such groups is an ongoing activity; improving the quality of the organisation's products, services and internal processes are central to this.

(c) **Innovative ability** is concerned with developing new products and services. For most organisations the ability to innovate is central to being able to compete effectively. Increasingly the ability to innovate requires organisations to work closely with suppliers and customers.

(d) **Possession of strategic assets** refers to those unique resources and competences that the organisation may have.

Stalk *et al* (1992) identify four principles of the resource-based view (referred to as **capabilities-based competition**):

(1) Advantage needs to be **based on business processes**, not products.
(2) Success derives from **converting these processes** into value-adding capabilities.
(3) These capabilities require **group-wide investment** (ie across functional boundaries).
(4) The **CEO needs to champion** this group-wide approach for it to be effective.

Stalk argues competitive advantage is derived by performing better than competitors in the following five ways:

(1) **Speed**. Organisations need to be able to respond quickly to changes in customer and market demand by introducing new technologies and fresh ideas into products.

(2) **Consistency**. Organisations need to produce products which satisfy customer expectations.

(3) **Acuity**. This refers to the ability of organisations to understand the competitive environment, in order to anticipate customers' evolving needs.

(4) **Agility**. Organisations need to be able to respond simultaneously to many business environments.

(5) **Innovativeness**. This refers to the ability of organisations to generate new ideas which can be combined with existing ways of working.

2.2.5 Assessing resource-based theory

(a) Core competences are **difficult to identify and assess**: a wrong appraisal could lead to the loss of wider competence or source of advantage by misdirected outsourcing.

(b) Attempts to apply core competences (or other resources) widely across a range of markets and operations may make the firm **vulnerable to more focused, single market operations**.

(c) The emphasis on unique resources is reminiscent of the 'product orientation' decried by marketing experts: competitors who are more in touch with **market requirements** may be more successful. On the other hand, a strategy based on a sequence of unique products, as in the pharmaceutical industry, can be successful.

(d) **Investors** may or may not be convinced by the resource-based view. Where there is a clear, identifiable and credible strategy, they may well maintain their support. However, a strategy based on exploiting existing markets may be more intuitively acceptable.

(e) The competence approach seems to support ideas such as cross-functional, activity-based management, team working and the use of network structures both within the organisation and in its relations with suppliers and customers. However, the need to safeguard core competence capability against erosion by staff turnover and direct sharing of know-how may lead to a **perceived need for close control of activities** and narrow limits on outsourcing.

Section summary

Organisations can attempt to adapt in an **ecological** way to their changing environment. A bottom-up, empowering philosophy is one approach.

The **positioning approach** suggests that the main source of competitive advantage lies in how the organisation fits its strategy to its external environment.

The **resource-based approach** suggests that the main source of competitive advantage lies in how the organisation exploits its distinctive internal competences and resources.

Exam alert

The different approaches to strategy may seem heavily theoretical, but they lend themselves to examination in various ways.

Question 1B.2

Resource-based approach

Learning outcome A1b

This question focuses on the Farmers case study that is set out at the front of this Study Text.

Farmers supermarkets is a successful retail chain. It is rapidly developing a strong reputation for innovation following the launch of its internet shopping site. The company provides value for money through the efficient use of operations and its relationship with suppliers, and its pursuit in adopting the latest technology and its strong customer focus have enabled it to gain a large share of the market in the UK.

Following detailed analysis, the senior management of Farmers has concluded that the market in the UK has reached saturation point and that the only opportunity for significant growth is to develop activities in new markets abroad.

Acting partly on the advice of the UK Government's Overseas Advisory Board, and using its own research team, Adrian Williams (Farmers' Managing Director) has recently announced the strategic decision to enter into a new market. The location selected for the first supermarket is in the suburbs of the French capital, Paris, where groceries, clothing and the other non-food products that Farmers intends to supply are currently provided by a large number of small shops.

Required

Discuss the resource-based approach to strategic management, making reference to the resources and competences that appear to give Farmers supermarkets competitive advantage.

2.3 Value chain analysis

Introduction

In addition to identifying the organisation's resources, it helps to determine how well they are being used, and how much value is added after those resources are acquired. One such technique is **value chain analysis**. Value chain analysis identifies the way in which the firm organises the business's activities. It was developed by Michael Porter in his book *Competitive Advantage*.

Before we go any further, keep in mind that, in Porter's analysis, **business activities** are **not** the same as **business functions.**

(a) **Functions** are the familiar departments of a business (eg the production function and the finance function) and reflect the formal organisation structure and the distribution of labour.

(b) **Activities** are what actually goes on, and the work that is done. A single activity can be performed by a number of functions in sequence. Activities are the means by which a firm creates value in its products. (They are sometimes referred to as **value activities.**) Activities incur costs and, in combination with other activities, provide a product or service that earns revenue.

Some examples should make this clear. An organisation needs many inputs of resources to function. It needs to secure resources from the environment. This activity can be called procurement. However, procurement will involve more departments than purchasing; accounts will certainly be involved and possibly production and quality assurance (QA).

'Firms create value for their buyers by performing these activities' (Porter). The ultimate value a firm creates is measured by the amount customers are willing to pay for its products or services above the cost of carrying out value activities. A firm is profitable if the realised value to customers exceeds the collective cost of performing the activities.

There are two points to note here.

(a) **The customers purchase value**, which they measure by comparing a firm's products and services with similar offerings by competitors.

(b) **The business creates value** by carrying out its activities either more efficiently than other businesses, or combined in such a way as to provide a unique product or service.

2.3.1 The value chain

KEY TERM

VALUE CHAIN. 'The sequence of business activities by which, in the perspective of the end-user, value is added to the products or services produced by an entity.' *(CIMA Official Terminology)*

Porter analysed the various activities of an organisation into a **value chain.** This is a model of value activities (that procure inputs, process them and add value to them in some way, to generate outputs for customers) and the relationships between them.

Here is a diagram of the value chain.

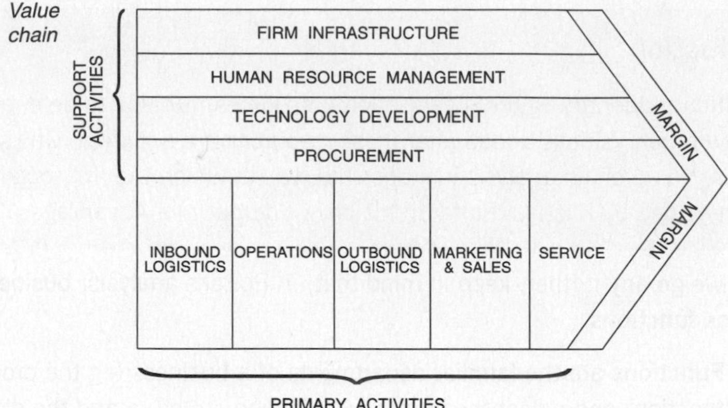

Let us examine some of these elements in turn.

2.3.2 Primary activities

The first distinction that can be made is that between **primary activities** and **support activities**.

Primary activities are those directly related to production, sales, marketing, delivery and services. The diagram shows five primary activities.

(a) **Inbound logistics** are those activities involved with receiving, handling and storing inputs to the production system.

(b) **Operations** are those activities that convert resource inputs into a final product. In a manufacturing firm, this is relatively easy to identify as the factory. In a service company, operations include those activities that make up the basic service.

(c) **Outbound logistics** are those activities relating to storing the product and its distribution to customers.

(d) **Marketing and sales** are those activities that relate to informing customers about the product, persuading them to buy it, and enabling them to do so.

(e) **After-sales service** includes activities such as installing products, repairing them and providing spare parts.

2.3.3 Support activities

Support activities are those that provide purchased inputs, human resources, technology and infrastructural functions to support the primary activities.

(a) **Procurement** consists of those activities that acquire the resource inputs to the primary activities (eg purchase of materials, subcomponents and equipment).

(b) **Technology development** (in the sense of apparatus, techniques and work organisation). These activities are related both to product design and to improving processes and/or resource utilisation.

(c) **Human resource management** is the activities of recruiting, training, developing and rewarding people.

(d) **Firm infrastructure**. The systems of planning, finance, quality control and management are activities that Porter believes are crucially important to an organisation's strategic capability in all primary activities.

2.3.4 Other elements

In addition to the categories described above, Porter identifies three further types of activity.

(a) **Direct activities** are concerned with adding value to inputs.

(b) **Indirect activities** enable direct activities to be performed (eg maintenance and sales force administration).

(c) **QA**. This type of activity monitors the quality of other activities, and includes inspection, review and audit (eg the quality of the financial records).

Linkages connect the interdependent elements of the value chain together. They occur when one element of the value chain affects the costs or effectiveness of another. They require co-ordination.

(a) More costly product design, or better quality production, might reduce the need for after-sales service.

(b) To deliver goods on time requires smooth functioning of operations, outbound logistics and service activities such as installation.

Question 1B.3 Activities

Learning outcome A1b

Which of the following is not a value chain primary activity?

A Inbound logistics
B Human resource management
C Marketing and sales
D Service

2.3.5 The value system

Activities that add value do not stop at the organisation's boundaries. For example, when a restaurant serves a meal, the quality of the ingredients – although they are chosen by the cook – is determined by the grower. The grower has also added value, and the grower's success in growing produce of good quality is as important to the customer's ultimate satisfaction as the skills of the chef. Consequently, a company's value chain is connected to what Porter describes as a **value system.**

Value system

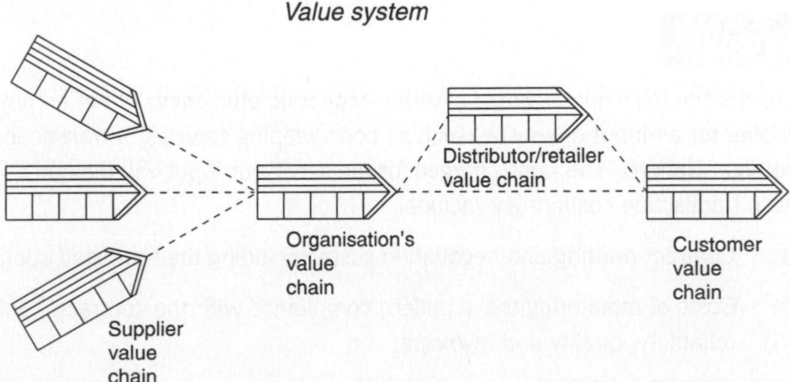

As well as managing its own value chain, a firm can secure competitive advantage by managing the linkages with its suppliers and customers. A company can create competitive advantage by making best use of these links and this means considering the value chains of these suppliers and customers. An example is a just-in-time system where close integration of the firm's operations with those of its suppliers is essential.

CASE STUDY

Toyota

Toyota is well known for close involvement with its suppliers. The company works with suppliers to improve its methods and the quality of its output; and to develop new, improved materials and components for input into its own operations. The relationship has benefits for all parties, but tends to be unequal, with Toyota dominating the operations of a large number of semi-captive suppliers.

Section summary

Value chain analysis identifies the way in which the firm organises the business's activities. It can be defined as 'the sequence of business by which, in the perspective of the end-user, value is added to the products or services produced by an entity'.

3 The transaction cost approach

Introduction

This is another theoretical approach, but bear with us! The **transaction cost approach** seeks to answer the question of why firms exist. Why not have individuals transacting with each other instead? Williamson answered the question by explaining that firms have advantages over individuals making contracts, which he explained by **uncertainty and bounded rationality**.

He then explained that firms are set up to allow **asset specificity** or using specialised assets in the business.

3.1 Markets and hierarchies

Transaction cost analysis is an aspect of economics that deals with the way resources are organised for production. It is an important contribution to thinking about the nature of business and has important implications for both business strategy and business structure. In its simplest form, this analysis is concerned with the question of why firms exist and grow; and why production is not undertaken by self-employed individuals contracting with one another for the supply of goods and services. This is sometimes referred to as the '**markets or hierarchies**' question.

Example

Consider the following example covering **economic efficiency**. When an organisation uses an outside supplier for an input or service, such as book-keeping services, a transaction will take place between the two organisations. The price charged for the service or input will include a number of transaction costs. These transaction costs might include:

(a) Contract drafting and negotiation costs, including the time staff spend on these tasks.

(b) Costs of monitoring the supplier's compliance with the contract. Factors considered will include reliability, quality and invoicing.

(c) Legal costs, if action needs to be taken against the supplier in the case of non-performance.

(d) Cancellation and penalty payments should problems or disputes arise.

KEY TERMS

A **TRANSACTION** is an economic event in which a good or service is transferred from one economic entity to another.

TRANSACTION COSTS are the costs associated with performing a transaction.

Ronald Coase addressed the question of why firms exist in his 1937 essay *The Nature of the Firm*. He suggested that, initially at least, an entrepreneur will find cost advantage in employing people and resources in a coherent business organisation. Later, as the firm grows, overhead costs also grow and mistakes in resource allocation increase. Under these conditions, the market approach may be preferable.

3.2 Problems with contracts

This basic idea was refined by Oliver Williamson. The market or contractual approach, he suggested, was hampered in the long term by a combination of **uncertainty** and **bounded rationality**.

(a) **Environmental uncertainty** means we must expect economic relationships to change as time passes.

(b) **Bounded rationality** is our acceptance of the fact that we cannot have perfect knowledge of those changes in advance.

Taken together, uncertainty and bounded rationality mean that in the longer term, satisfactory contracts are not feasible: the range of possibilities they must cover is impossibly large. The incessant search for economic advantage means that the contracting parties could not trust one another not to take advantage of a new opportunity to benefit at the other's expense.

Short-term contracts allowing for renegotiation when conditions change can overcome this problem to some extent, but they increase the associated transaction costs of negotiation and so on.

KEY TERM

A very important problem with the market approach lies in **ASSET SPECIFICITY**. Relationship-specific assets are those that have little or no application outside a given commercial relationship.

Example

For example, imagine a catering firm that contracts to supply meals to an airline. In the interests of speed of delivery, it builds a new kitchen at the airport used by the airline as its main operational base. So long as the contractual relationship continues, the kitchen is an important asset to the catering company. If, however, the contract is not renewed when it comes to an end, the asset may be worthless if it cannot be sold to a successful competitor and even then a good price with only one possible purchaser may be unobtainable.

Now, from the point of view of economic efficiency, it is often better to employ specialised assets rather than general purpose ones. The related disadvantage illustrated above can be overcome if the operations involved are undertaken by a single firm. Asset specificity has thus been suggested as a major driver of **vertical integration** in organisations.

There are six different types of asset specificity.

(a) **Physical asset** specificity arises from unique physical properties, such as rare mineral deposits. It must be distinguished from dedicated assets (see below).

(b) **Dedicated asset** specificity arises in a man-made asset that has only one application, such as the 'Guppy' aircraft built to ferry Airbus wings from the UK to France.

(c) **Site** specificity arises from location: the airport kitchen we described earlier is a good example.

(d) **Human asset** specificity arises from skills or knowledge that is relevant to the requirements of a single organisation.

(e) **Temporal** specificity arises from an ability that is constrained to a given time, such as a landing slot at an airport.

(f) **Brand name** specificity is **brand equity** that is not susceptible to **brand extension**: that is, the value of the brand will deteriorate if it is spread over too many products. Any well-known motor manufacturer's brand would be an example.

3.3 Problems with hierarchies

Williamson also pointed out problems with the hierarchy approach. He noted the tendency of managers to pursue personal or systems objectives (such as control and growth) rather than the overall corporate objective; the continued existence of inefficiency traceable to monopolistic practices; the limits to organisational size; hierarchical complexity imposed by communication; and control difficulties in large bureaucracies.

3.4 Insights

Transaction cost analysis has some important insights for the way firms go about their business.

KEY POINT

(a) There is the tendency to **vertical integration** discussed above.

(b) **Resource-based strategy** can be supported by transaction cost ideas: the acquisition and exploitation of distinctive capabilities is an obvious route to lower costs and greater control when compared with the purchase of the same thing on the open market.

(c) The whole field of **outsourcing**, **network organisations** and **virtual organisations** is also susceptible to transaction cost analysis. In essence, it is logical to suggest that a business should examine all of its processes to see if any can be performed at less cost by external contractors, with due consideration being given to problems of control, security and asset specificity.

(d) The **divisional form of organisation** was supported by Williamson as tending to reduce both the size of the operating bureaucracy (several small ones instead of one huge one) and the scope for managers to pursue personal or systems goals.

Section summary

Transaction cost analysis compares the relative cost advantage of organising production on either a **market** or a **hierarchy** basis. It suggests that **asset specificity** may drive vertical integration and that outsourcing every activity that is not a core competence should be considered.

4 Mission

Introduction

An organisation should have a **vision** of what it is trying to achieve overall. Such a vision, or **strategic intent**, is a kind of overall aspiration, perhaps with emotional overtones. It sets the scene for the development of a clear idea of what the mission is.

4.1 What is 'mission'?

KEY TERM

MISSION 'describes the organisation's basic function in society, in terms of the products and services it produces for its clients' (Mintzberg).

A broader definition of mission could include the following **four elements**.

Elements	Comments
Purpose	Why does the organisation exist and for whom (eg shareholders)?
Strategy	Mission provides the operational logic for the organisation: • What do we do? • How do we do it?
Policies and standards of behaviour	Mission should influence what people actually do and how they behave: the mission of a hospital is to save lives, and this affects how doctors and nurses interact with patients.
Values	What the organisation believes to be important: that is, its principles.

4.2 Mission statements

KEY TERM

A MISSION STATEMENT is a generalised statement of the overriding purpose of the organisation. It should cover the **purpose**, **scope**, **strategy** and **principles** of the organisation.

Mission statements might be reproduced in a number of places, such as at the front of an organisation's annual report, on publicity material, in the chairman's office and in communal work areas. There is no standard format, but they should have certain qualities.

(a) **Brevity** will make them easier to understand and remember.
(b) **Flexibility** will enable them to accommodate change.
(c) They should be **distinctive**, to make the firm stand out.

According to **Hooley *et al*** (1992), a mission statement should:

(a) Provide a basis for consistent decision making
(b) Assist in translating direction into objectives suitable for assessment and control
(c) Provide a consistent purpose between different interest groups (stakeholders)
(d) Establish organisational goals and ethics
(e) Improve understanding and support from key groups outside the organisation

Scott Adams, creator of Dilbert, defines a mission statement as 'a long awkward sentence that demonstrates management's inability to think clearly'. This illustrates the main problem with mission statements, which is getting people to take them seriously.

4.3 The role of mission

Although the mission statement might be seen as a set of abstract principles, it plays an important role in the planning process.

(a) **Planning**. Objectives should be set that support the mission: if an objective is attained, the mission should be forwarded. At the corporate appraisal stage, mission is an essential element in the definition of just what constitutes a strength, weakness, opportunity or threat: any factor only qualifies in one of these categories if it relates as such to the furtherance of the mission.

(b) **Evaluation and screening**. Mission acts as a **yardstick** by which plans are judged. Take the example of a financial services organisation that runs a number of ethical investment funds that exclude from their portfolios shares in firms involved in alcohol, tobacco and armaments. If a new fund manager proposed to invest in shares of a diversified company, it would be examined to see if its activities included those that the investment fund considered unethical. The investment strategy would be assessed with reference to the investment fund's mission. Mission helps to ensure **consistency in decisions**.

(c) **Implementation**. Mission also affects the implementation of a planned strategy and can be embodied in the **policies and behaviour standards** of the firm.

There is a clear link here with the standard criteria for strategy evaluation: sustainability, acceptability and feasibility.

Section summary

A **vision** is an overall aspiration for the future, as is strategic intent. **Mission** includes both the organisation's value system and an answer to the question 'What business are we in?'. A mission (sometimes referred to as 'official goals') is often embodied in a mission statement.

Exam alert

You may be asked to consider mission in the context of a rational approach to formulating strategy.

As a rule of thumb, if you have any difficulty, ask yourself 'What and whom is this organisation for?' and possibly 'What does this organisation do?'.

Mission is covered in more detail in the E3 Study Text.

5 Goals, aims and objectives

Introduction

Goals and objectives are derived from mission and should support it. They provide the detail of what must be done if mission is to be achieved. There should be a **hierarchy of objectives** (or goal structure), cascading downwards from the general to the specific, each level supporting the one above.

5.1 The nature of goals and objectives

Different terminology is used in this area. We will distinguish between terms, for clarity.

KEY TERM

GOALS. 'The intentions behind decision or actions' (Henry Mintzberg) or 'a desired end result' (*Shorter Oxford English Dictionary*)

There are two types of goal.

(a) Non-operational, **qualitative** goals (**aims**). For example, a university's goal may be: 'To seek truth'. (You would not see: 'To increase truth by 5%'.)

(b) Operational, **quantitative** goals (**objectives**).

Characteristics	Example
Objectives are SMART • Specific • Measurable • Achievable • Relevant • Time-bounded	• Operational goal: cut costs • Objective: reduce budgeted expenditure on office stationery by 5% by 31 December 2014

Exam alert

There are numerous versions of the SMART criteria (specific; measurable; agreed; achievable; attainable; relevant; results-orientated; time-bound). Candidates should consider as wide a range of criteria as possible when answering exam questions.

Here is an example to help clarify the distinction between mission, goals and objectives.

(a) **Mission**: deliver a quality service

(b) **Goal**: enhance manufacturing quality

(c) **Objectives**: over the next 12 months, reduce the number of defects to one part per million

Note that not all goals can be easily measured, or can ever be attained completely. **Customer satisfaction** is a goal, but satisfying customers and ensuring that they remain satisfied is a **continuous process** that does not stop when one target has been reached.

Question 1B.4 Aims and objectives

Learning outcome A1a

Most organisations establish closed or quantifiable objectives. Give reasons why aims (non-operational goals) might still be important.

5.2 The purpose of organisational objective setting

'Objectives are needed in every area where performance and results directly and vitally affect the survival and prosperity of the business' (Drucker). Objectives in these key areas should support management in:

(a) **Planning**. Objectives are the targets that the plan aims to meet.

(b) **Responsibility**. Objectives are given to individuals and departments for which they have responsibility.

(c) **Integration**. If objectives are consistent then they should aid goal congruence within an organisation.

(d) **Motivation**. The setting of targets (especially when success is linked to promotion or bonuses) may increase motivation.

(e) **Evaluation**. Senior management control the business by evaluating the performance of the managers responsible for each of its divisions.

(Note the acronym **PRIME** for learning the above.)

5.3 The hierarchy of objectives

There is a **hierarchy of objectives**, with one primary corporate objective (restricted by certain constraints on corporate activity) and a series of subordinate objectives/goals that should combine to ensure the achievement of the overall objective.

5.3.1 Primary objectives

People might disagree on the choice of the overall corporate objective, although for a business it must be a **financial objective**, such as profitability, return on capital employed or earnings per share.

Profit, in its broadest sense, measures the creation of value, the relationship of inputs to outputs. It thus integrates cost behaviour and revenue performance for the whole organisation. Profit is also a key indicator for shareholders, and one of several measures that can be compared across organisations. However, profit has limitations as a measure of success.

(a) It is an **accounting convention** and is subject to technical **adjustment** and managerial **manipulation**.

(b) It is a **retrospective**, **annual measure**: it does not necessarily reflect current strategy and is anyway short term in its focus.

(c) It is of little use as a measure of success in the **early years** of a business venture (as is cash flow measures) because of the heavy investment normally required at this stage.

5.3.2 Secondary objectives

Secondary or subordinate goals and objectives support the primary goal. They can be listed under the following broad headings.

(a) **Market position**. Total market share of each market; growth of sales, customers or potential customers; the need to avoid relying on a single customer for a large proportion of total sales; what markets should the company be in?

(b) **Product development**. Bring in new products; develop a product range; investment in research and development; provide products of a certain quality at a certain price level.

(c) **Technology**. Improve productivity; reduce the cost per unit of output; exploit appropriate technology.

(d) **Employees and management**. Train employees in certain skills; reduce labour turnover; create an innovative, flexible culture; employ high-quality leaders.

Question 1B.5 Primary and secondary objectives

Learning outcome A1a

Review the list of secondary objectives above. How do you think each of them relates to financial objectives?

5.3.3 Objectives in not for profit organisations

Organisations such as charities and public sector organisations do not make a profit and, as such, have a different set of objectives to those set by commercial organisations. Objectives will not be based on profit achievement but rather on achieving a particular response from various target markets.

This also has implications for reporting of results. The organisation will need to be open and honest in showing how it has managed its budget and allocated funds raised.

One approach for the setting of objectives in this sector focuses on the Audit Commission's 3 Es approach, which we will look at below with the example of a police service.

(a) **Economy**. This focuses on inputs. For example, objectives may focus on reducing costs to a minimum. This might involve comparing the annual spend on providing training to police officers, or the amount spent per year on new uniforms or equipment.

(b) **Effectiveness**. This focuses on the outputs, ie the overall goals or objectives of the organisation. For the police service, this would involve looking at key targets, for example has the crime rate been reduced? What percentage of reported crimes have been solved?

(c) **Efficiency**. This focuses on the relationship between the inputs and the outputs, ie an efficient process would generate maximum outputs from minimal inputs. To achieve this, the organisation will require strong internal processes. For example, what was the average cost per arrest?

There are a number of different audiences that not for profit organisations may serve. The objective-setting process must **balance** the interests and concerns of these audiences, which may result in a **range of objectives**, rather than a single overriding one.

In addition, a not for profit organisation may face a number of other challenges in relation to the setting, and meeting, of their objectives:

(a) Providers of funds have potentially greater influence than members or beneficiaries and may have different objectives.

(b) There is no overall profit motive. There is often a conflict between delivering a profit and achieving social responsibilities.

(c) Priorities may change rapidly as circumstances change, such as when a natural disaster occurs or a government changes.

All the factors above make it easier for powerful insiders to pursue their personal objectives for power or recognition.

5.3.4 Strategy development in different contexts

CASE STUDY

Key differences between commercial and not for profit organisations

The following case study draws together the key differences between an organisation's mission, goals and objectives in both a commercial and not for profit setting.

	Commercial organisation	Not for profit organisation	Not for profit organisation
	Leading supermarket	*International charity (Stop Poverty)*	*(Top-tier international university)*
Mission	'Our mission is to be our customers' shop of choice providing them with a wide range of quality products, whilst also providing a great environment for our staff to work in'	'The charity's mission is to help improve the lives of people around the globe who are unable to help themselves'	'The university is committed to attracting the best students from around the world. We proudly recognise the diversity of our student body. It is our aim that all students realise their full potential'
Goals	'Our goal is improve the lives of customers and the communities in which we operate, through providing great service at reasonable prices'	'Our goal is to champion the rights of people everywhere to enjoy a better standard of living'	'Our goal is to is nurture our students through their studies and to help them to achieve the knowledge that will create the foundation for their future careers'
Objectives	Increase food sales by 5% over the next 12 months	To help move 300,000 people out of poverty over the next 12 months in some of the world's most impoverished regions	To increase the number of students attending from disadvantaged backgrounds by 1% over the next three years
Internal appraisal (internal strengths and weaknesses)	**Strengths.** Well-recognised brand image, that customers trust **Weakness.** Limited number of suitable internal candidates to promote to the board	**Strengths.** Strong established mechanisms in place for accepting donations (ie via the internet, mobiles, shop displays and own charity stores) **Weakness.** Charity shop operations are dependent on the use of volunteers; these individuals have no obligation to help	**Strengths.** Strong academic track record enables the university to access different types of funding **Weakness.** Limited number of student spaces available

	Commercial organisation	Not for profit organisation	Not for profit organisation
	Leading supermarket	*International charity (Stop Poverty)*	*(Top-tier international university)*
Environmental analysis (external threats and opportunities)	**Threat**. The growing emergence of discount retailers **Opportunities**. The continuing obesity epidemic in Western countries is increasing demand for healthier food products	**Threat**. Economic recession reducing the amount of disposable income that people are prepared to donate **Opportunities**. New mobile technologies allow for mobile donations to be taken	**Threat**. Increasing tuition fees in the university's home country may deter prospective students from applying **Opportunities**. Use the university's stature and recognisable image to establish satellite campuses around the world

The above illustration follows the strategic analysis stage from the rational model to strategic development. Although the organisations featured are pursuing different corporate aims, we can clearly see that in each case strategic development stems from the entities' overarching mission. Once the mission is set, goals and objectives are then formed. Objectives can be used by management in determining whether the organisation has achieved its stated objectives.

Once complete, this enables management to draw together the corporate appraisal, which details its strengths and weaknesses (driven by the organisation's internal capabilities) and its opportunities and threats (which come from the external environment). We consider the role of the corporate appraisal in more detail later in this Study Text.

At this point, senior management are now in a position to generate a range of strategic options.

5.3.5 Balanced scorecard

Kaplan and Norton suggested the **balanced scorecard** approach that looks at the business in four perspectives; performance in all must be satisfactory if the business is to prosper.

(a) The **financial perspective**, or 'how do we look to shareholders?'
(b) The **customer perspective**, or 'how do customers see us?'
(c) The **internal business perspective**, or 'what must we excel at?'
(d) The **innovation and learning perspective**, or 'can we continue to improve and create value?'

It is necessary for each business to set **goals** and establish **performance measures** for each perspective. Some will be fairly simple and traditional. For instance, shareholders will want to see their company survive and grow; suitable measures here might be cash generation and profits respectively. The internal perspective will vary widely between companies but will concentrate on efficiency goals and measures. Measuring customer satisfaction can be done in a variety of ways, such as counting complaints and starting a programme of interviews. The innovation and learning perspective will, perhaps, be the most difficult to handle. Kaplan and Norton give the example of an electronics company with several goals in this perspective; one is technology leadership and the chosen measure is how long it takes to develop a new generation of product.

5.4 Trade-off between objectives

When there are several key objectives, some might be achieved only at the expense of others. For example, attempts to achieve a good cash flow or good product quality, or to improve market share, might call for some sacrifice of profits.

There will be a trade-off between objectives when strategies are formulated, and a choice will have to be made. For example, there might be a choice between the following two options.

Option A 15% sales growth, 10% profit growth, a £2m negative cash flow and reduced product quality and customer satisfaction.

Option B 8% sales growth, 5% profit growth, a £500,000 surplus cash flow, and maintenance of high product quality/customer satisfaction.

If the firm chose Option B in preference to Option A, it would be trading off sales growth and profit growth for better cash flow, product quality and customer satisfaction. Note that the long-term effect of reduced quality has not been considered.

5.4.1 Long-term and short-term objectives

Objectives may be long term or short term.

(a) A company that is suffering from a recession in its core industries and making losses in the short term might continue to have a primary objective in the long term of achieving steady growth in earnings or profits, but in the short term its primary objective might switch to survival.

(b) Secondary objectives will range from the short term to the long term. Planners will formulate secondary objectives within the guidelines set by the primary objective, after selecting strategies for achieving the primary objective.

For example, a company's primary objective might be to increase its earnings per share from 30p to 50p over the next five years. Strategies for achieving the objective might include those below.

(a) Increasing profitability in the next 12 months by cutting expenditure
(b) Increasing export sales over the next 3 years
(c) Developing a successful new product for the domestic market within 5 years

Secondary objectives might then be reassessed.

(a) Improving manpower productivity by 10% within 12 months

(b) Improving customer service in export markets with the objective of doubling the number of overseas sales outlets in selected countries within the next 3 years

(c) Investing more in product-market research and development, with the objective of bringing at least 3 new products to the market within 5 years

5.4.2 Cyert and March's organisational coalition model

The American management writers Cyert and March suggest that traditional ideas on organisational objectives are too simplistic and do not recognise managerial and economic reality.

(a) The firm is **an organisational coalition** of stakeholders: shareholders, managers, employees, suppliers and customers.

(b) This network has **potentially competing goals and interests.** There is a need for 'political' compromise in establishing the goals of the firm. Each group must settle for less than it would ideally want to have. Shareholders must settle for less than maximum profits, managers for less than maximum utility, and so on.

(c) Organisations have **responsibilities** to (and constraints imposed by) various stakeholder groups. These may be **internal** considerations, based on stakeholder influence and the organisation's values. They may also be **external** considerations, such as legislation. (We will look at this further.)

Cyert and March conclude that 'organisations cannot have objectives, only people have objectives'.

5.4.3 How trade-offs are made

There are conflicts between different types of goals (eg long term vs short term). Daft indicates four ways of dealing with **goal conflict**.

(a) **Bargaining**. Managers with different goals will compete with each other, and will form alliances with other managers to achieve them.

(b) **Satisficing**. Organisations do not aim to maximise performance in one area if this leads to poor performance elsewhere. Rather they will accept satisfactory, if not excellent, performance in a number of areas.

(c) **Sequential attention**. Goals are dealt with one by one, as it were, in a sequence.

(d) **Priority setting**. Certain goals get priority over others. This is determined by senior managers, but there are quite complicated systems to rank goals and strategies according to certain criteria.

Question 1B.6 Trade-offs

Learning outcome A1a

What type of trade-off mechanisms are being used in the following cases?

(a) 'Next year, we'll flood the market with the stuff. But we've got to get the quality right first.'
(b) 'Don't bother about the third coat of varnish, as long as we get the job done by Saturday.'

5.5 Goal structure

If an organisation is to achieve its corporate objectives, the individuals and groups within it need goals that are relevant to their own roles, but that are co-ordinated with each other and that contribute towards overall objectives. There is said to be a 'cascade' of objectives from the organisational level to the individual level.

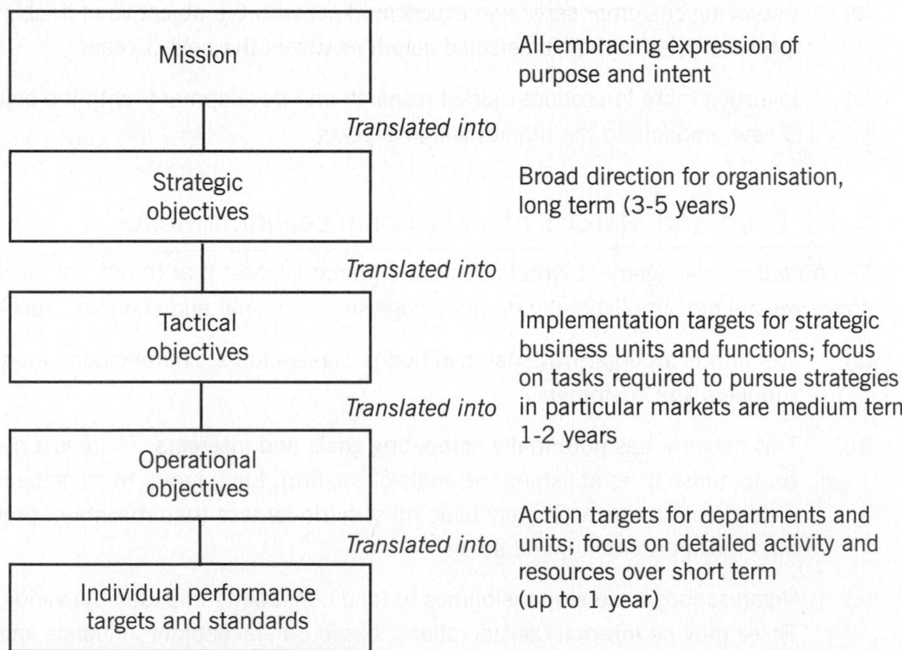

This flow-down of objectives and plans is designed to ensure:

(a) **Vertical alignment**. Lower-level objectives are designed to further corporate objectives and mission, so that there is unity of direction.

(b) **Horizontal alignment**. The objectives of different groups and functions dovetail with each other, so that there is co-ordinated effort, and so that the organisation presents a coherent and consistent face at its points of contact with the outside world.

5.5.1 Goal structure in action – management by objectives (MbO)

The diagram of the hierarchy of objectives above shows a cascade of objectives from the organisation to the individual. Integrating all these objectives is not always easy to achieve. However, a method of doing so was suggested by proponents of **management by objectives (MbO)** (originally, Peter Drucker).

Exam alert

Note that MbO is an 'integrating' topic: understanding the role that objectives play throughout modern organisations is very important from the point of view of your E2 studies, and is closely linked to the topics of managerial control and performance management, which are covered later in this Study Text.

MbO is a process whereby individual goals are integrated with the corporate plan, as part of an ongoing programme of goal setting and performance review involving all levels of management. The stages in developing such a programme are as follows.

Clarifying **organisational goals and objectives**. MbO will only be effective within the framework of a coherent strategic plan.

Collaboratively defining each individual's major **areas of responsibility** and their purpose within the corporate plan.

Jointly defining and agreeing the **key tasks** that are directly related to the achievement of objectives, and in which any performance shortfall would negatively impact on the organisation's effectiveness.

Jointly defining and agreeing **key results** (that must be achieved in order for the key tasks to be successfully performed and objectives met) and methods of monitoring and measuring performance in these areas.

Agreeing individual **performance improvement plans** for a defined planning period: selecting specific improvement objectives for each key task and formulating an action plan to achieve those objectives. This will include measures to be taken by the jobholder, resources to be provided by superiors (eg guidance and training) and dates for review.

Monitoring, self-evaluation and review of performance at agreed intervals, with revision of objectives, targets and action plans as required.

Periodic review of performance against individual improvement objectives and key results (reflected at the organisation level in a review of performance against the corporate plan).

A fresh cycle of planning and control would then continue the process.

5.5.2 Evaluating MbO

There are a number of **advantages** to an MbO programme.

(a) Clarifying organisational and sub-unit **goals**. This is crucial in establishing direction and co-ordination. It helps to focus organisation structures according to defined responsibilities. The goal clarification exercise may also encourage the flow of multidirectional communication and identify needs for innovation, change and development.

(b) Focusing organisational attention on **key tasks**, results and problem areas, for more efficient targeting of effort.

(c) Systematically converting strategic plans into **co-ordinated** managerial action plans and budgets. Each individual manager knows clearly what is expected of them, while retaining a big-picture perspective and unity of purpose.

(d) Securing the **commitment** of individuals to defined targets and areas of accountability, as well as potentially improving morale and motivation through greater involvement and discretion in performing tasks (within defined targets).

(e) **Systematic information** for managerial planning and control, individual performance appraisal, reward and development planning.

There are **disadvantages** too.

(a) Potential **rigidity**. Individual objectives must be set and, once set, are not changed because the overall plan is difficult to revise. There must be **flexibility**, especially:

  (i) In flexible working environments where individual 'jobs' are no longer rigidly defined

  (ii) Where individual results are less relevant (or measurable) because of team working

  (iii) Where a less hierarchical management authority structure is preferred (eg self-managed team working)

  (iv) Where jobs are less amenable to measurement and the setting of specific quantitative targets (eg interpersonal roles such as counselling)

(b) Potential requirement for a significant **change** in attitudes, the style of leadership and organisation structure. This may involve time and labour costs of change management – and may ultimately be unsuccessful if not supported (and sustained) by senior management.

(c) Potential for **conflict** and demotivation. Staff may perceive increasing accountability for defined results as a command and control pressure tactic, thinly disguised as involvement/empowerment.

5.6 Critical success factors (CSFs)

This topic is covered in more detail in the E3 Study Text.

KEY TERM

CRITICAL SUCCESS FACTORS (CSFs) are a small number of areas in which (a) satisfactory results will enable successful competitive performance and (b) an organisation **must** excel in order to outperform competition. Control and improvement can be achieved by setting **key performance indicators (KPIs)** in these areas, and monitoring progress against targets.

As an alternative to a systematic goal-structured approach, an organisation may focus on CSFs. Having determined its competitive strategy, the organisation identifies those factors that are essential and effective in delivering competitive advantage (CSFs). It can then identify the business processes and activities that yield each CSF: this focuses on the organisation's core competences. For each of these processes and activities, KPIs can be defined in order to evaluate and measure performance in delivering the CSFs.

5.6.1 CSF analysis

Johnson and Scholes describe six stages in the process of managing strategy using CSFs.

Identify the **CSFs**. This will require both experience of the organisation and its activities, and sound judgement. The emphasis is not on what activities must be undertaken, but on what must be achieved in broad terms. Johnson and Scholes recommend that the number of CSFs identified should be restricted to six or fewer.

Identify the **competences** that must be displayed if the CSFs are to be achieved. Note that the emphasis has now changed from what must be achieved (CSFs) to the special skills and processes that will enable the required achievement (core competences).

The core competences identified must then be considered to determine whether they are adequate to provide genuine **competitive advantage**, or whether they must be improved or supplemented.

A **KPI** must be identified for each competence so that strategic control may be exercised.

When we discussed **resource-based strategy** earlier, we noted that core competences were defined as 'the skills and abilities by which resources are deployed through an organisation's activities and processes such as to achieve competitive advantage in ways that others cannot imitate or obtain'. The fifth step is to ensure that this is, in fact, the case. If it is not, competitive advantage will not be achieved.

Competitors' responses must be monitored and their effects on the CSF structure forecast.

Section summary

Goals give flesh to the mission. They can be quantified (**objectives**) or not quantified (**aims**). Most organisations use a combination of both. Quantified or specific objectives have **SMART** characteristics.

There is a **hierarchy of objectives**. A primary objective of a business might be profit; secondary objectives relate to ways to achieve it.

Objectives are sometimes in **conflict**. In such a case, managers can adopt four ways of reconciling them.

- Internal bargaining
- Satisficing
- Sequential attention
- Priority setting

The term **goal structure** is given to the hierarchy of objectives whereby mission flows down to strategic objectives, which in turn are translated into tactical, operational and individual objectives.

Techniques have been suggested to break down organisational goals into targets for departments and individuals. **Management by objectives** is one such technique.

The identification of **critical success factors (CSFs)** provides a flexible basis for identifying strategic goals, as an alternative to a comprehensive hierarchy of objectives.

6 Implementation

Introduction

The formulation of strategic plans is one thing: implementing them is quite another. **It is impossible to plan for every eventuality**. Some decisions of strategic importance may not be anticipated in the strategic plan. Implementation often involves adjusting the plan in the light of changed conditions.

The relative abstraction of the strategy is made real by the work of many individuals, sometimes in isolation, sometimes in small teams, sometimes in large organisational formations.

KEY POINT

Implementation of strategy is a ground level issue. An organisation has to decide how its resources are deployed.

(a) At **corporate level** (between different businesses)
(b) At **unit level** (between functions, departments and so forth)

6.1 Resource planning

Resource planning involves allocating the resources (and identifying potential resources) of the undertaking in order that the defined and agreed corporate objectives may be achieved. At operational level, there are four stages in resource planning.

(a) Establishing currently available and currently obtainable resources (by category) and details of any that are not available or readily obtainable – making a resource audit

(b) Estimating what resources would be needed to pursue a particular strategy and deciding whether there would be enough resources to pursue it successfully

(c) Assigning responsibilities to managers for the acquisition, use and control of resources

(d) Identifying all constraints and factors exerting an influence on the availability and use of resources (internal and external environments)

Resource plans can be prepared in detail, providing organisations know what they need to achieve.

(a) **CSFs** 'are those factors on which the strategy is fundamentally dependent for its success'.

(b) **Key tasks** are what must be done to ensure each CSF is achieved.

(c) **Priorities** indicate the order in which tasks are achieved.

6.2 Operations planning

Linneman says operations planning has two aspects.

(a) Deciding what is to be accomplished, by whom and when, and at what cost
(b) Setting up control points and methods of measuring and monitoring performance

This planning process spans plans at the corporate level, for product-market areas (subsidiaries or divisions), for functional areas and for lower echelons of management.

Operations plans are relatively short. Major items would need to be quantified – such as sales, cost of sales, operating profit, other income, non-current asset details, inventory levels, working capital investment and production targets (if appropriate). Budgets add flesh and muscle to the bones of these skeleton operations plans.

Plans for functional departments must also be prepared, below the overall corporate level. In a manufacturing company, major functional plans will be for **marketing** and **production**.

6.3 Review and control

Successful implementation of the corporate plan demands the continued interest of senior management.

(a) Strategic plans must be converted into action plans (ie operations plans and budgets).

(b) Responsibilities must be allocated and authority given to individual managers to use resources (eg spend money sufficient to allow them to achieve their individual targets).

(c) Checkpoints must be established to monitor activities.

(d) Pressure must be exerted for control action where necessary, to ensure that things get done according to the aims of the corporate plan.

Control checkpoints or milestones should monitor factors such as those below.

(a) Have deadlines been met and are future deadlines going to be met?

(b) Are any targets in danger of being missed?

(c) Will the required resources be available to make the products/services?

(d) Will the products be available in sufficient numbers to achieve the aims of the product-market plan?

A control system requires organisation.

(a) The responsibilities of divisions, departments and individual managers must be documented.

(b) Responsibility charts for managers at divisional, departmental and subordinate levels must be prepared.

(c) Activity schedules for managers at divisional, departmental and subordinate levels must be prepared.

Section summary

Implementation requires detailed planning and hands-on management of resources and operations. Progress and performance must be properly measured and reported.

Chapter Summary

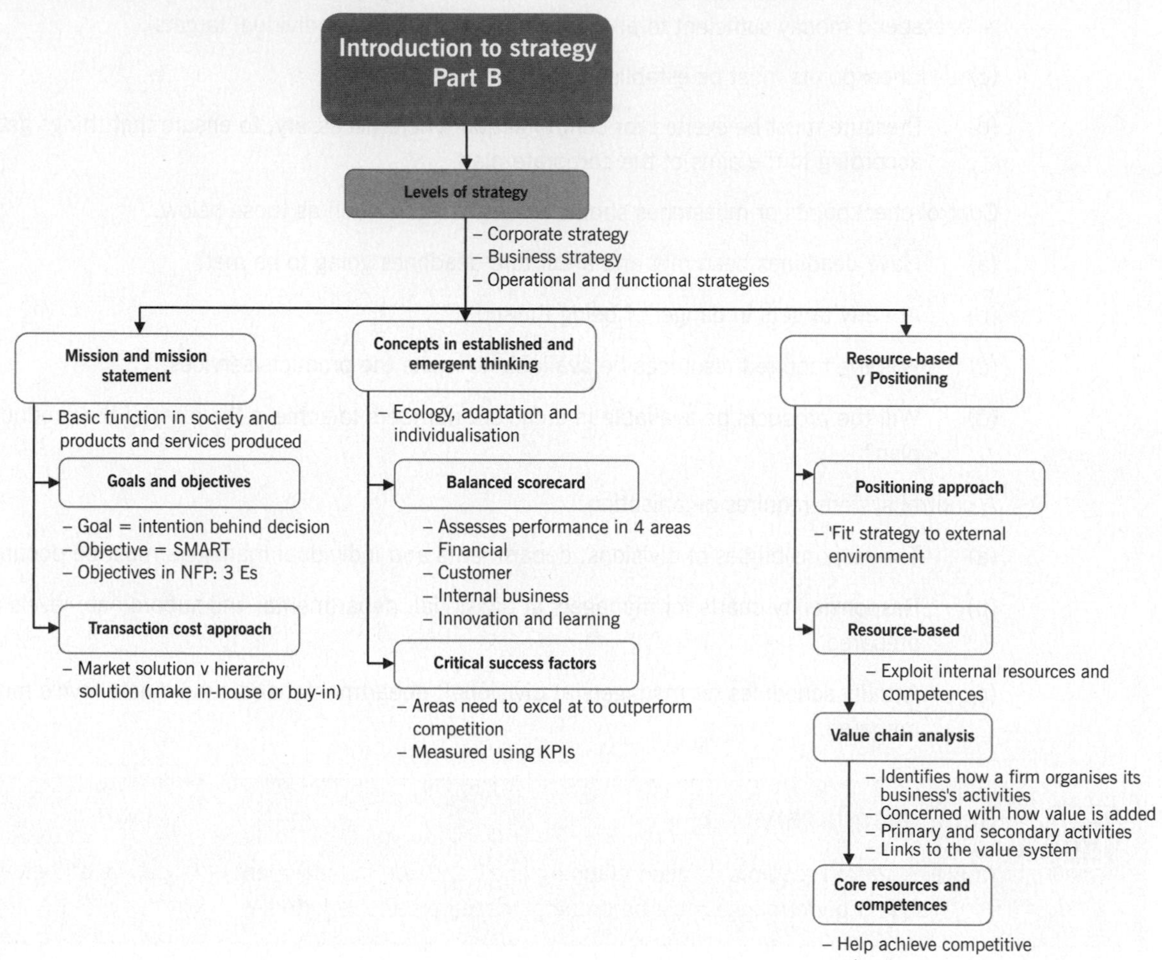

Introduction to strategy Part B
Levels of strategy
– Corporate strategy
– Business strategy
– Operational and functional strategies
Mission and mission statement
– Basic function in society and products and services produced
Goals and objectives
– Goal = intention behind decision
– Objective = SMART
– Objectives in NFP: 3 Es
Transaction cost approach
– Market solution v hierarchy solution (make in-house or buy-in)
Concepts in established and emergent thinking
– Ecology, adaptation and individualisation
Balanced scorecard
– Assesses performance in 4 areas
– Financial
– Customer
– Internal business
– Innovation and learning
Critical success factors
– Areas need to excel at to outperform competition
– Measured using KPIs
Resource-based v Positioning
Positioning approach
– 'Fit' strategy to external environment
Resource-based
– Exploit internal resources and competences
Value chain analysis
– Identifies how a firm organises its business's activities
– Concerned with how value is added
– Primary and secondary activities
– Links to the value system
Core resources and competences
– Help achieve competitive advantage

Quick Quiz

1 Complete the statement below by using one of the list of phrases given in brackets.

'A strategy of vertical integration is likely to be supported by …'

(core competences; bounded rationality; transaction cost analysis; system goals)

2 An approach to strategy that works 'from the inside out, seeking to identify strategic activities for which the organisation is best equipped', is called:

A A positioning approach

B A resource-based approach

3 'Procurement is a primary activity in the value chain.' True or false?

4 What do you understand by the acronym SMART?

5 How must objectives be interlocked?

Answers to Quick Quiz

1 Transaction cost analysis

2 B This is a resource-based approach.

3 False Procurement is a support activity.

4 Specific, measurable, achievable, relevant, time-bounded

5 Vertically; horizontally (across departments); over time

Answers to Questions

1B.1 Levels of strategy

The corporate objective is profit growth. The corporate strategy is the decision that this will be achieved by entering new markets, rather than producing new products. The business strategy suggests that those markets include Latin America. The operational or functional strategy involves the decision to invest in new plant (the production function) which is to be financed by shares rather than loans (the finance function).

1B.2 Resource-based strategy

Much strategic thinking is based on adapting the organisation's characteristics to match the demands of its environment; that is, to the exploitation of opportunities and the avoidance of threats. The resource-based approach shifts the emphasis towards the organisation's strengths and weaknesses, and proceeds on the basis that competitive advantage comes from the possession of **scarce resources** and the exploitation of **unique competences**.

This approach is therefore equally applicable to organisations that have **favoured access** to material resources such as vital raw materials; those that possess a specific but intangible protected **intellectual property** such as a patent on a drug; and those whose advantage consists of the **experience and expertise of its staff and the capabilities of its systems**. The advantage of firms in the last category is based on what are now known as **core competences**. Apple is often cited as an example of a firm that creates industries through leverage of core competences in innovation and design of mobile devices, eg iPhone, iPad and iPod.

Johnson and Scholes define core competences as those that both **outperform competitors** and are **difficult to imitate**. Organisations must achieve an acceptable or **threshold** level of competence in all their activities, but it is core competences that give a lasting competitive edge. Indeed, the exploitation of such core competences is potentially a more durable source of competitive advantage than more specific assets such as raw materials and intellectual property. Raw material sites become exhausted and patents expire, but good management can maintain a technical lead almost indefinitely, by paying proper attention to innovation and the nurturing of what the firm does well.

Possible **disadvantages** of a resource-based strategy include the following.

(a) The difficulty of assessing core competences
(b) The risk of losing skills that fall within core competences if staff leave
(c) Investors may prefer a strategy of exploiting existing markets

Farmers supermarkets: resources and core competences

We do not have a great deal of information on Farmers supermarkets, other than that it is a very successful supermarket chain with a large share of its domestic market. We know that it is customer focused; provides value for money; is operationally efficient; and uses the latest technology. It is also innovative and has launched internet shopping services and clothing ranges.

We might, if we were pushed, make some tentative suggestions about the firm's resources and core competences.

(a) **Costs**

Farmers' size should give it extensive purchasing power and enable it to achieve significant **economies of scale** even though the company is recognised as paying its suppliers better prices for produce than its rivals.

(b) **Customer focus**

Customer focus is valuable in any business, but it is essential in a retailer; the examples of Woolworths, Comet and Blockbuster illustrate what happens when previously successful retailers lose touch with their customers. As Farmers is committed to good customer service, this should show in such areas as: continuing successful new product development, a high degree of customer satisfaction and differentiated product offerings in geographical areas that vary in socio-demographic make-up.

(c) **Technology**

Farmers is keen to innovate, and uses the latest technology. This does not just have the potential to cut costs, as in Wal-Mart's introduction of radio frequency identification tags; it also has the potential to achieve important improvements in customer focus through the use of **loyalty cards**. Effective use of this technology is very difficult, simply because of the volume of data involved, but Tesco has used it with great success in such areas as targeted price cuts, response to emerging preferences and effective promotions.

(d) **Innovation**

Farmers' customer focus has no doubt helped it in its introduction of new products that challenge traditional notions of what the grocery business is about. Introduction of more new products and new product categories is an obvious route to continued turnover growth. We may assess the ability to make regular and successful product launches to be a core competence of the organisation and one that it should sustain and exploit.

1B.3 Activities

B. Human resource management

1B.4 Aims and objectives

Aims can be just as helpful: customer satisfaction, for example, is not something that is achieved just once. Some goals are hard to measure and quantify, for example 'to retain technological leadership'. Quantified objectives are hard to change when circumstances change, as changing them looks like an admission of defeat: aims may support greater flexibility.

1B.5 Primary and secondary objectives

(a) Markets are customers. Customers are sources of revenue. Markets are where organisations compete with each other. Gaining market share now helps future profitability – but may be expensive in the short term.

(b) Product development is another way of competing, to make profits to satisfy the corporate objectives.

(c) Technology and (d) employees and management relate to organising the production process, making operations efficient and effective.

1B.6 Trade-offs

(a) Sequential attention
(b) Satisficing

Now try these questions from the Practice Question Bank

Question	Level
1B.1 – 1B.5	Practice
Mission statement	Practice

GENERAL ENVIRONMENT

In the last two chapters we considered models of strategy and managing strategy. Now we move on to look at the **external environment** in which the organisation is managed.

Organisations interact with their environment, and you should expect the environment to have a significant effect on the organisation. The rational model of strategy making includes an analysis of the environment, and is highly dependent on this information to make decisions. Other strategy models are less formal in their use of this knowledge but will use it as they emerge/muddle through or make incremental decisions.

PEST is the best known of the external environmental analyses. It scans the environment by considering political, economic, social and technological factors. Variants on PEST include **PESTEL**, which adds environmental and legal factors. A **LoNGPEST** analysis views PEST factors from three levels: local, national and global.

Stakeholder **mapping** considers the stakeholders who are the constituency of the organisation. They have an influence on and an interest in what the organisation does.

In Section 7, on **the competitive advantage of a nation's industries**, we learn how the domestic origins of an industry can affect its competitive success. The chapter finishes with an exploration of new and emerging markets.

Topic list	Learning outcomes	Syllabus references	Ability required
1 Relating the organisation to its environment	A2a	A2(i), (ii)	Comprehension
2 The political and legal environment	A2a	A2(iii), (iv)	Comprehension
3 The economic environment	A2a	A2(i)	Comprehension
4 The social and cultural environment	A2a	A2(i)	Comprehension
5 The technological environment	A2a	A2(i)	Comprehension
6 Stakeholder goals and objectives	A2a	A2(i)	Comprehension
7 The competitive advantage of a nation's industries – Porter's diamond	A2a	A1(v), (vi)	Comprehension

Chapter Overview

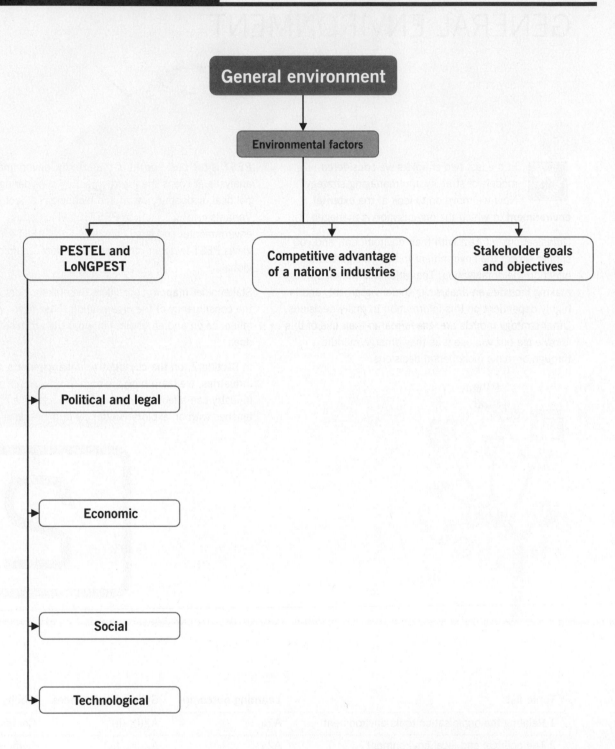

General environment
- Environmental factors
  - PESTEL and LoNGPEST
    - Political and legal
    - Economic
    - Social
    - Technological
  - Competitive advantage of a nation's industries
  - Stakeholder goals and objectives

1 Relating the organisation to its environment

Introduction

It is usual to consider an organisation as having boundaries that separate it from its environment. You must remember that it can be useful to regard the organisation and environment as inextricably linked to one another in a wide range of ways. This is consistent with the modern emphasis on stakeholders, organisational networks and the strategic importance of human resource management.

Exam alert

The use of PEST and stakeholder analysis could be examined in the context of a scenario question. It is important that you are happy with the key concepts covered in this chapter, as you may be required to use your knowledge of these models when attempting longer-form objective test questions.

1.1 Environmental factors

Organisations exist within an environment which strongly influences what they do and whether they survive and develop. Strategic planners must take account of potential environmental impacts in order to produce plans that are realistic and achievable. Where international or even global operations are undertaken, it is important to understand that there may be important differences between the environments present in the various regions and countries involved.

The environment of an organisation is everything outside its boundaries. It may be segmented according to the diagram below.

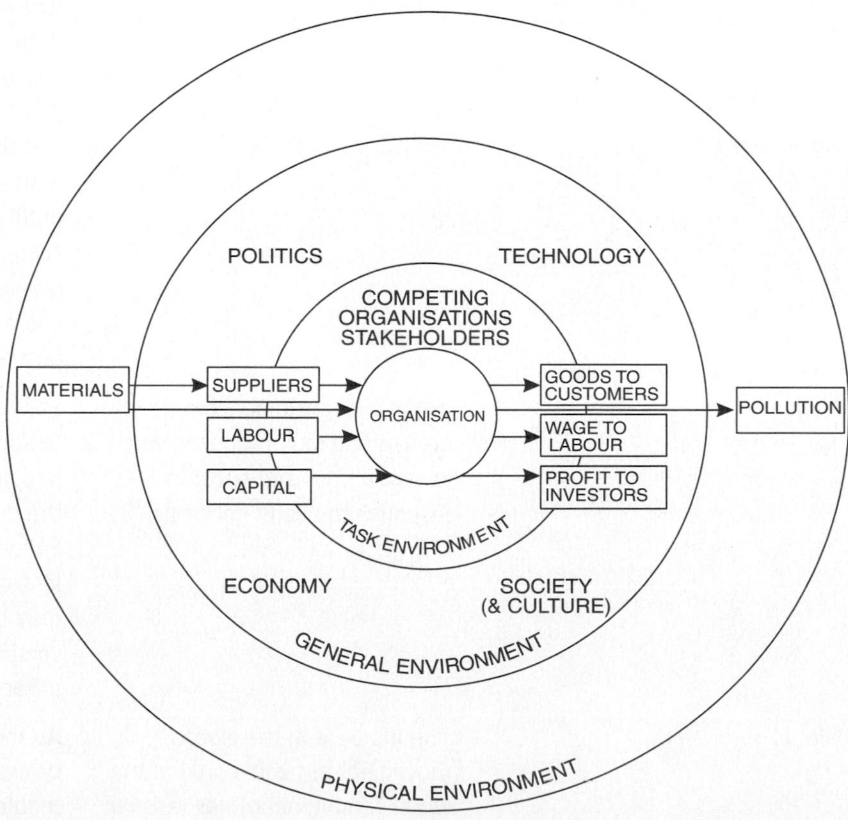

KEY TERMS

The **GENERAL ENVIRONMENT** covers all the political/legal, economic, social/cultural and technological (**PEST**) influences in the countries an organisation operates in.

The **TASK ENVIRONMENT** relates to factors of particular relevance to a firm, such as its competitors, customers and suppliers of resources.

The mnemonic PEST is often used in environmental analysis. **PEST** stands for political, economic, social and technological; legal matters are considered under the political heading, and cultural matters under the social heading. Increasing public concern for the natural environment and corporate sensitivity about protest groups has led in recent years to the inclusion of a second 'E' in the mnemonic, to stand for environment. This has given rise to new arrangements such as **STEEPLE** and **PESTEL**.

The PEST model can also be extended to create a **LoNGPEST** analysis. A LoNGPEST analysis considers the traditional PEST factors that impact an organisation, but views them at three different levels: local, national and global. This method is particularly useful for management when attempting to understand the key external influences on the organisation. Once the influences that are considered most important are known, the decision on how to respond can be made.

Below is an example of LoNGPEST analysis covering social factors applied to the Farmers supermarket chain. The Farmers case study can be found in the front of this Study Text.

Level	Social issue	Impact on organisation
Local (individual store)	Customers demand fresh produce to be available in-store bought from local farms.	The Farmers supermarket may choose to exploit this opportunity by building new relationships with local suppliers to stock locally grown produce. Alternatively, Farmers may choose to concentrate on offering products purchased from large suppliers that can be sold at lower prices due to the chain's ability to achieve economies of scale. However, this seems unlikely, given the company's commitment to supporting UK farmers.
National	In the UK, customers are now demanding food products with lower salt, fat and sugar in response to health concerns.	Farmers supermarkets may need to source its products from more suppliers committed to reducing the reliance on such ingredients. Failure to do so may result in a loss of customers. Equally, there may be scope to offer healthier versions of existing products to attract shoppers.
Global	The increase in the global movement of people around the world (immigration) has resulted in a more diverse range of shoppers visiting the supermarket's stores.	An increase in the ethnic diversity of shoppers is likely to require a broader range of 'world foods' to be stocked in every store to appeal to buyers.

Exam alert

The PEST model is a useful checklist for general environmental factors – remember that in the real world they are **interlinked**, and any given environmental development is likely to qualify under two or more of the PEST or PESTEL headings.

1.2 Environmental fit

One approach to strategy is to seek **environmental fit**, relating a company to its environment.

Any strategy is made in conditions of **partial ignorance**. The environment is a major cause of such 'ignorance'.

(a) It contains **opportunities and threats** that may influence the organisation's activities and may even threaten its existence.

(b) The environment is sometimes so **varied** that many organisations will find it difficult to discern its effects on them.

(c) Firms can conduct **audits** to identify which of the many different sorts of environmental factors have had a significant influence.

(d) Environmental conditions **change**.

1.3 Complexity and dynamism

Johnson and Scholes contrast the concepts of **environmental complexity** (how many influences and the interrelationships between them) and **environmental dynamism** (the rate of change).

Together, complexity and dynamism create **uncertainty**.

1.3.1 The strategic impact of uncertainty

A high degree of uncertainty can have an important impact on the strategic management of a business.

(a) There is likely to be a wish for **more and better information** in order to enhance the likelihood of making useful forecasts. The difficulty of achieving this is likely to lead to a **close planning time horizon**.

(b) Decisive moves to new strategies are unlikely: strategy is likely to be **conservative**, and new ideas may only appear as **emergent strategies**.

1.4 Time horizon

You should bear in mind which environmental issues are of:

- **Long-term impact**, which can be dealt with in advance
- **Short-term impact**, which require crisis management

1.5 Environmental interactions

We will use the PEST approach to give structure to much of the rest of this chapter. It is very important that you understand that **this framework is merely one of convenience**.

Environmental influences on business do not appear in neatly packaged groups: they interact and take effect in complex ways. A good example is the way in which **government policy affects economic factors**. Policy is by definition a political matter, but it is inevitable that economic conditions and developments will be heavily influenced by policy developments. Similarly, policy itself is likely to evolve in the face of demographic change or the development of opinion in society.

Advanced nations are currently very concerned about the ageing of their populations, for example, while the growth of concern over green issues has led to subsidy for power generation that does not produce carbon dioxide.

Section summary

The environment exists outside an organisation's boundaries, and organisations survive and prosper in this context. To secure **environmental fit**, an analysis of the environment is therefore required. PEST and LoNGPEST are useful mnemonics to discuss these issues. Uncertainty in the environment arises from complexity and dynamism.

2 The political and legal environment

Introduction

The **political environment** affects the firm in a number of ways.

- A basic legal framework generally exists.
- The Government can take a particular stance on an issue of direct relevance to a business or industry.
- The Government's overall conduct of its economic policy is relevant to business.

Exam alert

PEST analysis is a useful tool to employ as an initial survey of conditions and options. But remember that the real world doesn't have neatly defined categories like a model does; for example, political and economic factors often overlap. This may be a particularly useful model to use when attempting your Management Level integrated case study, to help generate ideas, but do not be too concerned with attributing factors to a specific category: identifying relevant factors is more important.

2.1 The political and legal environment

Laws come from common law, parliamentary legislation and government regulations derived from it, and obligations under treaties such as those establishing the European Union (EU).

Some legal factors affect all companies, for example tax law (corporation tax, sales tax and income tax); employment law; health and safety law; and company law that governs directors and their duties, reporting requirements, takeover proceedings and shareholders' rights.

CASE STUDY

The Competition and Markets Authority

The activity of the Competition and Markets Authority in the UK is a good example of the way governments may approach the problem of monopoly. The Competition and Markets Authority (CMA) has the power to investigate if it appears that competition is being prevented, distorted or restricted in a particular market. The Secretary of State may do the same if any proposed takeover or merger would create a firm that controlled 25% or more of the market and where a merger appears to lead to a substantial lessening of competition in one or more markets. The Authority will then investigate the proposed merger or takeover and recommend whether or not it should be allowed to proceed.

Source:

Competition and Markets Authority (2014) *Mergers Guidance on the CMA's jurisdiction and procedure*. [Online]. Available from: https://www.gov.uk/government/uploads/system/uploads/attachment_data/file/384055/CMA2__Mergers__Guidance.pdf [Accessed 27 September 2016].

Other legal and regulatory factors affect **particular industries**, where the public interest is served by doing so. For example, electricity, gas, telecommunications, water and rail transport are subject to **regulators** (Ofgem, Ofcom, Ofwat, ORR) which have influence over market access, competition and pricing policy (they can restrict price increases).

This is because either:

- The industries are, effectively, monopolies; or
- Large sums of public money are involved (eg in subsidies to rail companies).

2.2 The impact of government

Porter notes several ways whereby the **Government** can directly affect the **economic structure** of an industry. They are explained below.

Capacity expansion	Government policy can encourage firms to increase or cut their capacity. (a) The UK tax system offers 'capital allowances' to encourage investment in equipment. (b) A variety of incentives, funded by the EU and national governments, exist for locating capacity in a particular area. (c) **Incentives** are used to encourage investment by overseas firms. Different countries in the EU have 'competed' for investment from Japan, for example.
Demand	(a) The Government is a major customer. (b) Government can also influence demand by legislation, tax reliefs or subsidies.
Divestment and rationalisation	In some European countries, the State takes many decisions regarding the selling-off or closure of businesses, especially in sensitive areas such as defence.
Emerging industries	Can be promoted by the Government or damaged by it.
Entry barriers	Government policy can discourage firms from entering an industry, by restricting investment or competition or by making it harder, by use of quotas and tariffs, for overseas firms to compete in the domestic market.

Competition		
	(a)	The Government's **purchasing decisions** will have a strong influence on the strength of one firm relative to another in the market (eg armaments).
	(b)	**Regulations and controls** in an industry will affect the growth and profits of the industry – eg minimum product quality standards.
	(c)	As a supplier of **infrastructure** (eg roads), the Government is also in a position to influence competition in an industry.
	(d)	Governments and supra-national institutions such as the EU might impose policies that keep an industry **fragmented**, and prevent the concentration of too much market share in the hands of one or two producers.

In some industries, governments regulate the adoption of **new products**. This is well illustrated by the **pharmaceuticals industry**, where new drugs or medicines must in many countries undergo stringent testing and obtain government approval before they can be marketed.

National and EU institutions also affect the operating activities of some organisations, for example:

- Anti-discrimination legislation
- Health and safety legislation
- **Product safety and standardisation** (especially EU standards)
- Workers' rights (eg unfair dismissal, maternity leave)
- Training and education policies (which can determine the 'standard' of recruits)

Question 2.1 Government impact

Learning outcome A2a

List five ways in which government policy affects the pharmaceutical industry in your country.

2.3 Influencing government

Businesses are able to influence government policies in a number of ways.

(a) They can employ **lobbyists** to put their case to individual ministers or civil servants.

(b) They can give MPs **non-executive directorships**, in the hope that the MP will take an interest in all legislation that affects them.

(c) They can try to **influence public opinion**, and hence the legislative agenda, by advertising.

Of particular importance is the need to influence the decision-making processes of the European Commission. EU regulations, for practical purposes, take priority over national law. They are arrived at after a great deal of negotiation and, for this reason alone, are difficult to change. It is therefore much better to influence the **drafting process** of new regulations than to try to get them changed once they have been implemented.

The EU will have an increasing role in the conduct of **European businesses** in:

(a) Product standards
(b) Environmental protection
(c) Monetary policy (the **European Central Bank** might set interest rates)
(d) Research and development
(e) Regional policy
(f) Labour costs (wages and pensions)

2.4 Political risk and political change

Changes in UK law are often predictable. A government will publish a **green paper** discussing a proposed change in the law, before issuing a **white paper** and passing a bill through Parliament. Plans should be formulated about what to do if the change takes place.

The political environment is not simply limited to legal factors. Government policy affects the whole **economy**, and governments are responsible for enforcing and creating a **stable framework** in which business can be done. A report by the World Bank indicated that the quality of **government policy is important in providing the right**:

(a) Physical infrastructure (eg transport)
(b) Social infrastructure (education, a welfare safety net, law enforcement)
(c) Market infrastructure (enforceable contracts, policing corruption)

However, it is **political change** that complicates the planning activities of many firms. Many economic forecasts ignore the implications of a change in government policy.

(a) At **national level**, political influence is significant and includes legislation on trading, pricing, dividends, tax and employment as well as health and safety (to list but a few).

(b) Politics at **international level** also has a direct bearing on organisations. EU directives affect all countries in the EU.

The **political risk** in a decision is the risk that political factors will invalidate the strategy and perhaps severely damage the firm. Examples are wars, political chaos and regime change, social unrest, corruption and nationalism.

2.4.1 Political risk checklist

A political risk checklist was outlined by Jeannet and Hennessey. Companies should ask the following six questions.

(1) How stable is the host country's political system?

(2) How strong is the host Government's commitment to specific rules of the game, such as ownership or contractual rights, given its ideology and power position?

(3) How long is the Government likely to remain in power?

(4) If the present Government is succeeded, how would the specific rules of the game change?

(5) What would be the effects of any expected changes in the specific rules of the game?

(6) In the light of those effects, what decisions and actions should be taken now?

It is also important to remember that there are many countries that do not conform to the Western model of the **rule of law**. Political power may well be extra legal, with the legal system being manipulated or even ignored by government or by other powerful groups such as political parties.

Question 2.2 Political risk

Learning outcome A2a

For a business of your choice, identify the most significant areas of political risk.

2.5 Globalisation

KEY TERM

GLOBALISATION refers to the growing interdependence of countries worldwide through increased trade, increased capital flows and the rapid diffusion of technology.

In this section we consider the factors that led to the globalisation of world trade and the implications this has had on the wider political and economic environment.

You may be familiar with the term 'globalisation', as it has been a common term in the business world over the last 30 years. It is focused on the growing convergence of national cultures, economies and political systems.

Features of globalisation include:

(a) The ability of individuals to enter into transactions with individuals and organisations based in other countries

(b) The increased importance of global economic policy relative to domestic policy

(c) The rise of globally linked and dependent financial markets

(d) The reduction in importance of local manufacturing

(e) Reduced transaction costs through the developments in communications and transport

(f) The rise of emerging, newly industrialised nations

2.5.1 Factors encouraging the globalisation of world trade

(a) Financial factors such as debt of developing countries. Often, lenders require the initiation of economic reforms as a condition of the loan.

(b) Country/continent alliances. Earlier in this chapter we discussed the impact of bodies such as the EU on organisations.

(c) Legal factors such as patents and trademarks, which encourage the development of technology and design.

(d) Markets trading in international commodities. Commodities are not physically exchanged, only the rights to ownership. A buyer can, thanks to efficient systems of trading and communications, buy a commodity in its country of origin for delivery to a specific port.

2.5.2 International trade

The political environment is of particular importance in **international trade**. Such trade is governed by an extra layer of legislation contained in treaties and agreements, and is potentially subject to a **higher level of political risk**. This may be manifested in a variety of ways, such as taxation law, labour regulation and economic policy on such matters as ownership. At worst, there is a threat of expropriation or nationalisation. Failure to repress lawlessness and corruption are further complicating factors, as is open or covert refusal to consider international bidders for government contracts.

2.6 Global business regulation

The wider political and legal environment interacts with the immediate task environment in the sphere of business regulation. Here, industry-specific rules are laid down and enforced.

Braithwaite and Drahos, in their book *Global Business Regulation*, discuss the way that the development of globally effective regulation has taken place. They argue that, while laws are passed by national legislatures, the rules they embody are actually created by discussion, negotiation and agreement among a **variety of expert bodies** including states, corporations and international bodies.

The emergence of global regulation does not necessarily march in step with the globalisation of either markets or business organisations. Gambling, for example, via the internet, is a global market, but it is regulated in different ways by different states. By contrast, regulations relating to prescription drugs are now largely global in effect, but national markets are kept isolated from one another by differences in government policy on medicine as a welfare benefit. Pharmaceutical firms, however, are among the best-established of global businesses.

2.6.1 Common features in global regulation

The processes that result in developments in global regulation are complex and vary from industry to industry. But some common features emerge.

(a) **Power of individual countries**. The **US** has huge influence over the globalisation of regulation; the **EU** is beginning to have similar influence. Among individual countries, the **UK** is second to the US in influence.

(b) **International organisations** such as the World Trade Organization, the International Monetary Fund (IMF) and the International Chamber of Commerce also have extensive power to influence the development of regulations.

(c) **US corporations** are very effective at enrolling the power of their own government and international bodies to promote their interests. For example, at one time, the technical committees of the International Telecommunications Union nearly all had chairmen and vice-chairmen that had been nominated by US companies. As a result, US-patented systems became global standards.

(d) Change in global regulatory regimes often results from two contrasting sequences: the proactive and the reactive.

  (i) The **proactive** sequence involves the promotion of regulatory innovation to one or more early mover organisations: these organisations will initially suffer a cost disadvantage but if the new standard is globalised, they will enjoy early mover benefits.

  (ii) The **reactive** sequence starts with a disaster, followed by media hypes and public unrest: subsequent adoption of regulation placates the public.

However, despite any changes in the level at which regulation is made, it is still in the interests of businesses to **remain alert to the general thrust of regulation** as it affects their industries, and to participate in the processes of lobbying and representation in order to preserve their self-interest.

Section summary

Government policy influences the economic environment, the framework of laws, industry structure and certain operational issues.

Political instability is a cause of risk. Different approaches to the political environment apply in different countries.

Globalisation is the term that refers to the growing interdependence of countries worldwide through increased trade, increased capital flows and the rapid diffusion of technology.

International trade is governed by international law and associated regulations.

3 The economic environment

3.1 The importance of the economic environment

Introduction

The economic environment is an important influence at local and national level. Here are some factors that firms must attend to.

Factor	Impact
Overall growth or fall in gross domestic product (GDP)	Increased/decreased demand for goods (eg dishwashers) and services (holidays)
Local economic trends	Type of industry in the area; office/factory rents; labour rates; house prices
National economic trends:	
Inflation	Low in most countries; distorts business decisions; wage inflation compensates for price inflation
Interest rates	How much it costs to borrow money affects **cash flow**. Some businesses carry a high level of debt. How much customers can afford to spend is also affected as rises in interest rates affect people's mortgage payments.
Tax levels	Corporation tax affects how much firms can invest or return to shareholders. Income tax and sales tax affect how much consumers have to spend, hence demand.
Government spending	Suppliers to the Government (eg construction firms) are affected by spending.
The business cycle	Economic activity is always punctuated by periods of growth followed by decline, simply because of the nature of trade. The UK economy has been characterised by periods of 'boom' and 'bust'. Government policy can cause, exacerbate or mitigate such trends, but cannot abolish the business cycle. (Industries that prosper when others are declining are called counter-cyclical industries.)
Productivity	An economy cannot grow faster than the underlying growth in productivity, without risking inflation. UK manufacturing productivity is still lower than that of its main competitors but, in services, the UK is relatively efficient.

The **forecast state of the economy** will influence the planning process for organisations that operate within it. In times of boom and increased demand and consumption, the overall planning problem will be to **identify** the demand. Conversely, in times of recession, the emphasis will be on cost effectiveness, continuing profitability, survival and competition.

3.1.1 Growth of the service sector

There is a trend in many developed economies, such as the UK and the US, for **services** to account for a growing proportion of national economic activity and employment. The **service sector** accounts for most output. Services include activities such as restaurants, tourism, nursing, education, management consultancy, computer consulting, banking and finance. Manufacturing is still important, especially in exports, but it employs fewer and fewer people.

KEY TERM

SERVICES are value-creating activities that in themselves do not involve the supply of a physical product. Service provision may be subdivided into:

(a) **Pure services**, where there is no physical product, such as consultancy
(b) **Service with a product attached**, such as the design and installation of a computer network
(c) **Products with services attached**, such as the purchase of a computer with a maintenance contract

3.1.2 Impact of international factors on a country's economy

Factor	Impact
Exchange rates	Cost of imports, selling prices and value of exports; cost of hedging against fluctuations
Characteristics of overseas markets; different rates of economic growth and prosperity, tax etc	Desirable overseas markets (demand) or sources of supply
Capital flows and trade	Investment opportunities, free trade, cost of exporting
Globalisation	Increased competition; increasing prosperity

3.2 Government economic policy

Governments generally accept that they have a role to play in the management of the macroeconomy. Their objectives are generally to achieve satisfactory and stable **growth**, while controlling **inflation** and avoiding significant changes in the value of their **currencies**. Growth is required, since it enhances general economic **wellbeing** and provides for high levels of **employment**.

A government can use various policy tools as follows.

Fiscal policy	• Taxation and other sources of income • Government spending • Borrowing whenever spending exceeds income • Repaying debt when income exceeds expenditure
Monetary policy	• Interest rates • Exchange rates or exchange controls • Control of the money supply • Controls over bank lending and credit (rarely used nowadays)

Businesses are affected by a government's tax policy (eg corporation tax rates), and monetary policy (high interest rates increase the cost of investment, or depress consumer demand).

In practice, governments are making use of these tools in different ways.

In the UK, the US and the Eurozone, control of **monetary policy** (interest rates) is set by independent bodies (the Bank of England, the Federal Reserve, the European Central Bank), over which governments have little direct influence. In other countries, this is not the case.

Some countries use exchange rate policy and exchange controls to affect economic activity. Not all currencies are fully convertible into others. The Government of Malaysia used this approach, by restricting the import and export of Malaysian ringgit, in the financial crises of Asia in the late 1990s.

Finally, there is pressure in some jurisdictions for co-ordination of fiscal policies.

3.2.1 Government spending

Governments nationally and locally spend money on the following.

- Payments of wages and salaries to employees, and of pensions to old-age pensioners
- Payments for materials, supplies and services
- Purchases of capital equipment
- Payments of interest on borrowings and repayments of capital

Tax and spending decisions have the effect of increasing or decreasing the amount that consumers have to spend generally, and **reallocating resources** in the economy to the public sector activities.

3.2.2 Involvement of the private sector

In many countries, various areas of the public sector have been delivered to the private sector in a process of **privatisation**. Where these were utilities, these organisations are regulated by bodies such as Ofcom. This process has had a number of sometimes conflicting objectives.

(a) **Reductions in public sector borrowing** and expenditure to finance tax cuts and/or spending.

(b) **Greater investment** that the Government is unwilling or unable to fund from its own resources. Privatised utilities are then **free to borrow**.

(c) **New management practices** are introduced.

(d) Privatisation can encourage **competition**, but some utilities have been sold off as **monopolies**, subject to a regulator.

Privatisation is now relatively uncontroversial in the UK, but still causes political hostility in the developing world.

The blurring of boundaries between public and private sector continues.

(a) **Contracting out**. Some work that was previously done by government employees has been contracted out to firms in the private sector.

(b) **Welfare spending**. Government policy has been to shift some welfare spending to individuals, for example in personal pensions.

(c) **Private finance initiative**. In the UK, the private sector is involved in financing public projects, such as roads and hospitals.

In some countries, therefore, government policy has been to purchase welfare services from private sector suppliers rather than manage them directly.

3.2.3 Inflation and interest rates

Inflation can be a deterrent to real economic growth, creating expectations of further inflation and undermining business confidence. The consequences include the following.

(a) A demand for **higher money wages** to be paid to employees to compensate for the fall in value of their wages.

(b) A demand for **high interest rates**, so that investors can be compensated for inflation and borrowers are deterred.

3.2.4 The housing market

An important feature of the UK and other countries is the **housing market**. For a number of years, events from the 2007 'credit crunch' affected the ability to borrow to buy a house. This meant many young buyers with limited funds were unable to borrow enough to buy a house. In early 2014, it was reported that this trend was gradually starting to reverse, with house prices rising. This was due in part to banks offering lower mortgage rates coupled with the UK Government's 'Help to Buy' scheme.

(a) The **housing market** is a key factor for people in the UK and many other countries. Most houses are owner-occupied, and most people's wealth is tied up in their homes. UK borrowers generally borrow at variable rates of interest, so are vulnerable to changes in interest rates.

(b) **Rising prices** encourage people to take out extra loans to spend on other things. This was held to lead to inflation.

(c) Most of the debt owed by UK borrowers is at **variable rate**. Changes in interest rates have an immediate effect on people's pockets. This is not necessarily the case elsewhere.

3.3 International trade and exchange rates

International trade and finance consists of:

- Trade in goods and services, forming the **balance of trade**
- Long-term and short-term **investments** from other countries and into other countries
- Movements in a government's **official reserves** of foreign currency, gold etc

Faced with a **trade deficit**, a government might once have considered **protectionist measures** (protectionism aims to restrict trade with one or more other country to protect home country producers from overseas suppliers) and, in the case of developing countries, **exchange controls**.

However, a government's long-term strategy for a balance of trade deficit should be to improve conditions in the domestic economy.

(a) The improvements required could include bringing inflation under control, encouraging investment in domestic industries and depressing consumer demand.

(b) The **quality** of the deficit is an important consideration. If capital goods are imported, this might mean only a short-term deficit, as the machinery enhances the productivity and export capacity of domestic firms in the long term. If consumer goods are imported, this might not be as sustainable in the long run.

Question 2.3 Single currency

Learning outcome A2a

For the purpose of this question, assume that the UK is considering joining the 'single European currency', the euro.

Required

Consider the implications of the UK adopting the euro for the following UK businesses.

(a) A package holiday firm, mainly selling holidays to France and Germany
(b) An exporter of power station generating equipment to developing countries in Asia
(c) An importer of wine from Australia

3.4 Economic factors and the Management Accountant

As we shall discuss in greater detail later in this Study Text, the role of the Management Accountant may be extended to help estimate the effect of particular economic factors on the firm's operations.

(a) **Interest rates**

(i) A rise might increase the cost of any borrowing the company has undertaken, thereby reducing its profitability. It also has the possible effect of raising a firm's cost of capital. An investment project therefore has a higher hurdle to overcome to be accepted. If, on the other hand, a firm has surplus cash, this can be invested for a higher return.

(ii) Interest rates also have a general effect on consumer confidence and liquidity, and hence demand, especially in relation to the housing markets.

(b) **Inflation**. For an economy as a whole, inflation works as a 'tax on savers', given that it reduces the value of financial assets and the income of those on fixed incomes.

(i) It requires high **nominal interest rates** to offer investors a real return.

(ii) Inflation makes it hard for businesses to plan, owing to the uncertainty of future financial returns. Inflation and expectations of it help explain '**short-termism**'.

(iii) Inflation has a number of effects on how firms report their performance and how they plan.

Exchange rate volatility affects the cost of imports from overseas, and the prices that can be charged to overseas customers. A high value to the pound means that customers must be charged more in their local currencies – and imports are cheaper.

Exchange rates do not only affect imports and exports. Many firms invest large sums of money in factories in overseas markets.

(a) The **purchasing power parity** theory of exchange rate suggests that, in the long term, differences in exchange rates caused by inflation or higher interest rates will even out. It looks at what people can buy in their own country and uses this to compare economic performance. The Chinese economy, measured in US dollars, is much smaller than the US economy: the difference in size is not so marked when purchasing power parity is used for comparisons.

(b) Firms are very vulnerable to changes in exchange rates over the short to medium term, especially as a subsidiary's reported profit can affect the reported profit of the holding company and hence, by implication, its share price. Firms can guard against the risk of exchange rates by a number of financial instruments such as **hedges**.

Section summary

Economic factors include the overall level of growth, the business cycle, official monetary and fiscal policy, exchange rates and inflation.

4 The social and cultural environment

Introduction

Social change involves changes in the nature, attitudes and habits of society. Social changes are continually happening, and trends can be identified, which may or may not be relevant to a business. Culture is often spoken of as 'the way we do things round here', certainly in organisations. In society, however, culture is broader than this and encompasses customs, attitudes, characteristic ways of viewing the world and behaviour. Most countries contain several subcultures.

4.1 Demography

KEY TERM

DEMOGRAPHY is the study of populations and communities. It provides analysis of statistics on birth and death rates, age structures of populations, ethnic groups within communities and so on.

Demography is important for the following reasons.

- Labour is a factor of production.
- People create demand for goods, services and resources.
- It has a long-term impact on government policies.
- There is a relationship between population growth and living standards.

Here are some statistics, which might help to explain the importance many businesses are placing on overseas markets. The figures are taken from *Social Trends*, published by the Office for National Statistics (ONS).

	1994 population Millions	*2025 population* (estimated) Millions	*Increase 1994–2025* %
World population	5,665.5	8,472.4	49
Europe (including the Baltic states)	512.0	541.9	5
Former USSR (excluding the Baltic states)	284.5	344.5	21
Canada and the US	282.7	360.5	27
Africa	681.7	1,582.5	132
Asia	3,233.0	4,900.3	52
Latin America	457.7	701.6	53
Oceania (including Australia)	27.5	41.3	50

The following demographic factors are important to organisational planners.

Factor	Comment
Growth	The rate of growth or decline in a national population and in regional populations.
Age	Changes in the age distribution of the population. In the UK, there will be an increasing proportion of the national population over retirement age. In developing countries, there are very large numbers of young people.
Geography	The concentration of population into certain geographical areas.
Ethnicity	A population might contain groups with different ethnic origins from the majority. In the UK, about 5% come from ethnic minorities, although most of these live in London and the South East.
Household and family structure	A household is the basic social unit and its size might be determined by the number of children, whether elderly parents live at home etc. In the UK, there has been an increase in single person households and single parent families.
Social structure	The population of a society can be broken down into a number of subgroups, with different attitudes and access to economic resources. Social class, however, is hard to measure (as people's subjective perceptions vary).
Employment	In part, this is related to changes in the workplace. Many people believe that there is a move to a casual flexible workforce; factories will have a group of **core employees**, supplemented by a group of insecure **peripheral employees**, on part-time or temporary contracts, working as and when required. Some research indicates a 'two-tier' society split between 'work-rich' (with two wage-earners) and 'work-poor'. However, despite some claims, most employees are in permanent, full-time employment.
Wealth	Rising standards of living lead to increased demand for certain types of consumer good. This is why developing countries are attractive as markets.

4.1.1 Implications of demographic change

(a) **Changes in patterns of demand**. An ageing population suggests increased demand for healthcare services: a 'young' growing population has a growing demand for schools, housing and work.

(b) **Location of demand**. People are moving to the suburbs and small towns.

(c) **Recruitment policies.** There are relatively fewer young people, so firms will have to recruit from less familiar sources of labour.

(d) **Wealth and tax**.

4.2 Culture

We will look at organisational culture in a later chapter. We now look at culture in the context of the society that an organisation exists and operates in.

KEY TERM

CULTURE is used by sociologists and anthropologists to encompass 'the sum total of the beliefs, knowledge, attitudes of mind and customs to which people are exposed in their social conditioning'.

Through contact with a particular culture, individuals learn a language, acquire values and learn habits of behaviour and thought. Culture has the following characteristics.

(a) **Beliefs and values**. Beliefs are what we feel to be the case on the basis of objective and subjective information (eg people can believe the world is round or flat). Values are beliefs that are relatively enduring, relatively general and fairly widely accepted as a guide to culturally appropriate behaviour.

(b) **Customs**. These are modes of behaviour that represent culturally accepted ways of behaving in response to given situations.

(c) **Artefacts**. These are all the physical tools designed by human beings for their physical and psychological wellbeing: works of art, technology, products.

(d) **Rituals**. A ritual is a type of activity that takes on symbolic meaning, consisting of a fixed sequence of behaviour repeated over time.

The learning and sharing of culture is made possible by language (both written and spoken, and verbal and non-verbal).

4.2.1 Importance of culture for business

Knowledge of the culture of a society is clearly of value to businesses in a number of ways.

(a) **Marketers** can adapt their products accordingly, and be fairly sure of a sizeable market. This is particularly important in export markets, as globalisation has led to a convergence of consumer tastes around the world. As a result, products have become more homogenised and are capable of being sold in more countries.

(b) **Human resource managers** may need to tackle cultural differences in recruitment. For example, some ethnic minorities have a different body language from the majority, which may be hard for some interviewers to interpret.

Culture in a society can be divided into **subcultures** reflecting social differences. Most people participate in several of them.

Subculture	Comment
Class	People from different social classes might have different values reflecting their position in society.
Ethnic background	Some ethnic groups can still be considered a distinct cultural group.
Religion	Religion and ethnicity are related.
Gender	Some products are targeted directly to women or to men.
Geography or region	Distinct regional differences might be brought about by the past effects of physical geography (socioeconomic differences etc). Speech accents noticeably differ most.
Age	Age subcultures vary according to the period in which individuals were socialised to an extent, because of the great shifts in social values and customs in this century ('youth culture'; the 'generation gap' etc).
Work	Different organisations have different corporate cultures, in that the shared values of one workplace may be different from another.

Cultural change might have to be planned for. There has been a revolution in attitudes to female employment, despite the well-publicised problems of discrimination that still remain.

Question 2.4

Social trends

Learning outcome A2a

Club Fun is a UK company, which sells packaged holidays. It offers standard 'cheap and cheerful' package holidays to resorts in Spain and the Greek islands. It was particularly successful at providing holidays for the 18–30 age group.

Required

What do you think the implications are for Club Fun of the following developments?

- A fall in the number of school leavers
- The fact that young people are more likely now than in the 1960s to go into higher education
- Holiday programmes on TV that feature a much greater variety of locations
- Greater disposable income among the 18–30 age group
- Increasing levels of internet access

Section summary

Social and cultural factors relate to two main issues. **Demography** is the study of the population as a whole: its overall size; whether it is growing, stable, or falling; the proportion of people of different age groups – in industrial countries, the proportion of elderly people is increasing; where people live and work; ethnic origin. **Culture** includes customs, attitudes, characteristic ways of viewing the world and behaviour: most countries contain several subcultures.

5 The technological environment

Introduction

In the most general sense, technology contributes to overall **economic growth**. Consider the **production possibility curve**, which describes the total production in an economy. Technology can shift this curve, increasing total output, by enabling:

- Gains in productivity (more output per units of input)
- Reduced costs (eg transportation technology, preservatives)
- New types of product

Technological change is rapid, and organisations must adapt themselves to it. Technological change can affect the activities of organisations as follows.

(a) **The type of products or services that are made and sold**. For example, consumer markets have seen the emergence of personal computers, tablets and smartphones; and industrial markets have seen the emergence of custom-built microchips, robots and local area networks for office information systems.

(b) **The way in which products are made**.

(i) Modern production equipment reduces the need for labour.

(ii) Technology can also develop new raw materials.

(c) **The way in which services are provided**, for example travel agencies over the internet. The case study below highlights how changes in technology have impacted newspaper readership numbers in Scotland.

(d) **The way in which markets are identified**. Database systems make it much easier to analyse the marketplace.

(e) **The way in which firms are managed.** IT has helped in the 'delayering' of organisational hierarchies (in other words, the reduction of management layers between the senior managers and the workforce), but requires greater workforce skills. Using technology often requires changes in working methods. Information technology, in particular, requires skills at manipulating and interpreting abstract data.

(f) **The means and extent of communications with external clients.**

CASE STUDY

The decline of the Scottish newspaper industry

This case study illustrates the importance of adapting to technological environmental changes.

In August 2013, the BBC reported on the continued decline of the Scottish newspaper industry. The Audit Bureau of Circulation (ABC) confirmed that Scottish newspaper sales had fallen by 11% in the preceding 12 months. Several newspapers have seen their sales fall by more than half in the past decade.

The decline in sales of *The Scotsman* newspaper have left it classed as being a 'regional' title. Interestingly, online readership of the *Scotsman.com* has increased though. 'The free-to-access web service saw a rise in daily browsers of 13%, according to ABC, reaching 120,000. The failure to convert the increase in online readers into increased advertising revenue had led to a decline in the value of the titles owned by Johnston Press, the Edinburgh-based company which includes *The Scotsman* among more than 200 mainly local titles. Johnston Press recently announced that it is writing down the asset valuation of its newspapers by nearly £200m'.

John McLellan, of the Scottish Newspaper Society said, 'some titles have been responding to changing market conditions for 20 years of the digital revolution. The truth is that while we can't deny there are challenges, so far as hard copy sales are concerned, the journalism produced by all newspaper companies is being accessed by more people than ever'.

Professor Raymond Boyle, a communications expert at Glasgow University, commented on the state of the industry: 'Traditionally, Scottish newspapers have been a very important part of Scottish national identity. That's changed over the past 10 to 15 years. Certain sectors remain very strong; sport, for example, and football remains an important part of Scottish newspapers and their identity. But the sense of newspapers being carriers of national identity is no longer sustainable'.

Source:

Fraser, D. (2014) *Further decline in Scottish newspaper sales.* [Online]. Available from: http://www.bbc.co.uk/news/uk-scotland-scotland-business-26366464 [Accessed 27 September 2016].

The impact of technological change also has potentially important **social consequences**.

(a) Whereas people were once collected together to work in factories, **home working** will become more important.

(b) Certain sorts of skill, related to **interpretation** of data and information processes, are likely to become more valued than manual or physical skills.

(c) Technology increases manufacturing productivity, so that more people will be involved in **service** jobs.

It is extremely difficult to **forecast** developments beyond more than a few years. For example, many of the current developments in information technology would have seemed almost impossible not much more than a decade ago.

(a) **Futurology** is the science and study of sociological and technological developments, values and trends, with a view to planning for the future.

(b) The **Delphi model** involves a panel of experts providing views on various events to be forecast, such as inventions and breakthroughs, or even regulations or changes over a time period into the future.

(c) In some cases, instead of technological developments being used to predict future technologies, future social developments can be predicted, in order to predict future **customer needs**.

It is also possible that one particular invention or technique will have wide-ranging applications. Such a technology might be called a **meta-technology**.

CASE STUDY

Meta-technology

An example of a meta-technology might be the technology behind lasers. Lasers are used for a huge variety of jobs.

- Eye surgery
- Industrial cutting
- Illuminating public monuments at night
- Reading data from DVDs
- Nightclubs

Section summary

Technological factors have implications for economic growth overall, and offer opportunities and threats to many businesses. Meta-technologies are technologies that are applicable to many applications.

6 Stakeholder goals and objectives

KEY TERM

STAKEHOLDERS are 'those persons and organisations that have an interest in the strategy of an organisation. Stakeholders normally include shareholders, customers, staff and the local community'.

(*CIMA Official Terminology*)

Introduction

There are three broad types of stakeholder in an organisation, as follows.

- **Internal** stakeholders (employees, management)
- **Connected** stakeholders (shareholders, customers, suppliers, financiers)
- **External** stakeholders (the community, government, pressure groups)

6.1 Internal stakeholders: employees and management

Because **employees and management** are so intimately connected with the company, their objectives are likely to have a strong influence on how it is run. They are interested in the following issues.

(a) The **organisation's continuation and growth**. Management and employees have a special interest in the organisation's continued existence.

(b) Managers and employees have **individual interests** and goals that can be harnessed to the goals of the organisation.

Internal stakeholder	Interests to defend	Response risk
Managers and employees	• Jobs/careers • Money • Promotion • Benefits • Satisfaction	• Pursuit of 'systems goals' rather than shareholder interests • Industrial action • Negative power to impede implementation • Refusal to relocate • Resignation

6.2 Connected stakeholders

Writing in *Management Accounting* (November 1997), Malcolm Smith stated that increasing shareholder value should assume a core role in the strategic management of a business. If management performance is measured and rewarded by reference to changes in **shareholder value**, then shareholders will be happy, because managers are likely to encourage long-term share price growth.

Connected stakeholder	Interests to defend	Response risk
Shareholders (corporate strategy)	• Increase in shareholder wealth, measured by profitability, price/earnings ratios, market capitalisation, dividends and yield • Risk	• Sell shares (eg to predator) or remove management
Bankers (cash flows)	• Security of loan • Adherence to loan agreements	• Denial of credit • Higher interest charges • Receivership
Suppliers (purchase strategy)	• Profitable sales • Payment for goods • Long-term relationship	• Refusal of credit • Court action • Wind down relationships
Customers (product-market strategy)	• Goods as promised • Future benefits	• Buy elsewhere • Sue

6.3 External stakeholders

External stakeholder groups – the Government, local authorities, pressure groups, the community at large, professional bodies – are likely to have quite diverse objectives.

External stakeholder	Interests to defend	Response risk
Government	• Jobs, training, tax	• Tax increases • Regulation • Legal action
Interest/pressure groups	• Pollution • Rights • Other	• Publicity • Direct action • Sabotage • Pressure on government

6.4 The nature of stakes

Stakes may be analysed in several ways:

(a) Local, national or international

(b) Single or multiple issues

(c) Economic or social (ie financial – or concern-based: the latter would include interests such as equal opportunities)

(d) Concrete or symbolic: symbolic stakes are hard to define but important to the persons concerned and include general concern, anxiety and the need for respect

6.5 Primary and secondary stakeholders

Stakeholders may also be analysed by reference to whether they have a **contractual relationship** with the organisation. Stakeholders who have such a relationship are called **primary stakeholders**, while those who do not are known as **secondary stakeholders**. The primary stakeholder category thus includes **internal** and **connected** stakeholders, while the secondary stakeholders category equates to **external** stakeholder status.

6.6 Stakeholder conflicts

The analysis above demonstrates that conflict is likely between stakeholder groups simply because of the divergence of their interests. The picture is complicated when individuals are members of more than one stakeholder group and when members of the same stakeholder group do not share the same principal interest. Both cases are illustrated by considering a workforce, some of whose members are also shareholders and some of whom are not.

6.7 Dependency

A firm might depend on a stakeholder group at any particular time.

(a) A firm with persistent cash flow problems might depend on its bankers to provide it with money to stay in business at all.

(b) In the long term, any firm depends on its customers.

The degree of dependence or reliance can be analysed according to these criteria.

(a) **Disruption**. Can the stakeholder disrupt the organisation's plans (eg a bank withdrawing overdraft facilities)?

(b) **Replacement**. Can the firm replace the relationship?

(c) **Uncertainty**. Does the stakeholder cause uncertainty in the firm's plans? A firm with healthy, positive cash flows and large cash balances need not worry about its bank's attitude to a proposed investment.

The way in which the relationship between a company and stakeholders is conducted is a function of the parties' **relative bargaining strength** and the philosophy underlying **each party's objectives**. This can be shown by means of a spectrum.

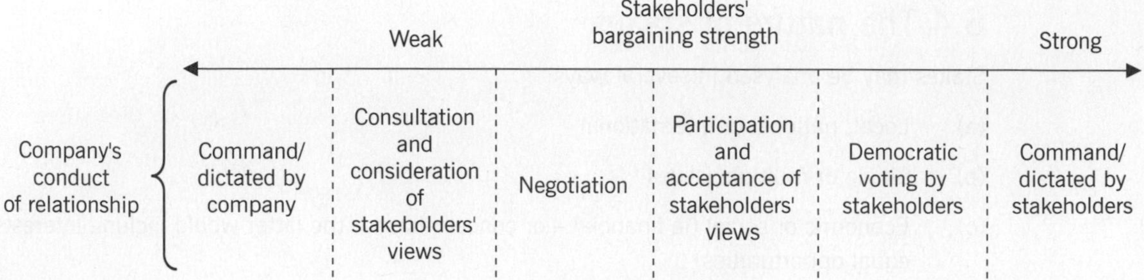

6.8 Stakeholder mapping: power and interest

A useful tool that you need to be familiar with when assessing stakeholder power is that of Mendelow's model of stakeholder mapping. The model helps organisations to better understand what different groups want from it, expressed as their level of interest. Interest is compared to the level of power that different stakeholders hold over the organisation. Power is often regarded as the ability to interfere or to potentially disrupt activities. Once an organisation understands these two variables, it is better placed to manage these groups.

Level of interest

Power	Low	High
Low	A	B
High	C	D

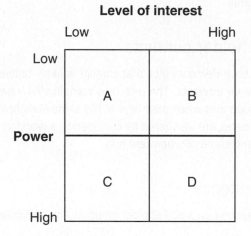

(a) **Key players** are found in Segment D: strategy must be **acceptable** to them, at least. An example would be a major customer.

(b) Stakeholders in Segment C must be treated with care. While often passive, they are capable of moving to Segment D. They should, therefore, be **kept satisfied**. Large institutional shareholders might fall into Segment C.

(c) Stakeholders in Segment B do not have great ability to influence strategy, but their views can be important in influencing more powerful stakeholders, perhaps by lobbying. They should therefore be **kept informed**. Community representatives and charities might fall into Segment B.

(d) Minimal effort is expended on Segment A.

Building on the work of Mendelow, Johnson and Scholes propose four strategies that organisations should look to use when seeking to manage stakeholder relations:

(a) **Low interest** and **low power** stakeholder groups can be managed through a process of **direction** where the organisation uses its authority over such groups to influence their opinions and behaviours.

(b) **High interest** and **low power** groups should be managed carefully. A focus on **education** and **communication** is likely to be appropriate here to avoid such groups attempting to increase their level of influence over the organisation. Activities here may involve regular communications with stakeholders to keep them up to date on the organisation's strategy or general plans.

(c) **Low interest** and **high power** stakeholder groups can be managed through regular **interventions**. The aim of the organisation is to stop such stakeholders becoming key players. Intervention may take the form of regular communications and face to face meetings with stakeholders to reassure and explain the consequences of an organisation's plans in advance of their implementation.

(d) **High interest** and **high power** stakeholder groups should be actively allowed to **participate** in the organisation's activities that affect them. Failure to effectively manage 'key player' stakeholders increases the scope for such groups to oppose the organisation's plans.

A single stakeholder map is unlikely to be appropriate for all circumstances. In particular, stakeholders may move from quadrant to quadrant when different potential future strategies are considered.

Stakeholder mapping is used to assess the **significance** of stakeholder groups. This in turn has implications for the organisation.

(a) The framework of **corporate governance** should recognise stakeholders' levels of interest and power.

(b) It may be appropriate to seek to **reposition** certain stakeholders and discourage others from repositioning themselves, depending on their attitudes.

(c) Key **blockers** and **facilitators** of change must be identified.

Stakeholder mapping can also be used to establish political priorities. A map of the current position can be compared with a map of a desired future state. This will indicate critical shifts that must be pursued.

In *Power In and Around Organizations*, Mintzberg identifies groups that not only have an interest in an organisation but also power over it.

The external coalition	The internal coalition
• Owners (who hold legal title) • Associates (suppliers, customers, trading partners) • Employee associations (unions, professional bodies) • Public (government, media)	• The Chief Executive and board at the strategic apex • Line managers • Operators • The technostructure • Support staff

Each of these groups has three basic choices.

(a) **Loyalty**. They can do as they are told.

(b) **Exit**. For example by selling their shares, or getting a new job.

(c) **Voice**. They can stay and try to change the system. Those who choose **voice** are those who can, to varying degrees, influence the organisation. Influence implies a degree of power and willingness to exercise it.

Existing structures and systems can channel stakeholder influence.

(a) They are the **location of power**, giving groups of people varying degrees of influence over strategic choices.

(b) They are **conduits of information**, which shape strategic decisions.

(c) They **limit choices** or give some options priority over others. These may be physical or ethical constraints over what is possible.

(d) They **embody culture**.

(e) They **determine the successful implementation** of strategy.

(f) The **firm has different degrees of dependency** on various stakeholder groups. A company with a cash flow crisis will be more beholden to its bankers than one with regular cash surpluses.

Question 2.5 — Stakeholder influences

Learning outcome A2a

Ticket and Budget International is a large multinational firm of accountants. The firm provides audit services, tax services and consultancy services for its many clients. The firm has a strong technical department that designs standardised audit procedures. The firm has just employed a marketing manager. The Marketing Manager regards an audit as a 'product', part of the entire marketing mix including price (audit fees), place (usually on the client's premises) and promotion (advertising in professional journals). The Marketing Manager is held in high regard by the firm's Senior Partner. The Marketing Director and the Senior Partner have unveiled a new strategic plan, drawn up in conditions of secrecy, which involves a tie-up with an advertising agency. The firm will be a 'one-stop shop' for business services and advice to management on any subject. Each client, or 'customer', will have a dedicated team of auditors, consultants and advertising executives. Obviously, a member of staff will be a member of a number of different teams.

The firm has recently settled a number of expensive lawsuits for negligence (which it has, of course, 'contested vigorously') out of court, without admitting liability. The technical department is conducting a thorough review of the firm's audit procedures.

Required

In the light of what we have covered in this section, what do you think will be the organisational and stakeholder influences on the proposed strategy?

So, different stakeholders will have their own views as to strategy. As some stakeholders have **negative power**, in other words power to impede or disrupt the decision, their likely response might be considered.

Exam alert

In your Objective Test exam, you may have to:

- Identify the stakeholders in the scenario
- Identify what their particular interests are

You may also have to:

- Identify the importance of developing and maintaining relationships with them
- Explain how their varying interests may be reconciled

A scenario question may require you to choose the right word(s) from a number of options and to use these to fill in the blanks in a sentence concerning the stakeholders featured.

6.9 The strategic value of stakeholders

The firm can make strategic gains from managing stakeholder relationships. Studies have revealed the following correlations.

(a) A correlation between **employee** and **customer loyalty** (eg reduced staff turnover in service firms generally results in more repeat business).

(b) **Continuity** and **stability** in relationships with employees, customers and suppliers is important in enabling organisations to respond to certain types of change, necessary for business as a sustained activity.

Responsibilities towards customers are mainly those of providing a product or service of a quality that customers expect, and of dealing honestly and fairly with customers.

Responsibilities towards suppliers are expressed mainly in terms of trading relationships.

(a) The organisation's size could give it considerable power as a buyer. One ethical guideline might be that the organisation should not use its power unscrupulously.

(b) Suppliers might rely on getting prompt payment in accordance with the terms of trade negotiated with its customers.

(c) All information obtained from suppliers and potential suppliers should be kept confidential.

6.10 Measuring stakeholder satisfaction

If it is accepted that stakeholders other than shareholders have a legitimate interest in what the firm does, it is appropriate to consider measuring the degree of success it achieves in satisfying those interests.

We have already considered ways in which stakeholders may be classified and given some instances of their probable interests. Measuring the satisfaction of stakeholder interests is likely to be difficult, since many of their expectations relate to **qualitative** rather than **quantitative** matters. It is, for example, difficult to measure good corporate citizenship. On the other hand, some of the more important stakeholder groups do have fairly specific interests, the satisfaction of which should be fairly amenable to measurement. Here are some examples of possible measures.

Stakeholder group	Measure
Employees	Staff turnover; pay and benefits relative to market rate; job vacancies
Government	Pollution measures; promptness of filing annual returns; accident rate; energy efficiency
Distributors	Share of joint promotions paid for; rate of stock-outs

Paper E3 requires you to be able to recommend how to manage relationships with stakeholders.

Section summary

Stakeholders are those individuals or groups that, potentially, have an interest in what the organisation does. Different stakeholder groups have different degrees of power and interest, and management must respond to each in a different way.

7 The competitive advantage of a nation's industries: Porter's diamond

Introduction

Michael Porter's *The Competitive Advantage of Nations* suggests that some nations' industries succeed more than others in terms of international competition. UK leadership in some industries (eg ship-building) has been overtaken (by Japan and Korea).

Porter does not believe that countries or nations as such are competitive, but he asks:

(a) 'Why does a **nation become the home base** for successful international competitors in an industry?'

(b) 'Why are firms based in a particular nation able to create and **sustain competitive advantage** against the world's best competitors in a particular field?'

(c) 'Why is **one nation** often the home for **so many of an industry's world leaders**?'

The original explanation for **national** success was the theory of **comparative advantage**. This held that relative **factor opportunity costs** in countries determined the appropriateness of particular economic activities in relation to other countries. (In other words, countries should concentrate on what they are best at, in relation to other countries.)

Porter argues that **industries that require high technology and highly skilled employees are less affected** than low-technology industries by the relative costs of their inputs of raw materials and basic labour as determined by the national endowment of factors.

Comparative advantage is too **general a concept** to explain the success of **individual companies and industries.** If high technology and global markets allow firms to circumvent (or ignore) the constraints (or advantages) of their home country's endowment of raw materials, cheap labour, access to capital and so forth, how can they be successful internationally?

Porter identifies determinants of national competitive advantage, which are outlined in the diagram below. Porter refers to this as the **diamond.**

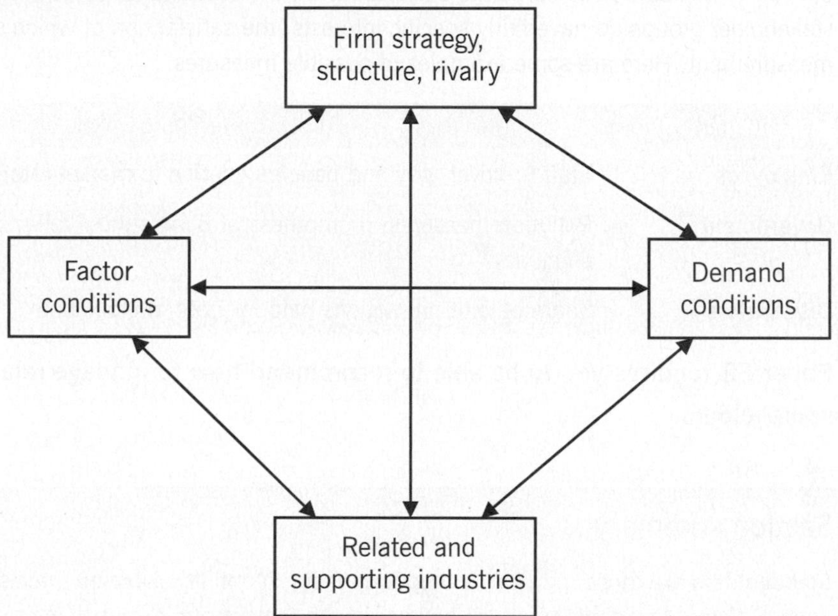

Each element of the diamond is capable of enhancing national competitive advantage. Conversely, a nation that enjoys competitive advantage will find it diminishes if the elements cease to work positively.

7.1 Analysing the diamond

7.1.1 Factor conditions

Factor conditions are a country's endowment of inputs to production.

(a) **Human resources** (skills, motivation, industrial relations)
(b) **Physical resources** (land, minerals, climate, location relative to other nations)
(c) **Knowledge** (scientific and technical know-how, educational institutions)
(d) **Capital** (amounts available for investment, how it is deployed)
(e) **Infrastructure** (transport, communications, housing)

Porter distinguishes between the following:

(a) **Basic factors**. Natural resources, climate, semi-skilled and unskilled labour. Basic factors are inherited, or at best their creation involves little investment.

(b) **Advanced factors**. These include modern digital communications and highly educated personnel research laboratories. They are necessary to achieve high-order competitive advantages such as differentiated products and proprietary production technology.

Inappropriate decisions and economic policy, in particular, can lead to erosion of advantageous factor conditions. This is particularly true of advanced factor conditions, which require significant investment,

but even the advantage provided by basic physical factors can be eroded if markets change significantly. For example, there is plenty of coal left under England, but it is difficult to work underground and open-cast extraction is politically unacceptable because of its environmental effects.

KEY POINT

An abundance of factors is not enough. It is the efficiency with which they are deployed that matters. The former USSR had an abundance of natural resources and a fairly well-educated workforce, but was an economic catastrophe.

7.1.2 Demand conditions: the home market

The **home market determines how firms perceive, interpret and respond to buyer needs**. This information puts pressure on firms to innovate, and provides a launch pad for global ambitions.

(a) There are **no cultural impediments** to communication.

(b) The **segmentation** of the home market shapes a firm's priorities: companies will be successful globally in segments that are similar to the home market.

(c) **Sophisticated and demanding buyers** set standards. ('The British are known for gardening, and British firms are world class in garden tools.')

(d) **Anticipatory buyer needs**. If consumer needs are expressed in the home market earlier than in the world market, the firm benefits from experience.

(e) The **rate of growth**. Slow-growing home markets do not encourage the adoption of state of the art technology.

(f) **Early saturation** of the home market will encourage a firm to export.

(g) Serving a substantial home market allows the attainment of **economies of scale**.

Advantage here can be eroded if a gap emerges between local and foreign demand.

7.1.3 Related and supporting industries

Competitive success in one industry is linked to success in related industries. Domestic suppliers are preferable to foreign suppliers, as 'proximity of managerial and technical personnel, along with cultural similarity, tends to facilitate free and open information flow' at an early stage. However, it is easy for this aspect of the diamond to lose its advantage if individual companies do not remain competitive or mutually supportive.

7.1.4 Firm strategy, structure and rivalry

Structure. National cultural factors create certain tendencies to orientate businesspeople to certain industries. German firms, according to Porter, have a strong showing in 'industries with a high technical content'.

Strategy. Industries in different countries have different **time horizons**, funding needs and so forth.

(a) **National capital markets** set different goals for performance. In some countries, banks are the main source of capital, not equity shareholders.

(b) When an industry faces difficult times, it **can either innovate within the industry**, to sustain competitive position, or **shift resources from one industry to another** (eg diversification).

Domestic rivalry is important because:

(a) With little domestic rivalry, firms are happy to rely on the home market

(b) Tough domestic rivals teach a firm about competitive success

(c) Each rival can try a different strategic approach

If rivalry collapses, perhaps because of consolidation, standards are likely to slip, reducing competitiveness.

7.1.5 Losing competitive advantage

It is important to remember that the factors that create competitive advantage are dynamic, and so over time they may deteriorate, eroding a nation's competitive advantage.

(a) Factor conditions may deteriorate due to a lack of investment in technology or education.

(b) Demand conditions may deteriorate due to a recession or deflationary government policies.

(c) Supporting clusters may collapse as firms diversify and therefore stop concentrating on their own business.

7.2 Influencing the diamond

7.2.1 Interactions between the determinants

The factors in the diamond are interrelated. Competitive advantage rarely rests on only one element of the diamond.

(a) **Related industries** affect **demand conditions** for an industry. An example from the context of international marketing is piggy-back exporting in which an exporting company also exports some of the products of related industries.

(b) **Domestic rivalry** can encourage the **creation of more specialised supplier industries**.

Porter says that a nation's competitive industries are **clustered**. Porter believes clustering to be a key to national competitive advantage. A cluster is a linking of industries through relationships that are either vertical (buyer-supplier) or horizontal (common customers, technology, skills). For example, the UK financial services industry is clustered in London.

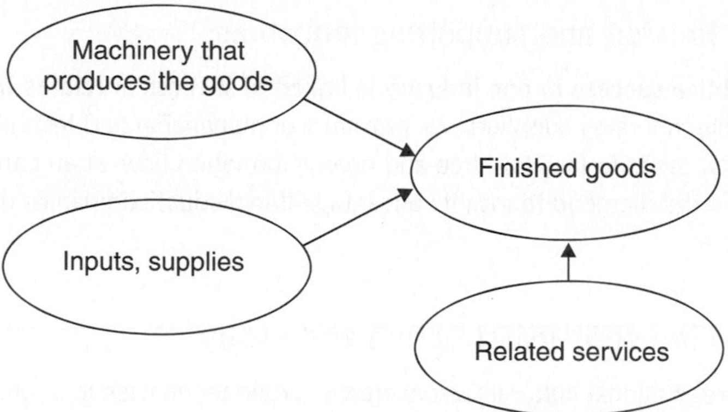

The **individual** firm will be more likely to succeed internationally if there is a **supporting cluster**. Such a cluster can lead to lower costs or the achievement of differentiation; the presence of advanced factors such as skilled labour and digital infrastructure; the transfer of expertise; and a degree of vertical integration through the development of network relationships among the organisations concerned.

Silicon Valley

The concept of clustering in certain industries is not a new phenomenon. Clusters were commonplace in during the industrial revolution in England. Places such as Staffordshire became renowned for the skilled potters working in the regions many potteries, whereas places such as Nottingham built a reputation for lace-making.

Today one of the world's most famous clusters of companies is the iconic Silicon Valley in San Francisco, California. Silicon Valley is home to hi-tech innovators including Apple and Cisco Systems, Google,

Facebook and eBay. Setting up operations close to firms operating in similar industries allows new firms to achieve economies of scale which may not have been available to them elsewhere. New start-ups benefit from the Valley's pool of highly skilled workers with expertise in innovation. Companies in Silicon Valley are able to capitalise on their close proximity to Stanford University, which provide a readily available source of new graduates in hi-tech specialisms. A number of the graduates from Stanford University have gone on to start up their own businesses in Silicon Valley, such as Hewlett-Packard. The appeal of working for hi-tech companies saw 'around 20% of American business-school graduates' going to work for technology firms in 2014. (*The Economist* 2015).

The Economist (2015) reported that in the Valley 'every year ideas grow from specks to spectacular' as new start-up companies are very common. Sander Daniels, the founder of an app that matches skilled labourers with tasks that suit them, notes that living in San Francisco today, with its bustle and big ideas, feels like 'living in Florence during the Renaissance'.

Recently, Airbnb a company set-up in Silicon Valley in 2008 – which operates a website for people to list, find and rent lodgings – was valued at $26 billion.

Source:

The Economist (2015) *To fly, to fall, to fly again.* [Online]. Available from: http://www.economist.com/news/briefing/21659722-tech-boom-may-get-bumpy-it-will-not-end-repeat-dotcom-crash-fly [Accessed 27 September 2016].

7.2.2 Government policy

Porter also points out the importance of **government policy** in nurturing all four of the diamond factors by means of education, subsidy and the provision of services. He also reminds us that **chance** plays an important part.

7.2.3 Overcoming lack of advantage

If a UK firm wishes to compete in an industry in which there is no national competitive advantage, it can take a number of steps to succeed.

(a) **Compete in the most challenging market**, to emulate domestic rivalry and to obtain information.

(b) **Spread research and development** activities to countries where there is an established research base or industry cluster already.

(c) Be prepared to **invest heavily in innovation**.

(d) **Invest in human resources**, both in the firm and the industry as a whole.

(e) **Look out for new technologies** that will change the rules of the industry.

(f) **Collaborate with foreign companies.** US motor companies successfully learned Japanese production techniques.

(g) **Supply overseas companies**. Japanese car plants in the UK have encouraged greater quality in UK components suppliers.

(h) **Source components from overseas**. In the UK **crystal glass industry**, many firms buy crystal glass from the Czech Republic, and do the cutting and design work themselves.

(i) **Exert pressure on politicians** and opinion formers to create better conditions for the diamond to develop (eg in education).

Question 2.6 National advantage

Learning outcome A2a

The Republic of Albion, an island in the North-East Atlantic inhabited by about 40 million people, has a climate that is plagued by fog, damp and rain. Life is a battle to keep dry. In this battle, the Republic has set up 20 research institutes to focus on water and aridity studies. A variety of companies compete in devising new ways of keeping houses (and their owners!) dry, involving advanced technology. A recent innovation is the ionising umbrella, with an electric field that drives away water particles. The country imports most of its raw materials. The water problem is so bad that the country has a network of canals taking surplus water to the sea, through a network of hydroelectric turbines.

Required

What do you think are the possible competitive advantages of the industries of the Republic of Albion?

7.3 The diamond and competitive strategy

Porter's description of the diamond is more a piece of positive economic theory than a useful strategic tool. Individual companies cannot rely on favourable diamond conditions to provide them with competitive advantage. Countries with extremely favourable national conditions still have their share of poor companies.

(a) In international trade, it is essential to study and analyse environmental conditions within the **target nation**, as discussed earlier.

(b) The theory of the diamond is largely based on exporting manufacturing industry: it is less relevant to service industries and any industry that expands internationally by setting up local production or provision of services.

7.4 Emerging markets

Introduction

As we have seen in this chapter, traditionally the largest and most **powerful economies** in the world were those of the **US**, **Japan** and **Western Europe**. These countries were the first to become developed, and therefore they had a 'head start' on the rest of the world. However, in recent years, a number of **other countries** have begun to **compete** with them.

7.4.1 Newly industrialising and emerging markets

Newly industrialising and **emerging** nations (**NIEs**) are countries that are grouped together by virtue of the fact that their economies have grown significantly in recent years and they are becoming increasingly important in the world economy.

NIEs are often (but not always) located in Asia and Latin America and include the so-called 'BRICS' economies of Brazil, Russia, India, China and South Africa (see below) and other countries such as Argentina, Mexico, South Korea, Taiwan and Singapore.

7.4.2 The BRICS economies

Brazil, **R**ussia, **I**ndia, **C**hina and **S**outh Africa have all experienced rapid economic growth in recent years, partly as a consequence of globalisation. When combined, the BRICS economies have a bigger share of world trade than the US.

China has attracted most attention. China is now the second largest economy in the world (behind the US). An article published on the Ernst & Young website entitled *Emerging markets increase their global power* (www.ey.com) predicts that by 2020 the BRICS economies will contribute nearly 50% of global GDP growth.

Key factors influencing the growth of the BRICS economies include the following.

(a) **Increased economic activity**

(b) **Abundance of natural and low-cost labour resources**. Brazil has a vast array of natural resources. It produces sugar, oil and beef, and is the largest grower of coffee beans in the world.

(c) **Increased education standards**. One recent report highlighted plans by the Indian Government to increase the number of young people going to university from 12% to 30% by 2025. The move is regarded as being necessary to sustain India's economic growth.

(d) **Free market philosophy encouraged**. This is particularly evident in the formerly communist country of Russia, where Western multinational companies such as Coca-Cola have established bases.

(e) **Foreign direct investment (FDI)**. According to Reuters, China received $117.6bn of FDI in 2013. This has largely funded the growth in Chinese manufacturing and telecommunications.

FDI is now global in nature, with investment flows becoming more multidirectional. China's rapid growth has enabled the country to invest heavily in other parts of the world, in particular African countries with vast quantities of natural commodities for use in Chinese production facilities.

It is important to note that FDI can take a number of forms, but two of the most common are to **acquire an existing organisation** in the local market or to develop new production facilities (known as **greenfield investment**).

7.4.3 Second-tier emerging nations

Many other countries are often referred to as 'emerging nations'. Examples are Vietnam, Columbia and Ukraine (which is also a transition economy, a term we shall explore later in more detail).

CASE STUDY

The Mint countries

The following case study considers the increasing importance of emerging nations.

In January 2014, the BBC reported on the emergence of four prospective economic superpowers known as the 'Mint' countries. Jim O'Neill, who in 2001 created the 'BRIC' terminology (South Africa was admitted to the BRIC grouping in 2010), highlighted the rise of Mexico, Indonesia, Nigeria and Turkey, also known as 'Mint' nations.

O'Neill suggested that the emergence of these countries is based on a range of factors that are likely to support economic growth in the long term. He noted that 'what they really share beyond having a lot of people, is that at least for the next 20 years, they have really good "inner" demographics – they are all going to see a rise in the number of people eligible to work relative to those not working'.

Furthermore, each of the 'Mint' countries is supported by its geographical positioning to enable easier access to some of the world's most successful markets; 'Mexico is next door to the US, but also Latin America. Indonesia is in the heart of South-East Asia but also has deep connections with China. Turkey is in both the West and East. Nigeria is not really similar in this regard for now, partly because of Africa's lack of development, but it could be in the future if African countries stop fighting and trade with each other'.

Source:

O'Neill, J. (2014) *The Mint countries: Next economic giants?*. [Online]. Available from: http://www.bbc.co.uk/news/magazine-25548060 [Accessed 27 September 2016].

7.5 Types of economic system

There are four main types of economic system in operation in the world – planned, free market, mixed and transition.

Exam alert

It is important that you understand the key differences between the four main economic systems, as Objective Test questions could easily test your ability to distinguish between these.

Type of economy	Impact
Planned economy	Economic activity is controlled by the Government. The State fixes the price of goods and services, and makes all the decisions regarding how resources are allocated.
Free market economy	Opposite of a planned economy. Prices and the allocation of resources are not controlled by the State or any individual, but by market forces and the actions of producers and suppliers.
Mixed economy	There are no true free market economies, as governments tend to have some input into the economy to influence the actions of private sector organisations. This leads to a halfway alternative, known as a mixed economy.
Transition economy	This often applied to the countries that abandoned the Soviet-type political and planned economic system at the end of the 20th century. Examples are the Russian Federation, Poland, Hungary, Romania, the Czech Republic and Ukraine. A number of these countries have completed their transition to a market economy and have become members of the EU.

It is worth noting that the term is sometimes used with a wider meaning, referring to any country emerging from a socialist-type economy towards a market-based economy (eg China). This means that in general usage, there is overlap between transition economies and emerging economies.

7.6 Industrialisation strategies

Successful emerging nations follow **three main strategies**:

- Export of natural commodities
- Import-substitution
- Export-led industrialisation

Export of natural commodities

Countries are endowed with **natural resources** in various degrees; for example, oil, precious metals such as gold, and fertile agricultural land. The first stage of industrialisation is to simply sell natural resources to foreign countries. This generates **income** for the country, which can be used to invest in infrastructure (such as education and technology) and develop the economy. However, the country must import products that it cannot produce domestically.

Import-substitution

Once the economy has created wealth through exporting natural resources, it begins to invest in **new industries**, which produce the more advanced products that it needs. Historically, to **protect** these fledgling industries so that they can be developed and to reduce the country's dependence on foreign imports, protectionist measures were used (eg import tariffs and quotas).

Export-led industrialisation

Protecting and developing new industries was the only perceived method of creating an industrial base up until the 1960s. However, with the **liberalisation of economic systems** came an alternative – an export-centred, outward-looking strategy. Governments realised that the key to rapid economic growth was to **increase exports** – and that by doing so, the wealth of the country would be substantially improved.

Section summary

Four factors support **competitive success** in a nation's industries: factor conditions, demand conditions, related and supporting industries, and firm strategy, structure and rivalry.

Newly industrialising and **emerging** nations (**NIEs**) are countries that are grouped together by virtue of the fact that their economies have grown significantly in recent years. These include the 'BRICS' countries.

Chapter Summary

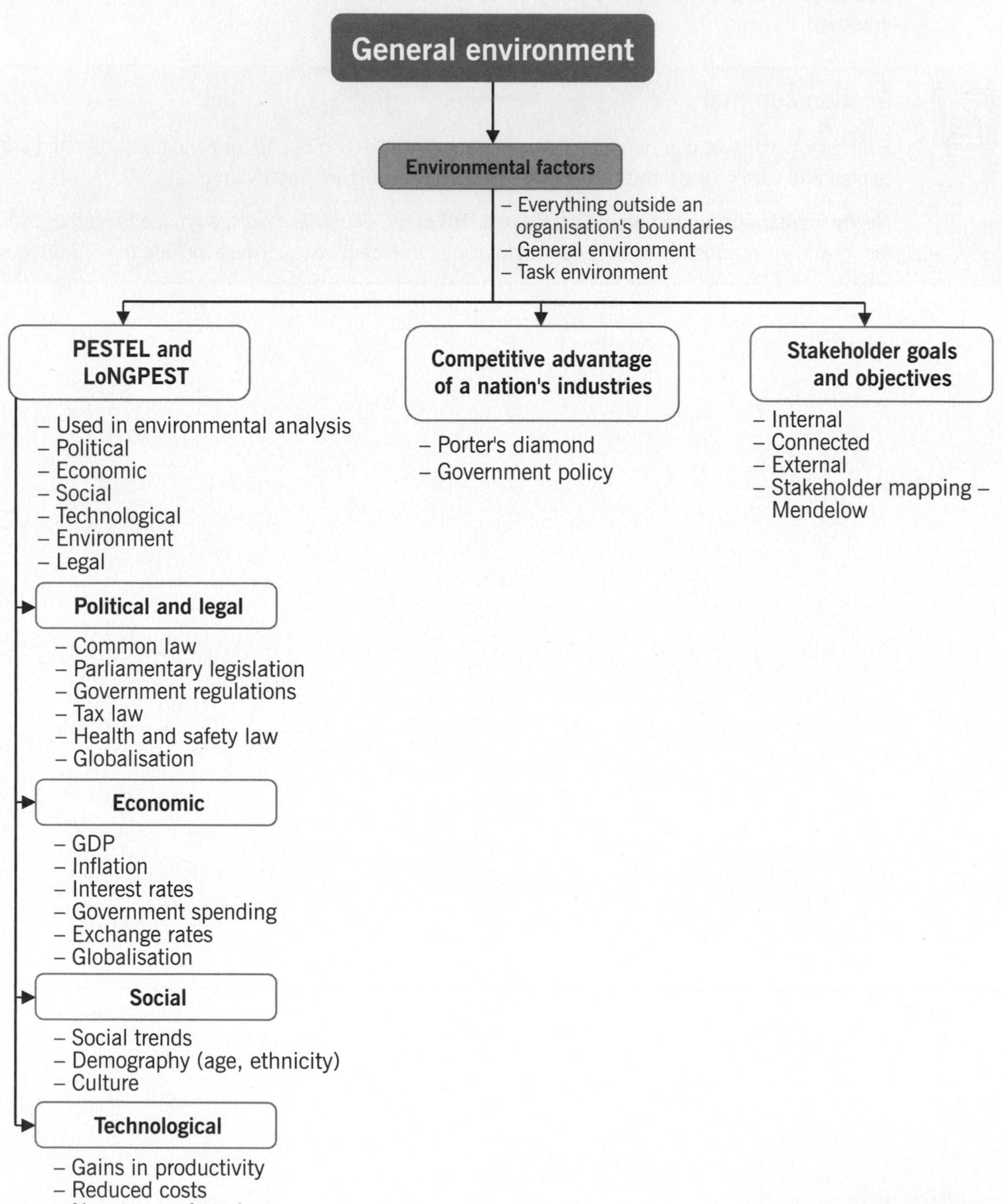
General environment
Environmental factors
– Everything outside an organisation's boundaries
– General environment
– Task environment
PESTEL and LoNGPEST
– Used in environmental analysis
– Political
– Economic
– Social
– Technological
– Environment
– Legal
Political and legal
– Common law
– Parliamentary legislation
– Government regulations
– Tax law
– Health and safety law
– Globalisation
Economic
– GDP
– Inflation
– Interest rates
– Government spending
– Exchange rates
– Globalisation
Social
– Social trends
– Demography (age, ethnicity)
– Culture
Technological
– Gains in productivity
– Reduced costs
– New types of product
Competitive advantage of a nation's industries
– Porter's diamond
– Government policy
Stakeholder goals and objectives
– Internal
– Connected
– External
– Stakeholder mapping – Mendelow

Quick Quiz

1 What does PEST stand for?

2 Distinguish between the general environment and the task environment.

3 What is political risk?

4 Are the following related to government **fiscal** or **monetary** policy?

(a) Taxation
(b) Borrowing
(c) Interest rates
(d) Control of the money supply
(e) Exchange rates
(f) Government spending

5 How can technological change affect the activities of organisations? (List four ways.)

Answers to Quick Quiz

1 Political, economic, social and technological – factors that shape an organisation's environment.

2 The general environment covers all the political/legal, economic, social/cultural and technological (PEST) influences in the countries that an organisation operates in.

The task environment relates to factors of particular relevance to a firm, such as its competitors, customers and suppliers of resources.

3 The political risk in a decision is the risk that political factors will invalidate the strategy, and perhaps severely damage the firm. Examples are wars, political chaos, corruption and nationalisation.

4 (a) Fiscal
(b) Fiscal
(c) Monetary
(d) Monetary
(e) Monetary
(f) Fiscal

5 Any four from the following.

- It can affect the type of products or services that are made and sold.
- It can affect the way in which products are made.
- It can affect the way in which services are provided (especially with the growth of the internet).
- It can affect the way in which markets are identified.
- It can affect organisational structure and the way firms are managed.
- It can affect the way organisations communicate with their customers or suppliers.

Answers to Questions

2.1 Government impact

Using the example of the UK:

(a) The Government must authorise most new drugs (eg for safety before they can be sold).

(b) The UK Government is a major purchaser of pharmaceuticals for the National Health Service, and so has significant buying power.

(c) Health education policies affect consumer demand.

(d) Funding of universities affects the science base for recruitment.

(e) Employment practices, such as working hours, are influenced by EU employment directives.

2.2 Political risk

Answers will differ depending on the nature of the business chosen. However, your answer should include reference to some of the risks identified on the political risk checklist in Section 2.4.1.

2.3 Single currency

There is no definitive right or wrong answer to questions like this, but here are some points to consider.

(a) For companies trading primarily within the EU, such as the package holiday firm, adopting the euro will mean a reduction in exchange rate volatility. In these markets, businesses will be able to compete on the essentials of cost and productivity, rather than being subject to exchange rate movements outside of their control. An analogy is the US – although there are many 'states', there is only one currency (others may argue that, as the US does not represent a union of nation states, it is not a valid analogy).

(b) and (c)

Companies trading outside the Eurozone would remain subject to exchange rate risk, although this would be based on the euro rather than the current UK currency, sterling. Implications will depend on exchange rates and how the European Central Bank manages the euro. If the euro had a relatively 'high' value, then overseas consumers would have to pay more for UK exports. On the other hand, imports to the UK from overseas suppliers would be cheaper.

A related factor is that, if the UK adopted the euro, some commentators believe this would enable the UK to more readily influence the monetary policies of other euro countries. As these policies affect the UK economy and UK businesses, some would argue that this would bring benefits to the UK economy.

2.4 Social trends

The firm's market is shrinking. There is an absolute fall in the number of school leavers. Moreover, it is possible that the increasing proportion of school leavers going on to higher education will mean there will be fewer who can afford Club Fun's packages. That said, a higher disposable income in the population at large might compensate for this trend. People might be encouraged to try destinations other than Club Fun's traditional resorts if these other destinations are publicised on television. Growing access to the internet makes it easier for other suppliers to compete.

2.5 Stakeholder influences

Accountants have divided loyalties – to their firm, and to their profession.

The technical department will almost certainly resist such a change, as the proposals devalue audit to being one of many business services to management. An audit is undertaken for the benefit of shareholders, not the company management. The technical department (the firm's **technostructure**) is also powerful, as enforcement of the standards it will suggest should reduce professional negligence costs. The technostructure will thus exert a powerful influence over the strategy and business practices. External influences include **professional associations**, which have a technostructural influence on the profession as a whole. The Marketing Manager may also be misled as to the degree to which **customers** want a 'one-stop shop' for accounting and advertising services. Perhaps the Marketing Manager is overestimating the power of this factor in the external coalition.

2.6 National advantage

The only **basic factor** endowment appears to be rain. **Advanced factors** include the research institutes. The country also has very sophisticated demand conditions for umbrellas and waterproof items. There seems to be domestic competition in the industry. In addition to umbrellas, you would expect related industries (such as high-technology waterproof raincoats) to appear. The country's firms could compete successfully in global markets for waterproof materials.

It is possible that the country's inhabitants would also have certain expertise in building technologies (eg damp proofing), which could be exported to the construction industry. Finally, hydro-electric turbines **might** be a source of advantage: but the amount of water for energy is so plentiful that only the simplest technology need be used to harness it.

Now try these questions from the Practice Question Bank

Question	Level
2.1 – 2.5	Practice
National advantage	Practice

COMPETITIVE ENVIRONMENT

Chapter 2 dealt with general environmental factors in the external environment (**macro environment**). There we looked at trends that affect most organisations to some extent.

We now narrow our focus to consider the **micro environment** or the immediate small-scale environment of the organisation.

We start by considering how an organisation might go about analysing its competition and what data it would need to do so.

Then we move on to consider the sources of data and the role of **big data** in modern business.

Most businesses compete with other firms but have a limited number of direct competitors. Competitors are a vital influence on decision making, and we discuss the five competitive forces underlying a particular industry.

Consideration is then given to Porter's generic competitive strategies. These are strategies that organisations adopt for competitive advantage. This discussion then leads us to the work of Ansoff and the **growth vector matrix**, a framework which highlights four strategies for organisational growth.

We end this chapter by considering the importance of interpreting competitor data. This is a critical skill that you will need to develop in advance of attempting your Integrated Case Study exam. The final question in this section draws together a number of the themes covered in the chapter.

Topic list	Learning outcomes	Syllabus references	Ability required
1 Competitor analysis	A2b	A2(i), (ii)	Analysis
2 Accounting for competitors	A2b	A2(iii)	Analysis
3 Sources, availability and quality of data for environmental analysis	A2b	A2(iii), (iv)	Analysis
4 Information for planning and control	A1a	A1(i)	Analysis
5 Environmental information and analysis	A2b	A2(iii), (vi)	Analysis
6 The competitive environment – the five forces	A2a	A2(i), (vii)	Analysis/ comprehension
7 Competitive strategies	A1c	A1(i), (ii), (iv)	Comprehension
8 Product-market strategies: direction of growth	A1c	A1(ii), (iv)	Comprehension
9 Methods of growth	A1c	A1(ii), (iv)	Comprehension

Topic list	Learning outcomes	Syllabus references	Ability required
10 Corporate appraisal (SWOT)	A1a	A1(ii)	Analysis
11 Analysing and interpreting competitor data	A2b	A2(v)	Analysis

Chapter Overview

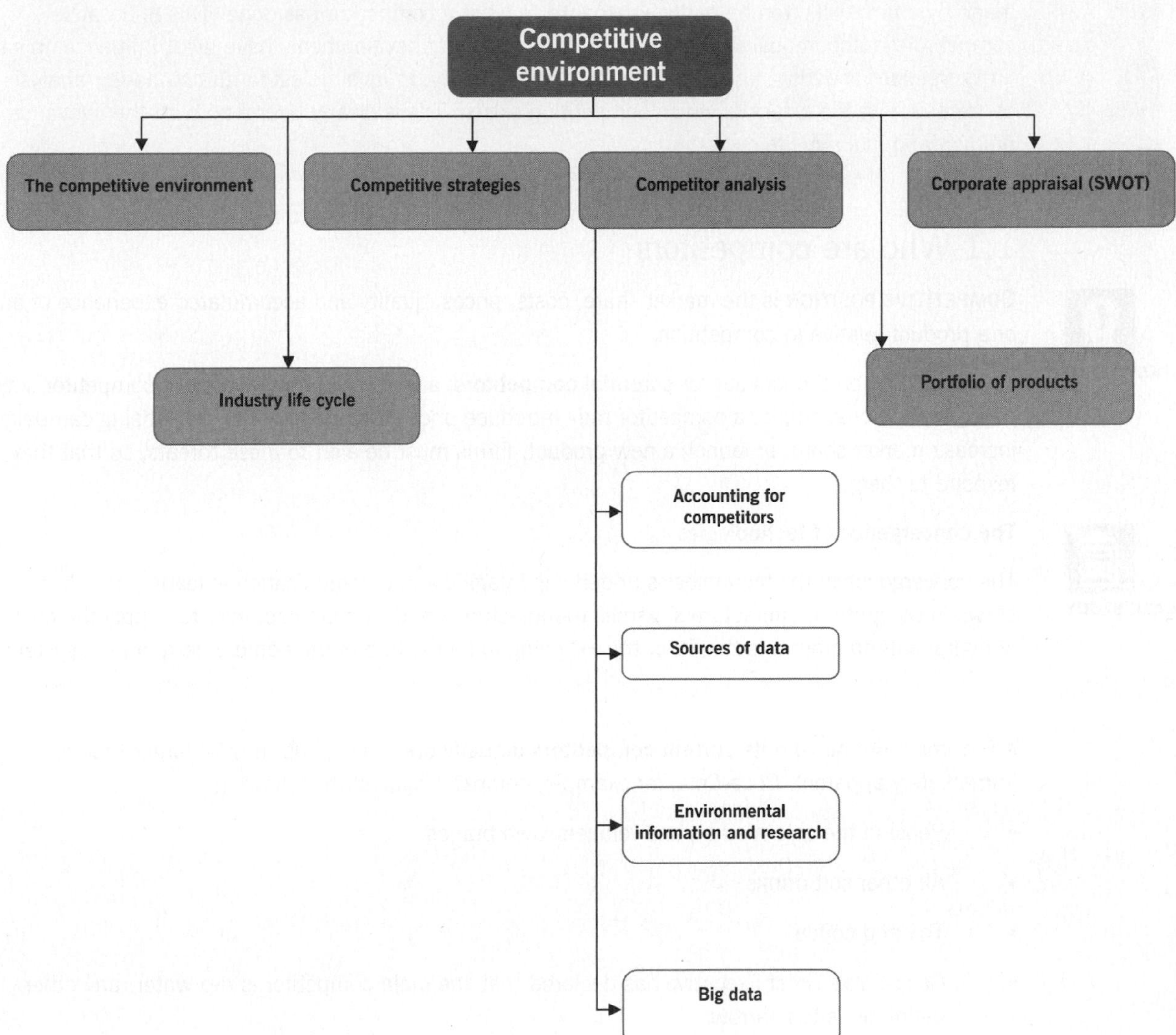
Competitive environment
The competitive environment
Competitive strategies
Competitor analysis
Corporate appraisal (SWOT)
Industry life cycle
Portfolio of products
Accounting for competitors
Sources of data
Environmental information and research
Big data

1 Competitor analysis

Introduction

In any market where there are significant competitors, the strategic decisions and marketing decisions made by a firm will often be partly a response to what a competitor has done. This is because competitors' autonomous policies and reactions to market developments have great influence on each firm's freedom of action, and ultimately on its profitability. In its simplest form, competitor analysis will be concerned with the extent to which competition exists. This is clearly bound up with the relevance of product and industry life cycles.

1.1 Who are competitors?

KEY TERM

COMPETITIVE POSITION is the market share, costs, prices, quality and accumulated experience of an entity or a product relative to competition.

Firms must be on the lookout for **potential competitors**, and the potential impact of competitor actions on their profits. For example, a competitor may introduce price cuts or aggressive advertising campaigns to increase market share, or launch a new product. Firms must be alert to these threats, so that they can respond to them.

CASE STUDY

The convergence of technologies

The convergence of the technologies underlying imaging and communication is leading to a battle between computer manufacturers, games manufacturers and TV manufacturers to supply the environment of digital entertainment. Is the TV or the PC going to be the hub of the home entertainment system?

A firm must **define who its current competitors actually are**. This group may be larger than is immediately apparent. Coca-Cola, for example, competes against the following:

- Pepsi in the cola market, and retailers' own brands
- All other soft drinks
- Tea and coffee
- Coca-Cola's Chief Executive has declared that 'the main competitor is tap water: any other definition is too narrow'

1.1.1 Types of competitor

Kotler lists four kinds of competition.

(a) **Brand competitors** are similar firms offering similar products: for example, McDonald's and Burger King.

(b) **Industry competitors** have similar products but are different in other ways, such as geographical market and range of products: for example, Amazon and HMV, or British Airways and American Airways.

(c) **Generic competitors** compete for the same disposable income with different products; for example, home improvements versus foreign vacations.

(d) **Form competitors** offer products that are technically significantly different, but satisfy the same needs; for example, manufacturers of matches and cigarette lighters.

1.2 Analysing competitors: the main issues

KEY TERM

COMPETITOR ANALYSIS is the 'identification and quantification of the relative strengths and weaknesses (compared with competitors or potential competitors), which could be of significance in the development of a successful competitive strategy'. (*CIMA Official Terminology*)

An important initial variable is **industry structure**. A fragmented industry with many small players is unlikely to be highly competitive overall, since most firms will seek to pursue a **niche strategy**. The situation is the opposite in a **consolidated industry**, where a small number of firms are striving for a dominating market share and **cost leadership**.

Some industries cannot easily be consolidated, and the niche structure may continue indefinitely.

An organisation should look at four key factors when undertaking competitor analysis.

Factor	Comment
The competitor's goals (the firm as a whole and the business unit)	• What are the business's **stated financial goals**? What trade-offs are made between long-term and short-term objectives? • What is the competitor's attitude to **risk**? • Do **managerial beliefs** (eg that the firm should be a market leader) affect its goals? • **Organisation structure**. What is the relative status of functional areas? • What **incentive systems** are in place? • What are the **managers** like? Do they favour one particular type of strategy? • To what extent does the business **cross-subsidise** others in the group if the business is part of a group? What is the purpose of the business: to raise money for the group?
The competitor's assumptions about the industry	• What does a competitor believe its **relative position** in the industry (in terms of cost, product quality) to be? • Are there any **cultural or regional differences** that indicate the way managers are likely to respond? • What does the competitor believe about the **future** for the industry? • Does the competitor accept the industry's '**conventional wisdom**'?
The competitor's current and potential situation and strategy	• Distribution • Operations • Overall costs • Marketing and selling • Financial strengths • Organisation • Research and engineering • Managerial ability • Products
The competitor's capability	• The **competitor's core competences**. In other words, what does the competitor do distinctively well? • Does the competitor have the **ability to expand** in a particular market? • What **competitive advantages and disadvantages** does the competitor possess?

1.2.1 Market size, market growth and market share

When analysing competitors, it is important to distinguish between three connected concepts relating to the market.

(a) **Market size**. It is useful to get an idea of the size of the market, based on total sales volume or sales value of all competitors. In some cases, it may prove difficult to define the market. For example, is Travelodge in the hotel market or the budget hotel market?

(b) **Market growth**. Another important consideration when analysing competitors is how fast the market has grown in recent years, particularly over the last year. A company's strategy will affect its decision to get involved in a fast-growing or more gradually developing market.

(c) **Market share**. Market share is the proportion of a market that is being serviced by an organisation. Increased market share is not necessarily the same, as a market can grow as more competitors come into it, so that an organisation's market share declines even if the organisation itself is growing. It is generally considered to be of strategic advantage to have a large and growing share of a particular market for a number of reasons:

(i) Economies of scale
(ii) Leverage over suppliers
(iii) Greater influence over prices

1.2.2 Competitor response profiles

All these are combined in a **competitor response profile**. This indicates the competitor's vulnerability and the right 'battleground' on which to fight.

KEY POINT

Kotler lists four response profiles.

- The **laid back** competitor does not respond.
- The **tiger** responds aggressively to all opposing moves.
- The **selective** competitor reacts to some threats in some markets, but not to all.
- The **stochastic** competitor is unpredictable.

The reasons for these observed profiles may be complex. An effort should be made to understand them and how they fit into the competitor's overall strategy.

Information for strategic uses can be gathered from the following sources.

- Financial statements
- Information from common customers and suppliers
- Inspection of a competitor's products
- Information from former employees
- Job advertisements

1.2.3 Competitive significance

Competition is likely to be intense when firms have strategic similarities in such matters as those below.

- Technology used
- Management skills
- Distribution channels
- Products offered
- Geographical coverage

Even when current products are dissimilar, similarities in other areas may well see new competition emerging, as for instance when Marks & Spencer, an own-brand clothes retailer, started selling own-brand food.

1.2.4 Exit barriers

Exit barriers are those that **prevent a firm from leaving an industry**, or increase the cost of so doing. Cost-related exit barriers include the following.

(a) **Vertically integrated companies** producing products for many markets. Exiting one market would not significantly alter its cost structure. In global commodity markets, inability to buy cheaply on spot markets can be a severe hindrance to competitive pricing, as is seen for example in the UK petrol market, where supermarkets have greater flexibility than the major integrated companies which are committed to selling their own oil through their own filling stations.

(b) **Common administrative costs** might be shared over a number of different businesses. This might result in a high overhead charge but, while the apportionment might turn one of the businesses into a loss, closing the business down might save little of the overhead expenditure.

Question 3.1 Competitor analysis

Learning outcome A2b

Jot down a list of items of information that might be obtained from an environmental analysis of competitors. The list can be a long one!

1.2.5 The Boston classification

The **Boston Consulting Group classification** (the BCG matrix) classifies products in terms of their capacity for growth within the market and the market's capacity for growth as a whole. A firm should have a balanced **portfolio of products**. The GE business screen and the Shell matrix are similar tools.

The **BCG matrix** assesses a company's products in terms of potential cash generation and cash expenditure requirements. Products or strategic business units (SBUs) are categorised in terms of **market growth rate** and a firm's **relative market share**.

KEY TERM

RELATIVE MARKET SHARE. One entity's sales of a product or service in a specified market, compared to the total sales earned by the largest entity offering that product or service.

(a) The rate of **market growth** depends on market conditions. No single percentage rate can be set, since new markets may grow explosively while mature ones grow hardly at all. A high market growth rate can indicate good opportunities for profitable operations. However, intense competition in a high-growth market can erode profit, while a slowly growing market with high barriers to entry can be very profitable.

(b) **Relative market share** is assessed as a ratio: it is market share compared with the market share of the **largest competitor**. A relative market share greater than one indicates that the product or SBU is the market leader. The BCG matrix use market share to estimate costs associated with given products. This is used because there is a connection between lower costs and higher market share. However, **correlation does not prove causation.**

(c) Note that there is an unspoken assumption that the **market** itself is easily defined. This may not be the case and it is likely that much thought will have to be given to this problem, even if only to decide whether the analysis should be in terms of brand, generic product or product form.

(d) Be aware also that the **matrix ignores potential links between products**. However, it is important to consider such links; for example, if a firm stops producing one product, will it have a knock-on effect on other products?

		Relative market share: *High*	Relative market share: *Low*
Market growth	*High*	Stars	Question marks/ problem children
	Low	Cash cows	Dogs

The product portfolio should be balanced, with cash cows providing finance for stars and question marks, and a minimum of dogs.

(a) **Stars**. In the short term, these require capital expenditure in excess of the cash they generate, in order to maintain their market position, but promise high returns in the future. Strategy: **build.**

(b) **Cash cows**. In due course, stars will become cash cows. Cash cows need very little capital expenditure and generate high levels of cash income. However, apparently mature products can be invigorated, possibly by competitors, who could come to dominate the market. Cash cows can be used to finance the stars. Strategy: **hold**, or **harvest** if weak.

(c) **Question marks**. Do the products justify considerable capital expenditure in the hope of increasing their market share, or will they be squeezed out of the expanding market by rival products? Strategy: **build** or **harvest**.

(d) **Dogs**. They may be ex-cash cows that have fallen on hard times. Although they will show only a modest net cash outflow, or even a modest net cash inflow, they are cash traps that tie up funds and provide a poor return on investment. However, they may have a useful role, either to complete a product range or to keep competitors out. There are also many smaller niche businesses in market that are difficult to consolidate that would count as dogs but which are quite successful. Strategy: **divest** or **hold**.

Although developed for use with a **product** portfolio, the BCG matrix is also used in diversified conglomerates to assess the strategic position of subsidiary **SBUs**. This is an important point to note: the BCG matrix can be applied either to a **product portfolio** or to a **business portfolio**.

The BCG matrix offers management a simple and convenient way of looking at a diverse range of businesses and products, within a single overall portfolio. In doing so, it encourages management to look at the portfolio as a whole, rather than simply assessing the needs and performance of each unit independently. For example, the portfolio would allow a group of companies to consider the cash flow requirements of the group as a whole, rather than focusing on individual units in isolation.

Also, the BCG matrix should help management with long-term strategic planning; for example, by highlighting the need for new question marks or stars to be developed, to eventually replace the current crop of cash cows.

However, critics argue the axes are too simplistic.

(a) A high market share is assumed to indicate competitive strength but this is not necessarily true.

(b) A strong brand may yield competitive strength despite a relatively low market share.

(c) High market growth is deemed to indicate an attractive industry. But fast-growing industries are likely to require significant investment, so they may not be attractive to a firm with limited available capital.

(d) The requirement that firms have a high relative market share is justified by the ability of large producers to benefit from scale economies and experience effects, and thereby to assist in surviving price pressure in late life cycle markets. However, following a **differentiation** strategy or a **niche** strategy allows a firm to prosper even with a small relative share.

(e) The approach sees the board as working on behalf of shareholders as a super-investor seeking to balance the demands of cash returns now with future growth, to make the firm's equity attractive. This overlooks other synergies from combining businesses together in the same portfolio, such as cross-selling, supply and demand integration and knowledge spreading.

Section summary

Firms should **analyse their competitors** and build models of how they might react based on their future goals, assumptions, capability and current situation.

2 Accounting for competitors

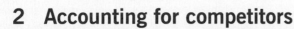

Introduction

Competitive strategies can be analysed in financial terms, as we know, using simple techniques such as net present value. However, simple models really require a consideration of likely competitive response if they are to be useful in forecasting the likely return on a strategic investment.

2.1 Competitor response

In practice, anticipated **competitor actions** are dealt with indirectly in the planning process. The management accounting system may not be able to identify those deficiencies in performance arising from competitors' activities **after** the plan has been implemented.

A few detergent companies own many of the brands offered to the market. This deters competitors. How do you evaluate, financially, a strategy such as this?

(a) The expenditure to **maintain market share** and sustain brands is a known cost. However, the benefit is not known exactly.

(b) There might be a variety of **assumptions** about market size, market shares and the profit assumptions of a number of the scenarios identified.

(c) There are problems with forecasting the future cash flows of market share estimates.

A useful approach to take is to **analyse the anticipated loss** caused by **not** undertaking a particular course of action: the present value of this loss becomes, effectively, the maximum size of the investment. For example, A Ltd is worried that a competitor will shift the market dynamics from I to II.

	Market state	
	I	II
A Ltd's market share	20%	15%
Present value of future cash flows	£1m	£800,000

(a) There is a present value loss of £200,000. If a marketing manager suggested that spending £100,000 would see off the competitor, this action would be worth taking.

(b) There is still the problem of estimating the difference between market states I and II; after all, the marketing campaign might deter **other** competitors, or create an increase in demand. It is also impossible to be certain that the competitor will in fact be deterred by an advertising campaign.

2.2 Competitor modelling

2.2.1 Sources of information

Data sources include: published accounts and annual reports; market research reviews and reports (eg by the Economist Intelligence Unit); investment analysts' notes; industry experts and consultants; suppliers; shared customers; the competitor's marketing strategy; public communications (magazines, journals and newsletters); and the internet.

A great deal can be gleaned from using one's own company as a model, and adjusting it for significant differences in competitors' businesses. For example, a firm might make some sub-components in-house, whereas a competitor might buy them on the open market.

2.2.2 Cost structures

Important differences between firms include the following.

- Absolute cost levels
- The proportion of fixed to variable costs
- The strategic impact of outsourcing decisions on competitive flexibility
- The sales price in relation to costs, and unit costs (this will affect a firm's ability to respond to a competitor's price cut)
- Not all businesses require the same rate of return
- Exit costs (if a firm has high exit costs, it is likely to stay in an industry and compete aggressively, rather than leave the industry)

2.2.3 Barriers to entry

Competitor analysis should also consider the costs that any potential new entrant to the industry will incur to overcome barriers to entry. (We discuss the nature of barriers to entry later in this chapter, when we consider Porter's five forces model.)

Comparing entry costs with the present value of the returns the entrant could achieve will indicate the likelihood of new entrants. If revenues exceed costs, the market is financially attractive to new entrants; if costs exceed revenues, the threat of new entrants is reduced.

Exam alert

It is important to remember that competitor analysis does not simply involve finding out information about competitors. An organisation should also consider how it can use the information it has gained to shape its own strategies.

KEY POINT

If the market appears attractive to new entrants, an organisation should compare the cost of raising new barriers (for example, by spending on a brand) to the potential loss of revenue if a new competitor does enter the market. If the potential loss of revenue from a new competitor entering the market exceeds the cost of raising new barriers, the organisation should look at raising new barriers to entry.

Section summary

The **management accountant's techniques** are useful in competitor analysis (eg by analysing how a competitor's cost structure influences the options available to it) and by modelling the impact of different strategies.

3 Sources, availability and quality of data for environmental analysis

Introduction

Data and information come from sources both inside and outside an organisation, and can be qualitative or quantitative. An organisation's information systems should be designed so as to obtain – or **capture** – all the relevant data and information required.

3.1 Internal information

Capturing data and information from **inside** the organisation involves designing a system for collecting or measuring data, and information that sets out procedures for:

(a) What data and information is collected
(b) How frequently
(c) By whom
(d) By what methods
(e) How data and information is processed, filed and communicated

The accounting ledgers provide an excellent source of financial information.

3.2 External information

Formal collection of data from outside sources includes the following.

(a) A company's **tax specialists** will be expected to gather information about changes in tax law and how this will affect the company.

(b) Obtaining information about any new legislation on health and safety at work, or employment regulations, must be the responsibility of a particular person – for example, the company's **legal expert** or **company secretary** – who must then pass on the information to other managers affected by it.

(c) Research and development (R&D) work often relies on information about other R&D work being done by another company or by government institutions. An **R&D official** might be made responsible for finding out about R&D work in the company.

(d) **Marketing managers** need to know about the opinions and buying attitudes of potential customers. To obtain this information, they might carry out market research exercises.

Informal gathering of information from the environment occurs naturally, consciously or unconsciously, as people learn what is going on in the world around them – perhaps from newspapers, television reports, and meetings with business associates or the trade press.

Organisations hold external information such as invoices, letters and advertisements **received from customers and suppliers**. But there are many occasions when an active search outside the organisation is necessary.

KEY TERM

The phrase ENVIRONMENTAL SCANNING is often used to describe the process of gathering external information, which is available from a wide range of sources.

Sources of external information include:

(a) The Government
(b) Annual reports and press statements of competitors or other firms
(c) Advice or information bureaux
(d) Consultants

(e) Newspaper and magazine publishers

(f) Market research and other reports, for example from Mintel or the Economist Intelligence Unit

(g) **Libraries** and information services

(h) Other organisations' systems, for instance via extranets or **electronic data interchange (EDI)**.

(i) Many of the sources mentioned above, and others, are available in digital (electronic) format.

 (i) Information services such as **Prestel** offer a very large bank of information gathered from organisations such as the Office for National Statistics, newspapers and the British Library. **Topic** offers information on the stock market. Companies like **Reuters** operate primarily in the field of provision of information.

 (ii) The **internet** is a vast source of information, for example company websites, and there are a huge number of journals and articles published online.

Question 3.2 Decisions

Learning outcome A2b

Information is often required by people **outside** the organisation for making judgements and decisions relating to an organisation. Give four examples of decisions that may be taken by outsiders.

3.3 Qualitative research

KEY TERM

QUALITATIVE RESEARCH involves collecting and analysing non-numerical data, and is useful for understanding behaviours and attitudes.

For example, qualitative data that could inform competitor analysis might relate to brand awareness or why customers prefer one scent or product over another. Qualitative research is by nature subjective and can be complex, time consuming and expensive. However, it can play a significant role in decision making. There are several ways in which qualitative research could be carried out.

Observation. The way in which the product is sold by competitors and/or the way customers use the product can be observed. This can be done either with or without the knowledge of the competitors or customers.

Interviews. The company could directly interview its customers about their perceptions of the products and their preferences. Interviewing past employees of competitors may also be possible but confidentiality rules must not be breached.

Online surveys (feedback). Data could be collected from website visitors using online surveys and tools such as Google Analytics.

Focus groups. This is particularly useful in relation to new products. It involves selecting and questioning a group of individuals who are representative of the target market in order to determine their preferences.

Analysis. The qualitative data obtained via the methods above must then be analysed to convert the data into meaningful information that can be used to determine its strategy and to develop its products.

The types of qualitative data that a company could collect to inform its competitor analysis include:

(a) The products affected by the competitor including information such as the popularity, selling price and unique selling proposition of each of the products. Any products that are in direct competition should also be identified.

(b) Marketing strategies and approaches used by competitors should be identified. Branding of competitive products should be considered along with details of customer awareness and perceptions of brands.

(c) Customer profiling can be determined. Who buys the competitors' products? Are they the same people who purchase your products? What factors make them choose which products to buy and from whom?

(d) Customer value analysis could be carried out. What it is about the products of your company and competitors that customers value? Unique scents? Product design? Stylish packaging? And so on.

3.4 Quantitative research

KEY TERM

QUANTITATIVE RESEARCH is based on facts and numbers, and is objective. Ratios, trend analysis and other statistical methods can be used to convert the data into meaningful information.

The types of quantitative data that could be collected to inform competitor analysis include:

(a) Financial information. This can be undertaken through a review of the competitors' operating statements. Trend analysis of sales and profit margins should be reviewed and financial ratios such as earnings per share (EPS), return on investment (ROI) and liquidity could be calculated. This information can be compared to the company's own financial information and to industry standards.

(b) Time taken to dispatch goods ordered online, number of customer complaints, speed of resolution of complaints, and percentage of customers who reorder are all examples of quantitative data that can be used to determine the levels of customer satisfaction.

Section summary

An information system should be designed to obtain information from **all relevant sources** – both internal and external.

Qualitative research uses non-numerical data, and provides subjective responses and so is useful in understanding behaviour and attitudes. **Quantitative research** uses facts and figures and is objective.

Exam alert

Make sure the sources of information you recommend are practical and relevant to the context of the scenario.

4 Information for planning and control

Introduction

We now consider what sorts of decisions are made at the **strategic level** and the **operational level**. These decisions are affected by risk and uncertainty in the environment.

KEY TERM

STRATEGIC PLANNING is a process of deciding on objectives of the organisation, on changes in these objectives, on the resources used to attain these objectives and on the policies that are to govern the acquisition, use and disposition of these resources.

Strategic decision making:

(a) Is medium to **long term**
(b) Involves high levels of **uncertainty** and risk (the future is unpredictable)
(c) Involves situations that **may not recur**
(d) Deals with **complex** issues

KEY TERM

OPERATIONAL CONTROL ensures that specific tasks are carried out effectively and efficiently. It focuses on individual tasks, and is carried out within the strictly defined guidelines issued by strategic planning and tactical control decisions.

4.1 The decision-making process

The stages in making a decision are as follows.

Problem recognition

Problem definition and structuring

Identifying alternative courses of action

Making and communicating the decision

Implementing the decision

Monitoring the effects of the decision

Information and decision making

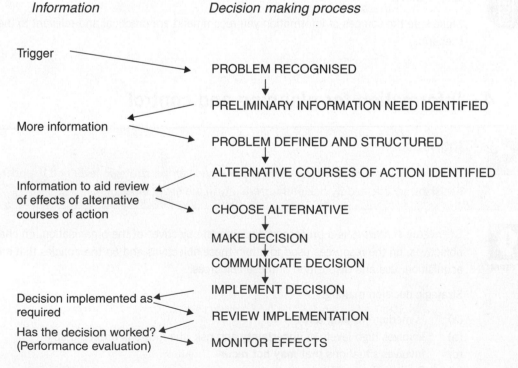

Information	*Decision making process*
Trigger →	PROBLEM RECOGNISED
←	PRELIMINARY INFORMATION NEED IDENTIFIED
More information →	PROBLEM DEFINED AND STRUCTURED
←	ALTERNATIVE COURSES OF ACTION IDENTIFIED
Information to aid review of effects of alternative courses of action →	CHOOSE ALTERNATIVE
	MAKE DECISION
	COMMUNICATE DECISION
←	IMPLEMENT DECISION
Decision implemented as required →	REVIEW IMPLEMENTATION
Has the decision worked? (Performance evaluation) →	MONITOR EFFECTS

4.1.1 Problem recognition

Decisions are not made without **information**. The decision maker needs to be informed of a problem in the first place. This is sometimes referred to as the **decision trigger**.

4.1.2 Problem definition and structuring

Normally, **further information** is then required. This further information is **analysed** so that the problem can be **defined** precisely.

Consider, for example, a company with falling sales. The fall in sales would be the **trigger**. **Further information** would be needed to identify where the deficiencies were occurring. The company might discover that sales of product X in area Y are falling, and the problem can be **defined** as:

'Decline of sales of product X in area Y due to new competitor: how can the decline be reversed?'

One of the purposes of **defining** the problem is to identify the **relationships** between the **various factors** in it, especially if the problem is complex.

4.1.3 Identifying alternative courses of action

Where alternative courses of action are identified, **information** is needed about the likely effect of each, so that they can be assessed.

As a simple example, if our company wishes to review the price of product X in area Y, information will be needed as to the effect of particular price levels on demand for the product. Such information can include external information such as market research (demand at a particular price) and the cost of the product, which can be provided internally.

4.1.4 Making and communicating the decision

The decision is **made** after review of the information relating to alternatives. However, the decision is useless if it is not **communicated**. So, in our example, if the **Marketing Director** decides to lower the price of product X and institute an intensive **advertising** campaign, nothing will happen unless the advertising department is informed, and also the **manufacturing** department, which will have to prepare new packaging showing the lower price.

4.1.5 Implementation of the decision

The decision is then **implemented**. For large-scale decisions (for example, to relocate a factory 100 miles away from its current site), implementation may need substantial **planning**, detailed information and very clear communication.

4.1.6 Monitoring the effects of the decision

Once a decision has been implemented, information is needed so that its effects can be **reviewed**. For example, if a manufacturing organisation has installed new equipment in anticipation of savings in costs, then information will need to be obtained as to whether these are achieved in practice.

Exam alert

You could use this six-stage process as a means of analysing an exam question scenario in your Integrated Case Study. What is the problem; what are the alternatives; how will your solution be implemented; and so on.

4.2 Risk and uncertainty in decision making

Decision making involves **making decisions now about what will happen in the future**. Obviously, decisions can turn out badly, or actual results can prove to be very different from the estimates on which the original decision was made because the necessary **information is not available** when the decision is made.

KEY TERMS

RISK involves situations or events that may or may not occur, but whose probability of occurrence can be calculated statistically and the frequency of their occurrence predicted from past records.

UNCERTAINTY involves situations or events whose outcome cannot be predicted with statistical confidence.

The Management Accountant, who must present relevant cost and revenue data to assist a manager who is about to make a decision, should consider two things.

(a) If the figures are **only slightly in doubt** or the amounts themselves are not material, a **best estimate** with a note that the figures are not certain may be good enough.

(b) If the amount or the **degree of uncertainty was large**, to present just one set of forecast figures would be unwise. For example, if a forecast of sales demand is 'anywhere between 1,000 and 10,000 units', it would be naive and unhelpful to prepare a **single point estimate** of sales – just one forecast figure – of, say, 5,000 units.

If the uncertainty in a situation does warrant special attention in the figures, the next problem is **how the uncertainty** in the figures should be presented.

There are various methods of bringing uncertainty and risk analysis into the evaluation of decisions. They include the following.

(a) **Conservative estimates**. Estimating outcomes in a conservative manner in order to provide a built-in safety factor.

(b) Looking at the **worst possible** and **best possible** outcomes, as well as the most likely outcome, and reaching a decision that takes these into account.

(c) **Sensitivity analysis**. Any technique that tests decision options for their vulnerability to changes in a 'variable' such as expected sales volume.

(d) Assessing **probabilities** and calculating, for each decision alternative, either the **expected value** of costs or benefits with, possibly, the standard deviation of the possible outcomes, or a probability distribution of the possible outcomes. **Decision trees** might be used to illustrate in a 'pictorial' or 'graphical' form the alternatives facing the decision maker.

4.3 Perfect information

KEY TERMS

PERFECT INFORMATION is information that predicts the future with perfect accuracy.

IMPERFECT INFORMATION is information that cannot be guaranteed to be completely accurate. Almost all information is therefore imperfect – but may still be very useful.

Obtaining more information first about what is likely to happen can sometimes reduce the uncertainty about the future outcome from taking a decision. We can categorise information depending on **how reliable** it is likely to be for predicting what will happen in the future and hence for helping managers to make better decisions.

Section summary

Control information, to be useful, must aid the decision-making process.

5 Environmental information and analysis

5.1 Environmental analysis and uncertainty

KEY POINT

Introduction

Johnson and Scholes suggest that a firm should conduct an **audit of environmental influences**. This will identify the environmental factors that have had a significant influence on the organisation's development or performance in the past.

In this section, we shall explore the role of big data. Big data analytics is a term used to describe the extraction of meaning from vast quantities of data. Many organisations have turned to its use to identify trends and correlations in the data that they collect and store, with the aim of putting this to commercial use.

Consideration is also given to Laney's 3 Vs definition of big data, followed by a case study illustrating the role that big data is now playing in competitor analysis. Finally, we look at some of the criticisms surrounding the increasing usage of big data analytics.

Strategic decisions are made in partial ignorance, as we have seen, because the environment is **uncertain**. As we mentioned earlier, uncertainty arises from the **complexity and dynamism** of the environment.

(a) **Complexity** arises from:

(i) The **variety of influences** faced by the organisation. The more open an organisation is, the greater the variety of influences. The greater the number of markets the organisation operates in, the greater the number of influences to which it is subject.

(ii) The amount of **knowledge** necessary. All businesses need to have knowledge of the tax system, for example, but only pharmaceuticals businesses need to know about mandatory testing procedures for new drugs.

(iii) The **interconnectedness** of environmental influences. Importing and exporting companies are sensitive to exchange rates, which themselves are sensitive to interest rates. Interest rates then influence a company's borrowing costs.

(b) **Dynamism**. Stable environments are unchanging. Dynamic environments are in a state of change. The computer market is a dynamic market because of the rate of technological change, for example.

Question 3.3 — Contrasting environment

Learning outcome A2b

Analyse the environments of the two situations below, according to the criteria given above.

(a) A new product has just been introduced to a market segment. It is proving popular. As it is based on a unique technology, barriers to entry are high. The product will not be sold outside this market segment.

(b) A group of scientists has recently been guaranteed, by an EU research sponsoring body, funds for the next ten years to investigate new technologies in the construction industry, such as 'smart materials' (which respond automatically to weather and light conditions). This is a multi-disciplinary project with possible benefits for the construction industry. A number of building firms have also guaranteed funds.

The implication is that the type of business strategy adopted, and indeed the approach to making business strategy, will depend on the type of environment the firm inhabits.

5.2 Impact of uncertainty

If an organisation is operating in a highly uncertain environment, this will affect its strategy.

(a) **The planning horizon will be shortened** because the uncertainty will mean that management will not dare plan too far ahead.

(b) **Strategies may be more conservative** because management are unlikely to risk anything new. However, the counter argument to this is that management may want to try something new, because the uncertainty could mean that the existing strategies will no longer work.

(c) **Emergent strategies may be encouraged**, instead of planned strategies. Advocates of emergent strategies argue they are more appropriate to periods of uncertainty because of their adaptability to changing circumstances.

(d) **Increased information requirements**. Management will require more regular information to allow them to monitor and assess the changing conditions. Uncertainty will make forecasting harder, so management will need more information to gauge their strategic position.

(e) **Firms may follow multiple strategies**. Firms may respond to risk and uncertainty by trying to develop a number of alternative options. For example, in the current climate of uncertainty surrounding oil reserves and production, oil firms may try to develop multiple sources of oil around the world, to avoid being dependent on a particular region or a particular extraction technology.

5.3 Forecasts

KEY TERM

A **FORECAST** is 'a prediction of future events and their quantification for planning purposes'.

(*CIMA Official Terminology*)

Forecasting attempts to reduce the uncertainty that managers face. In **simple/static conditions, the past is a relatively good guide** to the future. Techniques are:

(a) **Time series analysis.** Data for a number of months/years is obtained and analysed. The aim of time series analysis is to identify:

  (i) Seasonal and other cyclical fluctuations
  (ii) Long-term underlying trends

  An example of the use of this approach is the UK's monthly unemployment statistics, which show a 'headline figure' and the 'underlying trend'.

(b) **Regression analysis** is a quantitative technique to check any underlying correlations between two variables (eg sales of ice cream and the weather). Remember that the relationship between two variables may only hold between certain values.

(c) **Econometrics** is the study of economic variables and their interrelationships.

  (i) **Leading indicators** are indicators that change before market demand changes. For example, a sudden increase in the birth rate would be an indicator of future demand for children's clothes.

  (ii) The ability to predict the span of time between a change in the indicator and a change in market demand. Change in an indicator is especially useful for demand forecasting when they reach their highest or lowest points (when an increase turns into a decline or vice versa).

In **dynamic/complex conditions**, the picture is different.

- **Future developments** – the past is not a reliable guide.
- Techniques such as **scenario building** are useful, as they can propose a number of possible futures.
- **Complex environments** require techniques to reduce the effects of complexity on organisational structure and decision making.

Some firms aim to deal with planning in complex environments by techniques such as scenario building.

5.4 Strategic intelligence

If a key task of strategic management is to ensure environmental fit, managers need a willingness and an ability to understand the environment and to anticipate future trends.

- A separate strategic planning department collects data on trends.
- The marketing department identifies customer needs.
- The R&D department identifies new technology.
- The production department suggests process innovation.

Arguably, as strategy is about the whole organisation, there are dangers in restricting the gathering of strategic information to functional departments. The whole firm needs to be aware of **strategic intelligence**.

KEY TERM

STRATEGIC INTELLIGENCE, according to Donald Marchand, is defined as 'what a company needs to know about its business environment to enable it to anticipate change and design appropriate strategies that will create business value for customers and be profitable in new markets and new industries in the future'.

A model of the process of creating strategic intelligence is outlined below.

Sensing	Identify appropriate external indicators of change
↓	↓
Collecting	Gather information in ways that ensure it is relevant and meaningful
↓	↓
Organising	Structure the information in the right format
↓	↓
Processing	Analyse information for implications
↓	↓
Communicating	Package and simplify information for users
↓	↓
Using	Apply strategic intelligence

Key dimensions of strategic intelligence

Information culture	What is the role of information in the organisation? Is it only distributed on a 'need to know' basis or do people have to give specific reasons for secrecy?
Future orientation	Is the focus on specific decisions and trade-offs, or a general attitude of enquiry?
The structure of information flows	Is communication vertical, up and down the hierarchy, or lateral?
Processing strategic intelligence	Are 'professional' strategists delegated to this task or is it everybody's concern?
Scope	Is strategic intelligence dealt with by senior management only, or is intelligence built throughout the organisation?
Time horizon	Short-termist or orientated towards the long term?
The role of IT	Some firms are developing sophisticated knowledge management systems to capture the information needed.
Organisational 'memory'	In other words, do managers keep in mind the lessons of past successes or failures?

There are many **sources** of strategic intelligence.

(a) **Internal sources** or sources relatively close to the company.

(i) The **sales force** deals with customers, and so is in a position to obtain customer and competitor information.

(ii) Many companies conduct **market research**. Although generally this deals with specific issues, it can indicate general environmental concerns (eg consumers' worries).

(iii) The management information system may generate information about the environment, although its main focus is internal.

(b) **External sources** of environmental data are various.

(i) **Media**. Newspapers, periodicals and television offer environmental information.

(ii) Sometimes, more detailed country information is needed than that supplied by the press. **Export consultants** might specialise in dealing with particular countries, and so can be a valuable source of information. The **Economist Intelligence Unit** offers reports into particular countries.

(iii) Academic or **trade journals** might give information about a wide variety of relevant issues to a particular industry.

(iv) **Trade associations** also offer industry information.

(v) The Government can be a source of statistical data relating to money supply, the trade balance and so forth, which is often summarised in newspapers. The Department for Business, Innovation and Skills offers a variety of services to UK companies looking at exporting overseas.

(vi) Sources of technological environmental information can include the **Patent Office**.

(vii) **Stockbrokers** produce investment reports for the clients that involve analysis into particular industries.

(viii) Specialist **consultancy firms** (eg CACI census data) provide information.

(ix) The **internet**.

5.5 Database information

A **management information system** or **database** should provide managers with a useful flow of relevant information that is easy to use and easy to access. Information is an important corporate resource. Managed and used effectively, it can provide considerable competitive advantage, and so it is a worthwhile investment. Large-scale databases are created and stored on **computer systems**, using **database application packages** such as **Microsoft Access**.

It is now possible to access large volumes of generally available information through databases held by public bodies and businesses.

(a) Some **newspapers** offer free or paid-for access on the web to both current and archived editions, with search facilities looking for information on particular companies or issues.

(b) Public databases are also available for inspection. **Dun & Bradstreet UK** provides general business information. **AC Nielsen** operates online information regarding products and market share.

(c) Developments in information technology allow businesses to have access to the databases of **external organisations**. Reuters, for example, provides an online information system about money market interest rates and foreign exchange rates to firms involved in money market and foreign exchange dealings, and to the treasury departments of a large number of companies. The growing adoption of technology at **point of sale** provides a potentially invaluable source of data to both retailer and manufacturer.

CASE STUDY

CACI

CACI is a company that provides market analysis, information systems and other data products to clients. It advertises itself as 'the winning combination of marketing and technology'.

As an illustration of the information available to the marketing manager through today's technology, here is an overview of some of their products.

AnaBase	This is an Address Management software tool that enables companies to improve direct mail marketing campaigns. The software works by validating the correct addresses for target recipients.
People UK	This is a mix of geodemographics, life stage and lifestyle data. It is person rather than household specific and is designed for those companies requiring highly targeted campaigns.
InSite	This is a geographic information system. It is designed to assist with local market planning, customers and product segmentation, direct marketing and service distribution.
ACORN	This stands for A Classification of Residential Neighbourhoods, and has been used to profile residential neighbourhoods by postcode since 1976. ACORN classifies people in any trading area or on any customer database into 54 types.

Source:

CACI, (n.d) *Products and Services*. [Online]. Available from: https://www.caci.co.uk/products [Accessed 27 September 2016].

Legislation and regulation exists to protect consumers from misuse of **personal details** held on computer, unsolicited mail and invasion of privacy.

(a) There are now stringent trading practices and regulations in the direct mail industry, administered by the **Direct Mail Services Standards Board** and **Mail Order Protection Scheme** (for display advertisements in national newspapers that ask for money in advance).

(b) The **Mailing Preference Service** allows customers to state whether they would – and more often, would not – be willing to receive direct mail on a range of specific areas.

(c) The **Data Protection Act 1998** provides that data users (organisations or individuals who control the contents of files of personal data and the use of personal data) must register with the Data Protection Registrar. They must limit their use of personal data (defined as any information about an identifiable living individual) to the uses registered.

5.5.1 Environmental data

Nine areas of environmental data that ought to be included in a database for strategic planners could be as follows.

(a) **Competitive data**. This would include information derived from an application of Porter's five forces analysis.

(b) **Economic data**. Details of past growth and predictions of future growth in GDP and disposable income, the pattern of interest rates, predictions of the rate of inflation, unemployment levels and tax rates, developments in international trade and so on.

(c) **Political data**. The influence that the Government is having on the industry.

(d) **Legal data**. The likely implications of recent legislation, legislation likely to be introduced in the future and its implications.

(e) **Social data**. Changing habits, attitudes, cultures and educational standards of the population as a whole, and customers in particular.

(f) **Technological data**. Technological changes that have occurred or will occur, and the implications that these will have for the organisation.

(g) **Geographical data.** Data about individual regions or countries, each of them potentially segments of the market with their own unique characteristics.

(h) **Energy suppliers data**. Energy sources, availability and price of sources of supply generally.

(i) **Data about stakeholders in the business.** Employees, management and shareholders, the influence of each group, and what each group wants from the organisation.

In other words, data that covers the key elements of the general and market environment should be included in a database for strategic and marketing planners.

As well as obtaining data from its own internal database system, an organisation can obtain it from an **external database** operated by another organisation.

5.5.2 A word of caution

Most external databases are online databases, which are very large computer files of information, supplied by **database providers** and managed by **host** companies whose business revenue is generated through charges made to **users**.

Information sources have to be used with caution. The internet, in particular, has made data more available, but this data is unvetted and often unmediated.

5.5.3 Big data

'Big data is a popular term used to describe the exponential growth and availability of data, both structured and unstructured. Big data may be as important to business and society as the internet has become.' (*Big Data – What it is and why it matters*. [Online] SAS. www.sas.com)

5.5.4 What is it?

In a commercial setting 'big data' is being used to identify trends that may exist in vast quantities of data in the pursuit of value creation. Historically, organisations have been restricted as to the amount of data that they can process due to the storage limitations of existing computer systems.

Due to the emergence of 'cloud based' data storage providers and improved computer technologies, these problems are gradually being overcome.

CASE STUDY

The rise of big data

In March 2014, the BBC's Matthew Wall reported on the growing emphasis that big business is now placing on the role of 'big data'.

It's not big, it's just bigger

Laurie Miles, Head of Analytics for big data specialist SAS, explains 'the term big data has been around for decades, and we've been doing analytics all this time. It's not big, it's just bigger'. Miles highlights that, for many years, organisations held traditional structured data, which could be neatly stored and organised in databases. However, over the last 20 years, the rise of the internet has led to a 'proliferation of so-called unstructured data, generated by all our digital interactions, from email to online shopping, text messages to tweets, Facebook updates to YouTube videos'. This has resulted in increasingly large and complex data sets, which have become harder to analyse. It is predicted that 90% of all the data in existence today has been created in the past few years.

The big challenge

The challenge for big business has been to capture and analyse these vast quantities of data, which may be of use in a commercial context. Miles notes 'data is only as good as the intelligence we can glean from it, and that entails effective data analytics and a whole lot of computing power to cope with the exponential increase in volume'.

Wall reports that a significant number of large entities have already turned to 'big data analytics' with the aim of gaining a competitive advantage over their rivals. Proponents of 'big data analytics' argue that the insights gained may lead to improvements throughout the entire organisation. 'Practically, anyone who makes, grows and sells anything can use big data analytics to make their manufacturing and production processes more efficient and their marketing more targeted and cost-effective.'

The article draws an important distinction between the role of 'big data analytics' and historic data analysis. 'Big data' is not just about understanding historic business intelligence, but instead combines several 'real time' data sets, which make it increasingly useful to big businesses.

The big questions

It should be noted that the rise of 'big data' has had its implications. Organisations looking to exploit the opportunities presented have encountered a significant shortage of individuals with the required skills in the job market to analyse the data. As Duncan Ross, Director of Science at Teradata, highlights, 'big data needs new skills, but the business and academic worlds are playing catch up. The job of the data scientist didn't exist five years or ten years ago'.

Questions have also been raised over who ultimately owns the data that organisations hold and who is responsible for keeping such data safe from hackers. Does it belong to the individual or customer, the company, the service provider hosting the data or the national jurisdiction where the data is held? Such questions are unlikely to go away in the short term; as Miles highlights, it is a 'legal minefield'.

Source:

Wall, M. (2014) *Big Data: Are you ready for blast-off?* [Online]. Available from: http://www.bbc.co.uk/news/business-26383058 [Accessed 27 September 2016].

5.5.5 Vs

Laney suggests that 'big data' can be defined by considering the 3 Vs: volume, velocity and variety.

	Comment
Volume	The volume of data generated is a key feature of 'big data'. The quantity of data now being produced is being driven by social media and transactional-based data sets recorded by large organisations, for example data captured from in-store loyalty cards and till receipts. Data is also now being derived from the increasing use of 'sensors' in business. See the Tesco case study later in this chapter.
Velocity	Velocity refers to the speed at which 'real time' data is being streamed into the organisation. To make data meaningful, it needs to be processed in a reasonable time frame.
Variety	Modern data takes many different forms. Structured data may take the form of numerical data, whereas unstructured data may be in the format of email or video. This presents a challenge for organisations, as processing varied forms of data requires significant investment in people and IT infrastructure.

5.5.6 Big data and competitor analysis

Large organisations have taken to using 'big data analytics' in competitor analysis. The following case study outlines how companies are now using data about their customers to analyse their competitors.

CASE STUDY

Supermarkets and big data

In 2013, Donna Ferguson, writing in *The Guardian* newspaper, illustrated how a number of major supermarket chains have taken to using 'big data' as a means to better understand their rivals.

The use of in-store loyalty cards, as a means of capturing data about customers and their shopping habits to enable the effective targeting of shoppers with promotions, is not a new occurrence. Tesco's Clubcard and Sainsbury's Nectar card schemes have been in existence for many years.

Today, retailers have started to exploit data about their shoppers by tracking purchases made by individual debit and credit cards. As Guy Montague-Jones of *The Grocer* highlights, retailers are able to 'build up a demographic profile of you, and collect data about how loyal you are, what you buy and how much you spend'.

Retailers that operate online shops are now able to use data about a shopper's previous purchasing behaviour to target individuals with particular products when they log on. Analysis of shopping patterns is now even being used to help store managers decide what items to stock. Ferguson notes that 'Sainsbury's discovered that a cereal brand called Grape-Nuts was worth stocking – despite weak sales – because the shoppers who bought it were extremely loyal to Sainsbury's, and were often big spenders'.

Furthermore, following extensive data analysis, Sainsbury's purchased the remaining 50% of Sainsbury's Bank, which it did not own, as those individuals who used the bank's services were found to 'become more loyal and spend more in-store'.

Competitor analysis

Establishing new stores

The supermarket chain Waitrose has taken to using shoppers' Visa card data obtained in-store to analyse which competing stores customers are using when not frequenting a Waitrose outlet. This data has been used to help the company decide where to locate new stores. The article highlights that the data analytics firm Beyond Analytics was hired by Waitrose to integrate 'Visa transaction data with Waitrose's own data to figure out what proportion of potential customers were buying groceries from other supermarkets, and the general locations of these competitors'.

Trends in shopping patterns

Rival supermarket Morrisons has historically shunned loyalty card schemes; however, it recently confirmed that it will 'buy in' demographic data about its shoppers to extrapolate trends in shopping patterns to help it target offers at customers. Clearly, if Morrisons' rivals are aware of the data that the company is buying in, then they will be able to target existing customers with their own promotional offers in a bid to undermine competing moves.

Selling data

Ferguson notes that big brands have become increasingly prepared to pay 'a lot of money' to purchase data about shopping patterns from the major supermarkets. 'A brand of, say, coffee will approach Sainsbury's, Morrisons or Tesco and ask to buy access to customers purchasing rival brands, so it can put an offer to these customers.'

Source:

Ferguson, D. (8 June 2013) How supermarkets get your data – and what they do with it. *The Guardian.* [Online]. Available from: https://www.theguardian.com/money/2013/jun/08/supermarkets-get-your-data [Accessed 27 September 2016].

5.5.7 Benefits of 'big data' analytics

There are a number of potential benefits to organisations undertaking big data analytics.

Benefits	Comment
Examine vast quantities of data relatively quickly	Big data analytics allows for large quantities of data to be examined to identify trends and correlations, eg shopper buying habits.
Improves organisational decision making	Better data analysis helps management to take advantage of current social trends by introducing new products to meet customers' needs.

Benefits	Comment
Greater focus on the individual customer	Organisations can target special offers or discounts directly to individual customers to entice repeat business.
Cost reduction	Improved data about customers and internal operations may help to reduce costs – this is illustrated in the following case study.

CASE STUDY

Big data in action

In May 2013 Tesco, the market-leading supermarket chain, unveiled plans to save €20m a year by exploiting the use of 'big data analytics' to help ensure that its in-store refrigerators operate at the right temperature. A report by Computerweekly.com highlighted the findings of a joint project between Tesco Ireland and IBM aimed at 'optimising the performance of its in-store refrigerators'. The project used highly sophisticated computer systems to analyse Tesco's refrigeration data. As Goodwin highlights, 'without realising it, many Tesco stores in Ireland were running their refrigerators at a lower temperature than necessary'. John Walsh, Tesco's Energy and Carbon Manager in Ireland, noted 'ideally, we keep our refrigerators at between –21°C and –23°C, but in reality we found we were keeping them colder. That came as a surprise to us'.

Tesco was able to capture this data from in-store sensors that monitor the performance of individual refrigeration units. The sensors then process 'the data in real time, and display the results on a Google map that shows the performance of refrigerators in more than 120 Irish stores', says Goodwin.

As the article highlights, Tesco has achieved maintenance cost savings, as engineers are now able to investigate potential faults remotely, 'diagnose the problem and turn up with the right part. Previously, engineers would turn up to the store, diagnose the problem and have to return to the depot to collect the equipment they needed'.

Source:

Goodwin, B. (2013) *Tesco uses big data to cut cooling costs by up to €20m*. [Online]. Available from: http://www.computerweekly.com/news/2240184482/Tesco-uses-big-data-to-cut-cooling-costs-by-up-to-20m [Accessed 27 September 2016].

5.5.8 Criticisms of 'big data'

An article in the *Financial Times* entitled 'Big data: are we making a big mistake' raised a number of criticisms over the ability of 'big data' to deliver the anticipated benefits.

Critics argue:

(a) 'Big data' is simply a buzzword, a vague term that has turned into an obsession in large organisations and the media. Very few examples exist where analysing vast amounts of data have resulted in significant new discoveries.

(b) There is a focus on finding correlations between data sets and less of an emphasis on causation. Critics suggest that it is easier to identify correlations between two variables than to determine what is actually causing the correlation.

Farmers example

The Store Manager in the Farmers supermarket store in Canterbury decided to reduce prices on bakery products. After a week, the Store Manager noticed an increase in bakery product sales. This represents a correlation between the selling prices and the quantities sold. However, during the same week, the Farmers chain also undertook a nationwide television and social media promotional marketing campaign, advertising its stores.

This makes it difficult for the Store Manager to fully understand what exactly caused the increase in bakery product sales, as causation may have been driven in part by the price reduction and the advertising campaign combined.

(c) A failure to understand the factors giving rise to a correlation means that analysts have no idea what factors may cause the correlation to break down.

(d) Analysing a data set regardless of its size is not necessarily representative of the entire data population as a whole. The *Financial Times* suggests that, if an organisation wishing to understand the public mood solely used the social networking site Twitter to analyse all the tweets made, this would not represent the views of all members of society. Research indicates that Twitter users tend to be young, urban individuals.

5.5.9 Risks with big data

A number of further risks have also been linked with big data, including:

(a) **Shortage of workers with the required skills** needed to operate big data systems. The evolving nature of information systems capable of storing and analysing big data sets means that many data analysts do not have the necessary skills needed to extract meaning from the data sets analysed.

(b) **Data security**. As organisations are able to capture and store increasing quantities of data this highlights the need for adequate data security measures to protect against data getting lost or damaged. It also highlights the issue of data ownership; if an organisation holds customer data who does this belong to?

(c) **Measuring everything**. Given the vast quantities of data available to modern organisations there is a strong temptation to try to capture, store and measure lots of different data sets, some of which may not reveal any meaningful insights.

(d) **Integrating big data systems**. The cost and time of purchasing and integrating new information systems to capture and store data sets may be prohibitive.

(e) **Change in perspective**. In order for organisations to gain meaningful insights from big data this will require a change in management perspective to ensure that value can be extracted from processed data.

Section summary

A company's response to the environment is influenced by its complexity and its dynamism. The value of forecasts varies according to these factors.

An organisation should plan to obtain **strategic intelligence** as a basis for future strategies. Internal and external databases should be maintained, and the data they contain assessed and applied.

Big data analytics is a term used to describe the extraction of meaning from vast quantities of data. Organisations are particularly interested in identifying trends and correlations in the data that they collect and store, with the aim of putting this to commercial use.

Laney suggests that big data is composed of 3 Vs (volume, velocity and variety).

Big data analytics is now being used by a number of organisations in competitor analysis.

Although the rise of big data analytics brings benefits, critics argue that it simply represents the latest buzzword and has not delivered the groundbreaking discoveries initially thought possible.

6 The competitive environment – the five forces

Introduction

Porter suggests that five **competitive forces** influence the state of competition in an industry, which collectively determine the **profit** (ie long-run return on capital) potential of the industry as a whole. Read the following section, learn what the forces are, and then note the evaluation of the model at the end. Always apply these models with a critical eye and an appreciation of their limitations.

We must make a basic distinction between the **market** and the **industry**.

KEY TERMS

A MARKET comprises the customers or potential customers who have needs that are satisfied by a product or service.

An INDUSTRY comprises those firms that use a particular competence, technology, product or service to satisfy customer needs.

Question 3.4 — Industries and markets

Learning outcome A2a

Assume that you are based in London and that you need to attend a meeting in Glasgow. Which industries can satisfy your need to attend the meeting?

KEY TERM

COMPETITIVE FORCES/FIVE FORCES. CIMA defines these as 'external influences upon the extent of actual and potential competition within any industry which in aggregate determine the ability of firms within that industry to earn a profit'. Porter argues that a firm must adopt a strategy that combats these forces better than its rivals' strategies if it is to enhance shareholder value.

KEY POINT

In discussing competition, Porter (*Competitive Strategy*) distinguishes between factors that characterise the nature of competition.

(a) **In one industry compared with another** (eg in the chemicals industry compared with the clothing retail industry). These factors relate to making one industry as a whole potentially more profitable than another (ie yielding a bigger ROI).

(b) **Within a particular industry**. These relate to the competitive strategies that individual firms might select.

Porter suggests that five **competitive forces** influence the state of competition in an industry, which collectively determine the profit (ie long-run return on capital) potential of the industry as a whole. **Learn them**:

- The threat of **new entrants** to the industry
- The threat of **substitute** products or services
- The bargaining power of **customers**
- The bargaining power of **suppliers**
- The **rivalry** amongst current competitors in the industry

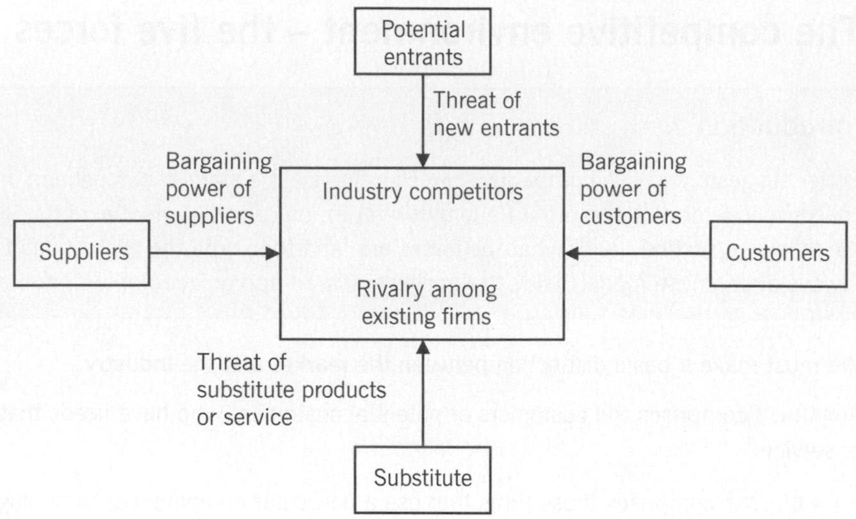

Source: adapted from Porter's *Competitive Strategy* (1980)

Exam alert

This model is fundamental to business strategy. You must know it and be able to apply it to circumstances as set out in questions. Not all five forces will necessarily be represented in a scenario, and so it may not provide an exhaustive answer. However, it should provide a good framework to build on.

6.1 The threat of new entrants (and barriers to entry to keep them out)

A new entrant into an industry will bring extra capacity and more competition. The strength of this threat is likely to vary from industry to industry, depending on:

- The strength of the **barriers to entry**. Barriers to entry discourage new entrants.
- The likely **response of existing competitors** to the new entrant.

Barriers to entry	Comment
Scale economies	As scale of operations increases, unit costs tend to fall. This means that new entrants must start their operations on a large scale or suffer a vast disadvantage. A high level of fixed costs, with a consequent high breakeven point, also requires entry on a large scale. If the market as a whole is not growing, the new entrant has to capture a large slice of the market from existing competitors.
Product differentiation	Existing firms in an industry may have built up a good brand image and strong customer loyalty over a long period of time. A few firms may promote a large number of brands to crowd out the competition.
Capital requirements	When capital investment requirements are high, the barrier against new entrants will be strong, particularly when the investment would possibly be high risk.
Switching costs	Switching costs refer to the costs (time, money and convenience) that a customer would have to incur by switching from one supplier's products to another's. Although it might cost a consumer nothing to switch from one brand of frozen peas to another, the potential costs for the retailer or distributor might be high.
Access to distribution channels	Distribution channels carry a manufacturer's products to the end buyer. New distribution channels are difficult to establish, and existing distribution channels hard to gain access to.

Barriers to entry	Comment
Cost advantages of existing producers, independent of economies of scale	Include: • Patent rights • Experience and know-how (the learning curve) • Government subsidies and regulations • Favoured access to raw materials

6.1.1 Lowering entry barriers

Entry barriers might be **lowered** by:

(a) Changes in the environment
(b) Technological changes
(c) New and creative distribution channels for products or services

6.2 The threat from substitute products

A **substitute product** is a good/service produced by **another industry** that satisfies the same customer needs.

CASE STUDY

The Channel Tunnel

Passengers have several ways of getting from London to Paris, and the pricing policies of the various industries transporting them there reflect this.

(a) 'Le Shuttle' carries cars in the Channel Tunnel. Its main competitors come from the **ferry** companies, offering a substitute service. Therefore, you will find that Le Shuttle sets its prices with reference to ferry company prices, and vice versa.

(b) Eurostar is the rail service from London to Paris/Brussels. Its main competitors are not the ferry companies but the **airlines**. Initially, prices on the London–Paris air routes fell with the commencement of Eurostar services, and some airlines curtailed the number of flights they offer. Low-cost airlines have changed this equation by offering a cheaper alternative.

6.3 The bargaining power of customers

Customers include both the **ultimate consumer** and the buyers forming the **distribution channel**. Customers want better-quality products and services at a lower price. Satisfying this want might force down the profitability of suppliers in the industry. The strength of the position of customers is dependent on several factors.

(a) How much the **customer buys**
(b) How **critical** the product is to the customer's own business
(c) **Switching costs (ie the cost of switching supplier)**
(d) Whether the products are **standard items** (hence easily copied) or specialised
(e) The **customer's own profitability**
(f) The customer's **ability to bypass** the supplier or take over the supplier
(g) The **skills** of the customer **purchasing staff**, or the price awareness of consumers
(h) The importance of **product quality** to the customer

6.4 The bargaining power of suppliers

Suppliers can exert pressure for higher prices, but this is dependent on several factors.

(a) Whether there are just **one or two dominant suppliers** to the industry, able to charge monopoly or oligopoly prices

(b) The threat of **new entrants** or substitute products to the **supplier's industry**

(c) Whether the suppliers have **other customers** outside the industry, and do not rely on the industry for the majority of their sales

(d) The **importance of the supplier's product** to the customer's business

(e) Whether the supplier has a **differentiated product** that buyers need to obtain

(f) Whether **switching costs** for customers would be high

6.5 The rivalry among current competitors in the industry

The **intensity of competitive rivalry** within an industry will affect the profitability of the industry as a whole. Competitive actions might take the form of price competition, advertising battles, sales promotion campaigns, introducing new products to the market, improving after-sales service or providing guarantees or warranties.

The intensity of competition will depend on the following factors.

Factor	Comment
Market growth	Rivalry is intensified when firms are competing for a greater market share in a total market where growth is slow or stagnant.
Cost structure	High fixed costs are a temptation to compete on price, as in the short run any contribution from sales is better than none at all.
Switching	Suppliers will compete if buyers switch easily (eg Coca-Cola vs Pepsi).
Capacity	A supplier might need to achieve a substantial increase in output **capacity**, in order to obtain reductions in unit costs.
Uncertainty	When one firm is not sure what another is up to, there is a tendency to respond to the uncertainty by formulating a more competitive strategy.
Strategic importance	If success is a prime strategic objective, firms will be likely to act very competitively to meet their targets.
Exit barriers	Make it difficult for an existing supplier to leave the industry. • Fixed assets with a low break-up value (eg there may be no other use for them, or they may be old) • The cost of redundancy payments to employees • If the firm is a division or subsidiary of a larger enterprise, the effect of withdrawal on the other operations within the group

6.6 Complements

An important aspect of industries is the existence of **complements**. This is a concept you should recall from your basic economics studies: a complement is a product that is consumed at the same time as another one, and both are, therefore, required. For example, a DVD player is useless without DVDs.

In modern high-technology industries, the existence of such complements is very important and fundamental to growth. The existence or otherwise of complements may almost be regarded as another competitive force, in that the more of them there are, the better for all concerned. Thus, the growth of IT-based industries requires a kind of mutual support between telecoms companies, mobile phone manufacturers, chip manufacturers, software houses and so on. This implies that **collaboration** and **co-operation** are important aspects of strategy in these industries.

6.7 The impact of information technology on the competitive forces

6.7.1 Barriers to entry and IT

(a) **IT can raise entry barriers** by increasing economies of scale, raising the capital cost of entry or effectively colonising distribution channels by tying customers and suppliers into the supply chain or distribution chain.

(b) **IT can surmount entry barriers**. An example is the use of telephone banking.

6.7.2 Bargaining power of suppliers and IT

(a) **Increasing the number of accessible suppliers**. IT enhances supplier information available to customers.

(b) **Closer supplier relationships**. Suppliers' power can be shared. Computer-aided design can be used to design components in tandem with suppliers. Such relationships might be developed with a few key suppliers.

(c) **Switching costs**. Suppliers can be integrated with the firm's administrative operations, by a system of EDI.

6.7.3 Bargaining power of customers

IT can 'lock customers in'.

(a) IT can raise switching costs.

(b) Customer information systems can enable a thorough analysis of marketing information so that products and services can be tailored to the needs of certain segments.

6.7.4 Substitutes

In many respects, **IT itself is 'the substitute product'**. Here are some examples.

(a) Video-conferencing systems might substitute for air transport in providing a means by which managers from all over the world can get together in a meeting.

(b) IT is the basis for leisure activities (eg games) that substitute for TV, cinema, music or other pursuits.

(c) Email might substitute for some postal deliveries and phone calls. Mobile text messages can substitute for email.

(d) Digital cameras, with output via computer, can substitute for traditional film and film processing labs.

6.7.5 IT and the state of competitive rivalry

(a) IT can be used in support of a firm's **competitive** strategy of cost leadership, differentiation or focus. These are discussed later in this Text.

(b) IT can be used in a **collaborative** venture, perhaps to set up new communications networks. Competitors in the financial services industry share the same automated teller machine network.

6.8 Evaluation of the five forces model

The five forces model offers a comprehensive framework into which appropriate aspects of economic theory, such as scale economies, may be fitted alongside elements of commercial practice, such as price negotiations. **Segmental analysis models** such as the five forces and PEST and its variants have much to offer the business strategist.

(a) They point out **key strategic uses**.
(b) They permit strategic analysis to be **divided up** among staff.
(c) Their wide acceptance provides a **clear basis for discussion**.
(d) They provide for **comprehensive analysis**.

Nevertheless, Porter's five forces model has **come in for criticism**.

(a) The model relies on a **static picture of the competition** and therefore plays down the role of innovation.

(b) It overemphasises the importance of the **wider environment** and therefore ignores the significance of possible individual company advantages with regard to resources, capabilities and competence.

(c) Its model of government is essentially **passive** – as a referee in the competitive battle – rather than an active agent and shaper of the competitive environment.

6.9 Negotiation with customers and suppliers

To survive and prosper, a business must **create value** on a long-term basis; this ultimately boils down to operating profitably. Costs and revenues have obvious impact on profitability and, therefore, purchasing and selling prices must be managed appropriately.

The strategic control of a business requires a firm control of trading relationships. This can only be achieved through **negotiation**, unless the business is in a position simply to accept the terms it is offered: this will anyway be impracticable for firms selling to the general public.

(a) Terms of business are usually drafted to confer maximum advantage on the drafting organisation; they will often clash with those of trading partners and when this cannot be resolved by simple insistence, **mutually agreeable terms** must be arranged. This is particularly important when considering payment terms and the passing of property and risk in goods.

(b) Trading relationships between **unequal partners** are frequently one-sided. The weaker partner must be sure that the terms and their impact are understood in detail.

(c) Price structures can be made deliberately complex and difficult to understand: **quantity and settlement discounts** must be managed with care.

(d) Price is an important aspect of the marketing mix and, especially in consumer markets, can send important messages about **quality**.

(e) Weaker partners can gain advantage from membership of **purchasing and selling consortia**.

6.10 The industry life cycle

We have already defined an industry earlier in this section. It may be possible to discern an **industry life cycle**, which will have wider implication for the nature of competition and competitive advantage. This cycle reflects changes in demand and the spread of technical knowledge among producers. Innovation creates the new industry, and this is normally **product innovation**.

Later, innovation shifts to processes in order to maintain margins. The overall progress of the industry life cycle is illustrated below.

	Inception	Growth	Maturity/shakeout	Decline
Products	Basic, no standards established	Better, more sophisticated, differentiated	Superior, standardised	Varied quality but fairly undifferentiated
Competitors	None to few	Many entrants Little concentration in industry	Competition increases, weaker players leave	Few remain Competition may be on price
Buyers	Early adopters, prosperous, curious must be induced	More customers attracted and aware	Mass market, brand switching common	Enthusiasts, traditionalists, sophisticates
Profits	Negative – high first-mover advantage	Good, possibly starting to decline	Eroding under pressure of competition	Variable
Strategy	Dominate market, build quality	React to competitors with marketing spend	Cost reductions sought	Control costs

6.11 Survival and success factors

We have already made reference to critical success factors (CSFs). **Survival and success factors** (SSFs) are rather different. While CSFs are vital aspects of an individual organisation's activity, SSFs relate to a **complete industry**. If an organisation wishes to operate in an industry at all, it must deploy survival factors; if it wishes to succeed, it must deploy success factors. Generally, survival and success will represent two different degrees of achievement in similar fields. Thus, in a technically complex manufacturing industry, a survival factor would be technical competence with existing technology, while the equivalent success factor might be the ability to introduce technical innovations on a continuing basis.

The identification of SSFs should be one of the outcomes of environmental analysis.

Section summary

A market is a group of customers with needs to satisfy. An industry is the companies that use similar technologies to satisfy those needs. For any industry, **five forces** determine its profitability: 'threat of new entrants, substitute products, customers, suppliers and the intensity of competition'.

Trading relationships have strategic impact and, while mutual benefit may be desirable, they must be firmly managed.

Industries may display a **life cycle**: this will affect and interact with the five forces.

7 Competitive strategies

Introduction

In any market where there are competitors, strategic and marketing decisions will often be in response to what a competitor has done.

Competitive advantage is anything that gives one organisation an edge over its rivals. Porter argues that a firm should adopt a competitive strategy that is intended to achieve some form of competitive advantage for the firm. A firm that possesses a **competitive advantage** will be able to make profit exceeding its cost of capital: in terms of economic theory, this is '**excess profit**' or '**economic rent**'. The existence of excess profit tends to be temporary because of the effect of the **five competitive forces**. When a company can continue to earn excess profit despite the effects of competition, it possesses a **sustainable competitive advantage**.

KEY TERM

COMPETITIVE STRATEGY means 'taking offensive or defensive actions to create a dependable position in an industry, to cope successfully with ... competitive forces and thereby yield a superior return on investment for the firm. Firms have discovered many different approaches to this end, and the best strategy for a given firm is ultimately a unique construction reflecting its particular circumstances'. (Porter)

7.1 The choice of competitive strategy

Porter believes there are three **generic strategies** for competitive advantage. To be successful, Porter argues, a company must follow only one of the strategies. If the company tries to combine more than one, it risks losing its competitive advantage and becoming 'stuck in the middle'.

KEY TERMS

COST LEADERSHIP means being the lowest cost producer in the industry as a whole.

DIFFERENTIATION is the exploitation of a product or service that the **industry as a whole** believes to be unique.

FOCUS involves a restriction of activities to only part of the market (a segment) through:

- Providing goods and/or services at lower cost to that segment (**cost-focus**)
- Providing a differentiated product or service to that segment (**differentiation-focus**)

Cost leadership and differentiation are industry-wide strategies. Focus involves segmentation but involves pursuing, within the segment only, a strategy of cost leadership or differentiation.

7.1.1 Cost leadership

A cost leadership strategy seeks to achieve the position of lowest-cost producer in the **industry as a whole**. By producing at the lowest cost, the manufacturer can compete on price with every other producer in the industry, and earn the higher unit profits, if the manufacturer so chooses.

Ways in which an organisation could achieve cost leadership include:

- Set up production facilities to obtain **economies of scale**
- Using **new technology**
- Exploit the **learning curve effect**
- Concentrate on **improving productivity**
- **Minimise overhead costs**
- **Get favourable access to sources of supply**
- **Relocate to cheaper areas**
- Use **IT** to record and analyse costs

7.1.2 Differentiation

A differentiation strategy assumes that competitive advantage can be gained through **particular characteristics** of a firm's products. Products may be categorised as:

(a) **Breakthrough products** offer a radical performance advantage over competition, perhaps at a drastically lower price (eg float glass, developed by Pilkington).

(b) **Improved products** are not radically different from their competition but are obviously superior in terms of better performance at a competitive price (eg microchips).

(c) **Competitive products** derive their appeal from a particular compromise of cost and performance. For example, cars are not all sold at rock-bottom prices, nor do they all provide immaculate comfort and performance. They compete with each other by trying to offer a more attractive compromise than rival models.

Ways in which an organisation may differentiate include:

(a) Build up a brand image
(b) Give the product special features to make it stand out
(c) Exploit other activities of the value chain such as marketing and sales or service
(d) Use IT to create new services or product features

Advantages and disadvantages of industry-wide strategies

Competitive force	Advantages		Disadvantages	
	Cost leadership	Differentiation	Cost leadership	Differentiation
New entrants	Economies of scale raise entry barriers	Brand loyalty and perceived uniqueness are entry barriers		
Substitutes	Firm is not as vulnerable as its less cost-effective competitors to the threat of substitutes	Customer loyalty is a weapon against substitutes		
Customers	Customers cannot drive down prices further than the next most efficient competitor	Customers have no comparable alternative Brand loyalty should lower price sensitivity		Customers may no longer need the differentiation factor Sooner or later, customers become price sensitive
Suppliers	Flexibility to deal with cost increases	Higher margins can offset vulnerability to supplier price rises	Increase in input costs can reduce price advantages	
Industry rivalry	Firm remains profitable when rivals go under through excessive price competition	Unique features reduce direct competition	Technological change will require capital investment, or make production cheaper for competitors Competitors learn via imitation Cost concerns ignore product design or marketing issues	Imitation narrows differentiation

7.1.3 Focus (or niche) strategy

In a focus strategy, a firm concentrates its attention on one or more particular segments or niches of the market, and does not try to serve the entire market with a single product. IT can be useful in establishing the exact determining characteristics of the chosen niche, using existing customer records.

(a) A **cost-focus strategy**. Aim to be a cost leader for a particular segment. This type of strategy is often found in the printing, clothes manufacture and car repair industries.

(b) A **differentiation-focus strategy**. Pursue differentiation for a chosen segment. Luxury goods suppliers are the prime exponents of such a strategy. Ben & Jerry's ice cream is a good example of a product offering based on differentiation-focus.

Porter suggests that a focus strategy can achieve competitive advantage when '**broad-scope**' businesses fall into one of two errors.

(a) **Underperformance** occurs when a product does not fully meet the needs of a segment and offers the opportunity for a **differentiation-focus** player.

(b) **Overperformance** gives a segment more than it really wants, and provides an opportunity for a **cost-focus** player.

Advantages of a focus strategy

(a) A niche is more secure, and a firm can insulate itself from competition.
(b) The firm does not spread itself too thinly.

Drawbacks of a focus strategy

(a) The firm sacrifices economies of scale that would be gained by serving a wider market.

(b) Competitors can move into the segment, with increased resources (eg the Japanese moved into the US luxury car market, to compete with Mercedes and BMW).

(c) The segment's needs may eventually become less distinct from the main market.

7.2 Which strategy?

Although there is a risk with any of the generic strategies, Porter argues that a firm must pursue one of them.

A **stuck in the middle** strategy is almost certain to make only low profits. 'This firm lacks the market share, capital investment and resolve to play the low-cost game, the industry-wide differentiation necessary to obviate the need for a low-cost position, or the focus to create differentiation or a low-cost position in a more limited sphere.'

CASE STUDY

Tesco: Stuck in the middle?

The troubles at UK retailer Tesco have been well documented in recent times. The retailer had prided itself for many years on its ability to offer different ranges of Tesco branded groceries to different buyer groups. Perhaps the two most notable Tesco brands are the company's Finest and Everyday Value ranges, both of which are designed to meet the needs of customers with different shopping budgets. The Tesco Finest range offers customers differentiated products and is designed to compete with food retailers such as Waitrose who sell higher quality, higher priced items.

By contrast the Everyday Value range is designed to appeal to price conscious shoppers, who tend be interested in basic products due to having a smaller budget. Competitors at this end of the market include discount retailers. It could be argued that Tesco's approach goes against the logic of Michael Porter who famously argued that firms should ideally only pursue one generic strategy if they wanted to ensure success. Porter suggests that a failure to do this increases the risk of becoming 'stuck in the middle'.

An article by Jennifer Rankin in *The Guardian 'What's gone wrong with Tesco',* suggests that Tesco's problems are due in no small part to better positioning by competitors. Andrew Stevens, a retail analyst with Verdict suggests that Tesco is 'stuck in the middle', he argues 'the problem is that it [Tesco] is trying to be everything for everyone. But there is someone in each tier who is doing it better'. (*The Guardian*, 2013).

As Andrew Stevens notes being 'a jack of all trades and a master of none' can be particularly troublesome.

Source:

Rankin, J. (4 December 2013) What's gone wrong with Tesco. *The Guardian*. [Online] Available from: https://www.theguardian.com/business/2013/dec/04/tesco-whats-gone-wrong-uk-largest-supermarket [Accessed 27 September 2016].

Question 3.5

Hermes

Learning outcome A1c

The Managing Director of Hermes Telecommunications plc is considering their corporate strategy.

Hermes has invested a great deal of money in establishing a network that competes with that of Telecom, a privatised utility.

Initially, Hermes concentrated its efforts on business customers in the large capital city, where it offered a lower cost service to that supplied by Telecom.

Recently, Hermes has approached the residential market (ie domestic telephone users), offering a lower-cost service on long-distance calls from landlines, together with competitively priced mobile phone deals.

Technological developments have resulted in the need for faster mobile phone networks, able to support streaming of content to mobile phones and other devices such as iPads.

The contract to develop this service has been awarded to Gerbil Communications, which is installing transmitters across the country.

Required

What issues of competitive strategy have been raised in the above scenario, particularly in relation to Hermes Telecommunications plc?

In practice, it is rarely simple to draw hard and fast distinctions between the generic strategies, as there are conceptual problems underlying them.

(a) **Problems with cost leadership**

(i) **Internal focus**. Cost refers to internal measures, rather than the market demand. It can be used to gain market share; but it is the **market share that is important**, not cost leadership as such. Economies of scale are an effective way to achieve low costs, but they depend on high volumes. In turn, high volumes may depend on low prices which, in turn, require low costs. There is a circular argument here.

(ii) **Only one firm**. If cost leadership applies across the whole industry, only one firm will pursue this strategy successfully.

(iii) **Higher margins can be used for differentiation**. Having low costs does not mean you have to charge lower prices or compete on price. A cost leader can choose to 'invest higher margins in R&D or marketing'. Being a cost leader arguably gives producers more freedom to choose other competitive strategies.

(b) **Problems with differentiation**. Porter assumes that a differentiated product will always be sold at a higher price.

(i) However, a **differentiated product** may be sold at the same price as competing products in order to **increase market share**.

(ii) **Choice of competitor**. Differentiation from whom? Who are the competitors? Do they serve other market segments? Do they compete on the same basis?

(iii) **Source of differentiation**. This includes **all** aspects of the firm's offer, not only the product. However, it is difficult to achieve differentiation purely by **promotion**, though some managers think it can be done this way.

Focus probably has fewer conceptual difficulties, as it ties in very neatly with ideas of market segmentation. In practice, most companies pursue this strategy to some extent, by designing products/services to meet the needs of particular target markets.

'Stuck in the middle' is therefore what many companies actually pursue quite successfully. Any number of strategies can be pursued, with different approaches to **price** and the **perceived added value** (ie the differentiation factor) in the eyes of the customer.

7.3 Limitations of the generic strategy approach

Porter's model depends on clear notions of what the **industry** and **firm** in question are. However, this may not be clear, since many companies are part of larger organisations and many 'industries' have boundaries that are hard to define.

Also, there is the question of whether strategies should be pursued at SBU or corporate level, and in relation to exactly which category of products. For example, Procter & Gamble have a huge range of products and brands: should it follow the same generic strategy with all of them?

There have been several criticisms of Porter's approach. One is that it does not allow for **expansion into new industries**, perhaps as the result of creative innovation. This is not really valid: Porter may be silent on this topic, but his model does not preclude it.

A second criticism is to see the model as dividing products into basic goods and luxury goods. This oversimplifies the model. Cost leadership might well be pursued over a wide range of product quality, though it seems likely that the emphasis will shift to differentiation where the higher-quality products are concerned.

A further questionable point that may be raised is that the model does not allow for technical obsolescence and the introduction of new products. This is simply incorrect, as shown by Black & Decker's regular new product launches. These, generally, are marketed on the basis of high volume and low price, economies of scale being the basis of the business model.

7.4 The strategy clock

The strategy clock develops Porter's theory, analysing strategies in terms of **price** and **perceived value added**. Porter's basic concept of generic strategies has been the subject of further discussion. Johnson, Scholes and Whittington, quoting Bowman, describe the strategic options using the **strategy clock**.

The eight strategies shown on the clock represent different approaches to creating value for the customer and each customer will buy from the provider whose offering most closely matches their own view of the proper relationship between price and perceived benefits.

Positions 1 and 2 will attract customers who are price conscious above all, with position 2 giving a little more emphasis to serviceability. These are typical approaches in commodity markets. By contrast, strategies 4 and 5 are relevant to consumers who require a customised product.

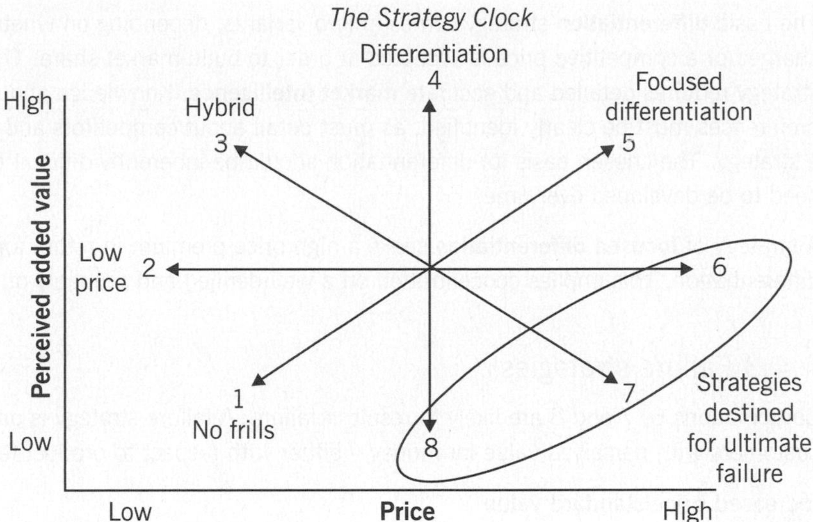

7.4.1 Price-based strategies

Strategies 1 and 2 are price-based strategies.

A **no-frills** strategy is appropriate under several conditions. It can be used for commodity-like products and the most price-conscious customers. It is also suitable where customers' switching costs are low and where there is little opportunity for competition on product features.

This strategy may be used for market entry, to gain experience and build volume. This was done by Japanese car manufacturers in the 1960s, and is now being seen in the airline industry, with companies such as EasyJet and Ryanair successfully adopting a no-frills approach. The no-frills airlines sell tickets at low prices but with limited customer services, and with a focus on keeping costs low at all times. They fly to less-congested, secondary airports, outside peak times, to reduce landing fees; they have fast turnaround times to maximise aircraft usage, and they make ticket sales over the internet to avoid travel agents' commissions. They have no reserved seats to encourage customers to turn up early to prevent delays, and do not offer complimentary food and drink like premium carriers, but instead generate ancillary revenue through in-flight sales.

A **low price** strategy offers better value than competitors. This can lead to price war and hence to reduced margins and lack of reinvestment for all players. Porter's generic strategy of **cost leadership** is appropriate to a firm adopting this strategy.

7.4.2 Differentiation strategies

Strategies 3, 4 and 5 are all differentiation strategies. Each one represents a different trade-off between market share (with its cost advantages) and margin (with its direct impact on profit). Differentiation can be created in three ways:

(a) Product features
(b) Marketing, including powerful brand promotion
(c) Core competences

The **hybrid** strategy seeks both differentiation and a lower price than competitors. The cost base must be low enough to permit reduced prices and reinvestment to maintain differentiation. This strategy may be more advantageous than differentiation alone under certain circumstances:

(a) If it leads to growth in market share
(b) If differentiation rests on core competences and costs can be reduced elsewhere
(c) If a low price approach is suited to a particular market segment
(d) Where it is used as a market entry strategy

The basic **differentiation** strategy comes in two variants, depending on whether a price premium is charged or a competitive price is accepted in order to build market share. The pursuit of a differentiation strategy requires detailed and accurate **market intelligence**. Knowledge about customers and their preferences must be clearly identified, as must detail about competitors and their likely responses to such a strategy. The chosen basis for differentiation should be inherently difficult to imitate, and will probably need to be developed over time.

A strategy of **focused differentiation** seeks a high price premium in return for a high degree of differentiation. This implies concentration on a well-defined and probably quite restricted market segment.

7.4.3 Failure strategies

Combinations 6, 7 and 8 are likely to result in failure. A failure strategy is one which does not provide customers with perceived value for money – either with respect to product features, or price, or both.

Increased price/standard value

The logic here is to increase margins by increasing price while keeping costs (and by inference, value) constant. Firms pursuing this strategy may be able to enjoy higher profitability, but this is likely to only last in the short term.

Increased price/low value

Position 7 on the clock is even more likely to result in failure than option 6. A strategy which sees a firm increasing its prices while lowering the value it offers its customers would be expected to result in that firm losing all its customers to its competitors. Position 7 on the clock is only likely to be feasible in a monopoly situation.

Low value/standard price

Again, the logic here is to increase margins, effectively by cutting costs (reducing value) but keeping price the same. However, this strategy is again likely to lead to a loss of market share as customers become aware of the reduction in value, and switch their purchases to competitors whose products or services cost the same but offer greater value.

Section summary

Porter suggests there are three generic strategies: **cost leadership**, **differentiation**, and **focus**.

Bowman's strategy clock develops Porter's theory and analyses strategies in terms of **price** and **perceived value added**.

8 Product-market strategies: direction of growth

Introduction

Product-market strategies involve determining which products should be sold in which markets, by market penetration, market development, product development and diversification. Diversification is assumed to be risky, especially diversification that is entirely unrelated to current products and markets.

8.1 Product-market mix

Ansoff drew up a **growth vector matrix**, describing how a combination of a firm's activities in current and new markets, with existing and new products can lead to **growth**. Ansoff's original model was a four-cell matrix based on product and market, shown as the heart of the diagram below.

Ansoff's competitive strategies (Ansoff matrix)

		Products	
		Existing	New
Markets	Existing	Market Penetration	Product Development
	New	Market Development	Diversification

8.1.1 Current products and current markets: market penetration

Market penetration. The firm seeks to do four things.

(a) **Maintain or increase its share** of current markets with current products, eg through competitive pricing, advertising, sales promotion

(b) Secure dominance of growth markets

(c) Restructure a mature market by driving out competitors

(d) Increase usage by existing customers (eg airmiles, loyalty cards)

This is a relatively **low-risk** strategy since it requires no capital investment. As such, it is attractive to the unadventurous type of company.

8.1.2 Present products and new markets: market development

Market development is the process by which the firm seeks new markets for its current products. There are many possible approaches. Here are some examples:

(a) **New geographical areas** and export markets (eg a radio station building a new transmitter to reach a new audience)

(b) **Different package sizes** for food and other domestic items so that both those who buy in bulk and those who buy in small quantities are catered for

(c) **New distribution channels** to attract new customers (eg organic food sold in supermarkets, not just specialist shops)

(d) **Differential pricing policies** to attract different types of customer and create **new market segments**. For example, travel companies have developed a market for cheap long-stay winter breaks in warmer countries for retired couples.

This approach to strategy is also low in risk since it requires little capital investment.

8.1.3 New products and present markets: product development

Product development is the launch of new products to existing markets. This has several advantages:

(a) The company can exploit its existing marketing arrangements such as promotional methods and distribution channels at low cost.

(b) The company should already have good knowledge of its customers and their wants and habits.

(c) Competitors will be forced to respond.

(d) The cost of entry to the market will go up.

This strategy is **riskier** than both market penetration and market development since it is likely to require **major investment** in the new product development process and, for physical products, in suitable production facilities.

8.1.4 New products: new markets (diversification)

Diversification occurs when a company decides to make **new products for new markets**. It should have a clear idea about what it expects to gain from diversification.

(a) **Growth.** New products and new markets should be selected which offer prospects for growth which the existing product-market mix does not.

(b) **Investing surplus** funds not required for other expansion needs, bearing in mind that the funds could be returned to shareholders.

Diversification is a high-risk strategy, having many of the characteristics of a new business start-up. It is likely to require the deployment of **new competences**.

Section summary

Ansoff's growth vector matrix considers how a combination of a firm's activities in current and new markets, with existing and new products can lead to growth. Ansoff suggests four strategies: **market penetration**, **market development**, **product development** and **diversification**.

9 Methods of growth

Introduction

Once an organisation has selected an appropriate competitive strategy, consideration needs to be given to the method it will use to deliver it. In this section we consider a range of different approaches an organisation can use to grow.

The **method of growth** can vary.

- Companies can grow organically, building up their own products and developing their own market.
- They may choose to acquire these ready-made by buying other companies. Acquisitions are risky because of the incompatibility of different companies.
- Many firms grow by other means, such as joint ventures and alliances.

9.1 Organic growth

Organic growth (sometimes referred to as **internal development**) is the primary method of growth for many organisations, for a number of reasons. Organic growth is achieved through the development of internal resources.

9.2 Acquisitions and mergers

9.2.1 The purpose of acquisitions

(a) **Marketing advantages**

(i) Buy in a new product range
(ii) Buy a market presence (especially true if acquiring a company overseas)
(iii) Unify sales departments or rationalise distribution and advertising
(iv) Eliminate competition or protect an existing market

(b) **Production advantages**

(i) Gain a higher utilisation of production facilities
(ii) Buy in technology and skills
(iii) Obtain greater production capacity
(iv) Safeguard future supplies of raw materials
(v) Improve purchasing by buying in bulk

(c) **Finance and management**

(i) Buy a high-quality management team, which exists in the acquired company
(ii) Obtain cash resources where the acquired company is very liquid
(iii) Gain undervalued assets or surplus assets that can be sold off
(iv) Obtain tax advantages (eg purchase of a tax loss company)

(d) **Risk spreading**

(e) **Independence**. A company threatened by a takeover might take over another company, just to make itself bigger and so a more expensive target for the predator company.

(f) **Overcome barriers to entry**

9.3 Other approaches

Short of mergers and takeovers, there are other ways by which companies can co-operate.

(a) **Consortia:** Organisations co-operate on specific business areas such as purchasing or research.

(b) **Joint ventures:** Two firms (or more) join forces and establish a new company. Each has a share in both the equity and the management of the business. A joint venture may be set up to undertake R&D activities to benefit the founding firms.

(i) **Share costs**. As the capital outlay is shared, joint ventures are especially attractive to smaller or risk-averse firms, or where very expensive new technologies are being researched and developed (such as in the civil aerospace and petrochemical industries).

(ii) **Cut risk**. A joint venture can reduce the risk of government intervention if a local firm is involved (eg *Club Mediterranée* pays much attention to this factor).

(iii) Participating enterprises **benefit from all sources of profit.**

(iv) **Close control** over marketing and other operations.

(v) Overseas joint ventures provide **local knowledge, quickly**.

(vi) **Synergies**. One firm's production expertise can be supplemented by the other's marketing and distribution facility.

(c) A **licensing agreement** is a commercial contract whereby the licenser gives something of value to the licensee in exchange for certain performances and payments.

(i) The licenser may provide rights to produce a patented product or to use a patented process or trademark as well as advice and assistance on marketing and technical issues.

(ii) The licenser receives a **royalty**.

(d) **Subcontracting** is also a type of alliance. Co-operative arrangements also feature in supply chain management, just-in-time and quality programmes.

9.4 Alliances

Organisations can also enter into contractual arrangements with one another in the form of strategic alliances. A strategic alliance does not involve the establishment of a new company such as a joint venture. Some firms enter long-term **strategic alliances** with others for a variety of reasons.

(a) They share development costs of a particular technology.

(b) The regulatory environment prohibits takeovers (eg most major airlines are in strategic alliances because in most countries – including the US – there are limits to the level of control an 'outsider' can have over an airline).

(c) Complementary markets or technology.

(d) **Learning**. Alliances can also be a 'learning' exercise in which each partner tries to learn as much as possible from the other.

(e) **Technology**. New technology offers many uncertainties and many opportunities. Such alliances provide funds for expensive research projects, spreading risk.

(f) **The alliance itself can generate innovations.**

(g) The alliance can involve **'testing' the firm's core competence** in different conditions, which can suggest ways to improve it.

(h) Regulation may prevent takeover.

Strategic alliances only go so far, as there may be disputes over control of strategic assets.

Alliances have some limitations:

(a) **Core competence**. Each organisation should be able to focus on its core competence. Alliances do not enable it to create new competences.

(b) **Strategic priorities**. If a key aspect of strategic delivery is handed over to a partner, the firm loses flexibility. A core competence may not be enough to provide a comprehensive customer benefit.

Section summary

Organisations can pursue a range of methods to achieve growth. These include:

- Organic growth
- Acquisitions and mergers
- Joint ventures
- Alliances

10 Corporate appraisal (SWOT)

KEY TERM

CORPORATE APPRAISAL. 'Critical assessment of the strengths and weaknesses, opportunities and threats (**SWOT** analysis) in relation to the internal and environmental factors affecting an entity in order to establish its condition prior to the preparation of the long-term plan.'

(*CIMA Official Terminology*)

Introduction

Corporate appraisal centres on a consideration of internal **strengths** and **weaknesses**, and external **opportunities** and **threats**. This is known, unsurprisingly, as **SWOT analysis**.

10.1 Internal appraisal – strengths and weaknesses

A strengths and weaknesses analysis will identify two things.

(a) The areas of the business that have **strengths** that should be exploited by suitable strategies
(b) The areas of the business that have **weaknesses** that need strategies to improve them

The strengths and weaknesses analysis is internal to the company, and intended to shape its approach to the external world. For instance, the identification of shortcomings in skills or resources could lead to a planned acquisition programme or staff recruitment and training. The strengths and weaknesses part of the SWOT analysis involves looking at the findings of the position audit. At the end of the internal appraisal, a firm should have some ideas as to its core competences.

10.2 External appraisal: opportunities and threats

An **external appraisal** is required to identify profit-making opportunities that can be exploited by the company's strengths and also to anticipate environmental threats against which the company must protect itself. The external appraisal is the **opportunities and threats** part of SWOT analysis.

Opportunities

(a) What opportunities exist in the business environment?
(b) What is their inherent profit-making potential?
(c) Can the organisation exploit the worthwhile opportunities?
(d) What is the comparative capability profile of competitors?
(e) What is the company's comparative performance potential in this field of opportunity?

Threats

(a) What threats to the company or its business environment might arise?
(b) How will competitors be affected?
(c) How will the company be affected?

10.3 Resource-based and positioning-based strategies

The SWOT analysis can be used in one of two ways.

(a) The firm can develop **resource-based strategies** that depend on two things.

   (i) What the firm is good at, and what its strengths and competences are
   (ii) Where these strengths can be deployed

   This is common in retailing, for example, as supermarket chains extend their own brands from food to pharmaceuticals.

(b) The firm can develop **positioning-based strategies**. These are based on product-market opportunities; in other words identifying what opportunities are available and what the firm has to do to align its resources with environmental conditions.

SWOT can usefully be combined with a **comparative analysis** of performance.

(a) **Anticipated** and **past** performance can be compared.

(b) A company's performance can be assessed in relation to its **competitors** and **industry norms**.

(c) Industry **best practice** can be used as a yardstick, perhaps via the techniques given below.

   (i) **Competitor profiles** – analysis of the performance of key competitors.

   (ii) **Benchmarking**. Benchmarks are goals of performance that an organisation wishes to achieve in particular value activities. A benchmark for quality would be so many rejected parts per million. This is to identify best practice and so achieve it. Benchmarks are often based on the most efficient competitors.

Section summary

The environmental assessment and the analysis of internal resources and capabilities are summarised in a **corporate appraisal**, or **SWOT** analysis. This stage explores the interplay between these factors preparatory to the generation of possible strategic courses of action.

11 Analysing and interpreting competitor data

Introduction

The final section of the chapter explores the need for organisations to be capable of analysing and interpreting competitor data.

Exam alert

As part of your Integrated Case Study at the Management Level, you may be required to analyse a scenario that details the performance of a company or competitor entity in a particular industry. The difference between a satisfactory answer and a great answer is the ability to interpret the information and data provided. Data is likely to take the form of financial statement information concerning the featured organisation. CIMA has highlighted that students will not be required to prepare financial information but must be confident in extracting meaning from the data provided.

11.1 Understanding competitor performance

So far in this chapter, we have explored various techniques and models that organisations use when attempting to analyse the position of competitors. However, key to being able to fully understand competitor performance and market position is interpreting financial data.

In your Integrated Case Study, you may be required to:

- Compare an entity's performance with previous period financial statements
- Compare key performance indicators with a similar entity
- Assess an entity's performance using industry benchmark information

Tasks are likely to require you to present your answer in a prescribed format; this could include a report, email or presentation.

When tackling 'interpretation' questions, it is important that you consider the following.

(a) The content of any accompanying commentary on the financial and non-financial information provided

(b) The age and nature of the company and its assets, the make-up of its workforce and customers

(c) Current and future developments in the company's markets

11.2 Approach to interpretation questions

(a) Read the requirements (identify the format required for the solution). If you are asked to analyse the position of an entity featured, you should consider any theories or models that may help you to structure your response.

(b) Read the question and analyse the data (look for obvious changes and differences in the financial and non-financial data).

(c) With financial data, consider the key categories of, for example, profitability, liquidity and gearing.

(d) Write up your answer, summarising the performance.

   (i) Structured using your categories

   (ii) Comment on main features first (eg the type of strategy the company is following)

   (iii) Bring in any relevant movements in the non-financial and financial data to support your argument

   (iv) Suggest reasons for key changes and the potential causes (eg if sales have gone down, this may be due to the loss of a major customer or a recession)

   (v) Use any information given in the question (eg what will key stakeholders think of a drop in sales?)

The next question requires you to use some of the skills that we have discussed in this section. It is strongly recommended that you take the time to attempt this question fully, as it will serve as good practice for your Integrated Case Study.

Question 3.6

Farmers – environmental analysis

Learning outcome A2b

At a recent board meeting at Farmers supermarkets, Managing Director Adrian Williams declared the need for the company to improve its understanding of its domestic market. In particular, he stressed the need for Farmers to pay closer attention to two rival retailers, Euro-Store and Turners, which have regularly featured in the business press in recent months. He has identified the following information about each retailer.

Euro-Store

Euro-Store is a large, low-price supermarket operating in the UK. It is owned by a German family and has similar operations in other European countries including its native Germany, France, Sweden and Hungary. Its stores sell a range of household and grocery products. Each Euro-Store shop offers a limited selection of frozen products, and only sells a basic range of fresh and chilled produce such as fruit, vegetables and meats. Customer choice in-store tends to be limited to one or two lines, to allow for greater quantities of inventory to be stored on the shop floor. Many of the items sold are well-known European brands that are not widely heard of in the UK.

Traditional supermarket shelving is not used. Instead, inventory that is received from one of the company's five regional depots is stacked on wooden pallets on the shop floor for customers to access. All Euro-Store outlets are of the same design and size, with limited warehousing. Profit margins tend to be low, and operating costs are kept to a minimum. It is company policy to only employ a skeleton staff: very often each outlet will only have one checkout in operation. Another checkout will only be opened when there is a queue of seven or more customers.

Brian Mitchell, Head of Euro-Store's UK operations, recently summed up the company as being 'a no-frills supermarket where people and their families pay sensible prices'. Euro-Store's UK success to date has been largely driven by the global 'credit crunch', which led to many customers switching from traditional supermarkets in pursuit of lower-priced groceries.

Turners

Turners was established in 1983 by Richard and Beverley Beaumont. The founders are still actively involved in the running of the business. In a recent television interview, Richard Beaumont stated that 'we opened our original Turners store because we realised that UK grocery retailing needed something special, it needed a Turners'.

Turners is a relatively small chain of high-end, small-format food stores. Each outlet incorporates a cafe for customers to enjoy. Every Turners store is based in a prosperous and wealthy area throughout the country, with each store located in a building once of historical importance; for example, the Turners store in Cheltenham was once a disused church. The majority of Turners shoppers tend to come from the company's target market, who are individuals of 50 years of age and older, who are prepared to pay higher than average prices.

The company does not sell household cleaning products or associated items, but is focused on selling foods from around the world. Some of the items sold include Italian meats and continental (and UK-produced) cheeses. A significant attraction for many shoppers is the in-store bakery, which produces over 50 different types of world breads on a daily basis. The quality of the experience has been designed to complement the produce sold. Every store has been given a rustic appearance to remain in keeping with its surroundings. Due to the popularity of the Turners brand, on busy trading days it is not uncommon for customers to wait for up to 20 minutes before the store opens.

The table below shows key performance data between 20X3 and 20X4.

	20X4	*20X3*	*20X4*	*20X3*
	Euro-Store		*Turners*	
Financials				
Inventory days	9 days	9 days	28 days	32 days
Sales ($m)	8,294	8,513	853	797
Profit for period ($m)	531	596	93	75
Operations				
Queuing times at till	8 mins	8 mins	3 mins	5 mins
Ave. number of staff on duty	5	6	12	10
Ave. age of employees	22 years	24 years	51 years	51 years
Most common complaint between 20X3 and 20X4	Poor customer service		Lack of space to shop	
What customers value the most between 20X3 and 20X4	Low prices		Quality service	
Number of outlets in UK	283	276	63	61

Required

Using the information and performance data provided, analyse the performance and market position of both Euro-Store and Turners.

Note. Although it was not mentioned in the scenario, you should take a moment to consider whether there are any theories or models discussed in this or earlier chapters that may help you to answer the question.

Section summary

In order for organisations to outmanoeuvre their rivals, detailed competitor analysis is needed. Central to this analysis is **interpreting** competitor data. Such data can come in both a financial and non-financial form.

Chapter Summary

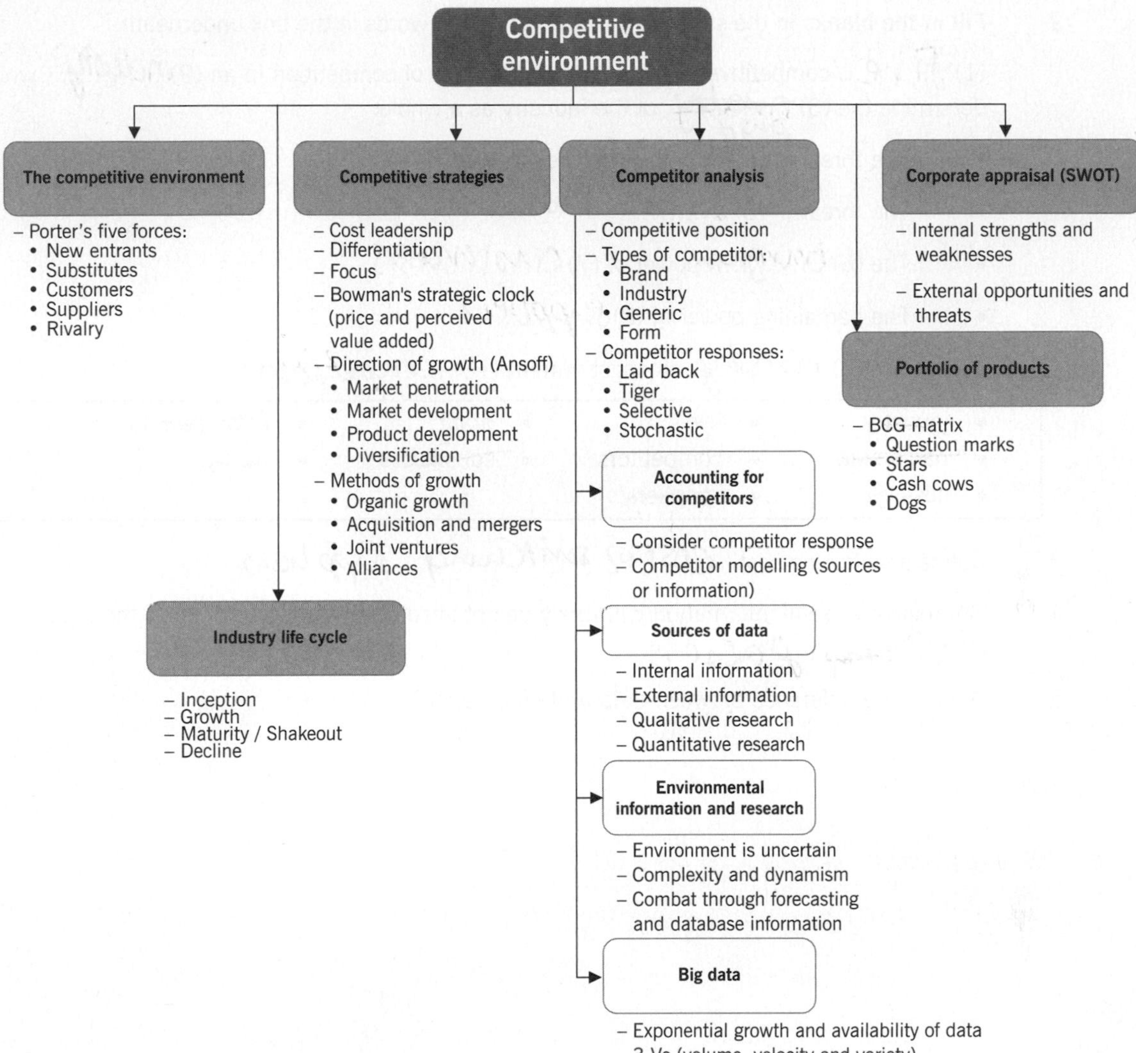
Competitive environment
The competitive environment
– Porter's five forces:
• New entrants
• Substitutes
• Customers
• Suppliers
• Rivalry
Competitive strategies
– Cost leadership
– Differentiation
– Focus
– Bowman's strategic clock (price and perceived value added)
– Direction of growth (Ansoff)
• Market penetration
• Market development
• Product development
• Diversification
– Methods of growth
• Organic growth
• Acquisition and mergers
• Joint ventures
• Alliances
Industry life cycle
– Inception
– Growth
– Maturity / Shakeout
– Decline
Competitor analysis
– Competitive position
– Types of competitor:
• Brand
• Industry
• Generic
• Form
– Competitor responses:
• Laid back
• Tiger
• Selective
• Stochastic
Accounting for competitors
– Consider competitor response
– Competitor modelling (sources or information)
Sources of data
– Internal information
– External information
– Qualitative research
– Quantitative research
Environmental information and research
– Environment is uncertain
– Complexity and dynamism
– Combat through forecasting and database information
Big data
– Exponential growth and availability of data
– 3 Vs (volume, velocity and variety)
Corporate appraisal (SWOT)
– Internal strengths and weaknesses
– External opportunities and threats
Portfolio of products
– BCG matrix
• Question marks
• Stars
• Cash cows
• Dogs

Quick Quiz

1 Distinguish 'market' from 'industry'.

2 **Fill in the blanks** in the statement below, using the words in the box underneath.

(1) .... competitive forces influence the state of competition in an (2) ...., which collectively determine the (3) .... of the industry as a whole:

- The threat of (4) .... to the industry
- The threat of (5) ....
- The (6) .... power of (7) ....
- The bargaining power of (8) ....
- The (9) .... amongst current (10) ....

• industry	• five	• profit	• new entrants
• bargaining	• competitors	• substitutes	• rivalry
• customers	• suppliers		

3 Define a switching cost.

4 'Strategically useful information will rarely be obtained from sources internal to the organisation.' True or false?

5 What is the difference between data and information?

Answers to Quick Quiz

1 The market comprises the customers or potential customers who have needs that are satisfied by a product or service.

The industry comprises those firms that use a particular competence, technology, product or service to satisfy customer needs.

2 (1) five (2) industry (3) profit (4) new entrants (5) substitutes (6) bargaining (7) customers (8) suppliers (9) rivalry (10) competitors

3 Switching costs refer to the costs (time, money and convenience) that a customer would have to incur by switching from one supplier's products to another's.

4 False. Many organisations possess large amounts of strategically useful information in their internal records.

5 Information is data that is organised in some useful way.

Answers to Questions

3.1 Competitor analysis

(a) Who are the existing competitors? How much of the market do they hold in each segment of the markets (eg in each particular region or country)?

(b) Who are potential competitors? How soon might they enter the market?

(c) How profitable are existing competitors? What is their earnings per share (EPS), dividend yield and return on capital employed (ROCE) etc?

(d) What do the goals of each competitor appear to be, and what strategies have they adopted so far?

(e) What products/services do they sell? How do they compare with the organisation's own products or services?

(f) How broad is their product line? (For example, are they upmarket high quality, or downmarket low quality, low price and high volume producers?)

(g) What is their distribution network?

(h) What are their skills and weaknesses in direct selling, advertising, sales promotions, product design etc?

(i) What are their design skills or R&D skills? Do they innovate or follow the market leader with new product ideas?

(j) What are their costs of sales and operational capabilities, with respect to equipment, technology, intellectual property etc?

(k) What are their general managerial capabilities? How do these compare with those of the organisation?

(l) Financial strengths and weaknesses. What is the debt position and financial gearing of each competitor? Do they have easy access to sources of new finance? What proportion of profits do they return in the business in order to finance growth?

(m) How is each competitor organised? How much decentralisation of authority do they allow to operating divisions, and so how flexible or independent can each of the operating divisions be?

(n) Does the competitor have a good spread or portfolio of activities? What is the risk profile of each competitor?

(o) Does any competitor have a special competitive advantage – eg a unique government contract or special access to government authorities?

(p) Does any competitor show signs of changing strategy to increase competition to the market?

3.2 Decisions

There are many possible suggestions, including those given below.

(a) The organisation's **bankers** take decisions affecting the amount of money they are prepared to lend.

(b) The **public** might have an interest in information relating to an organisation's products or services.

(c) The **media** (press and television etc) use information generated by organisations in news stories, and such information can adversely or favourably affect an organisation's relationship with its environment.

(d) The **Government** (for example the Department for Business, Innovation and Skills) regularly requires organisational information.

(e) **HM Revenue & Customs** requires information for taxation and VAT assessments.

(f) An organisation's **suppliers** and **customers** take decisions about whether or not to trade with the organisation.

3.3 Contrasting environment

(a) The environment is simple, as the product is only being sold in one market. The environment is dynamic, as the product is still at the introduction stage and demand might be predicted to increase dramatically.

(b) The environment is complex, but stable. The knowledge required is uncertain, but funds are guaranteed for ten years.

3.4 Industries and markets

(a) The airline industry. A number of airlines will compete to fly you from London to Glasgow.

(b) The railways. It is possible that two railway companies will compete to take you there.

(c) The car industry, if you have purchased a car.

(d) The bus industry. Several bus firms will compete to drive you to Glasgow.

(e) The telecommunications industry. You may not need to travel at all, if the conference can be held via a video-conferencing system or even something simpler, like a 'conference call'. Telecommunications firms might compete to provide this service.

3.5 Hermes

(a) Hermes initially pursued a cost-focus strategy, by providing a lower-cost service to the business segment.

(b) Hermes now seems to be moving into a cost leadership strategy over the whole market, although its competitive offer, in terms of lower costs for mobile calls, is incomplete.

(c) The barriers to entry to the market have been overcome by Gerbil Communications, as they have the technological know-how and have won a contract to provide a new, faster network based on new technology. Gerbil could be expected to gain a significant share of the mobile market. Hermes could perhaps consider some sort of relationship or joint venture with Gerbil.

3.6 Farmers – environmental analysis

Note. The answer provided here may be longer than that achievable within the time constraints of your examination. It is included as a learning tool.

Market position

Euro-Store is pursuing a cost leadership strategy, as defined by Michael Porter. This is evident, as the company offers low price, basic products as part of its 'no-frills' approach to business. Furthermore, Euro-Store does not offer customers as wide a selection of products as could be found in a standard supermarket, which historically appears to have been something consumers have been prepared to accept in exchange for lower prices.

Unlike Turners, Euro-Store does not aim to provide shoppers with a unique 'shopping experience', but instead promotes the fact that its prices are lower than competing stores by stacking products on wooden pallets as opposed to shelves. Coupled with its stores' standard design format, its insistence on only employing a 'skeleton' staff has enabled Euro-Store to cut its running costs.

The company's position in the UK appears to have been largely supported by its ability to realise economies of scale through purchasing products from existing suppliers to its European operations.

By contrast, Turners has adopted a differentiation-focus approach, as the business was founded on a belief that UK retailing needed something 'special'. Unlike Euro-Store and other traditional supermarkets, Turners only sells high-end food products. The company is focused on serving customers in its target market of 50 year olds and upwards. Each Turners store is unique, as every outlet is a former building of historical interest: this would appear to enhance the company's brand among shoppers.

Turners' shoppers are prepared to pay greater than average prices to use its stores; this is likely to be due to a number of combining factors such as: the quality of service received, the ability to use the cafe and the variety of world foods available (eg over 50 types of freshly baked breads).

Five forces analysis

The bargaining power of customers

Euro-Store's customers, as individuals, are unlikely to be able to exert significant power over the chain. However, as a collective, this group is likely to be very powerful. Power is increased because there is very little to stop shoppers using other supermarkets. This is particularly evident, as Euro-Store was able to attract shoppers to use its own stores during the 'credit crunch'. Although pursuing a different generic strategy, Turners' customers are likely to have a similar degree of power. It has long been the practice of established supermarkets to attract customers through the use of branding in-house products to appeal to buyer groups with different attitudes to price and quality. This represents a threat to both retailers.

The bargaining power of suppliers

Euro-Store's suppliers are likely to be in a weak bargaining position, as the company appears to be using the suppliers to its European stores to stock its UK operations. As Euro-Store only achieves low profit margins on the products it sells, it is highly likely that suppliers are only realising small profits themselves and may therefore be in a weak position to exert any influence.

Individual suppliers to Turners may hold a slightly greater degree of bargaining power, particularly if they sell one of Turners' bestselling cheeses or meats. However, Turners will most probably be able to reduce this threat due to the likely significant size of the orders it places with specialist food producers.

The threat of new entrants and the threat from substitutes

The threat posed by potential new entrants at either end of the supermarket industry is likely to be low. This is due to the initial high set-up costs of establishing a new chain and the need to be able to command almost instant economies of scale.

The threat from substitutes is also likely to be low, as consumers need to get their groceries from somewhere. Depending on how substitutes are viewed, it could be argued that farms that predominantly grow fresh produce and that also have a farm shop may represent a substitute threat. As we have already discussed, a substitute product is a good/service produced by another industry that satisfies the same customer needs, therefore farms could be regarded as being a substitute industry. However, this threat would appear to be insignificant to both Euro-Stores and Turners.

Rivalry among existing firms

As mentioned in the Farmers case study in the front of the Study Text, competition in the UK supermarket sector is intense, with a variety of different outlets for shoppers to choose from, including national discount chains and warehouse stores. This represents a significant threat to both Euro-Store and Turners.

Analysis of performance

Financials

Sales and profitability

Between 20X3 and 20X4, Euro-Store sales reduced by 2.6% ($219m). This may be due in part to an improvement in the overall state of the economy. Many shoppers switched to Euro-Store from traditional supermarkets during the onset of the 'credit crunch' in pursuit of paying lower prices for groceries. As the economy gradually moves out of recession, it seems plausible that shoppers may now be returning to their previous supermarkets, where they can purchase a greater range of groceries and non-food products (eg clothes, toys and books).

Unsurprisingly, sales per outlet reduced over the period, from $30.8m to $29.3m. This fall is in line with the overall drop in sales and is coupled with the fact that Euro-Store increased the number of UK stores it operates by seven. As would be expected, profitability has also suffered over the period, falling by $65m, a drop of 10.9%. This potentially represents a worrying development for the company, should this trend continue. The increase in the number of stores and associated costs (eg extra staff wages and property rentals) and falling sales has eroded net profit, as Euro-Store's net profit margin is now 6.4%, down from 7%.

Turners has enjoyed a much better 12 months of trading, with the company's sales up by $56m (7% on the previous year). This has most likely been helped in part by the opening of two new stores in the period. However, it seems likely that Turners will not have benefited from the full effects of having two new stores if they only opened partway through the year. Sales are likely to have been improved as a result of the UK's ageing population, especially as Turners' target market is those shoppers who fall into the 50 years plus age category. Turners' net profit has increased by $18m (24%) and this is reflected by the company's net profit margin, which is up to 10.9% from 9.4% in 2013. The ability to generate more profit from the sales made suggests that Turners may now be in a better position to control its costs, or is using its increased size to command better prices from its suppliers.

Inventory

Euro-Store's inventory days have remained constant at nine days; this is in keeping with the company's profile as a 'no-frills' retailer where products are brought straight onto the shop floor on pallets to reduce the amount of time it takes to sell these items. By contrast, Turners takes longer to turn over its inventory. This has, however, fallen by 28 days down from 32, which is most likely attributable to increasing awareness of the Turners brand among shoppers. Turners' higher selling prices may mean that shoppers do not make all their food purchases in the store, but instead go in for a selection of specialist food items to complement a big shop that they undertake in a rival supermarket.

Operational

Customers most value the level of service they receive when they shop at Turners. This is evidently part of the chain's differentiation strategy and has been something that the company has attempted to build on by employing more staff in-store. The impact of this move appears to have resulted in a reduction in the amount of time shoppers spend queuing at the tills. The fact that the average age of a Turners employee is 51 years suggests that the company has actively tried to recruit individuals who are going to appeal to the target market.

By contrast, Euro-Store's customers complain about the level of service they receive. This will most likely be due to the company's policy of only having a 'skeleton' staff on duty at any one time. It may help to explain Euro-Store's drop in sales and profitability. However, it is interesting to note that the amount of time customers spend at the till has remained constant over the period, while the number of staff on duty has fallen. Had Euro-Store not opened seven new outlets, the company would have reported a fall in staff wages, which may have supported its financial performance.

Appendix

Euro-Store	$m	%
Change in sales		
$m change in sales (8,294 – 8,513)	(219)	
% change in sales (8,294 – 8,513 ÷ 8,513) × 100		(2.57%)
20X4 sales ($m) per outlet		
(8,294 ÷ 283)	29.3	
20X3 sales ($m) per outlet		
(8,513 ÷ 276)	30.8	
Change in profit for the period		
$m change in profit (531 – 596)	(65)	
% change in profit (531 – 596 ÷ 596) × 100		(10.9%)
20X4 net profit margin		
Profit for the period ÷ sales × 100		6.4%
(531 ÷ 8,294) × 100		
20X3 net profit margin		7%
Profit for the period ÷ sales × 100		
(596 ÷ 8,513) × 100		
Turners		
Change in sales		
$m change in sales (853 – 797)	56	
% change in sales (853 – 797 ÷ 797) × 100		7%
20X4 sales ($m) per outlet		
(853 ÷ 63)	13.5	
20X3 sales ($m) per outlet		
(797 ÷ 61)	13.1	
Change in profit for the period		
$m change in profit (93 – 75)	18	
% change in profit (93 – 75 ÷ 75) × 100		24%
20X4 net profit margin		
Profit for the period ÷ sales × 100		10.9%
93 ÷ 853 × 100		
20X3 net profit margin		
Profit for period ÷ sales × 100		9.4%
75 ÷ 797 × 100		

Now try these questions from the Practice Question Bank

Question	Level
3.1 – 3.5	Practice
X Company (part a)	Practice

THE HUMAN ASPECTS OF THE ORGANISATION

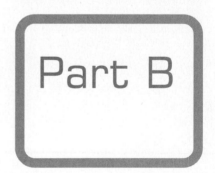

Part B

KEY CONCEPTS IN MANAGEMENT

In the opening chapters, we explored the role of senior management in setting strategy in a modern organisation. As discussed, in order for a strategy to be successfully realised, it must be implemented at all levels in the organisations.

It therefore falls on the role of the manager to co-ordinate the resources needed to implement the element of the corporate plan related to their area of responsibility.

'The human aspects of the organisation' is Part B of your syllabus. This chapter introduces a number of key concepts in management, leadership and organisation culture. Each concept underpins core aspects of the syllabus – whether you are managing people, managing a project or developing strategy.

We start by looking at what a manager does. This is fundamental in understanding why there are managers in organisations.

Then we explore the nature of **power and authority relationships** in organisations. These concepts give managers the right to manage – and leaders the ability to lead. They underpin our later discussion of project and stakeholder management too, because managers need to be able to influence others in contexts where they **do not** necessarily have direct 'line' authority.

We also discuss delegation and responsibility in this section, as they are allied to power and authority. These topics introduce the formal relationships and activities in the organisation.

We go on to look at the nature of **leadership**, why it might be different to management, and the different ways in which it can be exercised. You should be able to link this learning to our later coverage of the 'people' aspects of leading projects, and the wider issues of different cultures and how they affect organisations.

Bureaucracy is looked at briefly. You need to understand why bureaucracy developed and why it can be efficient in certain organisations.

Managers need to manage within the law, and we continue by analysing how managers and subordinates relate in areas as diverse as discipline, grievance, health and safety and equal opportunities.

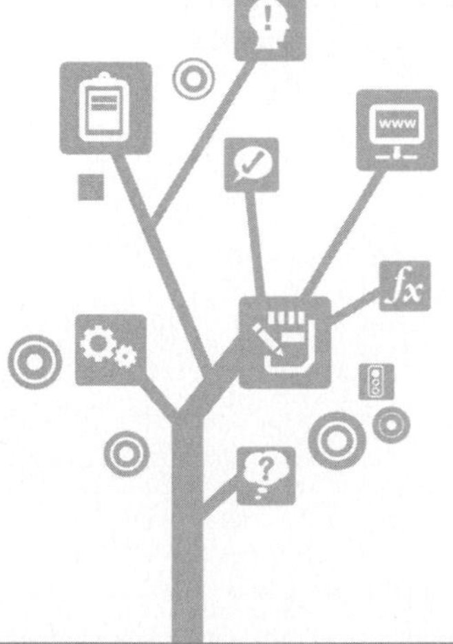

Topic list	Learning outcomes	Syllabus references	Ability required
1 Role of the manager	B1a	B1(i)	Analysis
2 Power, authority, responsibility and delegation	B1a	B1(ii)	Analysis
3 Management and leadership	B1a	B1(iii), (iv)	Analysis
4 Organisational flexibility	B1a	B1(i)	Analysis
5 Discipline	B1b	B1(v)	Analysis
6 Grievance	B1b	B1(v)	Analysis
7 Termination of contract	B1b	B1(vi)	Analysis
8 Equal opportunities	B1b	B1(iv)	Analysis
9 The practical implications of legislation	B1b	B1(i)	Analysis
10 Diversity	B1b	B1(iv)	Analysis

Chapter Overview

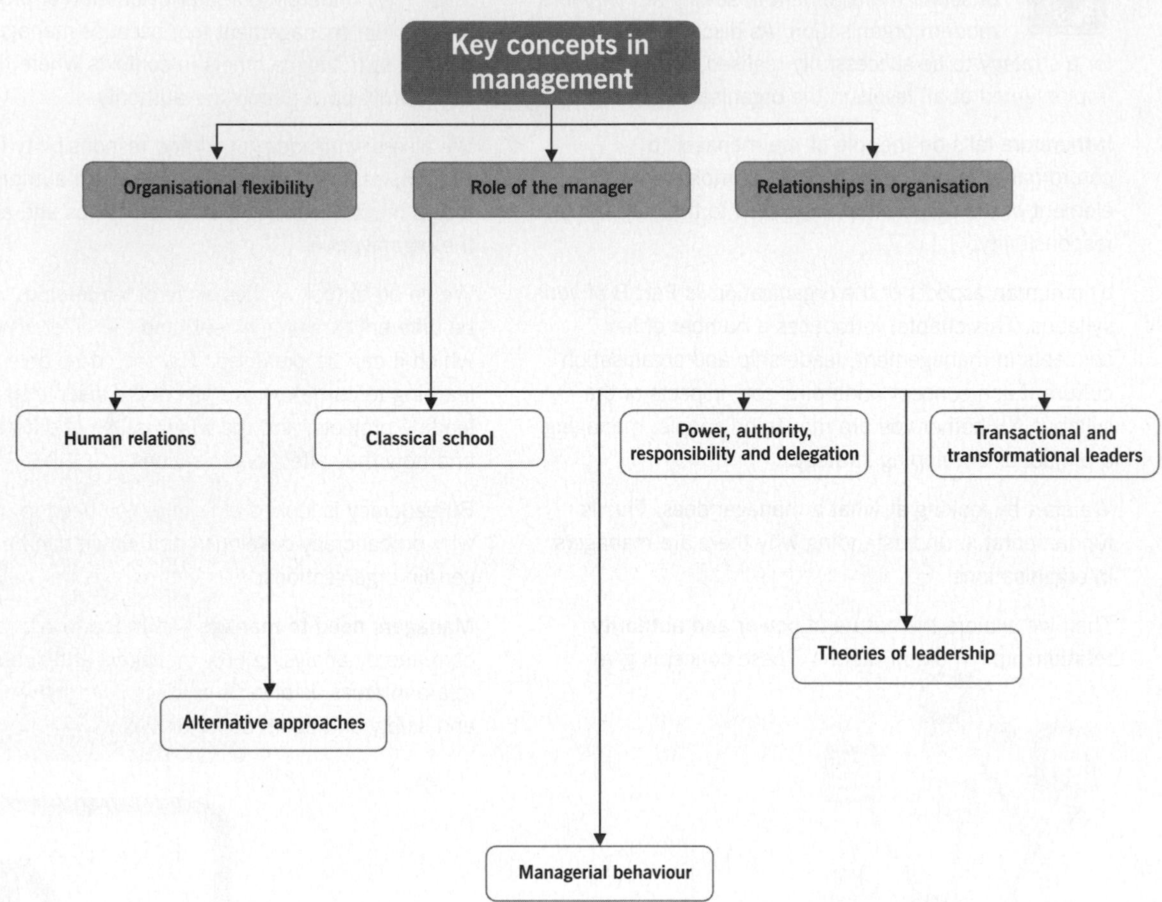

Key concepts in management
Organisational flexibility
Role of the manager
Relationships in organisation
Human relations
Classical school
Power, authority, responsibility and delegation
Transactional and transformational leaders
Theories of leadership
Alternative approaches
Managerial behaviour

1 Role of the manager

1.1 Management

Introduction

Managers manage resources to get things done. In most organisations, it is impossible for one person to do every job, and so managers also need to co-ordinate the actions of others to get things done.

KEY TERM

MANAGEMENT may be defined, most simply, as 'getting things done through other people' (Stewart).

Why is it that organisations have to be managed, and what is the purpose of management?

An organisation has been defined as 'a social arrangement for the controlled performance of collective goals'. This definition suggests the need for management.

(a) **Objectives** have to be set for the organisation.
(b) Somebody has to **monitor progress and results** to ensure that objectives are met.
(c) Somebody has to communicate and sustain **corporate values**, ethics and operating principles.
(d) Somebody has to look after the interests of the **organisation's owners** and other **stakeholders**.

Question 4.1

Management structure

Learning outcome B1a

John, Paul, George and Ringo set up a business together as repairers of musical instruments. Each has contributed £5,000 as capital for the business. They are a bit uncertain about how they should run the business and, when they discuss this in the pub, they decide that attention needs to be paid to planning what they do, reviewing what they do and controlling what they do.

Required

Suggest two ways in which John, Paul, George and Ringo can manage the business, assuming that no other personnel are recruited.

Different organisations have different structures for carrying out management functions. For example, some organisations have separate strategic planning departments. Others do not.

In a **private sector business**, managers act, ultimately, on behalf of shareholders. In practical terms, shareholders rarely interfere, as long as the business delivers profits year on year.

In a **public sector organisation**, management acts on behalf of the Government. Politicians in a democracy are in turn accountable to the electorate. More of the objectives of a public sector organisation might be set by the 'owners' – ie the Government – rather than by the management. The Government might also tell senior management to carry out certain policies or plans, thereby restricting management's discretion.

KEY POINT

Later in the chapter, we contrast **management** with **leadership**. The two activities are different. Management broadly focuses on maintaining the 'steady state' in the organisation, while leadership drives the organisation forward. Leadership also only affects people while management deals with all resources.

1.2 Classical school – Henri Fayol: five functions of management

Exam alert

The theories of Taylor, Fayol and Weber are collectively known as the '**classical theories**'. Emphasis is placed on **rules**, **specialisation**, **hierarchies** and **obedience**. It is important that you understand the distinction between the work of each theorist, as it could easily form the basis of a question in your E2 exam.

Fayol (1841–1925) was a French industrialist who put forward and popularised the concept of the '**universality of management principles**': in other words, the idea that all organisations could be structured and managed according to certain rational principles. Fayol himself recognised that applying such principles in practice was not simple: 'Seldom do we have to apply the same principles twice in identical conditions; allowance must be made for different and changing circumstances'.

Fayol classified five **functions of management** that apply to any organisation.

Function	Comment
Planning	This involves determining **objectives**, and strategies, policies, programmes and procedures for achieving those objectives, for the organisation and its sub-units.
Organising	Establishing a **structure of tasks** that need to be performed to achieve the goals of the organisation; grouping these tasks into jobs for individuals or teams; allocating jobs to sections and departments; **delegating** authority to carry out the jobs; and providing **systems of information** and communication, for the co-ordination of activities.
Commanding	Giving **instructions** to subordinates to carry out tasks, for which the manager has authority (to make decisions) and responsibility (for performance).
Co-ordinating	**Harmonising** the goals and activities of individuals and groups within the organisation. Management must reconcile differences in approach, effort, interest and timing, in favour of overall (or 'super-ordinate') shared goals.
Controlling	**Measuring** and **correcting** the activities of individuals and groups, to ensure that their performance is in accordance with plans. Deviations from plans are identified and corrected.

Question 4.2

Fayol

Learning outcome B1a

Group the activities of a manager in your organisation into Fayol's five functions. What do you think is left out from Fayol's list? What do you think is wrong or inadequate about it?

This reflects the **classical view** of the function of management as a matter of controlling resources and processes rather than people: an awareness of management as first of all an **interpersonal** process, involving communication and influence, only developed later, as we will see.

1.2.1 Fourteen general principles of management

Fayol also developed 14 general principles of management, based on his experiences. These principles provide modern-day managers with general guidelines on how a supervisor should organise their department and manage their staff.

(a) **Division of labour**. Division of work and specialisation produces more and better work with the same effort.

(b) **Authority and responsibility**. Authority is the right to give orders and the power to exact obedience. A manager has official authority because of their position, as well as personal authority based on individual personality, intelligence and experience. Authority creates responsibility.

(c) **Discipline**. Obedience and respect within an organisation are absolutely essential. Good discipline requires managers to apply sanctions whenever violations become apparent.

(d) **Unity of command**. An employee should receive orders from only one superior.

(e) **Unity of direction**. Organisational activities must have one central authority and one plan of action.

(f) **Subordination of individual interest to general interest**. The interests of one employee or group of employees are subordinate to the interests and goals of the organisation. This is necessary to maintain unity and to avoid friction among the employees.

(g) **Remuneration of personnel.** Salaries – the price of services rendered by employees – should be fair, and provide satisfaction both to the employee and employer.

(h) **Centralisation**. The objective of centralisation is the best utilisation of personnel. The degree of centralisation varies according to the dynamics of each organisation.

(i) **Scalar chain**. A chain of authority exists from the highest organisational authority to the lowest ranks.

(j) **Order**. Organisational order for materials and personnel is essential. The right materials and the right employees are necessary for each organisational function and activity.

(k) **Equity**. In organisations, equity is a combination of kindliness and justice. Both equity and equality of treatment should be considered when dealing with employees.

(l) **Stability of tenure of personnel**. To attain the maximum productivity of personnel, a stable workforce is needed.

(m) **Initiative**. Thinking out a plan and ensuring its success is an extremely strong motivator. Zeal, energy and initiative are desired at all levels of the organisational ladder.

(n) ***Esprit de corps***. Teamwork is fundamentally important to an organisation. Work teams and extensive face to face verbal communication encourages teamwork.

1.3 Classical school – F W Taylor: scientific management

Frederick W Taylor (1856–1915) pioneered the **scientific management** movement in the US. He was among the first to argue that management should be based on 'well-recognised, clearly defined and fixed principles, instead of depending on more or less hazy ideas'. Taylor was a very skilled engineer, and he took an engineering efficiency approach to management.

Principles of scientific management include the following.

(a) The development of a true **science of work**. 'All knowledge which had hitherto been kept in the heads of workmen should be gathered and recorded by management. Every single subject, large and small, becomes the question for scientific investigation, for reduction to law.'

(b) The **scientific selection** and **progressive development** of workers: workers should be carefully trained and given jobs to which they are best suited.

(c) The application of techniques to **plan, measure and control work** for maximum productivity.

(d) The constant and intimate **co-operation between management and workers**: 'the relations between employers and men form without question the most important part of this art'.

In practice, scientific management techniques included the following key elements.

(a) **Work study techniques** were used to analyse tasks and establish the most efficient methods to use. No variation was permitted in the way work was done, since the aim was to use the 'one best way'.

(b) **Planning and doing were separated**. It was assumed that the persons who were intellectually equipped to do a particular type of work were probably unlikely to be able to plan it to the best advantage: this was the manager's job.

(c) Jobs were **micro-designed**. They were divided into single, simple task components that formed a whole specialised 'job' for an individual, rather than permitting an individual to perform whole or part-task processes. (Task 'meaning' and 'significance', now considered essential to job satisfaction, had not yet emerged as important values.)

(d) Workers were **paid incentives** on the basis of acceptance of the new methods and output norms; the new methods greatly increased productivity and profits. Pay was assumed to be the only important motivating force.

Scientific management as practised by Taylor and contemporaries such as Gilbreth and Gantt was very much about **manual work**. However, elements of scientific management are still practised today, whenever there is a concern for productivity and efficiency.

Persistent Taylorism?

It has been argued that elements of Taylorism – maximising managerial control through the micro-design of jobs, automation and close supervision – can be seen in the management of junior staff in businesses such as:

(a) Large fast-food franchises (such as McDonald's)

(b) Call centres, where calls are scripted, timed and monitored – and (in some reported cases) staff must ask permission to leave the 'floor' to go to the toilet

1.4 Human relations – Elton Mayo

Exam alert

By the 1920s, the assumptions of the classical theorists were being challenged by Mayo and Herzberg with their 'human relations' theories. These place emphasis on employee **motivation** and **task commitment**.

In the 1920s, research began to show that managers needed to consider the complexity of **human behaviour**. It was recognised that an exclusive focus on technical competence (under scientific management) had resulted in social incompetence: managers were not taught how to manage people. At the same time, it emerged that being a 'small cog in the machine' was experienced as alienating and demoralising by workers – whatever the financial incentives offered. A more complex picture of human motivation began to emerge.

Elton Mayo was Professor of Industrial Research at the Harvard Business School. He was involved in a series of large-scale studies at the Western Electric Company's Hawthorne works in Chicago, between 1924 and 1932. These studies were originally firmly set in the context of scientific management, in that they began with an experiment into the effect of lighting on work output. However, it rapidly became

apparent that **worker attitudes** and **group relationships** were of greater importance in determining the levels of production achieved than the lighting itself.

An important element in the Hawthorne studies was the investigation of the dynamics of work groups. The group was very effective in enforcing its behavioural norms in such matters as 'freezing out' unpopular supervisors and restricting output. It was concluded that people are motivated at work by a variety of psychological needs, including social or 'belonging' needs. This became the basis of the **human relations school** of management theory.

1.4.1 Neo-human relations

Later writers (such as Maslow and Herzberg) focused on a wider variety of workers' 'higher-order' needs, including the need for challenge, responsibility and personal development in the job. This became known as the **neo-human relations school**, which proposed important theories of motivation and job satisfaction.

The human relations approaches contributed an important awareness of the influence of the human factor at work (and particularly in the work group) on organisational performance. Most of its theorists attempted to offer guidelines to enable practising managers to satisfy and motivate employees and so (theoretically) obtain the benefits of improved productivity.

However, the approach tends to emphasise the importance of work to the workers without really addressing the economic issues: there is still no proven link between job satisfaction and motivation, or either of these and productivity or the achievement of organisational goals.

Herzberg identified two groups of work-related factors that caused satisfaction and dissatisfaction respectively. He called those factors **motivators** and **hygiene factors**.

KEY TERMS

MOTIVATORS produced satisfaction when present, and were capable of motivating the individual.

HYGIENE FACTORS (or **MAINTENANCE FACTORS**) could not give satisfaction or provide motivation when present. Their absence, however, caused dissatisfaction.

In his book *Work and the Nature of Man*, Herzberg distinguished between **hygiene factors** and **motivator factors**, based on what he saw as two separate 'need systems' of individuals.

(a) There is a **need to avoid unpleasantness**. This need is satisfied at work by hygiene factors. Hygiene satisfactions are short-lived: individuals come back for more, in the nature of drug addicts.

(b) There is a **need for personal growth**, which is satisfied by motivator factors, and not by hygiene factors.

A lack of motivators at work will encourage employees to focus on poor hygiene (real or imagined) and to demand more pay, for example. Some individuals do not seek personal growth: these are 'hygiene seekers' who may be able to be satisfied by hygiene factors.

Hygiene or **maintenance** factors include:

- Company policy and administration
- Salary
- The quality of supervision
- Interpersonal relations
- Working conditions
- Job security

Hygiene factors are essentially **preventative**. They prevent or **minimise dissatisfaction** but do not give satisfaction, in the same way that sanitation minimises threats to health, but does not give 'good' health. They are called 'maintenance' factors because they have to be continually renewed to avoid dissatisfaction.

Motivator factors create job satisfaction and are effective in motivating an individual to superior performance and effort. These factors give the individual a sense of self-fulfilment or personal growth.

- Status (although this may be a hygiene factor as well as a motivator factor)
- Advancement
- Gaining recognition
- Being given responsibility
- Challenging work
- Achievement
- Growth in the job

Herzberg suggested that if there is sufficient **challenge**, **scope** and **interest** in the job, there will be a lasting **increase in satisfaction** and the employee will work well: productivity will be above normal levels.

The extent to which a job must be challenging or creative to a motivator-seeker will depend on each individual's ability and their tolerance for **delayed success.**

1.4.2 Maslow's hierarchy of needs

Maslow identified a hierarchy of needs which an individual will be motivated to satisfy, progressing towards higher-order satisfactions, such as self-actualisation (self-fulfilment). Abraham Maslow described five innate human needs, and put forward certain propositions about the motivating power of each need.

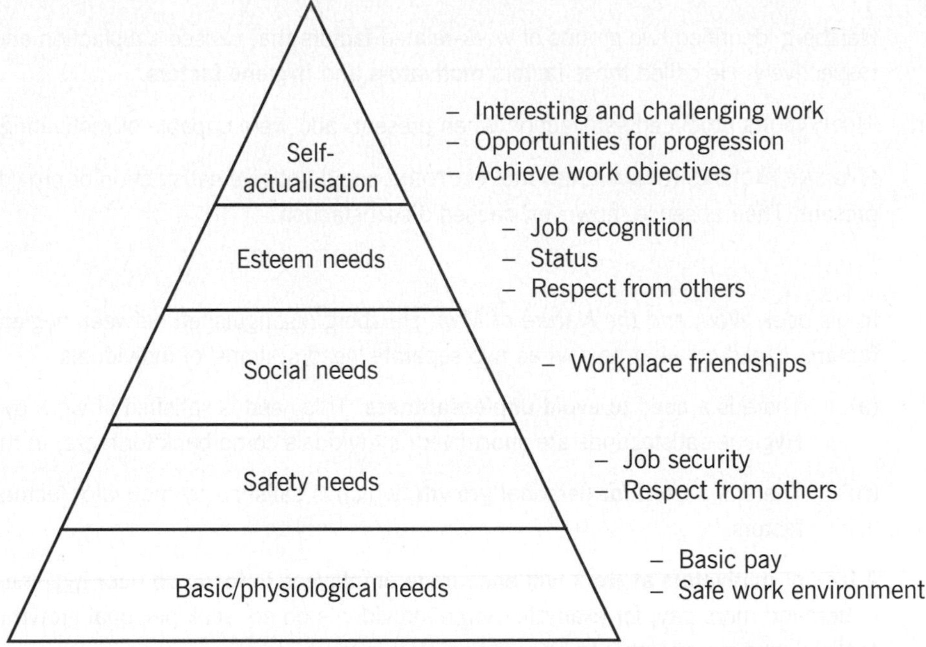

An individual's needs can be arranged in a **'hierarchy** of relative pre-potency' (as shown). Each level of need is **dominant until satisfied**; only then does the next level of need become a motivating factor. A need which has been satisfied no longer motivates an individual's behaviour. The need for self-actualisation can rarely be satisfied.

In addition, Maslow described:

(a) Freedom of enquiry and expression needs (for social conditions encouraging fairness and honesty)
(b) Knowledge and understanding needs (to gain knowledge of the environment, to explore, learn)

Evaluating Maslow's theory

Maslow's hierarchy is only a theory and has been shown to have several major limitations.

(a) An individual's behaviour may be in response to **several needs**, and the same need may cause **different behaviour** in different individuals, so it is difficult to use the model to explain or predict an individual's behaviour in response to rewards.

(b) The hierarchy ignores the concept of **deferred gratification** (by which people are prepared to ignore their current position for the promise of future benefits) and **altruistic behaviour** (by which people sacrifice their own needs for others).

(c) **Empirical verification** of the hierarchy is hard to come by.

(d) Research has revealed that the hierarchy reflects UK and US **cultural values**, which may not transfer to other contexts.

1.5 Modern writers on management

In the second half of the 20th century, writing on management became more diverse.

(a) The early emphasis on the organisation of work has been continued in the field of **supervisory studies** and the development of specific management techniques such as **project management**. The search for efficiency continues in the field of **work study** and **industrial engineering**.

(b) Human relations theory has been enhanced by developments in the study of motivation, group and individual behaviour, leadership and other aspects of **industrial psychology**.

(c) There has been much new writing on the nature of the **manager's task**: what it is to be a manager and what managers do, in increasingly complex and chaotic business environments.

1.6 Peter Drucker – the management process and management by objectives

KEY POINT

Drucker introduced the idea of management by objectives in the 1950s. At the time, the idea of involving all employees in the strategy and goals of the organisation was a radical one. This is now commonplace and unremarkable.

Drucker argued that organisational performance could be improved by aligning personal and departmental objectives with key business objectives. These are **profitability**, **management performance**, **worker performance** and **public responsibility**.

1.6.1 Management tasks

Drucker described the jobs of management within the basic function of economic performance as follows.

(a) **Managing a business**. The purposes of the business are to create a customer and innovation.

(b) **Managing managers**. The requirements here are:

- (i) Management by objectives (or performance management)
- (ii) Proper structure of managers' jobs
- (iii) Creating the right spirit (culture) in the organisation
- (iv) Making a provision for the managers of tomorrow (managerial succession)
- (v) Arriving at sound principles of organisation structure

(c) **Managing workers and work**. Planning, control, organising, motivating and developing people.

A manager's performance in all areas of management, including management of the business, can be enhanced by a study of the principles of management, the acquisition of 'organised knowledge' (eg management techniques) and systematic self-assessment.

1.6.2 Management processes

Later, Drucker grouped the work of the manager into five categories.

(a) **Setting objectives for the organisation**. Managers decide what the objectives of the organisation should be and quantify the targets of achievement for each objective. They must then communicate these targets to other people in the organisation.

(b) **Organising the work**. The work to be done in the organisation must be divided into manageable activities and manageable jobs. The jobs must be integrated into a formal organisation structure, and people must be selected to do the jobs.

(c) **Motivating** employees, and communicating information to them to enable them to do their work.

(d) **The job of measurement**. Management must:

  (i) Establish **objectives** or yardsticks of performance for all personnel

  (ii) Analyse **actual performance**, appraise it against the objectives or yardsticks that have been set, and analyse the comparison

  (iii) **Communicate** the findings and explain their significance both to subordinate employees and also to superiors

(e) **Developing people**. The manager brings out what is in their employees or stifles them. The manager strengthens their integrity or corrupts them.

Every manager performs all five functions listed above, no matter how good or bad a manager they are. However, a bad manager performs these functions badly, whereas a good manager performs them well. Unlike Fayol, Drucker emphasised the importance of **communication** in the functions of management.

1.7 Mintzberg – the manager's role

Henry Mintzberg (1989) did a study of a relatively small sample of US corporations to see how senior managers actually spend their time. He suggests that in their daily working lives, managers fulfil three types of **managerial role**.

Role category	Role	Comment
Interpersonal Based on manager's formal authority or position	**Figurehead** (or ceremonial)	A large part of a chief executive's time is spent representing the company at dinners, conferences and so on.
	Leader	Hiring, firing and training staff, motivating employees, and reconciling individual goals with the objectives of the organisation.
	Liaison	Making contacts outside the vertical chain of command. Some managers spend up to half their meeting time with their peers rather than with their subordinates.
Informational Based on managers' access to: • Upward and downward channels • Many external contacts	**Monitor**	The manager monitors the environment, and receives information from subordinates, superiors and peers in other departments. Much of this information is of an informal nature, derived from the manager's network of contacts.
	Spokesperson	The manager provides information on behalf of the unit and/or organisation to interested parties.

Role category	Role	Comment
	Disseminator	The manager disseminates relevant information to subordinates.
Decisional Based on the manager's formal authority and access to information, which allow them to take decisions relating to the work of the department as a whole	**Entrepreneur**	A manager initiates projects to improve the department or to help it react to a changed environment.
	Disturbance handler	A manager has to respond to unexpected pressures, taking decisions when there is deviation from plan.
	Resource allocator	A manager takes decisions relating to the mobilisation and distribution of limited resources to achieve objectives.
	Negotiator	Both inside and outside the organisation, negotiation takes up a great deal of management time.

Mintzberg's research challenged the classical view of the manager as separate to, or above, the routine demands of day to day work.

(a) Managers are not always able to be reflective, systematic planners.

(b) Managerial work is disjointed and discontinuous.

(c) Managers do have routine duties to perform, especially of a ceremonial nature (receiving important guests) or related to authority (signing cheques as a signatory) – contrary to the myth that all routine work is done by juniors.

(d) Managers prefer verbal and informal information to the formal output of management information systems. Verbal information is 'hotter' and probably easier to grasp.

(e) Management cannot be reduced to a science or a profession. According to Mintzberg, managerial processes cannot be analysed scientifically or codified into an examinable body of theory.

Mintzberg states that general management is, in practice, a matter of **judgement and intuition**, gained from **experience** in **particular situations** rather than from abstract principles. 'Fragmentation and verbal communication' characterise the manager's work.

Question 4.3 Mintzberg and classical management theory

Learning outcome B1a

'Mintzberg's findings completely invalidate the notion that there are distinct management functions.' Discuss.

1.8 The systems approach

KEY POINT

An organisation can be viewed as an **open system**, interacting with its environment.

The **systems approach** sees organisations, more dynamically, in terms of a system: 'an entity which consists of interdependent parts'. Rather than focus on administrative structures, this approach views the organisation as an **open system**, which is connected to and interacts with its environment. It takes in inputs from its environment and, through various organisational processes, converts them into outputs.

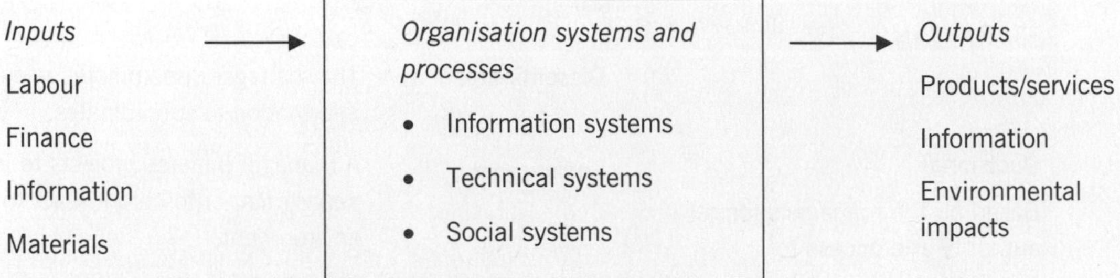

As an open system, an organisation must remain sensitive to **changes in its external environment**. It must also make **internal adjustments** in order to remain **stable**.

The systems approach is helpful in:

(a) Drawing attention to the dynamic nature of organisations

(b) Creating an awareness of subsystems that must be integrated (eg the needs of task processes may conflict with the human needs of workers)

(c) Focusing attention on the relationship of the organisation with its environment (Outward focus is particularly important for customer satisfaction: a shortcoming of the inward and process-focused bureaucratic approach.)

1.8.1 Socio-technical systems

KEY POINT

Trist and Bamforth highlighted the importance of balancing the **social** and **technical** requirements of the job.

CASE STUDY

Trist and Bamforth studied the effect of the introduction of new technology in coal mining.

The traditional method was based on a small, integrated work group consisting of a skilled man, his mate and one or two labourers. There was a high degree of autonomy at the work group level and close working relationships. It was usual for the group to be paid for its work as a group. The work was hard, the conditions unpleasant and there was often conflict, and even violence between work groups. However, 'the system as a whole contained its bad in a way that did not destroy its good'.

The introduction of large-scale coal-cutting machinery created a need for larger, more specialised groups. A single cycle of mechanised production might extend over three 7.5 shifts, each performing a separate process and made up of 10 to 20 men. The members of each shift would be spread over about 200 yards of coal face tunnel. This physical dispersion and the spread of the work over three shifts destroyed the previous close working relationships. Many symptoms of social stress appeared, including scapegoating across shifts, formation of cliques and absenteeism.

Trist and Bamforth studied the new technology and found that it was possible to organise its use in such a way that some of the social characteristics of the traditional method were preserved. The use of this new method led to greater productivity, lower cost, considerably less absenteeism and accidents, and greater work satisfaction.

Trist introduced the concept of the organisation as a **structured socio-technical system**, with at least two major sub-systems:

(a) **Technology**, including task organisation and methods (not just machinery and tools)

(b) **People** and their social arrangements – personal factors and interpersonal interactions

The socio-technical systems approach to organisation suggested that organisations should aim to find a 'fit' that will maximise efficiency (through use of technology) while at the same time ensuring member satisfaction and commitment (through meeting workers' social and psychological needs).

Section summary

Management is responsible for using the organisation's resources to meet its goals. It is accountable to the owners: shareholder in a business, or government in the public sector.

The earliest contributions on the science of management were offered by Fayol. His definition of management may be remembered by the '**POCCC**' mnemonic.

Taylor was an engineer, and sought the most efficient methods of work organisation and control, forming the basis of what became known as the scientific management school.

Mayo and his colleagues investigated individual and group behaviour at work, as a factor in productivity. This became the focus of the human relationship school of management.

Subsequent writers have taken a more **flexible** view of what managers do.

Mintzberg described managerial roles, arguing that management is a disjointed, non-systematic activity – unlike classical descriptions of a separate, reflective planning role.

An organisation can be viewed as an **open system** interacting with its environment.

Trist and Bamforth highlighted the importance of balancing the **social** and **technical** requirements of the job.

2 Power, authority, responsibility and delegation

Introduction

We look at four aspects of the relationship between managers and others in the organisation in this section. These aspects cover 'getting the work done'.

Make sure you are clear on the characteristics of each type of relationship, which are covered in the key point below.

KEY POINT

Ensure that you can distinguish clearly between the various terms. **Power and authority** are features of all organisations. They are exercised over others. **Responsibility** falls on any individual to complete their own tasks. **Delegation** is where authority is passed down to make decisions.

An organisation can be reviewed as an open **system** interacting with its environment.

2.1 Power

KEY TERM

POWER is the **ability** to get things done.

Power is not something a person 'has' in isolation: it is exercised over other individuals or groups, and – to an extent – depends on their **recognising** the person's power over them.

2.1.1 Types of power

French and Raven classified power into six types or sources.

Type of power	
Coercive power	The power of physical force or punishment. Physical power is rare in business organisations, but intimidation may feature, eg in workplace bullying.
Reward (or resource) power	Based on access to or control over valued resources. For example, managers have access to information, contacts and financial rewards for team members. The amount of resource power a person has depends on the scarcity of the resource, how much the resource is valued by others, and how far the resource is under the manager's control.
Legitimate (or position) power	Associated with a particular position in the organisation. For example, a manager has the power to authorise certain expenses, or issue instructions, because the authority to do so has been formally delegated to them.
Expert power	Based on experience, qualifications or expertise. For example, accountants have expert power because of their knowledge of the tax system. Expert power depends on others recognising the expertise in an area that they need or value.
Referent (or personal) power	Based on force of personality, or 'charisma', which can attract, influence or inspire other people.
Negative power (Handy)	The power to disrupt operations; for example, by industrial action, refusal to communicate information, or sabotage.

2.1.2 Influence

KEY TERM

INFLUENCE is the process by which one person modifies the behaviour or attitude of another.

Influence, the act of directing or modifying the behaviour of others, may be achieved in a variety of ways.

(a) The application of force, such as physical or economic power

(b) The establishment of rules and procedures that are enforced through position and/or resource power

(c) Bargaining and negotiation, which depend on the relative strengths of each party's position

(d) Persuasion

2.2 Power centres

The **degree** of power that people exercise, and the **types** of power they are able to exploit, differs depending in part on their position in the organisation's hierarchy.

2.2.1 Senior management

Senior managers enjoy **high position power**: in theory they take the major decisions and set constraints over the decisions taken by other people. In practice, however, this power is never absolute. Senior managers depend on decisions and information supplied by subordinates, and it is quite possible that the information is shaped at a lower level. Informal leaders may have upward or sideways influence (eg experts and front-line workers).

Senior managers have **high resource powers**, which they exercise over budget allocations and strategic direction.

2.2.2 Middle managers

Middle managers have **limited reward power** over their own subordinates; expert power and some decisions; and perhaps **negative power** to delay or subvert decisions taken by senior managers. They need **legitimate power**, hence the need for formal job descriptions, authorisation limits and so on. They may also gain influence from networking: tapping into valued sources of information, or influential mentors and coalitions.

2.2.3 Interest groups

Formal interest groups are groups that represent the interests of their members, in order to wield greater power than their individual members. Examples include trade unions and occupational/professional associations.

2.2.4 Departmental power

Some departments in the organisation exercise power by the use of **functional authority**, for instance, by specifying procedures. Other departments are influential because they deal with **key strategic contingencies**: 'events and activities both inside and outside an organisation that are essential for attaining organisational goals'. They can arise in several ways.

(a) **Dependency**. A department that depends on another department may not be in a position to exercise power over that department, without support at a higher level. A department may use its resource power to make other departments dependent on it.

(b) **Financial resources**. This is another sort of dependency, but a department with a larger budget can spend it with more discretion.

(c) **Centrality**. How critical is the department in the primary activities of the organisation?

(d) **Non-substitutability**. Some departments cannot easily be broken up and their activities carried out elsewhere. This used to be the case with information systems departments, before the advent of cheap personal computers and software.

(e) **Uncertainty**. A department that reduces the levels of uncertainty faced by other departments (in dealing with key environmental variables) has a sort of expert power.

Section summary

Power is the ability to get things done. There are many types of power in organisations: position or **legitimate power**, expert power, personal power, resource power and negative power are examples.

2.3 Authority

KEY TERM

AUTHORITY is the right to do something, or to ask someone else to do it and expect it to be done. Authority is thus another word for **position or legitimate power**.

Power and influence can be exercised at any level of the organisation, and in any direction – not just 'downwards' (over direct reports and teams), but sideways (over peers and cross-functional colleagues) and even upwards (eg promoting an idea or course of action to your manager).

Authority generally flows downwards through the line or chain of command that is part of the formal organisation structure.

Max Weber (many years before French and Raven's work on power) proposed three ways in which managers exercised what he called legitimate power (or authority).

(a) **Charismatic authority** arises from the personality of the leader and their ability to inspire devotion through, for example, sanctity, heroism or example.

(b) **Traditional authority** rests on established belief in the importance of immemorial tradition and the status it confers.

(c) **Rational-legal** authority raises from the working of accepted normative rules, such as are found in organisations and democratic governments.

Managerial authority is exercised in such areas as:

(a) **Making decisions within the scope of authority** given to the position. For example, a manager's authority is limited to their team, and with certain limits. For items of expenditure over a certain amount, say, they may require authorisation from a higher manager.

(b) **Assigning tasks** to subordinates, and expecting satisfactory performance of these tasks.

2.3.1 Line and staff authority

When analysing the types of authority that a manager may have, the terms **line**, **staff** and **functional authority** are often used. The following illustration draws on the Farmers supermarket case study, as set out in the front of this Study Text.

KEY TERMS

LINE AUTHORITY is the authority a manager has over a subordinate, down the vertical chain (or line) of command. Katy is a supervisor in charge of the fresh food department in a Farmers supermarket. She has line authority over four shop floor assistants. Katy has the authority to set the daily workload of each subordinate, deciding which worker will handle the inventory replenishment for each section in her department.

STAFF AUTHORITY is the authority one manager or department may have in giving specialist advice to another manager or department, over which there is no line authority. Staff authority does not entail the right to make or influence decisions in the advisee department. The Farmers store in Dundee recently placed an advertisement for new shop floor staff. Having selected a number of candidates to attend an interview, Ross the HR Manager advises department managers on company policy regarding approved interviewing methods. The final decision on which candidate to recruit remains with the respective department manager.

FUNCTIONAL AUTHORITY is a hybrid of line and staff authority, whereby the expert/staff manager has the authority, in certain circumstances, to direct, design or control activities or procedures of another department. Mick, the manager in charge of Farmers' South-East regional payroll team, has the authority to require monthly staff overtime reports from all the local store managers.

Question 4.4 Line and staff authority

Learning outcome B1a

What sort of authority is exercised:

(a) By the Financial Controller over the Chief Accountant?

(b) By the Production Manager over the production workforce?

(c) By the Financial Controller over the Production Manager?

There are inevitable tensions involved in asserting staff authority. **Technostructure** is a term used by Mintzberg to describe individuals in the organisation who strive for efficiency and standardise work processes. These are typically planners, HR professionals and analysts.

Problem	Possible solution
The technostructure can **undermine** the **line managers'** authority, by empire building.	Clear demarcations of line, staff and functional authority should be created.
Lack of seniority. Middle line managers may be more senior in the hierarchy than technostructure advisers.	Use functional authority (via policies and procedures). Experts should be seen as a resource, not a threat.
Expert managers may **lack realism**, going for technically perfect but commercially impractical solutions.	Technostructure planners should be fully aware of operational issues, and communicate regularly with the middle line.
Technostructure experts **lack responsibility** for the success of their ideas.	Technostructure experts should be involved in implementing their suggestions and share accountability for outcomes.

Section summary

Authority is related to position power. It is the right to take certain decisions within certain boundaries.

2.4 Responsibility and accountability

KEY TERMS

RESPONSIBILITY is the **obligation** that a person has to fulfil a task that they have been given.

ACCOUNTABILITY is a person's **liability** to be called to account for the fulfilment of tasks they have been given.

The definitions given above are useful because the term 'responsibility' is used in two ways.

(a) A person is said to be responsible **for** a piece of work when they are required to ensure that the work is done.

(b) The same person is said to be responsible **to** a superior when they are given work by that superior: in this sense, the term 'accountable' is often used.

One is thus accountable **to** a superior **for** a piece of work for which one is responsible.

The principle of **delegation** (which we discuss below) is that a manager may make subordinates **responsible for** work, but remains **accountable to** their own superior for ensuring that the work is done. Appropriate decision-making authority must be delegated alongside the delegated responsibility.

2.4.1 Responsibility/authority mismatch

In practice, matters are rarely clear cut, and in many organisations responsibility and authority are ambiguous and shifting, for example due to departmental 'empire-building' or changes in jobs or structures.

Authority without responsibility is a recipe for arbitrary and irresponsible behaviour: the person has the right to make decisions – without being held accountable for them.

Responsibility without authority places a subordinate in an impossible and stressful position: they are held accountable for results over which they have no control.

Section summary

Responsibility is the obligation a person has to fulfil a task they have been given. Responsibility can be delegated, but the person delegating responsibility still remains accountable to their boss for completion of the task.

Authority/responsibility mismatch or **ambiguity** is stressful for the individual, and may be risky for the organisation's control over decision making.

2.5 Delegation

KEY TERM

DELEGATION of authority is the process whereby a superior gives to a subordinate part of their own authority to make decisions.

Delegation can be done via several different methods.

(a) **Abdication** involves just leaving issues, with no formal delegation. This is not usually a very effective method.

(b) **Custom and practice** involves building delegation into the fabric of the organisation, eg the most junior member of staff collects the mail.

(c) **Explanation** is where the delegator briefs the subordinate on the work that needs to be done.

(d) **Consultation** involves discussion before delegating. This can be an effective method in identifying the best way in which to get the work done.

2.5.1 Why delegate?

Delegation has several key benefits.

(a) There are **physical and mental limitations** to the workload of any individual or group in authority.

(b) Managers are freed up to concentrate on **higher-level tasks** (such as planning).

(c) The **increasing size and complexity** of some organisations calls for specialisation, both managerial and technical.

(d) Delegated authority contributes to the job **satisfaction and development** of lower levels of employees. Taking on progressive levels of responsibility supports training, appraisal and management succession planning.

(e) Delegation shortens the chain of decision making, and brings decisions closer to the situations that require them. This is particularly important in fast-changing business environments that require responsiveness to customer demands.

2.5.2 How to delegate

The process of delegation can be outlined as follows.

Specify performance in terms of the goals and standards expected of the subordinate, keeping in mind their level of expertise.

Formally assign tasks to the subordinate, who should formally agree to do them.

Allocate resources and authority to the subordinate to enable them to carry out the delegated tasks at the expected level of performance.

Back off and allow the subordinate to perform the delegated tasks.

Maintain contact, to review progress made, make constructive criticism and be available to give help and advice if requested.

KEY POINT

Delegation links to a range of potentially examinable issues, such as team working and management/leadership style (which, as we will see, is largely about the extent to which managers delegate).

When diagnosing potential 'people problems' in scenarios, don't forget delegation issues: failure to delegate, lack of trust, micro-management, lack of development opportunities etc.

Section summary

Delegation is the process whereby a superior gives a subordinate part of their own decision-making authority. It is an important component of time management and employee development.

Successful delegation requires that people have the right skills and the authority to do the job, and are given feedback. It also requires a balance of support and trust from the delegator.

2.6 Empowerment

KEY TERM

EMPOWERMENT is the term for making workers (and particularly work teams) responsible for achieving, and even setting, work targets, with the freedom to make decisions about how they are to be achieved.

Empowerment goes in hand in hand with:

(a) **Delayering**, or cutting the number of levels (and managers) in the chain of command, as responsibility previously held by middle managers is, in effect, being given to operational workers.

(b) **Flexibility**, as giving responsibility to the people closest to the products and customer encourages responsiveness – and cutting out layers of communication, decision making and reporting speeds up the process.

(c) **New technology**, as there are more '**knowledge workers**'. Such people need less supervision, being better able to identify and control the means to clearly understood ends. Better information systems also remove the mystique and power of managers as possessors of knowledge and information in the organisation.

The argument for empowerment, in a nutshell, is that by empowering workers (or 'decentralising' control of business units, or devolving/delegating responsibility, or removing levels in hierarchies that restrict freedom), not only will the job be done more effectively, but the people who do the job will also get more out of it.

'The people lower down the organisation possess the knowledge of what is going wrong with a process but lack the authority to make changes. Those further up the structure have the authority to make changes, but lack the profound knowledge required to identify the right solutions. The only solution is to change the culture of the organisation so that everyone can become involved in the process of improvement and work together to make the changes.' (Max Hand)

CASE STUDY

Harvester Restaurants

The validity of this view, and its relevance to modern trends, appears to be borne out by the approach to empowerment adopted by Harvester Restaurants. The management structure comprises a branch manager and a 'coach', while everyone else is a team member. Everyone within a team has one or more 'accountabilities' (these include recruitment, drawing up rotas and keeping track of sales targets), which are shared out by the team members at their weekly team meetings. All the team members at different times act as 'co-ordinator': the person responsible for taking the snap decisions that are frequently necessary in a busy restaurant. Apparently all the staff involved agree that empowerment has made their jobs more interesting, and has hugely increased their motivation and sense of involvement.

3 Management and leadership

KEY TERM

LEADERSHIP is the ability to get others to follow you willingly. Leadership theories fall under **personality traits**, **situational**, **contingency** and **transformational**. **Leadership** style theories are used to describe places on a continuum of **task** and **relationship** focus.

3.1 Management and leadership

Introduction

The terms 'management' and 'leadership' are often used interchangeably. In some cases, management skills and theories have simply been relabelled to reflect the more fashionable term. However, there have been many attempts to distinguish meaningfully between them.

(a) Kotter (2001) argues that leadership and management involve two distinct sets of action. Management is about coping with **complexity**: its functions are to do with logic, structure, analysis and control, and are aimed at producing order, consistency and predictability. Leadership is about coping with **change**: its activities include creating a sense of direction, communicating strategy, and energising, inspiring and motivating others to translate the vision into action.

(b) Yukl (1998) suggests that, while management is defined by a prescribed role and position in the structure of the organisation, leaders are given their roles by the perception of others, through election, choice or influence. Leadership is an interpersonal process. In other words, managers have **subordinates**, but leaders have **followers**.

(c) Zaleznik (1992) suggests that managers are mainly concerned with order and **maintaining the status quo**, exercising their skills in diplomacy and focusing on decision-making processes within the organisation. Leaders, in contrast, direct their energies towards introducing **new approaches and ideas**. They create excitement and vision in order to arouse motivation, and focus with empathy on the meanings of events and actions for people. Leaders search out opportunities for change.

(d) Katz and Kahn (1974) point out that while management aims to secure compliance with stated organisational objectives, leadership aims to secure willingness, enthusiasm and commitment. Leadership is the **influential increment** over and above mechanical compliance with the routine directives of the organisation.

Management can be exercised over resources, activities, projects and other essential non-personal things. Leadership can only be exercised over **people**.

3.2 Transactional and transformational leaders – Burns and Boyd

Some of the values used to distinguish between managers and leaders have also been identified as different styles of leadership (Burns).

(a) **Transactional leaders** see the relationship with their followers in terms of a trade: they give followers the rewards they want in exchange for service, loyalty and compliance.

(b) **Transformational leaders** see their role as inspiring and motivating others to work at levels beyond mere compliance. Only transformational leadership is said to be able to change team/organisation cultures and create a new direction.

Boyd suggests that the rapid change endemic in the current business environment mandates a new approach to management in order to achieve transformation within the organisation as a response. These transformational leaders will be skilled in areas that contrast with some older prescriptions.

(a) **Vision**. The leader will use example and persuasion to convince the group to pursue a new purpose.
(b) **Anticipation**. The leader will possess foresight.
(c) **Value-congruence**. The leader will understand and empathise with group members' needs.
(d) **Empowerment**. The leader will empower group members, so as to make the group more effective.
(e) **Self-understanding**. The leader will be aware of their own needs and goals.

3.3 How leadership occurs

It is important to recognise that people become leaders in a variety of different ways; these can include:

(a) **Election**. This is particularly true in the field of politics where politicians are required to be democratically elected in order to lead others. The same is also true of workplace trade union representatives.

(b) **Emergence**. Some individuals become leaders by garnering the popular support of others. This is often achieved through the possession of innate qualities eg charisma.

(c) **Appointment**. In the workplace it is common for individuals to be appointed to lead a team or even the entire organisation.

3.4 Why develop managers as 'leaders'?

Whether or not we make the distinction between management and leadership, attempts to define what makes leadership 'special' (such as those outlined above) have suggested some key points about the benefits that effective leadership can bring and why it is valuable.

(a) Leaders energise and support **change**, which is essential for survival in highly competitive and fast-changing business environments. By setting visionary goals, and encouraging contribution from teams, leaders create environments that:

    (i) Seek out new information and ideas
    (ii) Allow challenges to existing procedures and ways of thinking
    (iii) Invite innovation and creativity in finding better ways to achieve goals
    (iv) Support and empower people to cope with the turbulence

(b) Leaders secure **commitment**, mobilising the ideas, experience and motivation of employees, which contributes to innovation and improved quality and customer service. This is all the more essential in a competitive, customer-focused, knowledge-based business environment.

(c) Leaders set **direction**, helping teams and organisations to understand their purpose, goals and value to the organisation. This facilitates team working and empowerment (allowing discretion and creativity about how to achieve the desired outcomes) without loss of co-ordination or direction.

(d) Leaders support, challenge and develop **people**, maximising their contribution to the organisation. Leaders use an influence-based, facilitate-empower style rather than a command-control style, and this is better suited to the expectations of empowered teams and the need for information sharing in modern business environments.

Question 4.5

Leadership

Learning outcome B1a

Reflect on your own experience of working under the direction of others. Identify the 'best' leader you have ever 'followed'. Think about how this person behaved and interacted with you and others.

What qualities make you identify this person as a 'great leader', from your point of view as a follower?

3.5 Theories of leadership

There are three basic 'schools' of leadership theory.

School	Comment
Trait theories	Based on analysing the personality characteristics or preferences of successful leaders.
Style theories	Based on the view that leadership is an interpersonal process whereby different leader behaviours influence people in different ways. More or less effective patterns of behaviour (or 'styles') can therefore be adopted.
Contingency theories	Based on the belief that there is no 'one best way' of leading, but that effective leaders adapt their behaviour to the specific and changing variables in the leadership context: the nature of the task, the personalities of team members, the organisation culture and so on.

We will look at each of these in turn.

Exam skills

The volume of leadership theory means that questions could easily focus on this subject in your E2 Objective Test examination. Questions may require you to identify, and select from a range of options, the style of leadership illustrated in the scenario as defined by a particular theorist.

3.6 Trait theories of leadership

Various studies have attempted to determine exactly **which** traits are essential in a leader. One US study (cited by Rosemary Stewart) cites the following 15 traits.

Judgement	Initiative	Integrity	Foresight	Energy
Drive	Human relations skill	Decisiveness	Dependability	Emotional stability
Fairness	Ambition	Dedication	Objectivity	Co-operation

Trait theory has been more or less discredited.

(a) The premise that certain traits are absolutely necessary for effective leadership has never been substantiated.

(b) The lists of traits proposed for leaders have been vast, varied and contradictory.

(c) 'A person does not become a leader by virtue of the possession of some combination of traits, but the pattern of personal characteristics must bear some relevant relationship to the characteristics, activities and goals of the followers.' (Stodgill)

3.7 Style theories

There are various classifications of leadership style. Although the labels and definitions of styles vary, style models are often talking (broadly) about the same thing – a continuum of behaviours between:

(a) Wholly task-focused, directive leadership behaviours (representing high leader control) at one extreme; and

(b) Wholly people-focused, supportive/relational leadership behaviours (representing high subordinate discretion) at the other extreme.

3.7.1 A continuum of leadership styles

Tannenbaum and Schmidt proposed a continuum of behaviours (and associated styles) based on the degree of authority used by a manager and the degree of freedom for the team.

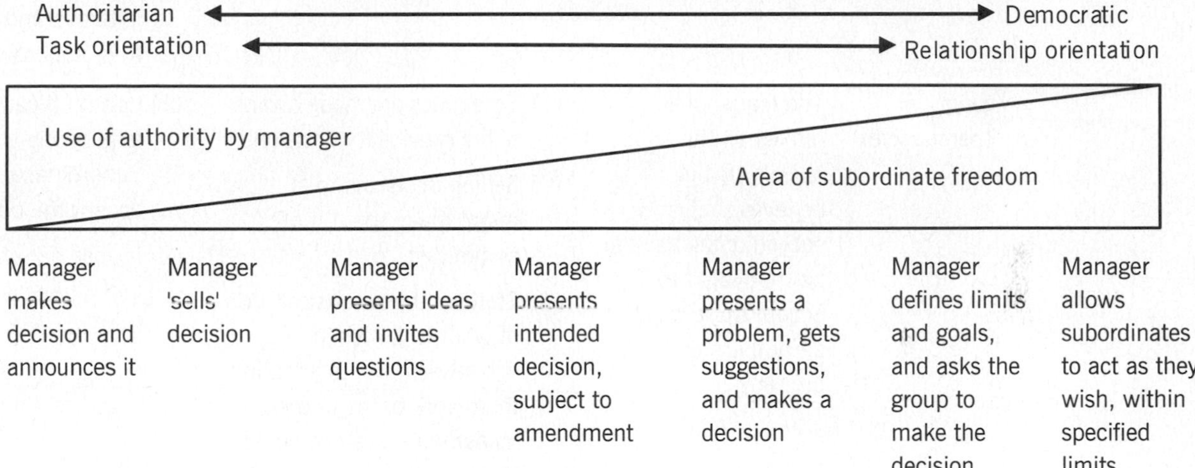

Manager makes decision and announces it	Manager 'sells' decision	Manager presents ideas and invites questions	Manager presents intended decision, subject to amendment	Manager presents a problem, gets suggestions, and makes a decision	Manager defines limits and goals, and asks the group to make the decision	Manager allows subordinates to act as they wish, within specified limits

3.7.2 The Ashridge Management College model

Developing the work of Tannenbaum and Schmidt, the Research Unit at Ashridge Management College distinguished four different management styles. (These are outlined, with their strengths and weaknesses, in the following table.) The researchers labelled their styles:

- Tells
- Sells
- Consults
- Joins

Other style models label similar styles as:

(a) Telling, selling, participating and delegating (Hersey and Blanchard)
(b) Telling, selling, consulting and join (Tannenbaum and Schmidt)

The Ashridge studies found that:

(a) In an ideal world, subordinates preferred the 'consults' style of leadership.

(b) People led by a 'consults' manager had the most favourable attitude to their work.

(c) Most subordinates feel they are being led by a 'tells' or 'sells' manager.

(d) In practice, **consistency** was far more important to subordinates than any particular style. The least favourable attitudes were found among subordinates who were unable to perceive any consistent style of leadership in their superiors.

Style	Characteristics	Strengths	Weaknesses
Tells (autocratic)	The leader makes all the decisions, and issues instructions that must be obeyed without question.	(1) Quick decisions can be made when speed is required. (2) It is the most efficient type of leadership for highly programmed routine work.	(1) It does not encourage subordinates to give their opinions when these might be useful. (2) Communication between the leader and subordinates will be one-way, and the leader will not know until afterwards whether the orders have been properly understood. (3) It does not encourage initiative and commitment from subordinates.
Sells (persuasive)	The leader still makes all the decisions, but believes that subordinates have to be motivated to accept them and carry them out properly.	(1) Employees are made aware of the reasons for decisions. (2) Selling decisions to staff might make them more committed. (3) Staff will have a better idea of what to do when unforeseen events arise in their work because the leader will have explained their intentions.	(1) Communications are still largely one-way. Subordinates might not accept the decisions. (2) It does not encourage initiative and commitment from subordinates.
Consults	The leader confers with subordinates and takes their views into account, but retains the final say.	(1) Employees are involved in decisions before they are made. This encourages motivation through greater interest and involvement. (2) An agreed consensus of opinion can be reached and, for some decisions, this can be an advantage (eg increasing ownership). (3) Employees can contribute their knowledge and experience to help solve more complex problems.	(1) It might take much longer to reach decisions. (2) Subordinates might be too inexperienced to formulate mature opinions and give practical advice. (3) Consultation can too easily turn into a facade, concealing a 'sells' style.
Joins (democratic)	The leader and followers make the decision on the basis of consensus.	(1) It can provide high motivation and commitment from employees. (2) It shares the other advantages of the consultative style (especially where subordinates have expert power).	(1) The authority of the leader might be undermined. (2) Decision making might become a very long process, and clear decisions might become difficult to reach. (3) Subordinates might lack experience.

Question 4.6 Styles of leadership

Learning outcome B1a

Suggest an appropriate style of leadership for each of the following situations. Think about your reasons for choosing each style in terms of the results you are trying to achieve, the need to secure commitment from others, and potential difficulties with both.

(a) Due to outside factors, the personnel budget has been reduced for your department, and 25% of your staff must be made redundant. Records of each employee's performance are available.

(b) There is a recurring administrative problem that is minor but irritating to everyone in your department. Several solutions have been tried in the past, but without success. You think you have a remedy that will work, but unknown problems may arise, depending on the decisions made.

3.7.3 Rensis Likert

Likert (*New patterns of Management*) also described a range of **four management styles** or 'systems':

(a) System 1: **exploitative authoritative**. The leader has no confidence or trust in their subordinates, imposes decisions, never delegates, motivates by threat, has little communication with subordinates and does not encourage teamwork.

(b) System 2: **benevolent authoritative**. The leader has only superficial trust in subordinates, imposes decisions, never delegates, motivates by reward and, though sometimes involving others in problem solving, is basically paternalistic.

(c) System 3: **consultative**. The leader has some confidence in subordinates, listens to them but controls decision making, motivates by reward and a level of involvement, and will use the ideas and suggestions of subordinates constructively.

(d) System 4: **participative**. The leader has complete confidence in subordinates, who are allowed to make decisions for themselves. Motivation is by reward for achieving goals set by participation, and there is a substantial amount of sharing of ideas, opinions and co-operation.

Likert's research suggested that effective managers naturally use a System 3 or System 4 style. Both are seen as viable approaches, **balancing** the needs of the organisation and the individual.

3.7.4 Lewin, Lippitt and White

In an early study using boys' clubs, Lewin, Lippitt and White identified three styles of leadership.

(a) **Authoritarian**. Giving orders, overseeing work activities and giving out criticism and praise on a whim. This style was found to lead to the highest productivity – but also hostility and discontent.

(b) **Democratic**. Showing concern for team members' welfare, participating in group activities, making suggestions as to what should be done, but allowing team members to make decisions. This kind of leadership was found to lead to the highest work-related communication, motivation and team satisfaction.

(c) **Laissez-faire**. Tending to be 'stand-offish', not getting involved in team activities or welfare, and more or less letting the group run itself. This style was least effective – suggesting the need for directing and facilitating/supporting behaviour.

3.8 Blake and Mouton's Managerial Grid

Blake and Mouton carried out research (The Ohio State Leadership Studies) into managerial behaviour, and observed two basic dimensions of leadership: **concern for production** (or task performance) and **concern for people**.

Along each of these two dimensions, managers could be located at any point on a continuum from very low to very high concern. Blake and Mouton observed that the two concerns did not seem to correlate, positively or negatively: a high concern in one dimension, for example, did not seem to imply a high or low concern in the other dimension. Individual managers could therefore reflect various permutations of task/people concern.

A questionnaire was designed to enable users to analyse and plot the positions of individual respondents on the grid. This was to be used as a means of analysing individuals' managerial styles and areas of weakness or 'unbalance', for the purposes of management development.

The managerial grid

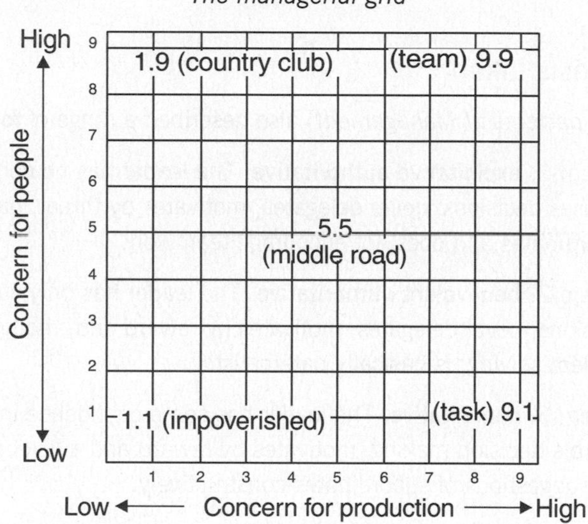

The extreme cases shown on the grid are:

(a) 1.1 **impoverished**. The manager is lazy, showing little interest in either staff or work.

(b) 1.9 **country club**. The manager is attentive to staff needs and has developed satisfying relationships. However, there is little attention paid to achieving results.

(c) 9.1 **task oriented**. Almost total concentration on achieving results. People's needs are virtually ignored.

(d) 5.5 **middle of the road** or the **dampened pendulum**. Adequate performance through balancing (or switching between) the necessity to get out work with team morale.

(e) 9.9 **team**. High work accomplishment through 'leading' committed people who identify themselves with the organisational aims.

3.8.1 Evaluating the managerial grid

The grid thus offers a number of useful insights for the identification of management **training and development** needs. It shows, in an easily assimilated form, where the behaviour and assumptions of a manager may exhibit a lack of balance between the dimensions and/or a low degree of concern in either dimension or both. It may also be used in team member selection, so that a 1.9 team leader is balanced by a 9.1 co-leader, for example.

However, the grid is a simplified model, and as such has practical limitations.

(a) It assumes that 9.9 is the desirable model for effective leadership. In some managerial contexts, this may not be so. Concern for people, for example, would not be necessary in a context of comprehensive automation: compliance is all that would be required.

(b) It is open to oversimplification. Scores can appear polarised, with judgements attached about individual managers' suitability or performance. The grid is intended as a simplified 'snapshot' of a manager's preferred style, not a comprehensive description of their performance.

(c) Organisational context and culture, technology and other 'givens' (Handy) influence the manager's style of leadership, not just the two dimensions described by the grid.

(d) Any managerial theory is only useful insofar as it is useable in practice by managers: if the grid is used only to inform managers that they 'must acquire greater concern for people', it may result in stress, uncertainty and inconsistent behaviour.

Question 4.7 The managerial grid

Learning outcome B1a

Steve Farmer (Head of HR at Farmers supermarkets) has observed that different managers across the company's operations adopt very different attitudes to attending corporate meetings. He has recently noted a number of comments made by different managers regarding such meetings. Which position on Blake and Mouton's grid do you think each might represent?

(a) I attend because it is expected. I either go along with the majority position or avoid expressing my views.

(b) I try to come up with good ideas, and push for a decision as soon as I can get a majority behind me. I don't mind stepping on people if it helps making a sound decision.

(c) I like to be able to support what my boss wants and to recognise the merits of individual effort. When conflict rises, I do a good job of restoring harmony.

3.9 Theory X and Theory Y

Douglas McGregor (*The Human Side of Enterprise*) suggested that managers (in the US) tended to behave as though they subscribed to one of two sets of assumptions about people at work: Theory X and Theory Y.

(a) **Theory X** suggests that most people dislike work and responsibility, and will avoid both if possible. Because of this, most people must be coerced, controlled, directed and/or threatened with punishment to get them to make an adequate effort. Managers who operate according to these assumptions will tend to supervise closely, apply detailed rules and controls, and use 'carrot and stick' motivators.

(b) **Theory Y** suggests that physical and mental effort in work is as natural as play or rest. The ordinary person does not inherently dislike work: according to the conditions, it may be a source of satisfaction or dissatisfaction. The potentialities of the average person are rarely fully used at work. People can be motivated to seek challenge and responsibility in the job, if their goals can be integrated with those of the organisation. A manager with this sort of attitude towards their staff is likely to be a consultative, facilitating leader, using positive feedback, challenge and responsibility as motivators.

Both are intended to be extreme sets of assumptions – not actual types of people. However, they also tend to be self-fulfilling prophecies. Employees treated as if Theory X were true will begin to behave accordingly. Employees treated as if Theory Y were true – being challenged to take on more responsibility – will rise to the challenge and behave accordingly.

Theory X and Theory Y can be used to heighten managers' awareness of the assumptions underlying their motivational style.

3.10 Limitations of style approaches

Perhaps the most important criticism of the style approach is that it does not consider all the variables that contribute to the practice of effective leadership.

(a) The manager's personality (or 'acting' ability) may simply not be **flexible** enough to utilise different styles effectively.

(b) The demands of the task, team, technology, organisation culture and other managers **constrain** the leader in the range of styles effectively open to them. (If their own boss practises an authoritarian style, and the team are incompetent and require close supervision, no amount of theorising on the desirability of participative management will make it possible ...).

(c) **Consistency** is important to subordinates. If a manager adapts their style to changing situations, their subordinates may simply perceive the manager to be fickle, or may suffer insecurity and stress.

Huczynski and Buchanan note that: 'There is therefore no simple recipe which the individual manager can use to decide which style to adopt to be most effective'.

It is the consideration of this wide set of variables that has led to the development of the contingency approach to leadership.

3.11 Contingency approaches to leadership

In essence, contingency theory sees effective leadership as being dependent on a number of variable or contingent factors. There is no one right way to lead that will fit all situations. Gillen (*Leadership Skills*) suggests that: 'Using only one leadership style is a bit like a stopped clock: it will be right twice a day but, the rest of the time, it will be inaccurate to varying degrees. Leaders need to interact with their team in different ways in different situations. This is what we mean by "leadership style"'.

3.11.1 F E Fiedler

Fiedler suggested that the effectiveness of a work group depends on the **situation**, made up of three key variables.

(a) The relationship **between the leader and the group** (trust, respect and so on)
(b) The extent to which the **task** is defined and structured
(c) The **power** of the leader in relation to the group (authority, and power to reward and punish)

A situation is **favourable** to the leader when:

(a) The leader is liked and trusted by the group
(b) The tasks of the group are clearly defined
(c) The power of the leader to reward and punish with organisation backing is high

Fiedler suggested that:

(a) A structured (or psychologically distant) style works best when the situation is either very favourable, or very unfavourable to the leader.

(b) A supportive (or psychologically close) style works best when the situation is moderately favourable to the leader.

(c) 'Group performance will be contingent upon the appropriate **matching of leadership styles** and the **degree of favourableness** of the group situation for the leader' (Fiedler).

This is summed up in the diagram below.

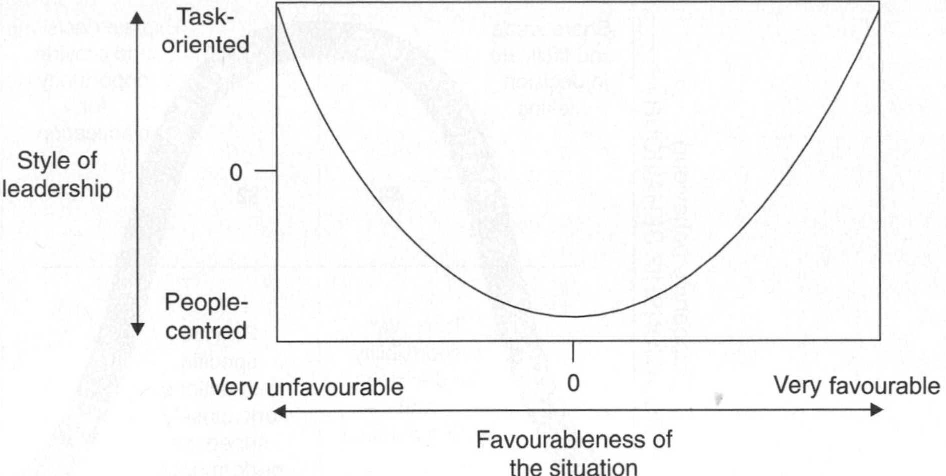

3.11.2 Hersey and Blanchard – situational leadership

In their influential **situational leadership** model, **Hersey and Blanchard** focus on the **readiness of the team members** to perform a given task, in terms of their **task ability** (experience, knowledge and skills) and **willingness** (whether they have the confidence, commitment and motivation) to complete the task successfully.

(a) **High-readiness:** Teams are able and willing. They do not need directive or supportive leadership: the most appropriate leadership style may be a joins or 'delegating' style.

(b) **High-moderate readiness:** Teams are able, but unwilling or insecure. They are competent, but require supportive behaviour to build morale: the most appropriate leadership style may be a consults or 'participating' style.

(c) **Low-moderate readiness:** Teams are willing and confident, but lacking ability. They require both directive and supportive behaviour to improve their task performance without damaging morale: the most appropriate leadership style may be a 'selling' style.

(d) **Low-readiness:** Teams are lacking ability and motivation/confidence. They require more directive behaviours in order to secure an adequate level of task performance: the most appropriate leadership style may be a 'telling' style.

Hersey and Blanchard also emphasise the relationship between three factors.

(a) **Task behaviour**. Does the leader provide direction as to how the followers should get the job done?
(b) **Relationship behaviour**. Does the leader communicate with their followers and provide support?
(c) The level of **task and relevant maturity** of the team.

Maturity is not defined by age and is not a matter of psychological stability. Rather, it consists of the following elements.

(a) Desire for achievement
(b) Willingness and ability to accept responsibility
(c) Education, experience and skills for the task

This can be summed up as follows (drawn from Hersey and Blanchard, 1988).

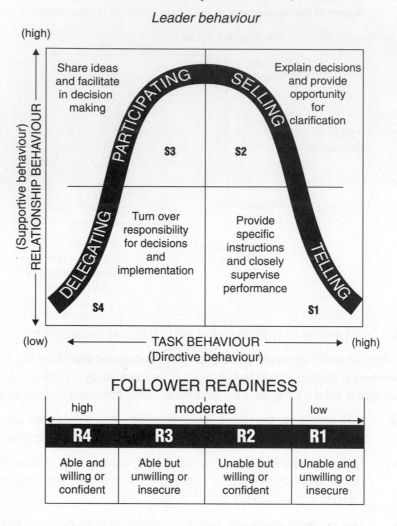

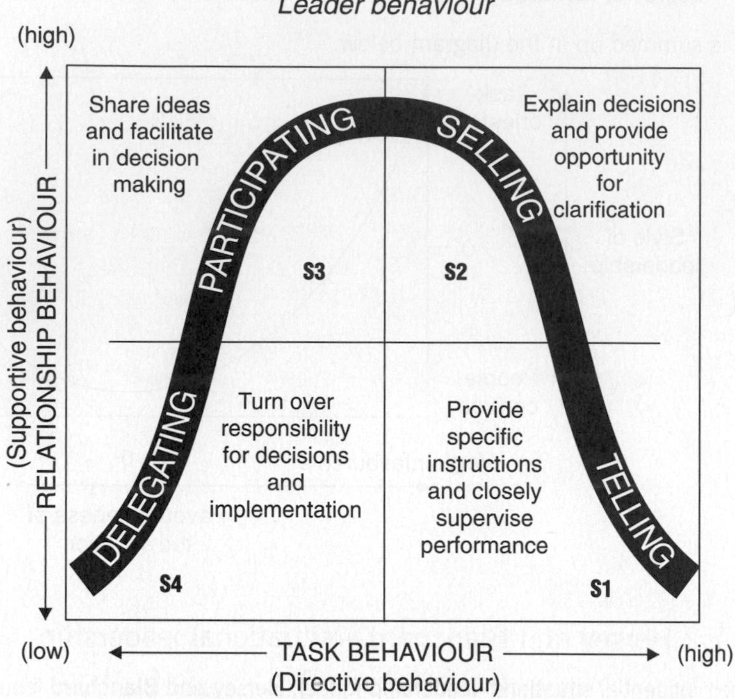

FOLLOWER READINESS

high	moderate		low
R4	R3	R2	R1
Able and willing or confident	Able but unwilling or insecure	Unable but willing or confident	Unable and unwilling or insecure

Question 4.8 Hersey and Blanchard

Learning outcome B1a

Diagnose the 'readiness' of a work or study group of which you are a member. What sort of leadership is likely to be most effective, according to Hersey and Blanchard's model? What sort of leadership does the team leader actually exercise?

3.11.3 John Adair – action-centred leadership

John Adair's model (variously called 'action-centred', 'situational' or 'functional') is part of the contingency school of thought, because it sees the leadership process in a context made up of three interrelated variables: **task** needs, the **individual** needs of group members and the needs of the **group** as a whole. These needs must be examined in the light of the **whole situation**, which dictates the relative priority that must be given to each of the three sets of needs. Effective leadership is a process of identifying and acting on that priority, exercising a relevant cluster of roles to meet the various needs.

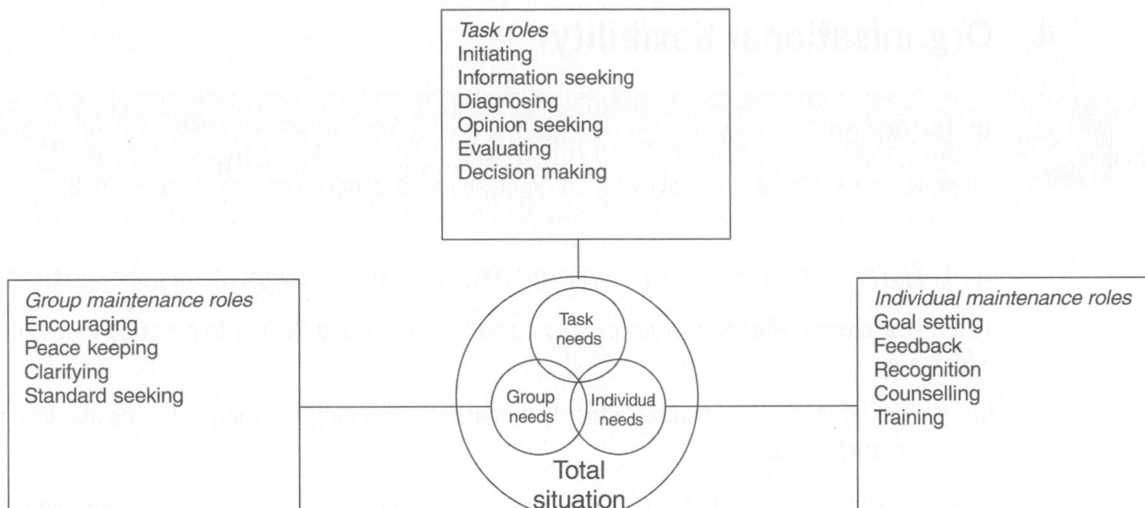

Exam alert

The general point of Adair's model – the three dimensions of effective team management – makes a good framework for analysing and discussing people management and project scenarios. This is something to watch out for when attempting your E2 exam and the Management Level Integrated Case Study.

Section summary

There are many different definitions of **leadership**. Key themes (which are also used to distinguish leadership from management) include: interpersonal influence; securing willing commitment to shared goals; creating direction and energy; and an orientation to change.

Leadership offers key **benefits** in a competitive, turbulent environment: activating commitment, setting direction, developing people and energising and supporting change.

There are three basic **schools of leadership theory**: trait theories, style theories and contingency theories.

Early theories suggested that there are certain personality characteristics common to 'great men' or successful leaders. In other words, **'leaders are born, not made'**.

Leadership styles are clusters of leadership behaviour that are used in different ways in different situations. While there are many different classifications of style, they mainly relate to the extent to which the leader is focused primarily on task/performance (directive behaviour) or relationships/people (supportive behaviour). Key style models include:

- The **Ashridge Model**: tells, sells, consults and joins
- **Likert**: exploitative authoritative, benevolent authoritative, consultative and participative
- **Lewin, Lippitt and White**: autocratic, democratic and laissez-faire
- **Blake and Mouton**'s **Managerial Grid**: concern for task and concern for people

McGregor suggested that a manager's approach is based on attitudes somewhere on a scale between two extreme sets of assumptions: Theory X (workers have to be coerced) and Theory Y (workers want to be empowered).

Leaders need to adapt their style to the needs of the team and situation. This is the basis of **contingency approaches** such as:

- **Fiedler**'s 'psychologically close' and 'psychologically distant' styles
- **Hersey and Blanchard**'s 'situational leadership' model
- **John Adair**'s 'action-centred' leadership model

4 Organisational flexibility

Introduction

There is no ideal level of flexibility for an organisation: it depends on the circumstances.

4.1 Burns and Stalker – mechanistic and organic organisation

The terms 'mechanistic' and 'organic' were coined by Burns and Stalker to describe forms of organisation which are:

(a) Stable, efficient and suitable for slow-changing operating environments (mechanistic organisations, or 'bureaucracies')

(b) Flexible, adaptive and suitable for fast-changing or dynamic operating environments (organic organisations)

Factor	Mechanistic	Organic
The job	Tasks are **specialised** and broken down into sub-tasks.	Specialist knowledge and expertise is understood to contribute to the **common task** of the organisation.
How the job fits in	People are concerned with completing the task **efficiently**, rather than how the task can be made to improve organisational **effectiveness**.	Each task is seen and understood to be set by the **total situation** of the firm: focus is on the task's contribution to **organisational effectiveness**.
Co-ordination	**Managers** are responsible for co-ordinating tasks.	People adjust and redefine their tasks through interaction and **mutual adjustment** with others.
Job description	There are **precise** job descriptions and delineations of responsibility.	Job descriptions are **less precise**: people do what is necessary to complete the task.
Commitment	**Doing the job** takes priority over serving the interests of the organisation.	**Commitment to the organisation** spreads beyond any technical definition of competence.
Legal contract vs common interest	**Hierarchical** structure of control. An individual's performance and conduct derive from a **contractual relationship** with an impersonal organisation.	**Network structure** of control. An individual's performance and conduct derive from a supposed **community of interest** between the individual and the organisation, and the individual's colleagues.
Decisions	Decisions are taken by **senior managers** who are assumed to know everything.	Relevant technical and commercial knowledge can be located **anywhere**.
Communication patterns	Communication is mainly **vertical** (up and down the scalar chain), and takes the form of **commands** and obedience.	Communication is **lateral** or networked, and communication between people of different rank represents **consultation**, rather than command.
Content of communications	Operations and working behaviour are governed by **instructions** issued by superiors.	Communication consists of **information and advice** rather than instructions and decisions.

Factor	Mechanistic	Organic
Mission	Insistence on **loyalty** to the concern and **obedience** to superiors.	Commitment to the organisation's **mission** is more highly valued than loyalty as such.
Internal vs external expertise	**Internal knowledge** (eg of the organisation's specific activities) is more highly valued than general knowledge.	'Importance and prestige attach to affiliations and expertise valid in the industrial, technical and commercial milieus **external** to the firm.'

4.2 Mechanistic organisations: bureaucracy

KEY TERM

A **BUREAUCRACY** is 'a continuous organisation of official functions bound by rules' (Weber).

- **Continuous organisation**. The organisation does not disappear if people leave: new people will fill their shoes.
- **Official functions**. The organisation is divided into areas (eg production and marketing) with specified duties. Authority to carry them out is given to the officials in charge.
- **Rules**. A rule defines and specifies a course of action that must be taken under given circumstances.

Weber was inclined to regard **bureaucracy** as the ideal form of organisation, because it is impersonal and rational and based on a set pattern of behaviour and work allocation, and does not allow personal issues to get in the way of achieving goals.

The characteristics of bureaucracy can be summarised as follows.

Characteristic	Description
Hierarchy of roles	An organisation exists even before it is filled with people. Each lower office is under the control and supervision of a higher one.
Specialisation and training	There is a high degree of specialisation of labour.
Professional nature of employment	Officials are full-time employees; promotion is according to seniority and achievement; pay scales are prescribed according to the position or office held in the organisation structure.
Impersonal nature	Employees work within impersonal rules and regulations, and act according to formal, impersonal procedures.
Rationality	The jurisdictional areas of the organisation are determined rationally. The hierarchy of authority and office structure is clearly defined. Duties are established and measures of performance set.
Uniformity in the performance of tasks	Procedures ensure that, regardless of who carries out tasks, they should be executed in the same way.
Technical competence	All officials are technically competent. Their competence within the area of their expertise is rarely questioned.
Stability	The organisation rarely changes in response to environmental pressures.

4.2.1 Bureaucracy – good or bad?

It is common to think of bureaucracy as an old-fashioned and dysfunctional form of organisation, but it has some **advantages**.

(a) Bureaucracies are ideal for **standardised, routine tasks**. For example, processing driving licence applications is fairly routine, requiring systematic work.

(b) Bureaucracies can be very **efficient**. Weber considered them the most effective organisational form, in stable environments.

(c) Rigid adherence to procedures may be necessary for **fairness**, adherence to the **law**, **safety** and **security** (eg procedures for data protection).

(d) Some people are **suited** to the structured, predictable environment. Bureaucracies tend to be long-lived because they select and retain bureaucratically minded people.

Stewart suggests that bureaucracy became the dominant organisational model because it was supported by increasing **organisation size and complexity** (requiring formalisation and standardisation) and increasing worker **demands for equitable treatment** (requiring impersonality).

In swiftly changing environments, however, the **dysfunctions** of bureaucracy become apparent.

(a) It results in **slow decision making**, because of the rigidity and length of authority networks and the use of committees.

(b) Uniformity creates **conformity**, inhibiting the personal development of staff.

(c) Bureaucracies suppress **innovation**. They can inhibit creativity, initiative and openness to new ideas and ways of doing things.

(d) Bureaucracies find it hard to **learn** from their mistakes, because of the lack of feedback (especially upwards): control systems are frequently out of date.

(e) Bureaucracies are **slow to change**. Crozier stated that 'a system of organisation whose main characteristic is its rigidity will not adjust easily to change and will tend to resist change as much as possible'. Environmental change therefore causes severe trauma.

(f) **Communication** is restricted to established channels, ignoring opportunities for networking, upward feedback and suggestions that may contribute to customer service and innovation.

(g) **Rules** may be functional in their impersonality and consistency, but they can be dysfunctional in encouraging employees to work only to the required minimum level of performance and permitting simplistic decision making (Gouldner).

4.3 Organic organisations

Organic organisations have their own structures and control mechanisms.

Control mechanism	Description
Status	Although organic systems are not hierarchical in the way that bureaucracies are, there are **differences of status**, determined by people's greater expertise, experience and so forth.
Commitment	The degree of **commitment** employees have to the goals of the firm and the team is more **extensive** in organic than in mechanistic systems.
Shared values and culture	Hierarchical control is replaced by the development of **shared beliefs and values**. In other words, corporate **culture** becomes a powerful guide to behaviour.

Burns and Stalker argued that organic (or organismic) structures are better suited to conditions of **change** – particularly where there is a need to respond to change by continuous innovation.

Note that the two approaches represent two ends of a spectrum: there are intermediate stages between bureaucratic and organic organisations. Different departments of a business may be run on different lines. For example, the payroll department of a firm has a well-defined task (eg paying salaries at the end of the month) with little variation. Controls are needed to ensure processing accuracy and to avoid fraud. A mechanistic system might be applied here. On the other hand, the 'creative department' of an advertising agency, with a number of professional experts (copywriters, graphic designers and account executives), may be run on an organic basis.

Question 4.9 Control

Learning outcome B1a

Complete the sentence below by inserting one of the words in brackets.

Control in a bureaucracy tends to depend on hierarchy and procedure, while in an organic organisation it depends largely on ....

(ambiguity, culture, seniority, loyalty)

4.4 Contingency theory – Woodward

Joan Woodward (1958) discovered that organisational structure was dependent on its 'technology' (ie ways of working). Woodward argued that organisations performed best when structured to fit their own particular way of working. Woodward identified that organisations could be grouped into one of three types based on their way of working:

(1) **Unit/small batch production**. This approach to working was generally found to exist in craft, 'cottage industries'. Organisational structures tended to encompass relatively small groups of highly skilled workers. Given the organisations' size, hierarchies were often short with managers remaining close to production work. Woodward identified that job satisfaction among these workers was generally medium to high.

(2) **Large batch/mass production**. This way of working was discovered in industries such as car manufacturing. The organisational structure was characterised by a large number of semi-skilled operatives. The high number of workers needed in this type of work meant that supervisors were often responsible for lots of employees which created a stressful work environment. As such, job satisfaction among workers was low.

(3) **Process production**. This approach was found to exist in highly mechanised environments such as in the oil industry. The structure was formed of skilled operatives, where technical expertise was highly valued. Control was exercised through the use of committees as opposed to direct instruction from a line manager. Job satisfaction was found to be high.

Woodward's work identified that four closely interrelated factors – structure, people, technology and the task undertaken – all impact on each other and need to be carefully managed to ensure optimal organisational performance.

4.5 The flexible firm

Modern businesses are often faced with fluctuations in the demand for labour and they cannot afford to employ a full-time workforce based on the best-case scenario or greatest demand. Indeed, in times of pressure to downsize the workforce, organisations prefer to increase their proportion of non-permanent labour, to avoid redundancies and layoffs during 'slack' times.

4.5.1 The flexible firm model

Atkinson developed an influential '**core-periphery**' **model** of the flexible firm.

(a) The **core group** is permanent and stable, based on: the lowest number of employees required by work activity at any given time throughout the year; and core tasks that are specific to the firm and require firm-specific skills and experience. This core group offers **functional flexibility**, by virtue of re-skilling or multi-skilling: training and deploying employees flexibly within core tasks.

(b) The **peripheral group** consists of full-time employees in areas where there is a high level of mobility and wastage/turnover (eg clerical/secretarial).

   (i) Workers on non-standard contracts (short-term contracts, part-time workers, job-share workers)

   (ii) 'Distance' workers not employed by the organisation, but contracted as required to supply services (agency workers, subcontracting/outsourcing and freelancers)

   This group is designed to offer **numerical** flexibility: the ability to meet short-term fluctuations of demand for skills that are not 'core' to the firm.

4.5.2 The Shamrock organisation

Handy (1989) puts forward the idea of the **shamrock** (or **clover-leaf**) organisation, giving examples such as Rank Xerox and IBM.

(a) The **professional core** are permanently employed people who represent the distinctive knowledge and competences of the firm. They are qualified professionals, technicians and managers. Their commitment is focused on their work and career within the organisation.

(b) The **flexible labour** force are temporary and part-time workers who can be brought in as and when needed – especially to meet peaks in the demand for services (since they have to be supplied in 'real time'). Their commitment is typically focused on the immediate job and work group, rather than career or the organisation. However, they are crucial in maintaining standards of service – so it is important for the firm not to treat them 'casually': they should receive fair and equitable treatment (now enshrined in employment law), adequate training and status.

(c) The **contractual fringe** are external providers (freelancers, consultants and subcontractors) who are able to undertake non-core activities and/or provide specialist services, more economically than the firm could manage internally. Their commitment is typically to achieving specified results in return for fees.

These represent three distinct labour forces, each with its own type of psychological (and legal) contract with the firm.

In addition, Handy notes the 'lucky' fourth leaf of the clover: the organisation may be able to 'subcontract' some sales, service and supply tasks – for free – to **customers**. Information and communication technology has supported a wide range of 'self-service' applications such as: internet/phone banking and automated teller machines; internet/telephone reservations and ticketing, in entertainment and travel; and online information services – in addition to traditional self-service retail and catering outlets, self-assembly products and so on. This should allow labour savings in other 'leaves' of the organisation.

Section summary

Burns and **Stalker** noted that **mechanistic** (or **bureaucratic**) organisations are stable and efficient in conditions of slow change, but that **organic** organisation is required for adaptation and responsiveness in fast-change environments.

Bureaucracy is 'a continuous organisation of official functions bound by rules' (Weber). It is a form of mechanistic organisation.

Organic organisations are controlled by mechanisms such as commitment and culture.

Woodward's contingency theory identified that organisational structure is dependent on the way of working.

The **flexible firm model** suggests a division of the firm into separate components, in which workers' experience and employers' expectations of them are differentiated as 'core' or 'peripheral'.

5 Discipline

Introduction

We now move on to consider how relationships in organisations are governed formally, ultimately by the law. Our discussion reflects UK legislation at a very basic level. You will not need to know all the names of Acts, but make sure you know what they generally aim to do. The principles used are what matters. You can use examples from other legal systems, if you are more familiar with these.

Disciplinary actions arise for a number of reasons and as such an organisation should prepare itself to deal with them. The **Advisory, Conciliation and Arbitration Service (ACAS) guidelines** set the benchmark in terms of legal compliance.

5.1 Positive and negative discipline

KEY POINT

The idea of 'positive' and 'negative' discipline makes the distinction between methods of maintaining sensible conduct and orderliness that are technically co-operative, and those based on warnings, threats and punishments.

(a) **Positive (or constructive)** discipline relates to procedures, systems and equipment in the workplace that have been designed specifically so that the employee has no option but to act in the desired manner to complete a task safely and successfully. A machine may, for example, shut off automatically if its safety guard is not in place.

(b) **Negative discipline** is the promise of sanctions designed to make people choose to behave in a desirable way. Disciplinary action may be punitive (punishing an offence), deterrent (warning people not to behave in that way) or reformative (calling attention to the nature of the offence, so that it will not happen again).

The best discipline is **self-discipline**. Even before they start to work, most mature people accept the idea that following instructions and fair rules of conduct are normal responsibilities that are part of any job. Most team members can therefore be counted on to exercise self-discipline.

KEY POINT

Do not confuse 'discipline' with 'punishment'. There is more to discipline than simply punishing people for 'doing things wrong'. More generally, be aware of the importance of encouraging discipline, and using fair and systematic disciplinary procedures, so that discipline is as 'positive' as possible and compliant with relevant law and codes of conduct.

5.2 Types of disciplinary situations

There are many types of disciplinary situation that require attention by the manager. Internally, the most frequently occurring are listed below.

(a) Excessive absenteeism
(b) Poor timekeeping
(c) Defective and/or inadequate work performance
(d) Poor attitudes that influence the work of others or reflect on the image of the firm
(e) Improper personal appearance or conduct (eg offensive humour or aggression)
(f) Breaking safety rules
(g) Other violations of rules, regulations and procedures
(h) Open insubordination, such as the refusal to carry out a work assignment

Managers might also be confronted with disciplinary problems stemming from employee behaviour off the job, such as alcohol or drug abuse. In such circumstances, whenever an employee's off the job conduct has an impact on performance on the job, the manager must be prepared to deal with such a problem within the scope of the disciplinary process.

The purpose of discipline is not punishment or retribution. Disciplinary action must have as its goal the improvement of the future behaviour of the employee and other members of the organisation.

5.3 The Employment Act 2002

The **Employment Act 2002** came into effect in October 2004. Among other matters, it aims to encourage internal resolution of workplace disputes, by introducing minimum internal disciplinary and grievance procedures, and encouraging employees to raise grievances with their employer before applying to an employment tribunal. It also requires details of disciplinary and grievance procedures to be included in the 'written particulars' given to new employees.

5.4 The Advisory, Conciliation and Arbitration Service (ACAS)

ACAS's role is (as its name implies):

(a) **Conciliation**. Getting conflicting parties together for informal discussion to resolve a dispute.

(b) **Mediation**. Providing a mediator or mediation board that hears arguments and makes proposals and recommendations as a basis for settlement.

(c) **Arbitration**. Assisting in the appointment of independent arbitrators who make a binding ruling.

5.5 Disciplinary procedures

The ACAS Code of Practice recommends the following criteria for an effective disciplinary procedure.

Good disciplinary procedures should:

- Be in writing
- Specify to whom they apply
- Be non-discriminatory
- Provide for matters to be dealt with without undue delay
- Provide for proceedings, witness statements and records to be kept confidential
- Indicate the disciplinary actions that may be taken
- Specify the levels of management that have the authority to take the various forms of disciplinary action

- Provide for workers to be informed of the complaints against them and, where possible, all relevant evidence before any hearing
- Provide workers with an opportunity to state their case before decisions are reached
- Provide workers with the right to be accompanied by a colleague or union representative
- Ensure that, except for gross misconduct, no worker is dismissed for a first breach of discipline
- Ensure that disciplinary action is not taken until the case has been carefully investigated
- Ensure that workers are given an explanation for any penalty imposed
- Provide a right of appeal – normally to a more senior manager – and specify the procedure to be followed

The **statutory disciplinary procedure** provides for the following minimal procedures to be in place.

The appropriate manager must write to the employee, stating why disciplinary action is being taken and inviting them to a meeting to discuss the matter. The employee has the right to be accompanied at the meeting.

At the meeting, the manager must explain the problem and allow the employee to respond. After the meeting, the manager should explain their decision, and inform the employee that they have the right to appeal.

The employee may appeal, and has the right to be accompanied to the appeal meeting, which should be with a different or more senior manager.

This procedure must be used if the manager is contemplating serious disciplinary action, such as dismissal.

5.6 Progressive discipline

KEY POINT

There are six broad stages of increasing formality and severity in disciplining an employee. These are intended to resolve any problems before they become so serious that dismissal is the only route. We have grouped them into three sets of two in this section, so we start with informal action, go on to warnings and end with dismissal.

5.6.1 Informal talk

Many minor cases of poor performance or misconduct are best dealt with by informal advice, coaching or counselling. An **informal oral warning** may be issued. None of this forms part of the formal disciplinary procedure, but workers should be informed clearly about what is expected and what action will be taken if they fail to improve.

When the facts of the case have been established, it may be decided that **formal disciplinary** action is needed. The Code of Practice divides this into three stages. These are usually thought of as consecutive, reflecting a **progressive response**. However, it may be appropriate to miss out one of the earlier stages when there have been serious infringements.

5.6.2 Warnings

A **first formal warning** could be either oral or written depending on the seriousness of the case.

(a) An **oral warning** should include the reason for issuing it, notice that it constitutes the first step of the disciplinary procedure and details of the right of appeal. A note of the warning should be kept on file but disregarded after a specified period, such as six months.

(b) A **first written warning** is appropriate in more serious cases. It should inform the worker of the improvement required, and state that a final written warning may be considered if there is no satisfactory improvement. A copy of the first written warning should be kept on file but disregarded after a specified period, such as 12 months.

If an earlier warning is still current and there is no satisfactory improvement, a **final written warning** may be appropriate.

5.6.3 Layoff, suspension, demotion and dismissal

The final stage in the disciplinary process is the **imposition of sanctions**.

(a) **Suspension without pay**. This course of action would be next in order if the employee has committed repeated offences and previous disciplinary steps were to no avail. Disciplinary layoffs usually extend over several days or weeks. Some employees may not be very impressed with oral or written warnings, but they will find a disciplinary layoff without pay a rude awakening. This penalty is only available if it is provided for in the contract of employment.

(b) **Demotion**. The employee is set back to a lower position and salary. This is not regarded as an effective solution, as it affects the employee's morale and motivation.

(c) **Dismissal**. Dismissal is a drastic form of disciplinary action, and should be reserved for the most serious offences. For the organisation, it involves waste of a labour resource, the expense of training a new employee, and disruption caused by changing the make-up of the work team. There may also be damage to the morale of the group.

KEY POINT

Think of the disciplinary procedure as a progressive, six-stage process as outlined in this section.

5.7 Relationship management in disciplinary situations

Even if the manager uses sensitivity and judgement, imposing disciplinary action tends to generate **resentment**. The challenge is to apply the necessary disciplinary action as constructively as possible.

(a) **Immediacy (the 'Hot Stove Rule')**. Immediacy means that after noticing the offence, the manager proceeds to take disciplinary action as **speedily** as possible, subject to investigations, while at the same time avoiding haste and on the spot emotions that might lead to unwarranted actions.

(b) **Advance warning**. Employees should know in advance (eg in a staff handbook) what is expected of them and what the rules and regulations are.

(c) **Consistency**. Consistency of discipline means that, each time an infraction occurs, appropriate disciplinary action is taken. Inconsistency in application of discipline lowers the morale of employees and diminishes their respect for the manager.

(d) **Impersonality**. Penalties should be connected with the act, and not based on the personality involved, and once disciplinary action has been taken, no grudges should be borne.

(e) **Privacy**. As a general rule (unless the manager's authority is challenged directly and in public) disciplinary action should be taken in private, to avoid the spread of conflict and the humiliation or martyrdom of the employee concerned.

Section summary

Discipline has the same end as **motivation**: to secure a range of desired behaviour from members of the organisation.

ACAS has published a **Code of Practice** for grievance and disciplinary procedures, as well as having a role in helping resolve industrial disputes.

Progressive discipline includes warnings and sanctions of increasing severity, in six broad stages: informal talk, oral warning, written/official warning, layoff or suspension, demotion and dismissal.

6 Grievance

KEY TERM

A GRIEVANCE occurs when an individual feels that they are being wrongly or unfairly treated by a colleague or supervisor, and wishes to assert their rights.

Make sure you can distinguish clearly between discipline (when an employee 'does wrong') and grievance (when an employee 'feels wronged'). This is a surprisingly common exam pitfall.

Fairness and equity are vital in ensuring that organisations are well ordered and workers are committed to their work. Read the relevant sections as background for the main topic of grievance.

6.1 Purposes of formal grievance procedure

Introduction

When an individual has a grievance, they should be able to pursue it and ask to have the problem resolved. Some grievances may be capable of solution informally by the individual's manager. However, if an informal solution is not possible, there should be a formal grievance procedure for the following reasons.

(a) To allow **objective grievance handling** – including 'cooling off' periods and independent case investigation and arbitration

(b) To **protect employees** from victimisation – particularly where a grievance involves their immediate superiors

(c) To provide **legal protection** for both parties, in the event of a dispute resulting in claims before an employment tribunal

(d) To **encourage grievance airing** – which is an important source of feedback to management on employee problems and dissatisfactions

(e) To **require full and fair investigation** of grievances, enabling the employer–employee relationship to be respected and preserved, despite problems

6.2 Elements of formal grievance procedures

A formal grievance procedure should:

(a) State the **rights** of the employee for each type of grievance. For example, an employee who is overlooked for promotion might be entitled to a review of their annual appraisal report, or to attend a special appeals promotion/selection board if they have been in their current grade for at least a certain number of years.

(b) State what the **procedures** for pursuing a grievance should be. The statutory procedure is as follows.

   (i) The individual should state **the grievance** in writing.

   (ii) The **first interview** will be between the immediate manager (unless they are the subject of the complaint, in which case it will be the next level up) and the employee, who has the right to be accompanied by a colleague or representative.

   (iii) If the immediate manager cannot resolve the matter, or the employee is otherwise dissatisfied with the first interview, the case should be **referred upwards** to their superior (and if necessary in some cases, to an even higher authority).

(c) Allow for the involvement of an individual's or group's **trade union or staff association representative**.

(d) State **time limits** for initiating certain grievance procedures and subsequent stages of them (such as communication of decisions and appeals).

(e) Require **written records** of all meetings concerned with the case to be made and distributed to all the participants.

6.3 Fairness and equity

It should be obvious that most grievances can be avoided if organisations treat their employees fairly, or with equity.

6.3.1 Psychological contracts

A **psychological contract** exists between individuals in an organisation and the organisation itself.

(a) The individual expects to derive certain benefits from membership of the organisation and is prepared to expend a certain amount of effort in return.

(b) The organisation expects the individual to fulfil certain requirements and is prepared to offer certain rewards in return.

Three types of psychological contract can be identified.

(a) **Coercive contract**. This is a contract in which the individual considers that they are being forced to contribute their efforts and energies involuntarily, and that the rewards they receive in return are inadequate compensation.

(b) **Calculative contract**. This is a contract, accepted **voluntarily** by the individual, in which they expect to do their job in exchange for a readily identifiable set of rewards. With such psychological contracts, motivation can only be increased if the rewards to the individual are improved. If the organisation attempts to demand greater efforts without increasing the rewards, the psychological contract will revert to a coercive one, and motivation may become negative.

(c) **Co-operative contract**. This is a contract in which the individual identifies themselves with the organisation and its goals, so that they actively seek to contribute further to the achievement of those goals. Motivation comes out of success at work, a sense of achievement, and self-fulfilment. The individual will probably want to share in the planning, and control decisions that affect their work, and co-operative contracts are therefore likely to occur where employees participate in decision making.

Employee commitment is secured when the psychological contract is viewed in the same way by the organisation and by the individual, and when both parties are able to fulfil their side of the bargain: the individual agrees to work, or work well, in return for whatever rewards or satisfactions are understood as the terms of the 'contract'.

6.3.2 Equitable pay

An important aspect of how employees perceive the equity of their relationship with their employers lies in the way they perceive their material rewards. Adams and Salomon suggest that this perception will always be coloured by comparisons with other people. Salomon shows the difficulty of achieving equity in a diagram that illustrates the factors on which an equitable relationship can be judged. These will differ between societies, cultures and work groups.

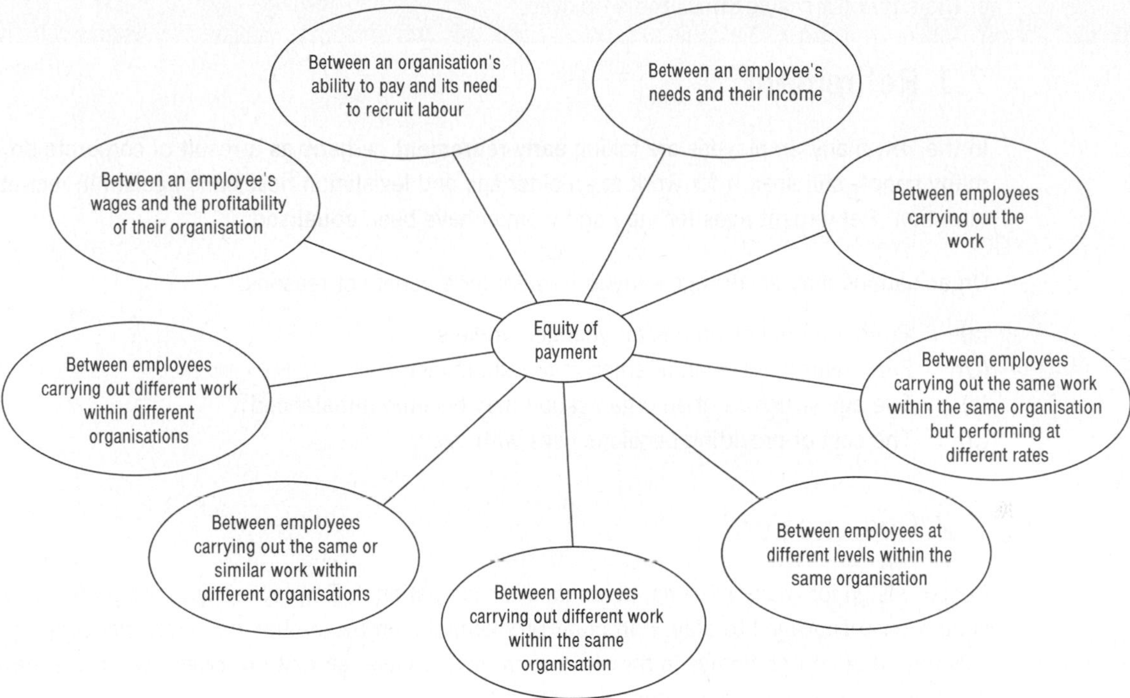

6.3.3 Commitment

KEY TERM

COMMITMENT has been defined as 'the relative strength of an individual's identification with an involvement in a particular organisation'. (Mowdray)

One of the key reasons to avoid grievance and conflict in an organisation is to secure the commitment of employees, which shows itself in:

(a) Productivity and timekeeping above the minimal standards set by compliance with rules
(b) Willingness to exert effort, creativity and initiative on behalf of the organisation's goals
(c) Positive, co-operative employee relations climate
(d) Strong morale and *esprit de corps*
(e) Lower levels of conflict, grievance and employee stress

Section summary

Grievance procedures embody employees' right to appeal against unfair or otherwise prejudicial conduct or conditions that affect them and their work.

Any staff **grievances** should be dealt with initially by line managers. Where this cannot be resolved, senior management and HR should be consulted. Most **disputes** arise where the employee feels they have been **treated unfairly**, often in respect of wages, responsibility and status.

7 Termination of contract

Introduction

Termination sounds very final, and it is indeed the ending of the formal relationship between the employer and the employee. It may come from the employee who hands in their notice, it may be required by law or the employer may dismiss the employee.

7.1 Retirement

In the UK, many employees are taking **early retirement** perhaps as a result of corporate downsizing, but many people still search for work at an older age and legislation now bans **ageism** in recruitment and retention. Retirement ages for men and women have been **equalised**.

Organisations may encourage early retirement for a variety of reasons.

(a) Promotion opportunities for younger workers.
(b) Early retirement is an alternative to redundancy.
(c) The age structure of an organisation may become unbalanced.
(d) The cost of providing pensions rises with age.

7.2 Resignation

People resign for many reasons, personal and occupational. Employees who are particularly valuable should be encouraged to stay. Particular problems the employee has been experiencing (eg salary) may be solvable, though not always in the short term. In any case, an **exit interview**, when the leaver explains the decision to go, is a valuable source of information.

The **period of notice** required for the employee to leave should be set out in the contract of employment, but some leeway may be negotiated on this.

7.3 Dismissal

There are three forms of termination that constitute dismissal under UK law.

(a) The termination of an employee's contract **by the employer**

(b) The ending of a fixed-term contract **without renewal** on the same terms

(c) Resignation by the employee where the employer's conduct breaches the contract of employment: **constructive dismissal**

The **statutory minimum** period of notice to be given is determined by the employee's length of continuous service in the employer's service. Longer periods may be written into the contract, at the employer's discretion, and by agreement. Either party may waive their right to notice, or accept payment in lieu of notice. An employee is entitled to a written statement of the **reasons** for dismissal.

7.3.1 Wrongful dismissal

Wrongful dismissal is dismissal that breaches the **contract of employment**. An example would be failure to give the contractual period of notice (assuming the circumstances did not justify summary dismissal).

7.3.2 Unfair dismissal

The legal concept of unfair dismissal gives protection to the employee against **arbitrary** dismissal; that is, dismissal without good reason. The basic principle is that any dismissal is potentially unfair: once the employee has proved that they have been dismissed, the onus is on the employer to prove that the dismissal was fair.

Potentially **fair** grounds for dismissal include:

(a) **Redundancy**, provided that the selection for redundancy was fair

(b) **Legal impediment**: the employee could not continue to work in their present position without breaking a legal duty or restriction

(c) **Non-capability**, provided adequate training and warnings had been given

(d) **Misconduct**, provided warnings suitable to the offence have been given

(e) **Other substantial reason**: for example, the employee is married to a competitor

Dismissal is regarded as **automatically unfair** by reason of:

(a) Unfair selection for redundancy
(b) Membership and involvement in a trade union
(c) Pregnancy
(d) Insisting on documented payslips and employment particulars
(e) Carrying out certain activities in connection with health and safety at work

The Conciliation Officer or **employment tribunal**, to whom a complaint of unfair dismissal is made, may order various **remedies**, subject to the circumstances of the case.

(a) **Reinstatement**. Giving the employee the old job back.
(b) **Re-engagement**. Giving the employee a job comparable to the old one.
(c) **Compensation**. This may include redundancy pay, breach of contract and punitive award.

In order to avoid claims of unfair dismissal, managers must:

(a) Ensure that **standards of performance and conduct** are set, clearly defined and communicated to all employees

(b) **Warn** employees where a gap is perceived between standard and performance

(c) Give a clearly defined and reasonable **period for improvement** – with help and advice where necessary, and clear improvement targets

(d) Ensure that **disciplinary procedures** are fairly and systematically applied

If such procedures are formulated, the employee will have been given every chance to redeem the situation, and the organisation will be in a strong position at an employment tribunal hearing.

Question 4.10 Dismissal

Learning outcomes B1b

An employer's treatment of an employee is so bad that eventually the employee resigns even though they liked their work. This would be an example of:

A Wrongful dismissal
B Potentially unfair dismissal
C Automatically unfair dismissal
D Constructive dismissal

7.4 Redundancy

Redundancy is defined as dismissal under two circumstances.

(a) The employer has ceased to carry on the business at all, or in the place where the employee was employed.

(b) The requirements of the business for employees to carry out work of a particular kind have ceased or diminished, or are expected to.

Compensation is a legal entitlement, and encourages employees to accept redundancy without damage to industrial relations.

The employee is **not entitled** to compensation in three circumstances.

(a) The employer has made an **offer of suitable alternative employment** and the employee has unreasonably rejected it.

(b) The employee is of **pensionable age** or over, or has less than two years' continuous employment.

(c) The employee's conduct merits **dismissal without notice**.

There are certain legal minimums for compensation offered, based on age and length of service.

7.4.1 Procedure for handling redundancies

From a purely humane point of view, it is obviously desirable to consult with employees or their representatives. Notice of impending redundancies is a legal duty for redundancies over a certain number.

The impact of a redundancy programme can be reduced in several ways.

(a) Retirement of staff over the normal retirement age
(b) Early retirement to staff approaching normal retirement age
(c) Restrictions on recruitment to reduce the workforce over time by natural wastage
(d) Dismissal of part-time or short-term contract staff
(e) Offering retraining and/or redeployment within the organisation
(f) Seeking voluntary redundancies

Where management have to choose between individuals doing the same work, the most equitable approach may be to dismiss the less competent (on carefully defined and measured criteria) or require people to reapply for the job. The last-in-first-out principle may be applied, so that newcomers are dismissed before long-serving employees, but care must be taken that this does not discriminate against women or ethnic minorities, for example.

Many large organisations provide benefits in excess of the statutory minimum, with regard to consultation periods, terms, notice periods, counselling and aid with job searching, training in job-searching skills and so on. Many firms provide advice and **outplacement** counselling to help redundant employees find work elsewhere.

Section summary

Termination of the employment relationship is the **last resort**, and alternatives such as **retirement** and **resignation** are preferable where possible.

8 Equal opportunities

Introduction

Equal opportunities tend to be preserved via legislation. **Diversity** represents a more positive, voluntary approach to avoid adverse working practices. We look at diversity in Section 10.

Our discussion uses UK legislation but refers to it at a very basic level. Make sure you know what each piece of legislation aims to do generally in terms of age, sex, race, disability or other aspects of equality in the workplace. You need a general awareness that there are laws governing these areas so that when you make decisions as a manager these are taken into account. We look at **codes of practice** in the next section, which are the practical implementation of the law on equality in organisations.

8.1 Equal opportunities

KEY TERM

EQUAL OPPORTUNITIES is an approach to the management of people at work, based on equal access and fair treatment, irrespective of gender, race, ethnicity, age, disability, sexual orientation or religious belief.

Equal opportunities employers will seek to redress inequalities (eg of access to jobs, training, promotion, pay or benefits) that are based around differences, where they have no relevance to work performance.

Certain aspects of equal opportunities (such as discrimination on the basis of sex, race or disability) are enshrined in law; others (such as, up to now, discrimination on the basis of age) rely on models of good practice.

Exam skills

Discrimination and equal opportunities are topics of great importance for managers in real life. We include them in this part of the Study Text because that is where the syllabus puts them. However, you should be aware that they are relevant to all aspects of management, and therefore, potentially, to **any question** in the examination. When attempting your E2 examination and Integrated Case Study, make sure that any strategies or actions you propose, in response to a scenario, are not discriminatory!

8.1.1 Why is equal opportunity an issue for employers?

Sound **business arguments** can be made for equal opportunities policy. Reasons argued for adopting non- or anti-discrimination measures include the following.

(a) Common decency and fairness, in line with business ethics

(b) Good HR practice, to attract and retain the best people for the job, regardless of race or gender

(c) Compliance with relevant legislation and codes of practice, which are used by employment tribunals

(d) Widening the recruitment pool in times of skill shortages

(e) Other potential benefits to the business through its image as a good employer, and through the loyalty of customers who benefit from (or support) equality principles

The Chairman of the Equality and Human Rights Commission, however, has criticised companies that do nothing except use 'equal opportunities designer labels' to make recruitment advertisements look good.

8.2 The legal framework on equality

In the UK, over the years a number of Acts have been passed to deal with inequality of opportunity and discrimination at work.

(a) The **Sex Discrimination Act 1986**, and the **Sex Discrimination and Equal Pay (Miscellaneous Amendments) Regulations 1996**, outlaw certain types of discrimination on the grounds of sex, marital status and sex change.

(b) The **Race Relations Act 1976**, as amended in 1996, outlaws certain types of discrimination on grounds of colour, race, nationality, or ethnic or national origin. The **Race Relations (Amendment) Act 2000** added the requirement that larger public organisations (with more than 150 employees) must draw up detailed plans for achieving racial equality in all employment practices.

(c) **Equal pay legislation** is intended to prevent discrimination as regards terms and conditions of employment between men and women, and provides that women have the right to equal pay for 'work of equal value' to that of a man in the same establishment (as defined by a job evaluation scheme).

(d) The **Disability Discrimination Acts 1995 and 2005** give disabled people (including those with HIV, cancer and multiple sclerosis) similar rights against discrimination to those already established in relation to sex and race. In addition, the employer has a duty to make 'reasonable adjustments' to working arrangements or premises where these constitute a disadvantage to disabled people.

(e) The **Employment Rights Act 1996** gives minimum rights to women during and after maternity.

(f) The **Employment Equality (Sexual Orientation) (Amendment) Regulations 2003** protect employees from direct and indirect discrimination, harassment and victimisation in employment and training on the grounds of sexual orientation.

(g) The **Employment Equality (Religion or Belief) Regulations 2003** protect employees from direct and indirect discrimination, harassment and victimisation in employment and training on the grounds of religion or belief.

(h) The **Employment Equality (Age) Regulations 2006**, introduced in October 2006, prohibit unjustified age discrimination in employment and vocational training; support later retirement and retirement planning; and remove upper age limits for unfair dismissal and redundancy rights.

The **Equality Act (2010)** brought the majority of the Acts outlined above together to form a stronger piece of legislation governing equal treatment and reduced the need for a vast array of complicated laws and regulations. The Equality Act (2010) has extended the range of protected characteristics which employers must abide by:

(a) Sex
(b) Sexual orientation
(c) Religion or belief
(d) Race
(e) Pregnancy and maternity
(f) Marriage and civil partnership
(g) Gender reassignment
(h) Disability
(i) Age

8.2.1 Types of discrimination

There are three types of discrimination under the Acts.

KEY TERMS

DIRECT DISCRIMINATION occurs when one interested group is treated less favourably than another (except for exempted cases).

INDIRECT DISCRIMINATION occurs when a policy or practice is fair in form, but discriminatory in operation: for example, if requirements or conditions are imposed, with which a substantial proportion of the interested group cannot comply, to their detriment.

VICTIMISATION occurs when a person is penalised for giving information or taking action in pursuit of a claim of discrimination.

In addition, **harassment** is the use of threatening, intimidatory, offensive or abusive language or behaviour. This is covered by UK law in relation to race, religious belief and sexual orientation: sexual harassment will also be covered in forthcoming legislation.

An employer must, if challenged, justify apparently discriminatory conditions on non-discriminatory grounds. It is often the case that employers are not aware that they are discriminating indirectly, and this concept was a major breakthrough when introduced by the Acts.

Question 4.11 Indirect discrimination

Learning outcomes B1b

Suggest four examples of practices that would constitute indirect discrimination on the grounds of gender.

Positive discrimination gives preference to a protected person, regardless of comparative suitability and qualification for the job. UK legislation does not (except with regard to training) permit positive discrimination. A number of countries in the world do use positive discrimination as an aspect of social policy to correct perceived disadvantages endured by various ethnic and other groups in society. (For example, in India scheduled castes are entitled to a proportion of government jobs.)

Section summary

Discrimination of certain types is illegal in the UK. The Equality Act 2010 governs the equal treatment of individuals in the workplace.

Employers should note the implications for both:

- **Direct discrimination** – less favourable treatment of a protected group
- **Indirect discrimination** – when requirements or conditions cannot be justified on non-discriminatory grounds, and work to the detriment of a protected group

9 The practical implications of legislation

Introduction

The practical implications of the legislation for employers are set out in **codes of practice**, currently issued by the Equality and Human Rights Commission. These do not have the force of law, but may be taken into account by employment tribunals, where discrimination cases are brought before them.

9.1 Formulating an effective equal opportunities policy

Some organisations make minimal efforts to avoid discrimination, paying lip service to the idea only to the extent of claiming 'we are an equal opportunities employer' on advertising literature. To turn such a claim into reality, the following are needed.

(a) **Support** from the top of the organisation for the formulation of a practical policy.

(b) A **working party** drawn from, for example, management, unions, minority groups, and the HR function and staff representatives. This group's brief will be to produce a draft policy and code of practice, which will be approved at senior level.

(c) **Action plans and resources** (including staff) to implement and monitor the policy, publicise it to staff, arrange training and so on.

(d) **Monitoring**. The numbers of women and ethnic minority staff can easily be monitored:

  (i) On entering (and applying to enter) the organisation
  (ii) On leaving the organisation
  (iii) On applying for transfers, promotions or training schemes

  (It is less easy to determine the ethnic origins of the workforce through such methods as questionnaires: there is bound to be suspicion about the questions' motives, and it may be offensive to some workers.)

(e) **Positive action**. This is the process of taking active steps to encourage people from disadvantaged groups to apply for jobs and training, and to compete for vacancies. (Note that this is not positive discrimination.) Examples might be: using ethnic languages in job advertisements, or implementing training for women in management skills. In addition, there may be awareness training, counselling and disciplinary measures to manage sexual, racial and religious harassment.

9.2 Recruitment and selection

There is always a risk that disappointed job applicants, for example, will attribute their lack of success to discrimination, especially if the recruiting organisation's workforce is conspicuously lacking in representatives of the same ethnic minority, sex or group. The following guidelines should be borne in mind.

(a) **Advertising**

  (i) Any wording that suggests preference for a particular group should be avoided (except for genuine occupational qualifications).

  (ii) Employers must not indicate or imply any 'intention to discriminate'.

  (iii) Recruitment literature should state that the organisation is an equal opportunities employer (where this can be justified).

  (iv) The placing of advertisements only where the readership is predominantly of one race or sex is construed as indirect discrimination. This includes word of mouth recruiting from the existing workforce, if it is not broadly representative.

(b) **Recruitment agencies**. Instructions to an agency should not suggest any preference.

(c) **Application forms**. These should include no questions that are not work related (such as domestic details) and that only one group is asked to complete.

(d) **Interviews**

  (i) Any non work related question must be asked of all subjects, if at all, and even then, some types of question may be construed as discriminatory. (You cannot, for example, ask only women about plans to have a family or care of dependants, or ask – in the most offensive case – about the contraceptive pill or premenstrual tension.)

(ii) It may be advisable to have a witness at interviews, or at least to take detailed notes, in the event that a claim of discrimination is made.

(e) **Selection tests**. These must be wholly relevant, and should not favour any particular group. Even personality tests have been shown to favour white male applicants.

(f) **Records**. Reasons for rejection, and interview notes, should be carefully recorded, so that in the event of investigation the details will be available.

9.3 Childcare

Although not specifically required to by law, many companies now find it beneficial to help their employees balance their working life with their responsibilities to care for children. The motivation is not humanitarian or altruistic. Some companies now regard childcare as something they must do to be competitive. Employees who have problems with childcare often fail to function effectively. In a nutshell: childcare affects the bottom line.

Benefits to a company of providing help with childcare are as follows.

(a) It **attracts employees** who would otherwise be deterred.

(b) Employees feel their employer **values them as people**, and are more likely to stay, thereby saving costs incurred by **staff turnover**.

(c) **Employee morale** is improved.

(d) The **company's reputation** is enhanced.

(e) **Productivity** is increased and **performance** enhanced.

(f) Employees are more prepared to be **flexible** if this is seen as a 'two-way street'.

Employees are important **stakeholders** in a company, and most employees have children.

9.4 Other initiatives

Measures such as the following may be used as positive action initiatives.

(a) Putting equal opportunities **higher on the agenda** by appointing equal opportunities managers (and even directors) who report directly to the HR Director.

(b) **Flexible hours** or part-time work, term-time or annual hours contracts (to allow for school holidays) to help women to combine careers with family responsibilities. Terms and conditions, however, must not be less favourable.

(c) **Career-break** or **return to work schemes** for women.

(d) **Fast-tracking school-leavers**, as well as graduates, and posting managerial vacancies internally, giving more opportunities for movement up the ladder for groups (typically women and minorities) currently at lower levels of the organisation.

(e) **Training for women-returners** or women in management, to help women to manage their career potential. Assertiveness training may also be offered as part of such an initiative.

(f) **Awareness training** for managers, to encourage them to think about equal opportunity policy.

(g) **Counselling and disciplinary policies** to raise awareness and eradicate sexual, racial and religious harassment.

(h) **Positive action** to encourage job and training applications from minority groups.

Section summary

Recruitment and selection are areas of particular sensitivity to claims of discrimination as well as genuine (though often unintended) inequality.

In addition to responding to legislative provisions, some employers have begun to address the **underlying problems** of discrimination.

10 Diversity

Introduction

Diversity in employment, as a concept, goes further than equal opportunities.

The ways in which people meaningfully differ in the workplace include not only race and ethnicity, age and gender, but personality, preferred working style, individual needs and goals and so on.

10.1 Managing diversity

A 'managing diversity' orientation implies the need to be proactive in managing the needs of a diverse workforce in areas (beyond the requirements of equal opportunity and discrimination regulations) such as:

(a) Tolerance of individual differences
(b) Communicating effectively with (and motivating) ethnically diverse workforces
(c) Managing workers with increasingly diverse family structures and responsibilities
(d) Managing the adjustments to be made by an increasingly aged workforce
(e) Managing increasingly diverse career aspirations/patterns, flexible working etc
(f) Dealing with differences in literacy, numeracy and qualifications in an international workforce
(g) Managing co-operative working in ethnically diverse teams

Section summary

The concept of '**managing diversity**' is based on the belief that the dimensions of individual difference on which organisations currently focus are crude and performance-irrelevant classifications of the most obvious differences between people.

Chapter Summary

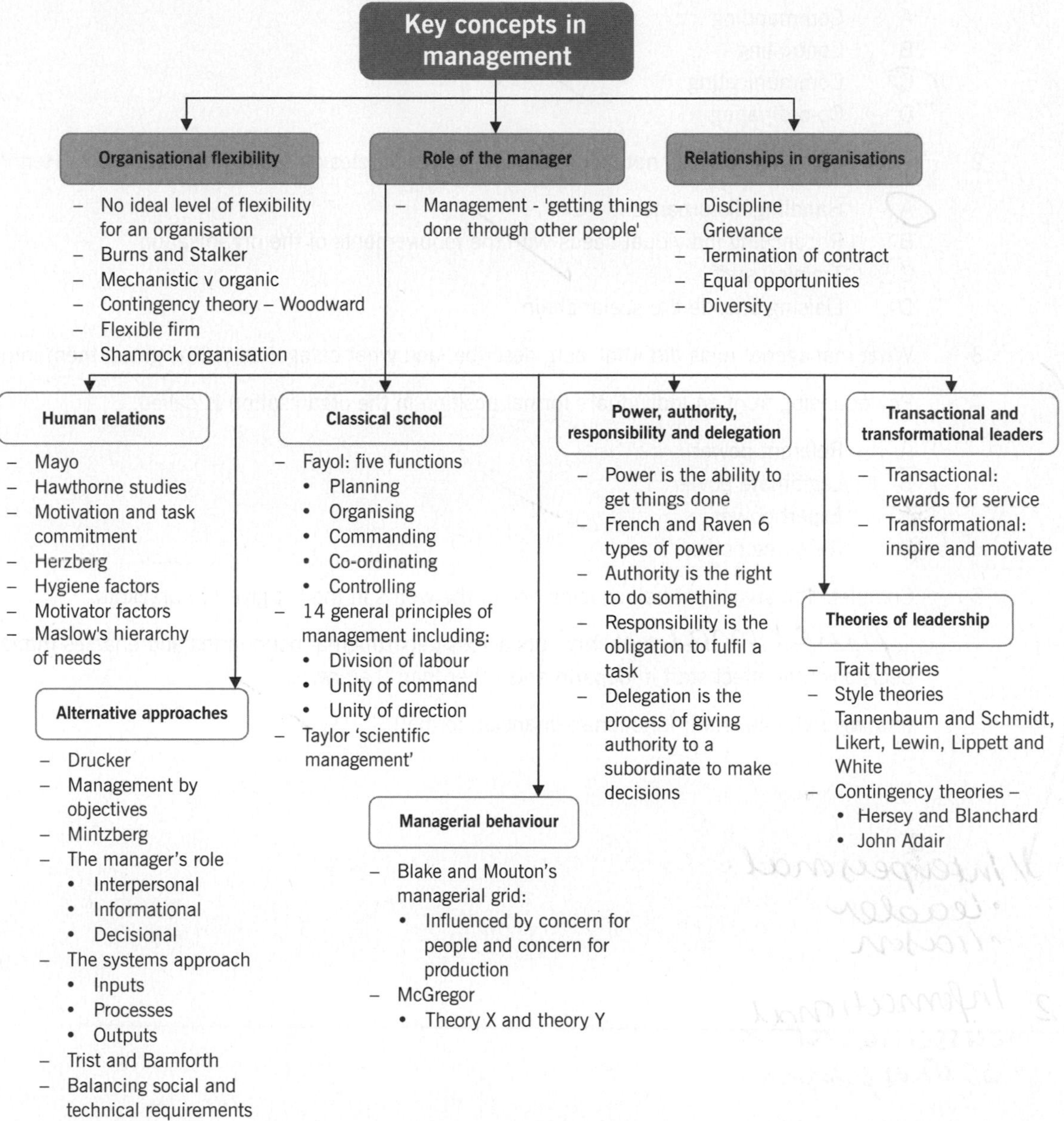
Key concepts in management
Organisational flexibility
- No ideal level of flexibility for an organisation
- Burns and Stalker
- Mechanistic v organic
- Contingency theory – Woodward
- Flexible firm
- Shamrock organisation
Role of the manager
- Management - 'getting things done through other people'
Relationships in organisations
- Discipline
- Grievance
- Termination of contract
- Equal opportunities
- Diversity
Human relations
- Mayo
- Hawthorne studies
- Motivation and task commitment
- Herzberg
- Hygiene factors
- Motivator factors
- Maslow's hierarchy of needs
Classical school
- Fayol: five functions
• Planning
• Organising
• Commanding
• Co-ordinating
• Controlling
- 14 general principles of management including:
• Division of labour
• Unity of command
• Unity of direction
- Taylor 'scientific management'
Power, authority, responsibility and delegation
- Power is the ability to get things done
- French and Raven 6 types of power
- Authority is the right to do something
- Responsibility is the obligation to fulfil a task
- Delegation is the process of giving authority to a subordinate to make decisions
Transactional and transformational leaders
- Transactional: rewards for service
- Transformational: inspire and motivate
Theories of leadership
- Trait theories
- Style theories Tannenbaum and Schmidt, Likert, Lewin, Lippett and White
- Contingency theories –
• Hersey and Blanchard
• John Adair
Alternative approaches
- Drucker
- Management by objectives
- Mintzberg
- The manager's role
• Interpersonal
• Informational
• Decisional
- The systems approach
• Inputs
• Processes
• Outputs
- Trist and Bamforth
- Balancing social and technical requirements to do a job
Managerial behaviour
- Blake and Mouton's managerial grid:
• Influenced by concern for people and concern for production
- McGregor
• Theory X and theory Y

Quick Quiz

1 Which of the following is **not** one of Fayol's five functions of management?

A Commanding
B Controlling
C Communicating
D Co-ordinating

2 Which of the following is **not** one of the interpersonal roles of managers identified by Henry Mintzberg?

A Handling disturbances
B Reconciling individual needs with the requirements of the organisation
C Training staff
D Liaising outside the scalar chain

3 What managerial roles did Mintzberg describe, and what categories did he group them into?

4 Power arising from an individual's formal position in the organisation is called:

A Referent power
B Legitimate power
C Expert power
D Resource power

5 Complete the statement below using one of the words in the list given in brackets.

'............................ authority cuts across departmental boundaries and enables managers to take decisions that affect staff in departments other than their own.'

(managerial, line, staff, functional, financial, formal)

Answers to Quick Quiz

1 C Communicating

2 A This is a decisional role. The 'disturbances' referred to are unpredictable situations that require managerial input to resolve.

3

Category	*Roles*
Interpersonal	Figurehead, leader and liaison
Informational	Monitor, spokesperson and disseminator
Decisional	Entrepreneur, disturbance handler, resource allocator and negotiator

4 B (Or 'position' power)

5 Functional

Answers to Questions

4.1 Management structure

The purpose of this exercise has been to get you to separate the issues of management functions from organisational structure and hierarchy. John, Paul, George and Ringo have a number of choices. Here are some extreme examples.

(a) All the management activities are the job of one person.

In this case, Paul, for example, could plan, direct and control the work, and the other three would do the work.

(b) Division of management tasks between individuals (eg repairing drums **and** ensuring plans are adhered to would be Ringo's job, and so on).

(c) Management by committee. All of them could sit down and work out the plan together etc. In a small business with equal partners, this is likely to be the most effective.

4.2 Fayol

From a more modern viewpoint, you may be struck by two key 'omissions' from Fayol's classification.

(a) '**Motivating**' is not mentioned. It is assumed that subordinates will carry out tasks when 'commanded' or instructed to do so, regardless of whether or how far they may 'want' to.

(b) '**Communicating**' is not mentioned, although it is implied by the process of commanding (giving instructions), co-ordinating (sharing information) and controlling (giving feedback).

4.3 Mintzberg and classical management theory

Managers still perform functions (in the way Fayol suggested, for example): Mintzberg's findings merely show that the functions are not as clear cut, or performed as systematically, as might be supposed from the classical literature.

4.4 Line and staff authority

(a) and (b) are both examples of line authority.

(c) is staff, or perhaps functional, authority.

4.5 Leadership

The answer to this is personal. The question was set to get you to think about good leadership.

4.6 Styles of leadership

(a) You may have to 'tell' here: nobody is gong to like the idea and, since each person will have their own interests at heart, you are unlikely to reach consensus. You could attempt to 'sell', if you can see a positive side to the change in particular cases: opportunities for retraining, for example.

(b) You could 'consult' here: explain your remedy to staff and see whether they can suggest potential problems. They may be in a position to offer solutions – and since the problem affects them too, they should be committed to solving it.

4.7 The managerial grid

(a) 1.1: low task, low people

(b) 9.1: high task, low people

(c) 1.9: high people, low task

4.8 Hersey and Blanchard

Answers will differ depending on the type of group chosen.

4.9 Control

Culture

4.10 Dismissal

D Little is certain in employment law but, on the face of it, this would seem to be a case of constructive dismissal. It may also turn out to be unfair dismissal. Wrongful dismissal is unlikely, as the employer may not have actually breached the contract of employment. It may emerge on investigation that the bad treatment of the employee was the result of one of the automatically unfair reasons for dismissal, such as membership of a trade union. However, on the facts we are given, option D is the best answer.

4.11 Indirect discrimination

(a) Advertising a vacancy in a primarily male environment, where women would be less likely to see it

(b) Offering less favourable terms to part-time workers (given that most of them are women)

(c) Specifying age limits that would tend to exclude women who had taken time out of work for child-rearing

(d) Asking in selection interviews about plans to have a family (since this might be to the detriment of a woman, but not a man)

Now try these questions from the Practice Question Bank

Question	Level
4.1 – 4.5	Practice
S and C	Practice

CULTURE

As we saw in the previous chapter, the approach that different managers and leaders adopt in the workplace is driven by a wide range of factors. Arguably, one of the most significant influences on how people behave comes from the organisation's culture.

Organisational culture is, broadly, the distinctive way an organisation does things: its particular 'style'.

We explore how this reveals itself in the first two sections of this chapter.

Culture is often discussed together with **structure**. Particular structures suit particular cultures (and vice versa). We look at an influential model of this in Section 3.

Then we consider how strategy and culture are linked too. We look at how different organisation cultures affect their approach to strategy.

The impact of **national culture** on organisational culture is important when discussing management in multinational and cross-cultural contexts. It may be particularly relevant in scenarios where a company is considering strategic options to start overseas operations.

This chapter underpins much of the rest of the syllabus.

Management/leadership style, team working and relationships, approach to project management and stakeholders, and organisational mission, objectives and strategy will all reflect the organisation's culture: 'the way we do things round here'.

Topic list	Learning outcomes	Syllabus references	Ability required
1 What is culture?	B2b	B2(i), (ii), (iii)	Comprehension
2 Organisation culture	B2b	B2(iv)	Comprehension
3 Culture and structure	B2b	B2(v)	Comprehension
4 Culture and strategy	B2b	B2(v)	Comprehension
5 Cross-cultural leadership	B2b	B2(vi)	Comprehension

Chapter Overview

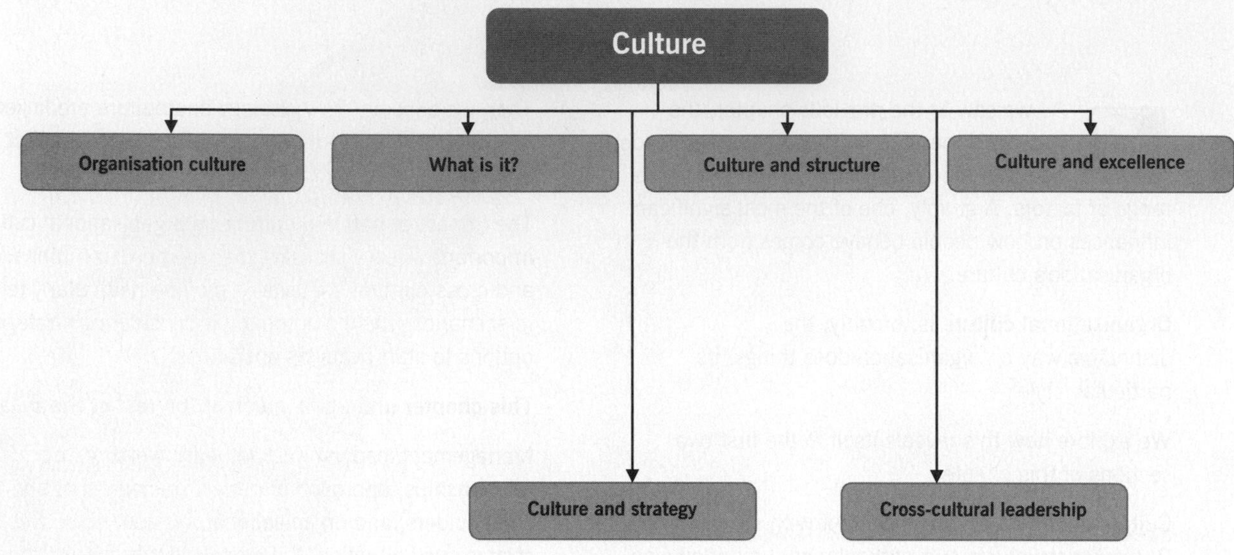

1 What is culture?

Introduction

We often think of culture as what you see in a museum, but for organisations it is 'the way we do things around here'. Culture is the ways of acting and thinking, shared by a group of people. Some of this culture can be hidden but is still influential. You may wish to think of culture in an organisation as an **iceberg** with a large part hidden below the surface.

1.1 Spheres of culture

KEY TERMS

HOFSTEDE (1984) summed up **culture** as 'the collective programming of the mind which distinguishes the members of one category of people from another'. Hofstede's model is explained in more depth later on in this chapter.

CULTURE may therefore be identified as ways of behaving, and ways of understanding, that are shared by a group of people. Schein referred to it as: 'The way we do things round here'.

Culture can be discussed on many different levels. The 'category' or 'group' of people whose shared behaviours and meanings may constitute a culture include:

(a) A nation, region or ethnic group
(b) Women versus men ('gender culture')
(c) A social class (eg 'working class culture')
(d) A profession or occupation
(e) A type of business (eg 'advertising culture')
(f) An organisation ('**organisational culture**')

If you are an accountant in an organisation operating in a given business sector in a particular region of your country of residence (which may not be your country of origin), you may be influenced by all these different spheres of culture!

CASE STUDY

Culture

Consider the case of a young French employee of Disneyland Paris.

(a) The employee speaks the French language – part of the national culture – and has participated in the French education system etc.

(b) As a youth, the employee might, in their spare time, participate in various 'youth culture' activities. Music and fashion are emblematic of youth culture.

(c) As an employee of Disneyland Paris, the employee will have to participate in the corporate culture, which is based on US standards of service, with a high priority put on friendliness to customers.

1.2 Elements of culture

Schein suggested that in fact there are different levels at which culture can be understood.

(a) The **observable**, expressed or 'explicit' elements of culture include:

(i) **Behaviour**. Norms of personal and interpersonal behaviour; customs and rules about behaviours that are 'acceptable' or unacceptable.

(ii) **Artefacts**. Concrete expressions such as art and literature, architecture and interior design (eg of office premises), dress codes, symbols and 'heroes' or role models.

(iii) **Rituals**. Patterns of collective behaviour that have traditional or symbolic value, such as greeting styles, business formalities, social courtesies and ceremonies.

(b) Beneath these observable phenomena lie **values and beliefs** that give the behaviours, artefacts and rituals their special meaning and significance. For example, the design of office space (artefact) may imply status and honour, or reflect the importance of privacy, or reflect spiritual beliefs (as in feng shui) within a culture: it 'means' more than the observable features. Values and beliefs may be overtly expressed in sayings, mottos and slogans.

(c) Beneath values and beliefs lie **assumptions**: foundational ideas that are no longer consciously recognised or questioned by the culture, but which 'programme' its ways of thinking and behaving. Examples include the importance of the individual in many Western cultures: this is taken for granted in designing human resources (HR) policies, for example.

1.3 The cultural iceberg

Various writers on culture have used the metaphor of an **iceberg** to describe the levels at which culture operates.

(a) The **overt** elements of culture are above the surface: differences can be observed, discussed and dealt with openly.

(b) The **covert** (hidden) elements of culture represent the larger part of the iceberg, which is below the water. They exert influence, without necessarily being openly expressed or even acknowledged.

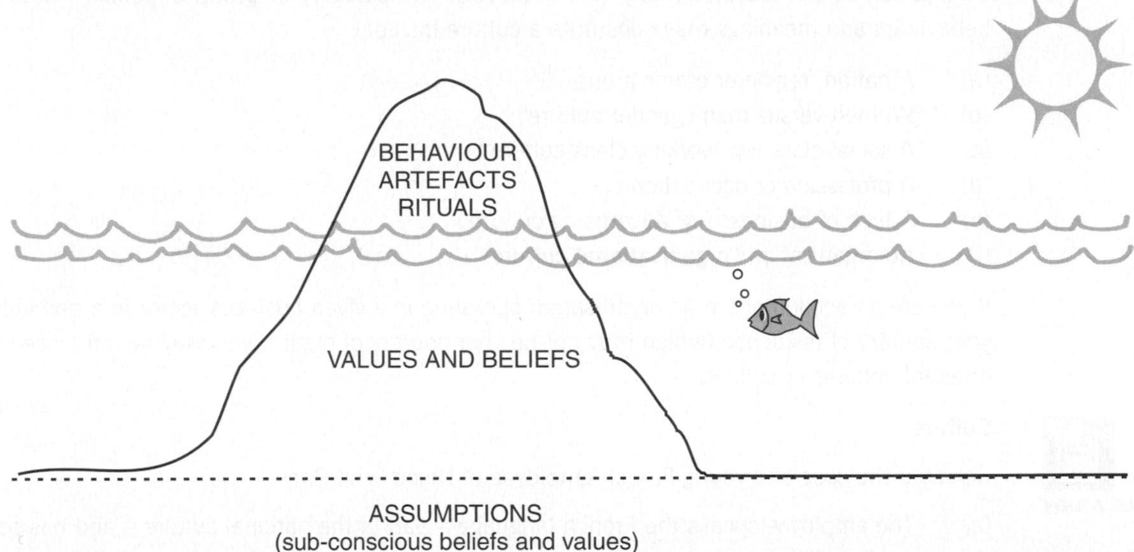

KEY POINT

Cultural assumptions, values and beliefs influence the behaviour of individuals, groups and organisations. They create a shared 'style' of operating within a given culture – but also the potential for misunderstanding and conflict **between** different cultural groups. An important aspect of culture management is to bring covert aspects of culture to the surface where they can be looked at and discussed: differences and influences can then be effectively understood and managed.

Section summary

Culture is 'the collective programming of the mind which distinguishes the members of one category of people from another' (Hofstede). It may be identified as ways of behaving, and ways of understanding, that are shared by a group of people.

Elements of culture include:

- Observable behaviour, artefacts, rituals and symbols
- Underlying values and beliefs that give meaning to the observable elements
- Hidden assumptions that unconsciously shape values and beliefs

2 Organisation culture

Introduction

We continue our study of culture by revisiting the iceberg and behaviour, artefacts and rituals from the last section. How do these explain culture in organisations? How would you as a manager be able to influence and interpret unseen cultural attitudes?

There are other models you can use to explain culture in organisations, including the '7 S' and cultural web.

Think of these as tools for explaining an organisation's culture which you could use to help you answer a question in your E2 exam or Integrated Case Study.

KEY TERM

ORGANISATION CULTURE may be defined as:

- 'The collection of traditions, values, policies, beliefs and attitudes that constitute a pervasive context for everything we do and think in an organisation' (Mullins)
- 'A pattern of beliefs and expectations shared by the organisation's members, and which produce norms which powerfully shape the behaviour of individuals and groups in the organisation' (Schwartz and Davies)
- 'The way we do things around here' (Schein)

2.1 Manifestations of culture in organisations

The following table provides **examples** of the organisational culture at Farmers supermarkets, applied to Schein's elements of culture.

Item	Example
Beliefs and values, which are often unquestioned	'The customer is always right.'
Behaviour	Every Farmers employee based in one of the company's stores is expected to wear the uniform provided. Those workers based at Farmers head office are permitted to participate in 'dress down Fridays', provided they comply with the company's rules on acceptable attire.
Artefacts	Every employee at Farmers supermarkets is made aware of the founder's background – 'the Nick Farmer story' – when they first join the organisation. This underlines how the business first started, and encourages employees to support the company in its aims of being a champion for UK farming.
Rituals	Many firms offer awards to outstanding staff members, given at a ceremony. At Farmers supermarkets, the company hosts an annual award ceremony, where those employees that are regarded as having 'gone above and beyond' in the performance of their role are recognised. Winners from across the business are awarded a 'Fantastic Farmers' award in a range of categories.
Symbols	Corporate logos are an example of symbols, but they are directed outwards. Within the organisation, symbols can represent power: dress, equipment and access to facilities can all be important symbols. In a typical Farmers store, every store manager is provided with a BMW car and is given their own office.

Manifestations of culture in an organisation may include:

(a) How formal the organisation structure is
(b) Communication: are senior managers approachable?
(c) Office layout
(d) The type of people employed
(e) Symbols, legends and corporate myths
(f) Management style
(g) Freedom for subordinates to show initiative
(h) Attitudes to quality
(i) Attitudes to risk
(j) Attitudes to the customer
(k) Attitudes to technology

Question 5.1 Manifestations of culture

Learning outcome B2b

What do you think would differentiate the culture of:

- A regiment in the army
- An advertising agency

2.2 The organisational iceberg

French and Bell (among others) apply the iceberg analogy specifically to organisations.

(a) **Overt aspects** (the tip of the iceberg) are the **formal aspects** of an organisation. These are financial resources, products, customers, formal structure, technology, policies, procedures and rules.

These are overt because they are visible (even to outsiders and new joiners), documented, controlled through formal management processes – and explicitly designed to support the mission of the organisation.

(b) **Covert aspects** (the larger, hidden part of the iceberg) are the **behavioural aspects** or culture. These include beliefs, assumptions and attitudes. Other covert aspects are informal communication patterns, informal team processes, informal influence and leadership, political behaviour and interpersonal relations.

These are not directly in control of management, not always supportive of the organisation's mission, and not readily visible to outsiders or new joiners.

KEY POINT

The challenge for managers is to be aware of covert cultural aspects and seek to influence them – as well as the more directly 'manageable' formal processes.

2.3 The McKinsey 7 S model

Another model, which depicts the interdependence of formal and cultural/behaviour elements in organisational management, is the McKinsey 7 S model.

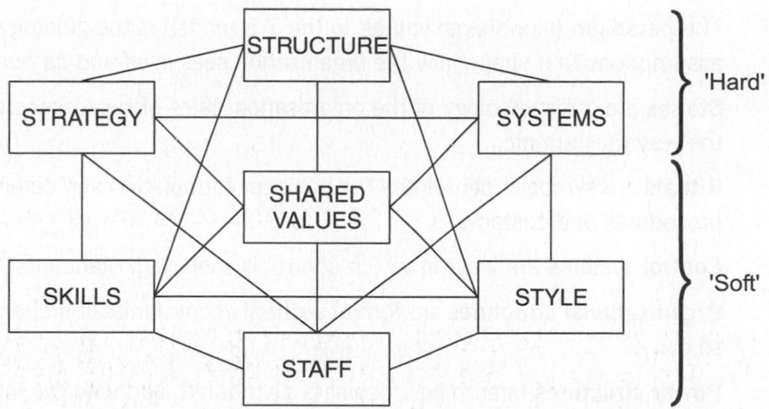

The important points to note here are that:

(a) Culture occupies a central position in the model, both in terms of style (corporate image, management style, patterns and norms of behaviour) and shared values (the underlying guiding beliefs and assumptions that shape the way the organisation sees itself and its purpose).

(b) All the elements are interlinked: altering any one variable will have an effect on the others and on the whole network.

Imagine that you wanted to reposition your organisation by offering unique levels of customer service in your industry (**strategy**). You might have to set up team working in customer-facing units to increase responsiveness (**structure**). You may have to recruit (**staff**) and train people in customer service skills (**skills**). They will also need new procedures and IT systems for better access to customer data (**systems**). Managers will have to adjust to empowering staff, and a new corporate image will be developed (**style**). But none of this will be sustainable unless there is also a fundamental shift in the organisation's values, to put the customer first (**shared values**).

KEY POINT

You may note from this example that culture (and each of the other elements) may both **shape strategy** – particularly in the resource-based view, where strategy is formulated on the basis of what the organisation is best (most competitive) at – and be **shaped by strategy** – particularly in a positioning view, where internal elements are adjusted to support strategic objectives.

2.4 The cultural web

Johnson and Scholes also use a 'web' as a way of representing 'the taken for granted assumptions, or paradigm, of an organisation, and the behavioural manifestations of organisation culture'.

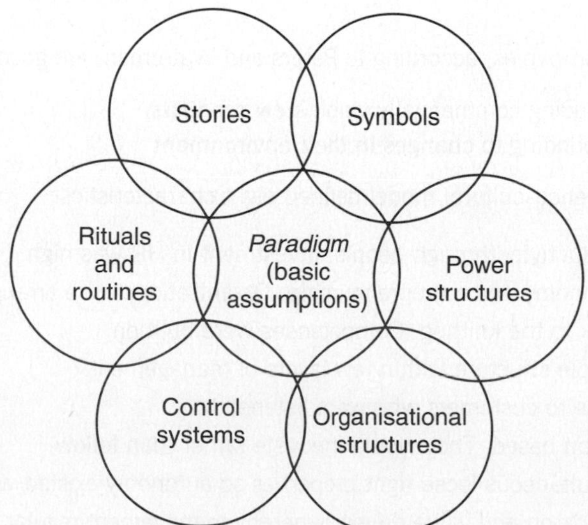

(a) The **paradigm** (like 'shared values' in the 7 S model) is the guiding set of beliefs, values and assumptions that shape how the organisation sees itself and its purpose.

(b) **Stories** are the 'mythology' of the organisation: tales of successes and failures, how things got to be the way they are etc.

(c) **Rituals** are symbolic behaviours (eg business formulation and ceremonies) and **routines** are formal procedures and customs.

(d) **Control systems** are ways in which control is exercised: standards, monitoring and supervision etc.

(e) **Organisational structures** are formal authority/communication channels, departments, teams and so on.

(f) **Power structures** refer to how power is distributed, and who the influential individuals and groups are.

(g) **Symbols** include formal logos and corporate identity, as well as things that take on symbolic value to people.

2.5 What shapes organisation culture?

Influences on organisational culture include:

(a) The organisation's **founder**. A strong set of values and assumptions is set up by the organisation's founder and, even after they have retired, these values have their own momentum. Or, to put it another way, an organisation might find it hard to shake off its original culture.

(b) The organisation's **history**.
  (i) Culture reflects the era when the organisation was founded.
  (ii) The effect of history can be determined by stories, rituals and symbolic behaviour. They legitimise behaviour and promote priorities.

(c) **Leadership and management style**. An organisation with a strong culture recruits and develops managers who naturally conform to it, who perpetuate the culture.

(d) The **organisation's environment**. As we have seen, nations, regions, occupations and business types have their own distinctive cultures, and these will affect the organisation's style.

2.6 Using and managing organisation culture

2.6.1 Culture and excellence

In 1982, Tom Peters and Robert Waterman published *In Search of Excellence.* Using an anecdotal approach, they set about describing and analysing what it was that made successful companies successful.

Excellent companies, according to Peters and Waterman, are good at two things:

(a) Producing commercially viable **new products**
(b) Responding to **changes in their environment**

Their 'excellence' cultural model defined eight characteristics:

(a) **P**roductivity through people. Investment in HR was high.
(b) **A**utonomy and entrepreneurship. Organisations were arranged in small, decentralised units.
(c) **S**tick to the knitting. Competences were built on.
(d) **S**imple structure within few layers of management.
(e) **C**lose to customers who were listened to.
(f) **A**ction based. They would innovate rather than follow.
(g) **S**imultaneous loose-tight properties so autonomy existed with centralisation.
(h) **H**ands-on and value driven, whereby management regularly met workers in the workplace.

These can be remembered by the **PASSCASH** mnemonic.

2.6.2 Cultural strength

Both Peters and Waterman and Deal and Kennedy argued that **cultural strength** is a powerful factor in shaping the behaviour and success of organisations. A 'strong' culture is one in which:

(a) Key values are widely shared and intensely held by employees.
(b) Employees allow themselves to be guided and motivated by these values.

Strong culture is said to improve overall business performance by:

(a) Replacing restrictive formal control systems. A few strong guiding values focus attention of strategic goals, empowering employees to take initiative and responsibility in pursuit of those aims. This in turn reduces rigidity, supports change and develops people.

(b) Increasing employee commitment, loyalty and job satisfaction.

You should be aware that, while this is an attractive and influential idea, empirical research has failed to show that strong-culture organisations are in fact any more successful in the long run than weak-culture organisations – or that culture is the determining factor in success (compared to other organisational, market or environmental factors).

2.7 Advantages and disadvantages of having a strong culture

An organisation's strategy and structure, and the relationship it has with its various stakeholders, will be significantly influenced by the organisation's culture.

A strong culture can bring thc following **advantages**.

(a) Provide a sense of identity and belonging
(b) Facilitate good internal communication and co-ordination
(c) Reduce differences between members of the organisation
(d) Regulate behaviour and norms
(e) Strengthen the dominant values and attitudes
(f) Reflect the philosophy of the organisation's founder or the dominant group
(g) Affect the organisation's strategy and ability to respond to change

However, a strong culture can also bring a number of **disadvantages**, including:

(a) Inflexibility; strong cultures can be deeply ingrained and difficult to change.

(b) Can create a blinkered view, preventing the organisation from learning new skills or taking on new challenges.

(c) If the strong culture is based on inappropriate values, it can cause the performance of the organisation to deteriorate.

(d) Effectiveness can be hindered if the strong culture does not have positive attributes in relation to stakeholders and change.

(e) Conflict can arise when two strong cultures come into contact, eg mergers.

(f) If the strong culture is out of synchronisation with the environment in which it operates, it will not be successful.

2.8 Changing corporate culture

So how can an organisation manage its culture, create a positive culture, or change a dysfunctional culture (or one that is unsuited to changing requirements)?

Models such as '7 S' and the cultural web suggests that any (ideally, all) elements of organisation can be manipulated to support cultural change. The key areas of leverage, however, are:

(a) **Changing the paradigm**. Changing underlying values and beliefs, through communication, education and involvement; spreading new values and beliefs and encouraging ownership (through the use of incentives, co-opting people to teach others and so on).

(b) **Top-down support**. Consistent, genuine expression, modelling and rewarding of new values and behaviour by senior management, leaders and influencers.

(c) **Reinforcement**. By human resource management (HRM) systems: including new values/behaviours in selection criteria, appraisal/reward criteria, and learning/developing planning.

Section summary

Organisation culture is '**the way we do things round here**'.

Cultural values can be used to guide organisational processes without the need for tight control. They can also be used to motivate employees, by emphasising the heroic dimension of the task. Culture can also be used to drive change, although – since values are difficult to change – it can also be a powerful force for preserving the status quo.

3 Culture and structure

Introduction

In this section, we look at the idea that culture can shape the structure of an organisation. The simplest example of this is the power culture (what Handy calls 'Zeus') where a strong individual dominates the culture of the organisation as founder. The organisation remains small and informal. There are three other cultural types of organisation described by Harrison and later Handy.

Remember that these are only indications of cultural types matching organisation structures, and may indeed only apply in parts of an organisation.

Writing in 1972, Harrison suggested that organisations could be classified into four types. His work was later popularised by Charles Handy in his book *Gods of Management*. The four types are differentiated by their structures, processes and management methods. The differences are so significant as to create **distinctive cultures**, to each of which Handy gives the name of a Greek god.

Zeus — **Power culture**	**Apollo** — **Role culture**
The organisation is controlled by a key central figure, owner or founder. Power is direct, personal and informal. Suits small organisations where people get on well.	Classical, rational organisation: bureaucracy. Stable, slow-changing, formalised and impersonal. Authority based on position and function.
Athena — **Task culture**	**Dionysus** — **Person culture**
Management is directed at outputs: problems solved and projects completed. Team based, horizontally structured, flexible and valuing expertise – to get the job done.	The purpose of the organisation is to serve the interests of the individuals who make it up: management is directed at facilitating and administering.

3.1 Power culture

Zeus is the god representing the **power culture** or **club culture**. Zeus is a dynamic entrepreneur who rules with snap decisions. Power and influence stem from a central source, perhaps the owner-directors or the founder of the business. The degree of formalisation is limited, and there are few rules and procedures. Such a firm is likely to be organised on a functional basis.

(a) The organisation is capable of adapting quickly to meet change.

(b) Personal influence decreases as the size of an organisation gets bigger. The power culture is therefore best suited to smaller entrepreneurial organisations, where the leaders have direct communication with all employees.

(c) Personnel have to get on well with each other for this culture to work. These organisations are clubs of 'like-minded people introduced by the like-minded people, working on empathetic initiative with personal contact rather than formal liaison'.

3.2 Role culture

Apollo is the god of the **role culture** or **bureaucracy**. There is a presumption of logic and rationality.

(a) These organisations have a formal structure, and operate according to well-established rules and procedures.

(b) Individuals are required to perform their job to the full, but not to overstep the boundaries of their authority. Individuals who work for such organisations tend to learn an expertise without experiencing risk; many do their job adequately, but are not overambitious.

(c) The bureaucratic style, as we have seen, can be very efficient in a stable environment, when the organisation is large and when the work is predictable.

3.3 Task culture

Athena is the goddess of the **task culture**. Management is seen as completing a succession of projects or solving problems.

(a) The task culture is reflected in **project teams** and task forces. In such organisations, there is no dominant or clear leader. The principal concern in a task culture is to get the job done. Therefore, the individuals who are important are the **experts** with the ability to accomplish a particular aspect of the task.

(b) Performance is judged by results.

(c) Task cultures are expensive, as experts demand a market price.

(d) Task cultures also depend on variety, and tapping creativity requires a tolerance of perhaps costly mistakes.

3.4 Person culture

Dionysus is the god of the **existential** or **person culture**. In the three other cultures, the individual is subordinate to the organisation or task. An existential culture is found in an organisation whose purpose is to serve the interests of the individuals within it. These organisations are rare, although an example might be a partnership of a few individuals who do all the work of the organisation themselves (with perhaps a little secretarial or clerical assistance): for example, barristers (in the UK) work through chambers.

Management positions in these organisations are often lower in status than the professionals and are labelled secretaries, administrators, bursars, registrars or clerks.

The organisation depends on the talent of the individuals; management is derived from the consent of the managed, rather than the delegated authority of the owners.

3.5 A contingency approach

When thinking about these four types of culture, remember that they do not necessarily equate to specific organisation types, though some styles of organisation culture may accompany particular organisation structures. Also, it is quite possible for different cultures to prevail in different parts of the same organisation, especially large ones with many departments and sites. In other words, as the contingency approach says: 'it all depends'.

CASE STUDY

Handy

Handy cites a pharmaceutical company that at one time had all its manufacturing subcontracted, until the turnover and cost considerations justified a factory of its own. The company hired nine talented individuals to design and run the factory.

(a) The **design team** ran on a task culture, with a democratic/consultative leadership style, using project teams for certain problems. This was successful while the factory was being built.

(b) After its opening, the **factory**, staffed by 400, was run on similar lines. There were numerous problems. Every problem was treated as a project, and the workforce resented being asked to help sort out 'management' problems. In the end, the factory was run in a slightly more autocratic way. Handy states that this is a classic case of a task culture (to set something up) being superseded by a role culture (to run it). Different cultures suit different businesses.

Handy also matched appropriate cultural models to Robert Anthony's classification of managerial activity.

(a) **Strategic management** (carried out by senior management) is concerned with direction setting, policy making and crisis handling. It therefore suits a **power culture.**

(b) **Tactical management** (carried out by middle management) is concerned with establishing means to the corporate ends, mobilising resources and innovating (finding new ways of achieving goals). It therefore suits a **task culture.**

(c) **Operational management** (carried out by supervisors and operatives) is concerned with routine activities to carry out tactical plans. It therefore suits a **role culture.**

Question 5.2 Classifications of culture

Learning outcome B2b

Review the following statements. Ascribe each of them to one of Harrison/Handy's four corporate cultures.

People are controlled and influenced by:

(a) The personal exercise of rewards, punishments or charisma

(b) Impersonal exercise of economic and political power to enforce procedures and standards of performance

(c) Communication and discussion of task requirements leading to appropriate action motivated by personal commitment to goal achievement

(d) Intrinsic interest and enjoyment in the activities to be done and/or concern and caring for the needs of the other people involved

Section summary

Harrison classified four types of culture, to which Handy gave the names of Greek deities.

- **Power** culture (Zeus) is shaped by one individual.
- **Role** culture (Apollo) is a bureaucratic culture shaped by rationality, rules and procedures.
- **Task** culture (Athena) is shaped by a focus on outputs and results.
- **Existential** or person culture (Dionysus) is shaped by the interests of individuals.

4 Culture and strategy

Introduction

If culture is the way things are done, perhaps it is not surprising that it can be aligned with the strategy an organisation adopts. Miles and Snow describe four types of culture in an organisation and how these exhibit certain strategies. Denison takes a different approach by classifying organisations according to internal/external strategic orientation and environmental stability/dynamism. He uses this classification to describe organisations as one of four cultural types.

Finally, Deal and Kennedy describe four cultures that arise out of a combination of risk taking and speed of feedback.

Use these models if you want to illustrate how strategy may be linked to the individual organisation and its culture.

4.1 Miles and Snow

Miles and Snow characterised four cultural types, and the kinds of strategies they are likely to support.

(a) **Defenders** like low risks, secure niche markets, and tried and trusted solutions. These companies have cultures whose stories and rituals reflect historical continuity and consensus. Decision taking is relatively formalised. (There is a stress on 'doing things right', ie efficiency.) Personnel are drawn from within the industry.

(b) **Prospectors** are organisations where the dominant beliefs are more to do with results (doing the right things, ie effectiveness). They seek to expand and increase market presence, and move into new areas.

(c) **Analysers** try to balance risk and profits. They use a core of stable products and markets as a source of earnings, like defenders, but move into areas that prospectors have already opened up. Analysers follow change, but do not initiate it.

(d) **Reactors** do not have viable strategies, other than living from hand to mouth: they simply respond to external demands and changes.

4.2 Denison

Denison's model uses a grid to assess the relationship of culture, strategy and the environment. There are two dimensions.

(a) How orientated is the firm to the environment rather than to its internal workings? (An internal orientation is not always a bad thing, eg maintaining the safety of a nuclear installation.)

(b) To what extent does the environment offer stability or change?

		Organisation's strategic orientation	
		Internal	External
Environmental responses required	Stability	Consistency	Mission
	Change/flexibility	Involvement	Adaptability

In Denison's analysis, there are thus four possible cultures.

(a) **Consistency culture**. This exists in a stable environment, and its structure is well integrated. Management are preoccupied with efficiency. Such cultures are characterised by formal ways of behaviour. Predictability and reliability are valued. This has some features in common with the Apollonian culture.

(b) **Mission culture**. The environment is relatively stable, and the organisation is orientated towards it (eg 'customers'). A mission culture, whereby members' work activities are given meaning and value, is appropriate. For example, hospitals are preoccupied with the sick: inevitably their values are 'customer' orientated. A church is concerned with saving souls.

(c) **Involvement culture**. The basic premise is that the satisfaction of employees' needs is necessary for them to provide optimum performance. An example might be an orchestra, whose performance depends on each individual. Involvement and participation are supposed to create a greater sense of commitment, and hence performance. For example, if you train people well enough, it is assumed that they will perform well. An involvement culture might take a 'human relations' approach to management.

(d) **Adaptability culture**. The company's strategic focus is on the external environment, which is in a state of change. Corporate values encourage inquisitiveness and interest in the external environment. Fashion companies are an example: ideas come from a variety of sources. Customer needs are fickle and change rapidly.

Question 5.3 — Contrasting cultural models

Learning outcome B2b

(a) What do you think is the most significant contrast between Denison's model and Harrison's model?

(b) Which is better?

4.3 Deal and Kennedy

Deal and Kennedy (*Corporate Cultures*, 1982) consider cultures to be a function of the willingness of employees to take **risks**, and how quickly they get **feedback** on whether they got it right or wrong.

High risk

Slow feedback	*Fast feedback*
BET YOUR COMPANY CULTURE ('Slow and steady wins the race') Long decision-cycles: stamina and nerve required eg oil companies, aircraft companies, architects	HARD 'MACHO' CULTURE ('Find a mountain and climb it') eg entertainment, management consultancy, advertising
PROCESS CULTURE ('It's not what you do, it's the way that you do it') Values centred on attention to excellence of technical detail, risk management, procedures, status symbols eg banks, financial services, government	WORK HARD/PLAY HARD CULTURE ('Find a need and fill it') All action – and fun: team spirit eg sales and retail, computer companies.

Low risk

Deal and Kennedy suggest that some companies blend elements of all four cultural types, and that this can enable them to respond well to environmental change. The stronger the culture, the more successful the company is likely to be, as discussed earlier.

Section summary

A model of culture that focuses specifically on a firm's approach to strategy was suggested by **Miles and Snow**, who outlined three strategic cultures, and a fourth 'non-strategic' culture.

Denison analyses cultural types on two axes: internal/external strategic orientation and environmental stability/dynamism.

Deal and Kennedy plot cultural types on two dimensions: willingness to take risks and speed of feedback on results.

5 Cross-cultural leadership

Introduction

Different countries have different ways of doing business, and different cultural values and assumptions that influence business and management styles.

Ouchi studied US and Japanese companies, and concluded that there was a 'third way' of management that combined the best of both cultures. He named this Theory Z.

Hofstede researched offices in a large multinational organisation in over 60 countries. From this, he identified four characteristics that differed according to the country and which affected the culture of the organisation in that country.

5.1 Ouchi – Theory Z

When the Japanese economy was performing well, a generation ago, it became fashionable to study Japanese management methods and promote them as a solution to the West's then seemingly intractable industrial problems. Profiling US management culture as 'Theory A' and typical Japanese management as 'Theory J', William Ouchi sought to synthesise the two, to propose a form of Japanese-style management that could be successfully applied in Western contexts. Ouchi called these methods 'Theory Z'.

The characteristics of a **Theory Z** organisation offer some interesting contrasts with the Western way of doing things, notably in key Japanese values such as consensus decision making and mutual loyalty in the employment relationship.

Ouchi described the Theory Z organisation as being characterised by:

(a) **Long-term employment, with slow-progressing managerial career paths** (as in the Japanese system, but with a more Western specialisation of skills)

(b) **Broad concern for employee welfare**, both inside and outside the work context (not just work performance, as in the Western system): commitment to the 'organisation family'

(c) **Implicit informal controls** (such as guiding values) alongside explicit, formal measures

(d) **Collective consensus decision-making processes** (Japanese), but with individual retention of ultimate responsibility for defined areas of accountability (Western)

(e) **Industrial relations characterised by trust, co-operation and mutual adjustment**, rather than unionisation, demarcation and artificial status barriers

Theory Z was welcomed as a more human, and therefore more effective, way of managing employee relations: Marks & Spencer in the UK has been cited as an organisation operating on principles akin to Theory Z. Elements of the approach have been incorporated into the HRM orientation to management, which regards committed people as the key resource of a business. However, it is less easy to transfer cultural values to foreign contexts than it is to apply methods and techniques: employee development programmes and quality circles have been adopted without necessarily being underpinned by Theory Z values.

5.2 The Hofstede model

Hofstede (1984) carried out cross-cultural research at 66 national offices of IBM, and formulated one of the most influential models of work-related cultural differences.

The Hofstede model describes four main dimensions of difference between national cultures, which impact on all aspects of management and organisational behaviour: motivation, team working, leadership style, conflict management and HR policies.

(a) **Power distance**. The extent to which unequal distribution of power is accepted.

  (i) **High PD cultures** (as in Latin, near Eastern and less developed Asian countries) accept greater centralisation, a top-down chain of command and closer supervision. Subordinates have little expectation of influencing decisions.

  (ii) **Low PD cultures** (as in Germanic, Anglo and Nordic countries) expect less centralisation and flatter organisational structures. Subordinates expect involvement and participation in decision making. (Japan is a medium PD culture.)

(b) **Uncertainty avoidance**. The extent to which security, order and control are preferred to ambiguity, uncertainty and change.

  (i) **High UA cultures** (as in Latin, near Eastern and Germanic countries and Japan) respect control, certainty and ritual. They value task structure, written rules and regulations, specialists and experts, and standardisation. There is a strong need for consensus: deviance and dissent are not tolerated. The work ethic is strong.

  (ii) **Low UA cultures** (as in Anglo and Nordic countries) respect flexibility and creativity. They have less task structure and fewer written rules; more generalists and greater variability. There is more tolerance of risk, dissent, conflict and deviation from norms.

(c) **Individualism**. The extent to which people prefer to live and work in individualist (focusing on the 'I' identity) or collectivist (focusing on the 'we' identity) ways.

  (i) **High individualism cultures** (as in Anglo, more developed Latin and Nordic countries) emphasise autonomy and individual choice and responsibility. They prize individual initiative. The organisation is impersonal and tends to defend business interests: task achievement is more important than relationships. Management is seen in an individual context.

  (ii) **Low individualism (or collectivist) cultures** (as in less developed Latin, near Eastern and less developed Asian countries) emphasise interdependence, reciprocal obligation and social acceptability. The organisation is seen as a 'family' and tends to defend employees' interests: relationships are more important than task achievement. Management is seen in a team context. (Japan and Germany are 'medium' cultures on this dimension.)

(d) **Masculinity**. The extent to which social gender roles are distinct. (Note that this is different from the usual sense in which the terms 'masculine' and 'feminine' are used.)

  (i) **High masculinity cultures** (as in Japan and Germanic and Anglo countries) clearly differentiate gender roles. Masculine values of assertiveness, competition, decisiveness and material success are dominant. Feminine values of modesty, tenderness, consensus, focus on relationships and quality of working life are less highly regarded, and confined to women.

(ii) **Low masculinity (or feminine) cultures** (as in Nordic countries) minimise gender roles. Feminine values are dominant – and both men and women are allowed to behave accordingly.

Question 5.4 National culture and management style

Learning outcome B2b

According to the Hofstede model, what issues might arise in the following cases?

(a) The newly appointed Spanish (more developed Latin) R&D manager of a UK (Anglo) firm asks to see the Rules and Procedures Manual for the department.

(b) A US-trained (Anglo) manager attempts to implement a system of management by objectives in Thailand (less developed Asian).

(c) A Dutch (Nordic) HR manager of a US (Anglo) subsidiary in the Netherlands is instructed to implement downsizing measures.

Exam alert

Questions in your E2 examination may focus on Hofstede's research and could require you to assess the compatibility of a corporation's intended **strategy** with the culture of a country in which it wanted to start to do business.

KEY POINT

Apart from these models, a manager operating in a cross-cultural or international environment will need to be **sensitive** to potential cultural assumptions and differences, and **flexible** in adapting to their demands. This will particularly be the case when working in **virtual teams** (geographically dispersed but collaborating using information and communications technology links). Project teams may now be global – and team leaders may have to deal with:

(a) Differences in cultural values (eg about seniority or the role of women)

(b) Differences in social and business customs (eg business gifts, religious observances)

(c) Differences in communication, negotiating and conflict resolution styles (eg different tolerance for challenging authority or displays of emotion)

(d) Language barriers

(e) Difference in education/qualifications

(f) Different time zones for communicating with team members

CASE STUDY

National culture

'French managers see their work as an intellectual challenge, requiring the remorseless application of individual brainpower. They do not share the Anglo-Saxon view of management as an interpersonally demanding exercise, where plans have to be constantly "sold" upward and downward using personal skills.

'Selection interviewers need to allow for cultural influences on interviewees' behaviour. For instance, Chinese applicants in Singapore tend to defer to the interviewer, whom they treat as "superior", and to focus on the group or family, besides avoiding self-assertion ... Hence, applicants from a Chinese background may be disadvantaged when being interviewed for jobs with multinational companies that are heavily influenced by Anglo-American culture.' (Guirdham)

Section summary

National culture (and other factors in the international environment) poses a challenge for managers working in **cross-cultural and international contexts**. **Ouchi** combined the US and Japanese ways of management in an ideal 'Theory Z' approach.

National culture influences organisation culture in various ways. One model of these effects is the 'Hofstede model', which describes four dimensions on which cultures differ:

- Power distance
- Uncertainty avoidance
- Individuality/collectivity
- Masculinity/femininity

Chapter Summary

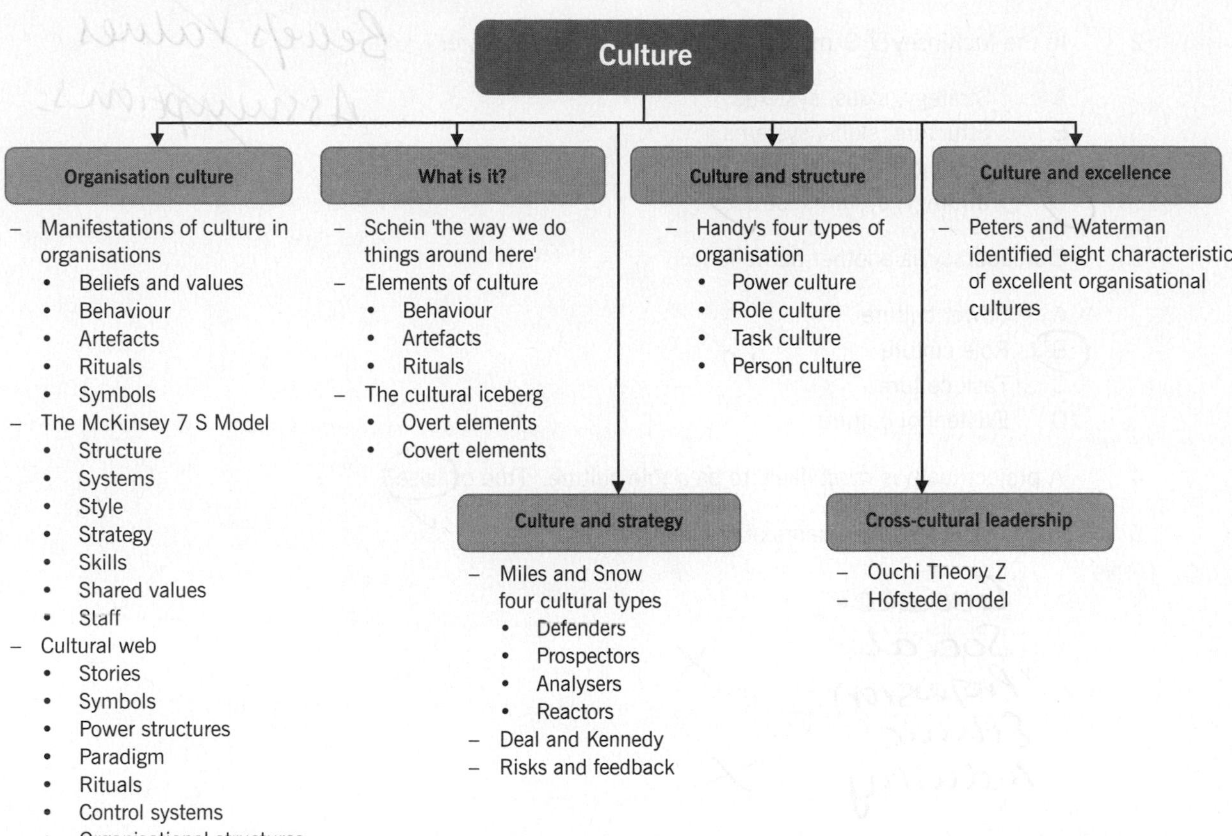
Culture
Organisation culture
– Manifestations of culture in organisations
• Beliefs and values
• Behaviour
• Artefacts
• Rituals
• Symbols
– The McKinsey 7 S Model
• Structure
• Systems
• Style
• Strategy
• Skills
• Shared values
• Staff
– Cultural web
• Stories
• Symbols
• Power structures
• Paradigm
• Rituals
• Control systems
• Organisational structures
What is it?
– Schein 'the way we do things around here'
– Elements of culture
• Behaviour
• Artefacts
• Rituals
– The cultural iceberg
• Overt elements
• Covert elements
Culture and structure
– Handy's four types of organisation
• Power culture
• Role culture
• Task culture
• Person culture
Culture and excellence
– Peters and Waterman identified eight characteristics of excellent organisational cultures
Culture and strategy
– Miles and Snow four cultural types
• Defenders
• Prospectors
• Analysers
• Reactors
– Deal and Kennedy
– Risks and feedback
Cross-cultural leadership
– Ouchi Theory Z
– Hofstede model

Quick Quiz

1 What are the elements of culture, according to Schein?

2 In the McKinsey '7 S' model, the three 'hard' elements are:

A Strategy, skills, systems
B Structure, skills, systems
C Strategy, skills, staff
D Strategy, systems, structure

3 'Bureaucracy' is another name for a:

A Power culture
B Role culture
C Task culture
D Existential culture

4 'A project team is most likely to be a role culture.' True or false?

5 Identify the seven elements of the cultural web.

Answers to Quick Quiz

1 Observable phenomena (behaviour, artefacts, rituals), values and beliefs, and assumptions.

2 D

3 B

4 False. It is most likely to be a task culture.

5 Paradigm, symbols, stories, rituals and routines, control systems, organisation structures, and power structures.

Answers to Questions

5.1 Manifestations of culture

Here are some hints. The army is very disciplined. Decisions are made by officers; behaviour between ranks is sometimes very formal. The organisation values loyalty, courage and discipline and teamwork. Symbols and artefacts include uniforms, medals, regimental badges and so on. Rituals include corporate expressions such as parades and ceremonies.

An advertising agency, with a different mission, is more fluid. Individual flair and creativity, within the commercial needs of the firm, is expected. Artefacts may include the style of creative offices, awards or prizes, and the agency logo. Rituals may include various award ceremonies, team meetings and social gatherings.

5.2 Classifications of culture

(a) Zeus/power culture
(b) Apollo/role culture
(c) Athena/task culture
(d) Dionysus/person culture

5.3 Contrasting cultural models

(a) Harrison's model places much more emphasis on organisation structure and systems, which both determine and are determined by culture. Harrison's model describes actual cultures. Denison's model describes **ideal** cultures, and is more concerned with the environment and a firm's external orientation than its structure. Denison suggests that if the environment is stable **and** the business is most effective with an internal orientation, **then** a consistency culture will be **best** and so on.

(b) It depends on what you wish to use each model for.

5.4 National culture and management style

(a) A high-UA manager, expecting to find detailed and generally adhered-to rules for everything, may be horrified by the ad-hocracy of a low-UA organisation: if they attempt to impose a high-UA culture, there may be resistance from employees and management.

(b) A high-individuality manager may implement MbO on the basis of individual performance targets, results and rewards: this may fail to motivate collectivist workers, for whom group processes and performance is more important.

(c) A low-masculinity manager may try to shelter the workforce from the effects of downsizing, taking time for consultation, retraining, voluntary measures and so on: this may seem unacceptably 'soft' to a high-masculinity parent firm.

Now try these questions from the Practice Question Bank

Question	Level
5.1 – 5.5	Practice
X Company (part b)	Practice
Corporate culture	Practice

MANAGING RELATIONSHIPS

Part C

COMMUNICATION, NEGOTIATION AND CONFLICT

As we saw in the previous chapter, the way in which people interact at work is influenced by the culture of the organisation. Communication is central to such interactions.

In this chapter, we continue our study into general management and leadership issues, looking at communication, negotiation and the role of conflict.

We start with communication, which is a key skill of anyone in an organisation. However, it can go wrong, so we spend some time looking at how it may be improved.

Negotiation is simply the process of meeting to achieve a mutually acceptable outcome. It is used in many workplace contexts, including agreeing contracts and trade union issues.

These topics could each be examined from a theoretical or practical point of view. They are also highly relevant to project management (communicating and negotiating with project stakeholders, for example) and specific projects (eg change management).

We then go on to look at conflict, which may be seen as a failure of control. However, some regard conflict as inevitable and useful in moving forward (evolution). Others see it as a symptom of failure in relationships. We consider both views in the chapter.

Conflict may arise from rivalry between peers, or vertically up and down the hierarchy. One of management's key roles is managing conflict between parties.

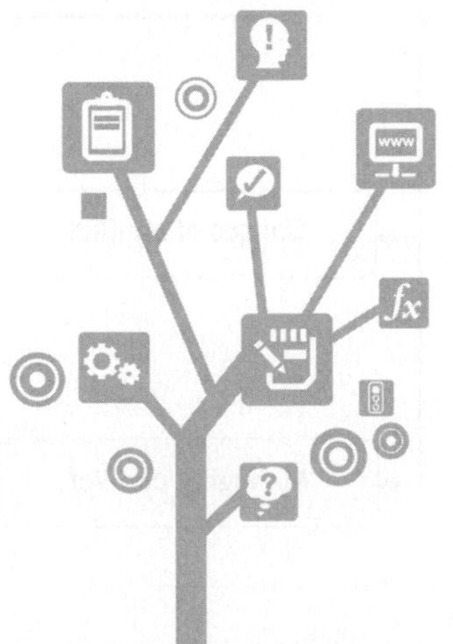

Topic list	Learning outcomes	Syllabus references	Ability required
1 Communication	C2a	C2(i), (ii), (iii)	Analysis
2 Negotiation	C2a	C2(iv), (v), (vi)	Analysis
3 The nature of conflict	C2b	C2(ii)	Analysis
4 Causes of conflict	C2b	C2(i)	Analysis
5 Managing conflict	C2b	C2(iii)	Analysis

Chapter Overview

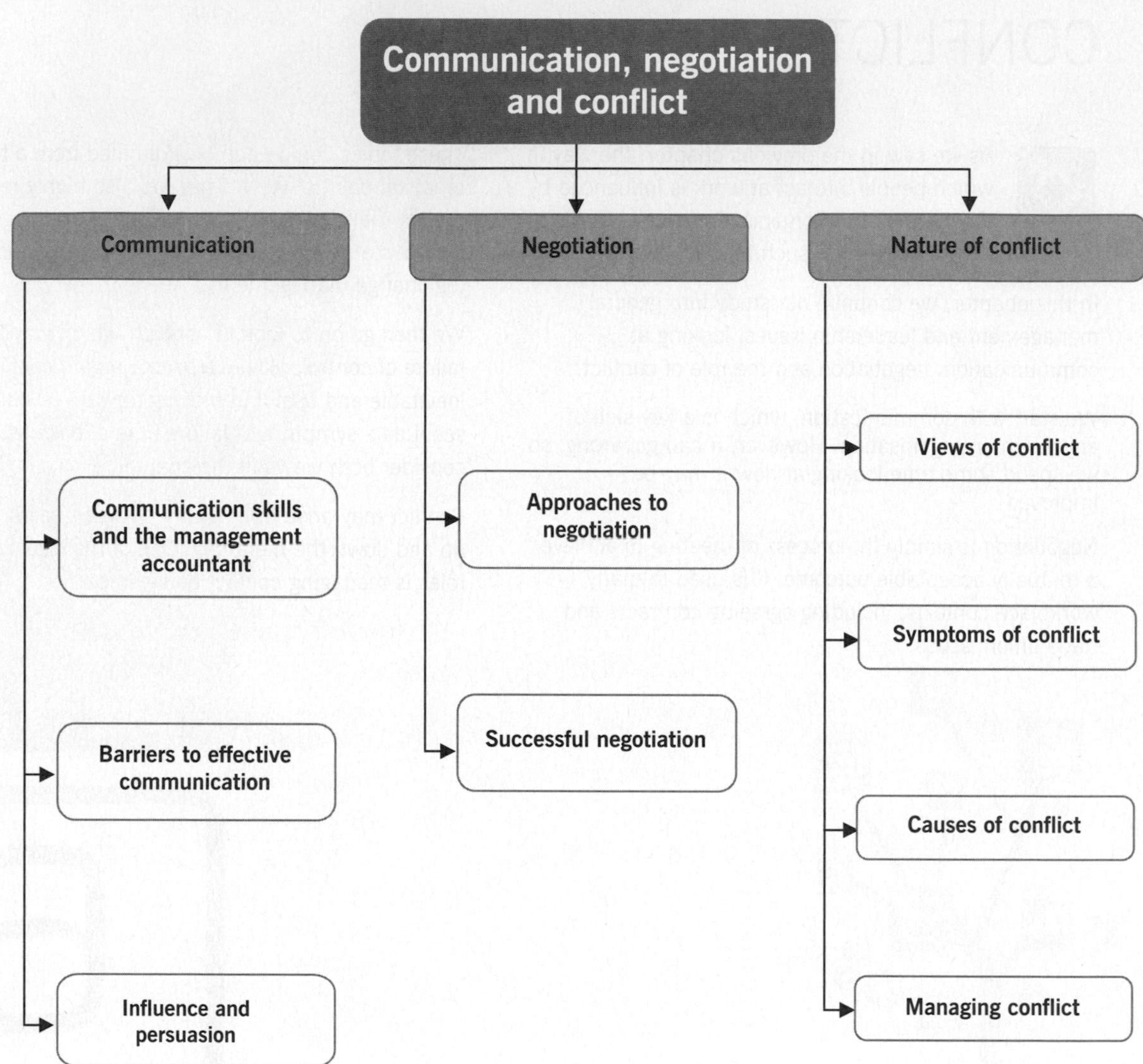

1 Communication

Introduction

We start this chapter with a run through of communication and how it works. As we shall discuss, the ability to communicate effectively is an important skill that the modern management accountant needs to develop. Communication has many forms, including non-verbal and written. You need to decide which method is most appropriate to your message and who is receiving it. A little thought and preparation will improve your communication skills. We explain how you can improve your message when it is misunderstood.

1.1 The purpose of communication

In an organisational context, communication has a wide variety of purposes (and specific aims). These can be broadly summarised as follows.

(a) Providing information to support managerial decision making, planning and control

(b) Providing information to co-ordinate the plans and activities of different units, functions and individuals

(c) Communicating organisational goals, plans and structure to those who will implement them

(d) Generating and exchanging ideas and knowledge for learning and innovation

(e) Gathering information from the external environment, and internal and external stakeholders, in order to shape strategy and managerial responses

(f) Providing information to external and internal stakeholders to secure awareness of, and 'buy-in' to, the organisation's plans

(g) Developing and maintaining relationships with network partners, stakeholders and employees

Managers (like management accountants) are a hub of information flow in the organisation.

1.1.1 Effective communication skills and the management accountant

The role of the finance function is intrinsic to the operation of most modern businesses. Today, the chartered management accountant often sits at the centre of the organisation's business dealings, which requires the possession of effective communication skills.

Need for effective communication skills	Comment
Wide range of users	Reports and financial data produced by the management accountant are likely to be used by a wide range of users, including managers at different levels within the organisation. As users have different requirements, it is important that the financial information communicated is targeted to the needs of the user in an appropriate manner to support their understanding. Effective communication for a management accountant involves recognising that not all users are accountants. Therefore, the use of unnecessary technical jargon should be kept to a minimum.

Need for effective communication skills	Comment
Assist the decision-making process	The effective communication of financial information should help users extract meaning from it, as opposed to merely reporting facts. For example, operational departments will require a benchmark to assess performance. The management accountant should provide reports, detailing actual performance, eg actual sales against budgeted sales, from which management can base future operational decisions.
Stakeholder interests	Key stakeholder groups are likely to be highly interested in the work of the management accountant. Investors will want to know how their investment is performing, and will spend time reviewing company financial statements. It is important that the management accountant accurately communicates the financial performance and position of the entity in a timely fashion, to support investors with investment decisions. Well-communicated information is likely to increase investor confidence in dealing with the organisation. Providers of finance such as banks will likely require regular reports on key financial metrics, including a breakdown of the entities' accounts receivables and cash position, as these may form the basis for decisions concerning future financial support, eg extending bank loans. The management accountant must therefore communicate such information clearly for use by the bank to secure finance. The management accountant may also play an important role in communicating the organisation's tax position to government authorities. The entity's tax position needs to be communicated by the necessary regulatory deadline and presented in the required format (eg written form) to ensure compliance with local tax laws.
Complex nature of accounting	The increasingly complex nature of global accounting transactions increases the need for effective communication skills. Management accountants are likely to need to prepare backup documentation and workings to help illustrate to certain users, eg management, how certain accounting figures were derived.

1.2 Direction of information flows

Formal channels of communication in an organisation may run in three main directions.

(a) **Vertical**, ie up and down the scalar chain.

   (i) **Downward** communication is very common, and takes the form of instructions, briefings, rules and policies, announcement of plans and so on, from superior to subordinate.

   (ii) **Upward** communication is rarer, but very important for the organisation. It takes the form of reporting back, feedback, suggestions and so on. Managers need to encourage upward communication to take advantage of employees' experience and know-how, and to be able to understand their problems and needs in order to manage better.

(b) **Horizontal or lateral** between people of the same rank, in the same section or department, or in different sections or departments. Horizontal communication between 'peer groups' is usually easier and more direct than vertical communication, being less inhibited by considerations of rank.

(i) **Formally**. To co-ordinate the work of several people, and perhaps departments, who have to co-operate to carry out a certain operation.

(ii) **Informally**. To furnish emotional and social support to an individual.

(c) **Diagonal**. This is interdepartmental communication by people of different ranks. Departments in the technostructure that serve the organisation in general, such as human resources and information systems, have no clear 'line authority' linking them to managers in other departments who need their involvement. Diagonal communication aids co-ordination, and also innovation and problem solving, as it puts together the ideas and information of people in different functions and levels. It also helps to bypass longer, less direct channels, avoiding blockages and speeding up decision making.

1.3 The communication process

The communication process can be broken down into five stages. It is important to note that a message can be in a variety of forms (written, oral and non-verbal) and can include a mixture of numbers and words.

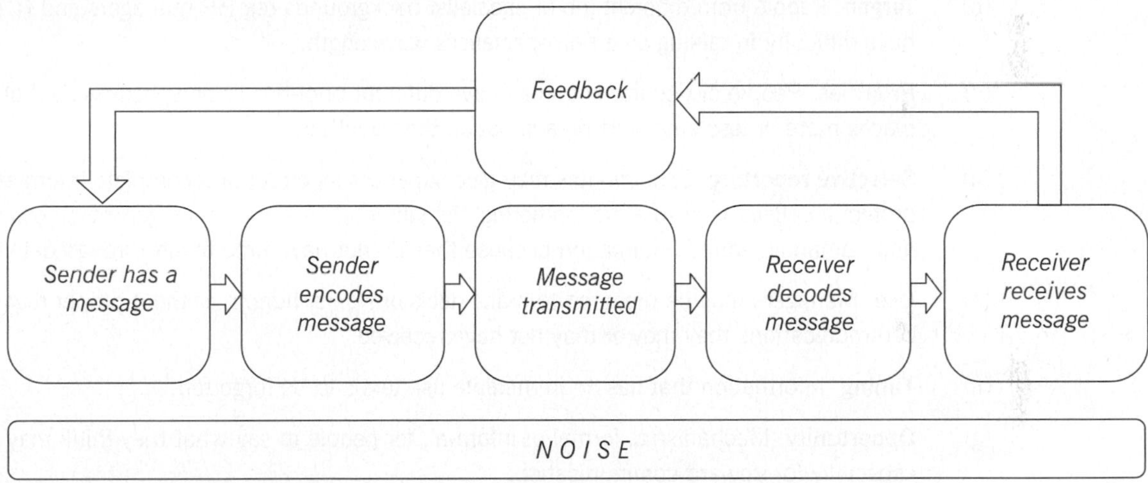

As the diagram illustrates, when a message is sent it passes through each of the stages outlined.

(1) Sender. The sender is the person or organisation that initially sends the message.

(2) Encoding the message. Encoding refers to the process of transferring the information the sender wishes to send into a given form, for example putting information into words.

(3) Message is transmitted. This stage is sometimes referred to as the channel as it relates to the medium used to send the message, for example, letter, email, meeting.

(4) Receiver. The receiver is the recipient of the message.

(5) Decoding the message. Decoding is the stage where the receiver processes the message into meaning.

(6) Feedback. This stage involves the receiver replying to the sender's message.

1.4 Barriers to effective communication

General problems that can occur in the communication process include:

(a) **Distortion**. A process by which the meaning of a message is lost 'in translation'. Misunderstanding may arise from technical or ambiguous language, misinterpretation of symbols etc.

(b) **Noise**. Interference in the environment of communication that prevents the message getting through clearly, eg due to physical noise, technical interference, or interpersonal differences making communication difficult.

(c) **Misunderstanding** due to lack of clarity or technical jargon.

(d) **Non-verbal signs** (gesture, facial expression) contradicting the verbal message.

(e) Failure to give or to seek **feedback**.

(f) **'Overload'**. A person being given too much information to digest in the time available.

(g) **Perceptual selection**. People hearing only what they want to hear in a message.

(h) **Differences** in social, racial or educational background.

(i) **Poor communication skills** on the part of the sender or recipient.

Additional difficulties may arise from the **work context**, including:

(a) **Status** (of the sender and receiver of information)

   (i) A senior manager's words are listened to closely and a colleague's perhaps discounted.

   (ii) A subordinate might mistrust their superior's intentions, and might look for 'hidden meanings' in a message.

(b) **Jargon**. People from different job or specialist backgrounds (eg HR managers and IT experts) can have difficulty in talking on a non-specialist's wavelength.

(c) **Priorities**. People or departments may have different priorities or perspectives so that one person places more or less emphasis on a situation than another.

(d) **Selective reporting**. Subordinates may give superiors incorrect or incomplete information (eg to protect a colleague or to avoid 'bothering' the superior). A senior manager may, however, only be able to handle edited information because they do not have time to sift through details.

(e) **Use**. Managers may be prepared to make decisions on a 'hunch', without proper regard to the communications they may or may not have received.

(f) **Timing**. Information that has no immediate use tends to be forgotten.

(g) **Opportunity**. Mechanisms, formal or informal, for people to say what they think may be lacking, especially for upward communication.

(h) **Conflict**. Where there is conflict between individuals or departments, communications will be withdrawn and information withheld.

(i) **Cultural values** about communication. For example:

   (i) **Secrecy**. Information might be given on a need to know basis, rather than considered as a potential resource for everyone to use.

   (ii) **Can't handle bad news**. The culture of some organisations may prevent the communication of certain messages. Organisations with a 'can-do' philosophy may not want to hear that certain tasks are impossible, for example.

Question 6.1 Communication

Learning outcome C2a

Is the statement below true or false?

'A clearly expressed verbal message will always be understood.'

1.5 Improving communication

Depending on the problem, measures to improve communication may be as follows.

(a) **Encourage, facilitate and reward** communication. Status and functional barriers (particularly to upward and interfunctional communication) can be minimised by improving opportunities for formal and informal networking and feedback.

(b) **Give training and guidance** in communication skills, including consideration of recipients, listening, giving feedback and so on.

(c) **Minimise the potential for misunderstanding**. Make people aware of the difficulties arising from differences in culture and perception, and teach them to consider others' viewpoints.

(d) **Adapt technology, systems and procedures** to facilitate communication: making it more effective (clear mobile phone reception), faster (laptops for emailing instructions), more consistent (regular reporting routines) and more efficient (reporting by exception).

(e) **Manage conflict and politics** in the organisation, so that no basic unwillingness exists between units.

(f) **Establish communication channels and mechanisms** in all directions: regular staff or briefing meetings, house journal or intranet, quality circles and so on. Upward communication should particularly be encouraged, using mechanisms such as inter-unit meetings, suggestion schemes, 'open door' access to managers and regular performance management feedback sessions.

Communication between superiors and subordinates will be improved when **interpersonal trust** exists. Exactly how this is achieved will depend on the management style of the manager, the attitudes and personality of the individuals involved, and other environmental variables. Peters and Waterman advocate 'management by walking around' and **informality in superior/subordinate relationships**, as a means of establishing closer links.

1.6 Communication methods and media

1.6.1 Written communication

A range of written communication media is used in business contexts, for one to one and one to group communication. Examples include: letters, reports, forms, notice boards, email, information leaflets, manuals and handbooks, and the minutes of meetings.

The key advantages of written formats are that:

(a) They focus the attention of the sender and receiver
(b) They enable subsequent and repeated reference to information and agreements
(c) They provide legally acceptable evidence of the information and agreements exchanged
(d) They enable both confidentiality (where required) and sharing/copying of information

1.6.2 Oral and face to face communication

Oral and face to face verbal media are also widespread in organisations, in forms such as: telephone calls or teleconferencing; discussions, meetings and interviews (and their electronic equivalents in webcasts and video-conferencing); brainstorming sessions, quality circles, team briefings; and large-scale public or shareholder meetings.

These kinds of media are particularly good for:

(a) Generating new ideas, because of their real-time information sharing and interactivity (as in brainstorming)

(b) Interactive feedback, exchange of views and questioning (without the lead time required for responses in writing)

(c) The availability of non-verbal cues (including tone of voice and, in face to face communication, body language) to support interpretation of underlying meaning and messages

(d) Personal interactions and relationship building (because of the ability to build rapport and be sensitive to the audience's needs and responses)

(e) Spreading information informally to large groups of people, with opportunities for interactive feedback and questions (as in briefings and public meetings)

Confirmation and reference material can often be provided in writing for, or following, conversations and meetings, in order to support more detailed and repeated reference, where necessary.

1.6.3 Non-verbal communication

Non-verbal communication (often called **body language**) consists of facial expression, posture, proximity, gestures and non-verbal noises (grunts, yawns etc).

Consciously or unconsciously, we send messages through body language during every face to face encounter. We can use it deliberately to **confirm** our verbal message – for example, by nodding and smiling as we tell someone we are happy to help them – or to **contradict** it, if we want to be sarcastic (saying 'How interesting!' with a yawn, for example).

More often, however, our body language contradicts our verbal message **without** our being aware of it, giving a 'mixed message' such as saying that you understand an instruction while looking extremely perplexed. Body language can also 'give away' messages that we would – for social or business reasons – rather not send, such as lack of interest and hostility.

Control and use of body language is needed to:

(a) Provide 'physical' feedback to the sender of a message (eg a nod of understanding)
(b) Create a desired impression (eg a confident posture)
(c) Establish a desired atmosphere or conditions (eg a friendly smile)
(d) Reinforce spoken messages with appropriate indications (eg nodding 'yes')

Reading other people's body language helps you to:

(a) Receive feedback from a listener and modify the message accordingly
(b) Recognise people's real feelings when their words are constrained by formalities
(c) Recognise existing or potential personal problems
(d) 'Read' situations in order to modify our own communication and response strategy

1.6.4 Electronic communication

The introduction of personal computer networks facilitates new sorts of communication, of which **email** is the most prevalent. It is particularly useful in organisations that are widely dispersed over several sites in one or more countries.

Email has many **advantages** over the telephone and paper memos, which explains why it has been so widely adopted.

(a) Emails can be sent to **large numbers of people at the same time** without having to be physically distributed on paper.

(b) Email messages **need not interrupt the recipient's flow of work**, unlike a phone call.

Email also has **drawbacks**, however.

(a) Some people use email when face to face contact is more appropriate.

(b) Although email can feel as informal as a spoken conversation, email records can be used in legal proceedings, eg for former employees suing the company for unfair dismissal. They may also be cited in defamation. ASDA was successfully sued by a disgruntled customer because untrue rumours that a customer was guilty of fraud had been circulated via the company's email system, for example.

(c) They contribute to information overload: there is a temptation to copy emails to people who do not really need to see it.

(d) If email is the main means of communication with external parties, the company's corporate identity may be compromised if people send emails in a variety of formats.

These problems emphasise the need for **internal guidance** on how email should be used. If email is used to communicate with other customers or suppliers, it should be treated in the same way as other business correspondence, including obtaining appropriate authorisation. The guidance should prohibit defamatory or other abusive messages. Above all, employees should be made aware that communication by email is permanent and not transitory in nature.

Electronic data interchange is a form of direct communication between computers, and may be used between organisations. For instance, production scheduling software may send orders directly to a supplier's stock handling computer via a telephone link.

1.6.5 Which medium should be used?

KEY POINT

The choice of medium (letter, memo, email, report, presentation, telephone call) and channel of delivery (telecom system, notice board, postal system, world wide web) depends on a number of factors.

(a) **Urgency**. The speed of transmission (eg phone or email as opposed to post)

(b) **Permanency**. The need for a written record for legal evidence, confirmation of a transaction or future reference

(c) **Complexity**. For example, the need for graphic illustration to explain concepts

(d) **Sensitivity/confidentiality** (eg a private letter)

(e) **Ease of dissemination**. Wide audience (eg a notice board)

(f) **Cost effectiveness** (taking into account all the above)

Question 6.2 Media

Learning outcome C2a

Mark Hutton, Store Manager of the Farmers supermarket store on Barry Island, is trying to decide on the best way to communicate a number of issues that have recently arisen at the store. He has asked you for some advice.

Indicate the most effective way in which the following situations should be communicated.

(a) Spare parts for the store's refrigerated food display units are needed urgently, as the cooling fans have stopped working.

(b) A corporate update on the company's performance this quarter from Managing Director Adrian Williams has been issued to store managers and needs to be relayed to staff.

(c) Fred, an employee working in the in-store bakery, has been absent five times in the past month.

(d) Mark needs information quickly from the Farmers regional payroll team, as two new store workers appear to have been underpaid.

(e) Mark needs to explain to the fresh food team some guidance received from Farmers' head office regarding the process for reducing perishable food products approaching their 'use-by date'. He regards the new process as being particularly complicated.

1.7 Influence and persuasion

In an earlier chapter we introduced the term influence. We build on this now by highlighting the importance of influence as a communication skill.

KEY TERM

INFLUENCE is the process by which one person modifies the behaviour or attitude of another.

Influence, the act of directing or modifying the behaviour of others, may be achieved in a variety of ways.

(a) The application of force, such as physical or economic power

(b) The establishment of rules and procedures that are enforced through position and/or resource power

(c) Bargaining and negotiation, which depend on the relative strengths of each party's position

(d) Persuasion

KEY TERM

PERSUASION is the ability to directly and intentionally influence the character, opinion or behaviour of a person or group.

1.7.1 Influence

The ability to influence others is a key communication skill. In an organisational context managers often need to influence others for a variety of reasons; for example, a manager may need to gain support for a new workplace initiative.

Robert Cialdini, author of *Influence: The Psychology of Persuasion*, identified six principles of influence, which can be used to influence others.

(1) **Reciprocity**. As human beings, people usually aim to treat others in accordance with the treatment they themselves receive; for example, a person may feel a sense of obligation to return a favour when they have received one in the past. As a result, we may feel obliged to help someone who has previously provided some form of support. When attempting to influence someone, a timely reminder of a prior favour performed may help to win them over.

(2) **Commitment (and consistency)**. Cialdini argues that as human beings we have a strong desire to be consistent in our actions. As a result, when we commit to something we may feel inclined to go through with it. For example, a worker may be more likely to support a colleague's proposal if they had shown some interest in it during preliminary discussions. The ability to influence others using this principle usually requires getting commitment from them during initial discussions.

(3) **Social proof**. This principle highlights that human beings are susceptible to the pressure of our peers. People generally like to conform to social norms; for example, a worker is more likely to work late if others in the same office do. Influencing a person here can be achieved by highlighting the support that you already have from others.

(4) **Liking**. Cialdini suggests people are much more likely to be influenced by people we like. How likeable a person is will be driven by a range of factors including how similar the person is, and whether they are friendly and approachable. Influencing others using the liking principle can take time as it may involve establishing relationships with the person or group you wish to influence first.

(5) **Authority**. The principle of authority is based on the notion that human beings are more likely to be influenced by those people perceived as being in a position of authority. The ability to influence others successfully using the principle of authority may require getting the support of senior managers to declare their backing for your plans.

(6) **Scarcity**. This principle suggests that a person's behaviour is influenced by the availability of a given item. In essence if a particular item or proposal has limited availability the more attractive it

becomes. This is driven by the desire not to lose out on an opportunity. The use of deadlines can be a powerful influencer of others. People are likely to act faster if they perceive that they could miss out if they fail to meet a deadline.

1.7.2 Persuasion

Persuasion differs from influence as it is always of a direct and deliberate nature. In essence persuasion is aligned to a particular objective which can only be achieved by gaining the support of others. It is important, however, to recognise that persuasion is not the same as commanding a person to do something, as it focuses on reaching agreement.

Section summary

Communication in an organisation **flows** downwards, upwards, sideways and diagonally.

The modern **management accountant** is expected to possess effective communication skills.

Barriers to communication include 'noise' (from the environment), poorly constructed or coded/decoded messages (distortion) and failures in understanding caused by the relative positions of senders and receivers.

A wide range of communication **methods and media** are available for use in organisations, including verbal (oral and written) and non-verbal methods.

Non-verbal communication (including **tone of voice** and **body language**) can support or undermine verbal messages: it needs to be carefully interpreted and managed.

Influence and **persuasion** are both key communication skills.

2 Negotiation

Introduction

We now look at negotiation, which is a means of communicating with the aim of reaching a mutual agreement. Negotiation is used for more complex communication where there is some uncertainty over the outcome. Professional negotiators work in areas such as government and trade unions, where communication takes place over difficult and complex issues.

The process of negotiation follows a number of stages, which are illustrated here. Much of the negotiation process is actually preparing before the meeting takes place, so that you know exactly what you want to achieve and how you intend to do this.

NEGOTIATION is, simply, a process whereby two parties come together to confer, with a view to concluding a jointly acceptable agreement.

Gennard and Judge (2003) suggest that this process involves two main elements:

(a) **Purposeful persuasion**. Each party attempts to persuade the other to accept its case by marshalling arguments, backed by factual information and analysis.

(b) **Constructive compromise**. Both parties accept the need to move closer towards each other's position, identifying the parameters of common ground within and between their positions, where there is room for concessions to be made while still meeting the needs of both parties.

Such an approach can be applied to a number of different situations.

(a) **Conflict resolution**. As we shall see later in the chapter, this aims to reduce resentment and preserve relationships, by allowing both parties to obtain at least some of their desired outcomes.

(b) **Group decision making** and **problem solving**. Integrating different viewpoints and interests so that the decision or solution is high on quality (from diverse relevant input) **and** acceptability (from joint consultation and commitment), enhancing the likelihood of effective implementation. People are increasingly expecting to participate in decisions that affect them, particularly at work.

2.1 Approaches to negotiation

There are two basic approaches to negotiation.

Distributive bargaining	Negotiation is about the distribution of finite resources. One party's gain is another's loss: a 'win-lose' or 'zero sum' equation. If a pay increase of, say, 10% is gained, where the management budget was 5%, the extra has to be funded from elsewhere – shareholders (reduced profits), customers (increased prices), other employee benefits (cuts in training) or whatever.
Integrative bargaining	Negotiation is about joint problem solving, aiming to find a mutually satisfying (or 'win-win') solution to problems. The aim is not just to get the best outcome for one's own party ('win-lose') or even compromise ('lose-lose') but to fulfil the needs of all parties as far as possible.

It is now generally recognised that integrative bargaining is the most constructive, sustainable and ethical approach to negotiation.

2.2 The negotiation process

The following is a general overview of the negotiation process. Any negotiation will involve the stages illustrated, although the duration and approach of each will vary according to the particular situation.

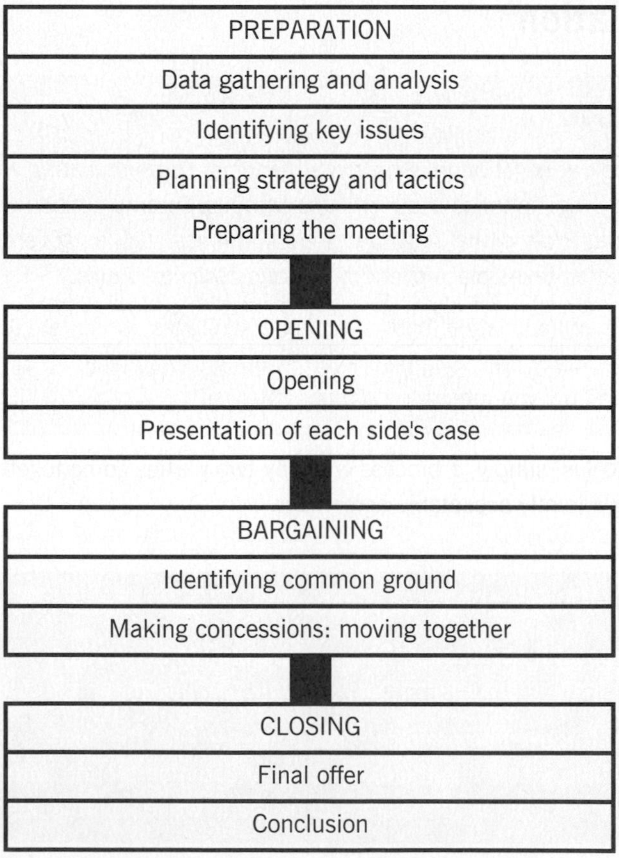

PREPARATION
Data gathering and analysis
Identifying key issues
Planning strategy and tactics
Preparing the meeting

OPENING
Opening
Presentation of each side's case

BARGAINING
Identifying common ground
Making concessions: moving together

CLOSING
Final offer
Conclusion

2.3 Preparing a negotiating strategy

Formal negotiations, as opposed to informal 'arrangements' you may come to, should follow broad guidelines.

(a) **Set objectives for the negotiation**. What you want to get out of it. These should be achievable and consistent with the organisation's policies.

(b) **Gather information** on the issues over which negotiations are going to be conducted: trends in union demands, market pay rates, case studies from similar organisations/sectors, relevant legislation and rules and so on. (Some information will have to be shared with the other party before the negotiation: this is the case in collective bargaining with trade union representatives, for example.)

(c) **Identify potential areas of conflict**. In integrative bargaining, each side accepts that the objectives and viewpoints of the other side are as real and legitimate as their own. Even in distributive bargaining, the outcome will have to be 'sold' to all parties. So recognition of the needs, wants and fears of the other party will help in devising a workable trade-off between different interests. It will also help you to anticipate counter-arguments and counter-proposals to your presentation.

(d) **Identify potential areas of movement**. Each party identifies the key issues or items likely to be on the table, and decides on which of these it will be willing to trade or make concessions. It also tries to anticipate the items on which the **other** party will be willing to trade or make concessions. Some may be amenable to movement on both sides, especially if they are identified as being relatively 'cheap' for one party to give up and relatively valuable for the other party to receive.

(e) **Formulate a negotiating strategy**. There are basically three possible outcomes.

(i) If we were to achieve all our objectives, what would be the **ideal settlement or outcome**?

'What I would really like is ...'

(ii) If we were able to make progress, but being realistic about the bargaining power of the other side, what is a **realistic settlement or outcome**?

'I could live with ...'

(iii) If we were to concede, what is an acceptable **fall-back position**: the least favourable outcome that can be accepted without failing to meet our objectives? (This may also represent the limit of our budget or authority.)

'My sticking point is ...'

Beyond this point, you cannot afford to concede or agree: the terms are unacceptable, and the only answer is: 'No way ...'. There may be costs to refusing to agree at this point, including sanctions and penalties that may be imposed by the other party: you should factor these costs in, when you decide where the 'no way!' line is ... .

A position for each side should be estimated for each of the above options – and areas of agreement concentrated on, as potential middle ground.

2.4 Preparing the meeting

The next part of your preparation focuses on the negotiation meeting itself.

Key elements	Comments
Purpose	What is the purpose or objective of the meeting? Is it about investigation or are you intending to finalise the negotiation?
Plan	Where will the meeting be held? How should the room be laid out? What facilities (eg side meeting rooms, visual aids) will be required? How will you structure the meeting? How long will it take?
Pace	About 5% of any meeting time should be given to breaking the ice and making introductions, before 'getting down to business'.
Personalities	With whom are you meeting? Are they experienced negotiators?

2.5 Conducting the negotiation – opening and bargaining

During the conduct of the negotiations themselves, participants should consider the following.

(a) **Opening presentation**. A broad statement of each side's ideal position or opening offer, explaining the rationale (and strength of feeling) behind the proposals, and supporting them with relevant objective data.

(b) **Fact-finding**. Each party should use the other party's presentation as an opportunity for fact finding, rather than point scoring or unconsidered ('knee-jerk') opposition. Negotiators should gain a better understanding of the other party's position **and** its strengths and weaknesses.

(c) **Identifying common ground**. Having established ideal (usually polarised) positions, the emphasis switches to exploring areas where agreement might be reached on realistic and fall-back positions.

(d) **Use of the negotiating strategy and bargaining power**. Items should be linked and packaged to achieve two-way momentum, so that no party gives away anything without getting something in return. Be firm on principles and flexible on details, so that there is room to move without compromising your priority objectives.

(e) **Considering** new proposals or counter-proposals. If new proposals are on the table, the meeting should be adjourned to give time for discussion: never do your thinking or strategising aloud in front of the other side!

(f) **Making concessions**. A concession is a 'revision of a position you have held previously and justified publicly' (Guirdham, 1995). Concessions are not easy to make without losing credibility – but they **must** be made in order to bring both parties progressively closer together. They should only be made in response to pressure or to offers in exchange from the other party – and only in small steps. You can encourage concessions from the other side by negatively reinforcing their present position (eg emphasising that it will not work) and positively reinforcing movement (eg offering options for them to move without losing face).

(g) **The negotiating team**. Members of the same negotiating team should not contradict one another or speak unless asked to do so by their leader. If there is an issue, pass a message to the leader, asking for an adjournment.

(h) **Effective communication skills**. Be brief and to the point: a businesslike approach encourages a similar response from the other side. Use language that everyone will be able to understand. Remember that assertiveness (an essential skill) is not the same as aggression: all parties should show respect for one another.

(i) **Leadership**. The meeting should be facilitated by an experienced chairperson, who will ensure that it is conducted in a courteous and effective manner: sticking to the agenda; giving alternating opportunities to speak (rather than a 'free for all'); and so on. All relevant details of the discussion should be recorded, in order to furnish minutes that can be used in formulating final agreements.

2.6 Closing the negotiation

Closing a negotiation is similar to closing a sale: it means attempting to bring the process to a conclusion. There are several techniques.

At the conclusion of negotiations, both parties must be satisfied that all issues have been discussed and that they understand exactly what has been agreed; the proceedings should be summarised and agreements 'played back' for confirmation by both sides. If any objectives are raised, negotiations should recommence.

Once there is oral agreement, the points should be written up as a signed 'draft agreement', which will be circulated and checked by both sides. When all clauses have been approved by both sides, the agreement can be printed, formally signed and communicated to those affected by its provisions.

Exam alert

You may be asked to identify the correct sequence of phases in the conduct of negotiation in a question.

2.7 Successful negotiation

John Hunt lists some characteristics of successful negotiators in his book *Managing People at Work*.

(a) They avoid direct confrontation.
(b) They consider a wide range of options.
(c) They hold back counter-proposals rather than responding immediately.
(d) They use emollient verbal techniques: 'would it be helpful if we ...?'.
(e) They summarise on behalf of all involved.
(f) They advance single arguments insistently and avoid long-winded, multiple reason arguments.

Negotiation skills are difficult to learn other than from experience. Role plays and simulations can help, but the best way is to attend live negotiations as a junior member of a team.

Section summary

The process of **negotiation** can be said to involve two main elements: purposeful persuasion and constructive compromise.

3 The nature of conflict

Introduction

The final section of the chapter builds on the issues that we have discussed so far, and considers a range of views on conflict. Some people believe any conflict is bad and that managers should act to eliminate it when it occurs. Others see conflict as inevitable, and even useful in helping the organisation to evolve.

KEY TERM

There are many definitions of **CONFLICT**. Huczynski and Buchanan (2001) usefully reflect the subjective dimensions of conflict (perceptions and values) in their definition:

'Conflict is a process that begins when one party perceives that another party has negatively affected, or is about to negatively affect, something the first party cares about. Typically, conflicts are based upon differences in interests and values, when the interests of one party come up against the different interests of another.' (p. 770)

3.1 Argument, competition and conflict

3.1.1 The 'happy family' view

The happy family view presents organisations as **essentially harmonious**.

(a) They are co-operative structures, designed to achieve agreed common objectives, with no systematic conflict of interest.

(b) Management power is legitimate.

(c) Conflicts are **exceptional** and arise from aberrant incidents, such as misunderstandings, clashes of personality and external influences.

Management literature often attempts to come up with training and motivational techniques for dealing with conflicts that arise in what are seen as potentially conflict-free organisations. Conflict is thus blamed on bad management, lack of leadership, poor communication, or bloody-mindedness on the part of individuals or interest groups that impinge on the organisation. The theory is that a strong culture, good two-way communication, co-operation and motivational leadership will eliminate conflict. **Co-operation is assumed to be desirable and achievable**.

3.1.2 The conflict view

In contrast, there is the view of organisations as **arenas for conflict on individual and group levels**. Members battle for limited resources, status, rewards and professional values. Organisational politics involves constant struggles for control, and choices of structure, technology and organisational goals are part of this process. Individual and organisational interests will not always coincide.

If a **pluralist view** is taken, organisations may be seen as **political coalitions** of individuals and groups, which have their own interests. Management has to create a workable structure for collaboration, taking into account the objectives of all the stakeholders in the organisation. A **mutual survival** strategy, involving the control of conflict through compromise, can be made acceptable in varying degrees to all concerned.

3.1.3 The evolutionary view

Conflict may be seen as a useful basis for **evolutionary** rather than revolutionary **change**. Conflict keeps the organisation **sensitive to the need to change**, while reinforcing its essential framework of control. The legitimate pursuit of competing interests can balance and preserve social and organisational arrangements. A flexible society benefits from conflict because such behaviour, by helping to create and modify norms, assumes its continuance under changed conditions.

KEY POINT

This **constructive conflict** view may be the most useful for managers. It neither attempts to dodge the issues of conflict, which is an observable fact of life in most organisations, nor seeks to pull down existing organisational structures altogether.

Managers have to get on with the job of managing and upholding organisational goals with the co-operation of other members. We will therefore look more closely at the idea of **managing conflict**.

3.2 Constructive and destructive conflict

If conflict is inevitable, there are two aspects of conflict that must be dealt with by the manager. They need to manage conflict where it is desirable and seek to eliminate the destructive elements in their workplace.

Conflict can be highly desirable. It can energise relationships and clarify issues. Hunt suggests that conflict can have constructive effects.

(a) It can introduce different solutions to problems.
(b) Power relationships can be defined more clearly.
(c) It may encourage creativity and the testing of ideas.
(d) It focuses attention on individual contributions.
(e) It brings emotions out into the open.
(f) It can release hostile feelings.

Conflict can also be **destructive**.

(a) It may distract attention from the task.
(b) It can polarise views and affect judgement.
(c) Objectives may be subverted in favour of secondary goals.
(d) It encourages defensive or spoiling behaviour, damaging co-ordination and co-operation.
(e) It may result in disintegration of the group.
(f) Losers may go into denial, look for scapegoats or withdraw from further participation.

CASE STUDY

Conflict

Tjosvold and Deerner researched conflict in different contexts. They allocated to 66 student volunteers the roles of foremen and workers at an assembly plant, with a scenario of conflict over job rotation schemes. Foremen were against, workers for.

One group was told that the organisational norm was to '**avoid controversy**'; another was told that the norm was '**co-operative controversy**', **trying** to agree; a third was told that groups were out to **win any arguments that arose**, '**competitive controversy**'. The students were offered rewards for complying with their given norms. Their decisions, and attitudes to the discussions, were then monitored.

(a) Where **controversy was avoided**, the foremen's views dominated.

(b) **Competitive controversy** brought no agreement, but brought out feelings of hostility and suspicion.

(c) **Co-operative controversy** brought out differences in an atmosphere of curiosity, trust and openness: the decisions reached seemed to integrate the views of both parties.

But can real managers and workers be motivated to comply with useful organisational 'norms' in this way?

3.3 Symptoms of conflict

Conflict may result in:

(a) Poor communications, in all directions
(b) Interpersonal friction
(c) Inter-group rivalry and jealousy
(d) Low morale and frustration
(e) Widespread use of arbitration, appeals to higher authority, and inflexible attitudes

The tactics of conflict include:

(a) **Withholding information** from others who need it.

(b) **Distorting information.** This will enable the group or manager presenting the information to get their way more easily.

(c) **Empire building.** A group (especially a specialist group such as accounting) that considers its influence to be neglected might seek to impose rules, procedures, restrictions or official requirements on other groups, in order to bolster its own importance.

(d) **Office politics.** A manager might seek to bypass formal channels of communication and decision making by establishing informal contacts and friendships with people in positions of importance.

(e) **Fault-finding** in the work of other departments.

Section summary

Argument (resolving differences by discussion) and **competition** can be distinguished from harmful expressions of difference as **conflict**.

Conflict can be constructive, if it introduces new information into a problem, if it defines a problem, or if it encourages creativity. It can be destructive if it distracts attention from the task or inhibits communication. **Conflict** may **manifest** itself in: poor communication; friction between individuals and groups; widespread use of arbitration and other conflict mechanisms; and various political games.

4 Causes of conflict

Introduction

Conflict can occur at many different levels:

- Within an individual (eg over two incompatible goals)
- Between two individuals (interpersonal conflict)
- Between groups or teams (eg because of competition for influence or resources, incompatible goals and schedules, or different cultures)
- Between different levels in the organisation hierarchy (eg workers and their trade unions versus management, or 'turf wars' between levels of management)

It may be helpful to distinguish between the following:

- **Horizontal conflict** between individuals and groups at the same broad level in the organisation. This is often based, as we will see, on competition for limited influence and resources.
- **Vertical conflict** between different levels in the organisation hierarchy. This is often based on conflict of interest and power imbalance.

We will look at the causes of conflict using this distinction.

4.1 Causes of horizontal conflict between departments/teams

It is possible to identify a number of typical sources of conflict between functions and groups in organisations.

(a) **Differences in goals**. Conflict may be caused by differences in the goals of different groups (or individuals). It is a function of management to create a system of planning whereby individual or group goals are formulated within the framework of a strategic plan and to provide leadership, and to encourage individuals to accept the goals of the organisation as being compatible with their personal goals.

(b) **Different business functions often differ in personality** or culture from those in other functions (eg sales staff and accountants). Different goals, attitudes, job roles, jargon and work styles create the potential for lack of understanding and frustration. This effect is worsened as the **size** of the organisation increases: informal interaction between the functions is reduced.

(c) **Task interdependence**. The dependence of one department on another (eg for resources or information) may be a cause of conflict if the relationship is badly managed. The **technology** in use can have a major influence on task interdependence, as in many manufacturing operations, where products flow from one department to another.

(d) **Scarcity of resources**. Resources are a source of power: managers fight for them. Departments may be given excessive targets and limited resources. This is another effect that can be amplified by growth and the establishment of specialist departments: staff are loyal to their colleagues and managers struggle to do their best for their staff in such matters as equipment and working conditions.

(e) **Power distribution**. Conflict may also be caused by disputes about the boundaries of authority. Staff managers may attempt to encroach on the roles of line managers and usurp some of their authority, while departments might start empire building and try to take over the work previously done by other departments.

(f) **Uncertainty**. Conflict can arise in times of change, where new problems arise. This may be particularly acute in **environments** posing threats through change, competition, resource scarcity and so on.

(g) The **reward system** can encourage conflict, for instance, if incentives are designed in a way that rewards one department while penalising another.

Question 6.3 Conflict

Learning outcome C2b

What kind of conflict issues, based on the same sources of conflict listed above, might arise within a **work or project team**?

4.2 Causes of vertical conflict

Vertical conflict is effectively entrenched in the **power imbalance** between those at higher levels of a hierarchy and those 'below' them. This may be seen (depending on ideology) as inherently inequitable – making conflict both inevitable and desirable, as in a Marxist view – or as a necessary order for the control of organisational performance – making conflict likely, but raising the possibility of compromise for mutual survival and benefit.

Vertical conflict is most visibly reflected in industrial relations (IR): the formal relationship between management and labour representatives. (We will look at IR in more detail later in the chapter.) The desire of employees to join trade unions and staff associations reflects significant sources of vertical conflict.

(a) **Resource distribution**. How will the value created by the organisation be shared between stakeholders and, in particular, between owners and the workforce?

(b) **Power**. The lack of power mentioned above can lead to workers joining a union and engaging in trials of strength.

(c) **Alienation**. Many workers have boring, repetitive jobs and do not identify with the organisation. This alienation can be exacerbated by management attitudes.

(d) **Politics**. In the sense of basic ideas about society and how it should work, politics is important, with workers seeking security and equality of outcome and managers being concerned to control costs and operate as freely as possible.

4.3 Organisational politics

Organisations are political systems in the sense that they are composed of individuals and groups who have their own interests, priorities and goals. Competition exists for finite resources, power and influence. There are cliques, alliances, pressure groups and blocking groups, centred on values, opinions and objectives which may be opposed by others.

Organisation politics reveals itself in various ways.

(a) **Individuals** wish to experience victory and avoid defeat. They have their own objectives, which are not always reconcilable with those of the organisation.

(b) There are inevitable **disparities of power and influence** in hierarchical organisations – and despite rational organisation designs, events are in reality decided by dominant individuals or coalitions within and/or outside the organisation. Other individuals tend to want to influence, join or overthrow the dominant coalition.

(c) Organisations are constantly involved in **compromise**, reconciling or controlling differences, and settling for reality rather than the ideal.

(d) **Territory** is a useful analogy for the jealousies and rivalries over boundaries of authority, specialisms and spheres of influence.

(e) Political behaviour might be characteristic of the **informal organisation**, where managers do each other favours in search of influence.

Mintzberg (*Power In and Around Organisations*) identifies various **political games**, which can be stimulating for the organisation, but can also degenerate into harmful, all-absorbing conflict.

(a) **Games to resist authority** – to sabotage the aims of superiors

(b) **Games to counter this resistance** – the imposition of rules and controls by superiors

(c) **Games to build power bases** – associating with useful superiors, forming alliances among colleagues, gaining the support of subordinates, getting control of information or resources

(d) **Games to defeat rivals** – inter-group or interdepartmental conflict

(e) **Games to change the organisation** – higher power struggles, or rebellion

Section summary

It may be helpful to distinguish between:

- **Horizontal conflict** between individuals and groups at the same broad level in the organisation. This is often based, as we will see, on competition for limited influence and resources.
- **Vertical conflict** between different levels in the organisation hierarchy. This is often based on conflict of interest and power imbalance.

Political behaviour is broadly concerned with competition, conflict, rivalry and power relationships in organisations.

5 Managing conflict

Introduction

In this section, we look at a model for classifying individual responses to conflict, based on assertiveness and co-operativeness. This maps five responses to conflict using these two factors. Then we look at ways managers can deal with conflict using a range of techniques. Finally, we consider how IR plays a part in resolving conflict.

5.1 Conflict-handling styles

Thomas (1976) suggests that individuals' conflict-handling styles can be mapped on two dimensions, according to the **intentions** of the parties involved. He labelled the two dimensions **assertiveness** (trying to satisfy one's own concerns) and **co-operativeness** (trying to satisfy the other party's concerns).

He describes five strategies for resolving conflict but feels, however, that **compromising** was the optimal solution.

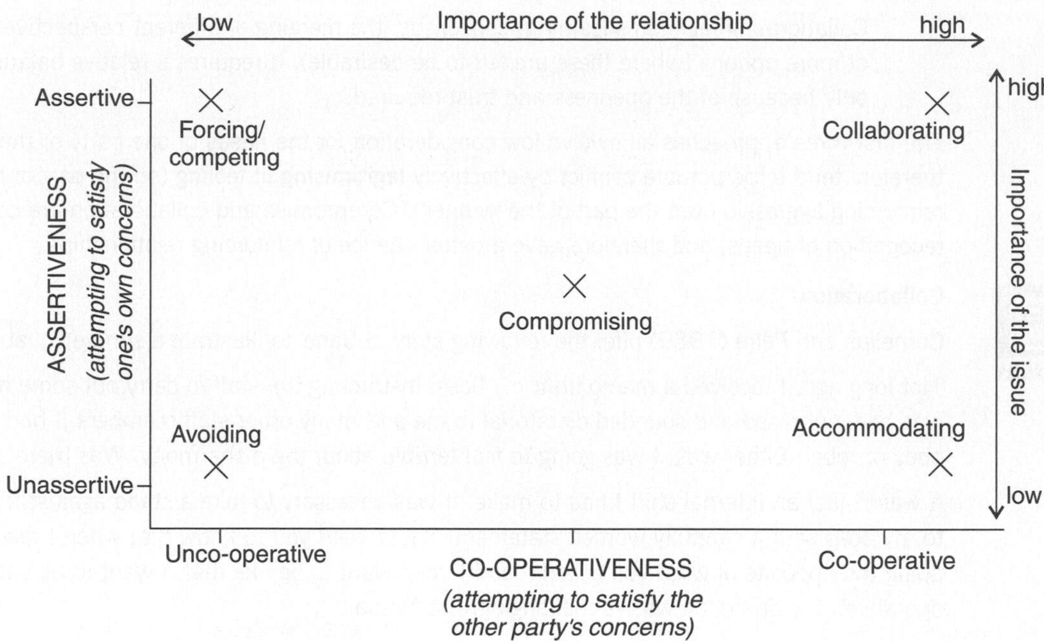

Source: Whetten and Cameron (2002), p. 359

(a) **Avoiding**. You withdraw from the conflict or deny/conceal the incompatibility ('sweeping it under the carpet'). This may be appropriate where the issue is trivial: it may simply blow over. Withdrawal is also a legitimate **short-term** response to more serious conflict, allowing tempers to cool and more information to be gathered. However, if underlying causes are not identified and addressed, the conflict may eventually re-emerge or escalate.

(b) **Accommodating**. You concede the issue to the other person, regardless of your own legitimate concerns. This may be appropriate where the relationship is the most important consideration. It may be the only option where you have relatively low power in the relationship, especially if the time constraints are tight. It may also be appropriate to allow the other person to 'win' (eg allowing a subordinate to learn from their own mistakes). However, your own legitimate interests are not served.

(c) **Competing/forcing**. You insist on your own concerns at the expense of others. This may be appropriate where the issue is the most important consideration: where it is necessary to solve ideological disputes, break down the inflexibility of others, implement unpopular measures or establish your autonomy. In other words, sometimes you just have to 'stick to your guns'. It is useful in emergencies, when quick, decisive action is required. It is facilitated where you have relatively high power in the relationship. The drawback is that the other person may feel defeated and humiliated, which may affect longer-term co-operation.

(d) **Compromising**. You trade concessions through (explicit or implicit) bargaining, negotiating and conciliating, so that each party makes some concessions in order to obtain some gains. This may be appropriate when the issue is not worth disruption of the relationship. It may be necessary where the power is evenly balanced and the parties have mutually exclusive goals that are equally important to them. If the issue is complex, compromise may be a temporary resolution while other options are explored: it may also be a 'fall-back' position if collaborating or forcing are unsuccessful. However, individuals often exaggerate their initial positions (to counteract the effect of compromise) and this may polarise the conflict unnecessarily. Compromise may also be perceived to weaken the value of the decision, perhaps reducing commitment to it on the grounds that 'it wasn't what we wanted'. (And this may be the position of both parties.)

(e) **Collaborating**. You work together with the other party in an attempt to find an outcome in which the assertively-stated needs of both parties are met as far as possible. Conflict handling is regarded as shared problem solving. This may be most appropriate when both the issues and the relationship are highly important to you, and time is not pressing: it is worth seeking an integrative solution because both sets of concerns are recognised as being too important to compromise.

Collaborating facilitates learning, consensus, the merging of different perspectives and the creation of more options (where these are felt to be desirable). It requires a relative balance of power, if only because of the openness and trust required.

The first three approaches all involve low consideration for the needs of one party or the other: they therefore tend to perpetuate conflict by effectively **legitimising** ill-feeling (on the part of the 'loser') and reinforcing aggression (on the part of the 'winner'). Compromise and collaboration are based on mutual recognition of needs, and therefore have a better chance of reinforcing relationships.

CASE STUDY

Collaboration

Cornelius and Faire (1989) offer the following story of 'Jane' to illustrate a simple collaborative approach.

'Not long ago, I received a memo from my boss, instructing the staff to carry out some new procedures. It was badly phrased and sounded dictatorial to me and many other staff members. I had two choices – to obey or rebel. Either way, I was going to feel terrible about the disharmony. Was there another way?

It wasn't just an internal shift I had to make. It was necessary to take a stand against that memo. I went to my boss with a carefully worded statement: "I just want you to know that when I read this I felt like doing the opposite of what you asked – and I don't want to be like that. I want to be supportive and co-operative". My approach wasn't challenging, but factual.

'My boss took it far better than I could have expected. He said, "That's interesting – which parts made you feel like that?". Then we talked about them. I got a different slant on the situation in this face to face friendly discussion. I left feeling I could now freely choose to follow the new procedures. My boss gained some helpful insights about approaching staff to implement his new plan.'

Exam alert

The Thomas model is an important model, which you need to be familiar with before attempting your E2 exam. Exam questions may require you to illustrate your understanding of the model by applying your knowledge to a scenario featuring some form of conflict between different parties. In cases where you are unsure of which model to use or no specific theory is mentioned in the question, then it is important that you try to use the clues in the scenario. A question may avoid the use of the term 'conflict-handling styles'; however, reference in the scenario to particular terms closely associated with the theory of conflict such as 'avoiding' and 'collaborating' may help to guide you to the required model. You will then know what general approach to take in answering a question on conflict.

Question 6.4 — Conflict handling

Learning outcome C2b

Becky, a worker in the Farmers supermarket store on Barry Island, has just finished replenishing the inventory in one of the fresh food refrigeration units, when the cooling fan suddenly stops working. The passing store manager, Mark Hutton, is holding a briefing on the shop floor with his management team when he notices the unit malfunction; he is particularly concerned that the produce in the unit will spoil if not relocated. Mark tells Becky to quickly remove all the produce that she has just put on display and to relocate it to a functioning unit.

Exasperated and upset, Becky tells Mark 'that he can do it, if he wants it moved'.

Required

Which would be the most appropriate conflict-handling style for Mark to use in this situation?

A Forcing
B Accommodating
C Collaborating
D Avoiding

5.2 Strategies for managing conflict

We now consider the work of Mainwaring who proposes four alternative strategies for managing conflict.

(a) **Conflict stimulation and orchestration**. This involves encouraging constructive conflict between individuals with the aim of getting people to generate ideas or to initiate change in the organisation. Clearly, artificially creating conflict needs to be carefully managed to avoid it turning into destructive conflict.

(b) **Conflict suppression**. This is a short-term approach to handling conflict. This commonly involves the threat of authority against those parties in conflict. It may involve suppressing the fact that a conflict has arisen, by downplaying the situation.

(c) **Conflict reduction**. This approach involves using strategies to bring conflicting parties towards shared objectives. Compromise and concessions are commonly used techniques.

(d) **Conflict resolution**. The focus of conflict resolution is to reach consensus among conflicting parties. This involves eradicating the original cause of the conflict. Co-operation and collaboration are both central to this approach.

5.3 Managing inter-group conflict

The conflict behaviour might be reduced in the following ways.

(a) **Structural separation**. Design the organisation's structure so that individuals, groups or departments in conflict have no dealings with each other. This is hardly a long-term solution: in most organisations, people need to work together.

(b) **Bureaucratic authority**. Conflict is controlled from above, by people with position power. Again, this is a short-term solution, as it will merely encourage political behaviour by the departments in conflict with each other.

(c) **Limited communication**. This is a short-term solution in which interdepartmental communications are restricted.

Co-operative behaviour might be encouraged in the following ways.

(a) **Integration devices**, such as joint problem-solving teams, force people to work together and, it is hoped, will encourage co-operative attitudes. A co-ordinator may be appointed.

(b) **Confrontation and negotiation** requires that the members in conflict are forced to hammer out a solution. It is important how the situation is presented to the conflicting parties. A **win-lose strategy** implies that there will be one winner and one loser. Each negotiating party will pursue solely its own interest, will be unwilling to negotiate and will be deceitful and manipulative. A **win-win strategy** presents the conflict as a problem to be solved, not a battle to be won by one of the parties.

(c) **Consultants** or third-party mediators/arbitrators can be brought in as objective catalysts for improving communications, exposing group think and stereotyping, and to act as an 'honest broker'. In the UK, the government-sponsored Advisory Conciliation and Arbitration Service has played this role.

(d) **Job rotation**. Personnel are seconded to other departments in order to break down communication barriers, eliminate negative stereotypes and create 'ambassadors' when conflict arises.

(e) **Super-ordinate goals**. Senior managers set shared, corporate objectives, overarching the agendas of the individual departments.

(f) **Inter-group training**. People from conflicting departments can be sent on joint training courses to break down barriers, encourage communication and emphasise shared goals and working styles.

(g) **Organisational adjustments**, such as improved procedure structures and workflow, can be used to minimise the frustration of interdependence, role ambiguity, authority overlaps and so on. One modern approach is to regard workflows in terms of total horizontal business processes, without vertical barriers between functions.

(h) Specific **issues** can be attacked and minimised by analysing them into components that can be dealt with separately and innovatively.

5.3.1 Environmental and ecological strategies

Charles Handy suggests two types of strategy that may be used to turn conflict into competition or argument, or to manage it in some other acceptable way.

(a) **Environmental ('ecological') strategies**. Such strategies involve:

   (i) Agreement of common objectives
   (ii) Reinforcing the group or 'team' nature of organisational life, via culture
   (iii) Providing feedback information on progress
   (iv) Providing adequate co-ordination and communication mechanisms
   (v) Sorting out territorial/role conflicts in the organisational structure

(b) **Regulation strategies**. Possible methods include:

   (i) The provision of arbitration to settle disputes
   (ii) The establishment of detailed rules and procedures for conduct by employees
   (iii) Appointing a person to 'manage' the area of conflict – a liaison/co-ordination officer
   (iv) Using confrontation, or inter-group meetings, to hammer out differences, especially where territorial conflicts occur
   (v) Separating the conflicting individuals
   (vi) Ignoring the problem, if it is genuinely likely to 'go away', and there is no point in opening fresh wounds

5.4 Industrial and employee relations

KEY TERM

INDUSTRIAL RELATIONS (IR) can be defined as 'all the rules, practices and conventions governing interactions between managements and their workforces, normally involving collective employee representation and bargaining'. (Graham and Bennett)

IR typically covers such areas as:

(a) **Individual and collective procedures for agreeing terms and conditions of work**. (The collective process is known as collective bargaining.)

(b) **Recognition of trade unions and/or alternative mechanisms for employee representation** and consultation. (This includes joint consultation committees, works councils and partnership agreements.)

(c) **Machinery for handling individual and collective grievance and disciplinary issues** (including third-party conciliation and arbitration if necessary). Detailed procedural agreements on disputes are generally made during collective bargaining or other non-union negotiated agreements.

5.4.1 Industrial relations (IR) orientations

The Industrial Relations Services has identified four approaches to IR (as cited by Armstrong, 2003).

(a) **Adversarial**. The organisation decides what it wants to do, and employees are expected to fit in. Employees only exercise power by refusing to co-operate.

(b) **Traditional**. A good day to day working relationship, but management proposes and the workforce reacts through its elected representatives.

(c) **Partnership**. The organisation involves employees in the drawing up and execution of the organisation's policies, but retains the right to manage.

(d) **Power sharing**. Employees are involved in both day to day and strategic decision making.

Some companies have taken an aggressive approach to dealing with union power.

(a) **Avoidance strategies** include complete derecognition of unions, shifting operations to new non-union sites and only allowing unions a presence in problem solving and not in the settlement of benefits.

(b) **Human resource management strategies** move away from dealing with staff collectively, establishing instead an individualistic approach to pay and benefits using such mechanisms as single status; appraisal and performance management; profit sharing; enhanced opportunities; and profit-related pay. Other, less confrontational approaches have emphasised problem solving, partnership, teamwork and policies based on a common interest in the success of the firm.

Many unionised firms, however, take a more **co-operative approach**, using mechanisms such as:

(a) Gain sharing, eg profit-related rewards.

(b) Partnership agreements: 'negotiated agreements in which both parties (management and the trade union) agree to work together to their mutual advantage and to achieve a climate of more co-operation and less adversarial industrial relations' (Armstrong). Shared goals may be defined in relation to such matters as: commitment to employment security; quality of working life; information sharing and consultation; and commitment to the survival and success of the enterprise.

(c) The use of labour-management teams to increase worker participation and involvement.

5.4.2 Employee relations

In line with other modern orientations in human resource management, the view of IR has shifted. IR has traditionally been adversarial, both in perception ('us and them') and in genuine conflict of interest. However, it has been recognised that employers and employees are interdependent: employee wellbeing depends on the continued prosperity of the organisation – and the continued prosperity of the organisation depends on the co-operation of the employees.

It has been argued that HR policies and management styles can capitalise on these shared interests and make traditional IR approaches (based on controlling conflict) largely irrelevant.

Employee relations are defined as 'all those areas of human resource management that involve general relationships with employees, through collective agreements where trade unions are recognised **and/or** through commonly applied policies for employee involvement and communications' (Armstrong).

Section summary

Thomas's model of conflict suggests that individuals' **conflict-handling styles** can be mapped on two dimensions, according to the **intentions** of the parties involved. He labelled the two dimensions **assertiveness** (trying to satisfy one's own concerns) and **co-operativeness** (trying to satisfy the other party's concerns). Mainwaring proposed four strategies for managing conflict; conflict stimulation and orchestration, suppression, reduction and resolution.

The solution to inter-group or horizontal conflict might be firstly to deal with the symptoms, by reducing conflict behaviour, and then deal with the causes of the conflict by encouraging co-operative attitudes.

Industrial relations typically cover:

- **Individual and collective procedures for agreeing terms and conditions of work**
- **Recognition of trade unions and/or alternative mechanisms for employee representation and consultation**
- **Machinery for handling individual and collective grievance and disciplinary issues**

Chapter Summary

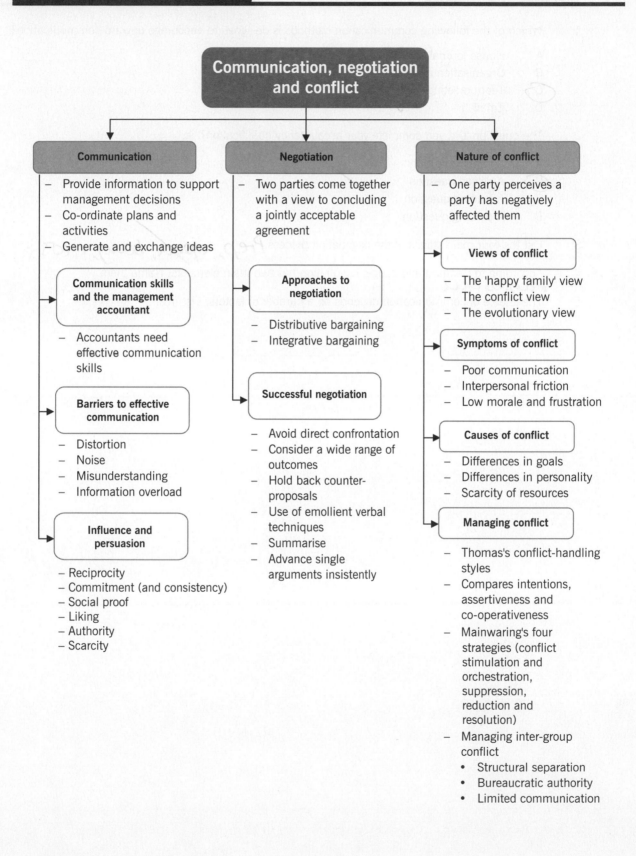

Communication, negotiation and conflict

Communication

- Provide information to support management decisions
- Co-ordinate plans and activities
- Generate and exchange ideas

Communication skills and the management accountant

- Accountants need effective communication skills

Barriers to effective communication

- Distortion
- Noise
- Misunderstanding
- Information overload

Influence and persuasion

- Reciprocity
- Commitment (and consistency)
- Social proof
- Liking
- Authority
- Scarcity

Negotiation

- Two parties come together with a view to concluding a jointly acceptable agreement

Approaches to negotiation

- Distributive bargaining
- Integrative bargaining

Successful negotiation

- Avoid direct confrontation
- Consider a wide range of outcomes
- Hold back counter-proposals
- Use of emollient verbal techniques
- Summarise
- Advance single arguments insistently

Nature of conflict

- One party perceives a party has negatively affected them

Views of conflict

- The 'happy family' view
- The conflict view
- The evolutionary view

Symptoms of conflict

- Poor communication
- Interpersonal friction
- Low morale and frustration

Causes of conflict

- Differences in goals
- Differences in personality
- Scarcity of resources

Managing conflict

- Thomas's conflict-handling styles
- Compares intentions, assertiveness and co-operativeness
- Mainwaring's four strategies (conflict stimulation and orchestration, suppression, reduction and resolution)
- Managing inter-group conflict
  - Structural separation
  - Bureaucratic authority
  - Limited communication

Quick Quiz

1 Which of the following communication methods is designed to encourage upward communication?

- A House journal
- B Organisation manual
- C Team meetings
- D Email

2 The question 'Did you complete your accountancy qualification?' is:

- A An open question
- B A closed question
- C A leading question
- D A probing question

3 List the four main stages of the negotiation process.

4 According to Gennard and Judge, negotiation has two main elements. Name them.

5 The choice of communication depends on a number of factors. List five.

Answers to Quick Quiz

1 C Options A and B primarily support downward communication; and option D primarily supports downward and lateral communication.

2 B (You might try to rephrase this question for the other types, for extra practice.)

3 Preparation, opening, bargaining and closing

4 They are: purposeful persuasion and constructive compromise.

5 Your list should include five of the following: urgency, permanency, complexity, sensitivity, ease of dissemination and cost effectiveness.

Answers to Questions

6.1 Communication

False. 'Clear expression' is a matter of opinion and perception or, in terms of the communications model, of coding and decoding. We must also consider the effect of noise, such as cultural differences.

6.2 Media

Communicating the situations given might best be done as follows.

(a) Telephone call to the local Farmers store engineer and an email message confirming in writing the need for urgent assistance.

(b) A notice board announcement or holding a general staff meeting.

(c) Face to face conversation with Fred. It would be a good idea to confirm the outcome of the meeting in writing, so that records can be maintained.

(d) Telephone call to the regional Farmers payroll team, or a face to face conversation, if possible. Due to the complex and confidential nature of payroll information, it is likely to be appropriate to email the payroll team with the details of the underpayment.

(e) Face-to-face team briefing to explain the new process to those staff required to carry it out.

6.3 Conflict

Similar conflict issues may arise within a work or project team, due to everyday factors such as:

(a) Disagreement about goals, priorities and interests, exacerbated by lack of direction and clarity from team leaders.

(b) Poor communication, leading to negative assumptions, stereotyping and misunderstandings (often the root of so-called 'personality clashes').

(c) Competition for resources such as recognition, office space and team-based rewards.

(d) Interpersonal issues, such as aggressive or argumentative communication styles, unfair treatment, and (in extreme cases) bullying or harassment.

(e) Dissatisfactions with pay and conditions, leadership and so on, which create grievances and spill over into interpersonal relations.

6.4 Conflict handling

A The seriousness of the outcome (in this case avoiding fresh produce being spoilt) means that avoiding and accommodating are not options. Collaborating would be a relationship-building, long-term approach within a team setting, but in this case the need for compliance is urgent, the Store Manager 'knows best', and his authority has been publicly challenged and potentially undermined by Becky's behaviour. Mark needs to reassert leadership and get the needed outcome, so forcing may be the immediate solution.

Now try these questions from the Practice Question Bank

Number	Level
6.1 – 6.5	Practice
Communication	Practice

CONTROL AND THE FINANCE FUNCTION

Control is one of the key functions of management. Control embraces a range of **approaches**, from financial controls determined by the finance function (a key part of a management accountant's technical role); to performance management (the use of contracts, performance appraisal, reporting and disciplinary processes to control individual and team performance); to regulatory controls (ensuring compliance with relevant law and regulation); and interpersonal control (the use of values and influence to regulate people's behaviour).

In this chapter, we look at key examples from each type of control. We begin with a model that helpfully highlights different **levels** at which control can be exercised.

This should help you to integrate your learning in this chapter across the syllabus, as you consider the application of controls at different levels.

The issues of corporate governance and business ethics (an important area of control) are discussed in the context of the business's obligations to its stakeholders.

We look at mentoring, which is an aspect of employee development that falls broadly under control.

Topic list	Learning outcomes	Syllabus references	Ability required
1 Theories of control	B2a	B2(i)	Analysis
2 The role of the finance function	C1b, C1c	C1(i), (ii), (iii)	Analysis
3 Internal control systems	B2a, C1c	B2(iii), C1(i)	Analysis
4 Performance management – controlling the individual	B1b, B2a	B1(ii), B2(ii)	Analysis
5 Controlling health and safety	B1b	B1(vii)	Analysis
6 Mentoring	B1b	B1(iii)	Analysis
7 Business ethics and corporate social responsibility (CSR)	B2a	B2(iii)	Analysis
8 Corporate governance	B2a, C1c	B2(iii), C1(i)	Analysis

Chapter Overview

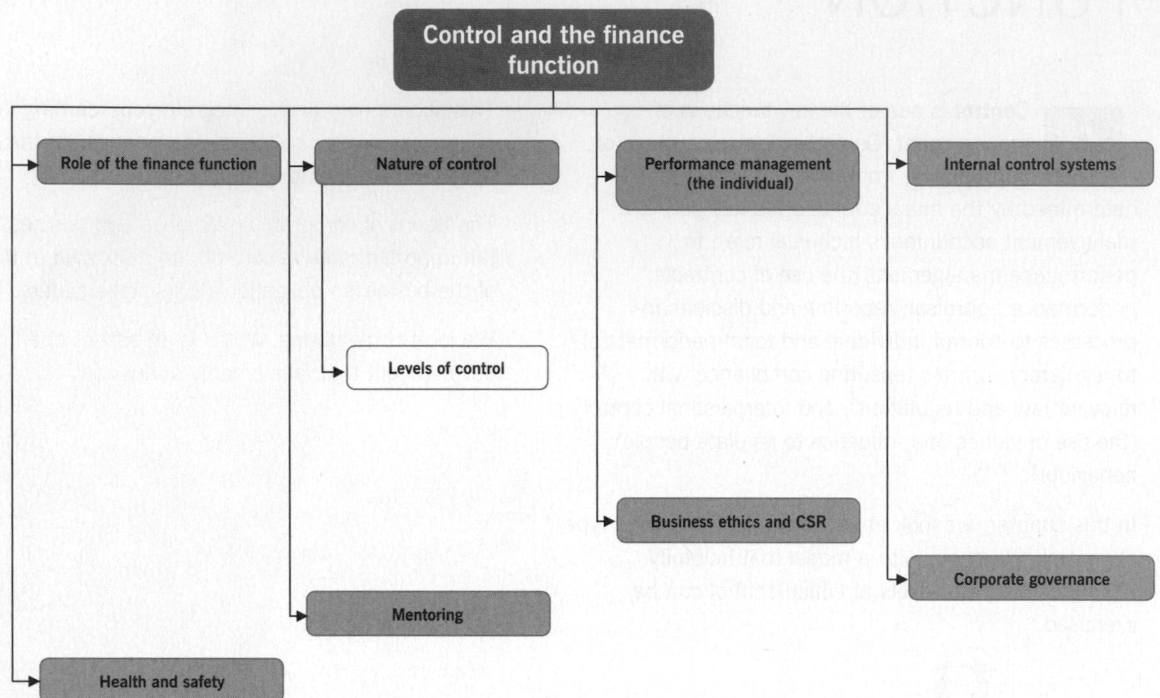

1 Theories of control

Introduction

Control is used at all levels of the organisation, from top-level management down to routine controls over operations. In this section, we look at what control systems need to be effective, or the 6 As. According to Ouchi, organisations employ three basic control strategies: market, bureaucratic and clan. Johnson and Scholes identify control processes in the organisation according to whether they focus on inputs or outputs and/or are direct or indirect.

1.1 The nature of control

The managers of a business organisation are responsible to its owners and stakeholders for the achievement of its goals. They need to find reliable and systematic ways of ensuring that:

(a) All individuals and units in the business understand their goals and objectives, within the overall direction of the enterprise.

(b) Resources are efficiently mobilised and utilised in pursuit of objectives, without undue risk or waste.

(c) Progress and performance can be continually compared to plans, in order to take corrective action where required.

(d) Performance can be periodically reviewed, in order to derive learning and planned improvements from any strengths and weaknesses identified.

Control is the overall process (or set of processes) whereby goals and standards are defined; performance is monitored and measured against the goals and plans for achieving them; and corrective action is taken, if necessary, to ensure that goals are being accomplished, either in the present planning cycle or in the next (through learning). This can be shown, simply, as follows.

Control system

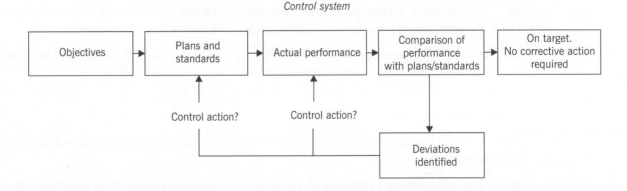

1.2 Levels of control

Robert Anthony classified managerial activity into three basic levels.

(a) **Strategic management** (carried out by the strategic apex): concerned with direction setting, policy making and crisis handling

(b) **Tactical management** (carried out by the middle line and techno structure): concerned with establishing means to corporate ends, mobilising and controlling resources, and innovating (finding new ways of achieving goals)

(c) **Operational management** (carried out by the operating core): concerned with routine activities to carry out tactical plans

1.2.1 Strategic control

At the strategic level, control involves activities such as:

(a) **Strategic planning**. Setting (and monitoring performance against) key objectives for the organisation as a whole, or organisational direction. This also includes environmental scanning, to identify opportunities and threats.

(b) Designing (or reviewing and redesigning) **organisational structures**. Decisions on downsizing, delayering, acquisition/merger, and divisionalisation and so on.

(c) Determining **policies** and **codes of conduct**, in a wide range of areas including: human resources (HR) (recruitment, training, reward, promotion, equal opportunities etc); the environment, ethics and corporate responsibility; risk appetite and risk management measures; and sourcing/procurement.

(d) **Organisation-wide initiatives**, such as business process re-engineering and total quality management.

(e) Monitoring of progress and performance against strategic plans at a high (non-detailed) level. This includes setting up a framework for management information and reporting.

(f) Managing **corporate governance**. Determining roles of the board of directors; taking board-level decisions; reporting to shareholders and so on.

1.2.2 Tactical control

Tactical control relates to the implementation of board-level decisions by functional managers. It involves activities such as:

(a) **Tactical planning**. In the case of a marketing manager, for example, this would include product/market planning and media scheduling. In the case of a production manager, it may include capacity planning, resource allocation and production scheduling.

(b) **Budgeting** and budgetary control for the function.

(c) The development and implementation of **procedures** (to fulfil policy requirements set at the strategic level). These would include recruitment, development and reward of functional staff. Other procedures include administrative procedures and systems, risk management, quality control and so on, within the scope of the function's activity.

(d) **Monitoring** compliance with plans and procedures within the function.

1.2.3 Operational control

Operational control relates to the control of relatively routine and repetitive activities, to ensure that pre-set plans and targets are met. At this level, little managerial intervention or discretion may be required: operational control systems are often automated, and generate reports only on identified deviations from plan, within pre-set tolerance limits.

Examples of operational control systems are credit controls (in accounting) and order processing, invoicing and delivery scheduling (in sales).

Exam alert

There are many models of control, but Anthony's three levels give a basic framework. You might be asked to analyse a production or HR system, using the three levels, or to recommend improvements to a specific system in a scenario.

1.3 Effective control systems – the 6 As

The effectiveness of any control procedure or system is likely to depend on the extent to which it satisfies six criteria. **We shall call these the 6 As.**

(a) **Acceptability** to the people who will operate it: a fit with their needs and expectations, and the culture of the unit.

(b) **Accessibility**, in terms of its ease of understanding and operation.

(c) **Adaptability** to changing conditions and demands.

(d) **Action orientation**, so that deviations trigger corrective action or improvements.

(e) **Appropriateness** to the circumstances, and skills and needs of the people operating it.

(f) **Affordability** or cost effectiveness: the cost of operating controls must be **less** than the costs associated with deviation or failure (which will be determined by risk analysis). In other words, prevention costs must be less than failure costs.

1.4 Control strategies and processes

There are various models describing how controls are applied in organisations. We will look briefly at two popular frameworks.

1.4.1 Market, bureaucratic and clan control

William Ouchi identified three basic control strategies used by organisations.

(a) **Market control** is the use of the price mechanism and related performance measures, internally and externally, to control organisational behaviour. It is used in loose organisational forms such as consortia and alliances, and in the construction industry when subcontractors are employed.

At corporate level, market control is always used: income statement (statement of comprehensive income), cash flow and balance sheet (statement of financial position) information is published, so the organisation's performance can be judged in comparison with other organisations, or with previous years. The market mechanism is provided by the capital markets and competitors.

At divisional level, market control may be relevant if there are separate divisions, which are established as **profit centres**, or **investment centres**.

At operational level, the price mechanism can be used as a means to control activities, for example in the use of target costing, competitive tendering for contracts (as in the UK public sector), or transfer pricing.

Market control can be regarded as a form of **output control**. Output control is focused on the achievement of outputs and results. Organisational performance is measured against predetermined standards and targets, for example achieving production or profitability targets. Output control facilitates increased levels of autonomy in working practices; once output targets have been determined and agreed with workers there is less need for bureaucratic control.

(b) **Bureaucratic control** uses an impersonal system of rules and reports to maintain control, which we discussed earlier in this Study Text.

The main mechanisms of control are policies, standard operating procedures, rules, statistical reports, budgets (and budgetary control), staff performance appraisal and a clear disciplinary framework.

(c) **Clan control** is based on corporate culture. It depends on shared values and standards of behaviour within the organisation, and assumes that employees 'buy in' to the purpose, goals and expectations of the organisation.

Ouchi suggested that all organisations use a mix of these strategies, but took a contingency view as to which control mechanism was likely to predominate in a given set of conditions.

Contingencies	Control strategies
• Routine technology • Stable environment • Large size • Functional structure	Mainly **bureaucratic** Some clan control is possible (eg top management, research and development)
• Priced internal outputs • Competition on price • Size – not relevant • Product/brand structure	Mainly **market** Bureaucratic or clan control may be used within profit centres
• Non-routine technology • Unstable environment • Small size • Matrix structure	Mainly **clan control** Bureaucratic control may be used in departments dealing with routine matters

Question 7.1

Control systems

Learning outcome B2a

What type of control would you expect to see in a large international airline?

A Contingency
B Market
C Clan
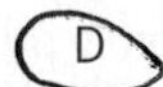
D Bureaucratic

Personal centralised control

We can extend Ouchi's work on control strategies by the inclusion of a form of control known as personal centralised control.

Personal centralised control is often found in owner-managed organisations; it shares some of the features of Handy's power culture (discussed in an earlier chapter). The key feature in personal centralised control is a central figure who acts as the main decision maker in the organisation. Control is achieved over activities by the owner personally overseeing the work of employees. The owner is able to enforce worker conformity through the issuing of rewards and punishment. Often the owner is able to command authority through a combination of personality and expertise. As the organisation grows, the owner is often no longer able to manage the day to day activities of the organisation in person and has to employ managers and supervisors. This gradual shift in control away from the owner tends to lead to a market (output) or bureaucratic control approach.

1.4.2 Control processes

In their influential work *Exploring Corporate Strategy*, Johnson and Scholes suggest that control processes can be classified as:

(a) **Input-focused** (controlling resources input to a given strategy) or **output-focused** (controlling the results and outcomes of a given strategy)

(b) **Direct** (using supervision, monitoring and behaviour-shaping) or **indirect** (creating environmental conditions within which the desired behaviour or results can be achieved)

They outline six controls using this framework. Again, organisations will use a mix of these processes, but some may dominate in a given organisation, depending on its culture, geography, technology and specific strategic challenges.

	Input-focused	Output-focused
Direct	• *Direct supervision* 'The direct control of strategic decisions by one or a few individuals, typically focused on the effort put into the business by employees.' Often the main control process in small organisations. • *Planning systems* Planning resource requirements and allocations, and monitoring their utilisation to identify variance and initiate corrective action. Eg budgetary control, standardisation of work processes, and centralised formulae for calculating resource allocations (such as marketing budget as a percentage of revenue).	• *Performance targets* Focus on outputs such as revenue, profitability, quality standards and other key performance indicators (KPIs). The organisation or strategic business unit's (SBU's) performance is evaluated against defined targets, allowing flexibility as to how they are achieved. Performance targets particularly suit large businesses, since they allow central control over results – without stifling the flexibility or initiative of SBUs in the face of changing 'local' demands.
Indirect	• *Social/cultural control* Norms, values and expectations of behaviour become standardised and accepted in the group or organisation, and individuals are 'brought into line' by group influence, education and training, rewards, involvement and so on. Particularly valuable in dynamic environments, because securing 'buy in' supports change.	• *Internal market mechanisms* A formalised system of 'contracting' for resources between units in an organisation, as internal market transactions between suppliers/customers. Units are required to earn revenue or achieve results in competition with external providers. Internal markets can foster integration and efficiency by

	Input-focused	Output-focused
	• *Self-control* Employees are given clear goals, performance feedback, incentives and leadership to support them in maintaining desired standards of conduct and performance without direct intervention. People behave in desired ways because they understand the need to do so, and are willing to commit themselves to the goals of the team.	encouraging an 'internal customer' orientation.

Section summary

Control systems exist to support the achievement of organisational objectives. They are of many types, both formal and informal.

Organisations require control at all levels of their operating framework: **strategic**, **tactical and operational**.

Control systems should be **acceptable**, **accessible**, **adaptable**, **action-oriented**, **appropriate** and **affordable**.

William Ouchi identified three broad **control strategies**: market control, bureaucratic control and clan control. Strategy gurus Johnson and Scholes outline a broader framework of **control processes**, both input- and output-focused and direct and indirect.

2 The role of the finance function

Introduction

For most organisations, the finance function represents a key control over its operations. In this section, we consider it useful to explain a little of the treasury function, as the two are often closely linked. As we shall discuss, the modern finance function is more than just a mechanism for reporting on performance, and in many organisations has taken on a broader advisory and strategic role.

2.1 Financial control and treasury

Although an organisation may operate a single finance function covering all its financial activities, within this function a distinction can be made between financial control activities and treasury activities.

Financial control activities involve the **allocation and effective use of resources**. This comprises:

(a) Advising on investment appraisal
(b) Analysing performance (management accounting)
(c) Reporting results (financial accounting)

The **treasury function** is involved in **obtaining suitable types of finance**. This includes:

(a) Advising on sources of finance and dividend policy
(b) Financial risk management (hedging)
(c) Liaising with financial stakeholders (banks / key shareholders)

Clearly, the two roles have many links. Treasury will use the detailed information prepared by the financial control function, and will in turn set down the parameters (major assumptions, cost of capital) that the financial control function will use in its detailed calculations.

Examples of interaction between the two functions are:

(a) **Financial control** reports on and identifies currency risk while **the treasury function** decides on hedging strategy.

(b) **The treasury function** assesses the cost of capital and **financial control**, and then applies it to proposed investments.

2.2 The roles of the financial controller

The specific activities and roles that may be expected from a financial control function include:

(a) **Processing** transactions, maintaining accounting records and delivering month-end reports at low cost and efficiently.

(b) **Communicating** results to internal and external stakeholders. (We explore the finance function's relationship with stakeholders later in the chapter).

(c) Ensuring the effective operation of **corporate governance and control**. This has become increasingly important in the wake of various financial scandals and the requirements of legislation such as the US Sarbanes-Oxley Act (which we will discuss later on).

(d) Acting as a **business partner** and adviser.

2.2.1 The finance function as business partner

The finance function has faced pressures to become **more actively involved** in business operations. Many finance functions have therefore refocused their roles as business partners, adopting a more **commercial, action-orientated approach**. This means gaining broad knowledge of the business, participating as full members of operational teams and bringing financial expertise to the management process. They are expected to **integrate management accounting information** with **strategic management accounting data**.

2.2.2 The hybrid accountant

This evolution in the role of the finance professional has led to the creation of the term the '**hybrid accountant**', which is now regarded as the modern model of an accountant. Growing numbers of management accountants spend the majority of their time as internal consultants or business analysts. They spend less time preparing standardised reports, but more time analysing and interpreting information. Moreover, many no longer work in an 'accounting department', but are based in the operating departments with which they work, meaning that they are increasingly involved with the operations of their business, and more actively involved in decision making.

Important areas where the finance function's role has developed have included:

- Providing more useful information on business units, projects, products and customers
- Supplying business cases for new investments
- Giving support in helping operational managers understand the information provided
- Collaborating in strategic planning and budgeting
- Designing information systems that provide greater support for operational managers

One example of where finance functions have been expected to assume a more active role is **investment appraisal**. Accountants are now often required to do more than state that the proposal does not meet financial criteria; they are expected to help develop and refine proposals.

Question 7.2 Sales support

Learning outcome C1b

In what ways can the finance function support the sales function?

2.2.3 Problems with the business partner model

Over the last couple of years, the business partner model has in turn faced criticism, due primarily to Enron and other financial scandals. Critics have questioned the **identification** of the finance function with **operational viewpoints** and the **loss of independence** of the finance function that has arisen from finance staff reporting to, and being accountable to, operational managers.

Critics also claim that the finance function has become too greatly diverted from delivering basic controls and safeguards and functions, providing prudent financial management and ensuring the **true and fair view** is given. The finance function has, critics suggest, lost sight of its role in governance and failed to protect shareholder and public interest.

2.2.4 Independent business partner

A new independent business partner model has therefore emerged, not losing sight of co-operation with operational managers, but also having at its heart **strict controls**, **safeguarding of assets** and **effective reporting**.

The independent business partner model stresses that the finance function should seek to **add** value, but its role is not to **create** value. The creation of strategy, ideas and opportunities is the responsibility of the operational departments. Finance's role is to **assess** and **validate** these ideas, taking a commercial view, but also ensuring that business plans and strategy are rigorously reviewed and challenged if necessary. Finance must also **review actual performance** rigorously and be prepared to challenge better than expected, as well as worse than expected, performance in order to minimise the risks of understatement.

2.2.5 Relationships between the finance function and key stakeholders

The growing importance placed on the role of the finance function emphasises the need to manage organisational relationships and to build collaborative working practices.

CASE STUDY

The finance function and organisational relationships

In 2010, ACCA published a report *Collaborative working: why relationships matter in finance*, written by Jamie Lyon. The report highlighted that the broadening remit of the finance function has led to an increase in the importance of the way in which the finance function manages the interactions it has with both internal and external stakeholders.

Internal relationships

The rise of business partnering has extended the role of the finance professional, with accountants now expected to play a greater role in supporting the business's operations. The drive towards business partnering has been partly driven by the recognition of the accountants' transferable skills that can be applied across the organisation, including project management, budgeting and business analysis. Accountants are no longer regarded as simply being 'number crunchers'.

Central to collaborative working across the organisation are the relationships that the finance function must build if it is to be successful in 'adding value' as a business partner. As Lyon highlights, these relationships can prove to be particularly important, as the finance function is expected to be at the heart of business change programmes, which may lead to resistance from those departments affected. For example, cost reduction programmes are likely to involve redundancies.

Organisational relationships are particularly important, as the finance function does not work in isolation. Finance professionals need to understand the contribution that other departments make to the role of the finance function. This is evident, as the finance function is dependent on the HR department to recruit the necessary finance staff. Lyon notes 'many HR departments have created HR or learning and development business partnering roles specifically for finance, so that the needs of finance can be better understood and delivered upon'.

External relationships

External stakeholders are likely to view the finance function and Chief Financial Officer (CFO) as representing the 'face of the business', acting as the interface between stakeholders and the entity. Due to factors including globalisation and increasing levels of corporate governance, most large organisations now have an increasingly diverse range of stakeholders to consider. Besides a primary responsibility to shareholders, CFOs are aware of the increasing importance of effective engagement with groups including tax authorities, auditors, regulators, investors, finance providers, customers and suppliers.

The ACCA report highlights that 'today's CFO is not only driving and shaping business strategy, but needs to work across the organisation to engage and bring on board partners such as HR, IT, marketing and sales, and other functions. A recent survey from the UK found that 34% of finance directors had responsibility for HR in their organisations, 49% had responsibility for IT systems, 50% were also company secretaries/heads of the legal function, and 41% had responsibility for property and facilities'.

Building relationships

Lyon highlights that building a collaborative culture to facilitate an effective business partnering relationship is key. An effective approach used by large organisations that have pursued business partnering involves specialist finance skills being deployed across the organisation's different activities. The proximity of these small units to the business's operations is believed to 'drive value'.

Operations are also supported by small centralised 'finance units', which standardise processes from transaction processing and outsourcing to investment appraisals. This approach often requires changes to be made to organisational design, eg restructuring the role of finance staff and the reassessment of training and IT capabilities across the organisation.

Collaborative relationships are intended to be beneficial for both the organisation and the individual, as they help to develop the careers of the finance professionals involved. Building closer links between the finance function and the entity's operations is believed to facilitate the sharing of experiences throughout the organisation, and help drive 'innovation by generating new ideas to take the business forward'. The report suggests that collaborative relationships can be established using a range of techniques:

(a) Talent programmes: which are aimed at identifying professionals from different business functions (including finance) who possess desired skills needed for the entity's future success. Such programmes often involve bringing together such individuals to build a 'collegiate spirit'.

(b) Multi-functional teams: where finance professionals increasingly work with individuals from other functions across the organisation on a variety of projects. This facilitates the flow of expertise and helps with relationship building.

(c) Job rotations: help to create a more collaborative culture as they allow finance professionals to interact with other parts of the business on a longer-term basis. Such experiential learning helps professionals to build a greater understanding of the organisation's operations.

(d) Coaching and mentoring programmes: 'afford the individuals the opportunities to develop the close and personal constructive working relationships that are the basis of any strong network'.

Source:

Lyon, J (2010) *Collaborative working: why relationships matter in finance.* [Online]. Available from: http://www.accaglobal.com/content/dam/acca/global/PDF-technical/finance-transformation/collaborative-working.pdf [Accessed 27 September 2016].

2.2.6 The finance function and external stakeholders

The case study above highlights the important role that the finance function plays in engaging with a range of external stakeholders. The nature of the finance function's relationships with certain external stakeholders is considered below.

External stakeholder groups that the finance function may interact with might include:

(a) External auditors
(b) Investors and providers of finance
(c) Tax authorities

External auditors

The objective of an audit of financial statements is to enable the auditor to express an opinion on whether the financial statements are prepared, in all material respects, in accordance with an applicable financial reporting framework. As a result, external audit work is concerned with the financial statements and associated accounting records.

A key part of the external auditors' work involves assessing the organisation's system of internal controls; this assessment drives the work required on the financial statements. The external auditor identifies weaknesses in the system of internal controls and presents these findings to the organisation's management, accompanied by recommendations on how current practices can be improved. This important exercise assists management in addressing the risk of internal control failure. The finance function should actively implement the external auditors' recommendations to reduce the scope of internal weaknesses impacting on the quality of financial information produced. This highlights the need for the finance function not to view the external auditors' work as being adversarial by nature, but instead as being a beneficial service.

Investors and providers of finance

Investors (shareholders) and providers of finance (banks) are often dependent on the output of the finance function when trying to assess the performance of their investment in the organisation. Information in the form of financial statements and performance forecasts are commonly used by such stakeholders when deciding whether to invest in more shares or provide additional funding. This illustrates the importance of the finance function in producing transparent, useful financial information.

Tax authorities

Local tax authorities require information from the finance function to enable the organisation to pay the correct amount of tax. This places a duty on the finance function to accurately prepare documentation to support submitted tax returns. The finance function needs to have up to date knowledge of statutory requirements to ensure compliance with the tax authorities.

2.2.7 The finance function and other parts of the organisation

As we have seen, the finance function is a crucial interface for external stakeholders; however, it is important not to overlook the role it plays in supporting the work of other departments throughout the organisation. In this section we consider how the finance function assists the procurement department and marketing department.

The finance function and procurement

The procurement department is involved in the placing and management of orders of supplies required by the organisation. The finance function is likely to interact with the procurement department in a number of ways, including:

- Liaising with suppliers on behalf of the procurement team to negotiate favourable credit terms
- Advising the procurement team on the prices that they can pay for certain supplies
- Making payments to suppliers for orders placed by the procurement team
- Advising the procurement team on inventory levels

The finance function and marketing

The marketing department aims to satisfy customer needs profitably. The finance function may engage with the marketing department in a number of ways, including:

- Assisting the marketing team in the establishment of advertising budgets
- Helping the marketing team to establish appropriate prices to charge customers for the organisation's goods and services
- Advising the marketing team on movements in the volume of sales for particular products to help determine market share

2.3 Assessment of the finance function

There has been increasing emphasis over the last few years on assessment of the contribution made by the finance function. Traditional measures of success have included the following.

2.3.1 Reliable information

A recent survey suggested that about four-fifths of CFOs rate **reliability of information** as their highest priority. Its importance has been enhanced by the recent financial scandals and the requirement of the US Sarbanes-Oxley legislation for CFOs to sign off personally their company's accounts.

As well as fulfilling legal requirements, finance departments must have regard for the information required by different **stakeholders**, the information that is **relevant** to their needs.

Organisations will need to develop processes to ensure that information is reliable. For the finance function, this means playing a key role in the development of technology that will **ensure information** is **reliable**, being available to answer queries and resolve problems and **educating** other staff to make sure that they are aware of the information needed, the accounting policies used by the company and the legal framework.

2.3.2 Flexibility

A very important aspect of the finance function's work is how it copes with **new developments and new financial reporting standards**. As well as coping with the technical issues, the finance function plays a vital role in **educating investors** on the language of new standards and their impact on the KPIs.

The management accounting function also needs to be flexible in **its response to users' requests** for information and reports.

2.3.3 Speed of reporting

The Sarbanes-Oxley legislation has also resulted in tighter reporting deadlines, with companies listed in the US being required to file quarterly accounts in 35 days rather than 45 days, and annual reports in 60 rather than 90 days. A European Union (EU) draft directive specifies 60 days for quarterly reports, with further reductions towards 35 days.

In addition, surveys suggest a possible link between market valuation and speed of reporting, with larger investors, in particular, viewing shorter reporting times as a sign that the company is well managed.

2.3.4 Efficiency

Pressure on the finance function to reduce costs and make greater use of resources, in particular speeding up basic processing functions, has greatly increased over the last few years. We shall see later in this chapter that this has led to pressure to **outsource** the basic functions, and let the finance function concentrate on more 'exciting' work.

Measures of efficiency include:

- The number of transactions processed per transaction-processing employee
- The cost of transactions processed as a percentage of revenue per transaction
- The time taken at period ends to report results

2.3.5 Balanced scorecard approach

As well as the traditional measures discussed above, many organisations have used a balanced scorecard approach to judge the work of the finance function, focusing not just on **traditional financial measures**, but also on other measures of concern to stakeholders. While many traditional measures focus purely on outcomes, balanced scorecard measures often go a stage back and measure the **factors** that will result in satisfactory outcomes.

(a) **Customer satisfaction**. This focuses on the strength of relationships between the finance function and other stakeholders, and whether the finance function is viewed as delivering the right mixture and quality of transaction processing, risk management and decision support.

(b) **Enhancement of internal processes**. These focus on the processes that the finance function must carry out efficiently and effectively in order to report accurately and give customer satisfaction.

(c) **Financial**. Success here could be measured by the frequency of forecasts and the average preparation times for key elements of the business planning process.

(d) **Learning and growth**. These measures concentrate on the organisation's ability to adapt to change, and also the development of finance staff's skills and competences. Possible measures include turnover of finance staff and what percentage of staff have a recognised financial qualification.

2.3.6 Benchmarking the finance function

One method of measuring the success of the finance function is to benchmark against finance functions elsewhere. With a large group, comparisons can be made of different finance functions within the same group. Alternatively, there are organisations which will bring finance directors together to compare best practice, or which offer databases of other departments.

Most benchmarking exercises have suggested that too much time is spent on transaction processing, and not enough time on value-added activities.

Problems with using benchmarking include the **money and time involved**. If the exercise is to be effective, data has to be collected for an organisation's own finance function as well as obtained for others.

2.4 Outsourcing and shared servicing

KEY TERM

OUTSOURCING is the contracting out of specified operations or services to an external vendor.

The arrangement varies according to the circumstances of both organisations.

	Outsourcing arrangement		
Feature	**Timeshare**	**Service**	**Facilities management (FM)**
What is it?	Access to an external processing system on a time-used basis	Focus on specific function, eg payroll	A outside agency manages the organisation's information systems (IS) and information technology facilities; the client retains equipment but all services provided by FM company
Management responsibility	Mostly retained	Some retained	Very little retained

	Outsourcing arrangement		
Feature	**Timeshare**	**Service**	**Facilities management (FM)**
Focus	Operational	A function	Strategic
Timescale	Short-term	Medium-term	Long-term
Justification	Cost savings	More efficient	Access to expertise; better service; management can focus on core business activities

Managing such arrangements involves deciding **what** will be outsourced, choosing a supplier and the supplier **relationship**.

2.4.1 How to determine what will be outsourced

(a) What is the system's **strategic importance**? A third-party IT specialist cannot be expected to possess specific business knowledge.

(b) Functions with only **limited interfaces** are most easily outsourced, eg payroll.

(c) Do we know enough about the system to manage the arrangement?

(d) Are our requirements likely to **change**?

The arrangement is incorporated in a contract sometimes referred to as the **service level contract** or **service level agreement** (SLA). The contract should cover the following elements.

Element	Comment
Service level	Minimum levels of service with penalties, for example: • Response time to requests for assistance/information • System 'uptime' percentage • Deadlines for performing relevant tasks
Exit route	Arrangements for an exit route, transfer to another supplier or move back in-house.
Timescale	When does the contract expire? Is the timescale suitable for the organisation's needs or should it be renegotiated?
Ownership	If outsourcing involved the development of software or new intellectual property, the agreement should cover ownership, licensing and copyright.
Dependencies	If related services are outsourced, the level of service quality agreed should group these services together.
Employment issues	If the organisation's IT staff move to the third party, employer responsibilities must be specified clearly.

2.4.2 Advantages of outsourcing arrangements

(a) Outsourcing can remove uncertainty about **cost**, as there is often a long-term contract where services are specified in advance for a **fixed price**.

(b) Long-term contracts (maybe up to ten years) encourage **planning** for the future.

(c) Outsourcing can bring the benefits of **economies of scale**. For example, an external outsourcer can provide financial processing activities (eg payroll services) at a lower cost than if these were retained in-house.

(d) A specialist organisation may have access to **best practice skills and knowledge**.

(e) New skills and knowledge become available. A specialist company can **share** staff with **specific expertise** between several clients.

(f) **Flexibility**. Resources may be scaled up or down, depending on demand.

2.4.3 Disadvantages of outsourcing arrangements

(a) Information and its provision is **an inherent part of business and management**. If the IS is outsourced, the organisation will have less control over the system. If controls are subsequently relaxed, or the quality of information falls, this could damage the organisation's competitive position.

(b) Information strategy can be used to gain **competitive advantage**. Opportunities may be missed if a third party is handling IS services.

(c) The organisation will lose the knowledge of key staff, which again may weaken its competitive position.

(d) An organisation may have highly **confidential information**, and to let outsiders handle it could be seen as **risky** in commercial and/or legal terms.

(e) An organisation may find itself **locked in** to an unsatisfactory contract.

2.4.4 Outsourcing the finance function

Even if the finance function has to refocus towards its more traditional roles, there will still be strong pressures to **outsource basic transaction processing functions**, payroll and expense management.

Exam alert

You will have covered outsourcing in other papers, and knowledge from these papers may be relevant to your E2 exam.

2.4.5 Shared servicing and shared service centres

An alternative to outsourcing is shared servicing, where shared service centres (SSCs) consolidate the **transaction-processing activities** of many operations within a company. Some organisations have decided to consolidate certain financial processing functions which had previously been nationally or internationally dispersed by bringing them together on one site. SSCs aim to achieve significant cost reductions while improving service levels through the use of standardised technology and processes, and SLAs.

Advantages to using this approach include:

(a) **Reduced headcount** due to economies of scale resulting from the single location centre

(b) Associated **reduction in premises** and other overhead costs

(c) Knowledge sharing should lead to an **improvement in quality** of the service provided

(d) Allows **standard approaches** to be adopted across the organisation, leading to more consistent management of business data

Disadvantages might include:

(a) **Loss of business specific knowledge**. For example, creating a consolidated finance function which broadly handles financial matters for the entire organisation may lack an understanding of specific finance issues affecting individual departments or business units.

(b) **Removed from decision making**. Building on from the point above, an SSC finance function is unlikely to be able to provide meaningful financial information for decision making if finance personnel are removed from the day to day realities facing a particular department or business unit.

(c) **Weakened relationships**. Geographical distance between the site of the SSC and the respective business areas it serves may weaken the relationships between the two.

Section summary

The financial control function is concerned with the **allocation and effective use of resources.**

The treasury function is concerned with **obtaining finance** and managing relations with financial stakeholders.

Basic processing tasks are now often **outsourced** or **concentrated** in **shared service centres.**

3 Internal control systems

Introduction

Internal controls cover policies, processes, tasks and behaviours (Turnbull). These controls enable a business to operate effectively, comply with laws and provide good-quality information from reports.

When you think about the **control framework**, you need to make a simple distinction between the **control environment** and **control procedures.**

KEY TERM

An INTERNAL CONTROL is any action taken by management to enhance the likelihood that established objectives and goals will be achieved. Management plans, organises and directs the performance of sufficient actions to provide reasonable assurance that objectives and goals will be achieved. Thus, control is the result of proper planning, organising and directing by management.

(*Institute of Internal Auditors*)

3.1 Purposes of an internal control system

The UK's Turnbull report provides a helpful summary of the main purposes of an internal control system.

Turnbull comments that internal control consists of the **policies**, **processes**, **tasks, behaviours** and other aspects of a company that, taken together:

(a) Facilitate its effective and efficient operation by enabling it to respond appropriately to significant business, operational, financial, compliance and other **risks** to achieving the company's objectives. This includes the safeguarding of assets from inappropriate use or from loss and fraud, and ensuring that liabilities are identified and managed.

(b) Help ensure the quality of internal and external **reporting**. This requires the maintenance of proper records and processes that generate a flow of timely, relevant and reliable information from within and outside the organisation.

(c) Help ensure **compliance** with applicable laws and regulations, and also with internal policies with respect to the conduct of businesses.

The Turnbull report goes on to say that a sound system of internal control reduces but does not eliminate the possibilities of poorly judged decisions, human error, deliberate circumvention of controls, management override of controls and unforeseeable circumstances. Systems will provide **reasonable (not absolute) assurance** that the company will not be hindered in achieving its business objectives and in the orderly and legitimate conduct of its business, but won't provide certain protection against all possible problems.

3.2 The control framework

Organisations need to consider the **overall framework of controls**, since controls are unlikely to be very effective if they are developed sporadically around the organisation, and their effectiveness will be very difficult to measure by internal audit and ultimately by senior management.

Perhaps the simplest framework for internal control draws a distinction between:

(a) **Control environment** – the overall context of control, in particular the attitude of directors and managers towards control. A 'strong' control environment is one in which clear strategies for dealing with risk are supported by policies and codes of conduct; clear definition of authority and responsibility; clear communication of expectations; and senior management commitment to competence, integrity and trust.

(b) **Control procedures** – the detailed controls in place, including measures such as financial controls, health and safety reporting, and quality monitoring.

3.3 Elements of effective internal control

One influential US guidance model (**Committee of Sponsoring Organizations of the Treadway Commission – or COSO**) recommends the following elements for effective internal control.

(a) A strong **control environment**, supportive of business objectives

(b) **Risk assessment** and **risk management** to identify areas of vulnerability and exposure (including a range of business, financial and compliance risks) as a basis for the objectives of the control system

(c) **A range of control activities**, such as segregation of duties, authorisation procedures, physical security measures, supervision, arithmetical and accounting checks/reconciliations and checking/development of personnel

(d) **Communication and information processes** to ensure that all levels of management receive appropriate progress reports

(e) Processes for **monitoring the continuing effectiveness** of the system and taking corrective action where required

Section summary

Internal controls should help organisations counter risks, maintain the quality of reporting and comply with laws and regulations. They provide reasonable assurance that organisations will fulfil their objectives.

Internal control frameworks include the **control environment** within which **internal controls** operate. Other important elements are the **risk assessment and response processes**, the **sharing of information** and **monitoring** the environment and operation of the control system.

4 Performance management – controlling the individual

Introduction

In this section we cover control, as this affects the individual employee. Performance management develops out of the organisation's business plan, as this is translated into individual performance targets. Employees are appraised on their performance in accordance with the plan and how they have performed. Employment contracts set out the expectations the organisation has regarding conduct and performance for the employee.

4.1 Human resource strategy

Although personnel control systems typically operate at the tactical level, the purpose of those controls will be to support control at the strategic level via human resource strategies and policies. Human resource policy will be determined with regard to matters such as:

(a) The number and type of skills required by the future plans of the organisation

(b) The organisation's commitment to equality of opportunity and diversity (with regard to recruitment and selection, development, promotion and so on)

(c) Training and development opportunities offered

(d) Promotion and management succession

(e) Flexible working, family-friendly policies, the use of non standard contract labour, outsourcing and so on

(f) Rewards and incentives, and how they are awarded and reviewed

(g) Codes of conduct, disciplinary and grievance processes and so on

These policy statements can then be translated into procedures at the tactical level.

4.2 Performance management

KEY TERM

PERFORMANCE MANAGEMENT is 'a means of getting better results ... by understanding and managing performance within an agreed framework of planned goals, standards and competence requirements. It is a process to establish a shared understanding about what is to be achieved, and an approach to managing and developing people ... [so that it] ... will be achieved'.

(Armstrong, *Handbook of Personnel Management Practice*, 2003)

The process of performance management can be outlined as follows.

From the **business plan**, identify the requirements and competences required to carry it out.

Draw up a **performance agreement**, defining the expectations of the individual or team, covering standards of performance, performance indicators and the skills and competences people need.

Draw up a **performance and development plan** with the individual. These record the actions needed to improve performance, normally covering development in the current job. They are discussed with jobholders, and will typically cover:

(a) The areas of performance the individual feels to be in need of development
(b) What the individual and manager agree is needed to enhance performance
(c) Development and training initiatives

Manage performance continually throughout the year, not just at appraisal interviews done to satisfy the personnel department. Managers can review actual performance, with more informal interim reviews at various times of the year.

(a) High performance is reinforced by praise, recognition, increasing responsibility. Low performance results in coaching or counselling.

(b) Work plans are updated as necessary.

(c) Performance problems are dealt with: identifying what they are, establishing the reasons for the shortfall, taking control action (with adequate resources) and providing feedback.

Performance review. At a defined period each year, success against the plan is reviewed, but the whole point is to assess what is going to happen in future.

Question 7.3 Performance management

Learning outcome B2a

Following a review of the customer satisfaction levels across all the Farmers outlets in the UK, it has come to light that one store is not meeting the company's high standards for customer service. Feedback from customers of the Farmers supermarket in Grimsby has revealed some interesting results. A number of customers regularly complain that staff do not seem to know where the fresh produce sold in-store comes from. This has raised some doubts among shoppers that the produce sold is not actually sourced locally, as Farmers claims. Other customers have also complained that store staff are often rude and unhelpful.

Steve Farmer, the Head of Human Resources, is keen to introduce a performance management system to help the Store Manager tackle the issues currently being encountered at the Grimsby store.

Required

What are the advantages to **employees** working at the Farmers store in Grimsby of introducing such a system?

4.3 Employment contracts

KEY POINT

As an alternative to negotiated agreements on performance, **contracts of employment** may be used to set out the organisation's expected standards of conduct and performance, as a basis for measurement and discipline/improvement planning.

A **contract of employment** may be written, oral or a mixture of both. There may be a standard form contract, exchange of letters, or terms agreed orally prior to engagement. As long as there is agreement on essential terms, such as hours and wages, a valid contract exists.

Under UK law, an employer must give employees a written statement of **particulars of employment**, within two months of starting work. This statement should identify:

(a) The names of the employer and employee, and the date on which employment began
(b) Pay, hours of work, holiday and sick leave entitlements and details of any pension scheme
(c) Length of notice of termination to be given on either side
(d) Details of disciplinary and grievance procedures and work rules
(e) Rules on health and safety at work (by custom)

The purpose of this is to ensure that employees have precise information about the terms on which they are employed. Note that this describes **mutual** expectations, rights and obligations: it can be used to control the performance both of the employee and of the organisation, in case of dispute.

4.4 Performance appraisal

KEY TERM

PERFORMANCE APPRAISAL is the systematic review and assessment of an employee's performance, potential and development or improvement needs.

4.4.1 The purpose of appraisal

The general purpose of any staff appraisal system is to improve the efficiency of the organisation by ensuring that the individuals within it are performing to the best of their ability and developing their potential for improvement. It has a number of aspects.

(a) **Reward review**. The appraisal should assess whether employees deserve bonuses or pay increases.

(b) **Performance review**. The appraisal can be used for planning and following up training and development programmes by identifying training needs and validating training methods.

(c) **Potential review**. This is an aid to planning career development and succession which attempts to predict the level and type of work the individual will be capable of in the future.

More specific objectives may include:

(a) **Establishing what the individual has to do** in a job in order that the objectives for the section or department are realised

(b) **Establishing the key or main results** that the individual will be expected to achieve in the course of their work over a period of time

(c) **Comparing the individual's level of performance against a standard**, to provide a basis for remuneration above the basic pay rate

(d) **Identifying the individual's training and development needs** in the light of actual performance

(e) **Identifying potential candidates for promotion**

(f) **Identifying areas for improvement**

(g) **Establishing an inventory of actual and potential performance within the undertaking** to provide a basis for manpower planning

(h) **Monitoring the undertaking's initial selection procedures** against the subsequent performance of recruits, relative to the organisation's expectations

(i) **Improving communication** about work tasks between different levels in the hierarchy

4.4.2 Benefits of appraisal

There are a number of benefits of the appraisal process, both to the organisation and to the employees themselves. These are summarised in the table below.

Benefits to the organisation	Benefits to the employees
• Provides a system for assessing the competence of employees • Identifies areas for improvement and training needs • Provides a fair basis for reward decisions • Identifies candidates for promotion • Improves communication between managers and subordinates • Allows individual targets to be linked to corporate objectives • Provides a basis for HR planning	• Provides a basis for remuneration • Can be an opportunity to discuss future opportunities and career development • Allows any training and development needs to be identified and addressed • Provides feedback about performance and competence via comparison against agreed targets and established standards • Identifies any particularly strong work carried out during the review period

Benefits to the organisation	Benefits to the employees
• Provides a method of monitoring recruitment and induction processes against results	

4.4.3 The process of appraisal

A typical appraisal system will consist of the following processes.

Identify criteria for assessment, perhaps based on job analysis, performance standards, and person specifications and so on.

Prepare an appraisal report. Traditional approaches focused on appraisal of a subordinate by their immediate superior, but modern approaches include:

(a) **Self-assessment**, to encourage self-awareness and learning

(b) **Upward appraisal**, to gather feedback from subordinates on the managerial style of their superiors

(c) **360-degree feedback**, to gather a rounded picture through feedback from superiors, subordinates, colleagues, customers and other relevant parties

Carry out an appraisal interview, for an exchange of views about the appraisal report, targets for improvement, solutions to problems and so on.

The assessor's superior reviews the assessment, so that the appraisee does not feel subject to one person's prejudices. Formal appeals may be allowed, if necessary to establish the fairness of the procedure.

Prepare and implement an action plan to achieve improvements and changes agreed.

Follow up the progress of the action plan.

Appraisal can thus be seen in terms of a basic control process, as follows.

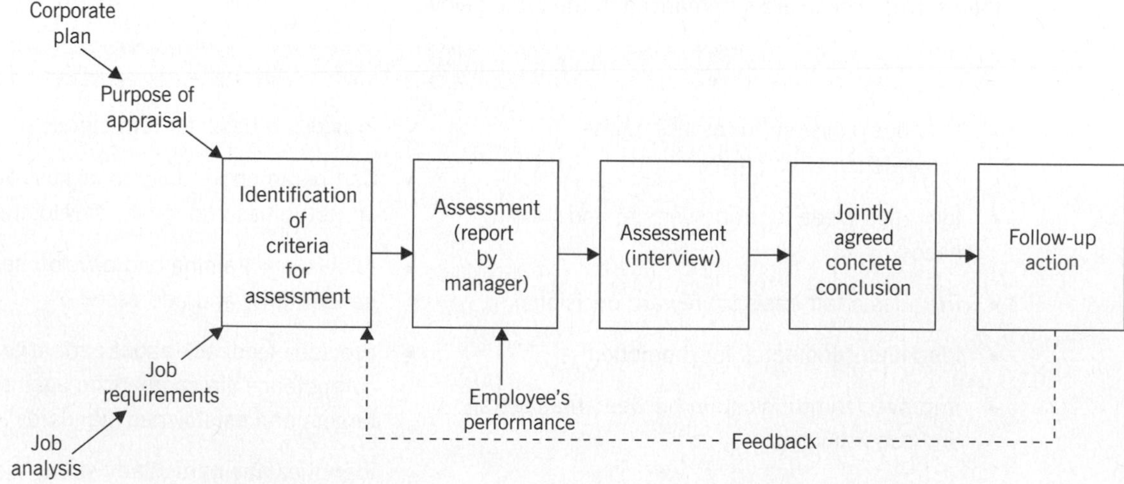

4.4.4 Improving appraisal

Even the most objective and systematic appraisal scheme is subject to **personal** and **interpersonal problems**.

(a) Appraisal is often **defensive on the part of the subordinate**, who believes that criticism may mean a low bonus or pay rise, or lost promotion opportunity.

(b) Appraisal is often **defensive on the part of the superior**, who cannot reconcile the role of judge and critic with the human relations aspect of interviewing and management.

(c) The superior might show **conscious or unconscious bias** in the appraisal or may be influenced by rapport (or lack of it) with the interviewee. Systems without clearly defined standard criteria will be particularly prone to the subjectivity of the assessor's judgement.

(d) The manager and subordinate may both **be reluctant to devote time and attention to appraisal**. Their experience in the organisation may indicate that the exercise is a waste of time (especially if there is a lot of form filling) with no relevance to the job, and no reliable follow-up action.

(e) The organisational culture may **simply not take appraisal seriously**: interviewers are not trained or given time to prepare, appraisees are not encouraged to contribute, or the exercise is perceived as a 'nod' to human relations with no practical results.

The appraisal scheme should itself be assessed (and regularly reassessed) for relevance, fairness, serious intent, co-operative orientation, positive outcomes and cost efficiency. Many of these issues have been addressed by modern approaches that emphasise multi-source feedback, a forward-looking improvement focus, collaborative discussion, and problem-solving and results-oriented appraisal criteria.

Question 7.4 Formal appraisal

Learning outcome B1b

List four disadvantages to the individual of **not** having a **formal** appraisal system.

Section summary

Performance management is an approach to controlling the conduct, performance and development of personnel in the organisation. Human resource control systems typically operate at the tactical level of control.

Contracts of employment may be used as the basis for controlling employee conduct and performance, by setting out the organisation's expectations.

There are a number of aspects to **performance appraisal**, including reward review, performance review and potential review. Appraisal is an important practical aspect of control in organisations.

5 Controlling health and safety

Introduction

Almost all industrialised countries have legislation covering governing health and safety in the workplace.

You need to know the main obligations of the employer and employee towards health and safety. Also, make sure you have a broad awareness of what the individual regulations cover, for instance visual display unit (VDU) usage, though you shouldn't need to know any detail for the exam.

Employers are obliged to report serious accidents under regulations known as RIDDOR (Reporting of Injuries, Diseases and Dangerous Occurrences Regulations) and to keep accident report books for all accidents that take place in the workplace.

5.1 Why is health and safety important?

Health, safety and wellbeing at work are important for several reasons.

(a) Employees should, as human beings, be **protected** from needless pain and suffering.

(b) Employers and employees have **legal obligations** to take reasonable measures to promote healthy and safe working.

(c) Accidents, illness and other causes of absence and impaired performance **cost** the organisation money.

(d) A business's **corporate image** and reputation as an employer (its **employer brand**) may suffer if its health and safety record is bad: this might alienate customers and potential employees.

5.2 The legal framework on health and safety

We look at the UK framework, as an example. The main UK legislation in this area is the **Health and Safety at Work Act 1974**, plus subsequent regulations and codes of practice issued under the Act, which implement the provisions of EU directives on health and safety issues.

However, it would be wrong to paint too optimistic a picture of employers' performance on health and safety.

(a) **Legislation sets bare minimum standards** for (and levels of commitment to) health and safety. ('The law is a floor.') It does not represent satisfactory, let alone best, practice for socially responsible organisations.

(b) Health and safety are still a **low priority** in some organisation (and even national) cultures. Provisions are costly, and have no immediately quantifiable benefit.

(c) **Positive discipline** (setting mechanisms and systems that theoretically prevent hazardous behaviour) only goes so far, and irresponsible or ignorant behaviour can still cause accidents.

(d) **New health and safety concerns** are constantly emerging, as old ones are eradicated.

   (i) New technology and ergonomics may make physical labour less stressful, but it creates new hazards and health risks, such as sedentary, isolated lifestyles, and problems associated with working long hours at VDUs.

   (ii) New issues in health are constantly arising, such as passive smoking in the workplace and alcohol abuse, with the increasing stress of work in highly competitive sectors.

Question 7.5 Disaster costs

Learning outcome B1b

How many notorious workplace disasters can you think of? What were the main costs to the organisations concerned?

5.3 The legal framework

Once again, if the UK is not your country of operation, you might like to use this checklist of basic issues and principles, which represent basic standards for ethical employment anywhere.

5.3.1 The Health and Safety at Work Act (HSWA) 1974

In the UK, the Health and Safety at Work Act (HSWA) 1974 provides for the introduction of a system of approved codes of practice, prepared in consultation with industry, so that employees, whatever their employment, should find that their work is covered by an appropriate code of practice.

Employers' responsibilities under the HSWA may be summarised as follows.

(a) To provide **safe systems** (work practices)
(b) To provide a **safe and healthy work environment** (well-lit, warm, ventilated, hygienic and so on)
(c) To maintain all **plant and equipment** to a necessary standard of safety
(d) To **support safe working practices** with information, instruction, training and supervision
(e) To consult with **safety representatives** appointed by a recognised trade union
(f) To appoint a **safety committee** to monitor safety policy, if asked to do so
(g) To **communicate safety policy** and measures to all staff, clearly and in writing

An **employee's responsibilities** under the Act include:

(a) Taking **reasonable care** of themselves and others affected by their acts or omissions at work

(b) **Co-operating** with the employer in carrying out their duties (including enforcing safety rules)

(c) **Not interfering** intentionally or recklessly with any machinery or equipment provided in the interests of health and safety

5.3.2 The Health and Safety Executive (HSE)

The Health and Safety Executive (HSE) is an independent body which is responsible for encouraging and enforcing employers to comply with the HSWA. It regularly conducts workplace inspections to ensure the main provisions of the law are being met. HSE has responsibility for investigating industrial accidents and major incidents.

5.3.3 The Management of Health and Safety at Work Regulations 1992

These regulations impose additional responsibilities on **employers** as follows.

(a) To carry out **risk assessment**, generally in writing, of all work hazards, on a continuous basis

(b) To introduce **controls** to reduce risks

(c) To assess the risks to **anyone else affected** by their work activities

(d) To **share hazard and risk information** with other employers, including those on adjoining premises, other site occupiers and all subcontractors entering the premises

(e) To initiate or revise **safety policies** in the light of the above

(f) To identify employees who are especially **at risk** (other legislation cites pregnant women, young workers, shift-workers and part-time workers)

(g) To provide **fresh and appropriate training** in safety matters

(h) To provide **information to employees** (including temporary workers) about health and safety

(i) To employ competent **safety and health advisers**

Employees have the additional responsibility under the regulations to inform the employer of any situation that may pose a danger to themselves or others.

5.3.4 Health and Safety (Consultation with Employees) Regulations 1996

Employers have the responsibility to consult all employees on health and safety matters, including the planning of health and safety training, changes in equipment and procedures that may substantially affect health and safety at work, or the health and safety consequences of introducing new technology.

5.3.5 The Workplace (Health, Safety and Welfare) Regulations 1992

These regulations provide for health and hygiene in work environments, including such aspects as the following.

(a) **Equipment** must be properly maintained.

(b) **Ventilation**. Air should be fresh or purified.

(c) **Temperature** must be 'reasonable' inside buildings during working hours.

(d) **Lighting** should be suitable and sufficient, and natural, if practicable.

(e) **Cleaning and decoration**. Floors, walls, ceilings, furniture, furnishings and fittings must be kept clean.

(f) **Room dimensions and space**. Each person should have at least 11 cubic metres of space.

(g) **Floors** must be properly constructed and maintained (without holes, not slippery, properly drained and so on).

(h) **Sanitary conveniences and washing facilities** must be suitable and sufficient.

(i) **Drinking water**. An adequate supply should be available with suitable drinking vessels.

5.3.6 The Manual Handling Operations Regulations 1992

The manual handling regulations cover heavy lifting – a major cause of industrial injury. They require employers, so far as is reasonably practicable, to avoid the need for employees to undertake any manual handling activities that will involve the risk of their becoming injured. However, if the cost of avoiding such risk is unreasonable, the employer will be required to carry out an assessment of all manual handling operations, and to take steps to reduce the risks.

5.3.7 The Health and Safety (Display Screen Equipment) Regulations 1992

If you have ever worked for a long period at a VDU, you may personally have experienced some discomfort. Backache, eye strain and stiffness or muscular problems of the neck, shoulders, arms or hands are frequent complaints. The common, if somewhat inaccurate, term for this is **repetitive strain injury** or **RSI**. The regulations address areas such as:

(a) Minimisation of glare and flicker from VDU screens
(b) Arrangement and flexibility of screens, keyboards, desks and chairs for comfortable working
(c) The provision of breaks
(d) Training and consultation to improve work practices

5.4 Accidents and other workplace hazards

5.4.1 Causes of accidents

Many accidents could be avoided by the simple application of common sense and consideration by employer and employee, and by safety consciousness encouraged or enforced by a widely acceptable and well-publicised safety policy.

Common causes of injury in administrative workplaces include falling/tripping, lifting and materials/equipment handling, related to hazards such as:

(a) Slippery or poorly maintained floors (eg frayed carpets)
(b) Trailing electric leads
(c) Obstacles in gangways or staircases
(d) Standing on chairs (particularly swivel chairs) to reach high shelving
(e) Lifting heavy items without bending properly
(f) Incorrect use of electrical machinery (including overloading power sockets)
(g) Removing the safety guard on a machine to free a blockage
(h) Incorrect labelling or storage of chemicals (that may burn, cause allergic reactions etc)

5.4.2 The cost of accidents

The costs of accidents to the employer are significant.

(a) **Time lost by the injured employee** and other employees who choose to, or must of necessity, stop work at the time of or following the accident

(b) **Time lost by management and technical staff** following the accident

(c) A proportion of the cost of **first aid materials and officers**

(d) The cost of **disruption to operations** at work

(e) The cost of any **damage** to the equipment or any cost associated with the subsequent modification of the equipment

(f) The costs associated with increased **insurance premiums**

(g) **Reduced output** from the injured employee on return to work

(h) The cost of possible **reduced morale**, increased absenteeism, increased labour turnover among employees

(i) The cost of recruiting and training a **replacement** for the injured worker

(j) The cost of **compensation payments** if employees sue for damages

Although the injured employee's damages may be reduced if their injury was partly a consequence of their own contributory **negligence**, due allowance is made for ordinary human failings.

(a) An employee is not deemed to consent to the risk of injury because they are aware of the risk. It is the employer's duty to provide a safe working system.

(b) Employees can become inattentive or careless in doing work that is monotonous or imposes stress. This factor too must be allowed for in the employer's safety precautions.

(c) It is not always a sufficient defence that the employer **provided** safety equipment and rules: the employer has some duty to encourage its proper **use**.

(d) Employees do not work continuously. The employer's duty is to take reasonable care for their safety in all acts that are normally and reasonably incidental to the day's work.

Question 7.6 — Responsibility for safe working

Learning outcome B1b

If a person went to wash a teacup after use, at their office, and slipped on a slippery surface in the kitchen and was injured, who would be at fault?

5.4.3 Preventing accidents

Some steps that might be taken to reduce the frequency and severity of accidents are as follows.

(a) Developing a **safety consciousness** among staff and workers and encouraging departmental pride in a good safety record: creating a culture of safety

(b) Developing effective **consultative participation** between management, workers and unions so that safety and health rules can be accepted and followed

(c) Giving **adequate instruction in safety rules** and measures as part of the training of new and transferred workers, or where working methods or speeds of operation are changed

(d) **Identified risks** (eg materials handling) to be minimised and designed as far as possible for safe operation

(e) Ensuring a **satisfactory standard** for both basic plant and auxiliary fittings (such as safety guards)

(f) **Proactive maintenance**: apart from making sound job repairs, temporary expedients to keep production going should not prejudice safety

In general, the appropriate code of practice for the industry/work environment should be implemented in full.

Question 7.7 Workplace hazards

Learning outcome B1b

What hazards can you identify in the following office scene?

5.4.4 Investigation and report of accidents

Safety inspections may be carried out as a comprehensive **audit**, working through a checklist, or by using **random spot checks**, regular checks of **particular risk points** or statutory inspections of particular areas, such as lifts, hoists, boilers and pipelines.

It is essential that checklists used in the inspection process should identify corrective action to be taken, and allocate responsibility for that action. There should be reporting systems and control procedures to ensure that inspections are taking place and that findings are being acted on.

Accident-reporting systems (eg using accident books) will be particularly important, but it must be emphasised to staff that the report is not an exercise in itself but a management tool, designed to:

(a) Identify problems
(b) Indicate corrective action

Serious accidents and dangerous occurrences (such as explosions) must be formally reported to the relevant authorities under the **Reporting of Injuries, Diseases and Dangerous Occurrences Regulations** (RIDDOR 1995).

5.5 Working time

The EU Working Time Directive was incorporated into UK law in the **Working Time Regulations 1998**. The regulations limit workers' hours to 48 hours per week (averaged over 17 weeks): individuals may agree in writing to work more than 48 hours per week, and a record of hours should be retained. There are also provisions for entitlement to work breaks and days off (24 hours' rest in every 7 days).

This is a health and safety issue, due to the dangers of overwork and inattention due to tiredness and monotony. It is also related to policies supporting work–life balance, and family-friendly working, by ensuring employees' entitlement to rest days.

5.6 Health and safety policy

A comprehensive health and safety policy can be depicted as follows.

Systematic approach to health and safety

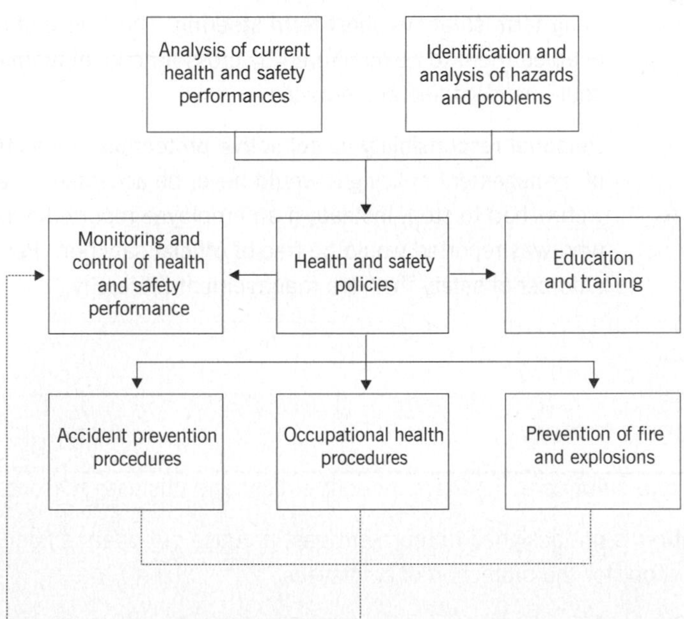

However, there is also a cultural element to health and safety. Staff education and training, appraisal and reward systems and role modelling by management all need to support safety values and compliance with policy and procedures.

CASE STUDY

Health & safety and corporate culture

Charles Hampden-Turner (in his book *Corporate Culture*) notes that attitudes to safety can be part of a **corporate culture**. He quotes the example of a firm called (for reasons of confidentiality) Western Oil.

(a) Western Oil had a bad safety record. 'Initially, safety was totally at odds with the main cultural values of productivity (management's interests) and maintenance of a macho image (the workers' culture) ... Western Oil had a culture which put safety in conflict with other corporate values.' In particular, the problem was with its long-distance truck drivers (who in the US have a culture of solitary independence and self-reliance) who drove sometimes recklessly with loads large enough to inundate a small town. The company instituted **operation integrity** to improve safety, in a lasting way, changing the policies and drawing on the existing features of the culture but using them in a different way.

(b) The **culture** had five dilemmas.

(i) **Safety-first vs macho-individualism**. Truckers see themselves as 'fearless pioneers of the unconventional lifestyle ... "Be careful boys!" is hardly a plea likely to go down well with this particular group'. Instead of trying to control the drivers, the firm recommended that they become **road safety consultants** (or design consultants). Their advice was sought on improving the system. This had the advantage that 'by making drivers critics of the system, their roles as outsiders were preserved and promoted'. It tried to tap their heroism as promoters of public safety.

(ii) **Safety everywhere vs safety specialists**. Western Oil could have hired more specialist staff. However, instead, the company promoted cross-functional safety teams from existing parts of the business, for example, to help in designing depots and thinking of ways to reduce hazards.

(iii) **Safety as cost vs productivity as benefit**. 'If the drivers raced from station to station to win their bonus, accidents were bound to occur ... . The safety engineers rarely spoke to the line manager in charge of the delivery schedules. The unreconciled dilemma between safety and productivity had been evaded at management level and passed down the hierarchy until drivers were subjected to two incompatible injunctions, work fast and work safely.' To deal with this problem, safety would be built into the reward system.

(iv) **Long-term safety vs short-term steering**. The device of recording 'unsafe' acts in operations enabled them to be monitored by cross-functional teams, so that the causes of accidents could be identified and reduced.

(v) **Personal responsibility vs collective protection**. It was felt that if 'safety' was seen as a form of management policing it would never be accepted. The habit of management 'blaming the victim' had to stop. Instead, if an employee reported another to the safety teams, the person who was reported would be free of **official** sanction. Peer presence was seen to be a better enforcer of safety than the management hierarchy.

Section summary

Health and safety are important for both ethical and business reasons.

Legislation is not designed to represent best practice but offers a floor below which standards of conduct cannot drop, for the protection of employees.

Health and safety legislation requires that the systems, environment, equipment and conduct of organisations be such as to minimise the risk to the health and safety of employees and visitors alike.

Employees **share responsibility** for health and safety with employers, although the latter take responsibility for the environment, systems, equipment and training.

Apart from obviously dangerous equipment in offices, there are many **hazards** to be found in the modern working environment.

The **prevention of accidents** requires effort on the part of employees and management.

Safety inspections should be carried out to locate and define faults in the system that allow accidents to occur.

6 Mentoring

Introduction

Both coaching and mentoring have become widely used approaches to continually develop people at work and encourage learning. We look at mentoring here.

Mentoring is a longer-term relationship, the purpose of which is primarily learning development and support for career development.

6.1 Mentoring

'Mentor' was the name of a character in ancient Greek literature (Homer's *The Odyssey*): an older man who acted as wise counsellor and trusted adviser to a young man, passing on the benefit of his knowledge and experience. The way the term is used in modern business still reflects these roots, to an extent.

KEY TERM

MENTORING is a long-term relationship in which a more experienced person acts as a teacher, counsellor, role model, supporter and encourager, to foster the individual's personal and career development.

Exam alert

Mentoring and how a **mentoring system** would aid a junior manager could easily be tested as part of an objective test question in your E2 exam or even feature in a longer question in your Integrated Case Study. It is important for your E2 exam that you are familiar with the functions and strengths of the mentoring relationship.

6.1.1 Functions of a mentor

Kram identifies two broad types of function for the mentor.

Career functions include:

(a) Sponsoring within the organisation and providing exposure at higher levels
(b) Coaching and influencing progress through appointments
(c) Protection
(d) Drawing up personal development plans
(e) Advice with administrative problems people face in their new jobs
(f) Help in tackling projects, by pointing people in the right direction

Psychosocial functions include:

(a) Creating a sense of acceptance and belonging
(b) Counselling and friendship
(c) Providing a role model

6.1.2 The mentoring relationship

From an HR practitioner's perspective, Armstrong (2003) describes the **function** of **mentors** as giving their allocated protégé(s):

(a) Advice in drawing up self-development programmes or learning contracts
(b) General help with learning programmes
(c) Advice on dealing with administrative, technical and people problems
(d) Information on 'the way things are done around here' (corporate culture and management style)
(e) Coaching in specific skills

(f) Guidance in tackling projects (ie helping protégés to help themselves)

(g) A listening 'ear' for aspirations, concerns and problems

Although every mentoring relationship will be different, depending on the approach followed and the personalities involved, the following may be a handy way of remembering the nature of the role.

Manage the relationship
Encourage the mentee
Nurture the mentee
Teach or coach the mentee
Offer mutual respect
Respond to the mentee's needs

6.2 Strengths of mentoring

Coaching and mentoring have particular strengths as a development approach. Many HR activities help individuals to identify **what they need to change**: appraisal, feedback, training needs analysis and so on. Coaching and mentoring, however, specifically focus on **facilitating and reinforcing actual changes** in a person's work style and habits: transferring learning to the job, putting action plans into practice – and providing ongoing support and feedback for lasting change and continuous development.

Zeus and Skiffington (2002) argue that coaches/mentors are ideally placed to implement **change**, because of their:

(a) **Communication skills**. Communication is essential to successful change management. Coaching and mentoring provide a trusting, open environment where individuals can share their fears or beliefs about change – and coaches can convey enthusiasm and conviction that the person **can** change, and that barriers can be overcome.

(b) **Orientation**. Change is always more successful where people's needs and goals are taken into account, so that change is seen as a 'win-win' for the individual and the organisation. This is the nature of a coaching/mentoring plan.

(c) **Empathy**. Change agents are most successful when they understand (and show that they understand) the difficulties of change for the individual – as well as being challenging and encouraging. These issues can be explored within the coaching/mentoring relationship.

(d) **Credibility**. Coaches and members are often in the position of role model, and therefore have the power to influence people to change.

Section summary

Mentoring is a development-focused relationship in which a more knowledgeable or experienced person supports the development of another person.

7 Business ethics and corporate social responsibility (CSR)

Introduction

Ethical and **social responsibility** are two key areas in which businesses have adopted non-financial objectives, taking into account stakeholder needs and interests, partly in response to political and consumer pressure. Contemporary thinking is that **shareholders' wealth and ethics need not be mutually exclusive**.

KEY TERMS

ETHICS are the moral principles by which people act or do business.

SOCIAL RESPONSIBILITY comprises those values and actions that the organisation is not obliged to adopt for business reasons, which it adopts for the good and wellbeing of stakeholders within and outside the organisation.

7.1 Why be socially responsible?

Social responsibility is concerned with the impact that an organisation has on stakeholders and on the wider community.

Managers need to take into account the effect of organisational outputs into the market and the wider **social community**, for several reasons.

(a) The modern **marketing concept** says that in order to survive and succeed, organisations must satisfy the needs, wants and values of customers and potential customers. Communication and education have made people much more aware of issues such as the environment, the exploitation of workers, product safety and consumer rights. Therefore, an organisation may have to be seen to be responsible in these areas in order to retain public support for its products.

(b) There are skill shortages in the labour pool, and employers must compete to attract and retain high-quality employees. If the organisation gets a reputation as a socially responsible employer, it will find it easier to do this, than if it has a poor '**employer brand**'.

(c) A business itself is a **social system**, not just an economic machine (Mintzberg). Organisations rely on the society and local community of which they are a part, for access to facilities, business relationships, media coverage, labour, supplies, customers and so on. Organisations that acknowledge their responsibilities as part of the community may find that many areas of their operation are facilitated.

(d) Social responsibility recognises **externalities**: the costs imposed by businesses on other people (but not included in the costing of their products and activities). For example, it is recognised that industrial pollution is bad for health.

(e) Law, regulation and codes of practice **impose** certain social responsibilities on organisations, in areas such as employment protection, equal opportunities, environmental care, health and safety, product labelling and consumer rights. There are financial and operational **penalties** for organisations that fail to comply.

The **stakeholder view** of organisations emphasises that they are not solely 'self-interested': other parties have an interest or 'stake' in the performance and practices of an organisation.

The stakeholder approach acknowledges that such parties have a **legitimate interest** – and may also have **influence** over the organisation. (Workers can withhold labour; customers can withhold business.) The objectives of the organisation should therefore take into account the needs and claims of influential stakeholder groups.

7.2 Areas of social responsibility

The perceived social responsibilities of a business, depending on the nature of its operations, may include the following matters.

(a) The impact of its operations on the **natural environment**

(b) Its **human resource management policies**: for example, the hiring and promotion of people from minority groups, policies on sexual harassment, refusal to exploit cheap labour in developing countries

(c) Non-reliance on contracts with **adverse political connotations**: sustainable business practices in developing countries, compliance with sanctions imposed by the international community and so on

(d) **Charitable support** and activity in the local community or in areas related to the organisation's field of activity

(e) **Above-minimum (legal) standards** of workplace health and safety, product safety and labelling, and so on

Question 7.8 Socially responsible activities

Learning outcome B2a

Using your knowledge of the Farmers supermarket chain, identify those activities that the company undertakes that could be classed as socially responsible activities.

7.3 Limits of CSR

According to Milton Friedman and Elaine Sternberg, 'the social responsibility of business is profit maximisation'; in other words, the only responsibility of a **business** organisation, as opposed to a public sector one, is to maximise wealth for its owners over the long term.

(a) Business profits are shareholders' wealth. Spending on other objectives **not** related to shareholders' wealth maximisation is irresponsible.

(b) The public interest is served because the State levies taxes: the State is a better arbiter of the public interest than a business.

(c) Without the discipline of shareholders, managers will simply favour their own pet interests. 'Managers who are accountable to everyone are accountable to none.'

'Consequently, the only justification for social responsibility is **enlightened self-interest**' (Friedman) on the part of the organisation. Socially responsible behaviour should be pursued for its **benefits** in employee recruitment, retention and commitment; customer retention; and public relations.

7.4 Ethics

The meanings of the words 'ethics' and 'morals' are similar and difficult to distinguish. For example, the *Concise Oxford English Dictionary* offers the following two definitions.

(a) **Morals** are 'standards of behaviour or principles of right and wrong'.

(b) **Ethics** are 'the moral principles governing or influencing conduct'.

Morals or ethics will also differ depending on the beliefs, value systems and norms of a particular society or culture. So, ethics might be considered to be **a system of behaviour that is deemed acceptable in the society or context under consideration.**

Blanchard and Peale suggest that, when faced with an ethical dilemma, individuals should ask themselves three questions:

(a) Is it legal?

(b) Is it balanced? (Ie is it fair to all parties involved?)

(c) Is it right? This is often related to your instinctive feeling about it. How would you feel if others knew you had taken this decision?

Ethics are a feature of business, as well as life, and managers are regularly faced with ethical issues. Examples might include the fair setting of pay and working conditions; non-exploitation of people or countries; honest advertising; effects of consuming products (eg tobacco and alcohol); and the management of redundancies.

Organisations may take a number of steps to assist management and others in dealing with ethics and making ethical decisions. These could include:

(a) Developing corporate ethical codes
(b) Setting up sustainability policies and strategies
(c) An analysis of the impact on the environment and on society of the activities of the organisation
(d) Building social responsibility into the organisation's strategy generation and planning systems

7.5 Business ethics

An organisation may have values to do with non-discrimination, fairness and integrity. It is very important that managers understand:

(a) The importance of ethical behaviour
(b) The differences in what is considered ethical behaviour in different cultures

Theorist Elaine Sternberg suggests that two **ethical values** are particularly pertinent for business, because without them business could not operate at all. These are:

(a) **Ordinary decency**. This includes respect for property rights, honesty, fairness and legality.

(b) **Distributive justice**. This means that organisational rewards should be proportional to the contributions people make to organisational ends. The supply and demand for labour will influence how much a person is actually paid but, if that person is worth employing and the job is worth doing, then the contribution will justify the expense.

Business ethics in a **global marketplace** are, however, far from clear cut. If you are working outside the UK, you will need to develop – in line with whatever policies your organisation may have in place – a kind of 'situational' ethic to cover various issues.

(a) **Gifts** may be construed as bribes in Western business circles, but are indispensable in others.

(b) Attitudes to **women** in business vary according to ethnic traditions and religious values.

(c) The use of **cheap labour** in very poor countries (eg through off-shoring) may be perceived as 'development' – or as 'exploitation'.

(d) The expression and nature of **agreements** vary according to cultural norms.

A business may operate on principles that strive to be:

(a) Ethical and legal (eg The Body Shop)
(b) Unethical but legal (eg arms sales to repressive regimes)
(c) Ethical but illegal (eg publishing stolen documents on government mismanagement)
(d) Unethical and illegal (eg the drugs trade, employing child labour)

7.5.1 Applying ethical principles

There are two basic approaches to the **management of ethics** in organisations.

(a) A **compliance-based approach** seeks to ensure compliance with law, regulation and rules of behaviour. It is based on the communication of clear rules, procedures and guidelines, which must be adhered to in given circumstances. Behaviour is monitored, and infringements of ethical codes are subject to disciplinary action.

(b) An **integrity-based approach** seeks to support members of the organisation in making their own ethical decisions in any situation they encounter. It is based on the communication and reinforcement of ethical values, and the creation of frameworks within which ethical issues and dilemmas can be freely discussed and resolved.

Using an integrity-based approach, a firm can embed ethical values in its culture and systems in the following ways.

(a) Include **value statements** in corporate culture, policy and codes of practice. (Professional staff should also be encouraged to adhere to the ethical codes of their professional bodies.)

(b) Ensure that **HR systems** (appraisal, training and rewards) are designed to support ethical behaviour.

(c) Identify ethical objectives in the **mission statement**, as a public declaration of what the organisation stands for.

(d) Establish **ethics committees** and discussion groups to encourage questioning and problem solving on ethical issues faced by staff.

(e) Provide confidential channels for '**whistle-blowing**' if staff feel that colleagues or the organisation is behaving illegally or unethically.

(f) Ensure that there is **top-down support** for, and modelling of, **ethical behaviour by managers**.

Exam alert

Social responsibility and ethics underpin issues such as corporate governance and also, for example, health and safety, equal opportunity and diversity and employee welfare. Organisational policies over and above legal requirements, in areas such as these, fulfil responsibility objectives.

7.6 *CIMA Code of Ethics for professional accountants*

If you are a CIMA-registered student, you are subject to CIMA's *Code of Ethics for professional accountants*.

CIMA's Code of Ethics is based on the International Federation of Accountants' Code of Ethics.

Fundamental principles

(a) **Integrity**
A professional accountant should be straightforward and honest in all professional and business relationships.

(b) **Objectivity**
A professional accountant should not allow bias, conflict of interest or undue influence of others to override professional or business judgements.

(c) **Professional competence and due care**
A professional accountant has a continuing duty to maintain professional knowledge and skill at the level required to ensure that a client or employer receives competent professional service based on current developments in practice, legislation and techniques. A professional accountant should act diligently and in accordance with applicable technical and professional standards when providing professional services.

(d) **Confidentiality**
A professional accountant should respect the confidentiality of information acquired as a result of professional and business relationships, and should not disclose any such information to third parties without proper and specific authority unless there is a legal or professional right or duty to disclose. Confidential information acquired as a result of professional and business relationships should not be used for the personal advantage of the professional accountant or third party.

(e) **Professional behaviour**
A professional accountant should comply with relevant laws and regulations, and should avoid any action that discredits the profession.

Conceptual framework

The conceptual framework sets out how **professional accountants** should comply with the fundamental principles. Specifically, they are required **to identify, evaluate and respond to threats to compliance with the fundamental principles**. When assessing the significance of a threat, they should take qualitative as well as quantitative factors into account.

There is a wide range of circumstances in which compliance with the fundamental principles may be threatened. Many **threats** fall into the following categories.

(a) **Self-interest threats**, which may occur as a result of the financial or other interests of a professional accountant or of an immediate or close family member

(b) **Self-review threats**, which may occur when a previous judgement needs to be re-evaluated by the professional accountant responsible for that judgement

(c) **Advocacy threats**, which may occur when a professional accountant promotes a position or opinion to the point that subsequent objectivity may be compromised

(d) **Familiarity threats**, which may occur when, because of a close relationship, a professional accountant becomes too sympathetic to the interests of others

(e) **Intimidation threats**, which may occur when a professional accountant may be deterred from acting objectively by threats, actual or perceived

Safeguards that may eliminate or reduce such threats to an acceptable level include safeguards **created by the profession, legislation or regulation**, such as the following.

(a) Educational, training and experience requirements for entry into the profession

(b) Continuing professional development requirements

(c) Corporate governance regulations

(d) Professional standards

(e) Professional or regulatory monitoring and disciplinary procedures

(f) External review by a legally empowered third party of the reports, returns, communications or information produced by a professional accountant

Safeguards may also be found in the **work environment**. Examples include the following.

(a) Effective, well-publicised complaint systems operated by the employing organisation, the profession or a regulator, which enable colleagues, employers and members of the public to draw attention to unprofessional or unethical behaviour

(b) An explicitly stated duty to report breaches of ethical requirements

Question 7.9 Acting ethically

Learning outcomes B2a

In order to motivate store staff to stay with Farmers supermarkets, the company runs a quarterly performance-related bonus scheme. Bonuses are determined by the sales revenue and net profit margin achieved at each store. The bonus is then paid quarterly to recognise the previous quarter's results.

Gemma Murphy works part time as an accounts and administrative assistant in the Farmers store in Newcastle. She is also a CIMA student, and is working towards achieving full membership. Her role involves dealing with local suppliers to the store, and the completion of monthly returns to Farmers' head office, which detail the supermarket's running costs. Gemma's role is regarded as an important position, as the submitted returns are used in determining whether the target net profit margin has been met for the quarter.

Last month, the Store Manager, Charles Barber, approached Gemma and suggested that certain expenses be omitted from the monthly return to ensure that the store hits its target profit margin. Gemma is aware that this course of action will trigger bonus payments to all staff in the Newcastle store in the following quarter. Charles Barber is responsible for approving Gemma's study leave when she sits her CIMA exams.

Required

(a) Which of CIMA's fundamental ethical principles would Gemma breach if she manipulated the monthly return?

(b) What type of threat(s) is Gemma facing?

(c) What action should Gemma take in response to the current situation?

Section summary

Business ethics are the values underlying what an organisation understands by socially responsible behaviour.

There is pressure towards **corporate social responsibility (CSR)** from law and regulation, market forces and the stakeholder perspective.

8 Corporate governance

Introduction

Corporate governance is an important area of control, and you need to be familiar with the provisions of the **UK Corporate Governance Code**. This prescribes rules covering the conduct of boards and their responsibilities for ensuring the good governance of organisations.

Read the first sections on background to set the scene, but you won't need to write on these in the exam. Consider the section on rules versus principles. Which seems the better approach?

Our discussion focuses on the UK but we have also mentioned the US guidance, which is enshrined in the Sarbanes-Oxley Act 2002, and South Africa's King report.

We cover this material at a fairly broad level here, as Paper P3 devotes a significant part of its syllabus to covering the issues of corporate governance.

KEY TERM

CORPORATE GOVERNANCE is the system by which organisations are directed and controlled.

8.1 Driving forces for governance development

Corporate governance issues came to prominence in the US during the 1970s, and in the UK and Europe from the late 1980s. There were several reasons why this happened.

(a) **Increasing internationalisation and globalisation** meant that investors, and institutional investors in particular, began to invest outside their home countries. This led to calls for companies to operate in an acceptable fashion and to report corporate performance fairly.

(b) Issues concerning **financial reporting** were raised by many investors and were the focus of much debate and litigation. Shareholder confidence in many instances was eroded and, while focus solely on accounting and reporting issues is inadequate, the regulation of practices such as off balance sheet financing has led to greater transparency and a reduction in risks faced by investors.

(c) An increasing number of **high-profile corporate scandals** and collapses, including Polly Peck International, BCCI, Enron and Maxwell Communications Corporation, prompted the development of governance codes in the early 1990s. However, the scandals since then, particularly in the banking sector, have raised questions about further measures that may be necessary.

8.2 Features of poor corporate governance

The scandals over the last 25 years have highlighted the need for guidance to tackle the various risks and problems that can arise in organisations' systems of governance.

(a) **Domination by a single individual**. A feature of many corporate governance scandals has been boards dominated by a single senior executive, with other board members merely acting as a rubber stamp. Sometimes the single individual may bypass the board to action their own interests. The report on the UK Guinness case suggested that the Chief Executive, Ernest Saunders, paid himself a £3m reward without consulting the other directors.

(b) **Lack of involvement of board**. Boards that meet irregularly or fail to consider systematically the organisation's activities and risks are clearly weak. Sometimes the failure to carry out proper oversight is due to a **lack of information** being provided.

(c) **Lack of adequate control function**. An obvious weakness is a lack of internal audit. Another important control is **lack of adequate technical knowledge** in key roles, for example in the audit committee or in senior compliance positions. A rapid turnover of staff involved in accounting or control may suggest inadequate resourcing, and will make control more difficult because of lack of continuity.

(d) **Lack of supervision**. Employees who are not properly supervised can create large losses for the organisation through their own incompetence, negligence or fraudulent activity. The behaviour of Nick Leeson, the employee who caused the collapse of Barings Bank, was not challenged because he appeared to be successful, whereas he was using unauthorised accounts to cover up his large trading losses. Leeson was able to do this because he was in charge of both dealing and settlement, a systems weakness or **lack of segregation of key roles** that featured in other financial frauds.

(e) **Lack of independent scrutiny**. External auditors may not carry out the necessary questioning of senior management because of fears of losing the audit, and internal audit do not ask awkward questions because the CFO determines their employment prospects. Often, corporate collapses are followed by criticisms of external auditors, such as the Barlow Clowes affair, where poorly planned and focused audit work failed to identify illegal use of client monies.

(f) **Lack of contact with shareholders**. Often, board members may have grown up with the company but lose touch with the interests and views of shareholders. One possible symptom of this is the payment of remuneration packages that do not appear to be warranted by results.

(g) **Emphasis on short-term profitability**. Emphasis on short-term results can lead to the concealment of problems or errors, or manipulation of accounts to achieve desired results.

(h) **Misleading accounts and information**. Often, misleading figures are symptomatic of other problems (or are designed to conceal other problems) but, in many cases, poor-quality accounting information is a major problem if markets are trying to make a fair assessment of the company's value. Giving out misleading information was a major issue in the UK's Equitable Life scandal, where the company gave contradictory information to savers, independent advisers, media and regulators.

8.3 Benefits of improving corporate governance

A number of benefits can accrue from improved governance.

(a) **Risk reduction**. Proper corporate governance reduces the risks of financial loss, compliance failure and reputational damage (and ultimately, business collapse) by aligning directors' interests with the company's strategic objectives and by providing for measures to reduce fraud.

(b) **Performance** should improve if accountabilities are made clear and directors' motivation is enhanced by performance-related remuneration. Also, the extra breadth of experience brought by non-executive directors should improve the quality of decision making at board level.

(c) **External support**. External perceptions of the company should be enhanced, leading to: improved ability to raise finance; improved corporate image with public and government; and improved relations with stakeholders such as customers and employees.

8.4 Reports on corporate governance

There were three significant corporate governance reports in the UK during the 1990s. The **Cadbury and Hampel reports** covered general corporate governance issues, while the **Greenbury report** concentrated on remuneration of directors.

The recommendations of these three reports were merged into a **Combined Code** in 1998, which was subsequently incorporated into the **UK Corporate Governance Code**, with which companies listed on the London Stock Exchange are required to comply. We look at the Corporate Governance Code in this section.

Since the publication of the **UK Corporate Governance Code** (formerly the **Combined Code**) a number of reports in the UK have been published about specific aspects of corporate governance.

- The **Turnbull report** focused on risk management and internal control.
- The **Smith report** discussed the role of audit committees.
- The **Higgs report** focused on the role of the non-executive director.

8.5 Approaches taken – principles vs rules

A continuing debate on corporate governance is whether the guidance should predominantly be in the form of principles, or whether there is a need for detailed laws or regulations.

The Hampel report in the UK came out very firmly in favour of a principles-based approach. The committee preferred to relax the regulatory burden on companies and was against treating the corporate governance codes as sets of prescriptive rules, and judging companies by whether they have complied ('box-ticking'). The report stated that there may be **guidelines** that will normally be appropriate, but the differing circumstances of companies meant that sometimes there are valid reasons for exceptions.

However, the Hampel report has been criticised for taking this approach. It has been commented that the principles set out in the Hampel report are so broad that they are of very little use as a guide to best corporate governance practice. For example, the suggestion that non-executive directors from a wide variety of backgrounds can make a contribution is seen as not strong enough to encourage companies away from recruiting directors by means of the 'old boy network'.

It has also been suggested that the Hampel comments about **box-ticking** are incorrect for two reasons. First, shareholders do not apply that approach when assessing accounts. Secondly, it is far less likely that disasters will strike companies with a 100% compliance record since they are unlikely to be content with token compliance, but will have set up procedures that contribute significantly to their being governed well.

8.6 Stock Exchange UK Corporate Governance Code

8.6.1 Directors

(a) **The board**
All listed companies should be led by an **effective board**. The board should meet regularly and have certain matters reserved for its decision. Directors should be able to obtain independent professional advice and have access to the services of the Company Secretary. The Company Secretary is responsible for ensuring that **board procedures and relevant regulations** are followed. The whole board should be responsible for removing the Company Secretary. Every director should use **independent judgement** when making decisions. Every director should receive appropriate **training**.

(b) The **Chairman and Chief Executive**
There are two leading management roles: running the board and running the company. A **clear division of responsibilities** should exist so that there is a balance of power, and no one person has unfettered powers of decision. Combination of the roles of Chairman and Chief Executive should be justified publicly. There should also be a **strong and independent** body of **non-executive** directors with a recognised senior member other than the Chairman.

(c) **Board balance**
The board should have a **balance of executive and non-executive directors** so that no individual or small group is dominant.

(d) **Supply of information**
The board should be **promptly supplied with enough information** to enable it to carry out its duties.

(e) **Appointment of directors**
There should be a **clear, formal procedure** for appointing new directors. A nomination committee should make recommendations about all new board appointments.

(f) **Re-election**
All directors should submit themselves for **re-election regularly**, and at least once every three years.

8.6.2 Directors' remuneration

(a) **Remuneration policy**
Remuneration levels should be sufficient to attract directors of **sufficient calibre** to run the company effectively, but companies should not pay more than is necessary. A proportion of remuneration should be based on **corporate and individual performance**.

(b) **Service contracts and compensation**
Boards' ultimate objectives should be to **set notice periods at one year or less**. Directors should consider whether to include compensation commitments in the contracts of service.

(c) **Procedure**
Companies should establish a formal and clear procedure for **developing policy on executive remuneration and for fixing the remuneration package of individual directors**. Directors should **not be involved in setting their own remuneration**. A remuneration committee, staffed by independent non-executive directors, should make recommendations about the framework of executive remuneration, and should determine specific remuneration packages. The board should determine the remuneration of non-executive directors.

(d) **Disclosure**
The annual report should contain a **statement about remuneration policy** and **details of the remuneration of each director**. The report should give details about **all elements of the remuneration package**, share options, pension entitlements and service contracts or compensation in excess of one year. Shareholders should approve all new long-term remuneration schemes.

8.6.3 Relations with shareholders

(a) **Institutional shareholders**
Companies should be prepared to **communicate with institutional shareholders**.

(b) **Use of the annual general meeting (AGM)**
The AGM should be a **means of communication** with **private investors**. Companies should count all proxies, and announce proxy votes for and against on all votes on a show of hands. Companies should propose a **separate resolution** on each substantially separate issue, and there should be a resolution covering the **board and accounts**.

8.6.4 Accountability and audit

(a) **Financial reporting**
The board should present a **balanced and understandable assessment** of the **company's position and prospects** in the annual accounts and other reports such as interim reports and reports to regulators.

(b) **Internal control**
A good system of control should be maintained. The directors should **review effectiveness** annually and report to shareholders that they have done so.

(c) **Audit committees and auditors**
There should be **formal and clear arrangements** with the **company's auditors**, and for applying the financial reporting and internal control principles. Companies should have an **audit committee** consisting of non-executive directors, the majority of whom should be independent. The audit committee should review the audit, and the independence and objectivity of the auditors. In particular, the committee should keep matters under review if the auditors supply significant non-audit services.

(d) **Shareholder voting**
Institutional shareholders should use their votes carefully and **disclose** how they have **voted** to their clients. They should also enter into a dialogue with companies, and should give appropriate weight to all relevant criteria when considering corporate governance arrangements.

8.6.5 Compliance with the Code

The UK Corporate Governance Code requires listed companies to include in their accounts:

(a) A narrative statement of how they **applied** the **principles** set out in the Corporate Governance Code. This should provide explanations that enable their shareholders to assess how the principles have been applied.

(b) A statement as to whether or not they **complied throughout** the **accounting period** with the provisions set out in the Corporate Governance Code. Listed companies that did not comply throughout the accounting period with all the provisions must specify the provisions with which they did not comply, and give **reasons** for **non-compliance**.

8.7 The US framework

Corporate scandals, particularly the Enron scandal, in the US over the last few years have led to the **Sarbanes-Oxley Act 2002** and consequent changes to the listing rules that companies quoted on Wall Street have to fulfil.

8.8 The South African framework

South Africa's major contribution to the corporate governance debate has been the **King report**, first published in 1994 and updated in 2002 to take account of developments in South Africa and elsewhere in the world.

The King report differs in emphasis from other guidance by advocating an integrated approach to corporate governance in the interest of a wide range of stakeholders – embracing the social, environmental and economic activities of a company. The report encourages activism by shareholders, business and the financial press and relies heavily on disclosure as a regulatory measure.

Section summary

Corporate governance in the UK is largely defined by the contents of the **Corporate Governance Code**. By providing guidance on areas such as **directors**, **remuneration**, **shareholder dialogue** and **internal controls**, it aims to reduce risk, improve performance and improve public perceptions.

There were three significant corporate governance reports in the UK during the 1990s. The **Cadbury and Hampel reports** covered general corporate governance issues, while the **Greenbury report** concentrated on remuneration of directors.

The recommendations of the three UK reports were merged into a **Combined Code** in 1998, which was subsequently incorporated into the **Corporate Governance Code** with which companies listed on the London Stock Exchange are required to comply.

Chapter Summary

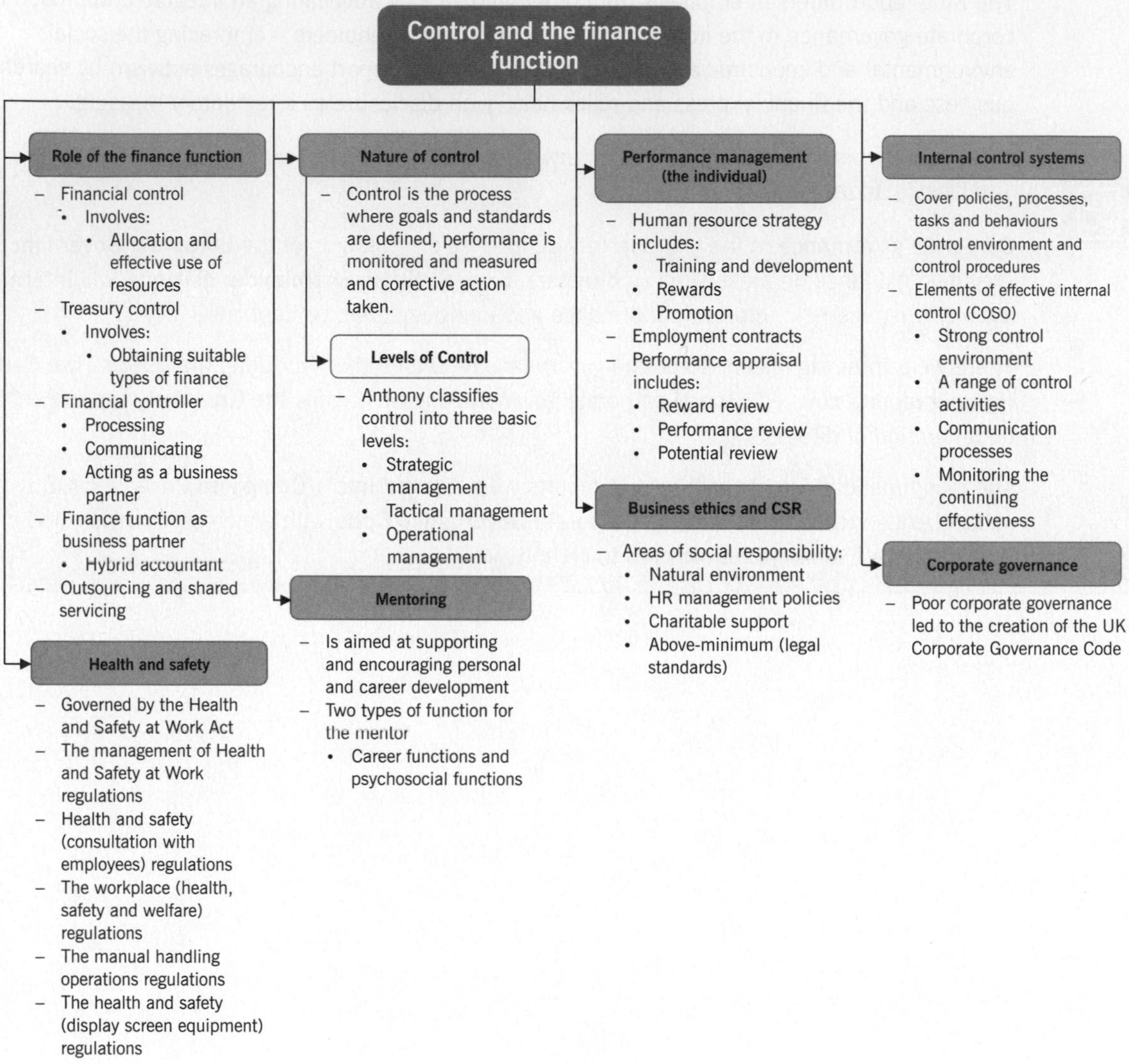

Control and the finance function

Role of the finance function

- Financial control
  - Involves:
    - Allocation and effective use of resources
- Treasury control
  - Involves:
    - Obtaining suitable types of finance
- Financial controller
  - Processing
  - Communicating
  - Acting as a business partner
- Finance function as business partner
  - Hybrid accountant
- Outsourcing and shared servicing

Health and safety

- Governed by the Health and Safety at Work Act
- The management of Health and Safety at Work regulations
- Health and safety (consultation with employees) regulations
- The workplace (health, safety and welfare) regulations
- The manual handling operations regulations
- The health and safety (display screen equipment) regulations

Nature of control

- Control is the process where goals and standards are defined, performance is monitored and measured and corrective action taken.

Levels of Control

- Anthony classifies control into three basic levels:
  - Strategic management
  - Tactical management
  - Operational management

Mentoring

- Is aimed at supporting and encouraging personal and career development
- Two types of function for the mentor
  - Career functions and psychosocial functions

Performance management (the individual)

- Human resource strategy includes:
  - Training and development
  - Rewards
  - Promotion
- Employment contracts
- Performance appraisal includes:
  - Reward review
  - Performance review
  - Potential review

Business ethics and CSR

- Areas of social responsibility:
  - Natural environment
  - HR management policies
  - Charitable support
  - Above-minimum (legal standards)

Internal control systems

- Cover policies, processes, tasks and behaviours
- Control environment and control procedures
- Elements of effective internal control (COSO)
  - Strong control environment
  - A range of control activities
  - Communication processes
  - Monitoring the continuing effectiveness

Corporate governance

- Poor corporate governance led to the creation of the UK Corporate Governance Code

Quick Quiz

1 Complete the table below, stating the control strategy most likely to be used in the given contingent cases.

Contingencies	Control strategy mainly:
Divisions trading with transfer prices and an overall product structure	
Large size, stable environment, functional structure	
Small entrepreneurial company with no professional managers	

2 Appraisal is an example of what level of control?

A Strategic
B Tactical
C Operational
D Clan

3 Delete the words that are not applicable in the following sentence: 'Performance targets are an example of direct/indirect, output/input-focused control'.

4 Assuming that an organisation has separate financial control and treasury functions, which is more likely to be responsible for currency management?

5 Which function is more likely to be responsible for preparation of quarterly accounts?

Answers to Quick Quiz

1

Contingencies	Control strategy mainly:
Divisions trading with transfer prices and an overall product structure	Market
Large size, stable environment, functional structure	Bureaucratic
Small entrepreneurial company with no professional managers	Personal centralised

2 B Tactical. (Note that 'clan control' is a type of control strategy: not a level of control.)

3 Direct/~~indirect~~, output/~~input~~-focused

4 Treasury function

5 Financial control function

Answers to Questions

7.1 Control systems

D Bureaucratic control is probably the most likely. Market control might be used for some operations, particularly where comparisons could be made with competitors, but the cost structures of aviation are so lacking in transparency that this would be rather rare. There may be some elements of clan control among highly trained specialists such as aircrew and engineers. Option A, 'contingency', is a red herring.

7.2 Sales support

Support could be provided in the following ways (this is not a definitive list).

(a) Profitability analysis on sales and discount decisions
(b) Developing finance deals for customers, such as leasing arrangements
(c) Planning and analysis of the costs and revenue outcomes of sales promotions and advertising campaigns
(d) Providing facilities for customers to review products, services and prices
(e) Setting up deals with other suppliers to provide facilities to simplify customer purchasing
(f) Developing product and service deals assisting the customer to improve processes and review their costs
(g) Building relationships and sharing information with customers, and assisting their financial planning
(h) Dealing with sales administration to enable sales staff to spend more time with customers

---

7.3 Performance management

The key to performance management is that it is forward looking and constructive. Objective setting gives employees the security of knowing exactly what is expected of them, and this is agreed at the outset with the manager. In this instance, the Store Manager of the Farmers supermarket in Grimsby should emphasise the importance to all staff of the need to improve the level of customer service provided. This standard can be regularly measured through the company's existing customer satisfaction survey. Furthermore, employees at the outset can indicate the resources needed to help them achieve the service level required. This may require staff to be provided with additional training on the store's procurement policy, and to be kept up to date with the details of local suppliers used.

7.4 Formal appraisal

Disadvantages to the individual of not having an appraisal system include: the individual is not aware of progress or shortcomings, is unable to judge whether they would be considered for promotion, is unable to identify or correct weaknesses by training and there is a lack of communication with the manager.

7.5 Disaster costs

You may have thought of the Bhopal chemical plant explosion, Chernobyl reactor explosion, Kings Cross station fire, Piper Alpha oil rig disaster, and so on. The main costs are reconstruction, compensation for death and injury, lost production, and loss of reputation.

7.6 Responsibility for safe working

Much would depend on why the surface was slippery. There have been cases where the employer has been found to be at fault, as they failed in their duty to take reasonable care to provide safe premises.

7.7 Workplace hazards

You may have spotted the following hazards (if not others as well ...)

(a) Heavy object on high (secure?) shelf
(b) Standing on swivel chair
(c) Lifting heavy object incorrectly
(d) Trailing wires
(e) Electric bar fire
(f) Open drawers blocking passage and risk toppling cabinet
(g) Unattended lit cigarette – passive smoking **and** fire hazard
(h) Overfull waste bin
(i) Overloaded electric socket
(j) Overloaded tray of hot liquids
(k) Dangerous spike and scissors
(l) Frayed carpet

7.8 Socially responsible activities

(a) Farmers is committed to buying certain fresh produce locally, with the aim of supporting local farmers. It has had relationships with a number of its suppliers for many years, which suggests that this approach is proving mutually beneficial.

(b) The founder of Farmers supermarket (Nick Farmer) believed that suppliers to large retailers were being treated badly. This belief forms part of the company's culture, as a policy which commits Farmers to pay fair prices to suppliers has been implemented.

(c) The company is involved in the global fair trade movement.

(d) Farmers sources more of its produce from the UK than competing supermarkets. This is positive, as it reduces the amount of pollution caused by transporting produce around the world.

(e) Staff working for Farmers supermarkets appear to be well paid, as high staff costs are given as a reason for lower profitability. Furthermore, all store staff receive a quarterly performance-related bonus, based on the previous quarter's results. Store managers also appear to be treated well, as they have been given responsibilities for local procurement and staffing.

7.9 Acting ethically

(a) If Gemma were to manipulate the return, she would breach the fundamental principles of integrity, objectivity and professional behaviour. Knowingly submitting an incorrect return would not be honest behaviour. Gemma's objectivity would be affected due to a conflict of interest; if she manipulated the figures, she would personally benefit from receiving the bonus. Clearly, such behaviour is likely to bring the accountancy profession into disrepute.

(b) Gemma is facing both a self-interest and intimidation threat. As mentioned above, Gemma is facing a self-interest threat, as she stands to benefit financially from the fraud. Due to Charles Barber's position as Gemma's manager, it is likely that she feels intimidated to act unethically. This situation is exacerbated because Charles is responsible for approving Gemma's leave to take her CIMA exams. Failure to participate may result in Charles refusing requests for leave.

(c) The most appropriate safeguard available to Gemma would be to refuse her manager's request on the grounds that it is clearly unethical. It may also be necessary for Gemma to inform management higher in the organisational hierarchy of the situation. Due to the nature of the proposed fraud, it is likely to be appropriate for Gemma to approach Helena Farmer, the Finance Director, to discuss her concerns.

Now try these questions from the Practice Question Bank

Question	Level
7.1 – 7.6	Practice
Performance appraisal systems	Practice
The accounting function	Practice

MANAGING CHANGE THROUGH PROJECTS

Part D

CHANGE MANAGEMENT

In this chapter, we move on to Part D, the final element of the E2 syllabus 'Managing change through projects'. This chapter brings us back to some of the themes we explored earlier in the Study Text. In the opening sections, we considered the importance of the rational model, which may be used by the board of directors in setting the organisation's strategy.

Here we consider the practical methods and processes used for implementing it. The influence of environmental developments is such that strategies will inevitably change and evolve; the only question is how rapid the change will be.

The management of change is an integral and important part of strategic management. Following the work of Johnson, Scholes and Whittington, we start by considering the **diagnosis of change requirements**. The work to be done here consists of establishing the type of change required; exploring the organisational context and the cultural influences involved; and analysing the forces that support or hinder the change required.

We will then examine the impact of **management style** and the **roles played by** managers and other **agents of change**. There are a number of **levers of change** that managers can use, and we consider these next. Finally, we consider the **common pitfalls** that have hampered change programmes in the past.

Topic list	Learning outcomes	Syllabus references	Ability required
1 Diagnosis – situation analysis for change	D1a	D1(i), (ii), (iii), (iv)	Analysis
2 Approaches to managing resistance to change	D1b	D1(i), (ii)	Evaluation
3 Change management roles	D1b	D1(iii)	Evaluation
4 Change management levers	D1a	D1(iv)	Analysis
5 Pitfall of change management	D1a	D1(iv)	Analysis

Chapter Overview

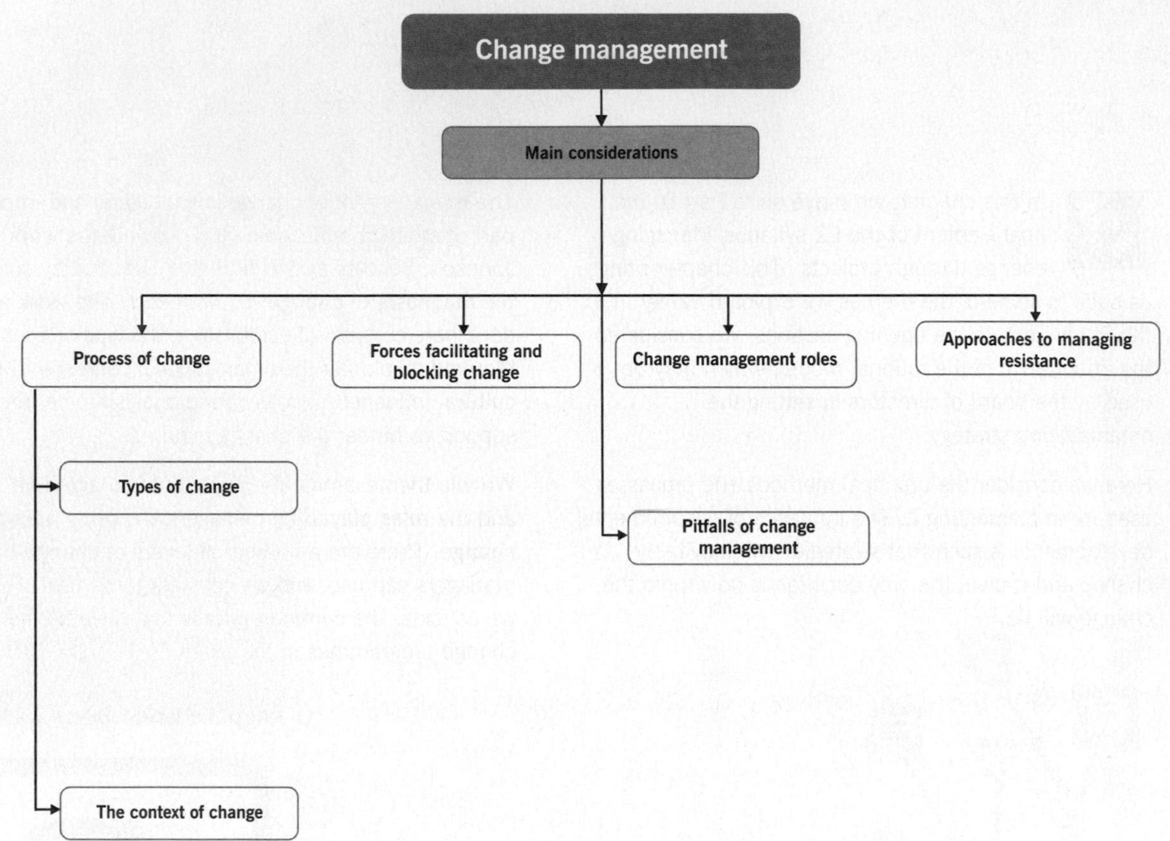
Change management
Main considerations
Process of change
Forces facilitating and blocking change
Change management roles
Approaches to managing resistance
Types of change
Pitfalls of change management
The context of change

1 Diagnosis – situation analysis for change

Introduction

Change and change management are important terms, which have featured heavily in the global business press in recent years. Earlier in the Study Text, we discussed the various stages that form the rational model to strategy setting. As we highlighted, the modern-day organisation is continually forced to respond to a range of internal and external pressures, the end result being the implementation of a selected strategy. Many of the change management issues raised in this chapter are central to strategy implementation. As we shall explore, change management is largely focused on the impact it has on people in the workplace.

There are three main change management considerations:

- The type of change required
- The wider context of change
- Forces facilitating and blocking change

A wide range of stimuli may lead an organisation's managers to recognise the need for strategic change. Consideration of the broader contexts of the **environment** and the organisation's **strategic capability** may show that large-scale developments are necessary; the need to put strategy into action may call for more detailed but no less far-reaching adjustment of processes, relationships, technologies and so on.

The process of change

The stimulus for organisational change is usually driven by some form of internal or external event. Such events are often referred to as '**triggers**'.

Triggers may include the following.

External events	Internal events
Increasing competition	Out of date working practices/processes
Changes in customer tastes and buying behaviour	Changes in organisational performance, eg reducing profitability
Social changes, eg demographics (age, income and gender)	Introduction of new technologies
Changes in the economic cycle (recession)	Changes in senior management
Political and legal pressures (new laws, regulations and tax rules)	High staff turnover
Increasing use of new technologies (internet and mobile technologies)	

Question 8.1 Triggers for change at Farmers supermarkets

Learning outcome D1a

As part of Adrian Williams' (Managing Director of Farmers supermarkets) review of Farmers' position in the UK supermarket sector, he has asked for your help in identifying the types of 'triggers' that could necessitate the need for change at the company.

Required

(a) Identify three internal 'triggers' for change at Farmers supermarkets **and** explain why this may lead to change.

(b) Identify three external 'triggers' for change at Farmers supermarkets **and** explain why this may lead to change.

1.1 Main considerations

In any event, the management of change starts with an understanding of **three main considerations**:

(a) The **type** of change required
(b) The **wider context** of the change
(c) **Forces facilitating** and **blocking** change

1.2 Types of change

Johnson, Scholes and Whittington (JS&W), quoting Balogun and Hope Hailey, analyse change on two axes: **scope** and **nature**.

The **scope** of change is its extent: the measure of scope is whether or not the methods and assumptions of the existing **paradigm** must be replaced.

The **nature** of change may be incremental and built on existing methods and approaches, or it may require a 'big bang' approach if rapid response is required, as in times of crisis.

		Scope of change	
		Realignment	Transformation
Nature of change	Incremental	Adaptation	Evolution
	'Big bang'	Reconstruction	Revolution

(a) **Adaptation** is the most common type of change. It does not require the development of a new paradigm and proceeds step by step.

(b) **Reconstruction** can also be undertaken within an existing paradigm, but requires rapid and extensive action. It is a common response to a long-term decline in performance.

(c) **Evolution** is an incremental process that leads to a new paradigm. It may arise from careful analysis and planning or may be the result of **learning processes**. Its transformational nature may not be obvious while it is taking place.

(d) **Revolution** is a rapid and wide-ranging response to extreme pressures for change. A long period of **strategic drift** may lead to a crisis that can only be dealt with in this way. Revolution will be very obvious and is likely to affect most aspects of both what the organisation does and how it does them.

Exam alert

Questions in your E2 exam may require you to identify and classify the type of change being detailed in a short scenario using Balogun and Hope Hailey's model. It is important that you spend some time learning this theory, as it also forms part of the syllabus for Paper E3.

CASE STUDY

Types of change and Farmers supermarket

Adaptation

Farmers supermarkets recently introduced a home delivery service to customers in the London area. This change is a form of adaptation, as the company is simply attempting to move with the times as competing supermarkets already offer this service. The fundamental nature of Farmers' culture and business model has not changed, as it is still operating as a supermarket.

Reconstruction

In the event that the UK economy went into a prolonged recession, Farmers supermarkets could be forced to undertake a rapid form of reconstruction. The impact of a significant fall in customer demand for the produce offered by Farmers may lead to the closure of the most unprofitable outlets. Making staff redundant in the affected stores would cause upheaval throughout the organisation but would not ultimately change Farmers' culture or business model.

Evolution

The decision to introduce the home delivery service may be part of a long-term plan to close down all the Farmers stores over a number of years with the view of becoming an online retailer only. Such an evolutionary change would lead to a change in the organisation's culture and business model.

Revolution

Revolutionary change at Farmers supermarkets would be driven by extreme pressures. An example would be the decision by Cherry Picker Holdings (CPH) to sell off its investment in Farmers to another conglomerate. A new parent company may move to instil its own culture throughout Farmers. Changes could result in the closure of existing stores or changes to Farmers' existing local, UK-based supply chain.

1.3 The context of change (contextual features model)

The context of change is provided by the organisational setting; this has many aspects and can therefore be very complex. However, this complexity can be approached in a manageable way by considering it under eight general headings proposed by Balogun and Hope Hailey. One of the eight headings is **scope**: this has already been discussed. The rest are discussed below.

The headings represent a wide range of influences, and the specific considerations affecting the impact of each may vary from organisation to organisation. For example, the first on the list, the **time available**, may be largely determined by stakeholder sentiment in one organisation and by anticipated political change in another, with different aspects of the market situation influencing both.

1.3.1 Aspects of context

(a) The **time available** may vary dramatically, but can often be quite limited when responding to competitive or regulatory pressure.

(b) The **preservation** of some organisational characteristics and resources may be required.

(c) **Diversity** of general experience, opinion and practice is likely to ease the change process: homogeneity in these factors is unlikely to do so.

(d) The **capability** to manage and implement change is obviously important. To a great extent, this depends on past experience of change projects, both among managers and among lower-level staff.

(e) **Capacity** to undertake change depends on the availability of resources, particularly finance, and information systems/information technology, and management time and skill. It is important to note that unrealisable or outdated systems could become a blockage in the change process.

(f) The degree of workforce **readiness** for change will affect its success. Readiness may be contrasted with **resistance** to change, which can exist at varying levels of intensity and may be widespread or confined to pockets.

(g) The **power** to effect change may not be sufficient to overcome determined resistance among important stakeholder groups. This can apply even at the strategic apex where, for example, major shareholders, trustees or government ministers may constrain managers' freedom of action.

1.3.2 Questions

An examination of context leads to four questions.

(a) Is the organisation able to **achieve** the change required?

(b) Does the context affect the **means** by which change should be achieved?

(c) Should the context itself be **restructured** as a preliminary to strategic change?

(d) Will constraints present in the context make it necessary to proceed in **stages**?

1.4 Forces facilitating and blocking change

1.4.1 The stage model of change

Lewin suggests that organisational change can be broken down into a three-stage process, '**unfreeze**', '**change**' and '**refreeze**'.

Figure: The unfreeze-change-refreeze model

1.4.2 Unfreeze

The first step is named the unfreeze stage, as it is focused on breaking the existing state of affairs and preparing the organisation for change. In many cases, the process of unfreezing existing approaches can be particularly difficult, as managing individual and group resistance to change proposals can create significant challenges, as we shall see later in this chapter.

Central to this stage is identifying those forces resisting change and by strengthening the position of those forces driving the need for change. The process of unfreezing the status quo will vary from organisation to organisation, but may involve the following approaches.

(a) Removing individuals resisting change from their current position and routines. This is aimed at breaking existing attitudes that are likely to hinder the successful implementation of the change. This may be achieved through making certain individuals redundant or promoting those opposed to change to a higher position within the organisation that requires the support for change.

(b) Staff affected by change may be encouraged to participate in the change process. Management may decide to consult individuals on proposals for change. This may help to reduce potential resistance and help to create staff 'buy-in' to the need for change.

(c) Management may decide to confront the perceptions that individuals hold towards a proposal for change. Engaging with people's emotions through direct, clear communication may reduce negative feelings towards change and help to 'clear the air' between management and employees.

(d) The creation of a positive agenda supporting the change is important. Building a climate for change can be achieved through positive reinforcement of the benefits that the change will bring. Efforts are likely to involve regular praise and recognition of those individuals supporting the change.

1.4.3 Change

At the change stage, the new working methods, systems and cultures are implemented. It is at this point that the organisation gradually makes the move towards its desired end state. This stage requires staff participation to help create the necessary 'buy-in' to the new status quo.

1.4.4 Refreeze

At the refreeze stage, this involves the new state being embedded. At this point, the difficulties of the transitional change stage should have ended. However, the process of embedding a change may take time, as staff need to become accustomed to the new state. A significant amount of management time will be spent reinforcing the adoption by staff of the new processes and working practices. Positive reinforcement may be achieved through the use of rewards, ie those employees that adopt the new process may receive bonus payments or be offered flexible working patterns to ensure their continued support.

In cases of non-compliance, management may use negative reinforcement as a means to punish those individuals failing to adopt the implemented change.

1.5 Culture and change

An important consideration in achieving a successful change focuses on the importance of organisational culture. If you think about the elements of context outlined earlier in this section, you will quickly realise that they are all affected to some extent by **cultural considerations**. For example, even the adequacy or otherwise of the time available may be affected by culturally influenced attitudes to speed of action, caution and risk.

The **cultural web** (which we have looked at earlier in this Study Text) may be used as a tool to establish specific implications of the desired overall strategic change by facilitating comparison between the current position and the desired future outcome. For example, consideration of **power structures** may make it clear that there should be a move away from some aspects of uncontrolled **devolution of power** and towards a **clearer definition of responsibility**. Similarly, it might be decided that dress is a powerful **symbol** and that a corporate livery should be provided for customer-facing staff.

1.6 Force field analysis

As we discussed earlier, when we explored the three-stage model of change, dealing with resistance is likely to be a common feature of most change projects.

Force field analysis consists of the identification of the factors that promote and hinder change. Central to this analysis is determining where the organisation wishes to be at the end of the change process; this is denoted below in the diagram by the 'ideal position' (or, as discussed earlier, the 'refreeze' stage). Promoting forces should be exploited and the effect of hindering forces reduced.

It is traditional to represent these forces by **arrows** whose individual dimensions correspond to their perceived strengths. Promoting and hindering forces are then shown pointing from opposite sides to a vertical linear datum line. This representation is useful for purposes such as brainstorming and staff briefings, but two lists in order of magnitude are just as useful for purposes of analysis. The example below concerns a public sector organisation that is introducing performance review.

Exam alert

It is important that you understand the connection between change management and project management (discussed later in this Study Text), as both areas could easily feature in your Integrated Case Study. Change management and project management are intimately linked: any project is quite likely to result in change, while change is often implemented through projects.

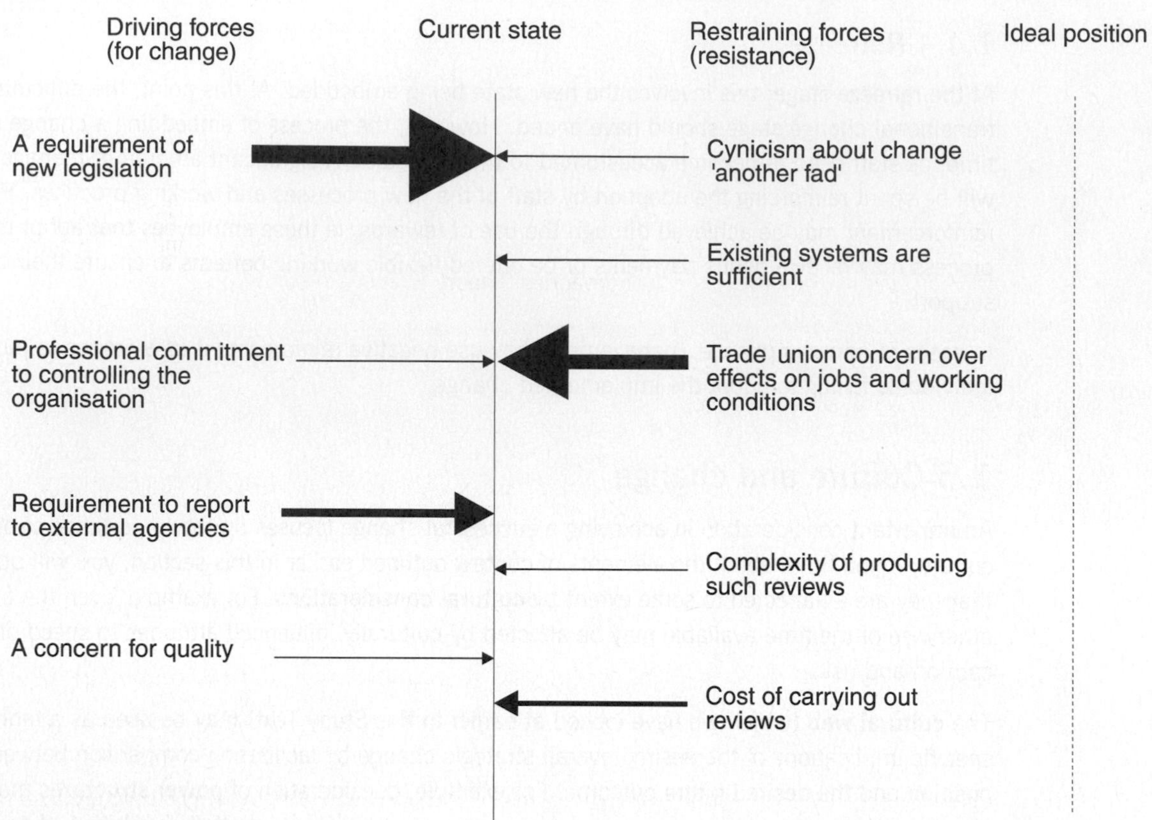

Question 8.2

Force field analysis at Farmers

Learning outcome D1b

Ross Halep, the Investment Director at CPH, is responsible for overseeing and managing the conglomerate's relationship with Farmers. During a recent board meeting at the supermarket, he proposed plans to investigate the viability of changing the company's existing milk suppliers.

He explained that 'a significant part of our store managers' time is spent dealing with local suppliers. I understand that sourcing produce locally has been part of Farmers' business model for many years, but maybe it is time for us to consider sourcing certain products that are common to all Farmers stores from a central supplier. All our major rivals use a national milk supplier, which has allowed them to realise significant economies of scale and reduce costs'.

Required

Identify those forces (driving forces) likely to be in favour of the Investment Director's proposal, and those forces likely to resist the change (restraining forces).

Senior (drawing on the advice of Carnall and Huczyuski and Buchanan) suggests a practical route to applying the force field analysis idea.

(a) Define the problem in terms of the current situation and the desired future state.

(b) List the forces supporting and opposing the desired change, and assess both the strength and the importance of each one.

(c) Draw the force field diagram.

(d) Decide how to strengthen or weaken the more important forces as appropriate, and agree with those concerned. Weakening might be achieved by persuasion, participation, coercion or bargaining, while strengthening might be achieved by a marketing or education campaign, including the use of personal advocacy.

(e) Identify the resources needed.

(f) Make an action plan including event timing, milestones and responsibilities.

JS&W state that, typically, elements of the **cultural web** emerge as important forces promoting or hindering change. The web can thus be used alongside force field analysis as a diagnostic tool.

1.7 Beer and Nohria – Theory E and Theory O

Beer and Nohria (writing in the *Harvard Business Review* in 2000) suggest that although each organisation's change is unique, each change is ultimately a variant of two underlying approaches. Beer and Nohria call these underlying approaches 'Theory E' and 'Theory O'.

Theory E starts from the premise that the purpose of change is to **increase economic value**, often expressed as shareholder value. Theory E changes usually involve the use of economic incentives, drastic layoffs, downsizing and restructuring.

Theory O is concerned with developing an organisation's **human capability** to implement strategy, and to develop corporate culture through **organisational learning**. The focus of change is on culture and cultural adjustment. The process is participative (rather than being top-down) with an emphasis on feedback and reflection.

These approaches have their drawbacks. Theory E approaches ignore the feelings and attitudes of employees, and may lead to a fall in motivation and commitment, and the loss of the creativity needed to sustain competitive advantage. By contrast, by trying to maintain positive relationships with staff, Theory O approaches may mean that organisations avoid taking difficult decisions; for example, decisions about how to reverse a decline in customer numbers or market share.

As a result Beer and Nohria argue that, in practice, organisations should implement both Theory E and Theory O at the same time. However, this then leaves managers with the problem of how to combine the relevant elements from both approaches, and to resolve the tension between Theories E and O in a way that obtains the benefits of each while minimising the negative consequences.

Yet at the same time, Beer and Nohria argue that this 'problem' should also be the objective of managers leading change. Their objective should be to integrate E and O in a way that resolves the tension between the two, allowing organisations to satisfy their shareholders and yet also have the capacity and capabilities to adapt and survive as viable institutions in the long run.

1.8 Reasons for resistance

An important aspect in successfully managing change centres on recognising the reasons why individuals resist change programmes. There are potentially many reasons for resistance.

Reason for resistance	Comment
High levels of uncertainty	Organisational change is likely to lead to uncertainty for those affected. Individuals may feel inclined to stick to the 'status quo' to avoid experiencing the uncertainty of the unknown.
Increase in workload	Management and those closely affected by a change programme are likely to experience a spike in their workload. Introducing a change will require management input in planning and testing new processes and systems. This may create resentment if staff are expected to carry out such work in addition to their everyday tasks.
Sense of embarrassment	Those management and staff associated with previous change initiatives that are now the focus of a change project may experience a sense of embarrassment or humiliation. The perception among others that the latest change project has been initiated to make up for the failings of previous projects may create a climate of resentment.

Reason for resistance	Comment
Rapid change	In cases of rapid, forced change this may strengthen resistance, as it does not allow time for those affected to understand the change or prepare themselves. Individuals may be more likely to oppose change than readily accept it, especially in instances where change was not anticipated.
Loss of autonomy	Individuals affected by organisational change may feel like they are losing control over their job remit. Feelings of helplessness are likely to increase resistance. Change inevitably requires different approaches to conducting business and job routines. Moving away from traditional routines increases the scope for confusion about how new processes should work.
Skills and competence	Change programmes that introduce new technologies may increase resistance among those expected to use the new system, as individuals may feel that they lack the skills to adapt to the new ways of working. There is a danger that individuals may experience feelings of inadequacy as their current skills are no longer required.

Section summary

There are three main change management considerations.

(a) The type of change required. Balogun and Hope Hailey classify change in one of four ways: adaptation, evolution, reconstruction or revolution. Each classification is determined by contrasting the scope and nature of the change.

(b) The wider context of change, including the time available; capability to implement change; capacity and readiness; and power.

(c) Forces facilitating and blocking change. To help better understand the stages involved in achieving a successful change programme, Lewin proposes the use of a three-stage model for change: unfreeze, change and refreeze. To help identify those factors driving and resisting change, it can prove particularly useful to conduct a force field analysis.

2 Approaches to managing resistance to change

Introduction

Kotter and Schlesinger have identified six approaches to managing resistance to change.

- Education and communication
- Participation and involvement
- Facilitation and support
- Negotiation and agreement
- Manipulation and co-operation
- Coercion, implicit and explicit

The approach (style) adopted by management will vary depending on the circumstances surrounding the type of change required.

2.1 Six approaches

We have looked at leadership earlier in this Study Text, and one of the aspects of a leader's role will be to implement strategic change. However, it is important that the style in which the change is managed is appropriate to the context.

Kotter and Schlesinger identify six approaches to overcoming staff resistance.

- **Education and communication**
- **Participation and involvement**
- **Facilitation and support**
- **Negotiation and agreement**
- **Manipulation and co-operation**
- **Coercion, implicit and explicit**

2.1.1 Education and communication

Education and communication is an approach based on persuasion; the reasons for change and the means by which it will be achieved are explained in detail to those affected by it. Change is effectively 'sold' to staff where the benefits of change are promoted to help create 'buy-in'. It is assumed that employee resistance to change is caused by ignorance.

2.1.2 Participation and involvement

Participation brings those affected by strategic change into the change management process. Participation involves bringing staff into issue identification, prioritisation and the creation of new routines to implement a newly established strategy, for example. It may improve decision quality by bringing wider experience and knowledge to bear. Bringing staff into the process may help to reduce resistance to change. This approach is both ethical and advantageous in practice, since it can nurture a positive attitude, thus building both **readiness** and **capability** for change.

2.1.3 Facilitation and support

Facilitation and support involves guiding people through the difficulties experienced during times of change. Support may take the form of offering staff counselling to discuss their concerns in a one to one environment. Management may establish an informal, open door policy that provides an opportunity for those affected by change to ask questions. In cases where change results in staff redundancies, support may involve offering generous redundancy packages and training to help in future careers.

2.1.4 Negotiation and agreement

Negotiation is likely to be appropriate when management have to deal with a strong trade union. Change programmes that impact on employee pay and workplace rights may require the use of incentives such as additional pay and flexible working hours, to get individuals and unions to support the change.

2.1.5 Manipulation and co-operation

Manipulation may be deemed appropriate in instances where there is significant resistance to change. Employee resistance may be undermined through the use of covert tactics including the manipulation of information and concealing the truth about the need for change. This is a high-risk strategy, as this may increase resistance if staff do not trust management. The use of manipulation also raises some ethical considerations.

2.1.6 Coercion, implicit and explicit

Coercion is an **extreme form of direction**, being based on the use of management power to impose change. It is likely to provoke opposition but may be the best approach in times of confusion or crisis.

2.2 Using the six approaches

There may be advantages to making use of more than one of the change management approaches outlined above.

2.2.1 Context

Specific aspects of the organisational context already discussed will influence the use that can be made of the six approaches. Clear and appropriate direction can be a strong motivating force and may enhance **readiness** to change, while **participation** and **facilitation** may help to build **capability** to change.

2.2.2 Scope and nature

Using Balogun and Hope Hailey's matrix of the scope and nature of change (discussed earlier in the chapter), we might suggest that progression down the list of approaches may correspond reasonably well with progression from the top left to the bottom right of the matrix. In **adaptation**, where time is not critical and the extent of the change required is small, styles from the participative-communicative end of the spectrum may be appropriate. **Revolution**, on the other hand, will require a great element of direction and even of **coercion**. The intermediate cases are likely to require a combination of participation and direction, with the emphasis on the former in **evolution** and on the latter in **reconstruction**.

2.2.3 Power structures

In many cases, it will be appropriate to **echo an organisation's normal power structure** when managing change. Direction or **coercion** are likely to be more suitable in a firmly hierarchical organisation than they would be in a network or learning organisation, except in time of crisis, for example.

2.2.4 Personality type

Management style is a tool. Good managers will be capable of using a **style appropriate to the conditions** they have to work in. However, many managers' personality types will incline them to the style with which they are most comfortable. This effect is likely to interact with the effect of power structure mentioned above.

2.2.5 Combining styles

It will often be appropriate to use a combination of styles in a change programme, taking different approaches with different stakeholders. Providers of capital are likely to respond better to **education and communication** than to direction, for example, while something approaching **coercion** may be necessary in some internal areas simply because of the pressure of time.

Section summary

Kotter and Schlesinger identified six different approaches to managing resistance to change. The type of approach adopted is dependent in part on the type of change required. In some instances, it may be appropriate to use more than one approach; this will be driven by a range of factors.

3 Change management roles

Introduction

In the next section, we shall consider the roles that individuals may undertake during the change process. It is important to note that some change management roles may be carried out by individuals external to the organisation.

KEY TERM

A **CHANGE AGENT** is an individual or group that helps to bring about strategic change in an organisation. (JS&W (amended))

Change agency is an activity that might be concentrated in one person, but which is just as likely to be spread among the members of a group, such as a project team or management staff generally. Outsiders, such as consultants, may share in change agency.

JS&W examine change agency by considering the roles played by three distinct groups.

- **Strategic leaders**
- **Middle management**
- **Outsiders**

3.1 Strategic leadership

KEY TERM

LEADERSHIP is the ability to get others to follow you willingly.

JS&W, quoting Farkas and Wetlaufer, identify **five approaches to strategic leadership**.

- **Strategy**
- **Human assets**
- **Expertise**
- **Control**
- **Change**

3.1.1 The strategy approach

The leader taking the strategy approach focuses on **strategic analysis** and the **formulation of strategy**. Other managers take responsibility for routine operations and for the management of change.

3.1.2 The human assets approach

The **development of the organisation's people** is the main activity of leaders who take the human assets approach: other managers take responsibility for strategic management. Such leaders are concerned to recruit the right people and to develop an appropriate **culture**. Their approach to change management is to recruit people to whom the responsibility can be devolved.

3.1.3 The expertise approach

The expertise approach focuses on some form of **technical expertise as a source of competitive advantage** and concentrates on building expertise through systems and procedures. This focus also forms the basis of change management. Other managers also concentrate on their areas of expertise.

3.1.4 The control approach

The control approach is also known as the 'box' approach. The strategic leader following this approach concentrates on setting **procedures and control measures**, and **monitoring performance** so as to achieve uniform, predictable performance. Other managers are expected to use this approach, and change management is based on **careful control**.

3.1.5 The change approach

The leader using the change approach focuses on **continual change**, and expends much effort on communication and motivation. Other managers are expected to act largely as **change agents**.

3.1.6 Transactional and transformational leadership

The five approaches outlined above may be fitted into the model of leadership we discussed earlier in this Study Text that recognises two general types: **transactional and transformational**.

(a) **Transactional leaders** focus on systems and controls, and generally seek improvement rather than change.

(b) **Transformational leaders** energise people and build a vision of the future. Change management is a natural part of what they do.

Using this analysis, we may say that the **control** approach is a form of **transactional leadership**, while the other four approaches fall into the **transformational** category.

3.2 Middle management

Strategic leaders pursuing change may see their middle managers as implementers at best and possibly as potential blockers. Their commitment to change is important and they have significant roles to play in change management.

(a) **Implementation** and **control** where change is introduced in a top-down way

(b) **Translation** of the overall change strategy into forms suited to specific local contexts: this may require **reinterpretation** and **adjustment** of strategic factors such as relationships with suppliers and customers

(c) Provision of **advice** to higher management on requirements for change and potential obstacles

3.3 Outsiders

Outsiders may contribute to the change process in a range of roles.

(a) A new **chief executive** may be appointed to bring a fresh point of view and break down the constraints of the existing paradigm. A **hybrid** chief executive is one who has appropriate experience of the industry, or even of the organisation, but is not part of the existing culture.

(b) New **managers** in other positions can enhance the capability to change and increase **diversity** of opinion and practice. However, their success is likely to depend on the visible backing of the chief executive.

(c) **Consultants** may be employed to fill a number of planning and facilitating roles. Like newly appointed managers, they bring a fresh approach and are not constrained by the existing paradigm. This enables them to challenge things that are taken for granted. Also, their appointment signals the importance of the change process.

(d) Other external **stakeholders** are capable of influencing change and may have a part to play.

3.4 Power skills of change agents

Kanter suggests that change agents require seven so-called 'power skills' to help overcome resistance to change:

(a) Ability to work independently, without management power, sanction and support
(b) An effective collaborator, able to compete in ways that enhance co-operation
(c) Ability to develop high-trust relationships, based on high ethical standards
(d) Self-confidence, tempered with humility
(e) Respect for the process of change as well as the content
(f) Able to work across business functions and units
(g) Willingness to stake reward on results and gain satisfaction from success

Section summary

A **change agent** is an individual or group that helps to bring about strategic change in an organisation.

Strategic leaders act as change agents in one of five styles.

- Strategy
- Human assets
- Expertise
- Control
- Change

Middle managers implement and control top-down change; translate overall change strategy for local contexts; and advise strategic managers.

Outsiders may be brought in at the strategic apex in order to remake the paradigm. New middle managers can enhance change capability; consultants can fill planning and facilitating roles.

4 Change management levers

Many of the levers that can be used to implement change are related to aspects of the **cultural web**. We will consider these in this section, but first we will consider the special case of **turnaround**. A turnaround strategy is required when a business is in terminal decline. Such a strategy uses its own change management techniques.

4.1 Turnaround

When a business is in terminal decline and faces closure or takeover, there is a need for rapid and extensive change in order to achieve cost reduction and revenue generation. This is a **turnaround strategy**. JS&W identify **seven elements of such a strategy**.

4.1.1 Crisis stabilisation

The emphasis is on reducing costs and increasing revenues. An emphasis on reducing direct costs and improving productivity is more likely to be effective than efforts to reduce overheads.

(a) **Measures to increase revenue**

- (i) Tailor marketing mix to key market segments
- (ii) Review pricing policies to maximise revenue
- (iii) Focus activities on target market segments
- (iv) Exploit revenue opportunities if related to target segments
- (v) Invest in growth areas

(b) **Measures to reduce costs**

- (i) Cut costs of labour and senior management
- (ii) Improve productivity
- (iii) Ensure clear marketing focus on target market segments
- (iv) Financial controls
- (v) Strict cash management controls
- (vi) Reduce inventory
- (vii) Cut unprofitable products and services

Severe cost cutting is a common response to crisis but it is unlikely to be enough by itself. The **wider causes of decline** must be addressed.

4.1.2 Management changes

It is likely that new managers will be required, especially at the strategic apex. There are four reasons for this.

(a) The old management allowed the situation to deteriorate and **may be held responsible by key stakeholders**.

(b) **Experience of turnaround management** may be required.

(c) Managers brought in from outside will not be **prisoners of the old paradigm**.

(d) A **directive approach** to change management will probably be required.

4.1.3 Communication with stakeholders

The support of key stakeholder groups – groups with both a high level of power and a high degree of interest in an organisation – such as the workforce and providers of finance is likely to be very important in a turnaround; it is equally likely that stakeholders did not receive full information during the period of deterioration. A **stakeholder analysis** (discussed earlier in this Study Text) should be carried out so that the various stakeholder groups can be informed and managed appropriately.

4.1.4 Attention to target markets

A **clear focus on appropriate target market segments** is essential; indeed a lack of such focus is a common cause of decline. The organisation must become customer-oriented and ensure that it has good flows of marketing information.

4.1.5 Concentration of effort

Resources should be concentrated on the best opportunities to create value. It will almost certainly be appropriate to **review products and the market segments** currently served, and eliminate any distractions and poor performers. A similar review of internal activities would also be likely to show up several candidates for **outsourcing**.

4.1.6 Financial restructuring

Some form of **financial restructuring** is likely to be required. In the worst case, this may involve trading out of insolvency. Even where the business is more or less solvent, capital restructuring may be required, both to provide cash for investment and to reduce cash outflows in the shorter term.

4.1.7 Prioritisation

The eventual success of a turnaround strategy depends in part on management's ability to **prioritise necessary activities**, such as those noted above.

4.2 Challenging the paradigm

The entrenched assumptions and habits of mind that JS&W refer to as **the paradigm** constitute an important obstacle to strategic change. The paradigm must, therefore, be **challenged** if change is to be achieved. There are several approaches to this process of challenge; JS&W give four examples.

(a) Newcomers to the organisation are likely to trust **objective evidence** that new conditions require new approaches. Unfortunately, evidence is rarely overwhelming, or even complete, and there is a natural tendency to reinterpret, discount or even deny it. Persistence is required when objective evidence is relied on.

(b) A **careful analysis** of just what is taken for granted, possibly through **workshop sessions**, may enhance an objective assessment of new ideas. The aim is to lead those involved to challenge their own assumptions.

(c) **Scenario construction** can be used to bring managers to a better understanding of changing conditions by presenting a range of possible futures and their implications for the organisation.

(d) It may be appropriate to take firm action to **bring senior managers close to the daily reality** of what the organisation does, perhaps by extended visits to places and processes with direct customer contact.

4.3 Changing routines

Routines are the **habitual behaviours** that members of the organisation display both internally and externally. They are **not** procedures or processes but the **wider ways of doing things** that are typical of the organisation. They are closely linked to the paradigm. The problem of routines is that they can subvert change efforts. For example, it is unlikely that simply explaining required new processes and procedures will lead to their effective adoption: existing routines will mould the way they are put into operation.

When a **top-down change programme** requires the introduction of new methods, the detail of implementation can be driven by the careful identification of **critical success factors** and the **competences** they demand.

When change is to be introduced in a **less directed** way, change agents may focus on routines, **extending** existing ways of doing things towards what is required and then '**bending** the rules of the game' when sufficient stakeholder support has been created.

4.4 Symbolic processes

Symbols were mentioned earlier in this Study Text, during our discussion of culture and the cultural web. Their importance in the context of change is that they can often be used as levers of change. However, it is important to understand that the significance of a given symbol may vary from person to person; this makes their use as a tool of management difficult.

(a) New **rituals** can be introduced and old ones abolished in order to communicate and implement change. For example, the replacement of a strictly hierarchical approach to management with a culture of coaching and empowerment can be signalled and reinforced by the introduction of social occasions such as office parties that will allow staff to meet relatively informally.

(b) Formal **systems and processes** can have symbolic aspects, typically when they signal status and power relationships, but also when they direct attention to new concerns, such as customer service.

(c) Changes to **physical aspects** of the workplace can have a strong symbolic effect as, for instance, when open-plan offices or hot desking are introduced.

(d) The **behaviour** of leaders and change agents has a very powerful symbolic effect and must reflect intended change if the intention is not to be undermined: staff will respond far better to example than to edict.

(e) **Language** can have symbolic significance beyond the bald meaning of the words used. Well-chosen words can inspire and motivate change; similarly, the use of badly chosen words can undermine their inherent meaning.

(f) **Stories** have an important symbolic role, but are not easy to exploit, since much corporate communication is automatically dismissed as mere marketing puff.

4.5 Power and politics

Politics is about the exercise of **power** and the use of **influence**. Managers and other important individual stakeholders establish and exploit **power structures** and **networks of influence** that are intertwined with both formal hierarchies and the informal aspects of the organisation's life. The implementation of strategy is inevitably influenced by the operation of these structures and networks. Change management is also, therefore, subject to political influence, and change managers should take due account of political processes.

JS&W suggest three objectives of **political activity** that may be sought by change managers.

- Building the **power base**
- Overcoming **resistance**
- Achieving **compliance**

Four **political mechanisms** may be used to exert influence in these areas.

- Manipulation of **resources**
- Relationships with **powerful groups and individuals** (elites)
- Exploitation of **subsystems**
- **Symbolic activity**

4.5.1 Resources

The ability to control the allocation of resources (or even merely to influence their allocation) is recognised as a distinct and important **form of power** within the organisation. It can be used both to **enable specific developments** in the change programme and, more subtly, to **build support and influence** that will assist with the processes of overcoming resistance and ensuring compliance.

4.5.2 Elites

Association with **respected and influential stakeholders** can enhance the personal status and thus the power base of the change agent. Similarly, association with a **high status change agent** can assist more junior managers to overcome resistance to change.

Sometimes it is necessary to **eliminate centres of resistance** by removing people from the organisation in order to ensure compliance with change requirements.

4.5.3 Subsystems

A power base can be established by building up **networks and alliances** among those sympathetic to change. It may then be possible to outmanoeuvre and marginalise the resistance. Equally, however, it may not; also, such manoeuvring by change agents may provoke stronger resistance. It will be useful to analyse power and influence using the stakeholder mapping model explained earlier in this Study Text.

4.5.4 Symbols

Change managers may utilise existing symbols and symbolic activities or challenge them, as appropriate.

4.6 Communication and monitoring

It is obvious that change management must include effective communication and explanation of the **need for change**, what the plan is intended to **achieve** and what it involves. Good communication is a very important factor in overcoming resistance to change, particularly in the matter of building trust. Strategic complexity may make this difficult, but a clear vision must be provided.

A wide range of **communication media** is available and it is important that **appropriate selections** are made. Media that provide richness, immediacy and interactivity are appropriate when complex and important material is to be communicated, while more routine matters can be dealt with in less complex ways. It is important for change agents to be aware that what seems simple and routine to them may have significantly greater importance for ordinary members of the organisation.

Communication efforts should include clear and plentiful opportunities and routes for **feedback**, so that omissions, poorly constructed messages, misunderstandings and anxiety can be dealt with.

Care must be taken with **emotional aspects** of communication so that appropriate media, language and symbols are used.

Monitoring of behaviour to ensure that required changes are not subverted is essential.

4.7 Tactics

The change process can be forwarded by the use of specific tactics of change management.

4.7.1 Timing

The time at which actions are taken can be selected for tactical effectiveness.

(a) A **crisis** can be used to justify extensive change, so monitoring a mounting crisis and delaying action until it is ripe may enhance acceptance.

(b) **Windows of opportunity** may occur as, for example, when a takeover occurs.

(c) **Messages** about timing must be coherent so that, for example, rapid action is not undermined by the retention of procedures that enforce long time frames.

(d) Fear and anxiety about change as such may be reduced if unpleasant consequences can be **decoupled in time** from the main change programme: an example would be a programme of redundancy that does not commence until other change objectives, such as the outcomes of product and market reviews, have been implemented.

4.7.2 Job losses

The threat of job losses associated with change is likely to be bad for morale and to provoke resistance. Redundancy programmes must be managed with care.

(a) A single, rapid and extensive round of cuts is preferable to a long drawn out programme of smaller reductions: the former can be stressful but the latter creates **long-term uncertainty and anxiety**.

(b) Where **delayering** is required, it may be possible to concentrate the job losses among managers identified as being opposed to change: these are likely to be more senior figures.

(c) Those who lose their jobs should be dealt with as sympathetically and **compassionately** as possible; the provision of services such as outplacement, counselling and retraining may help.

4.7.3 Quick success

Momentum for change can be created by putting simple but highly visible improvements into successful operation. Even where the overall position is difficult and requires a complex solution, such **quick wins** are often available: it is common for them to emerge in the form of suggestions from the lower echelons of the organisation.

Even where there are no obvious easy options, it may be possible to create some by **concentrating the available resources** on specific problems rather than spreading them thinly.

Section summary

Change management levers can be closely linked to key components of the cultural web. In extreme cases of change, an organisation may use a turnaround strategy. A **turnaround strategy** is aimed at saving the business from closure. Johnson, Scholes and Whittington identify seven elements of a turnaround strategy.

5 Pitfalls of change management

Introduction

In this final section, we consider some of the inherent pitfalls involved in the change management process. You may be able to relate some of the issues raised to your own experience of change in the workplace.

JS&W quote Harris and Ogbonna, who identify **eight unintended outcomes** of change programmes.

(a) **Ritualisation of change**. When change programmes extend into the longer term, there is a danger that organisation members will come to view the initiatives as mere ritual with little real significance.

(b) **Hijacked process of change**. Change initiatives can be hijacked for unintended purposes; for example, improved technology provided to improve performance may be used simply to cut staffing levels, defeating the overall objective.

(c) **Erosion**. The successful introduction of new initiatives may suffer erosion from the effects of other events and processes as, for example, when high staff turnover hampers staff development.

(d) **Reinvention**. Recalcitrant staff may reinvent the nature and implications of the change programme in a way that accommodates previous undesirable practices. This is a failure of monitoring and control.

(e) **Ivory tower change**. When change is imposed from the top down, its proponents may be seen as inhabiting an ivory tower, out of touch with operational reality and lacking in credibility as a result.

(f) **Lack of attention to symbols**. Change managers who pay insufficient attention to symbols can both fail to make the change relevant to day to day reality and succeed in sending the wrong messages.

(g) **Uncontrolled efforts**. If practical adjustments to systems, for example, do not fit well with the overall intent of the change programme, staff are likely to become confused and demotivated.

(h) **Behavioural compliance**. Apparent behavioural compliance may disguise lack of commitment. People may appear to comply with the changes, without actually 'buying into' them.

These problems underline the complexity of the change management task. JS&W identify four specific implications for change management.

(a) **Monitoring** and **control** are vital aspects of change management, as is the flexibility to adjust programmes as they unfold.

(b) It is essential to understand the **existing culture** and its effects, since they are highly likely to hinder planned change.

(c) It will generally be advantageous to **involve the organisation's people** in the change process.

(d) Change represents a **major challenge** and may be more difficult to implement than it seems at first.

Section summary

Change programmes may be subverted and lead to unintended consequences. This has four implications for change management.

- Monitoring and control are vital.
- The existing culture must be understood.
- The organisation's people should be involved in the change process.
- The extent of the challenge must be recognised.

Chapter Summary

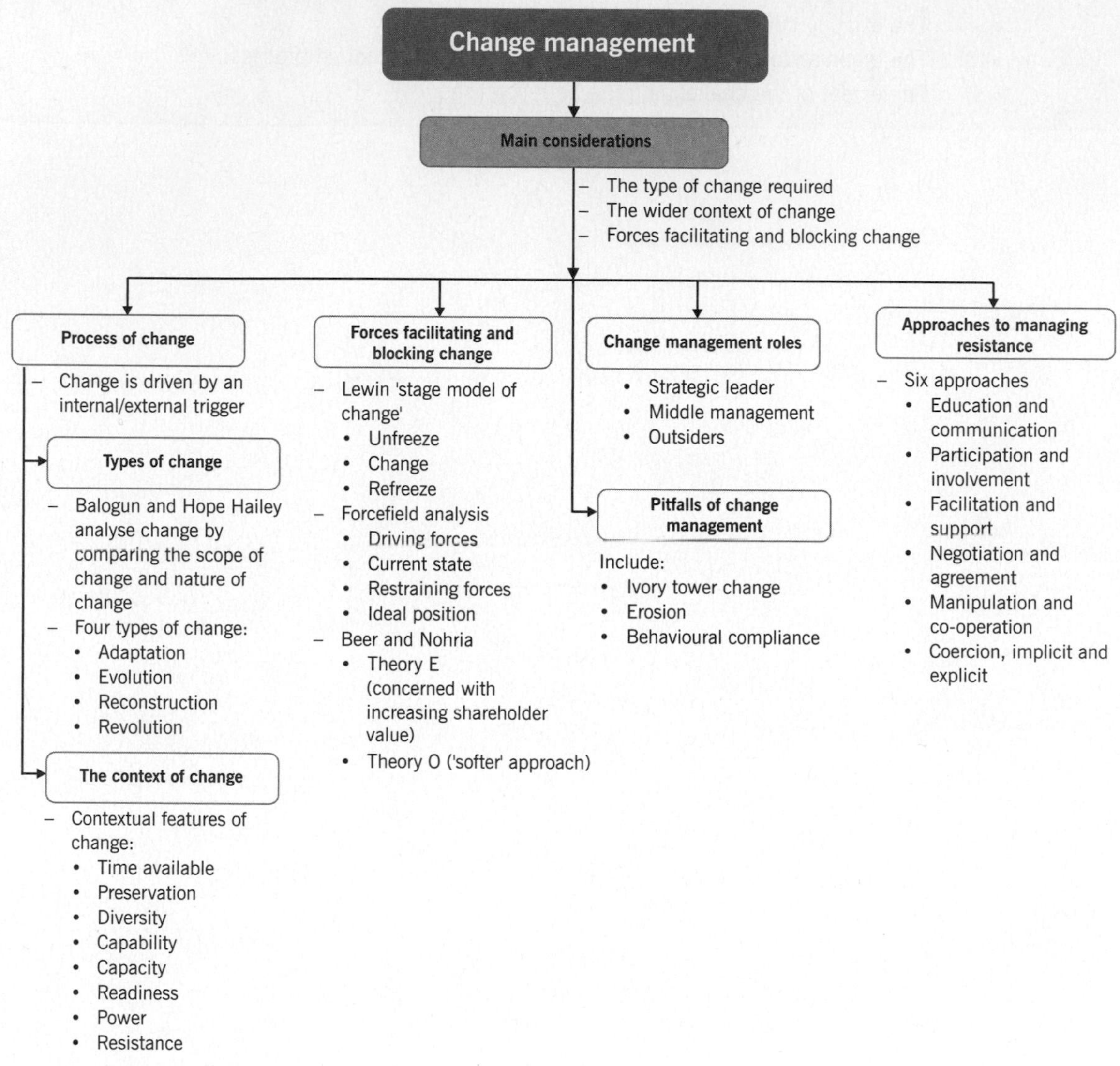

Quick Quiz

1. What is meant by the scope of change?
2. What is a change agent?
3. What is the difference between transformational leadership and transactional leadership?
4. What are the objectives of political activity that may be sought by change managers?
5. How can change managers create opportunities for early success?

Answers to Quick Quiz

1 The scope of change is the degree of change required – whether it can be transformational or whether a more fundamental realignment is required.

2 A change agent is an individual or group that helps to bring about strategic change in an organisation.

3 Transactional leaders focus on systems and controls, while transformational leaders seek to energise people and build a vision of the future.

4 Building a powerbase; overcoming resistance; and achieving compliance.

5 By concentrating resources on potentially solvable problems rather than spreading them thinly.

Answers to Questions

8.1 Triggers for change at Farmers supermarkets

Internal triggers

(a) The recent purchase of Farmers supermarkets by Cherry Picker Holdings (CPH) may lead to **changes in senior management** at the company in the future. At the present time this seems unlikely, as CPH is content to let Farmers carry on without interfering in the company's affairs; however, this could change if Farmers' performance deteriorates.

(b) Farmers recently introduced its own **home delivery service**. At the current time, this service is only available to customers based in the London area. Should the uptake of this service improve, then it is highly likely that Farmers may decide to offer this scheme nationally. The company would most likely need to undertake a change process to improve its delivery and website ordering infrastructure.

(c) **Reduction in employee performance**. At present, Farmers places a strong focus on providing shoppers with a good level of customer service. The level of service that customers receive is potentially very variable from outlet to outlet, and is dependent on the individual store worker. A drop in customer satisfaction is likely to require the implementation of some form of change process, eg company-wide customer service training.

External triggers

(a) **Economic downturn**. Although sales across the UK supermarket sector tend to be non-cyclical, an economic recession is likely to influence where those sales are made. Shoppers may be more inclined to choose supermarkets that offer discount brands or low-price special offers. As Farmers is committed to buying locally and accepts lower margins, the company may need to respond by introducing its own low-price products. This would facilitate the need to find suitable suppliers. This could be managed as part of a change project.

(b) **Competition in the industry is intense**. Farmers faces competition from other supermarkets in addition to discount chains and warehouse stores. Farmers needs to maintain its share of the market, which may require undertaking a change process to remain competitive, eg a new marketing campaign or, as mentioned in the case study, expanding its operations overseas.

(c) **Customer tastes change**. Farmers has been successful in offering customers a greater selection of produce that is grown locally to its supermarket outlets. However, changes in customer tastes may mean that fewer people demand traditional, locally grown produce in favour of a greater selection of 'world foods'. Responding to this change would require a change project to be undertaken to establish a new global supply chain.

8.2 Force field analysis at Farmers supermarket

Driving forces in favour of proposal

- Improve the returns generated from milk sales across all Farmers stores
- Using a central supplier may improve the certainty of supply
- Saves the Store Manager's time
- A central supplier should lead to consistency in the quality of the milk sold
- The proposal is being driven by the parent company

Restraining forces opposed to proposal

- Existing local farmers likely to feel betrayed
- Customers likely to feel betrayed, as the move represents a major shift in Farmers' approach to doing business
- Senior management will need to find a suitable new supplier (time and cost considerations)
- Negative press in the national media, giving up ethical procurement to increase profits

Now try these questions from the Practice Question Bank

Question	Level
8.1 – 8.5	Practice
Auto Direct	Practice

PROJECT MANAGEMENT – PART A

This chapter introduces the subject of project management. It is important that you take the time to go through this thoroughly, as the final two chapters build on the themes explored here.

We start our discussion by exploring the nature of project work and how this differs from ordinary day to day operations. We then explore the process for identifying suitable projects and outline the different methodologies that organisations may use in managing the projects they undertake.

In the following chapter, we look in more detail at the specific tools and techniques for planning and controlling projects. We end the chapter with a discussion on the importance of managing project risk.

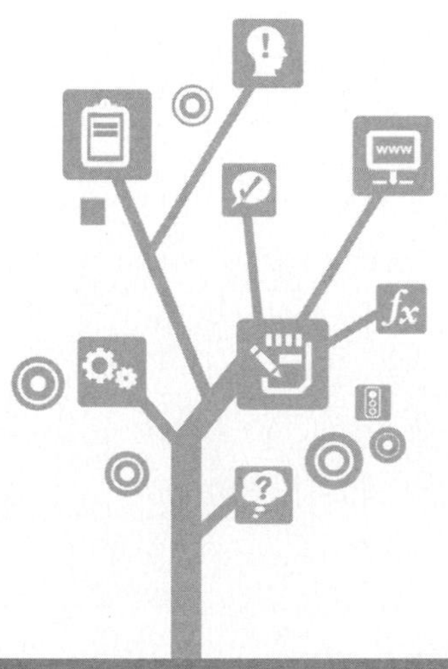

Topic list	Learning outcomes	Syllabus references	Ability required
1 The nature of project management	D2a	D2(i), (ii)	Analysis
2 Identifying projects	D2a	D2(iii)	Analysis
3 PRINCE2	D2a	D2(iv)	Analysis
4 The project life cycle	D2a	D2(iii)	Analysis
5 Managing project risk	D2b	D2(ii)	Application

Chapter Overview

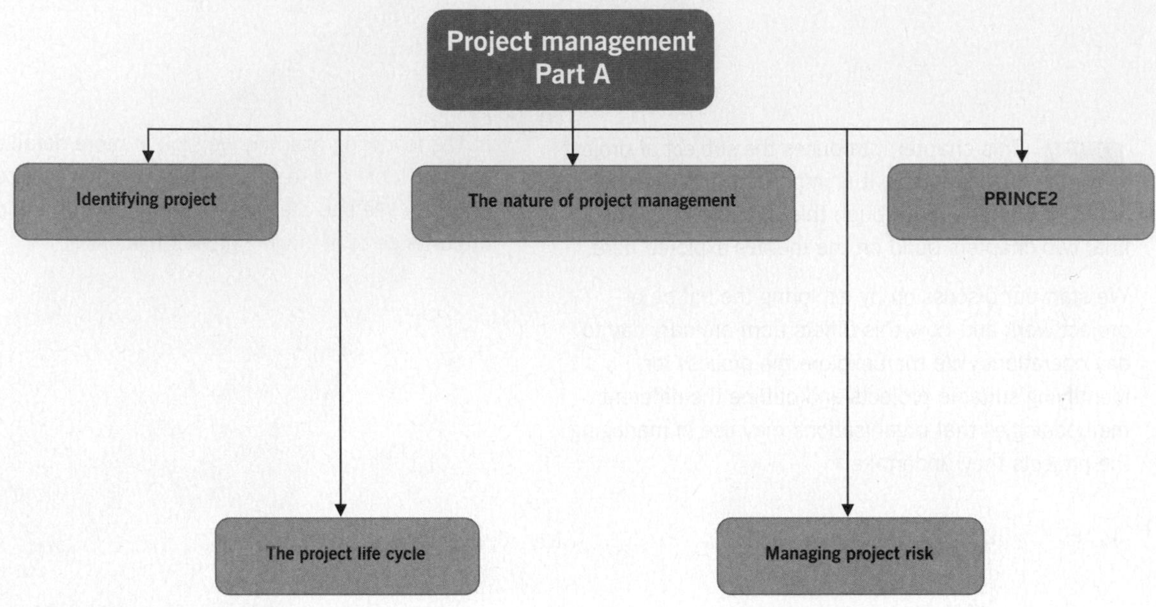

1 The nature of project management

Introduction

Welcome to project management! This section outlines how projects differ from ordinary work within the organisation. Projects tend to have their own deadlines, staff (at least temporarily) and resources and are intended to be one-offs. A typical project in an organisation would be installing a new IT system. This usually involves people from many departments, and has its own dedicated staff and resources running alongside the ordinary activities in the organisation.

Exam alert

The syllabus places a strong focus on project management, so every exam is likely to include a significant number of marks linked to project management. Some material covered elsewhere in this Study Text (for example, general management skills such as delegation and negotiation) can be applied in a project management setting. Remember that general management skills may be relevant in a scenario question covering project management.

1.1 What is a project?

To understand project management, it is necessary to first define what a project is.

KEY TERMS

A **PROJECT** is 'an undertaking that has a beginning and an end and is carried out to meet established goals within cost, schedule and quality objectives'. (Haynes, *Project Management*)

RESOURCES are the money, facilities, supplies, services and people allocated to the project.

1.1.1 How does project working differ from 'business as usual'?

In general, the work that organisations undertake involves either **operations** or **projects**. Operations and projects are planned, controlled and executed. So how are projects distinguished from 'ordinary work'?

Projects	Operations ('business as usual')
Have a defined beginning and end	Ongoing
Have resources allocated specifically to them, although often on a shared basis	Resources used 'full time'
Are often unique or intended to be done only once	Many recurring tasks
Follow a plan towards a clear intended end result	Goals and deadlines are more general
Often cut across organisational and functional lines	Usually follows the organisation or functional structure

An activity that meets the first four criteria above can be classified as a project, and therefore falls within the scope of project management. Whether an activity is classified as a project is important, as projects should be managed using **project management techniques**.

Common examples of projects include:

(a) Producing a new product, service or object
(b) Changing the structure of an organisation
(c) Developing or modifying a new information system
(d) Implementing a new business procedure or process

Maylor has described a project in **systems** terms as a process of conversion. This provides a useful overview of the concept.

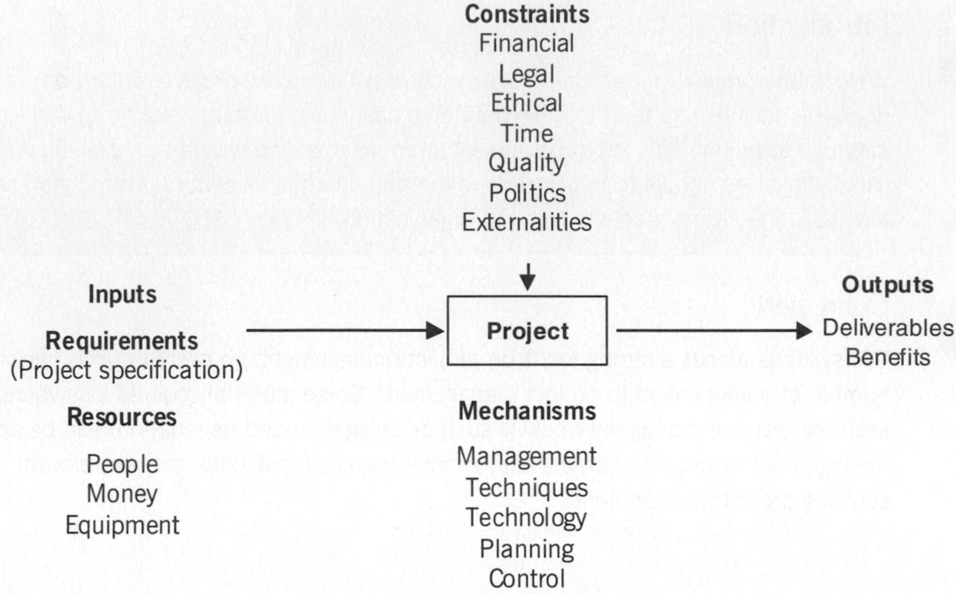

1.2 What is project management?

KEY TERM

PROJECT MANAGEMENT. Integration of all aspects of a project, ensuring that the proper knowledge and resources are available when and where needed, and above all to ensure that the expected outcome is produced in a timely, cost-effective manner. The primary function of a project manager is to manage the trade-offs between performance, timeliness and cost. *(CIMA Official Terminology)*

The objective of project management is a successful project. A project will be deemed successful if it is completed at the **specified level of quality**, **on time** and **within budget**. We revisit project objectives later in this Study Text, when we look at how these are balanced as competing objectives. This is known as the time/cost/quality or 'iron triangle'.

Constraint	Comment
Quality	The end result should conform to the project specification. In other words, the result should achieve what the project was supposed to do.
Budget	The project should be completed without exceeding authorised expenditure.
Timescale	The progress of the project must follow the planned process, so that the 'result' is ready for use at the agreed date. As time is money, proper time management can help contain costs.

Quality, **cost** and **time** are normally regarded as the yardsticks against which project success is measured. It is possible to add a fourth constraint: **scope** or **functionality**. This means that all the work that was specified has been done and all the deliverables have, in fact, been delivered. Under this analysis, the quality constraint is restricted to a slightly narrower meaning and the difference between scope and quality becomes the difference between doing a job and doing it well – or badly.

1.2.1 Management challenges of project working

Projects present some management challenges.

Challenge	Comment
Teambuilding	The work is carried out by a team of people often from varied work and social backgrounds. The team must 'gel' quickly and be able to communicate effectively with each other.
Expected problems	Expected problems should be avoided by careful design and planning prior to commencement of work.
Unexpected problems	There should be mechanisms within the project to enable these problems to be resolved quickly and efficiently.
Delayed benefit	There is normally no benefit until the work is finished. The 'lead in' time to this can cause a strain on the eventual recipient who is also faced with increasing expenditure for no immediate benefit.
Specialists	Contributions made by specialists are of differing importance at each stage.
Potential for conflict	Projects often involve several parties with different interests. This may lead to conflict.

Project management ensures responsibilities are clearly defined and that resources are **focused** on specific objectives. The **project management process** also provides a structure for communicating within and across organisational boundaries.

All projects share similar features and follow a similar process. This has led to the development of **project management tools and techniques** that can be applied to all projects, no matter how diverse. For example, with some limitations similar processes and techniques can be applied, whether building a major structure (eg the Millennium Dome) or implementing a company-wide computer network.

All projects require a person who is ultimately responsible for delivering the required outcome. This person (whether officially given the title or not) is the **project manager**.

1.2.2 Why do projects go wrong?

Many projects go wrong: this is usually manifested as a **failure to complete on time**, but this outcome can arise for a variety of reasons.

(a) **Unproven technology**
The use of **new technological developments** is likely to be a feature of any project. The range of such developments extends from fairly routine and non-critical improvements, through major innovations capable of transforming working practices, costs and timescales, to revolutionary techniques that make feasible projects that were previously quite impracticable. As the practical potential of a technical change moves from minor to major, so too moves its potential to cause disruption if something goes wrong with it. A classic example is Rolls-Royce's attempt to use carbon fibre in the design of the RB211 engine in the early 1970s. Not only did the project fail to meet its objectives, but its failure also led to the company's financial failure, which necessitated its rescue by government.

(b) **Changing client specifications**
It is not unusual for clients' notions of what they want to evolve during the lifetime of the project. However, if the work is to come in on time and on budget, they must be aware of what is **technically feasible**, reasonable in their **aspirations**, prompt with their **decisions** and, ultimately, prepared to **freeze the specification** so that it can be delivered. The failure of the TSR2 aircraft project 40 years ago was in large part caused by major, unrealistic changes to specification.

Note that the term 'client' includes **internal** specifiers.

(c) **Politics**

This problem area includes politics of all kinds, from those internal to an organisation managing its own projects, to the effect of national (and even international) politics on major undertakings. **Lack of senior management support** is an important political problem. This may be partly caused by:

(i) Lack of processes to evaluate potential projects and define a business case for the project

(ii) Reliance on informal measurement of project costs and benefits, rather than rigorous feasibility analysis and subsequent review and control

(d) **Poor project management**

This comes in several guises:

(i) **Overoptimism**. This can be particularly troublesome with new technology. Unrealistic deadlines may be accepted, for instance, or impossible levels of performance promised.

(ii) **Overpromotion of technical staff**. It is common for people with a high level of technical skill to be promoted. Only then is it made clear that they lack management and leadership ability. This is a particular problem with IT projects.

(iii) **Poor planning**. Realistic timescales must be established, use of shared resources must be planned and, most fundamental of all, jobs must be done in a sensible sequence.

(iv) **Poor control**. Progress must be under continuous review, and control action must be taken early if there are problems. The framework of control must provide for review at all levels of management and prompt reporting of problems. Communication and relationship skills must be deployed to a high standard by the project manager.

1.2.3 Project success factors

KEY POINT

An article in *Financial Management* helpfully summarises the factors that contribute to successful project delivery as follows.

(a) Proper planning with regard to time, cost and resource constraints

(b) The involvement of users (among other key stakeholders) in development and delivery processes, to ensure that their needs are met (without subsequent changes)

(c) Competent and committed project staff, with the right skills

(d) Ownership by senior managers on the basis of a clear business case

(e) Careful management of constraints: control procedures for monitoring the pace, money/resource usage and conformance of the project

(f) Risk assessment and management, allowing for risk reduction and contingency planning

(g) Clear criteria for business case and precise measurements of performance, so that project success can be evaluated and lessons learnt

Section summary

A **project** is an undertaking that has a beginning and an end, and is carried out to meet established goals within cost, schedule and quality objectives. It often has the following characteristics.

- A defined beginning and end
- Resources allocated specifically to it
- Intended to be done only once (although similar separate projects could be undertaken)
- Follows a plan towards a clear intended end result
- Often cuts across organisational and functional lines

Project management is the combination of systems, techniques and people used to control and monitor activities undertaken within the project. It will be deemed successful if it is completed at the specified level of **quality**, **on time** and within **budget**.

2 Identifying projects

Introduction

Projects should fit in with the strategies of the organisation. Once these have been drawn up and objectives identified, then a project may be the means by which an objective is achieved. A **feasibility study** will establish whether a project can achieve its objective in a cost-effective manner.

KEY POINT

A project will be initiated when an **objective** is identified that can only be achieved in this way. Where the objective is of **strategic importance**, a project set up to achieve it will amount to a **strategy**. Of course, not all strategic effort consists of projects, nor do all projects have strategic significance.

If an organisational objective emerges that can only be achieved by undertaking a project, this is often called the project **requirement**. (This is distinguished from the **project specification**: a detailed account of the nature of the project or the outcomes it is intended to deliver.)

Like all potential strategies, project proposals should be assessed for suitability, acceptability and **feasibility**. Feasibility will be particularly important when the project objective is innovative, complex or difficult to achieve, since such projects are likely to entail a high risk of failure or excessive expense. The mechanism employed for this area of assessment is the **feasibility study**.

2.1 The feasibility study

The purpose of the feasibility study is not so much to find out if a proposed project can achieve its objective, as to establish whether or not it can do so in a **cost-effective** manner. Given sufficient resources, most proposals that lie outside the realms of fantasy can be implemented but not all are worth undertaking. The feasibility study is the mechanism by which the organisation filters out proposed projects that would cost too much, cause too much disruption, make excessive demands on human and other resources, or have side effects whose undesirability outweighs their advantages. The assessment of feasibility can be broken down into a number of areas.

2.1.1 Technical feasibility

The assessment of technical feasibility will depend on the nature of the technology involved in the project: software would be a major part of an information systems (IS) project, for example, while materials and structures would be fundamental to a civil engineering project.

(a) Does all the necessary technology exist or is significant **innovation** required?
(b) Is the technology mature enough to use or is further **development** likely to be required?
(c) How **specialised** is the required technology and is **the expertise** to make use of it available?

Technical feasibility also includes **technical matters that do not relate to technology**; that is to say, matters of technical expertise, such as marketing, financial strategy and human resource management. We might wish to know, for example, whether it was feasible to communicate effectively with a particular identified market segment.

In this category of technical feasibility, assessment we would include **features analysis**, which is the process of identifying and prioritising those features of the project requirement that are critical to its success. This process can help to guide the allocation of project resources so that the importance of deliverable features is reflected in the resources expended on achieving them.

2.1.2 Social feasibility

Any project is likely to have effects on people, both those in the organisation concerned and those outside it. The social feasibility of a project depends on the nature and extent of those effects. There are obvious human resource management implications to most projects, in the area of forming, leading and motivating the project team. The progress and outcome of a project may also have important consequences for employees outside the team, such as increased demand for certain categories of staff, redundancies, training requirements and changed work patterns.

Outside the organisation, the undertaking of projects and their outcomes may have **wider social consequences**, such as the drain of public funds and disruption of transport systems confidently expected as a result of the staging of the 2012 Olympic Games in London.

2.1.3 Ecological (environmental) feasibility

Customers have become increasingly aware of environmental costs and the damage caused by organisations, and there is a growing trend and demand for products or services that are more ecologically sound. The following factors should be considered when determining the ecological feasibility of a project.

(a) Impact on the local community
(b) Pollution and the impact on the environment that could be caused by the project
(c) Reputational damage should the project not be perceived to be ecologically sound

2.1.4 Financial feasibility

It is appropriate to submit proposed projects to **cost-benefit analysis**, though this can be very difficult when the benefits are largely in intangible form. Part of the difficulty lies in identifying the benefits and part in assigning monetary values to them. Dealing with intangible or qualitative benefits is likely to be particularly important in the public and voluntary sectors, where objectives such as improved road safety and education are common.

The usual analysis of costs should be made.

(a) **Capital costs** are incurred in the purchase of assets.
(b) **Finance costs** are the charges made for the use of loan capital.
(c) **Revenue costs** are all other costs.

The financial feasibility of a project is assessed using the common techniques such as net present value, **payback period** and **accounting rate of return**.

Exam alert

A question in your E2 exam may ask you to identify the key components of a project feasibility study; it is important that you are familiar with the different types of feasibility that exist.

2.2 Risk

Risk differs from **uncertainty** in that risk can be quantified and managed.

Risk management is an important aspect of project management, and we will discuss it in more detail later. However, the assessment of risk is also important at the project appraisal stage.

(a) The risk may be so high as to make it imprudent to continue with the project.

(b) The process of **risk management** can begin straightaway, with appropriate steps being taken to mitigate the level of risk involved. Suitable strategies include **avoidance**, **transference**, **acceptance** or **reduction**.

2.3 SWOT analysis

We have already looked briefly at the assessment of strengths, weaknesses, opportunities and threats in the corporate appraisal stage of the rational model of strategy in an earlier chapter). This can also be used to evaluate and compare projects, particularly when there are a number of potential projects contending for funds. The strengths and weaknesses of each could be considered in relation to the opportunities and threats the organisation was facing at the time, and that it is likely to face in the future. An assessment of project strengths and weaknesses would include consideration of the deliverables and the factors revealed by the investigation of feasibility.

2.4 Selecting projects – a summary

List potential projects and for each one establish:

(a) Need or opportunity
(b) Financial and other resource requirements
(c) Overall feasibility
(d) Approximate duration
(e) Risk profile

Eliminate projects that are unsuitable, inappropriate and unfeasible.

Prioritise the remaining projects.

Question 9A.1 Projects

Learning outcome D2a

Give six examples of work that you would consider suitable for a project management approach.

Section summary

Projects may have **strategic significance**. As strategies, they should be subjected to the same **evaluation** for suitability, feasibility and acceptability as other strategies. SWOT should be used. Even where they do not constitute strategic action, proposed projects must be appraised for their value before they are started. **Feasibility studies** are a common approach: technical, social, environmental and financial feasibility are all assessed. An assessment of risk must also be made.

3 PRINCE2

Introduction

PRINCE2 is mentioned in the syllabus. It is a model built on eight components and eight processes. We suggest that you learn what is in each, as you are likely to have to use these in any question based on PRINCE2.

The acronym **PRINCE** stands for **PR**ojects **IN C**ontrolled **E**nvironments. The PRINCE project management methodology was developed by the UK Government. It was initially launched in 1989 as the government standard methodology for IS project management.

There is a useful article on the CIMA website called 'An introduction to the PRINCE2 methodology'; you are strongly advised to take the time to read this.

The latest version of PRINCE, **PRINCE2** is now the *de facto* UK standard for IS project management, and is widely used in other countries. The wide acceptance that PRINCE has achieved is itself an important advantage to its use for managing projects, since it provides a common language for all participants.

3.1 Main features of PRINCE2

(a) PRINCE2 may be used to manage any project of any size or complexity, since the system is **scaleable**.

(b) A clear **management structure** of roles and responsibilities within the system is defined; this may be adapted according to the skills available within the organisation and the nature of the project.

(c) The system focuses on **delivering results** (called 'products') rather than the technical processes of project management. The users of the final end product are actively involved in the project.

(d) It is a fundamental aspect of PRINCE2 that a project is driven by its **business case**; the continuing viability of the project is checked at regular intervals.

3.2 The PRINCE2 approach to project management

PRINCE2 uses its own terminology to describe its constituent parts; this terminology is not intuitive and can be difficult to grasp. However, it is precise in its meaning. The PRINCE2 methodology is built up mainly from **components** and **processes**.

3.3 Components

Components are rather conceptual in nature, being matters to which proper consideration must be given if the project is to succeed, but also varying widely in actual nature from project to project. There are **eight components**.

(a) **Business case**
(b) **Organisation**
(c) **Plans**
(d) **Controls**
(e) **Risk**
(f) **Quality**
(g) **Configuration management**
(h) **Change control**

3.3.1 Business case

A business case is not something that is confined to commercial organisations. The term may be understood as meaning a **reasoned account of what is to be achieved and why it will be of benefit**. As already mentioned, it is fundamental that a project is driven by its business case. Occasions when the business case must be referred to should be specified at the outset. This is to ensure focus on what the project is really supposed to be about. The business case may require updating as the project progresses.

3.3.2 Organisation

Management implies a structure of authority and accountability. PRINCE2 recognises four layers of management responsibility, though levels may be combined or eliminated if appropriate. A major project of strategic significance will be of interest to the organisation's **strategic apex**, or top-level decision makers, which may appoint one of its members or form a **steering committee** to set policy to support business objectives. An **executive committee** below strategic apex level may have the job of translating policies into specific projects that support them.

The top level of management for an individual project is the **project board**, chaired by the **executive**. This person provides overall guidance and must represent the business interests of the organisation. Two other constituencies may also be represented.

(a) The **senior user** represents the interests of those who are affected by the introduction of the new system and is accountable for the quality of the specification.

(b) The **senior supplier/senior technical** person represents those charged with implementing the project. This role may be filled by an external prime contractor or a person within the organisation such as the purchasing officer or, in the case of an IT project, for example, the senior IT person appointed to the project.

Day to day management of the project is the responsibility of the **project manager**, who is supported by one or more **stage managers** or **team managers**. The roles of project manager and stage or team manager may be combined. The **project team** reports to the stage manager. Also working for the project manager, but with a responsibility to the project board and representing the same three interests, is the **project assurance team**.

3.3.3 Plans

Clearly, projects must be planned if they are to succeed; we have already noted that PRINCE2 planning is based on products rather than processes. Planning is therefore based on **product breakdown structure** rather than work breakdown structure (see later in the Study Text).

3.3.4 Controls

Control is built into PRINCE2, using the normal cybernetic feedback control action approach discussed elsewhere in this Study Text. The project board restricts authorisation to one stage at a time and manages by exception.

3.3.5 Risk

Risk is analysed and managed throughout the project's life and reviewed at predetermined intervals.

3.3.6 Quality

Quality management is built into the management of the project, though PRINCE2 is not itself a quality management system, despite the prominence of quality products in the product breakdown. Further quality procedures may need to be introduced into a project if it is to satisfy ISO 9000, for example.

3.3.7 Configuration management

A **configuration** is a technical description, a complete specification of everything that is needed to bring a project to a successful conclusion. With complex projects, it is likely that frequent technical changes will be made: all these changes must be approved and documented. **Configuration management** controls the processes by which projects evolve.

3.3.8 Change control

Any project may be subject to changed conditions or requirements, such as failure to deliver by a supplier or new legislation. Changes to the project itself must be dealt with in a comprehensive and rational way, so that all concerned know what is going on and what the new plan is.

3.4 Processes

Project processes are more concrete than components, essentially being groups of linked activities. They are largely identifiable as approximately equivalent to stages of the project life cycle, which we will discuss in the next section of this chapter, though they also relate to aspects of continuing project management activity. There are eight processes.

(a) **Directing a project**
(b) **Starting up a project**
(c) **Initiating a project**
(d) **Planning**
(e) **Controlling a stage**
(f) **Managing stage boundaries**
(g) **Managing product delivery**
(h) **Closing a project**

3.4.1 Directing a project

Directing a project is the responsibility of the senior management team or project board. This process continues throughout the life of the project but is limited to higher aspects of control and decision making.

3.4.2 Starting up a project

Starting up a project is a short scene-setting pre-project process concerned with fundamentals such as the project's aims and the appointment of the project board and project manager.

3.4.3 Initiating a project

Initiating a project is an initial planning process that includes quality planning, setting up project controls and creating the **project initiation document**, which sets fundamental progress and success criteria. The first productive stage of the project is planned during this process.

3.4.4 Planning

Planning is a process that may be carried out at any time in order to satisfy the requirements of other processes. The PRINCE2 hierarchy of plans has up to four levels.

(a) The **project plan** is the overall plan and is produced at the beginning of the project. It will probably be in summary form.

(b) A **stage plan** is produced for each stage of the project.

(c) **Detailed plans** are produced if more detail is needed at any point in a stage.

(d) **Individual work plans** guide the activity of each team member.

Much past project planning has been based on the ideas embodied in **work breakdown structure (WBS)**, in which the processes required to complete the project are analysed into discrete, manageable units. PRINCE2, however, uses a **product-based** approach. This has the advantage of directing management attention to **what** is to be achieved rather than **how** to do it, thus providing an automatic focus on achieving the product goals. Also, it can be helpful in complex projects, where the processes involved may be unclear initially.

Under this approach, work breakdown is preceded by **product breakdown**. PRINCE2 starts this analysis by dividing the **project products** into three groups.

(a) **Technical products** are the things the project has been set up to provide to the users. For an IT system, for example, these would include the hardware, software, manuals and training.

(b) **Quality products** define both the quality controls that are applied to the project and the quality standards the technical products must achieve.

(c) **Management products** are the artefacts used to manage the project. They include the project management organisation structure, planning documentation and reports.

Each of these groups of products is then broken down into manageable components as part of the planning process, using the traditional WBS approach if the complexity of the project requires it. Project and stage plans may make use of the normal planning tools such as critical path analysis, Gantt charts and resource histograms (which we will discuss in greater detail later in the Study Text).

Plan text describes the plan, its assumptions, constraints and reporting structure. Cumulative costs and the status of major products are shown on the **resource plan graphical summary**.

An interesting feature of the PRINCE2 management approach is the use of **tolerances**. Project and stage managers may be authorised to make variations to the plan within stated tolerances of **time**, **cost** and **quality**, thus providing them with some flexibility of implementation. However, if it seems likely that the stated tolerances will be exceeded, the further approval of the project board must be sought for an **exception plan**.

3.4.5 Controlling a stage

Controlling a stage is the process undertaken by the project manager to ensure that any given stage of the project remains on course. A project might consist of just one stage, of course.

PRINCE2 project control includes a structure of reports and meetings.

(a) A **project initiation** meeting agrees the scope and objectives of the project and gives approval for it to start.

(b) The completion of each project stage is marked by an **end stage assessment**, which includes reports from the project manager and the project assurance team. The next stage does not commence until its plans have been reviewed and approved.

(c) **Mid-stage assessments** are optional and may arise if, for example, a stage runs for a particularly long time or it is necessary to start a new stage before the current one is complete.

(d) **Highlight reports** are submitted regularly to the project board by the project manager. These reports are the main overall routine control mechanism and their frequency (often monthly) is agreed at project initiation. They are essentially progress reports and should include brief summaries of project schedule and budget status.

(e) The **checkpoint** is the main control device used by the project team itself. Meetings are held more frequently than highlight reports are prepared (possibly weekly) and provide a basis for continuing progress review by team leaders and members.

3.4.6 Managing stage boundaries

Managing stage boundaries is the process that must be undertaken when a project has more than one stage. This process ensures that one stage is properly completed before the next one begins.

3.4.7 Managing product delivery

Managing product delivery is the process that controls work done by specialist teams by agreeing what work is to be done and ensuring that it is carried out to the proper standard.

3.4.8 Closing a project

Closing a project is the process by which the project manager brings the project to a conclusion. It consists of checking and reporting on the extent to which the project has been a success. The completion of the project is formally marked by the **project closure meeting**. This is held to ensure that all planned work has been carried out, including any approved variations to the plan, and that the work has been accepted.

3.5 PRINCE2 (2009 version)

The rate of change and advancements in technology and communication that have occurred since the introduction of PRINCE2 in 1996 has meant that project managers now face many challenges that did not exist, nor could have been predicted, when the framework was developed.

To address this, PRINCE2 underwent a significant refresh, resulting in an updated method that launched in June 2009. The main changes were:

(a) There are now two separate guides, one for project managers and people working on projects, and one for project sponsors and directors.

(b) The process model that describes the activities to be performed through the project has been simplified, with activities describing what needs to be done, by whom and when. The complex sub-process diagrams have also been removed.

(c) The eight components of the previous version are replaced by seven key themes. These themes are aspects of project management that need to be **continually addressed**.

(1) Business case
(2) Organisation
(3) Plans
(4) Risk
(5) Progress
(6) Quality
(7) Issues and changes

Configuration management, from the 'old' components, is incorporated into **Issues and changes**, while the 'old' **Controls** could be considered part of **Progress**. This refreshed version of PRINCE2 is considered to be simpler and more easily customised to an individual project's context. This should provide project managers and directors with a better set of tools for ensuring their projects are delivered on time, within budget and within the required quality constraints.

3.6 Alternatives to PRINCE2

It is important to note that alternative project management methodologies do exist; the US **Project Management Institute** and the **Guide to the Project Management Body of Knowledge** (PMBOK) are also widely used by specialists.

3.6.1 The Project Management Body of Knowledge (PMBOK)

The US Project Management Institute has published a guide to what it calls the **PMBOK**. This divides the process of project management into nine **key knowledge areas**.

PROJECT MANAGEMENT

Project Integration Management
Project plan development
Project plan execution
Integrated change control

Project Scope Management
Initiation
Scope planning
Scope definition
Scope verification
Scope change control

Project Time Management
Activity definition
Activity sequencing
Activity duration estimating
Schedule development
Schedule control

Project Cost Management
Resource planning
Cost estimating
Cost budgeting
Cost control

Project Quality Management
Quality planning
Quality assurance
Quality control

Project Human Resource Management
Organisational planning
Staff acquisition
Team development

Project Communications Management
Communications planning
Information distribution
Performance reporting
Administrative closure

Project Risk Management
Risk management planning
Risk identification
Qualitative risk analysis
Quantitative risk analysis
Risk response planning
Risk monitoring and control

Project Procurement Management
Procurement planning
Solicitation planning
Solicitation
Source selection
Contract administration
Contract closeout

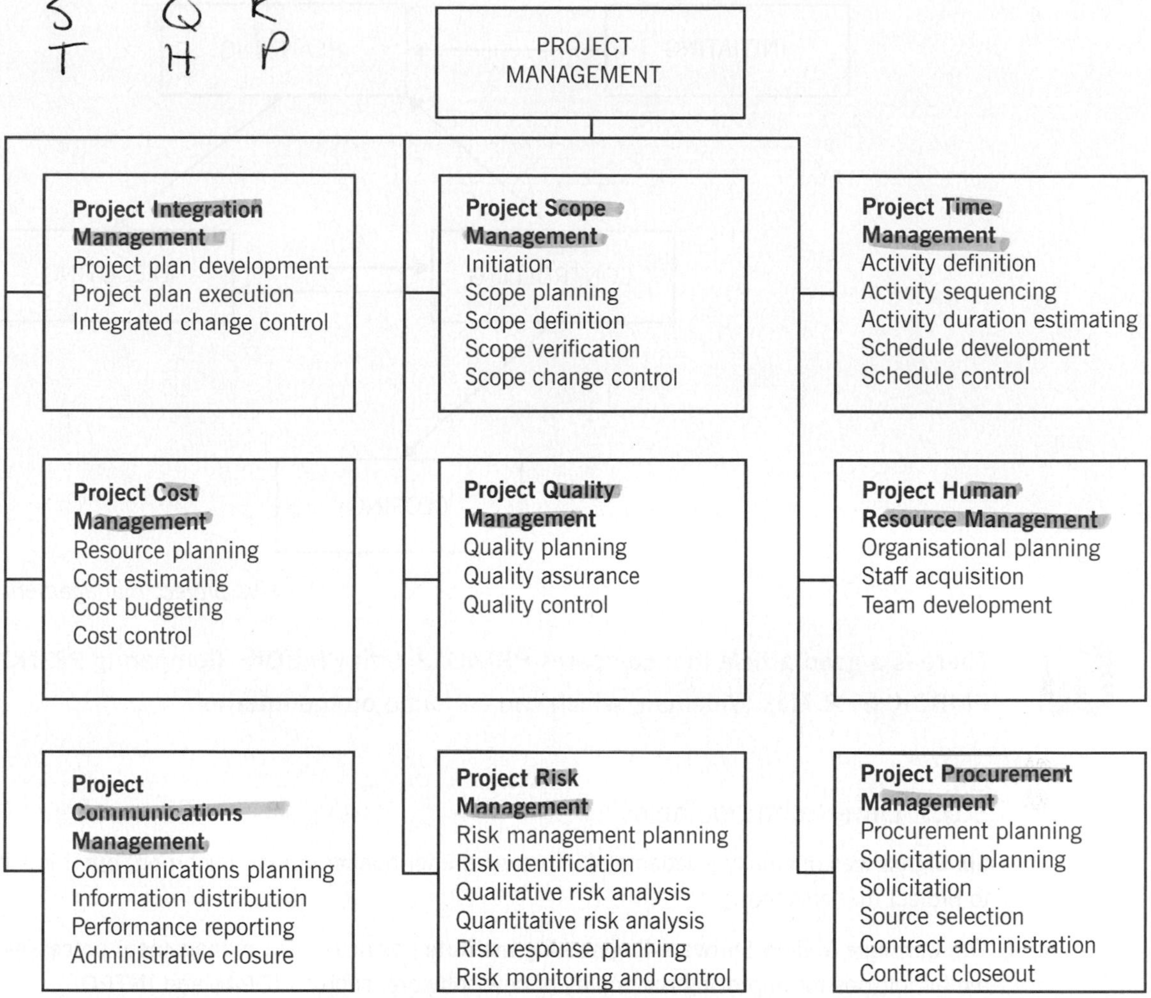

Project Management Knowledge Areas and Project Management Processes

The PMBOK approach is intended to act as a guide, helping the project manager to identify the activities that need to be conducted within each of the **five project management process areas (stages)**. These stages and the relationships between them are shown in the diagram below. You should be able to remember them using the mnemonic **IPECC**. (We explore the five project management process areas in greater depth later in the chapter.)

To illustrate the interaction between the PMBOK nine knowledge areas and the five project management process areas (stages) let us consider the work of the project manager at the planning stage of a new project. Work here is likely to require undertaking a combination of the activities listed under the scope, time and cost headings as outlined in the PMBOK diagram above.

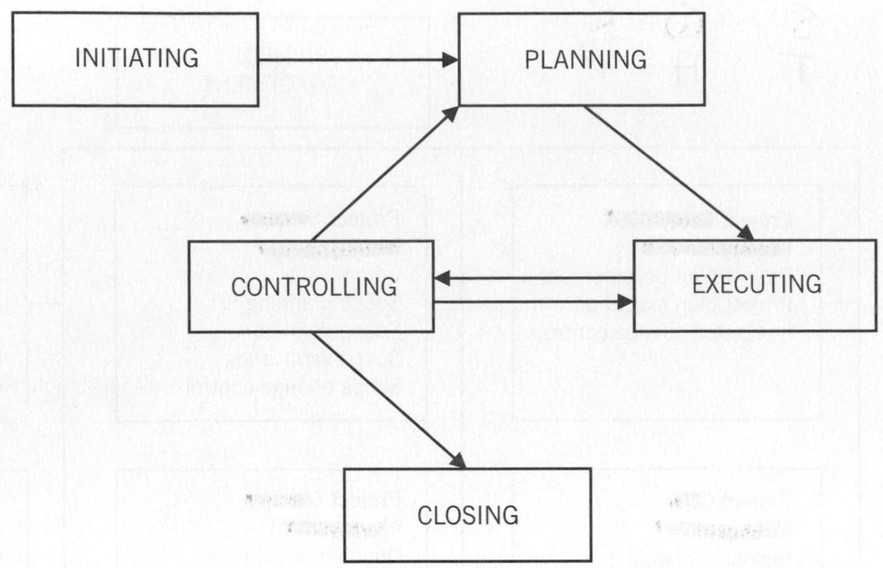

Five project management process areas

There is a good article that compares PRINCE2 with PMBOK: 'Comparing PRINCE2 with PMBOK' by R Max Wideman, which can be found on the internet.

3.6.2 Other methodologies

Six Sigma was originally a scheme of improvement for quality in manufacturing, but it has been adapted to project management.

The **Carnegie Mellon Software Engineering Institute** has developed management processes and methodologies for improving the quality of new software, such as **IDEAL** and **INTRO**.

Section summary

PRINCE2 is a widely accepted, standard method of project management. It offers clear management structures and planning and control methods, and is noteworthy for its focus on **outputs** rather than processes.

4 The project life cycle

Introduction

Projects are conventionally seen as having a **life cycle**, and this is particularly true of larger projects. The life cycle concept can be useful in the management of projects, since it breaks the whole down into more easily manageable parts. This is applicable to the **allocation and management of resources**, since their type and quantity vary from phase to phase.

The project life cycle can be seen as having **four main phases**. These can be shown diagrammatically.

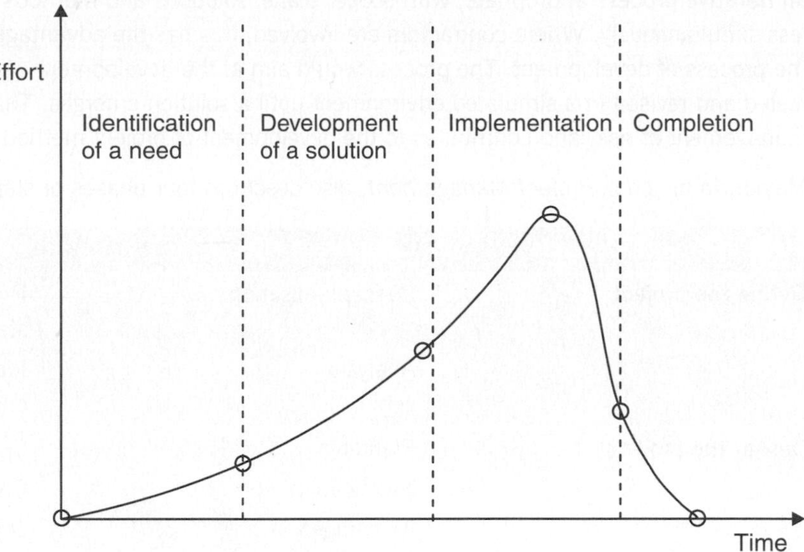

Identification of a need, a problem or an opportunity. This may lead to a **feasibility study**, possibly carried out internally to the organisation or possibly by external contractors in response to an invitation to tender or a request for proposal. If this process shows that the project has merit, a **project initiation document** is written and a **project team** established.

Development of a solution. There must be agreement on what is to be done. This may be through the medium of competitive bidding or by an internal process of iterative development.

Implementation. The proposed outcome must be delivered. This may involve further detailed planning and the achievement of agreed progress stages and, where contractors are involved, stage payments.

Completion. The success or otherwise of the project is assessed, documentation is completed and final payments are made.

4.1 Five project management process areas

Previously we introduced the five project management process areas. It was developed by the Project Management Institute (PMI) and breaks the main elements involved in project work into a five-step process. It is important to note that this model is simply an alternative to the project life cycle discussed above. The table below illustrates the main stages of the project life cycle mapped against the five PMI process areas.

Project Life Cycle	PMI Process	Description
Identification of need	Initiation	Goals and objectives are set
Development of a solution	Planning	Resources (finance, skills etc) are scheduled
Implementation	Execution	Using allocated resources to complete the tasks according to the schedule
	Control	Measuring progress against plan and taking corrective action where necessary
Completion	Closing	Ensure that the project is completed and meets the goals and objectives

KEY POINT

It is unlikely that there will be clear boundaries between the phases, and the various aspects may run in parallel to some extent.

Field and Keller suggest that uncertain requirements and the need to integrate a range of ideas may make an **iterative process** appropriate, with scope, plans, solutions and methods all being developed more or less simultaneously. Where contractors are involved, this has the advantage of involving the customer in the process of development. The process would aim at the development of a 'predictive model' that can be tested and revised in a simulated environment until a solution emerges. This approach helps in the management of risk, and contributes to the development of project methods and system integration.

Maylor, in his book *Project Management*, also describes four phases or stages: this is the **4D model**.

Stage in project life cycle	Component title	Activities
Define the project	Conceptualisation	Produce a clear and definitive statement of needs
	Analysis	Identify what has to be done and check its feasibility
Design the project	Planning	Show how the needs will be met
	Justification	Compute costs and benefits
	Agreement	Obtain sponsor agreement
Deliver the project (Do it!)	Start up	Assemble resources and people
	Execution	Carry out planned project activities
	Completion	Success or abandonment
	Handover	Output passed to sponsor/user
Develop the process	Review	Identify outcomes for all stakeholders
	Feedback	Document lessons and improvements for future use

Exam alert

Exam questions may refer to the '**project life cycle**' or **PLC**, or they may simply refer to '**stages**' in a project. Either way, they are asking for the same thing, and will generally refer specifically to a four-stage model (although there are alternative models).

4.2 Define the project

Exam alert

Exam questions may require you to identify the purpose of, and components that should be included in, a project initiation document.

A project starts when someone becomes aware of the need for one. This can occur at any level and in any context, though more formal business projects of management significance will normally be originated within the area of responsibility of the sponsoring manager. Larger projects are likely to involve the creation of a **project brief** or **terms of reference** for discussion. A **project initiation document** may be prepared, if it is decided to continue with the project. This will include a **statement of requirements**, a **statement of the vision** for the project and a **business case**.

At this early stage, one of the most important things to get under control is the **scope of the project**; that is, just what is included and what is not. A firm grasp of the agreed scope of the project must be maintained throughout its life.

Planning will start in this phase, but is unlikely to be completed until the end of the project. The aim should be to do enough planning to achieve three things.

(a) Avoid the chaos of unplanned activity
(b) Provide a basis for accepting or rejecting the project
(c) Identify problems in advance

More complex projects will have a greater requirement for detailed plans. **WBS** is the traditional method of planning a project. WBS is dealt with in the next chapter.

Larger projects will benefit from being broken down into phases. This assists the planning process and enhances the ability of those responsible to control progress. The boundary between one phase and the next is a suitable place to impose a review of progress, with the option of closing down the whole thing if it is proving unsatisfactory in any way. Established project management methods such as PRINCE2 incorporate review procedures for ensuring that phases are completed on time.

4.2.1 Identifying requirements

Project scope is all the things that have to be achieved if the project is to succeed: essentially it is all the work that has to be done. There are several ways of determining what has to be done if a project is to succeed. This is a necessary stage whatever approach is taken overall, be it iterative or linear.

(a) **Gap analysis**. Where a replacement or an upgrade is needed, a comparison can be made between what currently exists and what is desired. This is a common approach in IS projects.

(b) **Reverse engineering** identifies the features of an existing product or system by taking it apart.

(c) **Functional decomposition** is a process of analysis that starts with the desired end state and establishes what must be done to achieve it. The process starts in broad brush terms and continues in ever-finer detail until manageable tasks and elements are established.

4.3 Design the project

There are several aspects to detailed project planning. Maylor categorises the various techniques used for scheduling, such as network analysis and Gantt charts, as **time planning**. He also deals with the need to plan for **cost**, **quality** and **risk**.

4.3.1 Project planning

Exam alert

E2 exam scenario questions may require you to identify and evaluate potential problems that could result from poor project planning. If faced with a question such as this, make sure you **relate your knowledge of project planning to the scenario**. The main focus should be on what will happen in the absence of project planning, rather than the process of project planning itself.

The project manager will be responsible for producing plans and documentation for the project.

(a) The project charter or project initiation document
(b) Plan for time
(c) Plan for cost
(d) Plan for quality
(e) Plan for risk and contingencies

These aspects of planning are dealt with in a later chapter.

It may also be necessary to produce further plans.

(a) A **resource plan** specifies the resources of all types that are needed and how they will be used. The aim is to match resources smoothly to workload.

(b) A **communication plan** may be necessary when there are many and varied stakeholders needing different amounts and types of information.

4.4 Deliver the project

This is the **operational** phase of the project. Planning will continue as required in order to control agreed changes and to deal with unforeseen circumstances, but the main emphasis is on getting the work done.

There are several important themes.

(a) **Management and leadership**. People management assumes a greater importance as the size of the project workforce increases.

(b) **Control**. Time, cost and quality must be kept under control, as must the tendency for changes to proliferate.

(c) **Supply chain**. All the aspects of logistics management must be implemented, especially with projects involving significant physical output.

(d) **Problems and decisions**. Problems are bound to arise and must be solved sensibly and expeditiously. Complex problems will require careful analysis using the scientific tools of decision theory.

4.5 Develop the process

Because project management is episodic in nature, it is difficult to improve. The lack of continuous operation means that the skills and experience developed during a project are likely to fragment and atrophy after it is complete. This is especially true of organisations that do not have many projects or manage them on an *ad hoc* basis. Managers move around, projects are sponsored in different departments from time to time, and the pressure of normal work inhibits organisational learning. Even in project-based organisations, there can be a reluctance to devote resources to improving the corporate body of project management knowledge.

The completion and review phase involves a number of important but often neglected activities.

(a) **Completion** itself is often neglected. All activities must be properly and promptly finished; care must be taken that contractors do not either leave small things undone or, if paid by time, spin things out for as long as possible.

(b) **Documentation** must be completed. This is important on any project but it is vital if there are quality certification issues or it is necessary to provide the user with operating documentation. Indeed, these two types of documentation should be specified as deliverables at the outset. Contracts, letters, accounting records and so on must be filed properly.

(c) **Project systems** must be closed down, but in a proper fashion. In particular, the project accounts and any special accounting systems must remain in operation and under control until all costs have been posted, but must then be closed down to avoid improper posting.

(d) **Handover** must take place where the project has been managed for a client under contract. At some point, the client must formally accept that the contract is complete and take responsibility for any future action that may be required, such as the operation and maintenance of a system.

(e) **Immediate review** is required to provide staff with immediate feedback on performance and to identify short-term needs such as staff training and remedial action for procedure failures.

4.5.1 The review process

KEY POINT

A thorough review is the organisation's opportunity to make significant improvements in how it manages its projects. The review should cover all aspects of the project, possibly organised on a functional basis, and have clear **terms of reference** for each. This cannot be done on the cheap: appropriate quantities of management time and attention must be allocated to the review process and to the assimilation of its results and recommendations.

4.5.2 The project management maturity model

The concept of project management maturity (Maylor; Buttrick) suggests that some organisations have more developed capabilities to implement projects than others.

Different models focus on the **levels of development** or the **pace of improvement and learning**, but broadly:

(a) **Level 1 organisations** have little or no organisational processes or methodologies for project management. The delivery of cost, time and quality objectives depends on the efforts of the project manager and team.

(b) **Level 2 organisations** have developed an **agreed project methodology**, based on accumulated experience: new projects can now follow defined paths rather than individual initiative. Outcomes are more predictable.

(c) **Level 3 organisations** are not only able to implement projects successfully, but to realise significant **benefits** at the end. The focus has shifted from quality/cost/time objectives to intended benefits.

(d) **Level 4 organisations** integrate projects with **overall corporate strategy**. The entire project portfolio is selected and managed to support organisational strategy and add value to the organisation as a whole.

Project maturity models are used as a project control tool, to evaluate where the organisation has reached in the maturing process – and what steps might be needed to take it to the next stage.

Section summary

Projects may be perceived as having a **life cycle**. This is commonly seen as commencing with the identification of a need and progressing through the development of a solution, implementation and closure. Maylor suggests that the four phases of the project life cycle are **definition**, **design**, **delivery** and **development**. These phases constitute the **4D model**.

The definition phase includes consideration of the **scope** of the project and the production of initial plans. Detailed planning continues in the **design phase**.

The **operational management** of the project involves attention to people management, control requirements, logistics and problem solving.

The final phase of project management is **completion and review**. Work must be finished, documentation completed, systems closed down, deliverables handed over and proper review undertaken so that skills may be improved.

5 Managing project risk

Introduction

Projects don't always go according to plan. There is always a risk of something going wrong. Risk is the probability of an unwanted outcome happening.

Projects and other undertakings carry an element of risk, for example the risk of an inappropriate system being developed and implemented. Risk management is concerned with identifying such risks and putting in place policies to eliminate or reduce these risks. The identification of risks involves an overview of the project to establish what could go wrong, and the consequences.

5.1 Types of risk

Risk is, broadly, 'the **probability** of an **unwanted** outcome happening'.

(a) Some risks are **quantifiable**. Probability can be established by statistical analysis of past occurrences. The probability of a given loss can then be multiplied by its likely cost.

(b) Some risks are **unquantifiable**. This takes them into the area of **uncertainty**, which makes them difficult to manage. However, it may be possible to assign some estimation of probability and magnitude of loss to them.

(c) Attention must be given to **socially constructed risk**, which is an aspect of human psychology. People tend to be poor at the rational assessment of risk, downplaying some (particularly those they are familiar with) and being overconcerned about others. Since stakeholder views must be taken into account, **perceived** as well as **actual** risk must be managed: this may make it necessary to take precautions in some areas that are greater than are really warranted.

(d) Other classifications of risk include: **internal** (within the project process) and **external** (arising from the environment); and business, commercial, operational, environmental, compliance, technical and reputational (depending on which aspect of the process and outcomes is likely to be affected).

5.2 Risk management

KEY POINT

Risk management may be viewed as a five-stage process.

Stage 1 Identify and record risks, for example in a **risk register**

Stage 2 Assess risks and record this assessment

Stage 3 Plan and record risk strategies

Stage 4 Carry out risk management strategies

Stage 5 Review and monitor the success of the risk management approach

5.3 Risk analysis and assessment

Risk assessment is the process of assessing the likelihood and impact of a given risk event on the organisation.

The likelihood and consequences of risks can be plotted on a **matrix**. This approach allows unquantifiable risks to be considered alongside those to which a numerical value can be given.

Risk assessment matrix

Potential impact			
High	M	H	VH
Med	L	M	H
Low	VL	L	M
	Low	*Med*	*High*

Threat likelihood

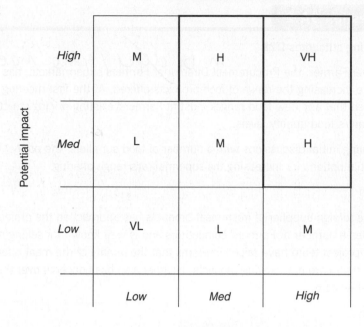

Developing a risk **contingency plan** that contains strategies for risks that fall into the VH quadrant should have priority, followed by risks falling into the two H quadrants. Following the principle of **management by exception**, which is focused on identifying those activities that might threaten the successful completion of a project, the most efficient way of dealing with risks outside these quadrants may be to do nothing unless the risk presents itself. Extra time and finance should be held in reserve for dealing with likely contingencies.

5.4 Responses to risk

KEY POINT

There are four basic responses to risk.

(a) **Avoidance**. The factors that give rise to the risk are removed, or the project is not undertaken.

(b) **Reduction** or **mitigation**. Measures taken to reduce the likelihood and/or the consequences of the risk event.

(c) **Transference**. The risk is passed on to, or shared with, another party (eg an insurer).

(d) **Absorption**. The potential risk is accepted in the hope or expectation that the incidence and consequences can be coped with if necessary.

These are sometimes relabelled as the four Ts: terminate, treat, transfer and tolerate.

Risk management is a continuous process. Procedures are necessary to regularly review and reassess the risks documented in the risk register. Each project risk should have an allocated '**owner**' to monitor and manage the risk.

Question 9A.2

Risk response

Learning outcomes D2b

Heather Farmer, the Procurement Director at Farmers supermarkets, has recently established a project to explore increasing the range of food products offered. At the first meeting with the project team, Heather stressed that any new food ranges must fit Farmers' existing pricing structure and must meet the company's food quality levels.

Following initial discussions with a number of food suppliers, the project team have identified four potential options for increasing the supermarket's range offering.

Option 1

A large foreign supplier of fresh meat products has approached the project team. The supplier currently supplies a number of Farmers' competitors and is well known for selling meat at very low prices. Members of the project team have raised concerns that the quality of the meat offered by the supplier is of a lower grade than Farmers' existing products. Heather also has concerns over the supplier's track record for animal welfare.

Option 2

A new, UK-based fruit supplier has recently started selling a unique range of high-quality pears. One of Farmers' main rivals has already made contact with the supplier with a view to agreeing a contract to secure exclusivity of supply. The pear supplier has mentioned that they would prefer to supply Farmers, due to the company's well-publicised ethical stance. The project team believe that a new line of unique pears would complement the company's existing pear and fruit offering. The only concern Heather has is whether a small supplier would be capable of maintaining supply to all Farmers' stores.

Option 3

One of Farmers' existing cheese suppliers has proposed offering a new range of smoked and strong flavoured cheeses, similar to those that are sold in continental Europe. If accepted, the supplier's proposal would significantly enhance Farmers' existing cheese offering. The project team is unsure how customers would react to a new range of cheeses.

Option 4

The project team have identified a supplier of high-quality fresh fish, located on a remote Scottish island. The supplier conforms to an international sustainable fishing initiative. The project team are keen to establish a supply arrangement with the supplier. Heather has raised concerns about physically getting the fish from the supplier's base to Farmers' various stores before it perishes.

Required

Recommend an appropriate risk response to the four options mentioned above. Justify your recommendation.

Section summary

Projects, being one-off activities, are particularly subject to risk. Risks must be identified in advance, recorded and managed using one of four strategies: **avoidance**, **reduction**, **transference** and **absorption**.

Exam alert

The concept of risk and how it can be managed in a project are key areas of project and business management – and highly examinable. Ensure that you understand and can apply the basic principles.

Chapter Summary

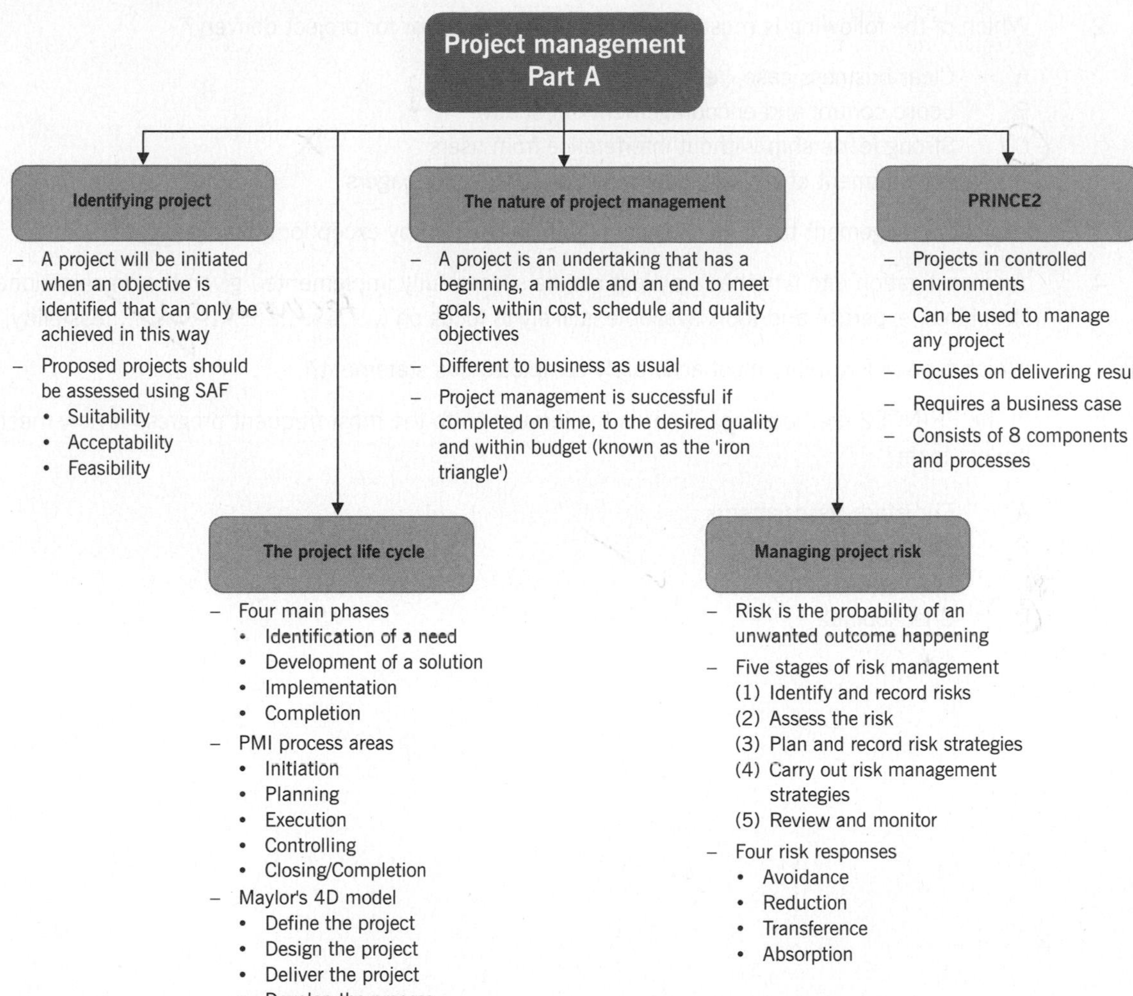

Project management Part A
Identifying project
– A project will be initiated when an objective is identified that can only be achieved in this way
– Proposed projects should be assessed using SAF
• Suitability
• Acceptability
• Feasibility
The nature of project management
– A project is an undertaking that has a beginning, a middle and an end to meet goals, within cost, schedule and quality objectives
– Different to business as usual
– Project management is successful if completed on time, to the desired quality and within budget (known as the 'iron triangle')
PRINCE2
– Projects in controlled environments
– Can be used to manage any project
– Focuses on delivering results
– Requires a business case
– Consists of 8 components and processes
The project life cycle
– Four main phases
• Identification of a need
• Development of a solution
• Implementation
• Completion
– PMI process areas
• Initiation
• Planning
• Execution
• Controlling
• Closing/Completion
– Maylor's 4D model
• Define the project
• Design the project
• Deliver the project
• Develop the process
Managing project risk
– Risk is the probability of an unwanted outcome happening
– Five stages of risk management
(1) Identify and record risks
(2) Assess the risk
(3) Plan and record risk strategies
(4) Carry out risk management strategies
(5) Review and monitor
– Four risk responses
• Avoidance
• Reduction
• Transference
• Absorption

Quick Quiz

1 What is a successful project?

2 Which of the following is most likely to be a success factor for project delivery?

A Clear business case
B Loose control and encouragement of initiative
C Strong leadership without interference from users
D Appointment of technical specialists as project managers

3 'Project management techniques encourage management by exception.' True or false?

4 'An investigation into whether a project can be successfully implemented given the organisational structures, expertise and tools available is likely to focus on .... feasibility.'

Which type of feasibility most accurately completes this statement?

5 In the PRINCE2 methodology, what is the term given to the most frequent progress review meetings of a project team?

A End stage assessments
B Milestones
C Highlight reports
D Checkpoints

Answers to Quick Quiz

1 One that is completed on time, within budget and to specification.

2 A Business case encourages ownership/support by senior management. The other options reflect common problems in project management. (Poor control, lack of stakeholder involvement and overpromotion of technical staff.)

3 True

4 Technical

5 D (Note that 'milestones' is general project management terminology for key points at which progress is reviewed for control: it is not unique to PRINCE2.)

Answers to Questions

9A.1 Projects

Common examples of projects include:

- Building a new national football stadium
- Producing a new product, service or object
- Changing the structure of an organisation
- Implementing a new service style
- Streamlining the company's ordering service
- Reorganising the company car park to maximise parking

9A.2 Risk response

Option 1

Farmers should avoid purchasing meat products from the foreign supplier.

The decision to use the foreign supplier would clearly go against Farmers' commitment to selling higher-quality food products, as the supplier produces lower-grade meats. It seems likely that Heather's concerns regarding the supplier's record for animal welfare could reflect badly on Farmers' brand image should it decide to use the supplier.

Option 2

Farmers should look to absorb the risk of purchasing pears from the supplier.

It seems likely that a decision by Farmers to start selling the unique pears offered by the supplier would lead to an increase in sales, especially as a rival supermarket chain is seeking to establish an exclusive agreement with the supplier. Furthermore, the unique pears would appear to meet Farmers' high-quality food standards and fit with the company ethos of purchasing from UK suppliers.

As Farmers supermarkets already sells pears, it seems unlikely that the supplier's failure to keep up with demand would be overly detrimental, as customers could still purchase the existing fruit lines offered.

In the event of this risk occurring, Farmers could look to offer the unique pears in selected stores, in a bid to ease demand on the supplier. Clearly, a fuller analysis of the supplier's capabilities would be required before committing Farmers to any formal supply arrangement.

Option 3

Farmers should look to mitigate (reduce) the risk that customers do not purchase the newly introduced continental cheeses.

This could easily be achieved by only placing orders for small quantities of the continental cheeses initially. This would ensure that Farmers supermarkets did not end up with perishable inventory that customers do not want. In the event that customers respond well and demand increases, then the quantities ordered could be revised.

Option 4

Farmers should look to transfer the risks associated with transporting the fresh fish to a third party.

Providing the cost implications are not prohibitive, there may be scope to use a specialist haulage firm to transport the fish from Scotland to Farmers' depots and stores. The agreement between Farmers and the haulage firm should include penalties for late deliveries to stores. This would ensure that Farmers supermarkets did not incur the expense of fish spoiling prior to delivery.

Now try these questions from the Practice Question Bank

Question	Level
9A.1 – 9A.5	Practice
C Hospital	Practice

PROJECT MANAGEMENT – PART B

In the last chapter, we looked at the phases of a project. Now we explore the key tools and techniques used in managing projects.

Project software is then explained, and its usefulness particularly with large projects and processing data.

Then we move on to review the documentation and reports used in projects.

Next, we look at different project control systems available to organisations and the challenges that projects bring. Particular consideration is given to the difficulties in managing the so-called 'iron triangle', which represents the key project objectives of time, cost and quality. The chapter concludes by exploring the importance of continuous improvement in the ways projects are managed.

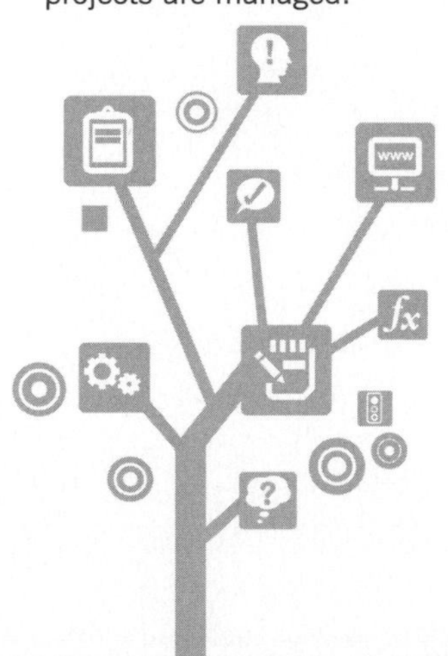

Topic list	Learning outcomes	Syllabus references	Ability required
1 Management tools and techniques	D2b	D2(i), (iii), (iv)	Application
2 Project management software	D2b	D2(v), (x)	Application
3 Documentation and reports	D2b	D2(i)	Application
4 Compare and contrast project control systems	D2a	D2(iv)	Analysis
5 Project troubleshooting	D2a	D2(ii)	Analysis
6 Projects and continuous improvement	D2a	D2(iii), (iv)	Analysis

Chapter Overview

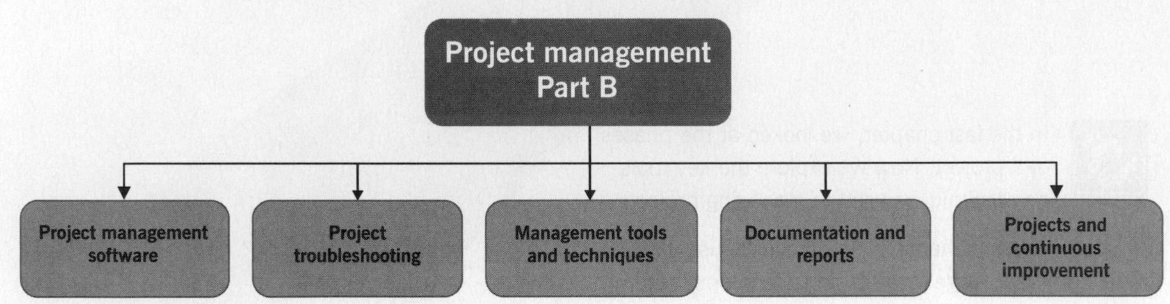

1 Management tools and techniques

Introduction

The tools for managing projects in this chapter measure the **time required** and **resources needed** to complete the project successfully. If you remember that, it will be easier to grasp what each tool is meant to do. They have two purposes then: **planning and control** of the project process.

Exam alert

Objective test questions built around a scenario may require you to identify how different tools and techniques could assist an organisation with project planning. Although PRINCE2 is a key part of your E2 syllabus, it is important that you have a wider understanding of other project management techniques that exist.

The techniques we discuss in this section are concerned with the fundamentals of planning projects and controlling their progress. As with most activities, it is difficult to separate the process of planning a project from that of controlling it: planning is likely to continue throughout the life of the project. A **baseline plan** will show the following.

(a) Start and end dates for the project and its major phases or activities
(b) The resources needed and when they are required
(c) Estimates of cost for the project and the major phases or activities

1.1 Work breakdown structure

Work breakdown structure (WBS) is fundamental to project planning and control. Its essence is the **analysis** of the work required to complete the project into **manageable components**. These are also known as **work packages**, which have defined outcomes and responsibilities.

A good way to approach WBS is to consider the **outputs** (or '**deliverables**') the project is required to produce. This can then be analysed into physical and intangible components, which can in turn be further analysed down to whatever level of simplicity is required. Working backwards in this way helps to **avoid preconceived ideas** of the work the project will involve and the processes that must be undertaken.

Example

For example, a simple domestic project might be to create a vegetable plot in a garden. The output would be a plot of cultivated, well-drained soil that was free of weeds, of a suitable level of fertility and with suitable exposure to sun and rain, together with protection from strong winds. This has obvious implications for what must be done. A plot must be selected; existing vegetation must be cleared; weeds must be dug out; the soil must be improved if necessary, by liming and composting; and a physical boundary or kerb must be provided to prevent invasion by creeping weeds such as grass.

The WBS can allow for several levels of analysis, starting with major project phases and gradually breaking them down into major activities, more detailed sub-activities and individual tasks that will last only a very short time. There is no standardised terminology for the various levels of disaggregation, though an **activity** is sometimes regarded as being composed of **tasks**.

The delivery phase of many projects will break down into significant stages or sub-phases. These are very useful for control purposes, as the completion of each stage is an obvious point for reviewing the whole plan before starting the next one.

1.1.1 Dependencies and interactions

A very important aspect of project planning is the determination of **dependencies** and **interactions**. At any level of WBS analysis, some tasks will be dependent on others; that is to say, **a dependent task cannot commence** until the task on which it depends is completed.

Example

In our vegetable plot example, it is quite obvious that thought must be given to selecting the site of the plot in order to achieve the necessary sun, rain and shelter **before** seizing a spade and starting to dig. Similarly, it would be physically impossible to apply fertiliser if it had not already been positioned at the site.

Careful analysis of dependencies is a major step towards a workable project plan, since it provides an **order in which things must be tackled**. Sometimes, of course, the dependencies are limited and it is possible to proceed with tasks in almost any order, but this is unusual. The more complex a project, the greater the need for analysis of dependencies.

Interactions are slightly different; they occur when tasks are linked but not dependent. This can arise for a variety of reasons: a good example is a requirement to share the use of a scarce resource.

Example

If we only possessed one spade to prepare our vegetable plot, we could not use it simultaneously both to cultivate the plot itself and to dig the trench in which we wish to place the kerbstones. We could choose to do either of these activities first, but we could not do them both at the same time.

The output from the WBS process is a list of tasks, probably arranged hierarchically to reflect the disaggregation of activities. This then becomes the input into the planning and control processes described in the rest of this section.

1.2 The project budget

KEY TERM

PROJECT BUDGET. The amount and distribution of resources allocated to a project.

Building a project budget should be an orderly process that attempts to establish a realistic estimate of the cost of the project. There are two main methods for establishing the project budget: **top-down** and **bottom-up**.

Top-down budgeting describes the situation where the budget is imposed 'from above'. Project managers are allocated a budget for the project based on an estimate made by senior management. The figure may prove realistic, especially if similar projects have been undertaken recently. However, the technique is often used simply because it is quick, or because only a certain level of funding is available.

In **bottom-up budgeting**, the project manager consults the project team, and others, to calculate a budget based on the tasks that make up the project. WBS is a useful tool in this process.

It is useful to collate this information on a **budgeting worksheet**.

Budgeting worksheet				
Project name ____________		**Date worksheet completed** ____________		
Project manager ____________				
Task (code)	Responsible staff member or external supplier	Estimated material costs	Estimated labour costs	Total cost of task

Estimates (and therefore budgets) cannot be expected to be 100% accurate. Business **conditions may change**, the project plan may be amended or estimates may simply prove to be incorrect.

Any estimate must be accompanied by some indication of expected accuracy.

Estimates can be **improved** by:

(a) **Learning** from past mistakes
(b) Ensuring sufficient design **information**
(c) Ensuring as **detailed a specification as possible** from the customer
(d) Properly **analysing the job** into its constituent units

The overall level of cost estimates will be influenced by:

(a) **Project goals**. If a high level of quality is expected, costs will be higher.

(b) **External vendors**. Some costs may need to be estimated by outside vendors. To be realistic, these people must understand exactly what would be expected of them.

(c) **Staff availability**. If staff are unavailable, potentially expensive contractors may be required.

(d) **Time schedules**. The quicker a task is required to be done, the higher the cost is likely to be – particularly with external suppliers.

The budget may express all resources in monetary amounts, or may show money and other resources – such as staff hours. A monetary budget is often used to establish the current cost variance of the project. To establish this we need:

(a) **The actual cost of work performed (ACWP)**. This is the amount spent to date on the project.

(b) **The budgeted cost of work scheduled (BCWS)**. The amount that was budgeted to be spent to this point on scheduled activities.

(c) **The budgeted cost of work performed (BCWP)**. This figure is calculated by pricing the work that has actually been done – using the same basis as the scheduled work.

BCWP – ACWP = the **cost variance** for the project

BCWP – BCWS = the **schedule variance** for the project

During the project, actual expenditure is tracked against budget on either a separate **budget report**, or as part of a regular **progress report**.

Budgets should be presented for approval and **sign-off** to the stakeholder who has responsibility for the funds being used.

Before presenting a budget for approval, it may have to be revised a number of times. The 'first draft' may be overly reliant on rough estimates, as insufficient time was available to obtain more accurate figures.

On presentation, the project manager may be asked to find ways to cut the budget. If they agree that cuts can be made, the consequences of the cuts should be pointed out – eg a reduction in quality.

It may be decided that a project costs more than it is worth. If so, scrapping the project is a perfectly valid option. In such cases, the budgeting process has highlighted the situation before too much time and effort has been spent on an unprofitable venture.

1.3 Gantt charts

A **Gantt chart**, named after the engineer Henry Gantt who pioneered the procedure in the early 1900s, is a horizontal bar chart used to plan the **timescale** for a project and to estimate the **resources** required.

The Gantt chart displays the time relationships between tasks in a project. Two lines are usually used to show the time allocated for each task, and the actual time taken.

A simple Gantt chart, illustrating some of the activities involved in a network server installation project, follows.

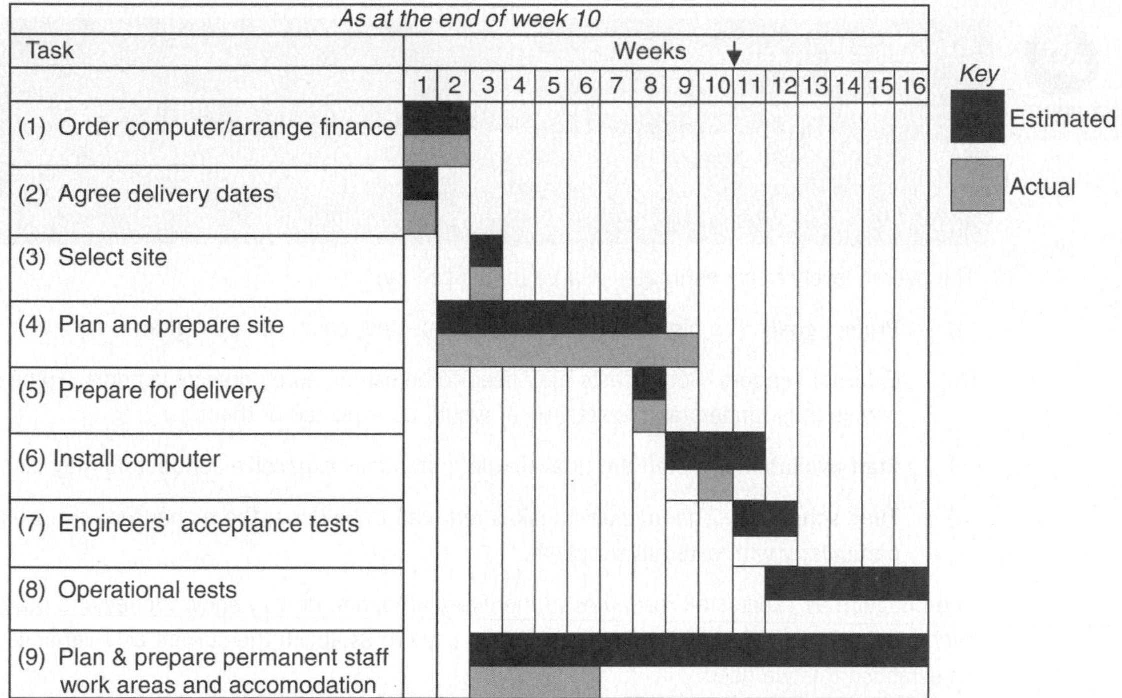

The chart shows that at the end of the tenth week, Activity 9 is running behind schedule. More resources may have to be allocated to this activity if the staff accommodation is to be ready in time for the changeover to the new system.

Activity 4 had not been completed on time, and this has resulted in some disruption to the computer installation (Activity 6), which may mean further delays in the commencement of Activities 7 and 8.

Gantt charts can be excellent tools for tracking projects and identifying potential problems or delays before the final deadline is compromised. However, its use will be limited for projects with a large project team. In addition, a Gantt chart does not show the interrelationship between the various activities in the project as clearly as a **network diagram** (covered later in this chapter). A combination of Gantt charts and network analysis will often be used for project planning and resource allocation.

For more complex projects, Gantt charts have a number of **additional limitations**.

(a) Gantt charts do not identify any potential **weak links** between phases.

(b) They do not indicate the need for resources to be co-ordinated or communication at critical phases of the schedule.

(c) They do not identify team problems that may occur due to unexpected delays.

(d) They do not show the degree of completion for each phase.

1.3.1 Milestones and control gates

A key reason for producing a Gantt chart is to improve the control of the project.

To help the project manager to retain control, a number of **milestones** are identified. These are clearly identifiable events that illustrate how far the project has progressed. Setting milestones involves breaking the project down into a number of segments or phases that can be easily defined by key events and unambiguous targets of what needs to be done, and the responsibilities for doing this.

These milestones should be set at the project planning stage. Monitoring the milestones helps the project manager to retain control and identify delays at the earliest opportunity.

Certain milestones, known as **control gates**, represent key points in the project's life cycle that allow the project sponsor or steering committee the opportunity to review project progress and make a decision as to whether to continue with, or terminate, the project. A control gate can only be 'passed' if specific predefined criteria have been met.

Question 9B.1 Terminology

Learning outcome D2b

What is the surname of the man who invented the resource planning chart a century ago?

A Gannt
B Gantt
C Ganntt
D Gant

1.4 Network analysis or critical path analysis (CPA)

Network analysis, also known as **critical path analysis** (CPA), is a useful technique to help with planning and controlling large projects, such as construction projects, research and development projects and the computerisation of systems.

KEY TERMS

NETWORK ANALYSIS requires breaking down the project into tasks, arranging them into a logical sequence and estimating the duration of each.

This enables the series of tasks that determines the minimum possible duration of the project to be found. These are the **CRITICAL ACTIVITIES**.

Exam alert

Network analysis is very easy to set practical questions on, and could feature in both your E2 exam and Integrated Case Study. You may be required to analyse a critical path diagram (to identify critical path, project duration, earliest start/end times and floats).

KEY POINT

CPA aims to ensure the progress of a project, so the project is completed in the **minimum amount of time**. It pinpoints the tasks that are **on the critical path**, ie those parts that, if delayed beyond the allotted time, would **delay the completion** of the project as a whole. The technique can also be used to assist in **allocating resources** such as labour and equipment.

CPA is quite a simple technique. The events and activities making up the whole project are represented in the form of a **diagram**. Drawing the diagram or chart involves the following steps.

Estimating the time needed to complete each individual activity or task that makes up a part of the project.

Sorting out what activities must be done one after another, and which can be done at the same time, if required.

Representing these in a network diagram.

Estimating the critical path, which is the longest sequence of consecutive activities through the network.

The duration of the whole project will be fixed by the time taken to complete the longest path through the network. This path is called the **critical path** and activities on it are known as **critical activities**. Activities on the critical path **must be started and completed on time**, otherwise the total project time will be extended. The method of finding the critical path is illustrated in the example below.

Network analysis shows the **sequence** of tasks and how long they are going to take. The diagrams are drawn from left to right. To construct a network diagram, you need to know the activities involved in a project, the expected duration of each and the order (or precedences, or dependencies) of the activities.

For example:

Activity	*Expected duration (days)*	*Preceding activity*
A	3	-
B	5	-
C	2	B
D	1	A
E	6	A
F	3	D
G	3	C, E

1.4.1 Activity-on-arrow presentation

Here is a network diagram showing our example in the form known as **activity-on-arrow**.

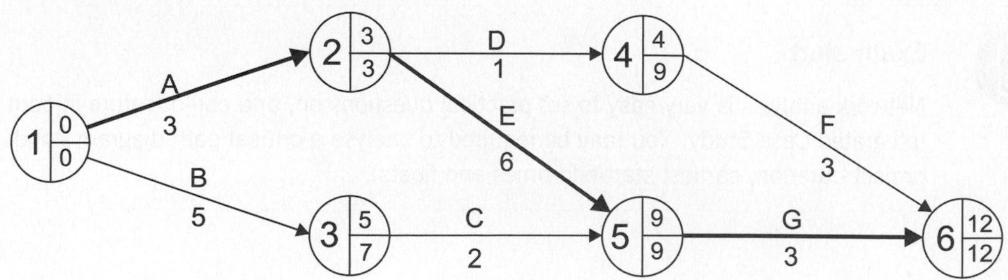

(a) The network is made up of **events and activities, represented by circles and arrows respectively**. The diagram is laid out to show the dependencies that exist between the activities, working from left to right. The first event is the start of the overall sequence of activities (or the project). Each subsequent event marks the beginning of at least one activity and, therefore, the end of any activities on which it is dependent. In the network diagram above, for example, event 5 marks the completion of activities E and C and the start of activity G.

(b) **Events are numbered, working from left to right** and the numbers are entered in the left-hand halves of the event circles. Also by convention, the events are numbered so that the event at the end of any activity has a higher number than the one at its start.

(c) **Activities are lettered, again working from left to right**. The duration of each activity is shown by a number entered against its identifying letter.

(d) When the basic information has been entered onto the network, it becomes possible to determine the **critical path** through it: this is the sequence of activities that takes the longest time and which therefore determines the overall expected duration of the project.

(e) A **forward pass** is made through the network and the **earliest event time** (EET) is entered in the upper-right quadrant of each event circle. This time depends on the duration of any sequence of activities leading to the event in question and therefore reflects the dependencies involved. In the diagram, event 5, for example, cannot occur (and activity G therefore cannot begin) until the sequences A–E and B–C are both complete. B–C takes (5 + 2) days, while A–E takes (3 + 6) days. The **EET** for event 5 is therefore 9 days. This is a general rule: the EET for any event shows the **longest duration sequence of activities leading to it**.

(f) When the forward pass is complete, a **rearward pass** is made, starting at the final event and working back to establish the **latest event time** (LET) for each event. The LET for an event is entered in the lower-right quadrant of its symbol. Like the EET, the LET depends on the longest sequence of activities involved, but this time it is the sequences of events that follow the event in question that are relevant, rather than the ones that precede it. In the example network diagram, event 2 is followed by sequences D–F and E–G with durations (1 + 3) days and (6 + 3) days respectively. If there is to be time to complete the longer sequence E–G, the LET for event 2 must be 3 days.

(g) When both forward and rearward passes are complete, the **critical path** is identifiable as the route through the network that links all the events that have LET equal to EET: there is no **float** on this path. We discuss float times later in this section. The critical path activities are highlighted on the diagram in some way, such as by using double lines or hash marks.

The **critical path** in the diagram above is AEG. Note the **float time** of 5 days for Activity F. Activity F can begin any time between days 4 and 9, thus giving the project manager a degree of flexibility.

(h) Sometimes it is necessary to use a **dummy activity** in a network diagram. Dummies indicate dependency, but they take no time. The need for them arises from the convention that activity arrows are always straight. Thus, if an activity, C, depends on both activity A and activity B, the presentation below is not used:

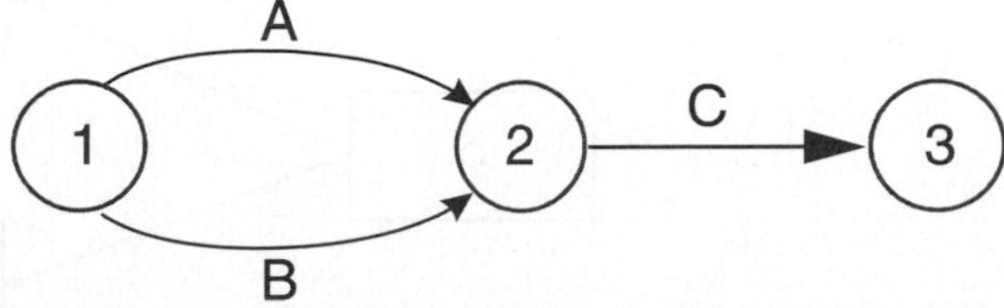

Instead, an extra event and a dummy are inserted:

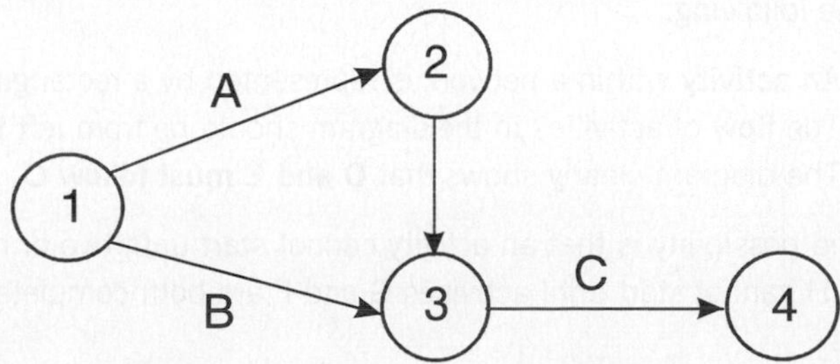

The dummy activity is shown as a broken line. Note also how the dummy starts at an event with a lower number than the one it ends at. Sometimes it is necessary to use a dummy activity not just to comply with the convention, but to **preserve the basic logic** of the network.

Question 9B.2

Dummy activity

Learning outcome D2b

Consider the following example of a project to install a new office telephone system.

Activity	*Preceding Activity*
A Buy equipment	–
B Allocate extension numbers	–
C Install switchboard	A
D Install wiring	B, C
E Print office directory	B

The project is finished when both D and E are complete.

Required

Identify why there may be a need for a dummy activity, and draw the basic network showing it.

Dummy activities are not required when the **activity-on-node** technique (discussed below) is used for drawing the network.

In our earlier example, if activity G had depended on activity D as well as on activities C and E, this would have been shown as a dummy running from event 4 to event 5.

1.4.2 Activity-on-node presentation

Network diagrams may also be drawn using **activity-on-node** presentation, which is similar in style to that used by the **Microsoft Project** software package.

1.5 Example – activity-on-node

Suppose that a project includes three activities: C, D and E. Neither activity D nor E can start until activity C is completed, but D and E could be done simultaneously if required.

This would be represented as follows.

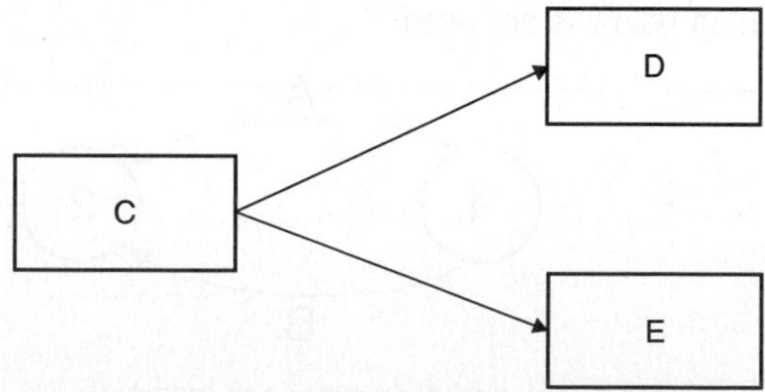

Note the following.

(a) An **activity** within a network is represented by a rectangular box. (Each box is a **node**.)

(b) The **flow** of activities in the diagram should be from **left to right**.

(c) The diagram clearly shows that **D and E must follow C**.

A second possibility is that an activity cannot start until two or more activities have been completed. If activity H cannot start until activities G and F are both complete, then we would represent the situation like this.

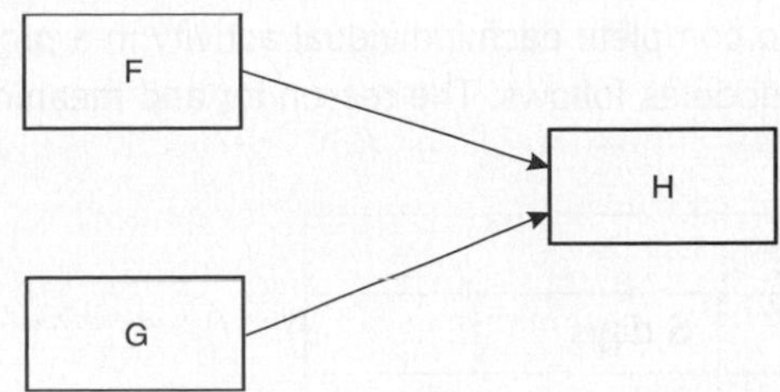

In some conventions, an extra node is introduced at the start and end of a network. This serves absolutely no purpose (other than to ensure that all the nodes are joined up), so we recommend that you do not do it. Just in case you ever see a network presented in this way, both styles are shown in the next example.

1.6 Example – starts and ends

Draw a diagram for the following project. The project is finished when both D and E are complete.

Activity	*Preceding activity*
A	–
B	–
C	A
D	B and C
E	B

Solution

Microsoft Project style

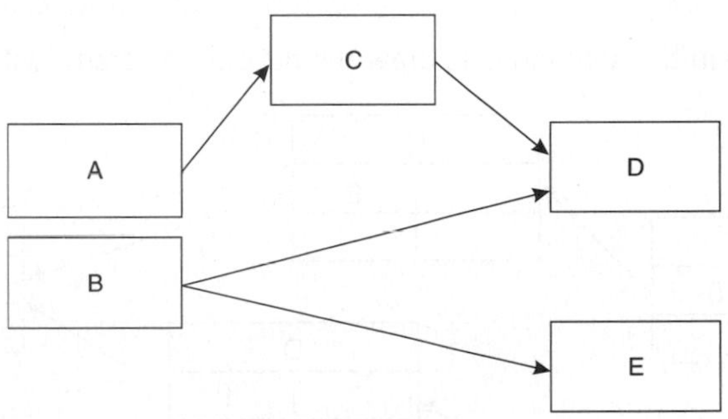

With start and end nodes

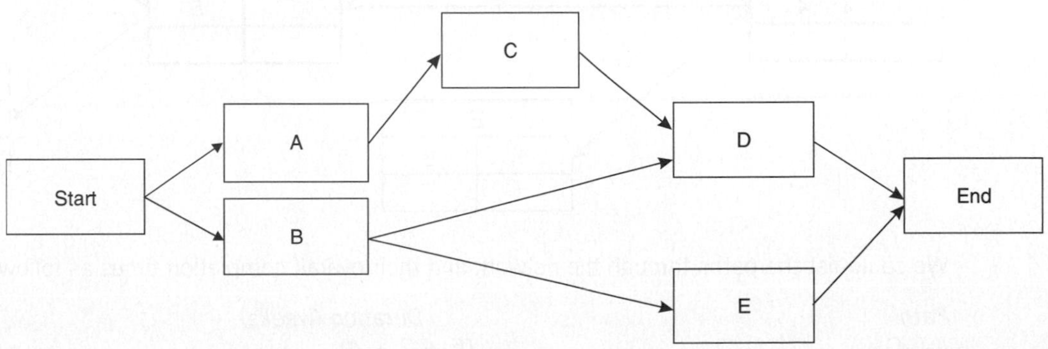

Any network can be analysed into a number of different paths or routes. A path is simply a sequence of activities that can take you from the start to the end of the network. In the example above, there are just three routes or paths.

(a) A-C-D
(b) B-D
(c) B-E

The time needed to complete each individual activity in a project must be estimated. This duration is shown within the node as follows. The reason for and meaning of the other boxes will be explained in a moment.

Task A	
	6 days

1.7 Example – the critical path

Activity	*Immediately preceding activity*	*Duration (weeks)*
A	–	5
B	–	4
C	A	2
D	B	1
E	B	5
F	B	5
G	C and D	4
H	F	3
I	F	2

(a) What are the paths through the network?
(b) What is the critical path and its duration?

Solution

The first step in the solution is to draw the network diagram, with the time for each activity shown.

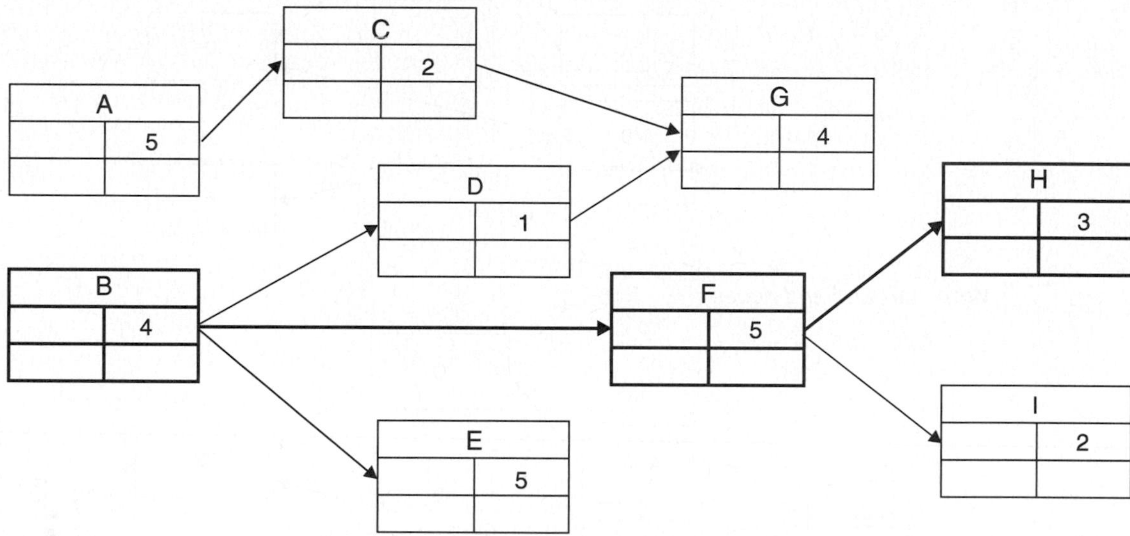

We could list the paths through the network and their overall completion times as follows.

Path	*Duration (weeks)*	
A-C-G	(5 + 2 + 4)	11
B-D-G	(4 + 1 + 4)	9
B-E	(4 + 5)	9
B-F-H	(4 + 5 + 3)	12
B-F-I	(4 + 5 + 2)	11

The critical path is the longest, B-F-H, with a duration of 12 weeks. This is the minimum time needed to complete the project.

The critical path is indicated on the diagram by drawing thick (or double-line) arrows, as shown above. In Microsoft Project, the arrows and the nodes are highlighted in red.

Listing paths through the network in this way should be easy enough for small networks, but it becomes a long and tedious task for bigger and more complex networks. This is why software packages are used in real life.

Project management software packages offer a much larger variety of techniques than can easily be done by hand. **Microsoft Project** allows each activity to be assigned to any one of a variety of types: 'start as late as possible', 'start as soon as possible', 'finish no earlier than a particular date', 'finish no later than a particular date', and so on.

In real life too, activity times can be shortened by working weekends and overtime, or they may be constrained by non-availability of essential personnel. In other words, with any more than a few activities the possibilities are mind-boggling, which is why software is used.

Nevertheless, a simple technique is illustrated in the following example.

1.8 Find the critical path

The procedure for finding the critical path is essentially the same as the one we used with the activity-on-arrow example earlier.

One way of showing earliest and latest **start** times for activities is to divide each event node into sections. This is similar to the style used in **Microsoft Project**, except that Project uses real dates, which is far more useful, and the bottom two sections can mean a variety of things, depending on what constraints have been set.

These sections record the following things.

(a) The **name** of the activity, for example Task A. This helps us to understand the diagram.

(b) An **ID number**, which is unique to that activity. This helps computer packages to understand the diagram, because it is possible that two or more activities could have the same name. For instance, two bits of research done at different project stages might both be called 'research'.

(c) The **duration** of the activity.

(d) The **earliest start time**. Conventionally, for the first node in the network, this is time 0.

(e) The **latest start time**.

(**Note.** Don't confuse start times with the '**event**' times that are calculated when using the **activity-on-arrow** method, even though the approach is the same.)

Task D	
ID number: 4	Duration: 6 days
Earliest start: Day 4	Latest start: Day 11

1.8.1 Earliest start times

To find the earliest start times, always start with activities that have no predecessors and give them an earliest starting time of 0. In the example we have been looking at, this is week 0.

Then work along each path from **left to right** through the diagram, calculating the earliest time that the next activity can start, just as with activity-on-arrow.

For example, the earliest time for activity C is week 0 + 5 = 5. The earliest time activities D, E and F can start is week 0 + 4 = 4.

To calculate an activity's earliest time, simply look at the box for the **preceding** activity and add the bottom-left figure to the top-right figure.

If **two or more** activities precede an activity, take the **highest** figure as the later activity's earliest start time: it cannot start before all the others are finished!

1.8.2 Latest start times

The latest start times are the latest times at which each activity can start **if the project as a whole is to be completed in the earliest possible time**; in other words, in 12 weeks in our example.

Work backwards from **right to left** through the diagram, calculating the latest time at which the activity can start, if it is to be completed at the latest finishing time. For example, the latest start time for activity H is 12 – 3 = week 9, and for activity E it is 12 – 5 = week 7.

Activity F might cause difficulties as two activities, H and I, lead back to it.

(a) Activity H must be completed by week 12, and so must start at week 9.

(b) Activity I must also be completed by week 12, and so must start at week 10.

Activity F takes 5 weeks, so its latest start time is either 9 – 5 = week 4, or 10 – 5 = week 5. However, if it starts in week 5, it will not be possible to start activity H on time and the whole project will be delayed. We therefore take the **lower** figure.

The final diagram is now as follows.

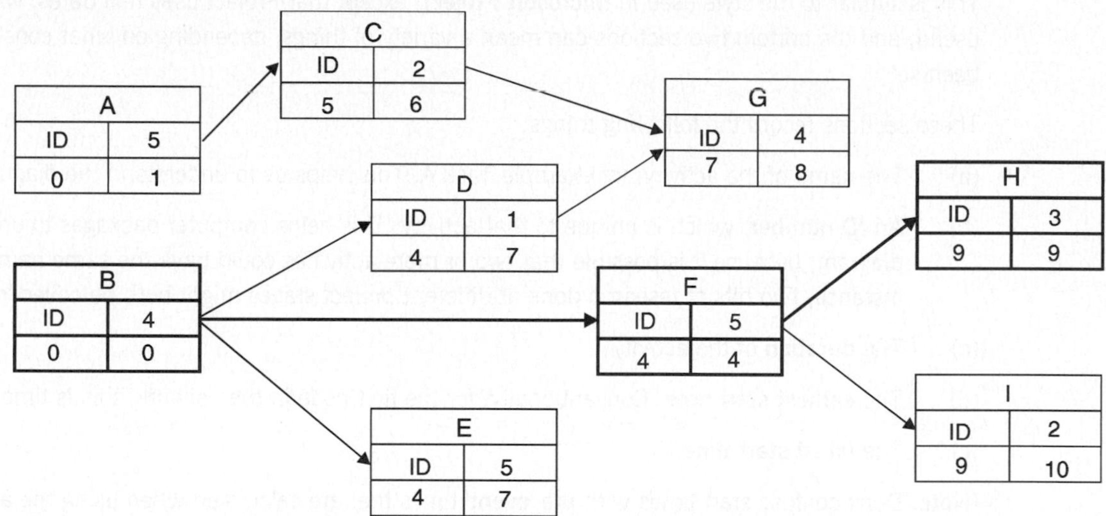

Critical activities are those activities that must be started on time, otherwise the total project time will be increased. It follows that each event on the critical path must have the same earliest and latest start times. The critical path for the above network is therefore B-F-H.

1.9 Float times

Float time is the time available for unforeseen circumstances.

(a) **Total float** on an activity is the time available (earliest start date to latest finish date) **less** the time needed for the job. If, for example, job A's earliest start time was day 7 and its latest end time was day 17, and the job needed 4 days, total float would be:

(17 – 7) – 4 = 6 days

(b) **Free float** is the delay possible in an activity on the assumption that all preceding activities start as early as possible and all subsequent activities also start at the earliest time.

(c) **Independent float** is the delay possible if all preceding jobs have finished as late as possible, and all succeeding jobs are to start as early as possible.

By definition, there is no float time on the critical path.

1.10 Criticisms of critical path/network analysis

KEY POINT

(a) It is not always possible to devise an effective WBS for a project.

(b) **It assumes a sequential relationship** between activities. It assumes that Activity B starts after Activity A has finished. It is not very good at coping with the possibility that an activity 'later' in the sequence may be relevant to an earlier activity.

(c) There are **problems in estimation**. Where the project is completely new, the planning process may be conducted in conditions of relative ignorance.

(d) Although network analysis plans the use of resources of labour and finance, it does not appear to develop plans for contingencies, other than crashing time.

(e) CPA **assumes a trade-off between time and cost**. This may not be the case where a substantial portion of the cost is **indirect overheads** or where the direct labour proportion of the total cost is limited.

1.11 Example – using Gantt charts and CPA

This example consolidates what we have learnt so far in this section, in a short example on Gantt charts and CPA.

A company is about to undertake a project about which the following data is available.

Activity	*Preceded by activity*	*Duration* Days	*Workers required*
A	–	3	6
B	–	5	3
C	B	2	4
D	A	1	4
E	A	6	5
F	D	3	6
G	C, E	3	3

There is a multi-skilled workforce of nine workers available, each capable of working on any of the activities.

Draw the network to establish the duration of the project and the critical path. Then draw a Gantt chart, using the critical path as a basis, assuming that jobs start at the earliest possible time.

Solution

Here are the diagrams.

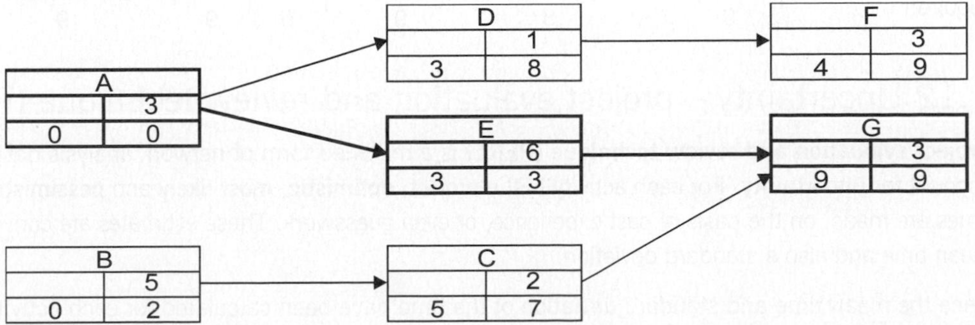

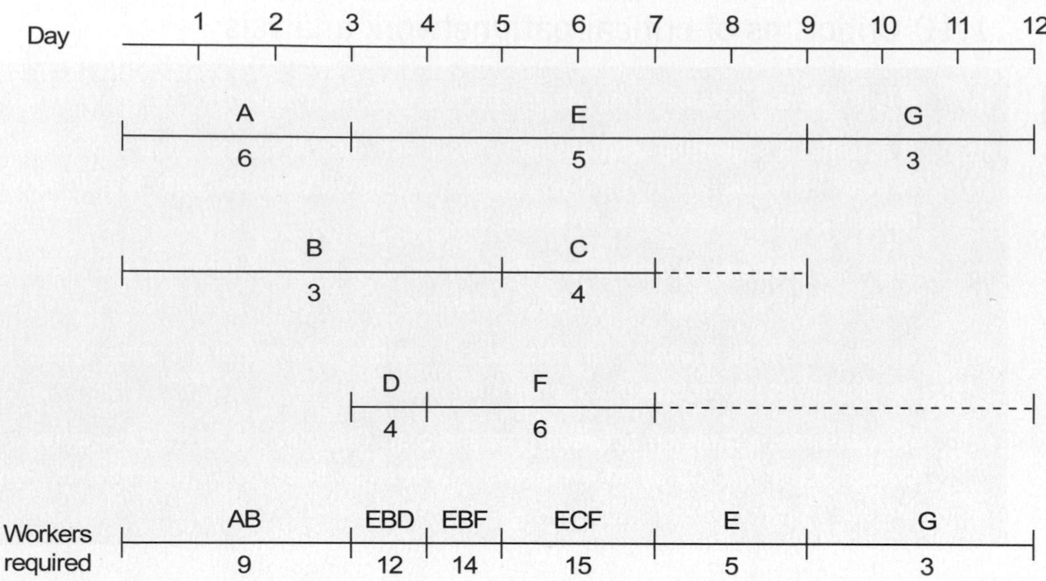

It can be seen that if all activities start at their earliest times, as many as 15 workers will be required on any one day (days 6–7) whereas on other days there would be idle capacity (days 8–12).

The problem can be reduced, or removed, by using up spare time on non-critical activities. Suppose we **deferred the start** of activities D and F until the latest possible days. These would be days 8 and 9, leaving 4 days to complete the activities by the end of day 12.

The Gantt chart would be redrawn as follows.

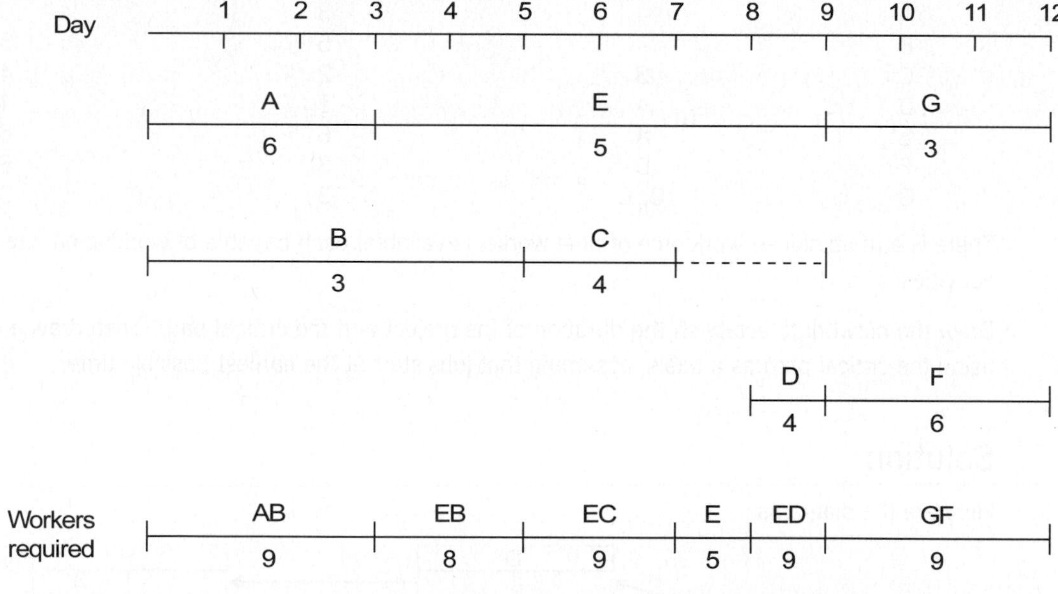

1.12 Uncertainty – project evaluation and review technique (PERT)

Project evaluation and review technique (PERT) is a modified form of network analysis designed to account for **uncertainty**. For each activity in the project, **optimistic**, **most likely** and **pessimistic** estimates of times are made, on the basis of past experience, or even guesswork. These estimates are converted into a mean time and also a standard deviation.

Once the mean time and standard deviation of the time have been calculated for each activity, it should be possible to do the following.

(a) Establish the duration of the critical path using **expected times**

(b) Calculate a **contingency time allowance**

1.12.1 Expected times

The **probable** time estimate is based on the assumption that **all relevant conditions are normal**. The **expected** time is a different concept: like an **expected value**, it is an estimate based on the use of probability.

$$\text{Expected time} = \frac{o + 4m + p}{6}$$

Where:

o = optimistic estimate
m = probable estimate
p = pessimistic estimate

1.12.2 Contingency time allowances

The standard deviation of the time required for the critical path activities is calculated.

Calculate the standard deviation for each critical activity time using the formula $\frac{p - o}{6}$.

Square the standard deviations to obtain the **variances**.

Sum the variances to give the total variance for the critical path.

Find the square root of the total variance to give the standard deviation of the duration of the critical path.

A contingency time allowance stated in terms of a number of **standard deviations** will indicate the probability of completion within the total time allowed, including contingency.

1.12.3 Costs

A similar approach may be employed to deal with uncertainty over costs.

1.12.4 Further analysis

Similar, slightly more complex statistical processes may be used to establish the probability that any given activity or sequence of activities will be completed by a given time. This is useful when **staged payments** or **time penalties** are involved.

1.13 Alternatives to PERT

Scenario planning is an alternative, and perhaps simpler, way of planning for risk. It involves identifying a number of alternative outcomes that may occur in addition to the expected outcome on which the budget has been based.

Each of these potential outcomes, or scenarios, is then tested to determine the likely impact they would have should they actually occur. **Contingency plans** for these scenarios can then be developed. These plans allow the project manager to quickly take the appropriate pre-planned action for whichever scenario was to arise.

Buffering is a method of attempting to incorporate a 'buffer' for risk by building slack into the plans. This involves padding and overestimating in order to allow for any unforeseen difficulties. This practice should be discouraged, as such a build-up of slack has the potential to lead to complacency.

1.14 Critical chain project management (CCPM)

Critical chain project management (CCPM) is a relatively new approach, which attempts to address some of the problems of time scheduling that arise with network analysis and WBS.

(a) Sequential scheduling (eg by CPA) tends to 'pad' the schedule. Safety margins are included in time estimates for tasks – but these are rarely used constructively, so that if a task is finished 'early', the next task can begin early. The safety margin often encourages people to begin tasks at the last moment – and then if problems occur, the task overruns! Moreover, as Parkinson's law states, 'work expands to fill the time available for it'.

(b) Delays in one task are passed on to the next – but time gains are usually wasted (eg to avoid appearing a poor estimator or to set harder standards for future timings).

CCPM overcomes these problems by:

(a) Allowing **no padding of time estimates**. The agreement of all estimates is sought for this, and the project manager accepts the likelihood that some tasks will be underestimated, leading to overruns.

(b) A **margin of safety** is built in at the final stages of the project, to counter the accumulated overrun – **not** at individual tasks, where they are likely to be wasted.

(c) Precedence relationships (the planned task sequence) is only regarded as a helpful overview: the emphasis is on **responding flexibly** to changes, constraints and problems as they occur.

When time becomes critical on a project, the traditional management approach is based on 'crashing' float activities: reducing their durations by injecting extra resources. The CCPM approach instead uses **buffers** – defined quantities of time applied to a project schedule to protect the promised due date from slippage.

(a) A **feeding buffer** is added to non-critical tasks where they feed into critical tasks, so that the critical task can begin on time.

(b) A **capacity buffer** is used in a multi-project programme, so that one project is not affected by variations in resource usage by another project.

(c) A **resource buffer** is added to key resources, so that they will not be in short supply when needed.

1.15 Resource histogram

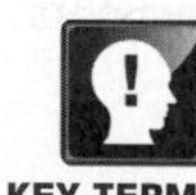

KEY TERM

A **RESOURCE HISTOGRAM** shows a view of project data in which resource requirements, usage and availability are shown against a timescale.

A simple resource histogram showing programmer time required on a software development program is shown below.

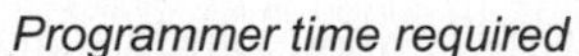

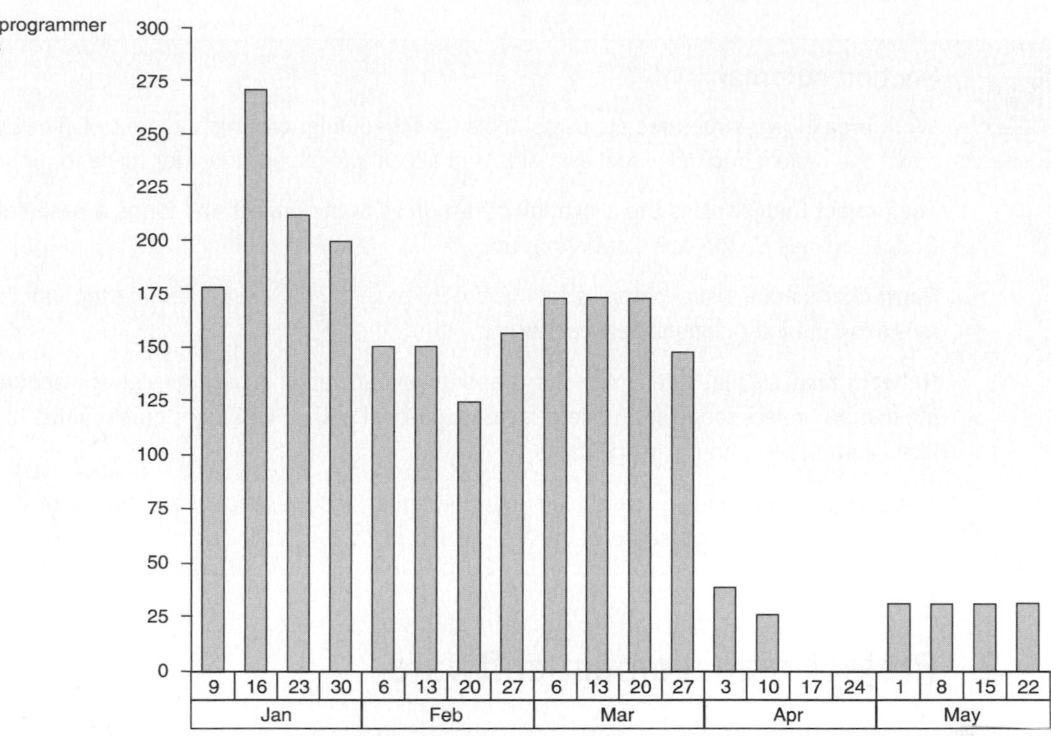

Some organisations add another bar (or a separate line) to the chart showing resource availability. The chart then shows any instances when the required resource hours exceed the available hours. Plans should then be made to either obtain further resource for these peak times, or to reschedule the work plan. Alternatively, the chart may show times when the available resource is excessive, and should be redeployed elsewhere. An example follows.

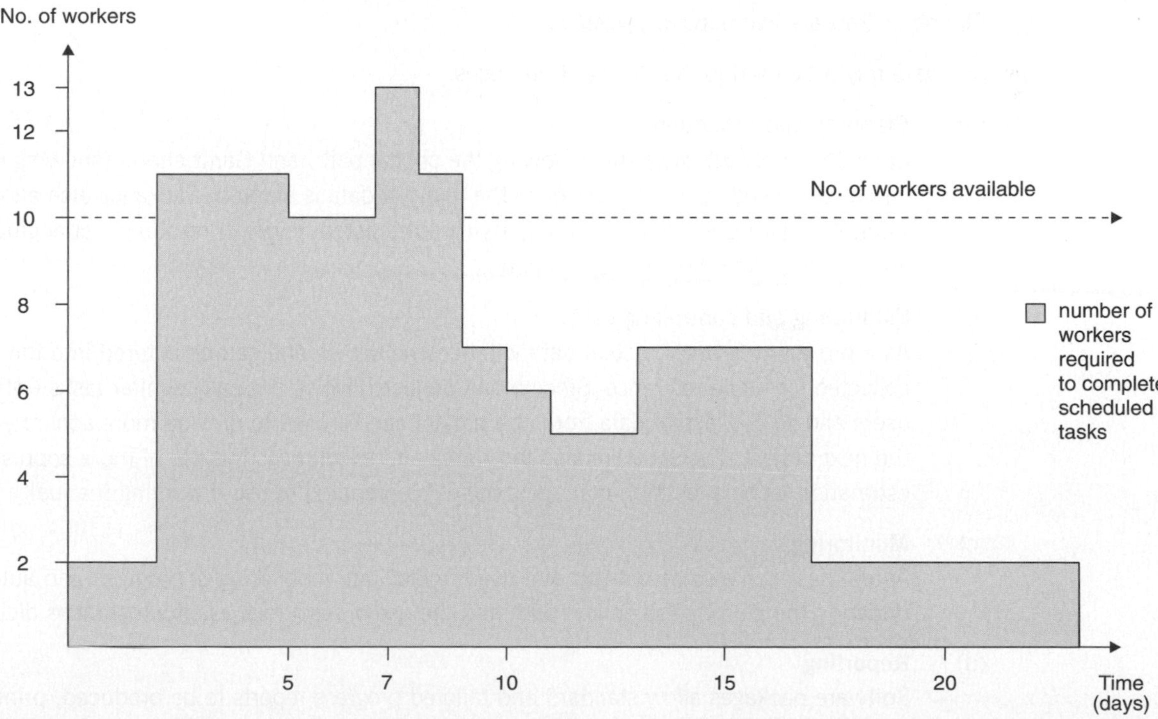

The number of workers required on the seventh day is 13. Can we reschedule the non-critical activities to reduce the requirement to the available level of 10? We might be able to rearrange activities so that we can make use of the workers available from day 9 onwards.

Using a **WBS** integrates work, schedule and cost data.

Section summary

Work breakdown structures are useful tools for **scheduling**, **costing** and **control**. They work by breaking down the project into individual elements and allocating responsibility for these to individuals.

The **project budget** plans the allocation of resources to the project and forms a basis for their control. Budgeting may be top down or bottom up.

Gantt charts are a **visual** planning tool useful for projects, but are limited in their use, as they do not recognise the interrelations between tasks.

Network analysis illustrates interactions and dependencies. It is used to plan the sequence of tasks making up project scope and to determine the **critical path**. **PERT** uses probabilities to make estimates of likely completion and milestone dates.

A **resource histogram** is a useful planning tool that shows the amount and timing of the requirement for a resource (or a range of resources).

2 Project management software

Introduction

Project software is useful when projects become complex. Computer programs allow project managers to calculate outcomes more quickly than manually, and to produce standardised reports. Beware of drawbacks though, which include human error in inputting and interpreting data.

Project management techniques are ideal candidates for computerisation. Inexpensive project management software packages have been available for a number of years. Microsoft Project and Micro Planner X-Pert are two popular packages.

Software might be used for a number of purposes.

(a) **Planning and scheduling**
Calendars, **network diagrams** (showing the critical path) and Gantt charts (showing resource use) can be produced automatically, once the relevant data is entered. Packages also allow a sort of 'what if?' analysis for initial planning, trying out different levels of resources, changing deadlines and so on, to find the best combination.

(b) **Estimating and controlling costs**
As a project progresses, actual data will become known and can be entered into the package and collected for future reference. Since many projects involve basically similar tasks (interviewing users and so on), actual data from one project can be used to provide more accurate estimates for the next project. The software also facilitates and encourages the use of more sophisticated estimation techniques than managers might be prepared to use if working manually.

(c) **Monitoring**
Actual data can also be entered and used to facilitate monitoring of progress and automatically updating the plan for the critical path and the use of resources as circumstances dictate.

(d) **Reporting**
Software packages allow standard and tailored progress reports to be produced, printed out and circulated to participants and senior managers at any time, usually at the touch of a button. This helps with co-ordination of activities and project review.

Most project management packages feature a process of identifying the main steps in a project, and breaking these down further into specific tasks.

A typical project management package requires four **inputs**.

(a) The length of **time** and the resources required for each activity of the project
(b) The **logical relationships** between each activity
(c) The **resources** available
(d) **When** the resources are available

The package is able to analyse and present this information in a number of ways.

The advantages of using project management software are summarised in the following table.

Advantage	Comment
Enables quick re-planning	Estimates can be **changed many times** and a new schedule produced almost instantly. Changes to the plan can be reflected immediately.
Document quality	Outputs are accurate, well presented and easy to understand.
Encourages constant progress tracking	Actual times can be captured, enabling the project manager to be able to compare **actual** progress against **planned** progress and investigate problem areas promptly.
'What if?' analysis	Software enables the effect of various scenarios to be calculated quickly and easily. Many project managers conduct this type of analysis using copies of the plan in separate computer files – leaving the actual plan untouched.
Complexity	Software can handle projects of size and complexity that would be very difficult to handle using manual methods.

The software also has several **disadvantages**, some of which also apply to manual methods.

(a) **Focus**. Some project managers become so interested in software that they spend too much time producing documents and not enough time managing the project. Entering actual data and producing reports should be delegated to an administrator.

(b) **Work practices**. The assumptions behind WBS are not always applicable: people tend to work in a more flexible way rather than completing discrete tasks one by one.

(c) **Estimates**. Estimation is as much an art as a science, and estimates can be wildly wrong. They are subject to the **experience** level of the estimator; influenced by the **need to impress clients**; and based on **assumptions** that can easily change.

(d) **Human factors**. Skill levels, staff turnover and level of motivation can have profound effects on performance achieved. Also, human variation makes rescheduling difficult because putting more people on to an activity that is running late may actually slow it down at first, while the newcomers are briefed and even retrained.

Section summary

Project management software can be used to produce detailed project planning documentation, to update plans and to produce reports. These will be faster and more accurate than non-automated tools. They will also suffer from a **lack of intelligence** and human error.

Exam alert

Perhaps the most likely questions on project software are how it might be used, and how it might help the project manager to successfully carry out a project.

3 Documentation and reports

Introduction

We will now look at the main **documents and reports** used in project management. The name allocated to documents will vary across different organisations. What is constant is the need for clear and relevant documentation that helps monitor and control the project.

Remember that reports are not a substitute for **face to face communication**. Too many (or too lengthy) reports will result in **information overload**.

When outlining possible content of documents, some **duplication** of items occurs. This does not mean that information should be repeated, but that the information may appear in one or other of the documents, depending on the format adopted by the organisation.

3.1 Project charter

KEY TERMS

The PROJECT CHARTER or PROJECT BRIEF or PROJECT AUTHORISATION or PROJECT INITIATION DOCUMENT is approved by the project board and provides the project manager with the authority to apply resources to project activities. It also defines the terms of reference for the project.

The project charter is presented at the **project initiation meeting**. This meeting agrees the project organisation structure and the initial project plans, which may then be incorporated into the project charter. The aim of the meeting is to ensure that everyone knows their role; all agree on what job is to be done; there are good business reasons for the project; and that any risks involved have been assessed.

It is likely that the charter will evolve as the project develops, until it is ultimately incorporated into the project management plan.

The project charter defines the **terms of reference** for the project. The charter should contain the statements of the project manager, team, stakeholders and sponsors about:

(a) Overview of the project including key dates
(b) The **scope** of the project – what it is intended to cover and what it is not
(c) The objectives for the team during the project, and for the completed project
(d) Project team organisation, roles and responsibilities

The charter is not likely to give many specifics about how the team and the project are to proceed. The **project management plan** will do that.

3.2 Project management plan

The project manager should also develop a **project management plan**. (In some organisations, what is described here as the project management plan would simply be called the project plan. In other organisations, the project plan refers only to the project schedule, usually in the form of a network diagram.)

KEY TERM

The PROJECT MANAGEMENT PLAN (also referred to as a **project quality plan**) is used as a reference tool for managing the project. The plan is used to guide both project execution and project control. It outlines how the project will be planned, monitored and implemented.

KEY POINT

The **project management** plan should include:

(a) Project objectives and how they will be achieved and verified
(b) How any **changes** to these procedures are to be **controlled**
(c) The **management and technical procedures**, and **standards**, to be used
(d) The **budget** and **timescale**
(e) **Safety**, health and environmental policies
(f) Inherent **risks** and how they will be managed

An example of a simple **project plan/project management plan** is shown below. This plan was produced by a US organisation, the Project Management Institute (PMI), to manage a project to produce formal project management principles.

The project plan **evolves** over time. A high-level plan for the whole project and a detailed plan for the current and following stage are usually produced soon after project start-up. At each subsequent stage, a detailed plan is produced for the following stage and, if required, the overall project plan is revised.

Project management plan	
Project name	The full name of this project is 'project management principles'.
Project manager	The Project Manager is Joe Bloggs. The Project Manager is authorised to (1) initiate the project, (2) form the project team and (3) prepare and execute plans and manage the project as necessary for successful project completion.
Purpose/business need	This project addresses a need for high-level guidelines for the project management profession through the identification and presentation of project management principles. The project sponsor and accepting agent is the PMI Standards Program Team (SPT). The principal and beneficial customer is the membership of PMI. Principles are needed to provide high-level context and guidance for the profession of project management. These principles will provide benefit from the perspectives of practice, evaluation and development.
Product description and deliverables	The final deliverable of this project is a document containing a statement of project management principles. The text is to be fully developed and ready for publication. As a research and development project, it is to be approached flexibly in schedule and resource requirements, with an initially proposed publication date of June 20X1.
Project management	The project team will use project methodology consistent with PMI standards. The project is to be managed with definitive scope and acceptance criteria fully established as the project progresses and the product is developed.
Assumptions, constraints and risks	The project faces some increased risk that, without a clearly prescribed definition of a principle, standards for product quality will be more difficult to establish and apply. To mitigate this risk, ongoing communication between the project team and the project sponsor on this matter will be required.
Resources	The PMI SPT is to provide the project team with the following. **Financial resources.** SPT will provide financial resources as available. The initial amount for the current year is \$5,000. The project manager must not exceed the allocated amount, and must notify the SPT when 75% of the allocation has been spent. **Explanation of standards programme**. SPT will provide guidance at the outset of the project, updates as changes occur, and clarifications as needed. **Personnel/volunteers**. SPT will recruit volunteer team members from within the membership of PMI through various media and liaisons. The project team is to consist of no less than ten members, including the project manager. General qualifications to be sought by SPT in recruiting will be:

Project management plan	
	Mandatory • Acceptance of the project plan • Demonstrated capability for strategic, generalised or intuitive thinking • Capability to write clearly on technical subject matter for general audiences • Capability to work co-operatively with well-developed interpersonal skills • Be conversant in English and be able to use telephone and internet email telecommunications **As possible** • **Time availability** (team members may contribute at different levels. An average of approximately five to ten hours per month is desired) • **Diversity** (team members collectively may represent diverse nationalities, types of organisations or corporate structure, business sectors, academic disciplines and personal experience) • **Travel** (as determined mutually by the project sponsor and manager, some travel for face to face meetings may be requested)
Approach	The project will progress through the following phases. **Phase 1. Team formation** – recruit and orient volunteer team members. Establish procedures and ground rules for group process and decision making. **Phase 2. Subject matter clarification** – identify and clarify initial scope and definitions of project subject matter. **Phase 3a. Exploration** – begin brainstorming (through gathering, sharing, and discussion) of data and views in an unrestricted, non-judgmental process. **Phase 3b. Selection** – conclude brainstorming (through evaluation and acceptance or rejection) of collected data and views. As the conclusion to this phase, the SPT will review as an interim deliverable the selection made by the project team. **Phase 4. Development** – conduct further research and discussion to develop accepted subject matter. **Phase 5. Articulation** – write a series of drafts to state the accepted and developed subject matter as appropriate for the project business need and product description. **Phase 6. Adoption** – submit product to SPT for the official PMI standards approval and adoption process. Revise product as needed. **Phase 7. Closeout** – perform closure for team and administrative matters. Deliver project files to SPT.
Acceptance	The project manager will submit the final product and any interim deliverables to the SPT for formal acceptance. The SPT may (1) accept the product as delivered by the project team, or (2) return the product to the team with a statement of specific requirements to make the product fully acceptable. The acceptance decision of the SPT is to be provided to the project manager in writing.
Change management	Requests for change to this plan may be initiated by either the project sponsor or the project manager. All change requests will be reviewed and approved or rejected by a formal proceeding of the SPT with input and interaction with the project manager. Decisions of the SPT will be documented and provided to the project manager in writing. All changes will be incorporated into this document, reflected by a new version number and date.

<table>
<tr><th colspan="2">Project management plan</th></tr>
<tr><td>Communication and reporting</td><td>The project manager and team will communicate with and report to the PMI SPT as follows.
Monthly status reports – written monthly status and progress reports are to include:
• Work accomplished since the last report
• Work planned to be performed during the next reporting period
• Deliverables submitted since the last report
• Deliverables planned to be submitted during the next reporting period
• Work tasks in progress and currently outside of expectations for scope, quality, schedule or cost
• Risks identified and actions taken or proposed to mitigate
• Lessons learnt
• Summary statement for posting on PMI website
Monthly resource reports – written monthly resource reports are to include:
Financial resources
• Total funds allocated
• Total funds expended to date
• Estimated expenditures for the next reporting period
• Estimated expenditures for entire project to completion
Human resources
• List of all volunteer team members categorised by current involvement (ie active, new (pre-active), inactive and resigned)
• Current number of new and active volunteer team members
• Estimated number of volunteer team members needed for project completion
Milestone and critical status reports – additional status reports are to be submitted as mutually agreed upon by SPT and the project manager, and are to include at least the following items.
• Milestone status reports are to include the same items as the monthly status reports, summarised to cover an entire project phase period since the last milestone report, or entire project to date.
• Critical status reports are to focus on work tasks outside of expectations and other information as requested by SPT or stipulated by the project manager.</td></tr>
<tr><td>Plan acceptance</td><td>Signature and date</td></tr>
<tr><td>By PMI SPT</td><td>______________________________12 July 20X0
Fred Jones – PMI Technical Research and Standards Manager</td></tr>
<tr><td>By project manager</td><td>______________________________20 July 20X0
Joe Bloggs – PMI Member</td></tr>
</table>

The format and contents of a project management plan will **vary** depending on the organisation involved and the complexity of the project. The contents page and introduction from a detailed project management plan relating to a software implementation project at a call centre follow.

CASE STUDY

Call centre software implementation – project management plan

CONTENTS		Page
1	INTRODUCTION	
2	PROJECT ROLES	
3	COMMUNICATIONS PLAN	
4	TRAINING PLAN	
5	CHANGE MANAGEMENT PLAN	
6	QUALITY MANAGEMENT	
7	PROJECT DOCUMENTATION	
8	FINANCIAL MANAGEMENT	
9	PROGRAMME MANAGEMENT	

SECTION 1

INTRODUCTION

1.1 Purpose of the project management plan

The purpose of this plan is to define the working relationship between Project Team (PT) and the Manager, Customer Centres Group (MCCG). It details the level of service to be provided by PT to the client and the associated cost. If the nature of the project changes, or if situations develop that indicate a need for modification, then this plan will be altered accordingly in consultation with the client. This plan details key milestones, the methods for delivering these milestones, and responsibilities of the project manager, project owner and the project team representatives.

1.2 Project objective

To develop and fully support a call centre environment that promotes the achievement of '80% of all incoming calls resolved at the first point of contact'.

1.3 Project deliverable

To deliver to the MCCG fully commissioned and operational system upgrades as defined within this project plan, including an appropriately skilled call centre team, by 15 April 20X0 at an estimated PT cost of $123,975.

Note. Only the contents page and introduction of this comprehensive plan are reproduced here.

3.3 Progress report

KEY TERM

A PROGRESS REPORT shows the current status of the project, usually in relation to the planned status.

The frequency and contents of progress reports will vary depending on the length of, and the progress being made on, a project.

The report is a **control tool** intended to show the discrepancies between where the project is, and where the plan says it should be.

A common form of progress reports uses two columns – one for **planned** time and expenditure and one for **actual**.

Any additional content will depend on the format adopted. Some organisations include only the 'raw facts' in the report, and use these as a basis for discussion regarding reasons for variances and action to be taken, at a project review meeting.

Other organisations (particularly those involved in long, complex projects) produce more comprehensive progress reports, with more explanation and comment.

The report should monitor progress towards key **milestones**.

A progress report may include a milestone slip chart, which compares planned and actual progress towards project milestones. Planned progress is shown on the X-axis and actual progress on the Y-axis. Where actual progress is slower than planned progress, **slippage** has occurred.

Milestone slip chart

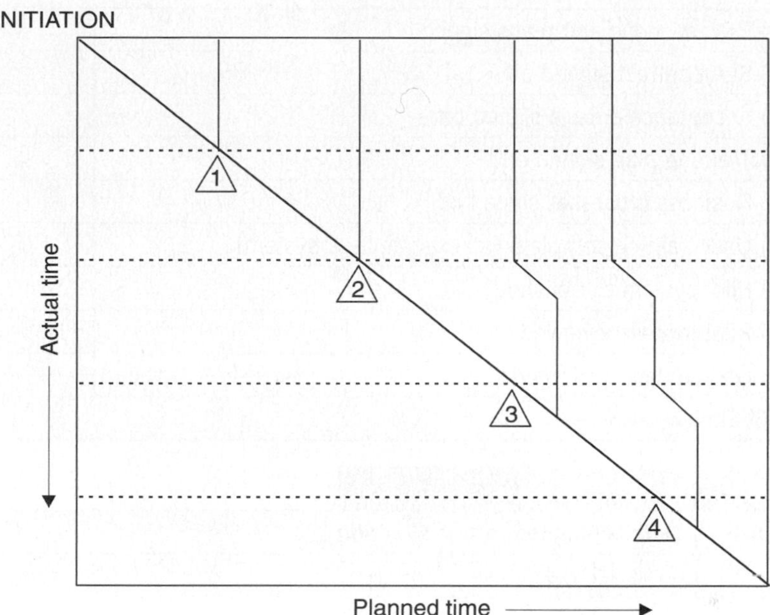

On the chart above, milestones are indicated by a triangle on the diagonal planned progress line. The vertical lines that meet milestones 1 and 2 are straight, showing that these milestones were achieved on time.

At milestone 3, some slippage has occurred. The chart shows that no further slippage is expected, as the progress line for milestone 4 is the same distance to the right as occurred at milestone 3.

We look at ways of dealing with slippage later in this chapter.

The progress report should also include an updated budget status – such a report could adopt the format shown in the following example.

PROJECT STATUS REPORT

Project title: software implementation **To date: 11 May 20X0**

OVERALL STATUS	**Behind XX days**	On target	Ahead........days

KEY MILESTONES

	Plan	**Actual**
(1) Project scope and plans signed off		
(2) SLA/contract signed off		
(3) Acceptance criteria signed off		
(4) Training plan signed off		
(5) Business processes signed off		
(6) User training complete (on existing 'test' system)		
(7) Pilot system established		
(8) Pilot system reviewed		
(9) Go live date confirmed		
(10) Go live		

IMPACT OF SLIPPAGES

M/s	**Details/planned remedial action**	**Date**

KEY RISKS

Ref	**Description**	**Management actions**	**Date**

KEY ISSUES

Ref	**Description**	**Resolve by date**

FINANCIAL STATUS

$'000	*(a)* *Initial budget*	*(b)* *Current budget (inc approved changes)*	*(c)* *Actual spend to date*	*(d)* *Forecast spend to complete*	*(e)* *Variance*	*Reason*
Capital						
Fixed						
Variable						
Ongoing						
Fixed						
Variable						
Total						

Note. Variance = (c + d) – b

Other comments (notable achievements/major changes/planned absences etc):

Project Manager..

Project Sponsor...

3.4 Completion report

The COMPLETION REPORT summarises the results of the project, and includes client sign-off.

On project completion, the project manager will produce the **completion report**. The main purpose of the completion report is to document (and gain client sign-off for) the end of the project.

The report should include a **summary** of the project outcome. The completion report should contain:

(a) Project objectives and the outcomes achieved

(b) The final project budget report, showing expected and actual expenditure (if an external client is involved, this information may be sensitive – the report may exclude or 'amend' the budget report)

(c) A brief outline of time taken compared with the original schedule

The completion report will also include provision for any **ongoing issues** that will need to be addressed after completion. Such issues would be related to the project, but not part of the project. (If they are part of the project, the project is not yet complete!) An example of an ongoing issue would be a procedure for any 'bugs' that become apparent **after** a new software program has been tested and approved.

Responsibilities and procedures relating to any such issues should be laid down in the report.

The manager may find it useful to distribute a provisional report and request **feedback**. This should ensure the version presented for client sign-off at the completion meeting is acceptable to all parties.

A more detailed review of the project follows a few months after completion: the post-completion audit.

3.5 The post-completion audit

The POST-COMPLETION AUDIT is a formal review of the project that examines the lessons that may be learned and used for the benefit of future projects.

The audit looks at all aspects of the project with regard to two questions.

(a) Did the end result of the project meet the **client's expectations**?

(i) The actual **design** and **construction** of the end product
(ii) Was the project achieved **on time**?
(iii) Was the project **completed within budget**?

(b) Was the **management of the project** as successful as it might have been, or were there bottlenecks or problems? This review covers two things.

(i) Problems that might occur on future projects with similar characteristics
(ii) The performance of the team individually and as a group

In other words, any project is an opportunity to learn how to manage future projects more effectively. It should be clear that the audit thus has the potential to reduce the costs associated with future projects. Where senior management are reluctant to incur the expense involved in an audit, a cost-benefit analysis may be carried out to demonstrate the likely effect on future costs.

The post-completion audit should involve **input from the project team**. A simple questionnaire could be developed for all team members to complete, and a reasonably informal meeting held to obtain feedback on what went well (and why), and what didn't (and why).

KEY POINT

This information should be formalised in a report. The **post-completion audit report** should contain the following.

(a) A **summary** should be provided, emphasising any areas where the structures and tools used to manage the project have been found to be **unsatisfactory**.

(b) A **review** of the end result of the project should be provided, and compared against the results expected. Reasons for any significant **discrepancies** between the two should be provided, preferably with suggestions of how any future projects could **prevent these problems recurring**.

(c) A **cost-benefit review** should be included, comparing the forecast costs and benefits identified at the time of the feasibility study with actual costs and benefits.

(d) **Recommendations** should be made as to any steps that should be taken to **improve** the project management procedures used.

3.6 Project meetings

The multidisciplinary nature of most larger projects makes frequent meetings unavoidable: they are essential for the proper management of project progress. There will be both scheduled, regular meetings and occasional meetings as required. They will be concerned with three main areas of project management.

(a) **Project design review meetings** are held to air technical problems and possible solutions, and to gain approval for design features and changes.

(b) **Project status review meetings** are held regularly to monitor progress and gain approval for schedule changes.

(c) **Problem-solving meetings** are held as required to investigate, define and solve (and gain approval for the solutions to) problems as they arise.

Section summary

A variety of **reports** and other **documentation** is used in project management. The **project charter** authorises the work and cost; various **planning documents** are produced; regular **progress reports** are submitted by the project manager and a **completion report** is produced when the objective has been realised. The post-completion audit should generate a report and recommendations.

Lessons learnt that relate to the way the **project was managed** should contribute to the smooth running of future projects.

A starting point for any new project should be a **review** of the documentation of any **similar projects** undertaken in the past.

4 Compare and contrast project control systems

Introduction

Organisations use a range of systems to control projects. We have already met **PMBOK and PRINCE2.** In this section, we also consider **Six Sigma** and end with a quick review of other systems.

4.1 Project Management Body of Knowledge (PMBOK) and PRINCE2

We have already mentioned the US **PMI** and the **Guide to the Project Management Body of Knowledge** (PMBOK). This is widely used by specialists.

4.2 Six Sigma

4.2.1 The search for perfection

Six Sigma was originally a scheme of improvement for quality in manufacturing, but it has been adapted to project management.

'Sigma' is a measure of statistical variation. Six Sigma indicates near perfection. It is a rigorous operating methodology aimed to ensure complete customer satisfaction by ingraining a culture of excellence, responsiveness and accountability within an organisation.

Six Sigma requires the delivery of **defect-free products or services** 99.9997% of the time. Thus, only three out of a million products or services offered would fail to meet the customer's expectations. The average company runs at around Three Sigma, or 66,800 errors per million.

This superior target for operations and product designs requires **Six Sigma programs** that constantly measure and analyse data on the variables in any process. These then use statistical techniques to understand what improvements will drive down defects.

These programs also incorporate a system for gathering customer feedback.

4.2.2 The five key steps

Six Sigma entails five key steps. These can be memorised as the acronym **DMAIC**. These are the steps an organisation should take when looking at **improving processes**.

Define. Identify the customer requirements, clarify the problem and set goals.

Measure. Select what needs to be measured, identify information sources and gather data.

Analyse. Develop hypotheses, identify the key variables and root causes.

Improve. Generate solutions and put them into action, either modifying existing processes or developing new ones. Quantify costs and benefits.

Control. Develop monitoring processes for continued high-quality performance.

Organisations can also apply Six Sigma to **new processes**, and the steps here are define, measure, analyse, design and verify or **DMADV**.

4.2.3 The benefits

Benefits claimed for Six Sigma include:

(a) **Making processes more rigorous** by using hard, timely data, not opinions or gut feel, to make operating decisions

(b) **Cultivating customer loyalty** by delivering superior value

(c) **Strengthening and rewarding teamwork** by aligning employees around complex processes whose performance can still be easily, clearly and empirically measured

(d) **Accustoming managers to operating in a fast-moving internal business environment** that increasingly mirrors marketplace conditions outside the company

(e) **Achieving quantum leaps** in product performance

(f) **Reducing variation in service processes**, such as the time from order to delivery, or offering a consistent, high-quality service experience

(g) **Improving financial performance**, through cost savings from projects, increased revenue from improved products and expanded operating margins

4.3 Other control systems

As we mentioned earlier in the Study Text, the **Carnegie Mellon Software Engineering Institute** has developed management processes and methodologies for improving the quality of new software, such as **IDEAL** and **INTRO**.

Section summary

Other systems which may be used to control projects can include Six Sigma, IDEAL and INTRO.

5 Project troubleshooting

Introduction

This is where project managers really earn their money, dealing with problems!

Project managers need to manage any number of conflicting requirements and trade-offs. These trade-offs concern time, cost and quality. One of the major problems a project manager must cope with is slippage where project targets begin to fall behind.

5.1 Project management problems

Project managers are often appointed from the ranks of technical experts. Technical ability is no guarantee of management skill – an individual might be highly proficient technically, but not a good manager.

The project manager has a number of **conflicting requirements**.

(a) The project sponsor wants the project **delivered on time**, to specification and within budget.

(b) **User** expectations may be misunderstood, ignored or unrealistic.

(c) The project manager has to plan and supervise the work of **experts** in fields about which they may have little knowledge.

(d) The project manager needs to develop an **appropriate management style**. What they should realise is the extent to which the project will fail if users are not consulted, or if the project team is unhappy. As the project manager needs to encourage participation from users, an excessively authoritarian style is not suitable.

(e) The project manager may accept **an unrealistic deadline** – the timescale is fixed early in the planning process. User demands may be accepted as deadlines before sufficient consideration is given to the realism of this.

(f) **Poor or non-existent planning** is a recipe for disaster. Unrealistic deadlines would be identified much earlier if a proper planning process was undertaken.

(g) A lack of **monitoring** and **control**.

(h) Users **change their requirements**, resulting in costly changes to the system as it is being developed.

5.2 Trade-offs in project objectives – the iron triangle

The relationship between key project objectives can be shown as a triangle.

The time/cost/quality triangle

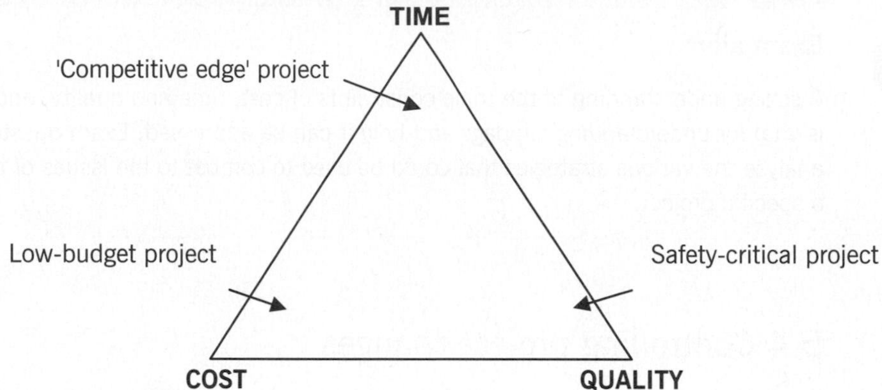

All three objectives are important: we would like our projects to finish on time, within budget **and** to the level of quality/performance required. However:

(a) The **relative importance** of each objective may depend partly on the type of project. Where a project is aiming to beat a competitor to market, or has a non-negotiable deadline (eg organising an event that has been advertised for a particular date) time will be a priority. In a low-budget or fixed-grant project, cost is a priority: once resources run out, the project ceases – complete or not! In a safety-critical project (such as building or aircraft construction) quality is a priority.

(b) This inevitably requires **trade-offs** between the three objectives. Schedule slippage could be brought back on track by extra expenditure, for example, or cost slippage could be brought back on track by 'cutting corners' on quality. Ideally, such decisions should be taken within a framework of stakeholder expectations and consultation.

The balance of time, cost and quality will influence decision making throughout the project – for example, whether to spend an extra $5,000 to fix a problem completely or only spend $1,000 on a quick fix and implement a user work-around.

5.3 Dealing with slippage

When a project has slipped behind schedule, there is a range of options open to the project manager. Some of these options are summarised in the following table.

Action	Comment
Do nothing	After considering all options, it may be decided that things should be allowed to continue as they are.
Add resources	If capable staff are available and it is practicable to add more people to certain tasks, it may be possible to recover some lost ground. Could some work be subcontracted?
Work smarter	Consider whether the methods currently being used are the most suitable – for example, could prototyping be used?
Replan	If the assumptions the original plan was based on have been proved invalid, a more realistic plan should be devised.
Reschedule	A complete replan may not be necessary – it may be possible to recover some time by changing the phasing of certain deliverables.
Introduce incentives	If the main problem is team performance, incentives such as bonus payments could be linked to work deadlines and quality.

Action	Comment
Change the specification	If the original objectives of the project are unrealistic given the time and money available, it may be necessary to negotiate a change in the specification.

Exam alert

A strong understanding of the triple constraints of cost, time and quality, and the trade-offs between them is vital for understanding slippage and how it can be addressed. Exam questions may require you to analyse the various strategies that could be used to combat to the issues of time, cost and quality within a specific project.

5.4 Controlling project changes

Some of the reactions to slippage discussed above would involve changes that would significantly affect the overall project. Other possible causes of changes to the original project plan include:

(a) The availability of new technology
(b) Changes in personnel
(c) A realisation that user requirements were misunderstood
(d) Changes in the business environment
(e) New legislation, eg data protection

The **earlier** a change is made, the **less expensive** it should prove. However, changes will cost time and money and should not be undertaken lightly.

When considering a change, **an investigation** should be conducted to discover:

(a) The consequences of **not** implementing the proposed change
(b) The impact of the change on **time, cost** and **quality**
(c) The expected costs and benefits of the change
(d) The risks associated with the change, and with the status quo

Furthermore, consideration needs to be given to a range of alternatives and their implications before selecting an appropriate course of action. Gido and Clements' **project control process** indicates the stages involved.

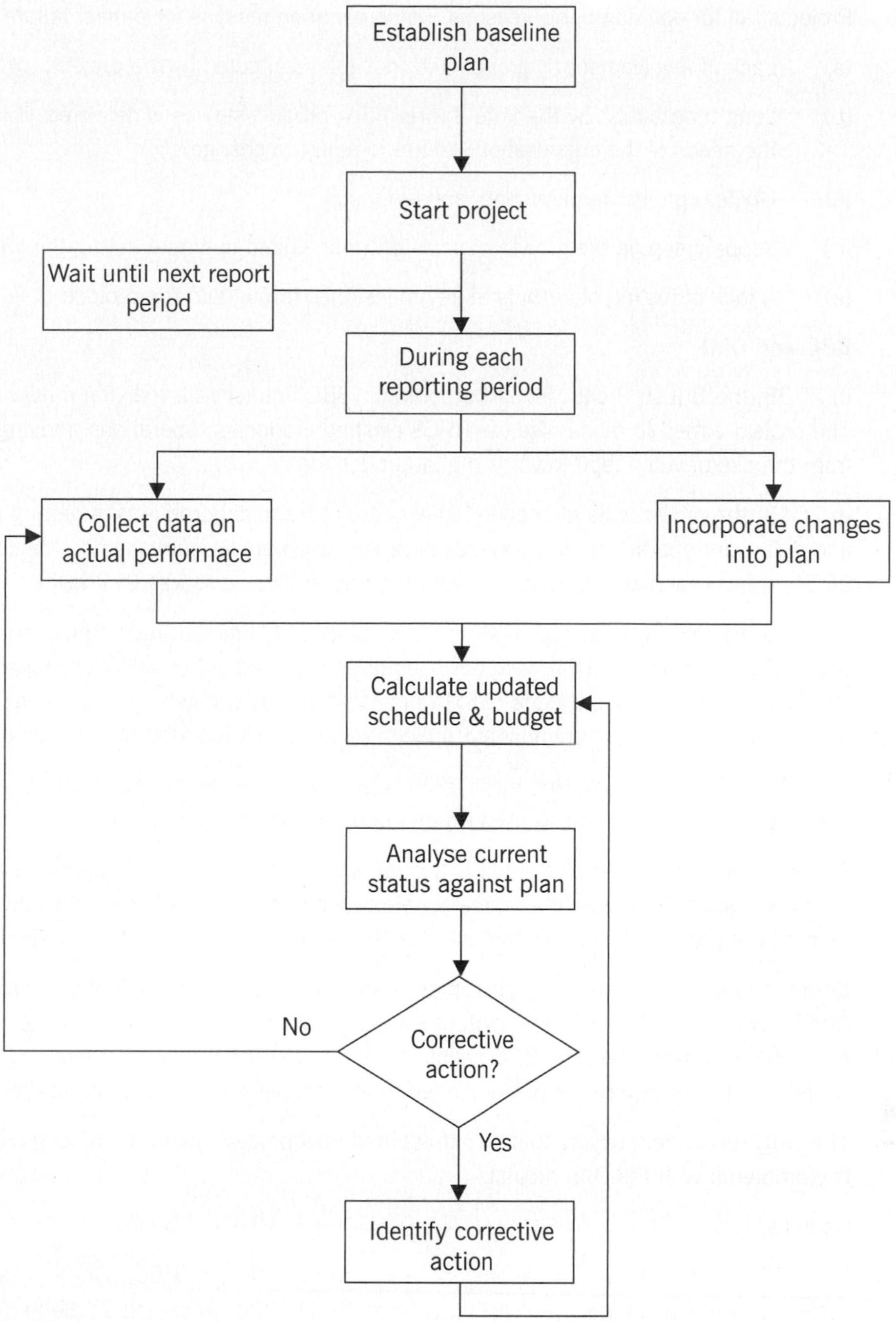

Establish baseline plan → Start project → During each reporting period → Collect data on actual performace / Incorporate changes into plan → Calculate updated schedule & budget → Analyse current status against plan → Corrective action? (No → Collect data on actual performace; Yes → Identify corrective action → Calculate updated schedule & budget). Wait until next report period → During each reporting period.

Project control process (Gido and Clements)

The process of ensuring that proper consideration is given to the impact of proposed changes is known as **change control**. The project manager will be responsible for this monitoring, as well as reporting it to key stakeholders such as the project sponsor. Planning tools such as Gantt charts and network charts will assist in identifying issues.

5.5 Project failure

A project fails if it is not delivered **on time**, **within budget** and to the **required level of quality**. In reality, the majority of projects fail in one or more of these criteria. Some projects fail so badly that they are cancelled before they are delivered.

Projects fail for any number of reasons. Some common reasons for project failure include:

(a) Lack of involvement by groups and individuals affected by the project.

(b) Long timescales. By the time the resulting product/service is delivered, it is no longer relevant to the needs of the organisation (failure to adapt to change).

(c) Unclear project requirements and planning.

(d) Scope creep, ie the growth in scale of the intended outcome during the life of the project.

(e) A lack of testing of outputs at key milestones throughout the project.

CASE STUDY

BBC and DMI

In 2008, the British Broadcasting Corporation (BBC) launched the digital media initiative (DMI) project. The project aimed to modernise the BBC's existing production operations, moving the corporation away from the use of video tape towards digital production.

In 2013, the project was abandoned after years of technical problems in getting the technology to work and delays in reporting on the project's progress. In an article published on the BBC website in February 2014, the corporation reported that the estimated project cost was £125.9m.

The Guardian newspaper, highlighting the findings of a National Audit Office inquiry, reported that the deteriorating fortunes of DMI were not adequately reported either within management or, critically, to the BBC Trust. For example, a 'code red' warning from the BBC's own internal project management office from February 2012 of the imminent project failure wasn't reported to the trust until July of that year.

The BBC Director General (the most senior executive officer at the organisation) at the time had believed that the technology was being used on programmes including the early-evening 'One Show'.

A later report by the 'National Audit Office reported that the BBC had hoped to save £98m by introducing the new system. However, the final estimate of the benefits it brought to the BBC was zero. The report blamed the project's failure on confusion, a lack of planning and insufficient scrutiny'.

Commenting on the National Audit Office report, Margaret Hodge, MP of the Public Accounts Committee (the body that oversees UK government spending), wrote: 'this report reads like a catalogue of how not to run a major programme. The BBC needs to learn from the mistakes it made and ensure that it never again spends such a huge amount of licence fee payer's money with almost nothing to show for it'.

The BBC responded, saying that it had adopted new procedures for managing big projects in the light of the problems with the DMI project.

Sources:

BBC (2014) *Mark Thompson apologises over project failure at BBC*. [Online]. Available from: http://www.bbc.co.uk/news/entertainment-arts-26016820 [Accessed 27 September 2016].

Hewlett, S (3 February 2014) BBC's Digital Media Initiative failed because of more than poor oversight. *The Guardian.* [Online] Available from: https://www.theguardian.com/media/media-blog/2014/feb/03/bbc-digital-media-initiative-failed-mark-thompson [Accessed 27 September 2016].

Section summary

Common problems in project management include conflicting requirements for time, cost and quality at the outset; changing user requirements; the need to supervise experts; poor planning; and poor control.

6 Projects and continuous improvement

Introduction

Continuous improvement applies to projects especially where they become a routine means of working in organisations. In that case project managers must think about how they might improve the way they run projects.

Project management can be a **core strategic competence** for companies working in such industries as consulting and construction. Such companies must ensure that they maintain and improve their project management abilities if they are to continue to be commercially successful. Failure to address weaknesses in an organisation's project management methodology increases the scope for errors and poor practice to occur again during future projects.

Continuous improvement requires that project management is placed at the centre of a single corporate methodology. This involves the development of an organisational culture which supports the need for continuous improvement to the way projects are managed.

The preparation of the project completion report and post-completion audit are important elements in the continuous improvement of projects. Undertaking these activities allows the project manager to reflect on those elements of the project that went well and those where lessons can be taken forward for future projects.

Section summary

Where project management is a core competence, **a continuous improvement** approach should be taken to developing and consolidating the methodology.

Chapter Summary

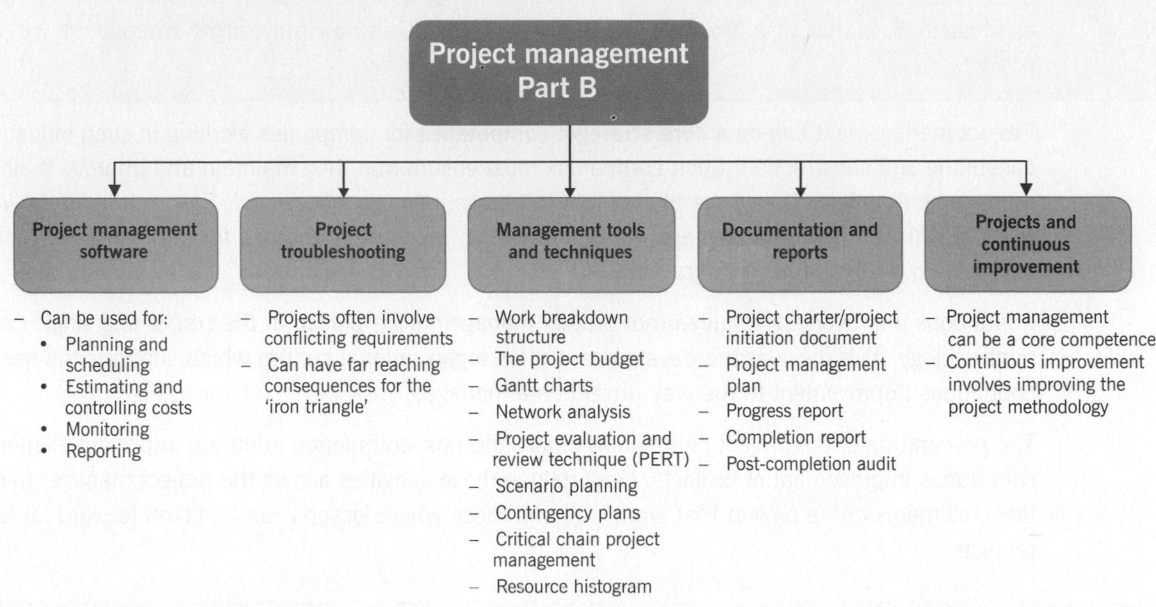

Project management Part B
Project management software
– Can be used for:
• Planning and scheduling
• Estimating and controlling costs
• Monitoring
• Reporting
Project troubleshooting
– Projects often involve conflicting requirements
– Can have far reaching consequences for the 'iron triangle'
Management tools and techniques
– Work breakdown structure
– The project budget
– Gantt charts
– Network analysis
– Project evaluation and review technique (PERT)
– Scenario planning
– Contingency plans
– Critical chain project management
– Resource histogram
Documentation and reports
– Project charter/project initiation document
– Project management plan
– Progress report
– Completion report
– Post-completion audit
Projects and continuous improvement
– Project management can be a core competence
– Continuous improvement involves improving the project methodology

Quick Quiz

1 What would you expect a project initiation document to contain?

2 What is work breakdown structure?

3 What is the purpose of a Gantt chart?

4 What is the project quality plan used for?

5 Why do many project managers prefer to use project management software?

6 An approach to project management that uses buffers to flexibly respond to the uncertainties of time estimating is:

A Critical path analysis
B Project management maturity
C Critical chain project management
D PERT

Answers to Quick Quiz

1 Contents could include: project objectives, the scope of the project, overall budget, final deadlines, the ultimate customer, resources, risks inherent in the project, a preliminary project plan (targets, activities and so on) and details of how the project is to be organised and managed.

2 Work breakdown structure (WBS) is the process of breaking down the project into manageable tasks.

3 A Gantt chart displays the time relationships between tasks in a project. It is a horizontal bar chart used to estimate the amount and timing of resources required.

4 The project quality plan is used to guide both project execution and project control. It outlines how the project will be planned, monitored and implemented.

5 A project management software package saves time and produces high-quality output. As with all software, it is dependent on the quality of the data fed into the package – the length of time required for each activity of the project, the logical relationships between each activity, the resources available and when the resources are available.

6 C (PERT has a similar orientation, in accounting for uncertainty, but is a very different approach.)

Answers to Questions

9B.1 Terminology

The answer is B: Gantt. Some people find this extremely difficult to get right.

9B.2 Dummy activity

The problem arises because D can only start when both B and C have been finished, whereas E is only required to follow B. The only way to draw the network is to use a dummy activity.

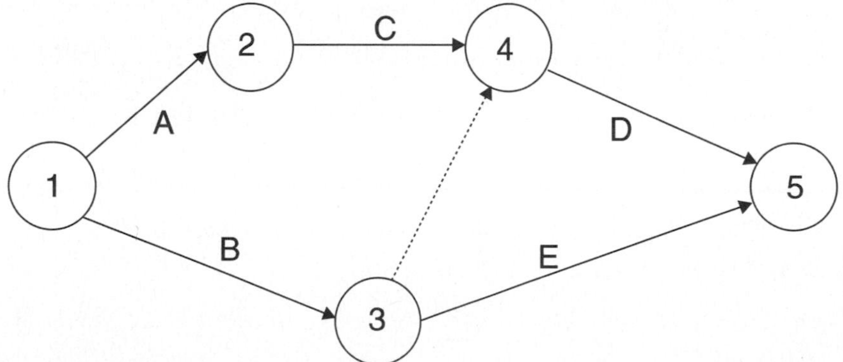

Now try these questions from the Practice Question Bank

Question	Level
9B.1 – 9B.5	Practice
Critical path analysis	Practice

THE PROJECT TEAM

The final chapter of the Study Text brings our discussion of project management to a close.

So far, we have looked at the technical practicalities involved in managing and controlling project work. In this chapter, we explore human aspects of project management.

We start the chapter by giving consideration to the role, responsibilities and skills of the project manager.

Then we briefly review the interaction between project work and organisational structure, before considering the impact that different stakeholders have on the outcome of the project.

The chapter finishes with a focus on the importance of teams and the role they play in project management.

Remember that this paper covers a number of integrated themes, so much of the material covered earlier in the Study Text can be directly applied to project working. So, for example, you need to think about leadership, and conflict in the context of a **project** team. We won't be repeating ourselves here and you can simply recap earlier chapters if you need to.

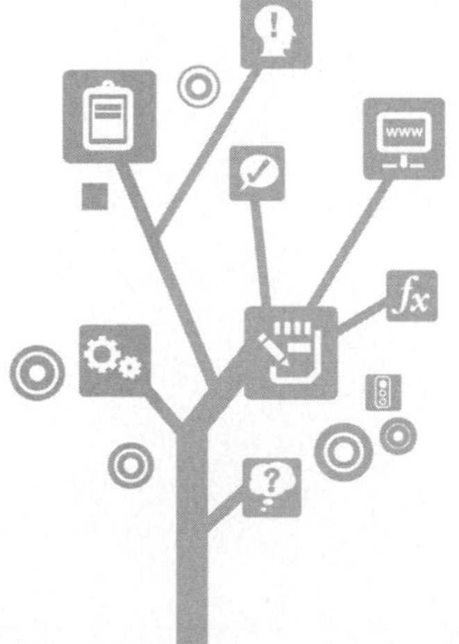

Topic list	Learning outcomes	Syllabus references	Ability required
1 The project manager	D2c	D2(ii)	Analysis
2 Projects and organisational structure	D2c	D2(i)	Analysis
3 Roles and management of project stakeholders	D2c	D2(iii), (iv), (v)	Analysis
4 Leading, managing and motivating teams	D2c C1a	D2(vi), (vii) C1(i), (ii), (iii), (iv), (v)	Analysis Evaluation

Chapter Overview

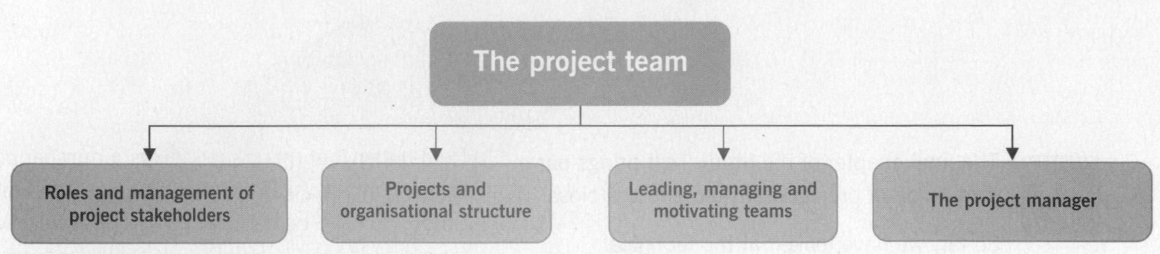

1 The project manager

Introduction

The project manager is dedicated to the running of the project as long as it is in existence. They have significant responsibilities covering task and people management. Often, large projects employ professional project managers who have experience in running projects, as their skills are transferable and they do not have to be a technical specialist.

Some project managers have the job title 'project manager'. These people usually have one major responsibility: the project. Most people in business will have 'normal work' responsibilities outside their project goals – which may lead to conflicting demands on their time. Anybody responsible for a project (large or small) is a project manager.

KEY TERM

The person who takes ultimate responsibility for ensuring the desired result is achieved on time and within budget is the **PROJECT MANAGER.**

The role a project manager performs is in many ways similar to those performed by other managers. There are, however, some important differences, as shown in the table below.

Project managers	Operations managers
Are often 'generalists' with wide-ranging backgrounds and experience levels	Usually specialists in the areas managed
Oversee work in many functional areas	Relate closely to technical tasks in their area
Facilitate rather than supervise team members	Have direct technical supervision responsibilities

A person should only take on the role of project manager if they have the time available to do the job effectively. Also, if somebody is to be held responsible for the project, they must be given the resources and authority required to complete project tasks.

1.1 Duties of a project manager

The duties of a project manager are summarised below.

Duty	Comment
Outline planning	Project planning (eg targets, sequencing) (a) Developing project targets such as the overall costs and timescale needed (eg project should take 20 weeks). (b) Dividing the project into activities and placing these activities into the right sequence; complicated tasks often overlap. (c) Developing a framework for procedures and structures needed to manage the project (eg decide, in principle, to have weekly team meetings, performance reviews and so on).
Detailed planning	Work breakdown structure, resource requirements, network analysis for scheduling.
Obtain necessary resources	Resources may already exist within the organisation or may have to be bought in. Resource requirements unforeseen at the planning stage will probably have to be authorised separately by the project board or project sponsor.
Teambuilding	Build cohesion and team spirit.

Duty	Comment
Communication	The project manager must let superiors know what is going on, and ensure that members of the project team are properly briefed.
Co-ordinating project activities	Between the project team and users, and other external parties (eg suppliers of hardware and software).
Monitoring and control	The project manager should estimate the causes for each departure from the standard, and take corrective measures.
Problem-resolution	Even with the best planning, unforeseen problems may arise.
Quality control	There is often a short-sighted trade-off between getting the project out on time and the project's quality.

Project management as a discipline developed because of a need to co-ordinate resources to obtain desired results within a set time frame. Common project management tasks include establishing goals and objectives, developing a work plan, scheduling, budgeting, co-ordinating a team and communicating.

The project management process helps project managers maintain control of projects and meet their responsibilities.

1.2 The responsibilities of a project manager

A project manager has responsibilities to both management and the project team.

Responsibilities to management:

(a) Ensure resources are used efficiently – strike a balance between cost, time and results

(b) Keep management informed with timely and accurate communications

(c) Manage the project to the best of their ability

(d) Behave ethically, and adhere to the organisation's policies

(e) Maintain a customer orientation (whether the project is geared towards an internal or external customer) – customer satisfaction is a key indicator of project success

Responsibilities to the project and the project team:

(a) Take action to keep the project on target for successful completion

(b) Ensure the project team has the resources required to perform tasks assigned

(c) Help new team members integrate into the team

(d) Provide any support required when members leave the team either during the project or on completion

1.3 The skills required of a project manager

To meet these responsibilities, a project manager requires a wide range of skills. The skills required are similar to those required when managing a wider range of responsibilities. Some of the skills required are described in the following table.

Type of skill	How the project manager should display the type of skill
Leadership and team building	A participative style of leadership is appropriate for much of most projects, but a more autocratic, decisive style may be required on occasion. Be **positive** (but realistic) about all aspects of the project. Understand where the project fits into the **big picture**. **Delegate** tasks appropriately – and do not take on too much personally. Build team spirit through **co-operation** and recognition of achievement. Do not be restrained by organisational structures – a high tolerance for ambiguity (lack of clear-cut authority) will help the project manager.
Organisational	Ensure all project **documentation** is clear and distributed to all who require it. Use project **management tools** to analyse and monitor project progress.
Communication and negotiation	**Listen** to project team members. Use **persuasion** to coerce reluctant team members or stakeholders to support the project. **Negotiate** on funding, timescales, staffing and other resources, quality and disputes. Ensure management is kept **informed** and is never surprised.
Technical	By providing (or at least providing access to) the **technical expertise** and experience needed to manage the project.
Personal qualities	Be **flexible**. Circumstances may develop that require a change in plan. Show **persistence**. Even successful projects will encounter difficulties that require repeated efforts to overcome. Be **creative**. If one method of completing a task proves impractical, a new approach may be required. **Patience** is required, even in the face of tight deadlines. The 'quick-fix' may eventually cost more time than a more thorough but initially more time-consuming solution.
Problem solving	Only the very simplest projects will be without problems. The project manager must bring a sensible approach to their solution, and **delegate** as much responsibility as possible to team members so that they become used to **solving their own problems**. By the nature of a project, there is always uncertainty and risk. The project manager needs to be able to react to these situations fast, and adopt an efficient problem-solving attitude, so as not to hold up the project at key moments.
Change control and management	Major projects may be accompanied by the kind of far-reaching **change** that has wide-ranging effects on the organisation and its people. Here, however, we are concerned with **changes to the project itself**. Changes can arise from a variety of sources (not least the intended end-users) and have the potential to disrupt the progress of the project. They must be properly authorised, planned and resourced, with records kept of their source, impact and authorisation if the project is not to become unmanageable. **Change control** is one of the components of the **PRINCE2** project management system.

1.4 Leadership styles and project management

As in other forms of management, different project managers have different styles of leadership. There is no 'best' leadership style, as individuals suit and react to different styles in different ways.

The leadership style adopted will affect the way decisions relating to the project are made. Although an autocratic style may prove successful in some situations (eg 'simple' or 'repetitive' projects), a more consultative style has the advantage of making team members feel more a part of the project. This should result in greater **commitment**.

Not all decisions will be made in the same way. For example, decisions that do not have direct consequences for other project personnel may be made with no (or limited) consultation. A **balance** needs to be found between ensuring decisions can be made efficiently, and ensuring adequate consultation.

The type of people that comprise the project team will influence the style adopted. For example, professionals generally dislike being closely supervised and dictated to. Some people, however, prefer to follow clear, specific instructions and not have to think for themselves.

Project management techniques encourage **management by exception** by identifying, from the outset, those activities that might threaten successful completion of a project.

Section summary

The person who takes ultimate responsibility for ensuring the desired result is achieved on time and within budget is the **project manager**.

Duties of the project manager include: planning, team building, communication, co-ordinating project activities, monitoring and control, problem resolution and quality control.

Project managers require the following **skills**: leadership and team building, organisational ability, communication skills (written, spoken, presentations and meetings), some technical knowledge of the project area and interpersonal skills.

2 Projects and organisational structure

Introduction

Projects are better suited to flatter organisational structures, where individuals opt in and out of the project as they are needed. The project can employ people as they are needed, which means they are a flexible labour force or it can use existing employees co-opted into the project for the time their skills are needed.

Traditional organisational structures are hierarchical with layers of management. Many modern organisations have undergone restructuring to cut out layers of management. These flatter structures are claimed to simplify decision making and will therefore affect how projects are managed in the organisation.

Project managers usually have to work within the structure that exists. Depending on their influence, they may have input in determining the structure in which the project is managed.

We outline a few organisational structures used in project management here.

2.1 Pure project organisation

This structure is described by Maylor in *Project Management*, 2003.

It is typical in the construction industry, where the workforce is flexible and changes over the project life cycle depending on the needs of the project. The project organisation consists of a project board, which is permanent, and made up of managers, directors and administration staff.

This board oversees the work of the project manager who co-ordinates the project team over the life of the project. The team will be *ad hoc*, brought together to compete tasks at certain stages in the project.

The organisation has **advantages** including:

(a) **A flexible labour force drafted in as needed**. So lawyers and architects would be engaged at the planning stage. Contractors would be used during the construction phase.

(b) **A saving on employment costs**, as the workforce is only engaged and paid at certain points in the project.

There are also **disadvantages**, including the **temporary nature of the team** which means there may be little commitment to success. Members of the team may not be able to pass on what they have learnt once they leave, and there is little continuity over the life of the project.

2.2 Matrix management

An alternative form of organisational structure is the matrix structure.

Matrix structures attempt to ensure co-ordination across functional lines by the embodiment of dual authority in the organisation structure. Matrix structures provide for the formalisation of management control between different functions, whilst at the same time maintaining functional departmentation. It can be a mixture of a functional, product and territorial organisation.

The matrix structure is particularly appropriate to project work, especially during the formation of project teams as it requires individuals with diverse skills from across the organisation (eg different departments) to be brought together. As the following diagram illustrates, project team members are expected to undertake a dual role, by undertaking their departmental duties and combining this with membership of the project team.

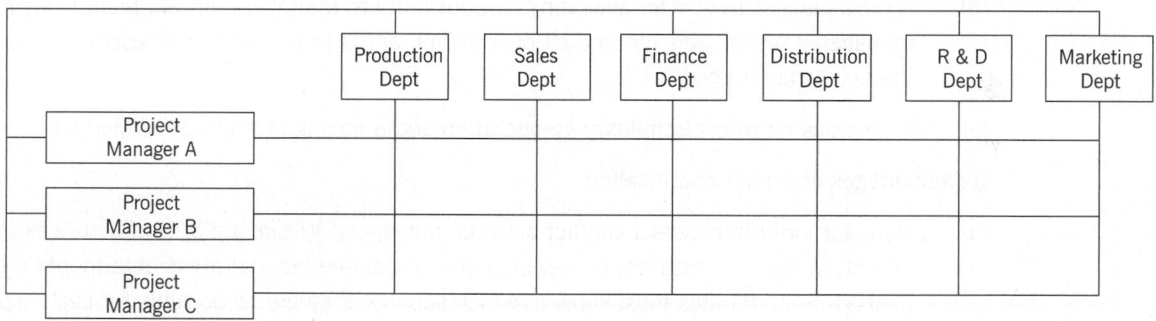

The diagram highlights the strong focus that the matrix structure places on both horizontal and vertical relations within the organisation. A key feature of this structure is that project team members are required to report to two managers (the project manager and head of department). Matrix structures are commonly found in organisations which are continually involved in project work; examples include the construction industry and audit (internal and external) and consultancy work.

The authority of project managers may vary from organisation to organisation. Once again, the division of authority between project managers and functional managers must be carefully defined. A matrix structure is most suitable in the following situations:

(a) There is a fairly large number of different functions, each of great importance.

(b) There could be communications problems between functional management in different functions (eg marketing, production, R&D, personnel, finance).

(c) Work is supposed to flow smoothly between these functions, but communications problems might stop or hinder the workflow.

(d) There is a need to carry out uncertain, interdependent tasks. Work can be structured so as to be **task centred**, with task managers (project managers) appointed to look after each task, and provide the communications (and co-operation) between different functions.

(e) Where projects are customer-facing it is important that the customer has a point of contact to deal with their queries.

2.2.1 Challenges of matrix management

Matrix management **challenges classical ideas** about organisational structure by rejecting the idea of one person, one boss. A subordinate cannot easily take orders from two or more bosses, and so an arrangement has to be established, perhaps along the following lines.

(a) A subordinate takes orders from one boss (the functional manager) and the second boss (the project manager) has to ask the first boss to give certain instructions to the subordinate.

(b) A subordinate takes orders from one boss about some specified matters and orders from the other boss about different specified matters. The authority of each boss would have to be carefully defined. Even so, good co-operation between the bosses would still be necessary.

2.2.2 Project achievement and matrix management

Advantages of a matrix structure

(a) It offers greater **flexibility**. This applies both to **people**, as employees adapt more quickly to a new challenge or new task, and develop an attitude which is geared to accepting change; and to **task and structure**, as the matrix may be formed for the short or long term.

(b) It should improve **communication** within the organisation.

(c) Dual authority gives the organisation **multiple orientation** so that functional specialists do not get wrapped up in their own concerns.

(d) It provides a **structure for allocating responsibility to managers for end results**. A product manager is responsible for product profitability, and a project leader is responsible for ensuring that the task is completed.

(e) It provides for **interdisciplinary co-operation** and a mixing of skills and expertise.

Disadvantages of matrix organisation

(a) Dual authority threatens a **conflict** between managers. Where a matrix structure exists it is important that the authority of superiors should not overlap and areas of authority must be clearly defined. Subordinates must know to which superior they are responsible for each aspect of their duties.

(b) One individual with two or more bosses is more likely to suffer **role stress** at work.

(c) It is sometimes more **costly** – eg project managers are additional jobs which would not be required in a simple structure of functional departmentation.

(d) It may be **difficult for the management to accept** a matrix structure. It is possible that a manager may feel threatened that another manager will usurp his or her authority.

(e) It requires **consensus** and **agreement** which may slow down decision making.

2.3 Types of matrix management

Maylor (ibid) notes that 'matrix management was invented as a way of achieving some of the benefits of the project organisation without the disadvantages'.

He describes three styles of matrix organisations used for project management. The advantages and disadvantages of each style are outlined. These stages represent a progression from an outline project team to a fully engaged project team.

2.3.1 Lightweight matrix

The **project manager co-ordinates the project and chairs meetings between the departments involved**. Responsibility for the success of the project is shared by the departments. **This structure has its disadvantages**, including a lack of commitment from the departments and the relative weakness of the project manager compared to departmental managers. These disadvantages may lead to the project being led off course or being neglected in departments with conflicting priorities.

2.3.2 Balanced model

This style of matrix organisation seeks to redress the relative powerlessness of the project manager described above. This is achieved by making part of the income earned by the department dependent on their involvement in the project.

However, the dual responsibilities of departmental managers to the project and their own department may lead to a conflict in loyalties.

Another disadvantage arises from there being a second line of command exercised by department managers in addition to the project manager.

2.3.3 Heavyweight matrix

Departmental members are **seconded to the project on a full-time basis**. They can then devote their time to the project without distraction. The project benefits from drafting in expertise as and when needed.

One disadvantage, however, is clearly to the sponsoring department, which loses its staff for their duration in the project team.

Section summary

Project managers must normally manage projects within the existing structure of their organisation. Certain organisational structures are more suited to project success than others.

3 Roles and management of project stakeholders

Introduction

One of the key roles a project manager has is to keep stakeholders informed and involved in a project. Some stakeholders are hands-off, whereas others are deeply involved in a project. See if you can work out which is which from the list below.

Ensure that you are clear about the differences between **process** and **outcome** stakeholders.

Mendelow's matrix provides a tool for **mapping** stakeholders and suggests strategies for managing them.

KEY TERM

PROJECT STAKEHOLDERS are the individuals and organisations who are involved in or may be affected by project activities.

Project stakeholders may be:

(a) **Process stakeholders**, with an interest in how the project process is conducted (eg those involved in it, those who want a say in it, and those who need to evaluate and learn from it)

(b) **Outcome stakeholders**, with an interest in the outcomes, results or deliverables of the project (eg users of the new system)

We will look at the role of the **project manager** and the **project team** later on. Other key stakeholders are defined as follows.

KEY TERMS

The **PROJECT OWNER** is the person for whom the project is being carried out (eg a client or senior manager), and is primarily interested in the deliverables achieved.

The **PROJECT SPONSOR** provides, and is accountable for, the resources invested into the project and is responsible for the achievement of the project's business objectives.

The **PROJECT BOARD** is the body to which the project manager is accountable for achieving the project objectives. It represents the interests of the project owner and sponsor.

The **PROJECT CHAMPION** represents the project to the rest of the organisation, communicating its vision and objectives, and securing commitment and resources.

PROJECT SUPPORT TEAM is a term used to designate the personnel working on a project who do not report to the project manager administratively.

USERS are the individuals or group that will utilise the end product, process (system), or service produced by the project.

RISK MANAGER. For large projects, it may be necessary to appoint someone to control the process of identifying, classifying and quantifying the risks associated with the project.

QUALITY MANAGER. For large projects, it may be necessary to appoint someone to write the quality plan and develop quality assurance and control procedures.

VENDORS. In any project, many of the components of the solution may be bought in from suppliers or vendors.

SPECIALISTS. Many complex projects will use specialists from within the organisation, eg specialists from human resources and engineering.

3.1 The role of the management accountant in project work

One specialist project stakeholder it is important not to overlook is the management accountant. The skills of the management accountant are well suited to supporting project teams, as they are able to monitor project progress from a financial perspective.

Management accountants are ideally placed to fulfil key project roles including:

(a) Project manager – management accountants possess a broad skill-set which lends itself to project work, including financial expertise and problem-solving skills, leadership and communication skills, all of which are key attributes of a good project manager.

(b) Project sponsor – management accountants can serve as the project sponsor by providing and monitoring the resources invested in the project.

(c) Project end user – management accountants may be affected by projects and will play a part in evaluating how a project will impact the finance function.

(d) Project team member – the management accountant may form part of the project team and play a significant role in analysing the project from a finance perspective and provide advice to the project manager on financial matters.

In the case of large-scale projects, it is common practice for the project team to be supported by a dedicated project accounting function distinct from the organisation's main finance department.

The management accountant can support the project team in a number of ways, including:

(a) Conducting a cost-benefit analysis of the project proposal as part of the feasibility study

(b) Working with the project manager to produce project budgets and forecasts

(c) Updating the project accounting system to ensure that accurate project information is recorded

(d) Maintaining a complete audit trail of project documentation to facilitate the post-completion audit

(e) Arranging stage payments to project suppliers

(f) Monitoring project progress against the budget and investigating variances

(g) Interpreting variance analysis and communicating this to the project manager to help avoid project slippage (ie cost overruns)

(h) Analysing and interpreting management reports for project team members to facilitate project decision making

(i) Liaising with the project sponsor to discuss additional project resource requirements

3.2 Differing stakeholder interests

Project stakeholders should all be **committed to a common goal** – successful project completion. The project plan should be the common point of reference that states priorities and provides cohesion.

However, the individuals and groups that comprise the stakeholders all have different roles, therefore are likely to have different points of view and perhaps also conflicting objectives (eg user needs vs cost reduction). There is therefore the potential for disagreements between stakeholder groups. The project manager should seek to manage stakeholder expectations and perceptions. Stakeholders must be identified and their interests assessed so that critical relationships may be managed. This is especially important when things go wrong.

Earlier in this Study Text, we discussed the importance of stakeholder mapping and we considered the use of the **Mendelow matrix. The Mendelow matrix** may be used to assist risk management, and focus attention. We cover this briefly below.

KEY POINT

The project manager should be aware of the following matters for each stakeholder or stakeholder group.

(a) Goals
(b) Past attitude and behaviour
(c) Expected future behaviour
(d) Reaction to possible future developments

Exam alert

You should be able to **identify** project stakeholders and what their role is, understand **why** it is important to consider the needs of different stakeholders in a project and suggest ways of **communicating** with stakeholders and securing their support for a project.

3.2.1 Managing stakeholder disputes

The first step is to establish a **framework** to predict the potential for disputes. This involves **managing risk**, since an unforeseen event (a risk) has the potential to create conflict, and **dispute management**: the managing of dispute procedures with minimum impacts on costs, goodwill and progress.

We have already discussed negotiation and resolution techniques in the context of general conflict earlier in this Study Text. Many of the principles discussed previously can be applied to stakeholder conflicts, although the relative positions of the stakeholders involved can complicate matters. Conflict between project stakeholders may be resolved by:

(a) **Negotiation**. The parties discuss the issue with a view to finding mutually acceptable solutions.

(b) **Mediation** (or assisted negotiation). A third party facilitates the negotiation process.

(c) **Partnering**. Creating communication links between project participants with the intention of directing them to a common goal – the project outcome – ahead of their own self-interest.

(d) **Arbitration**. A third party may be asked to intervene to impose a solution.

On very large projects, a **disputes review board** (DRB) may be formed. This may comprise persons directly involved in the project engaged to maintain a 'watching brief' to identify and attend to disputes as they arise. Usually there is a procedure in place that provides for the DRB to make an 'on the spot' decision before a formal dispute is notified so that the project work can proceed, and that may be followed by various rights of review at increasingly higher levels.

Question 10.1 Project board

Learning outcome D2c

What is the role of the project board?

A To represent the interests of the project to the rest of the organisation
B To represent the interests of the project sponsor
C To provide the resources needed to undertake the project
D To implement the project

3.3 Stakeholder power

How stakeholders relate to the management of the company depends very much on what **type** of stakeholder they are – internal, connected or external – and on the level in the management hierarchy at which they are able to **apply pressure**. In the case of projects, internal stakeholders will be employed by the company and so they have a strong interest in the success of the project. Vendors are probably connected stakeholders who would hope for repeat business if the project is successful.

Specific factors that influence stakeholders' power

(a) Seniority (managers)
(b) Reputation
(c) Social status
(d) Shareholding (directors)
(e) Volume of sales (customers)
(f) Volume of purchases (suppliers)
(g) Formal representation (eg trades union staff)
(h) Legal status

The way in which the relationship between a company and stakeholders is conducted is a function of the character of the relationship, the parties' relative bargaining strength and the philosophy underlying each party's objectives. This can be shown as a spectrum.

Spectrum of relationship between organisation and stakeholders

	Weak		*Stakeholders' bargaining strength*			Strong
Company's conduct of relationship	Command/ dictated by company	Consultation and consideration of stakeholders' views	Negotiation	Participation and acceptance of stakeholders' views	Democratic voting by stakeholders	Command/ dictated by stakeholders

3.4 Managing stakeholders – stakeholder mapping

Mendelow classifies stakeholders on a matrix whose axes are **power held** and **level of interest** in the organisation's activities. These factors will help define the type of relationship the project manager should seek with the project stakeholders.

We have already considered the factors that determine the level of power held by a stakeholder but, to plot the stakeholders on the matrix, we will also have to determine their level of interest. This is more difficult to assess, as it depends not only on **where their interests lie**, but also on **how interested they actually are**.

To determine where their interests lie, we would generally assume that most stakeholders would pursue self-interest. For example, we would expect customers to require good quality products or services at a reasonable price, and we would expect employees to require fair payment for their work, job security and good working conditions.

Determining how interested stakeholders actually are, however, can be tricky. Not all stakeholders have the time or the inclination to pay careful attention to the decisions taken by management.

Power \ Level of interest	Low	High
Low	A	B
High	C	D

(a) **Key players** are found in segment D: strategy must be **acceptable** to them, at least. These stakeholders may **participate** in decision making.

(b) Stakeholders in segment C must be treated with care. While often passive, they are capable of moving to segment D. They should therefore be **kept satisfied**.

(c) Stakeholders in segment B do not have great ability to influence strategy, but their views can be important in influencing more powerful stakeholders, perhaps by lobbying. They should therefore be **kept informed**.

(d) **Minimal effort** is expended on segment A.

It is not possible to produce a single, definite map: stakeholders are likely to move about the map as different issues are considered.

Stakeholder mapping is used to assess the significance of stakeholders. This in turn has implications for the organisation.

(a) The framework of **corporate governance** should recognise stakeholders' levels of interest and power.

(b) It may be appropriate to seek to **reposition** certain stakeholders and discourage others from repositioning themselves, depending on their attitudes.

(c) Key **blockers** and **facilitators** of change must be identified.

3.5 Conflicting stakeholder objectives

Since their interests may be widely different, conflict between stakeholders can be quite common. Project managers must take the potential for such conflict into account when setting policy and be prepared to deal with it if it arises in a form that affects the organisation.

Section summary

Project stakeholders are the individuals and organisations who are involved in, or may be affected by, project activities.

4 Leading, managing and motivating teams

Introduction

Paper E2 places a strong emphasis on the role of teams in modern business, as the topic appears in both parts C and D of the syllabus. In this section, we take a step back from project management and look at the importance of teams in a broader organisational setting. We start our discussion with a general look at some of the key issues involved in group work, before exploring the practical issues of team formation and management. We then tailor our review to consider the role of project teams in delivering a successful project.

A team is a form of group with a number of distinguishing features, including **common goals**, **norms** and **team loyalty**. Managers are often called on to lead and manage teams. In these circumstances, it is useful to know something about how teams work. This helps the manager in **selecting and building teams to make them more effective**.

Part of management is **evaluating the team's performance**, much as individuals are assessed on performance, so we have a section on **evaluation in here**.

It is also essential to motivate teams towards greater achievement, so we have included a short section on **team motivation**.

4.1 Groups

KEY TERM

A GROUP is 'any collection of people who perceive themselves to be a group'.

(Charles Handy, 1993)

4.1.1 Types of groups

Four types of group are commonly found in most organisations; these include the following:

(1) **Formal groups** are created by managers to meet specific organisational objectives.

(2) **Informal groups** develop out of individual relationships and are based on shared interests.

(3) **Reference groups** are those that a person wants to join but is not currently a member of.

(4) **Autonomous working groups** are experiments in improving productivity by getting individuals to work in small cells or teams.

4.2 Teams

KEY TERM

A TEAM is a 'small number of people with complementary skills who are committed to a common purpose, performance goals and approach for which they hold themselves mutually accountable'.

(Katzenbach and Smith, 1994)

It is important to note that teams are a type of group but not all groups are teams.

4.2.1 Strengths of team working

Teams are particularly well adapted to the following purposes.

Type of role	Comments
Work organisation	Teams combine the skills of different individuals. Teams are a co-ordinating mechanism: they avoid complex communication between different business functions.
Control	Fear of letting down the team can be a powerful motivator: team loyalty can be used to control the performance and behaviour of individuals.
Ideas generation	Teams can generate ideas, eg through brainstorming and information sharing.
Decision making	Decisions are evaluated from more than one viewpoint, with pooled information. Teams make fewer, but better-evaluated, decisions than individuals.

4.2.2 Limitations and problems of team working

Problems with teams include **conflict** on the one hand, and **groupthink** (excessive cohesion) on the other.

Teams and team working are very much in fashion, but there are potential **drawbacks**.

(a) **Conformity**. Individuals are pressured to agree with the majority against their better judgement.

(b) **The Abilene Paradox**. Group members accept an idea they don't like in the belief that everybody else supports it. In reality, nobody does.

(c) **Groupthink**. A strong culture of self-belief means that ideas generated by the group are not critically evaluated.

(d) **Risky shift**. Individuals recommend higher risk strategies than they normally would because accountability is diluted across the whole group.

(e) **Team working is not suitable for all jobs**: it should be introduced because it leads to better performance, not because people feel better or more secure.

(f) Team processes (especially excessive meetings and seeking consensus) can **delay decision making**: groups make fewer decisions than individuals.

(g) Social relationships might be maintained at the expense of other aspects of performance, or **inter-group conflicts** may get in the way of effective collaboration.

(h) **Group norms** may restrict individual personality and flair, or may suppress work output and performance (so that no individual 'shows up' the team by overproducing).

(i) Due to a process called **social facilitation**, performance of simple tasks at which people are relatively confident **improves** in the presence of other people – but performance of new, complex tasks is **hindered** by the presence of an audience (you may be familiar with this 'flustered' feeling).

4.3 Organising teamwork

Multi-disciplinary teams contain people from different departments, pooling the skills of specialists.

Multi-skilled teams contain people who themselves have more than one skill.

A team may be called together temporarily, to achieve specific task objectives (**project team**), or may be more or less permanent, with responsibilities for a particular product, product group or stage of the production process (a **product or process team**).

There are two basic approaches to the organisation of teamwork: multi-skilled teams and multi-disciplinary teams. Project teams may be of either type.

4.4 Who should be selected for a team?

Team members should be selected for their potential to contribute to getting things done (**task performance**) and establishing good working relationships (**group maintenance**). This may include:

(a) **Specialist skills**. A team might exist to combine expertise from different departments.

(b) **Power** in the wider organisation. Team members may have influence.

(c) **Access to resources**. Team members may contribute information, or be able to mobilise finance or staff for the task.

(d) The **personalities and goals** of the individual members of the team. These will determine how the group functions.

The blend of the individual skills and abilities of its members will (ideally) **balance** the team.

KEY POINT

You probably have had experience of being put into a group of people you do not know. Many teams are set up this way and it takes some time for the team to become effective. This is a highly relevant issue for project teams, in particular, as they are constantly being formed, disbanded and reformed.

4.5 Belbin: team roles

R Meredith Belbin (1981) researched business game teams at the Henley Management College and drew up a widely used framework for understanding roles within work groups.

Belbin insisted that a distinction needs to be made between:

(a) **Team (process) role** ('a tendency to behave, contribute and interrelate with others at work in certain distinctive ways')

(b) **Functional role** ('the job demands that a person has been engaged to supply the requisite technical skills and operational knowledge')

His model of nine roles addresses the mix of team/process roles required for a fully functioning team.

4.5.1 Nine team roles

Belbin identifies nine team roles.

Role and description	Team-role contribution	Allowable weaknesses
Plant		
Creative, imaginative, unorthodox	Solves difficult problems	Ignores details, too preoccupied to communicate effectively
Resource investigator		
Extrovert, enthusiastic, communicative	Explores opportunities, develops contacts	Overoptimistic, loses interest once initial enthusiasm has passed

Role and description	Team-role contribution	Allowable weaknesses
Co-ordinator (chairman) Mature, confident, a good chairperson	Clarifies goals, promotes decision making, delegates well	Can be seen as manipulative, delegates personal work
Shaper Challenging, dynamic, thrives on pressure	Has the drive and courage to overcome obstacles	Can provoke others, hurts people's feelings
Monitor-evaluator Sober, strategic and discerning	Sees all options, judges accurately	Lacks drive and ability to inspire others, overly critical
Team worker Co-operative, mild, perceptive and diplomatic	Listens, builds, averts friction, calms the waters	Indecisive in crunch situations, can be easily influenced
Implementer (company worker) Disciplined, reliable, conservative and efficient	Turns ideas into practical actions	Somewhat inflexible, slow to respond to new possibilities
Completer-finisher Painstaking, conscientious, anxious	Searches out errors and omissions, delivers on time	Inclined to worry unduly, reluctant to delegate, can be pedantic
Specialist Single-minded, self-starting, dedicated	Provides knowledge and skills in rare supply	Contributes only on a narrow front, dwells on technicalities, overlooks the 'big picture'

4.5.2 A balanced team

These team roles are not fixed within any given individual. Team members can occupy more than one role, or switch to 'backup' roles if required: hence, there is no requirement for every team to have nine members. However, since role preferences are based on personality, it should be recognised that:

(a) Individuals will be naturally inclined towards some roles more than others
(b) Individuals will tend to adopt one or two team roles more or less consistently
(c) Individuals are likely to be more successful in some roles than in others

The nine roles are complementary, and Belbin suggested that an 'ideal' team should represent a mix or balance of all of them. If managers know employees' team role preferences, they can strategically select, 'cast' and develop team members to fulfil the required roles.

Question 10.2 Belbin's team roles

Learning outcome C1a

The following phrases and slogans project certain team roles: identify which ones. (Examples are drawn from Belbin, 1993.)

(a) The small print is always worth reading.
(b) Let's get down to the task in hand.
(c) In this job you never stop learning.
(d) Without continuous innovation, there is no survival.
(e) Surely we can exploit that?

(f) When the going gets tough, the tough get going.
(g) I was very interested in your point of view.
(h) Has anyone else got anything to add to this?
(i) Decisions should not be based purely on enthusiasm.

4.6 Models of group functioning – Steiner

Steiner identifies four basic ways in which groups function.

(a) **Additive**. All members contribute, but no one member depends on others for their performance. Skills and output are simply pooled.

(b) **Conjunctive** (or co-ordination). There is a high degree of dependence between members' contributions, often in a defined sequence (as in assembly lines and office procedures).

(c) **Disjunctive** (or collaboration). Members contribute different skills and abilities, so that solutions are synergistic, reflecting the optimum contribution of each individual. This particularly suits problem-solving groups.

(d) **Complementary**. The task can be divided into separate parts and allocated to individuals with the skills needed for each. Members effectively work in parallel.

4.7 Team development

You probably have had experience of being put into a group of people you do not know. Many teams are set up this way and it takes some time for the team to become effective. This is a highly relevant issue for project teams, in particular, as they are constantly being formed, disbanded and reformed. In this section, we consider the effective life cycle of a team as it progresses through the stages of group development.

4.7.1 Tuckman's stages of group development

Four stages in group development were identified by Tuckman (1965).

Forming
The team is just coming together. Each member wishes to impress their **personality** on the group. The individuals will be trying to find out about each other, and about the aims and norms of the team. There will, at this stage, probably be wariness about introducing new ideas. The objectives being pursued may as yet be unclear and a leader may not yet have emerged.

Storming
This frequently involves more or less open conflict between team members. There may be changes agreed in the original objectives, procedures and norms established for the group. If the team is developing successfully, this may be a fruitful phase, as more realistic targets are set and trust between the group members increases.

Norming
A period of settling down: there will be agreements about work sharing, individual requirements and expectations of output. Norms and procedures may evolve that enable methodical working to be introduced and maintained.

Performing
The team sets to work to execute its task. The difficulties of growth and development no longer hinder the group's objectives.

Tuckman and Jensen later added two stages to Tuckman's model.

(a) **Dorming**. Once a group has been performing well for some time, it may get complacent, and fall back into self-maintenance functions, at the expense of the task.

(b) **Mourning/adjourning**. The group sees itself as having fulfilled its purpose – or, if it is a temporary project group, is due to physically disband. This is a stage of confusion, sadness and anxiety as the group breaks up. There is evaluation of its achievements, and gradual withdrawal of group members. If the group is to continue, going on to a new task, there will be a renegotiation of aims and roles: a return to the forming stage.

Exam skills

Look out for scenarios in which there is hesitancy, conflict or role negotiation in a newly set-up project team, as this may be a signal that Tuckman's model is relevant.

Question 10.3 — Team formation stages

Learning outcome D2c

Read the following descriptions of team behaviour and decide to which category they belong (forming, storming, norming, performing, dorming).

(a) Two of the group arguing about whose idea is best
(b) Progress becomes static
(c) Desired outputs being achieved
(d) Shy member of the group is not participating
(e) Activities being allocated

4.8 Building a team

KEY POINT

Team development can be facilitated by active **team building** measures to support team identity, solidarity and commitment to shared objectives.

Teams may have a natural evolutionary life cycle. However, not all teams develop into mature teams and might be stuck, stagnating, in an ineffective state.

So it often falls to a manager or project team leader to build the team. There are three main issues involved in team building.

Issues	Comments
Team identity	Get people to see themselves as part of the group eg by regular communication, shared mythology and perhaps a separate space (a personalised meeting room or intranet page, perhaps).
Team solidarity	Encourage loyalty so that members put in extra effort for the sake of the team. This may require encouraging relationships, controlling competition and perhaps injecting an element of competition with other teams.
Shared objectives	Encourage the team to commit itself to shared work objectives and to co-operate willingly and effectively in achieving them. This may involve a range of leader activity. • Clearly setting out the objectives of the team
Shared objectives	• Allowing the team to participate in setting objectives

Issues	Comments
(continued)	• Giving regular feedback on progress and results, with constructive criticism • Getting the team involved in providing performance feedback • Offering positive reinforcement (praise etc) for co-operative working and task achievement by the team as a whole (rather than just 'star' individuals) • Championing the success of the team within the organisation

Question 10.4 Group cohesion

Learning outcome C1a

Can you see any dangers in creating a very close-knit group? Think of the effect of strong team cohesion on:

(a) What the group spends its energies and attention on
(b) How the group regards outsiders, and any information or feedback they supply
(c) How the group makes decisions

Question 10.5 Team building

Learning outcome C1a

Why might the following be effective as **team-building exercises**?

(a) Sending a project team (involved in the design of electronic systems for racing cars) on a recreational day out karting.

(b) Sending two sales teams on a day out playing 'war games', each being an opposing combat team trying to capture the other's flag, armed with paint guns.

(c) Sending a project team on a conference at a venue away from work, with a brief to review the past year and come up with a vision for the next year.

4.9 Distributive leadership

In an earlier chapter we explored a variety of approaches that leaders may adopt to get the best from the teams they lead. Traditional leadership has been regarded as a role undertaken by a single individual who is responsible for a team of workers. However, this way of thinking is gradually changing.

Distributive leadership (sometimes referred to as shared leadership) is a form of leadership which spreads the role of leading the team among a number of team members, with power no longer solely residing with the appointed leader. This approach effectively allows team members to lead each other as they interact over time.

The creation of a distributive leadership approach can be encouraged by the presence of three elements:

- All team members clearly understand the team's main objective (**shared purpose**).
- The degree of **social support** (emotional and psychological) that team members provide each other.
- The level of involvement team members have in deciding how the team meets its objectives (**voice**).

4.10 Evaluating team effectiveness

KEY POINT

The task of the team leader is to build a 'successful' or 'effective' team. The criteria for team effectiveness include:

(a) **Task performance**. Fulfilment of task and organisational goals.

(b) **Team functioning**. Constructive maintenance of team working, managing the demands of team dynamics, roles and processes.

(c) **Team member satisfaction**. Fulfilment of individual development and relationship needs.

Some of the characteristics of **effective** and **ineffective** teams may be summarised as follows.

Factor	Effective team	Ineffective team
Quantifiable		
Labour turnover	Low	High
Accident rate	Low	High
Absenteeism	Low	High
Output and productivity	High	Low
Quality of output	High	Low
Individual targets	Achieved	Not achieved
Stoppages and interruptions to the workflow	Low	High (eg because of misunderstandings, disagreements)
Qualitative		
Commitment to targets and organisational goals	High	Low
Understanding of team's work and why it exists	High	Low
Understanding of individual roles within the team	High	Low
Communication between team members	Free and open	Mistrust
Ideas	Shared for the team's benefit	'Owned' (and hidden) by individuals for their own benefit
Feedback	Constructive criticism	Point scoring, undermining
Problem solving	Addresses causes	Only looks at symptoms
Interest in work decisions	Active	Passive acceptance
Opinions	Consensus	Imposed solutions
Job satisfaction	High	Low
Motivation in leader's absence	High	'When the cat's away ...'

4.11 High performance teams

Peter **Vaill** (1989) identified that high-performing teams have five common characteristics:

(a) Clarity of purpose and near-term objectives
(b) Commitment

(c) Teamwork is focused on the task
(d) Strong leadership
(e) High levels of creativity and the generation of new ways of doing things

4.12 Motivation and rewarding effective teams

Team-based rewards and incentives may be used to encourage co-operation and mutual accountability, as well as team performance. The manager needs to consider the desire of individuals to be recognised for their own contribution as well as the performance of the team.

Organisations may try to encourage effective team performance by designing reward systems that recognise team, rather than individual, success. Indeed, **individual performance rewards** may act **against** team co-operation and performance.

(a) They emphasise individual rather than team performance.

(b) They encourage team leaders to think of team members only as individuals, rather than relating to them as a team.

For team rewards and incentives to be effective, the team must have certain characteristics.

(a) Distinct roles, targets and performance measures (so the team knows what it has to do to earn the reward)

(b) Significant autonomy and thus influence over performance (so the team perceives that extra effort will be rewarded)

(c) Maturity and stability

(d) Co-operation

(e) Interdependence of team members (so that the team manages member contribution, everyone 'pulls their weight', no one feels they could earn higher rewards on their own)

4.13 The purpose of team meetings

Managers spend a large proportion of their working week in meetings, particularly with the rise of project working. Meetings are thus both a major cost to organisations, and a major context for **decision making, interpersonal influencing and team collaboration**.

4.13.1 General team meetings

Regular team meetings have particular purposes, over and above problem solving and decision making on any particular work-related issue.

(a) They provide an opportunity to review team working processes and appraise (formally or informally) how well they are working. Team members may raise problems of co-ordination or communication, for example.

(b) They reinforce the team's sense of itself as a team, drawing the team together to focus on its shared goals.

(c) They allow for goal reinforcement, progress feedback and information sharing, to ensure that team members are 'on the same page' with their efforts – especially if they do not directly work together (eg in dispersed or virtual project teams).

(d) They allow for all-member involvement and development in team decision making and information sharing processes. (Discussion leading and research/presentation roles might be rotated, for example, to facilitate this.)

(e) They allow for informal communication, which is important for working relations, ideas generation and information sharing. This can be built in at the beginning and end of meeting time.

4.13.2 Managing meetings effectively

KEY POINT

Effective meetings depend on: defined purpose; appropriate participants; a planned sequence of business; a well-facilitated process; and continual review and learning.

Whatever the purpose and level of formality of a given meeting, its effectiveness will broadly depend on the following.

(a) There is usually a discussion **leader**, chairperson, or at least an organiser, who guides the proceedings of the meeting and aims to maintain order.

(b) There is often a **sequence of business** or at least a list of items to be covered: topics of discussion or decisions to be reached. It is not essential to formalise this point with an **agenda**, but meetings usually do have one.

(c) The purpose of the meeting is achieved by reaching some **decision or expression of opinion** at the end of the discussion. In some circumstances, this may lead to taking a vote to determine what is the majority view. In other circumstances, the discussion may just be **summarised** by the leader and written confirmation of the decisions reached provided later for perusal by the various parties.

4.13.3 Conducting the meeting

Effective facilitation of a team meeting involves the following.

(a) Ensuring that **agreed decisions are accurately recorded** in the notes or minutes of the meeting, ideally with clearly defined responsibility for action. These should be distributed (eg by email) as soon as possible after the meeting.

(b) **Following up on decisions and action points from previous meetings**, to ensure that agreed action has been taken. (In formal meetings, this is done as part of the review of the previous minutes.)

Question 10.6 Meeting problems

Learning outcome C1a

What aspects of the following situations might be a problem for an effective team meeting? What might you, in the role of facilitator, do about it?

(a) One person suggests a revision to the agenda, a complex issue that the rest of the team is unprepared to discuss, and that two members are likely to feel is 'targeted' at them.

(b) The team has more items on its agenda than it can handle in a simple meeting.

(c) A team member has called ahead to say that she will be unavoidably late for a scheduled project team meeting.

4.14 The project team

4.14.1 Teams and team working

In this section, we offer some notes on aspects of team working and leadership that are particularly relevant to the project environment.

4.14.2 Building a project team

KEY TERM

The **PROJECT TEAM** comprises the people who report directly or indirectly to the project manager.

Project success depends to a large extent on the team members selected. The ideal project team achieves project completion on time, within budget and to the required specifications – with the minimum amount of direct supervision from the project manager.

The team will comprise individuals with **differing skills and personalities**. The project manager should choose a balanced team that takes advantage of each team member's skills, and compensates elsewhere for their weaknesses.

The project team will normally be drawn from existing staff, but highly recommended **outsiders with special skills** may be recruited. When building a team, the project manager should ask the following questions.

(a) **What skills** are required to complete each task of the project? This list will be based on the project goals established previously.

(b) **Who** has the talent and skills to complete the required tasks, whether inside or outside the organisation?

(c) Are the people identified **available**, **affordable**, and able to join the project team?

(d) What level of **supervision** will be required?

This information should be **summarised in worksheet format**, as shown in the following example.

Project skill requirements		
Project name ________	**Date worksheet completed** ________	
Project manager ________		
Task	Skill needed	Responsibility

The completed worksheet provides a document showing the skills required of the project team. Deciding who has the skills required for each task and if possible seconding those identified to the project team, should be done **as early as possible**. Team members should then be able to **participate** in the planning of schedules and budgets. This should encourage the acceptance of agreed deadlines, and a greater commitment to achieve project success.

The individuals selected to join the team should be told **why they have been selected**, referring both to their technical skills and personal qualities. This should provide members with guidance as to the role they are expected to play.

Although the composition of the project team is critical, project managers often find it is not possible to assemble the ideal team, and have to do the best they can with the personnel available. If the project manager feels the best available team does not possess the skills and talent required, the project should be **abandoned or delayed**.

Once the team has been selected, each member should be given a (probably verbal) project briefing, outlining the overall aims of the project, and detailing the role they are expected to play.

4.14.3 Managing the project team

Group cohesiveness is an important factor for project success. It is hoped that team members will **develop and learn from each other**, and solve problems by drawing on different resources and expertise.

The performance of the project team will be enhanced by the following.

(a) Effective communication
(b) All members being aware of the team's purpose and the role of each team member
(c) Collaboration and creativity among team members
(d) Trusting, supportive atmosphere in the group
(e) A commitment to meeting the agreed schedule
(f) Innovative/creative behaviour
(g) Team members highly interdependent, interface effectively
(h) Capacity for conflict resolution
(i) Results orientation
(j) High energy levels and enthusiasm
(k) An acceptance of change

Collaboration and interaction between team members will help ensure the skills of all team members are utilised, and should result in 'synergistic' solutions. Formal (eg meetings) and informal channels (eg email links, a bulletin board) of **communication** should be set up to ensure this interaction takes place.

4.14.4 Project team meetings

There are three basic types of meeting used in project management.

(a) **Status review meetings** used to control progress and maintain stakeholder communication. The purpose of such meetings, which may be held periodically and/or at defined project milestones and end of stages, is to:

   (i) Keep the team, project manager and key stakeholders informed about progress and current status (where the project is 'up to' in terms of planned schedule, cost and deliverables)

   (ii) Identify any problems, issues or changes that need to be resolved

   (iii) Develop action plans for the next period or stage of the project and/or authorise changes to the existing project plan in response to deviations or contingencies

(b) **Problem-solving meetings**, which may be called at any time an issue emerges in the course of the project. The meeting should involve those with a stake, competence and/or authority to make decisions and take corrective action (eg reallocate resources to the problem).

(c) **Post-project evaluation meetings**, used to review and derive learning from the project. Such a meeting should involve all relevant participants and stakeholders, to cover a range of issues, including the following. How effective was the project in attaining its objectives? How effectively was the project planned, managed and controlled? Are stakeholders satisfied with the deliverables and the process? What 'unfinished business' needs to be followed up? What lessons can be learned for future projects? And so on.

Section summary

A **team** is more than a group. It has joint **objectives** and **accountability** and may be set up by the organisation under the supervision or coaching of a team leader, although **self-managed teams** are growing in popularity.

Ideally, team members should perform a **balanced mix of roles**. **Belbin** suggests: co-ordinator, shaper, plant, monitor-evaluator, resource-investigator, implementer, team-worker, completer-finisher and specialist.

A team **develops in stages**: forming, storming, norming, performing (**Tuckman**) and dorming or mourning/adjourning.

Project success depends to a large extent on how the **project team** is selected, led and managed.

Chapter Summary

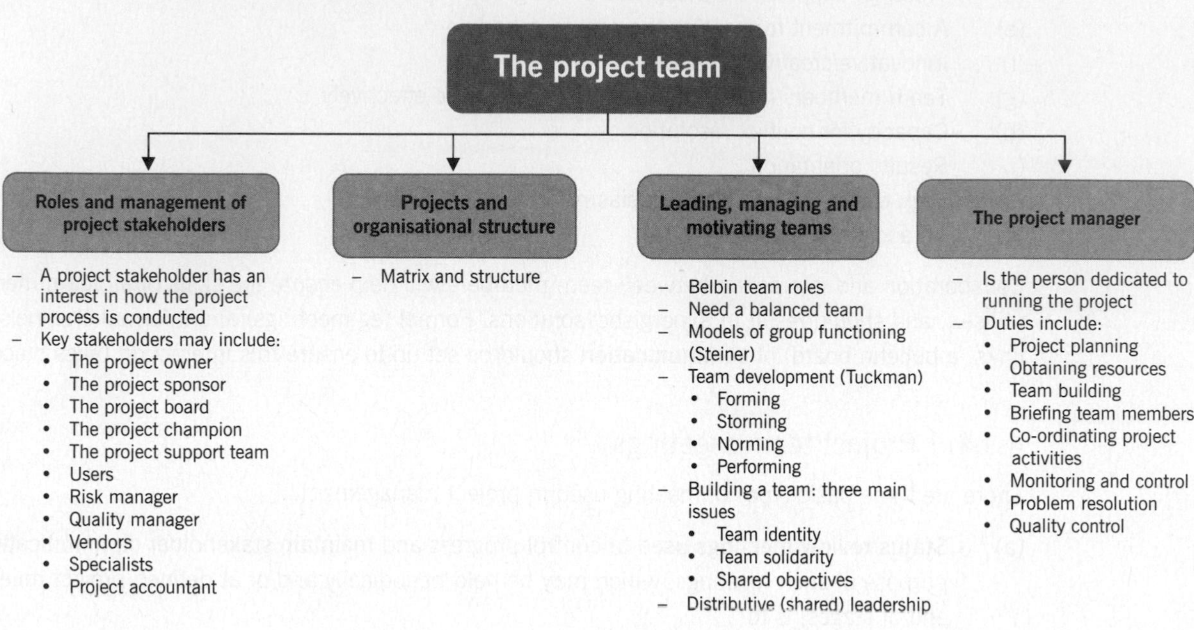

The project team
Roles and management of project stakeholders
Projects and organisational structure
Leading, managing and motivating teams
The project manager
– A project stakeholder has an interest in how the project process is conducted
– Key stakeholders may include:
• The project owner
• The project sponsor
• The project board
• The project champion
• The project support team
• Users
• Risk manager
• Quality manager
• Vendors
• Specialists
• Project accountant
– Matrix and structure
– Belbin team roles
– Need a balanced team
– Models of group functioning (Steiner)
– Team development (Tuckman)
• Forming
• Storming
• Norming
• Performing
– Building a team: three main issues
• Team identity
• Team solidarity
• Shared objectives
– Distributive (shared) leadership
– Is the person dedicated to running the project
– Duties include:
• Project planning
• Obtaining resources
• Team building
• Briefing team members
• Co-ordinating project activities
• Monitoring and control
• Problem resolution
• Quality control

Quick Quiz

1 List four areas that a project manager should be skilled in.

1 Communication
2 Efficiency of resources
3 Goal congruence
4 Motivating team/delegating

2 List four ways that a dispute between project stakeholders could be settled.

1 Negotiating
2 Partnering
3 Mediation
4 Arbitration

3 List five typical phases of a project.

1 Initiation
2 Plan
3 Execution
4 Control
5 Closing

4 Who is the project sponsor? Provides resources.

5 List Belbin's nine roles for a well-rounded team.

Answers to Quick Quiz

1 Four of the following: leadership, team building, organisational, communication, technical, personal.

2 Negotiation
Partnering
Mediation
Arbitration

3 Defining, planning, implementing, controlling, completing.

4 The project sponsor may be the owner, financier, client etc, or their delegate. The sponsor is accountable for the resources invested into the project and responsible for the achievement of the project's business objectives.

5 Co-ordinator (or chairman), shaper, plant, monitor-evaluator, resource-investigator, implementer (or company worker), team worker, completer-finisher, specialist.

Answers to Questions

10.1 Project board

The answer is B. Option A is the role of a project champion, option C is that of the project sponsor and option D is that of the project manager.

10.2 Belbin's team roles

(a) Completer-finisher
(b) Implementer/company worker
(c) Specialist
(d) Plant
(e) Resource investigator
(f) Shaper
(g) Team worker
(h) Co-ordinator/chairman
(i) Monitor-evaluator

10.3 Team formation stages

Categorising the behaviour of group members in the situations described results in the following: (a) storming, (b) dorming, (c) performing, (d) forming, (e) norming.

10.4 Group cohesion

Problems may arise in an ultra close-knit group because:

(a) The group's energies may be focused on its own maintenance and relationships, instead of on the task.

(b) The group may be suspicious or dismissive of outsiders, and may reject any contradictory information or criticism they supply; the group will be blinkered and stick to its own views, no matter what; cohesive groups thus often get the impression that they are infallible: they can't be wrong – and therefore can't learn from their mistakes.

(c) The group may squash any dissent or opinions that might rock the boat. Close-knit groups tend to preserve a consensus – falsely, if required – and to take risky decisions, because they have suppressed alternative facts and viewpoints.

10.5 Team building

(a) Recreation helps the team to build informal relationships: in this case, the chosen activity also reminds them of their tasks, and may make them feel special, as part of the motor racing industry, by giving them a taste of what the end user of their product does.

(b) A team challenge forces the group to consider its strengths and weaknesses, to find its natural leader. This exercise creates an 'us' and 'them' challenge: perceiving the rival team as the enemy heightens the solidarity of the group.

(c) This exercise encourages the group to raise problems and conflicts freely, away from the normal environment of work, and also encourages brainstorming and the expression of team members' dreams for what the team can achieve in the future.

10.6 Meeting problems

Agenda change. Propose the change to the team, and insist on getting a genuine response. If some members do not want to deal with the item, remind the meeting of the ground rules: consensus is required to put a new item on the agenda. It can be included in the next meeting.

Leftover items. The need here is to prevent frustration and loss of focus. You might assign each member an item and ask them to prepare and distribute information before the next meeting. Alternatively, you might keep a legible list of 'other agenda items'. So no one fears they will be forgotten.

Late attendance. The meeting should start on time, out of respect for the other team members. When the missing member arrives, this would be a good opportunity to summarise the discussion so far. If people are repeatedly late, however, this may need addressing.

Now try these questions from the Practice Question Bank

Question	Level
10.1 – 10.5	Practice
MFS	Practice
Z Company	Practice

PRACTICE QUESTION AND ANSWER BANK

What the examiner means

The table below has been prepared by CIMA to help you interpret exam questions.

Learning objectives	Verbs used	Definition
1 Knowledge		
What are you expected to know	• List	• Make a list of
	• State	• Express, fully or clearly, the details of/facts of
	• Define	• Give the exact meaning of
2 Comprehension		
What you are expected to understand	• Describe	• Communicate the key features of
	• Distinguish	• Highlight the differences between
	• Explain	• Make clear or intelligible/state the meaning of
	• Identify	• Recognise, establish or select after consideration
	• Illustrate	• Use an example to describe or explain something
3 Application		
How you are expected to apply your knowledge	• Apply	• Put to practical use
	• Calculate/ compute	• Ascertain or reckon mathematically
	• Demonstrate	• Prove with certainty or to exhibit by practical means
	• Prepare	• Make or get ready for use
	• Reconcile	• Make or prove consistent/compatible
	• Solve	• Find an answer to
	• Tabulate	• Arrange in a table
4 Analysis		
How you are expected to analyse the detail of what you have learned	• Analyse	• Examine in detail the structure of
	• Categorise	• Place into a defined class or division
	• Compare and contrast	• Show the similarities and/or differences between
	• Construct	• Build up or compile
	• Discuss	• Examine in detail by argument
	• Interpret	• Translate into intelligible or familiar terms
	• Prioritise	• Place in order of priority or sequence for action
	• Produce	• Create or bring into existence
5 Evaluation		
How you are expected to use your learning to evaluate, make decisions or recommendations	• Advise	• Counsel, inform or notify
	• Evaluate	• Appraise or assess the value of
	• Recommend	• Propose a course of action

Chapter 1A

Learning outcomes A1a and A1b

1A.1 Is the statement below true or false?

'Centralised control and functional departmentation are essential to the management of large diversified businesses.'

1A.2 The two diagrams below are diagrammatic expressions of which models?

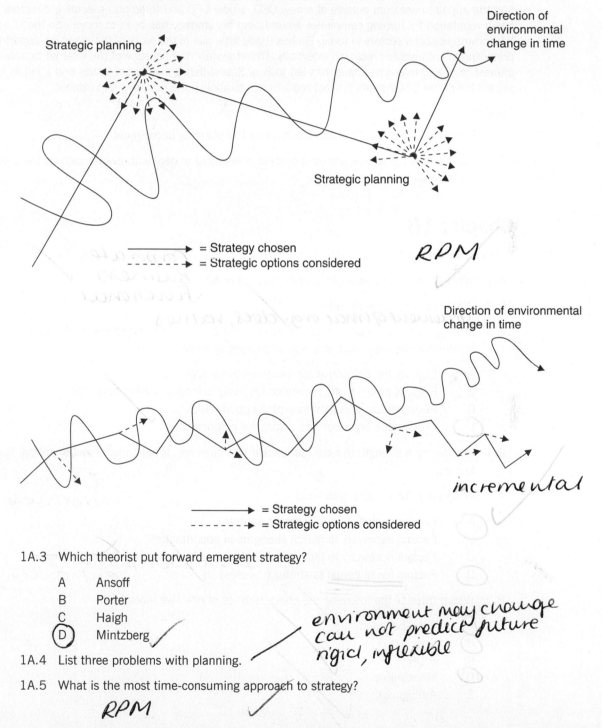

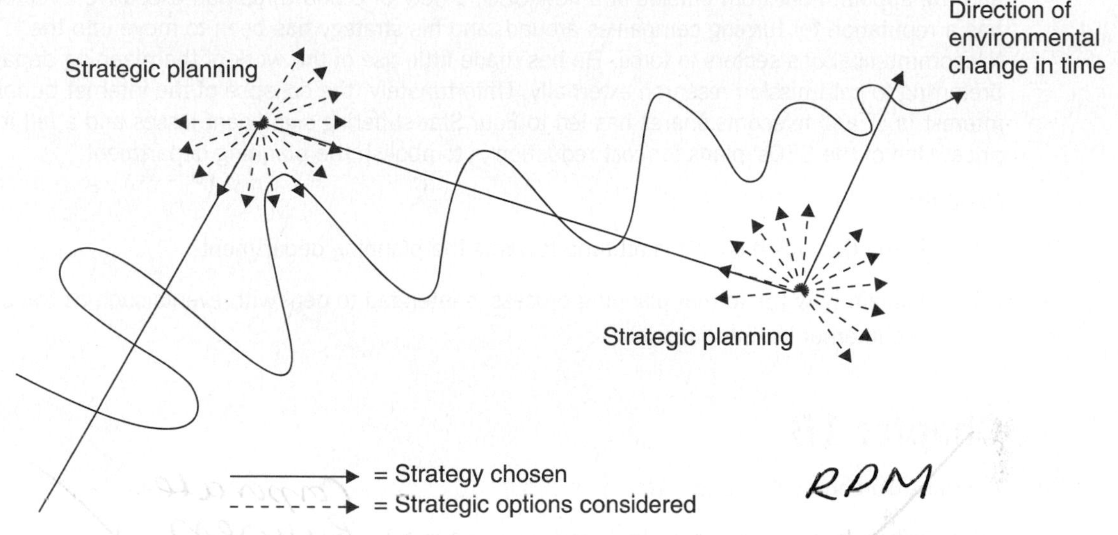

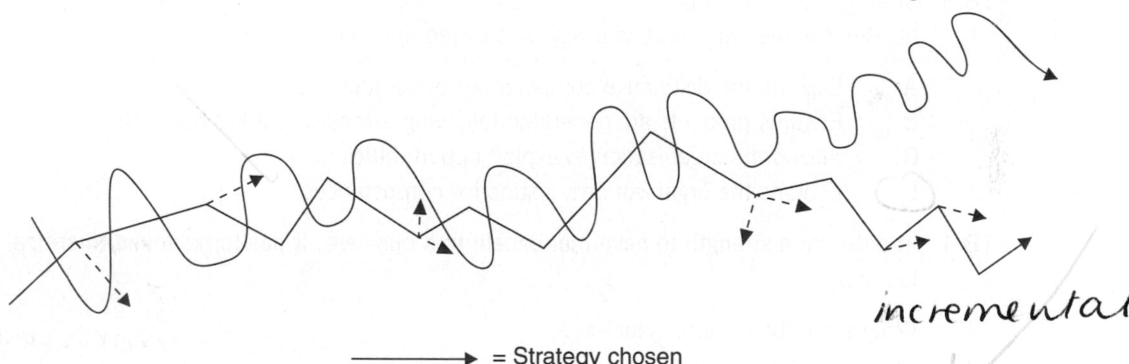

1A.3 Which theorist put forward emergent strategy?

A Ansoff
B Porter
C Haigh
D Mintzberg

1A.4 List three problems with planning.

1A.5 What is the most time-consuming approach to strategy?

Four Star Products

Learning outcome A1a

Four Star Products plc is a major manufacturing organisation with a range of consumer products. Founded over 70 years ago and run for many years by the founder and his family, the company was rather traditional in its strategy, tending to stick to the hardware and other household goods that it understood. A formal system of strategic planning was introduced in 1962 and remains in place today, with a 47-person planning department reporting to a planning director.

Since a financial crisis in 1994, the dominance of the founding family has been diluted by banker power and the appointment from outside of a new CEO, a new CFO and three non-executive directors. The CEO has a reputation for turning companies around, and his strategy has been to move into the IT and telecommunications sectors in force. He has made little use of the work of the planning department, preferring to commission research externally. Unfortunately, the collapse of the internet bubble and fall in interest in IT and telecoms shares has led to Four Star suffering significant losses and a fall in its share price. One of the CEOs' plans for cost reduction is to abolish the planning department.

Required

(a) Is the CEO justified in his attitude towards the planning department?

(b) Explain how the formal planning process is intended to deal with events such as the collapse of the internet business model.

Chapter 1B

Learning outcomes A1a and A1b

1B.1 What are the three levels that strategy is made at?

1B.2 What is a mission statement?

1B.3 Strategic direction has been described in terms of a resource-based approach and environmental fit. What is the advantage of a resource-based approach?

A Exploits the distinctive competences of competitors
B Ensures products are generated following extensive market research
C Allows the organisation to exploit opportunities
D Exploits the organisation's distinctive competences

1B.4 In order for a strength to have real benefit to a business, it has to be linked to critical success factors.

What are critical success factors?

A Factors contributing to strategic success
B Factors necessary to match strengths to opportunities
C Factors necessary to build on strengths
D Factors fundamental to strategic success

1B.5 Which three of the following are characteristics of effective objectives?

A Time-bounded
B Specific
C Risky
D Measurable
E Ambiguous

Mission statement

Learning outcome A1a

The managing director of TDM plc has recently returned from a conference entitled 'Strategic planning today'. While at the conference, she attended a session on corporate mission statements. She found the session very interesting, but it was rather short. She now has some questions for the accountant:

'What is a mission statement "for" and how does it fit with our strategic planning processes?'

'Where does our mission come from and what areas of corporate life should it cover?'

'If we were to develop a mission statement, what benefits would the company get from it?'

Required

Prepare a document that answers the managing director's questions.

Chapter 2

Learning outcome A2a

2.1 What are the two axes of Mendelow's matrix?

2.2 There are three broad types of stakeholder:

(1) ....

(2) ....

(3) ....

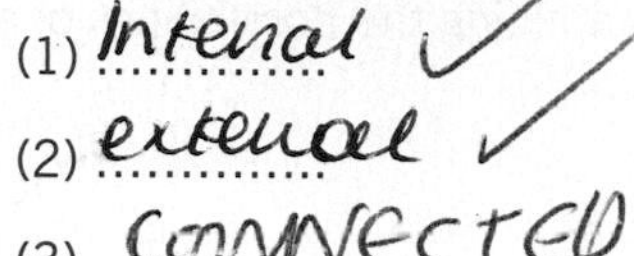

2.3 Fill in the diagram of Porter's diamond.

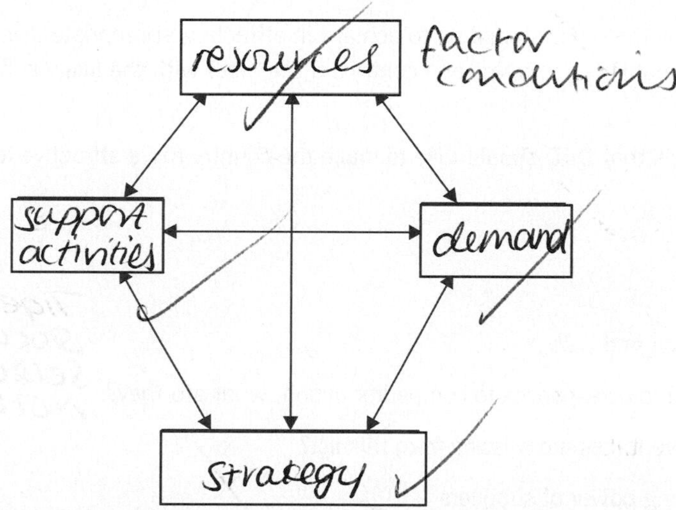

2.4 Which of the following statements does not explain why a country may be good at shipbuilding?

A Good coastline and waterways
B Low level of domestic competition
C Availability of steel
D Skilled shipbuilding labour force

2.5 Which of the following would you consider to be relevant to the social part of the PEST model?

A Changes in safety legislation
B Analysis of the population by age group
C Volatility of interest rates
D Effect of unemployment on demand
E Changes in leisure pursuits
F Religious affiliation and practices

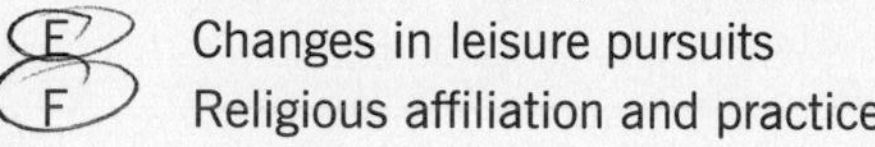

National advantage

Learning outcome A2a

D4D is a politically stable, developing country enjoying a temperate climate and a young, educated population, many of whom are educated to graduate level. Those who have studied at this level have tended to do so abroad, since there are limited opportunities to do so in D4D.

The economy is mixed, based on agriculture and some light manufacturing, but has enjoyed considerable revenue from oil exploration and production which is based offshore in its territorial waters. Some of this revenue is generated by providing services for the oil industry, but the majority comes from a tax on every barrel of oil that the foreign oil companies extract.

The Government has used the revenue to keep personal and property taxes low and to support the largely uneconomic local industry. It now recognises that, although politically popular, this decision might not have been in the best long-term interests of the country.

The Finance and Trade Minister of D4D is aware that the oil revenue may only last a further ten years. He wishes to build a competitive advantage over the neighbouring countries. The Prime Minister is sceptical, and has made the observation that 'companies have competitive advantages, not countries'.

As a management accountant within the Ministry of Finance and Trade, you have been asked to produce a number of documents, for both the Prime Minister and the Finance and Trade Minister, considering how competitive advantage could be achieved for D4D and examining the possibilities of attracting inward investment from foreign companies.

Required

(a) Using any models you consider appropriate, explain the factors that lead to competitive advantage being present in particular countries.

(b) Identify the aims that D4D should try to achieve in attracting appropriate investors into the country. You should also compare and contrast those aims with the likely aims of any company investing in D4D.

(c) Explain the steps that D4D should take to make the country more attractive to appropriate inward investment.

Chapter 3

Learning outcomes A2a and A2b

3.1 Kotler proposed four responses to competitor action, what are they?

3.2 Which of the five forces are missing from this list?

(1) Bargaining power of suppliers
(2) Bargaining power of buyers
(3) Rivalry among existing firms

3.3 Which of the following would result in a company's supplier having high bargaining power?

A The supplier operates in a highly competitive industry.
B The supplier is a monopolist or an oligopolist.
C The company in question is the supplier's sole customer.
D The components the supplier sells are generic rather than specialised.

3.4 Which three of the following changes will improve sales for a brewery?

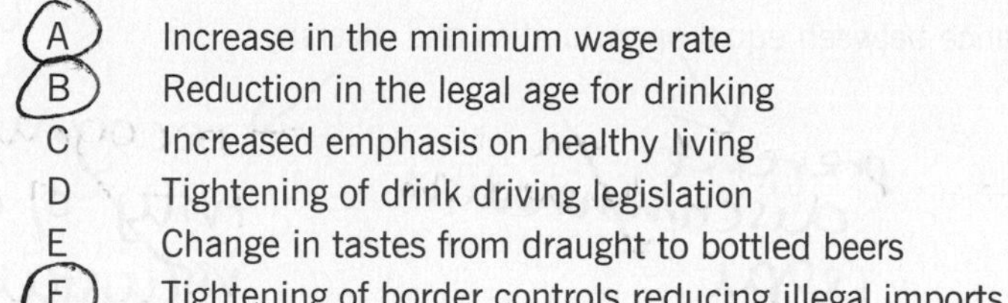

A Increase in the minimum wage rate
B Reduction in the legal age for drinking
C Increased emphasis on healthy living
D Tightening of drink driving legislation
E Change in tastes from draught to bottled beers
F Tightening of border controls reducing illegal imports

3.5 Porter's five forces model is used to analyse which of the following?

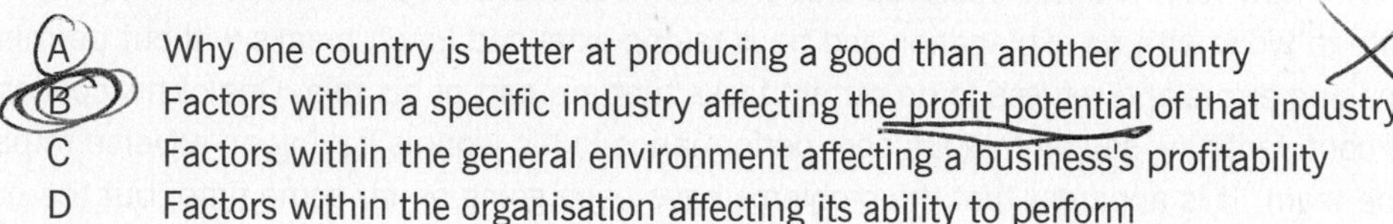

A Why one country is better at producing a good than another country
B Factors within a specific industry affecting the profit potential of that industry
C Factors within the general environment affecting a business's profitability
D Factors within the organisation affecting its ability to perform

X Company

Learning outcomes A2a and B2b

X Company is a manufacturer of non-alcoholic soft drinks, and has a well-established position and brand recognition in country Z. The potential for future growth in country Z is, however, limited, with the market reaching saturation. One option for expansion is to move into new markets in other countries offering its existing product range.

The business development team is evaluating this option and is currently working on proposals to sell the company's range of drinks in country Y. One possible strategy to achieve market entry that the team is investigating is through a joint venture with a company that is already established in country Y, and is in the drinks distribution business.

The board of X Company has given the business development team the task of undertaking a feasibility study to explore the viability of the proposed strategy. As part of the feasibility study, there needs to be some assessment of industry competition and the attractiveness of the market in country Y. The feasibility study also needs to assess the cultural compatibility of the ways of doing business in country Y compared to how X Company currently operates in country Z.

Required

(a) Advise the business development team on how Porter's five forces model could be used to assess industry competition in country Y.

(b) Discuss how Hofstede's research could be used to assess the compatibility of X Company's strategy with the culture of country Y.

Chapter 4

Learning outcomes B1a and B1b

4.1 'A manager might also be identified as a transformational leader.' True or false?

4.2 If a manager confers with subordinates, takes their views and feelings into account, but retains the right to make a final decision, this is a:

A Tells style
B Sells style
C Consults style
D Joins style

4.3 What is the most effective style suggested by Blake and Mouton's managerial grid? Why is it so effective in theory, and why might it not be effective in practice?

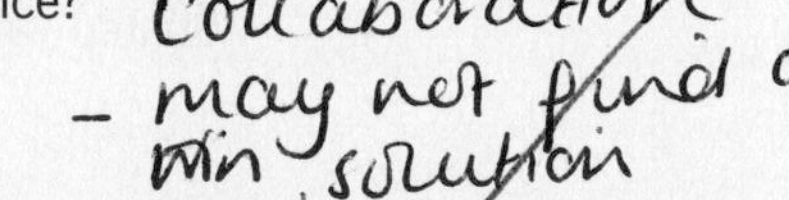

4.4 'A grievance occurs when an employee infringes organisational rules or expectations.' True or false?

4.5 What is the difference between equal opportunities and diversity?

S and C

Learning outcome B1b

S has recently been appointed as the Finance Department Manager in Z Company. During the first month in her new role, she has observed that one member of staff, C, is underperforming. C is frequently arriving late to work with no explanation and he is taking extended lunch breaks without permission. He is also making errors and refuses to do certain tasks that are part of his role. One of his colleagues has spoken to S confidentially, saying that C's poor performance in his work is having an adverse impact on the rest of the team. It is apparent that the problems have been going on for some time, but the previous manager had preferred to ignore them. S has decided that she must now take action on what appears to be a disciplinary case, but is unclear on how to deal with the situation.

Required

Explain to S the stages involved in taking disciplinary action against C.

Chapter 5

Learning outcome B2b

5.1 Whose cultural analysis identified defenders, prospectors, analysers and reactors?

A Miles and Snow
B Deal and Kennedy
C Denison
D Handy

5.2 Which of the following is not one of Handy's models of culture?

A Central
B Role
C Person
D Task

5.3 Which of the following does not describe corporate culture?

A The way we do things around here
B The degree of standardisation in an organisation
C The values, attitudes, norms and expectations of an organisation
D The personality or atmosphere of an organisation

5.4 In the following list, can you recognise three elements that help to make up the culture of an organisation?

A Symbols
B Ownership
C Customs
D Technology
E Beliefs and values

5.5 Which of the following is not one of the soft factors included in McKinsey's 7 S model?

A Systems
B Staff
C Skills
D Shared values

Corporate culture

Learning outcome B2b

Culture can be defined as 'the way we do things around here'.

Required

Explain what this definition means and how corporate culture develops. Then, identify the benefits and disadvantages of a strong corporate culture.

Chapter 6

Learning outcomes C2a and C2b

6.1 List four common sources of conflict in organisations.

6.2 Name three types of communication.

6.3 Name two of K Thomas's five strategies for handling conflict.

6.4 Vocabulary and style should contribute to the clarity of the message in a presentation. It is recommended that short simple sentences are used and the presenter should avoid certain expressions. Which three from the following list should be avoided?

A Mathematical expressions

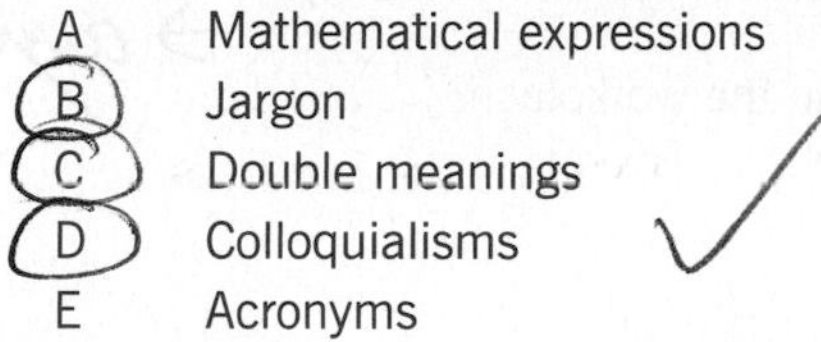

B Jargon

C Double meanings

D Colloquialisms

E Acronyms

6.5 Bob has been on a training course to help him develop his negotiation skills and learn some new techniques. He has been practising three of these back in the office – can you identify them?

A Create a trusting, supportive atmosphere

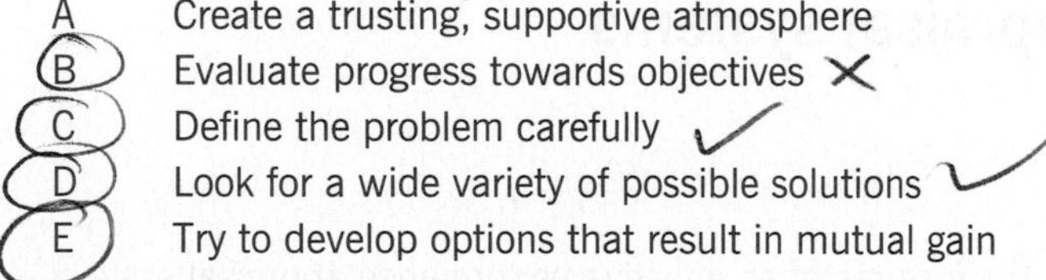

B Evaluate progress towards objectives

C Define the problem carefully

D Look for a wide variety of possible solutions

E Try to develop options that result in mutual gain

Communication

Learning outcome C2a

P is the project manager responsible for managing the relocation of H Company's head office to new premises. He thought everything was going well with the project, and is very surprised when he learns that various project stakeholders are complaining about his poor communication skills.

Some of the complaints made relate to the complex messages he sends and his use of very technical language associated with the project. While he feels that he is keeping the project team members up to date, they feel they are overloaded with emails covering lots of different issues, not all of which are relevant to them.

Required

Explain to P what he could do to ensure that his communications with stakeholders about the relocation project are more effective.

Chapter 7

Learning outcomes B1b and C1b

7.1 Name four measures that have traditionally been used to assess the work of the finance function.

7.2 Which of the following measures might be used to assess the work of the finance function using a balanced scorecard approach?

A Value enhancements
B Customer satisfaction
C Profits from investments
D Learning and growth

7.3 When a subordinate rates their superior's leadership skills, this is an example of:

A 360-degree feedback
B Performance management
C Upward appraisal
D Results-oriented appraisal

7.4 'An employer's responsibilities for health and safety apply solely to employees regularly working on the premises.' Is this statement true or false?

7.5 What are employees' legal duties with respect to health and safety?

7.6 Which of the following is a health hazard in the workplace?

A Uncollected waste paper
B Heavy objects
C Frayed carpet
D All of the above

Performance appraisal systems

Learning outcome B1b

Required

(a) Identify and explain the features of an effective performance appraisal system.
(b) Identify and explain the advantages and disadvantages of performance appraisal systems.

The accounting function

Learning outcome B1b

The accounting function is one of several key functions within an organisation, all of which integrate to ensure that the organisation is able to deliver its products or services as efficiently and effectively as possible.

Required

(a) Explain the purpose of the accounting function within an organisation, and identify and briefly describe how it interacts with **any two other** functional areas.

(b) Identify and describe the key factors that might affect the type of accounting system used within an organisation.

Chapter 8

Learning outcomes D1a and D1b

8.1 Lewin's force field analysis maps the forces that are pushing towards the preferred state (the driving forces) and the restraining forces, which are pushing back to the current state.

Which two of the following describe restraining forces?

A Fear of losing special privileges, such as concessionary prices for the organisation's products or services

B Fear that once higher output norms have been established, the organisation will expect such norms to be sustained permanently

C Response to pressure from the management and thus a desire to reduce that pressure to acceptable proportions

D Dislike of the work itself

E Fear of dismissal if output falls below a reasonably well-defined rate acceptable to or tolerated by the management

8.2 Ross Co is a manufacturing company which makes Venetian blinds. The company has operated from five factories for many years. Due to years of falling profitability, the management at Ross Co recently made the difficult decision to close one of its factories. Two hundred factory workers will be made redundant as a result.

Using Balogun and Hope Hailey's change matrix, which type of change is Ross Co undertaking?

A Reconstruction
B Evolution
C Adaptation
D Revolution

8.3 Balogun and Hope Hailey analyse change by reference to its scope and its nature. According to their change matrix, what type of change is an incremental process which leads to a new paradigm?

A Reconstruction
B Adaptation
C Transformation
D Evolution

8.4 If management wanted to change the culture of an organisation, the least direct way of doing so would be to alter which of the following features?

A Reward policies
B Management style
C Staff selection
D The product

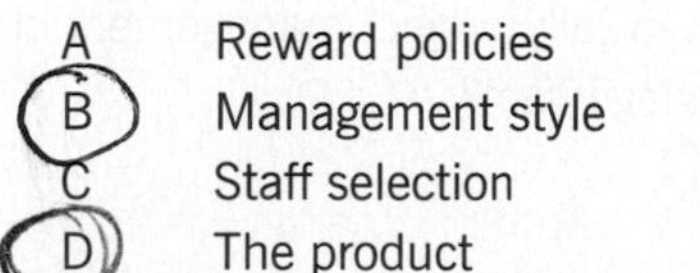

8.5 All the managers in SpendCo currently have personal assistants (PAs), but the new FD has suggested that this is not necessary, and the PAs should be removed. Not surprisingly, the managers have opposed this suggestion strongly.

Which aspect of the cultural web best explains the managers' opposition to the plan?

A Symbols
B Rituals
C Power structure
D Organisational structure

Auto Direct

Learning outcome D1a

B, Managing Director of Auto Direct, is a victim of his own success. B has created an innovative way of selling cars to the public which takes advantage of the greater freedom given to independent car distributors to market cars more aggressively within the European Union. This reduces the traditional control and interference of the automobile manufacturers, some of whom own their distributors. B has opened a number of showrooms in one of Europe's most prosperous countries and by 2004 Auto Direct had 20 outlets in and around the capital city. The concept is deceptively simple; B buys cars from wherever he can source them most cheaply and has access to all the leading volume car models. He then concentrates on selling the cars to the public, leaving servicing and repair work to other specialist garages. He offers a classic high volume/low margin business model.

B now wants to develop this business model onto a national and eventually an international basis. His immediate plans are to grow the number of outlets by 50% each year for the next three years. Such growth will place considerable strain on the existing organisation and staff. Each showroom has its own management team, sales personnel and administration. Currently, the 20 showrooms are grouped into a Northern and Southern Sales Division, with a small head office team for each division. Auto Direct now employs 250 people.

Required

Using appropriate strategies for managing change, provide B with a brief report on how he should pursue his proposed growth plans.

Chapter 9A

Learning outcome D2a

9A.1 How are projects distinguished from 'ordinary work'?

9A.2 List five management tasks undertaken by a project manager.

9A.3 Planning involves position analysis, options generation and option evaluation.

Which of the following techniques is usually applied to help these project stages?

A BCWS
B SWOT
C WBS
D CPA

9A.4 Projects present some management challenges.

Which two of the following would you say were typically project management challenges rather than challenges that occur during operations management?

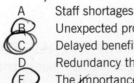

A Staff shortages
B Unexpected problems
C Delayed benefit
D Redundancy threats
E The importance of contributions made by specialists varies at different stages

9A.5 John has been informed by his manager that in order to complete his project he can follow a structured methodology. Which of the following is a recognised structured methodology useful when managing large-scale projects?

A PRINCE2
B PRINCESS 3
C KING 1
D CROWN 2

C Hospital

Learning outcome D2a

The main agenda item at the meeting of the executive board of C Hospital is to discuss the new pay and reward system. The hospital needs to make changes to the existing pay systems to respond to government requirements to reform reward systems as part of its pay modernisation agenda. The aim is to harmonise the payments systems for different categories of workers in the hospital onto one pay scale. This will mean that there is one pay scale for all employees of the hospital, including nurses, physiotherapists, radiographers, technicians and support staff (ie cleaners, porters and kitchen staff). The rationale for the new system is to achieve greater flexibility, to assist in recruitment and retention of staff and to reward people for their contribution to the achievement of hospital targets.

The hospital has 12 months in which to design and implement the new system in order to meet the government target of May 20X7. There is a huge amount of work that will need to be undertaken to deliver the new system, and a number of different stakeholders to satisfy.

At the meeting of the board, there was some discussion concerning who should be responsible for undertaking all tasks and activities associated with the development of the new system. The Human Resource (HR) Director proposed that a project manager should be appointed and a project team set up. While he would expect some members of his HR team to be part of the team, he is adamant that although his staff are responsible for administering the current payroll system and dealing with staff enquiries about pay and rewards, designing a new pay system should not form part of the 'business as usual' work for the HR department.

Required

(a) Describe the attributes of the proposed project in C Hospital that distinguish it from 'business as usual' work.

(b) Produce an outline of the different stages in the project to design and implement a new pay and reward system for C Hospital.

Chapter 9B

Learning outcome D2b

9B.1 What is the aim of critical path analysis?

9B.2 Construct a network analysis diagram from the following information, and identify the critical path.

Project data

Activity	*Preceding activities*	*Duration (days)*
A	-	3
B	-	5
C	B	2
D	A	1
E	D	6
F	C, E	3

9B.3 What is the purpose of a post-completion audit?

9B.4 What does a resource histogram show?

9B.5 Ralph's manager is explaining to him how he will rate his project's success. As this is the final project that Ralph will be responsible for, it is very important that he understands what is expected of him.

Which three of the following would be used as measurements of the success of a project?

A Quality
B Timescale
C Budget
D Use as few resources as possible
E Conflict-free implementation

Critical path analysis

Learning outcome D2b

You are the project manager responsible for a proposed new computer-based application for a medium-sized retail chain.

You have drawn up an outline timetable for the introduction of the new system. The first draft of this is shown below.

Task	*Description*	*Planned duration (weeks)*	*Preceding activities*
A	Communication – inform staff at each shop of the proposal and indicate how it will affect them	1	–
B	Carry out systems audit at each shop	2	A
C	Agree detailed implementation plan with board of directors	1	B
D	Order and receive hardware requirements	4	C
E	Install hardware at all shops	4	D
F	Install software at all shops	2	D
G	Arrange training	3	D
H	Test systems at all shops	4	E and F
I	Implement changeover at all shops	10	G and H

Required

Produce a critical path analysis of the draft implementation plan. (This should identify the critical path and the total elapsed time.)

Chapter 10

Learning outcomes C1a and D2c

10.1 What are the main categories of project stakeholders?

10.2 Why does a project manager require leadership skills?

10.3 Who described the stages of group development?

A Steiner
B Belbin
C Tuckman

10.4 Kelly is a supervisor in the accounts department of a food wholesaler.

The company wants to upgrade its information system and Kelly has been appointed the project manager.

Which two of the following management functions associated with projects will she find different from supervising an accounts section?

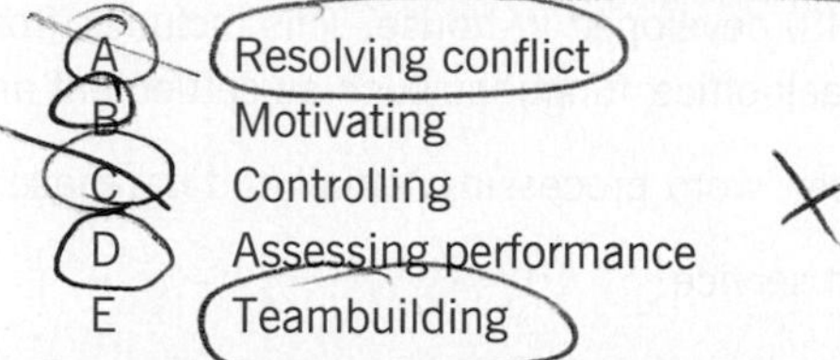

A Resolving conflict
B Motivating
C Controlling
D Assessing performance
E Teambuilding

10.5 Melissa has a list of the responsibilities associated with project management. For a job specification, she has been asked to distinguish between the responsibilities to management and the responsibilities to the project and the project team.

Which three of the following relate to the responsibilities to the project and the project team?

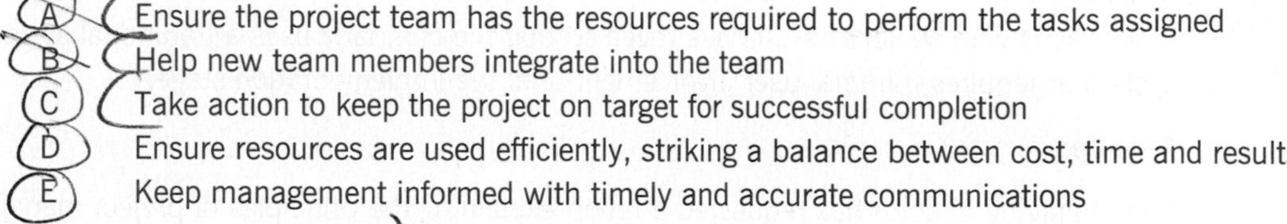

A Ensure the project team has the resources required to perform the tasks assigned
B Help new team members integrate into the team
C Take action to keep the project on target for successful completion
D Ensure resources are used efficiently, striking a balance between cost, time and results
E Keep management informed with timely and accurate communications

MFS

Learning outcome D2c

You are employed by Metropolitan Financial Services (MFS), a company employing 1,200 staff based in your own country. As a systems accountant, one of your responsibilities is to improve the systems development process. In particular, the managing director has expressed concern at the length of time that systems development takes. The managing director recently stated: 'we have highly trained staff with excellent technical skills but we still seem to fall behind schedule on all of our systems development projects'.

Current systems development

Most concern at the moment relates to a project agreed upon nine months ago. The project goal is to centralise the management information systems for the three operational units by the installation of a new centralised server, and the consolidation of each unit's IT staff into a new IT team based at head office. It was planned that the transition would be completed within 18 months. Interim plans were made to facilitate the change, for example one unit would deal with all payroll processing, one with all customer ledger activities and so on, using existing systems.

Problems encountered

At the end of the 9 months, it has become apparent that the 18-month time frame was over-optimistic.

The installation work on the new server at head office has progressed steadily, but the writing of the new software required for the centralised system is yet to start. As a result, a decision has been taken to defer the 'go live' date for the new system by six months, extending the transitional period to two years.

The redistribution of much of the back office and administrative work between units has proved difficult. The resulting operational problems have led to publication of regulatory body information being delayed. There is real concern that breaches of rules may occur.

Staff concerns

Senior management has been aware of the generally slow progress, and is now also becoming aware of the problems arising from the transitional arrangements.

In addition, users are concerned that they have had very little input to date on the development of new systems they will be dependent on. The disruption caused by the transitional arrangements has made users' jobs more difficult, for example staff often have to switch terminals depending on what type of information they need to access.

The three main areas affected by the changeover are:

(a) The management information system (MIS) developed in-house. This includes 'front-office' functions such as dealing/trading, and 'back-office' functions such as settlement and reporting.

(b) 'Office' type software including spreadsheet, word processing, email and database.

(c) Access to a third-party online information service.

The existing MIS has attracted user criticism. In particular, staff involved in dealing activities are unhappy with the way they have to navigate between screens when working in a high-pressure and fast-moving environment.

Users are satisfied with the office type software (running under Windows) and the access to, and information provided by, the third-party system.

Discussions with senior IT staff have revealed that the company uses a traditional systems development cycle that requires minimal user involvement until the implementation stage.

Required

The managing director has requested a report explaining the principles of project management and how these could be applied to systems development projects at MFS Ltd.

Z Company

Learning outcomes D2b and D2c

T has just returned to his job in the finance department of Z Company, having spent the last six months as a member of a project team working on the development of an educational visitor centre for the company.

Reflecting on his experiences while working on the project, he feels that most of his time was spent in meetings that did not achieve anything, but rather wasted his time. He also feels that the final stages of the project were not dealt with effectively, with the project members going back to their functional jobs without any discussion or feedback on the project performance and outcomes.

He has now been asked to take on the role of project manager for a new project, and is determined that he will improve the experience for his project team.

Required

(a) Discuss the problems that may be associated with project meetings. Make recommendations on the methods T could use to ensure that the meetings he arranges as project manager are effective.

(b) Evaluate the contribution of the various activities that should be carried out as part of project closure, the post-completion review and audit of the project.

Chapter 1A

1A.1 False. Such a business is almost certainly best organised into product-based autonomous divisions.

1A.2 (a) Rational planning model

(b) Incremental model

1A.3 D. Mintzberg

1A.4 (a) The assumption of formalisation – often strategy is inspirational.

(b) The assumption of detachment – that strategy formulation can be driven from considerations of implementation (top-down).

(c) Strategy is a learning process more than a planning process – a rigid process can become too bureaucratic.

(d) In dynamic environments, long-term plans may need changing frequently.

(e) Strategy set at a high level may find it difficult to gain commitment from lower levels.

1A.5 Rational model

Four Star Products

Part (a)

Answer plan

Note. This question is not so much about the planning department, as about what it does. Therefore, the answer requires critique of the formal planning approach.

Against

Difficulty of forecasting discontinuities
Linear approach – annual cycle
Isolation of planners from operations
Politics
Implementation
Learning

For

Systematic approach
Sets targets
Co-ordination of objectives, departments, activities
Organised attention to environment

Criticisms of the rational model concern both the theory behind it and how it has worked in practice. Empirical studies have not proved that formal planning processes contribute to success.

Planning theory assumes that the development of the business environment can be forecast, and to some extent controlled. In conditions of stability, forecasting and extrapolation make sense. But forecasting cannot cope with sudden **discontinuities** and **shocks**, such as the change from mainframe computing to PCs, which nearly destroyed IBM.

Part of the problem is the **linear approach** sometimes adopted, using an annual cycle. Unfortunately, strategically significant events outside the organisation are rarely synchronised with the annual planning cycle. Four Star's financial crisis in the early 1990s is, perhaps, an example.

Another problem is that formal planning can **discourage strategic thinking** among operational managers. Once a plan is locked in place, people are unwilling to question it. The internal significance of the chosen performance indicators leads managers to focus on fulfilling the plan rather than concentrating on developments in the environment. Strategy becomes something for specialists.

A complementary problem arises when the planners are separated from the operational managers; the implication is that the planners do not really need day to day knowledge of the product or market. However, small-scale developments can have important strategic influence and should not be ignored.

The rational model by definition assumes that an **objective approach** prevails. Unfortunately, no account is taken of the essentially political processes that determine many plans. There are also problems of implementation. Managers are not all-knowing, and there are limits to the extent to which they can control the actual behaviour of the organisation. This places limits on what can be achieved. Discovering strengths and weaknesses is a learning process. Implementing a strategy is necessary for learning – to see if it works.

On the other hand, we can discern an important role for **formal planning activities**. Apart from anything else, a desire to do things in a systematic way naturally leads to rational planning; deciding what to do, and when and how it should be done. Such an approach can make management control more effective by developing detailed and explicit targets. This shows managers at all levels where they fit in and forces them to confront the company's expectations of them.

The development of a plan for a large organisation such as Four Star includes an important element of **co-ordination**. Long-term, medium-term and short-term objectives, plans and controls must be made consistent with one another. Similarly, the activities of the different business functions must be directed towards a common goal.

Also, companies cannot remain static: they have to cope with and exploit changes in the **environment**. It is clear from the CEO's use of external agencies and his new strategy for Four Star that he understands this. We may speculate that he is not so much an enemy of strategic planning as much as he is unimpressed with the performance of the Four Star planning department.

Part (b)

Answer plan

Nature of environmental analysis
The environment – divisions
Desk research
Market research
Informal research
Technical nature of internet boom
Importance of judgement
Relationship of formal planning to strategic decision-making support

---

Environmental analysis is a fundamental part of strategic business management. The aim of the analysis is to identify opportunities and threats, and to assess their significance. The environment itself may be divided both according to its proximity to the organisation and according to its inherent features. Thus, the task environment, dealing with suppliers, customers, competitors and so on, may be differentiated from the wider, general environment and, indeed, from the global physical environment. The general, or macro, environment is often analysed under such headings as political, economic, social and technological.

The work of analysis can be carried on to a great extent by **desk research**. This may be quite adequate for keeping abreast of the more general aspects of the macro environment, and even for some parts of the task environment, such as changing labour costs and the fortunes of competitors. However, more complex and expensive methods, such as market research surveys, may be required for some aspects of the task environment, and more intuitive ones, such as personal contact between senior managers, for others.

In the case of the internet business model, which was given enormous publicity, it should have been easy to obtain a full understanding of both principle and technique by the methods outlined above. The problem with the collapse of confidence in the model was that foretelling was very much a matter of **judgement**. Extremely large sums of money were invested on quite rational grounds and very few commentators took a pessimistic view.

This is not a failure of the formal planning process as such, but rather a failure of strategic judgement at the highest levels of the organisations concerned. Planning techniques cannot foretell exactly what the future holds, let alone control it. Their purpose is to support those who must take strategic decisions, not to replace them.

Chapter 1B

1B.1 Corporate, business and functional.

1B.2 A mission statement sets out the main purpose or reason of an organisation.

1B.3 D. Exploits the organisation's distinctive competences.

A resource-based approach identifies distinctive competences within the company and then exploits these strengths to create sustainable competitive advantage that is difficult to imitate.

However, this is not enough to guarantee success. Every company should also consider environmental factors, adjusting its strategies to the opportunities and threats that it perceives around it.

1B.4 D. Factors fundamental to strategic success. There is little point in being good at something if it doesn't add value to your business.

1B.5 A, B, D (time-bounded, specific and measurable)

You can remember the characteristics of objectives by using the acronym SMART – specific, measurable, achievable, realistic and time-bounded.

Mission statement

To: Managing Director
From: Anne Accountant
Date: 29 February 20X0
Subject: Questions regarding mission statements

Introduction

A **mission statement** might be a short sentence, or a whole page, and should cover the following areas.

(a) **Purpose**

(i) The firm's purpose might be described in terms of more than just self-interest. A pharmaceutical company might define its corporate mission as 'the well-being of humanity'.

(ii) The firm's responsibility to its stakeholders.

(b) **Strategy**

(i) The statement should identify the type of business the firm is engaged in.

(ii) The statement should perhaps identify the strategy for competitive advantage the firm intends to pursue.

(c) **Values**

(i) The statement should identify values that link with the firm's purpose.

(ii) The values should reinforce the corporate strategy.

(d) **Behaviour standards**

(i) Defined standards of behaviour can serve as benchmarks of performance.
(ii) Individual employees should be able to apply these standards to their own behaviour.

(e) **Character**

(i) The statement should reflect the organisation's actual behaviour and culture, or at least its aspirations for improved behaviour and culture.

(ii) The statement should be easy to read.

Objectives, on the other hand, are the embodiment of a mission statement in a commercial context. They specify the meaning of a mission in a particular period, market or situation.

Mission statements and strategic planning

The relationship between mission statements and strategic planning is an ambiguous one. In some cases, the mission statement is prepared after the strategic plan is drawn up, as a sort of summary of it. However, this would only be done if there was a major change in the company's direction.

While the mission inspires corporate objectives, the strategy is a means for fleshing them out. The strategy also provides directions for specific context. The mission statement cannot institute particular strategies, but it can indicate priorities. Say that an investment company prided itself on investing funds in companies that it regarded as behaving ethically, and its mission statement contains a clause that says that the company is 'to invest clients' funds in companies whose products promote health'. It would be unlikely to invest in tobacco firms, but no indication is given as to which shares to buy, on which stock exchanges, when to sell, what returns to expect, and so forth.

Originating a mission statement

A mission statement originates at the highest levels of the organisation. It is meant to inspire as well as direct. Employees and other stakeholders may be consulted about developing or changing mission statements because, to be effective, mission statements need to reflect both the reality and the aspirations of an organisation.

The scope of mission statements

All areas of corporate life can be covered by a mission statement. This is because it is broadly based and, as a statement of an organisation's values and objectives, it should relate to everyone in the organisation.

For example, if a company's mission highlights the provision of **good quality** products and services, then this includes not only the way in which products are made and services delivered, but also the way in which commercial relationships are conducted.

The benefits of mission statements

The benefits of mission statements are that they:

(a) Describe what the company is about

(b) Provide a guiding philosophy where there are doubts about the direction a company should take, or a decision an individual manager or employee should make

(c) Display the area in which the company is operating

(d) Enable the communication of a common culture throughout the whole organisation

(e) Stimulate debate as to how the mission can be implemented

Chapter 2

2.1 Level of interest; power

2.2 (1) Internal
(2) Connected
(3) External

2.3

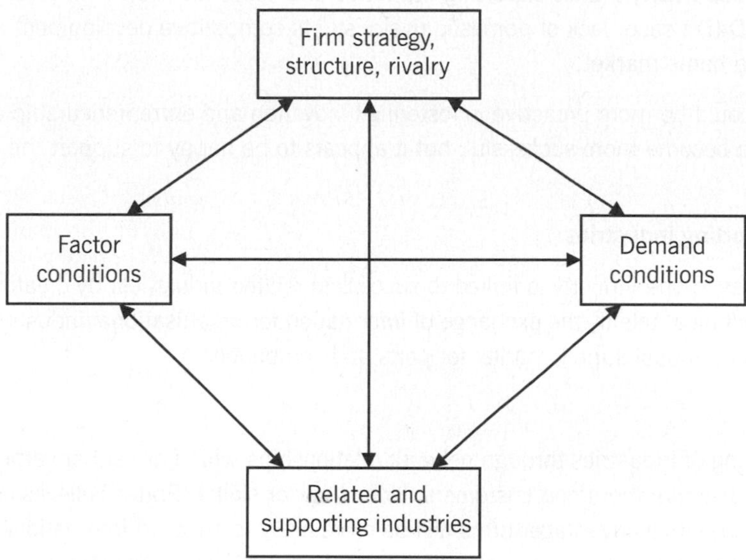

2.4 B. Low level of domestic competition

Porter's analysis of the competitive advantage of nations indicates that a high level of domestic competition promotes competence in an industry.

2.5 B, E, F. Analysis of the population by age group, changes in leisure pursuits, religious affiliation and practices.

National advantage

Part (a)

Porter notes that some nations' industries succeed more than others in terms of international competition. He does not suggest (as the D4D Prime Minister rightly notes) that countries as such are competitive, but that various factors support or inhibit the ability of the industries and firms **within** them to compete successfully on the international stage. Porter's 'diamond' model suggests that the degree of competitive advantage enjoyed by different nations results from the interaction of four basic factors.

Factor conditions

Factor conditions are a country's endowment of inputs to production. This includes **human resources**, **physical resources**, **knowledge**, **capital and infrastructure** (transport, communications etc). D4D appears to benefit from positive basic factor conditions (oil reserves and related revenues, a temperate climate, a young tertiary-educated population and political stability) – but there are limitations (eg lack of local education institutions) and risks (eg dwindling oil reserves). D4D does not currently have advanced factors which are necessary to achieve high-order competitive advantages such as their own production technologies.

Demand conditions

The home market determines how firms perceive, interpret and respond to buyer needs. Strong and sophisticated demand encourages **growth**, **high quality**, **innovation and economies of scale**: all these build competences for competing more effectively abroad. Given the recent revenue D4D has earned from oil, it is possible that it has not been focusing on demand conditions very closely. If that is the case, then the short-term benefits from oil could potentially be weakening its competitive advantage in the longer term.

Firm strategy, structure and rivalry

Capital markets, ownership structures, attitude to time horizons, degree of **innovation and entrepreneurship** vary from country to country. National cultures have been shown to orient business towards certain industries: in D4D's case, agriculture and light manufacturing.

Meanwhile, **domestic rivalry makes exporting attractive** and keeps firms on their toes, while the opposite is also true: as in D4D's case, lack of domestic rivalry stunts competitive development and encourages firms to rely on the home market.

The Government could be more proactive in fostering innovation and entrepreneurship among firms to encourage them to become more successful, but it appears to be happy to support the uneconomic local industry.

Related and supporting industries

Competitive success in one industry is linked to success in related industries, by creating a pool of managerial and technical talent, the exchange of information for organisational/industry learning and benchmarking, and a robust supply market for parts and components.

Clustering

A 'cluster' is a linking of industries through network relationships which are either vertical (within the supply chain) or horizontal (common customers, technology or skills). Porter believes clustering to be a key to national competitive advantage: firms will be more likely to succeed internationally if there is a supporting cluster that supports lower costs, infrastructure development, transfer of expertise and so on.

Part (b)

Aims of the D4D Government in attracting inward investment

D4D should be seeking to achieve:

(i) **Economic growth**, through additional economic activity and related investment in infrastructure. The latter may be particularly important to D4D in terms of information and communications technology (ICT) development, say, and the development of domestic higher education institutions.

(ii) **Technology and knowledge transfer**, through the importing of international managerial and technical expertise and proprietary technologies, and the technical training of domestic employees.

(iii) The creation of **well-paid and responsible employment** in a range of industries that have potential for further growth.

(iv) Related benefits through the production of **goods for export** and **increased domestic production** of goods that are currently imported. The Government should also aim to maximise the overall increase in national income resulting from the **multiplier effect**.

(v) **Minimisation of negative externalities** associated with economic growth: investment by firms with a good record of corporate governance, legal compliance, environmental protection, ethical employment practices and other indicators of corporate social responsibility.

(vi) **Positive public relations** with its own citizens and corporate sector, through proactive stakeholder consultation, marketing and issues management (eg with regard to the erosion of past protections for domestic industry, or the risk of cultural erosion).

Aims of companies considering investment in D4D

Companies considering investment in D4D will primarily be interested in:

(i) **Political and economic stability**, in order to minimise political and business risk to their investments

(ii) The **availability of human resources** (skills, educational levels and industrial relations climate) at competitive cost, since one of the principal attractions of off-shoring is economies through **low-cost labour**

(iii) **Supportive physical infrastructure** (transport, communications and education etc), political climatic (a government oriented towards facilitating business), legal and regulatory regime (without onerous constraints or duties) and tax regime

(iv) **Financial incentives and assistance** (eg tax breaks and regional development grants)

(v) **Developed business and trading networks** (particularly within neighbouring markets, supporting the use of D4D as an export base or 'hub')

(vi) Safe, attractive, economically viable **lifestyle and amenities** for foreign residents, to facilitate the posting of managerial and technical staff to D4D where necessary

Comparison and contrast

These aims are not all mutually incompatible. Indeed, in order for them to be achieved, there will have to be some dovetailing of aims towards a mutually satisfying 'win-win' outcome. D4D and potential foreign investors will have a 'symbiotic' relationship, in which the success of one depends on the success of the other. So for example:

(i) D4D's aim of increased economic activity and infrastructure is likely to be met **through** firms fulfilling their aims of successful trading and growth, while the firms' need for suitable infrastructure and human resources is likely to be met **through** fulfilling D4D's aims of attracting investment and knowledge sharing in those areas.

(ii) Political and economic stability are desired conditions for both parties.

The overall aim will thus be **mutual value gains** – but the aims of the two 'sides' also reflect a degree of competition for **share** of those value gains and, to this extent, the **sets of aims are somewhat different**. So, for example:

(i) D4D will want its people to be **paid as well as possible** (given the need for competitive HR costs); while firms will seek the **lowest possible wages cost** (given the need for ethical compliance).

(ii) D4D may be **relying on foreign investment to provide technical infrastructure**, while firms will be seeking an **existing supportive infrastructure** – unless competitive advantage can be gained by investment in its development (eg exclusive use or specificity/customisation creating barriers to entry to other firms, or concessions in other areas).

Negotiation will be required to attain a mutually satisfying set of outcomes.

Part (c)

Steps to make D4D more attractive to appropriate inward investment

Government can influence national competitive advantage both indirectly, by promoting the development of advanced factors, and directly, by supporting individual industries and companies with financial and other means such as business-friendly regulation. There are a number of related things the Government could do.

(i) **Developing a robust capital market within the country**

Promoting the development of liquid and flexible capital markets will benefit both domestic and arriving companies, and will encourage the local population to save and invest.

(ii) **Investment in infrastructure**

Direct investment in **transport infrastructure** will have wide benefits for agriculture and manufacturing industries, reducing costs associated with the supply chain and facilitating international trade.

Direct investment in the **digital communications infrastructure** would bring many related benefits such as cost reduction and improved innovation, as well as facilitating the growth of both domestic and international service and knowledge-based industries.

Incoming companies will require a significant local infrastructure of **supply and service industry**: this could be encouraged with government contracts and the provision of training within local firms. This would also help to strengthen the productivity and competitiveness of local firms, supporting business investment and skilling – and creating the 'clusters' regarded as key to national competitive advantage.

(iii) **Investment in education and training**

A particular need has been identified to **invest in domestic universities**, because most of D4D's graduates are currently being educated abroad, with the risk of a 'brain drain' if they choose to remain abroad. However, emphasis may also be required on vocational and professional education at all levels to **provide the skills required by potential investors.**

There may be potential for foreign companies to develop sponsorship or apprenticeship schemes, or R&D/learning partnerships with local universities. This should be supported by a robust **intellectual property protection** regime to reduce the business risk of knowledge/technology sharing.

(iv) **Investment-friendly tax regime**

The corporation and personal **tax regime** will be very important, as will the prospect of government incentives to business. Foreign investors will want to benefit from high public spending (on infrastructure etc) and low taxes.

However, while this may be a way of attracting foreign investment in the short term, in the longer term the Government will need to balance these incentives with its own economic constraints to achieve a balance between **business incentive** and **state activity**.

(v) **Legal/regulatory regime**

Since the aim is to promote 'appropriate' inward investment, D4D should protect its interests by ensuring that, while not unduly restrictive or onerous (which would deter investors), the law and regulations affecting business are ethical and adequate. This applies to areas such as planning, competition, the environment, health and safety, and employment rights. In addition to benefiting D4D, this should contribute to the foreign firms' management of ethical, compliance and reputational risk.

Chapter 3

3.1 Laid back, tiger, stochastic, selective

3.2 Substitute products and potential entrants

3.3 B. The supplier operates in a monopolistic or oligopolistic environment.

3.4 A, B, F, Reduction in the legal age for drinking, increase in minimum wage rate and tightening of border controls reducing illegal imports.

3.5 B. Factors within a specific industry affecting the profit potential of that industry

X Company

(a) **Using the five forces model to assess industry competition in country Y**

The level of competition that X Company and its joint venture partner will face in country Y will depend on the strength of the competitive forces at work in that country.

Michael Porter identified **five market factors**, or forces, that will drive the competitive position of a given supplier in a given market.

These five forces, taken together, will provide an overall assessment of X Company's competitive position in country Y. Entry into country Y would be suggested if, overall, the five forces were found to be weak and the prospective returns high.

Taking each force in turn:

Barriers to entry

X Company is considering **entry to the market** via a joint venture with a partner established in the drinks distribution business in country Y. This approach may facilitate its entry and enable it to overcome barriers to entry and commence operations relatively quickly.

Substitutes

Substitutes are products that differ from the product in question but provide similar satisfactions. In the case of soft drinks, substitutes might include some alcoholic drinks, such as beer; beverages such as tea and coffee; and small luxury or 'treat' items such as sweets and ice cream. X Company could use the experience of its partner to assess the importance of such substitutes.

Customers' bargaining power

Customers will be looking to achieve lower prices or to obtain a higher quality soft drink. If they have the power to get what they want, they will force down the profitability of the firms in the drinks industry.

The strength of the threat from the **bargaining power of customers** will depend on a number of factors.

(i) **The level of differentiation among soft drink manufacturers** (including 'intangible' aspects such as brand strength).

(ii) **The cost to the customer of switching from one supplier to another** – X Company's customers are likely to be retailers, in which case they will exercise considerable power via their ability to switch easily between suppliers.

(iii) **Whether a customer's purchases from the industry represent a large or small proportion of the customer's total purchases**. In this case, retailers could represent a material threat if – as in the UK – a small number of very large retailers account for a substantial proportion of soft drink sales and are in a position to drive a very hard bargain in relation to the prices paid to the manufacturers. X Company could seek to counter such a threat by investment in their brands.

Suppliers' bargaining power

Suppliers can influence the profitability of a firm by exerting pressure for higher prices or by reducing the quality of the goods and services that they supply.

The **bargaining power of the supplier** depends on a number of factors.

(i) The number of suppliers in the industry
(ii) The importance of the supplier's product to the firm
(iii) The cost to the firm of switching from one supplier to another

Given the widely available nature of the ingredients needed for soft drink manufacture, it is unlikely that suppliers to X Company will be limited and hence the power of suppliers is likely to be modest.

Competitive rivalry

The intensity of **competitive rivalry** within the soft drinks industry will be driven by the number of companies operating in this sector, the anticipated industry growth rates and the profitability of the industry as a whole. If the market is dominated by multinationals with strong brands and there are modest growth and profitability levels, this market will not be attractive to Company X. If at the other extreme a large number of small local suppliers dominate the marketplace, the margins being achieved are substantial and there are no well-established brands, the market opportunities for X Company could be significant.

(b) **Using the Hofstede model**

National cultures and **value systems** can be as distinctive as corporate cultures and value systems. It is potentially very important, therefore, for Company X to assess the compatibility of its strategy with the culture of country Y.

Hofstede sought to explain national differences by identifying key dimensions in the value systems of all countries. Each country is represented on a scale for each dimension so as to explain and understand values, attitudes and behaviour.

In particular, Hofstede pointed out that countries differ on the following dimensions.

(i) **Power distance**. This dimension measures how far superiors are expected to exercise power. In a high power-distance culture, the boss decides and people do not question. X Company needs to find out what organisations in country Y fit into this continuum, especially in relation to its current business model, and possibly modify its local operation accordingly.

(ii) **Uncertainty avoidance**. Some cultures prefer clarity and order, whereas others are prepared to accept novelty. This affects the willingness of people to **change** rules, rather than simply obey them. X Company may need to tailor its current operations to suit the way the local workforce makes decisions.

(iii) **Individualism-collectivism**. In some countries, individual achievement is what matters. In a collectivist culture, people are supported and controlled by their in-group and put the interests of the group first. For X Company, this means the local organisation would need to think about how important individual achievement, relationships in the organisation and achievement of the task is.

(iv) '**Masculinity**'. In 'masculine' cultures, assertiveness and acquisitiveness are valued. 'Masculine' cultures place greater emphasis on possessions, status and display as opposed to quality of life and caring for others. X Company needs to understand how local norms would alter its management of the local business and educate its managers to expect possible differences.

Hofstede grouped countries into **eight clusters** using these dimensions. Countries in the 'Anglo group' (the UK and the US), for example, were found to be comfortable with less direction and order than their counterparts in the 'more developed Asian group' (ie Japan). This suggests that typical UK management styles may not work well in Japan and vice versa.

Hofstede's work will be of particular relevance to X Company's intentions to joint venture with a company in country Y. Ideally, there should be minimal differences between the two cultures. Where differences are found to exist, plans should be made to overcome any problems that might result.

Chapter 4

4.1 False. Management is identified as 'transactional' leadership.

4.2 C. Make sure you can define the other styles as well.

4.3 9.9. It is effective if there is sufficient time and resources to attend fully to people's needs, if the manager is good at dealing with people and if the people respond. It is ineffective when a task has to be completed in a certain way or by a certain deadline, whether people like it or not.

4.4 False. This is a disciplinary action. (Try to define 'grievance' yourself.)

4.5 Equal opportunities tend to be presented via legislation. Diversity represents a more positive, voluntary approach to avoiding adverse working practices.

S and C

Disciplinary action is undertaken to improve future behaviour. It has considerable potential for creating serious disputes, so managers should always act consistently and in accordance with their organisation's established procedures. All disciplinary incidents should be **thoroughly investigated** and a written record kept by the manager concerned.

Stage – informal advice/coaching or counselling

Many minor cases of poor performance or misconduct are best dealt with by informal advice, coaching or counselling. S should certainly start by taking this course of action, using the medium of an **informal interview**. C should be informed that his behaviour has caused concern and be asked to account for it. This should focus his mind and reveal if there are any extenuating circumstances, such as illness or a family crisis. In the absence of such circumstances, C should be informed firmly that an improvement is required. A record should be made of the interview.

Stage – formal disciplinary procedures

Should there be no improvement, it may be necessary to deal with C through more formal disciplinary procedures. In the UK, such procedures are governed by the **ACAS Code of Practice** which, among other things, provides for full investigation, a right to be accompanied at any disciplinary proceeding and a right of appeal against sanctions. S, as a newly appointed manager, should take advice from HRM professionals within Z Company.

The next stage would be the issue of a warning. This could be oral or written.

(a) An **oral warning** should include the reason for issuing it; notice that it constitutes the first stage of the disciplinary procedure; and details of the right of appeal. A note of the warning should be kept on file but disregarded after a specified period, such as six months.

(b) A **first written warning** is appropriate in more serious cases. It should inform the employee of the improvement required and state that a **final written warning** may be considered if there is no satisfactory improvement. A copy of a first written warning should be kept on file but disregarded after a specified period, such as 12 months.

(c) A first written warning may also be appropriate if there has not been satisfactory improvement after an oral warning.

In the case of C, an oral warning is probably appropriate, as the disciplinary offences are fairly minor.

If the first warning is still current and there is no improvement, S may have to consider disciplinary sanction. Any sanction must be preceded by a **final written warning**.

The ultimate disciplinary sanction is dismissal. This is only appropriate for the most serious breaches of discipline. Demotion and suspension without pay are less drastic alternatives, but they must be provided for in the contract of employment.

Background material

In the UK, any imposition of disciplinary sanction must be in accordance with the statutory procedure introduced on 1 October 2004. This has three steps.

S writes to C, stating why disciplinary action is being taken and inviting him to a meeting to discuss the matter. C has the right to be accompanied by an adviser at the meeting.

At the meeting, S must explain the problem and allow C to respond. S must decide what is to be done and, after the meeting, explain her decision and inform C that he has the right to appeal to a different and preferably senior manager.

C may appeal and has the right to be accompanied by an adviser at the appeal meeting.

Chapter 5

5.1 A. Miles and Snow

5.2 A. Central

5.3 B. The degree of standardisation in an organisation

5.4 E, C, A. Beliefs and values, customs and symbols

5.5 A. Systems

Corporate culture

Defining culture

The definition neatly sums up the meaning of culture, which is the complex body of shared values and beliefs of an organisation.

Schein has defined culture in a more detailed way as 'the pattern of basic assumptions that a given group has invented, discovered or developed, in learning to cope with its problems of external adaptation and internal integration, and that have worked well enough to be considered valid and therefore, to be taught to new members as the correct way to perceive, think and feel in relation to these problems'.

IBM can be cited as a company with a strong culture. Other examples of 'the way we do things around here' can be found at Procter & Gamble and at Hewlett-Packard. At Procter & Gamble, all parts of the organisation's activities focus on product quality. At Hewlett-Packard, all employees are encouraged to be innovative and the culture is one that encourages individuals to experiment.

How a corporate culture comes into existence

Corporate culture develops along with the organisation as it grows. The development of a particular culture may be deliberate, perhaps through the issuing of policy documents and by selecting and retaining only certain types of employee. Alternatively, the culture may develop more naturally as a result of the leadership style of the organisation's senior managers.

It has been suggested that an **organisation's culture develops from three main sources**: the **organisation's origins**, its **technology** and the **dramatic events in its history**.

To demonstrate the effect of an organisation's **origins** on the development of culture, we can cite the two founders of Philips, who had distinct personal work preferences. One founder preferred technical work; the other concentrated on sales and commercial work.

An organisation's **technology** can give clues to the development of the underlying culture. For example, an engineering culture will be very different from mass production culture.

Dramatic events include events such as a recession, a major new product development and a significant layoff of staff, which could change or mould an organisation's set of shared values or beliefs.

The benefits of a strong corporate culture

A strong corporate culture exists where there is a very clear set of values and beliefs in the organisation. There are a number of benefits in this, and Peters and Waterman, in their book *In search of excellence*, found that '**dominance and coherence of culture**' was an essential feature of '**excellent**' companies. The benefits can be listed as follows.

(a) **Motivation and satisfaction of employees** may be improved by encouraging commitment to the organisation's values and objectives, fostering satisfying team relationships and using 'guiding values' instead of rules and controls.

(b) **The organisation will present a positive image in its environment**. The cultural attributes of an organisation will affect its appeal to potential customers and suppliers, employees, potential shareholders and so on.

(c) **An organisation's culture may encourage adaptability**, by supporting innovation, risk taking, willingness to embrace new methods and so on.

(d) **A background of unchanging values** (or values that change more slowly, over a longer timescale, as a result of more superficial changes) can act as a platform for change, and for the acceptance of change by individuals who may desire some familiarity and security to be retained.

The disadvantage of a strong corporate culture

(a) **Culture may be an obstacle to change because by its nature it is a force for continuity and cohesion**. If culture itself is continually adapting, there will be none of the sense of security and order and coherent self-image that Peters and Waterman observe in successful business cultures.

(b) **Culture establishes patterns of thought and behaviour as a basis for future action**. In other words, it establishes **attitudes**. Attitudes are notoriously hard to change – harder than behaviour.

(c) **Culture tends to be a force for cohesion and may cause a tendency for 'groupthink' or a cosy complacency**, a consensus that is resistant to outsider input and information that contradicts or threatens the group. This sense of infallibility and blindness to dangers in the present course can obviously be detrimental to an organisation's prospects of survival in a changing environment.

Chapter 6

6.1 (1) Poor relationships
(2) Poor communication
(3) Competition for power and resources
(4) Clashes of personality

6.2 (1) Vertical
(2) Horizontal
(3) Diagonal

6.3 Competing, collaborating, compromising, avoiding and accommodating

6.4 D, B, C. Colloquialisms, jargon and double meanings

6.5 E, D, C. Try to develop options that would result in mutual gain, look for a wide variety of possible solutions and define the problem carefully.

Communication

In an organisational context, communication has a variety of purposes. Among these is providing information to support managerial decision making and to co-ordinate the plans and activities of different units and functions. Project teams usually communicate laterally and the project manager needs to use communication to co-ordinate the work of several stakeholders who are individuals and possibly departments with a stake in the project.

There are certain general problems in communication that can arise. Based on the information in the scenario, relevant problems would include **distortion** whereby the meaning of a message is lost between sender and receiver. **Misunderstanding** is also arising due to lack of clarity or technical jargon. It also appears that **overload** is an issue whereby the recipients of the information are being given too much information to digest in the time available. Certainly, senior management would not be able to read detailed information and it would have to be edited for them. Timing may also be an issue here if information is being sent that has no immediate use. It is safe to say that there are also **poor communication skills** between P as sender and his audience, although it is unclear whether this is two-sided as the team have made the complaints but are unlikely to admit any fault in their part.

Given the problems identified, there are several suggestions to make communication more effective.

Give P training and guidance in communication skills, including how to consider the information needs of the recipients of his messages, listening to them and acting on their feedback. **P needs to encourage feedback**, as this is an important part of the communication process. **P also needs clear objectives about what he wants to achieve as a project manager** and this should frame his approach to communication. This would help P overcome problems with using inappropriate language unsuited to his audience; in his case, technical jargon.

It may be that P is uncomfortable with face to face communication. In this case, P could be given training on how to run meetings and make presentations. This would include looking at his non-verbal skills and giving him advice on how to make these cues consistent with the message he communicates verbally. In this way, he would also enhance personal interaction between the project team members, spread important information to all members at the same time and build relationships in a way that is not possible with remote ways of communicating.

Establish suitable communication channels and mechanisms that are suitable to all recipients. So the project group could agree to meet to update themselves if this was more suitable, or agree the timing and form of regular email updates to avoid the danger of becoming overloaded with information (or 'noise'). The most appropriate medium for updating the team depends on factors such as complexity (face to face is often better here), urgency (email is best here), permanency (any written form) and cost effectiveness. P needs to anticipate the reaction of those receiving the message, so that any bad news is probably better communicated face to face.

Chapter 7

7.1
- Reliability of information
- Flexibility
- Speed of reporting
- Efficiency

7.2 All of them apart from C, which is most likely to be used to assess the treasury function's work.

7.3 C. Upward appraisal.

7.4 False. The employer's responsibilities extend to visitors, contractors, and those on adjoining premises (where relevant).

7.5 To take reasonable care of themselves and of others. To allow the employer to discharge their duties. Not to interfere with any machinery or equipment.

7.6 D. Be aware of the range of common hazards!

Performance appraisal systems

(a) **Features of an effective performance appraisal system**

Most large firms have a regular system of appraising staff. **The objectives of staff appraisal systems** are to **help in developing staff members to their full potential** and **to enable the organisation to allocate their human resources in the most efficient way possible**. To achieve these objectives, an **effective appraisal system is likely to incorporate certain key characteristics**.

(i) **Reports on employees should be made out in writing and at fixed intervals**. Staff appraisal is a sensitive operation and a written record of the assessment may remove any doubts or uncertainties that arise at a later date. The report is part of a record, the personnel record, which charts an employee's progress within the organisation. The intervals at which the appraisal should be carried out depend on the nature of the employee's work. For specialist staff who move from one long-term assignment to another, appraisal may be appropriate after each assignment is completed. For staff engaged in more routine work, an interval of six months or a year may be suitable.

(ii) **Written reports should be objective**. An employee's superior may be inclined to assess harshly to excuse their own poor performance; alternatively, an easy-going relationship during day to day work may make a superior feel reluctant to be critical, especially if their subordinate's promotion prospects may be harmed. One way of improving objectivity is to make the assessment form very detailed: the more specific the assessor is required to be, the less margin there is for subjective responses.

(iii) **Appraisal should be consistent throughout the organisation**. This can cause problems in organisations which, like banks, have many semi-autonomous branches. Again, the use of detailed assessment forms (standard throughout the organisation) will help, but the assessment form is only the beginning of the appraisal process and care must be taken to ensure consistency in the later stages too.

(iv) **Assessments should be discussed with the person assessed**. If employees do not know what is being written about them, they will not be able to improve in areas where shortcomings have been noted. This could cause particular frustration if the assessment system is used as part of a process of selecting staff for promotion.

(v) **Persons conducting the appraisal interviews should be trained and experienced** in the necessary techniques.

(vi) **The employee should be encouraged to contribute to the appraisal process**. Ideally, they should have sight of the written assessment in time to consider their response before being called to interview. During the interview, the emphasis ought not to be on problems and obstacles, but on opportunities. The interviewee should be encouraged to talk about their career plans, their knowledge and skills and how they could be put to better use, and to make suggestions for improving the way their work is carried out.

(vii) **There should be adequate follow-up after the interview has taken place**. If the system is to be effective, staff must have confidence in it. This will only happen if results are seen to follow from the assessments.

(b) **Advantages of appraisal systems**

(i) **They enable the organisation to gather information about the skills and potential** of employees and to identify training needs.

(ii) **They provide a system on which salary reviews and promotions can be based**.

(iii) **They help to develop the employee's potential** by directing their attention to particular strengths and weaknesses.

(iv) **They allow the employee and their assessor to discuss and agree on personal objectives**.

(v) **They** may **contribute to staff motivation.**

Disadvantages of appraisal systems

(i) **The subjective element in such systems cannot be entirely eliminated.**

(ii) **They depend for their success on a mutual confidence** between the assessor and the employee assessed. In practice, it is difficult to achieve that confidence.

(iii) **It is difficult to go beyond appraisal of past performance**, which may be an inadequate guide to future performance in a different job. If an appraisal scheme is used as a guide to promotion potential, this is a serious disadvantage.

(iv) **They often do not lead to improvements in performance**. Criticism of areas where performance has been weak can lead to a defensive response, and future performance may actually deteriorate.

(v) **There are many posts, particularly in technical roles, where further promotion is impossible**, performance is standardised at a high level and experience is infinitely valuable. To the incumbents of such posts, a formal appraisal system may seem like a waste of time.

The accounting function

(a) **The work of the accounting function** can be seen as encompassing two areas of responsibility:

(i) **Handling the financial operations** of an organisation. This involves activities such as handling **receipts and payments**, receiving and checking **invoices from suppliers**, chasing payment from **customers**, accounting to the Government for **tax**, borrowing money and repaying loans and preventing errors or fraudulent practices.

(ii) **Providing information and advice** to the managers of other departments to help them to do their work better. The accounts department has to liaise with other departments all the time. Information may be required for planning, control and one-off decision-making purposes. In each case, information from other departments is necessary to carry out the accounting activity, and the procedures for interdepartmental communication may be formally set out.

Accounting management provides a good example of the need for close co-ordination.

Department	Accounts section	Relationship
Purchases dept (PD)	Purchase ledger (PL) Cashier (C)	PD advises PL of purchase orders PD indicates valid invoices C informs PD and PL of payment
Personnel dept	Payroll	Personnel gives details of wage rates, starters and leavers to payroll
Sales dept (SD) Credit control (CC)	Sales ledger (SL)	SD advises SL of sales order SL might give CC information about overdue debts SL might give details about debtors ageing and other reports
Operations, stock controllers	Cost accounting staff	Operations might give details of movements of stock, so that the accounts staff can value stock and provide costing reports
Senior management	Financial accounting and cost accounting staff	The accounts department as a whole produces management information for decision making and control

(b) **Key factors affecting the type of accounting system used in an organisation**

The accounting function is part of the broader business system, and does not operate in isolation. Accounts are produced to aid management in planning, control and decision making and to comply with statutory regulations. The accounting system must be adequate to fulfil these functions. An organisation's accounting systems are affected by the nature of its business transactions and the sort of business it is.

The key factors that might affect the type of accounting system used within an organisation are as follows.

(i) **Size**. A **small business** like a greengrocer will have a simple accounting system, where the main accounting record will probably be the till roll. A **large retail business**, such as a chain of supermarkets, will have elaborate accounting systems covering a large number of product ranges and sites.

(ii) **Type of organisation**. A **service business** might need to record the time employees take on particular jobs. Accounting on a **job or client basis** might also be a feature of service businesses. A **public sector organisation**, such as a government department, may be more concerned with the **monitoring of expenditure** against performance targets than recording revenue. A **manufacturing company** will account both for unit sales and revenue, but needs to keep **track of costs** for decision-making purposes and so forth.

(iii) **Organisation structure**. In a business managed by **area**, accounts will be prepared on an area basis. In a functional organisation, the accounts staff are in a separate department.

Chapter 8

8.1 B, D. Fear that once higher output norms have been established, the organisation will expect such norms to be sustained permanently and dislike of the work itself.

The other three forces describe the driving forces that the workers perceive to be threatening them, for example fear of dismissal if output falls, fear of losing special privileges and response to pressure from the management.

8.2 A. Reconstruction. This type of change is classified as reconstruction. Reconstruction involves maintaining the existing paradigm but requires rapid action. It is a common response to a long-term decline in performance. The decision to make staff redundant is a response to changing demand for Venetian blinds.

8.3 D. Evolution.

Evolution is an incremental process that leads to a new paradigm.

8.4 D. The product.

The specifications of the product itself are determined by other market and production factors. However, it is worth adding that the product can affect the culture indirectly. If, for reasons of market positioning, the product is improved, the changes will contribute to a culture where employees identify with the quality image of the product.

8.5 A. Symbols.

Having a PA is a status symbol for the managers within the organisation. Removing the PAs will therefore be opposed by the managers because it involves removing an important status symbol.

Auto Direct

Managing Director, Auto Direct

Date:

Report – change management strategies and methods

The change that you are contemplating, while extensive, is incremental and does not involve the transformation of your organisation. It therefore falls into the category of **adaptation**, which implies that you may proceed step by step, and leave your basic assumptions and approach unchanged.

It would be a very worthwhile exercise to consider some of the factors that might affect the success of your programme of change. Chief among these are likely to be the various human factors present in your staff.

Presumably you will include some element of promotion and cross-posting of your existing workforce in order to provide a basis of experience at your new sites, so you should consider the degree of **readiness** (or willingness) of your staff to undertake the development of your plan.

You should also consider your company's managerial **capability** and **capacity** in terms of resources to undertake change. The former depends largely on past experience.

While good **project management** of a programme of change is very important, it is the **human aspects of the change management process** that are crucial. This is because change will not happen unless people make it happen. A number of strategies are proposed for dealing with this aspect of change management.

Participation in decision making is sometimes recommended as a way of improving motivation generally, and may be useful in the context of change. It is probably advantageous to involve staff in decisions affecting them, their conditions and their work processes and at least hear what they have to say. However, participation is not a universal panacea and can be very **time consuming**. Also, the normal **management style and culture** of the organisation must be considered. It is probably inappropriate to promote participation exclusively in the context of change if staff are not used to it: their main reaction may be one of suspicious cynicism.

An **autocratic** approach, imposing change by means of **coercion**, can work reasonably well in some circumstances, especially where the staff expect nothing else. It has the benefit of saving time and is probably the **best approach in times of crisis**. However, it does have the weakness of ignoring the experience and knowledge that staff may be able to offer.

In any event, **communication** with staff about the proposed change is commonly regarded as an essential process. Ideally, information will be provided as early as possible, explaining why change is necessary and the course that will be followed. Anxiety, particularly over job security, is common during change, and a programme of communication and education can go a long way to allay it.

Sometimes neither participation nor coercion can resolve all problems, and **negotiation** may be required. This is often the case when the labour force is strongly organised and when there is disagreement between management factions as to the best course to follow.

This has been a brief overview of some approaches to change management. You will no doubt be in a position to decide which are most appropriate to the circumstances of Auto Direct.

Chapter 9A

9A.1 Defined beginning and end; resources specifically allocated; intended to be done as a one-off. Follows a plan towards a clear goal and cut across organisational and functional lines.

9A.2 Plan, monitor, control, co-ordinate and communicate.

9A.3 B. SWOT

A SWOT analysis is used to help with these project stages, by analysing internal strengths and weaknesses and external opportunities and threats. The other initials refer to other management tools. WBS – work breakdown structure, BCWS – the budgeted cost of work scheduled which is part of the project budget, and CPA – critical path analysis.

9A.4 C, E. Delayed benefit and the importance of contributions made by specialists varies at different stages.

For a project there is normally no benefit until the work is finished. Specialists are involved as team members on projects and their skills are called upon as and when they are needed. The other challenges – unexpected problems, redundancy threats and staff shortages – are typical challenges facing managers involved in operational or project work. They are not typically associated with projects.

9A.5 A. PRINCE2

This stands for PRojects In a Controlled Environment 2. This is a widely recognised methodology used to control large-scale projects.

C Hospital

(a) **Attributes of project working**

In general, the work that organisations undertake may be classified as either '**business as usual**' or **projects**. Whether an activity is classified as a project is important, as projects require management using specialised project management techniques.

A project has a number of attributes that distinguish it from 'business as usual'.

(i) **Projects have a defined beginning and end** – unlike operations which tend to be ongoing. So, for example, the C Hospital project has a defined duration of 12 months to meet its deadline of May 20X7. This often allows them to be perceived in terms of a 'life cycle' of defined stages, from project definition and planning through implementation and control to closure and review.

(ii) **Projects have resources allocated specifically to them**, although often on a shared basis. This is reflected in the HR Director's insistence on separating responsibility for the development of the new system, and staff involvement in it, from 'business as usual' working in the form of administering the system and dealing with staff enquiries. At the close of the development project, staff will return to their departments.

(iii) **Projects are often unique or 'one-off'**: intended to be done only once, in contrast to operations which involve recurring tasks. Thus the development of the new system is distinguished from its ongoing operation.

(iv) **Projects follow a specific plan towards a clear intended end result** (in this case, implementation of the new system), in contrast to operations for which goals and deadlines may be more general. There will be a specific schedule and resource plan for the system development project.

(v) **Projects often cut across organisational and functional lines**, while operations usually follow the organisation or functional structure. So, for example, the HR Director argues that HR staff will only be one part of the project team, since a number of other stakeholders will need to be involved (including, say, payroll and accounts, IT, worker representatives and hospital management).

(b) **Outline stages for the systems design project**

The life cycle of the project to design and implement a new pay and reward system for C Hospital will include the following four main phases.

Identification of a need

Projects start when someone becomes aware of the **need** for one. This can occur at any level and in any context, though more formal business projects of management significance will normally be originated within the area of responsibility of the sponsoring manager.

At C Hospital, the need has arisen as a result of the need to respond to government requirements to reform reward systems. A key first step is to **identify the goals and objectives** of the project – why we are doing it and what are we seeking to achieve. At this early stage, one of the most important things to get under control is the **scope** of the project; that is, just what is included and what is not. A firm grasp of the agreed scope of the project must be maintained throughout its life. Government requirements in relation to reward systems will play a major role in shaping the scope of the project.

The **project team** will also be assembled at this stage and should include representatives from HR, finance, and those who can speak on behalf of each of the employee groups affected. The **project manager** will take ultimate **responsibility** for ensuring the desired result is achieved on time and within budget. A person should only take on the role of project manager if they have the time available to do the job effectively. Since that person is to be held responsible for the project, they must be given the **resources** and **authority** to complete project tasks.

Development of a solution

Planning is a key duty of the project manager and the initial outline planning will include:

(i) Developing project targets such as overall costs and timescales

(ii) Dividing the project into activities and placing these activities into the right sequence

(iii) Developing a framework for procedures and structures needed to manage the project – this could include weekly team meetings and performance reviews

Detailed planning may include use of techniques such as work breakdown structure and network analysis in order to produce a schedule of activities to be undertaken.

Implementation

This is the **operational** phase of the project. Planning will continue as required in order to control agreed changes and to deal with unforeseen circumstances, but the main emphasis is on **getting the work done**.

There are several important aspects to this phase. **Management** and **leadership** assume a greater importance as the size of the project workforce increases. **Time**, **cost** and **quality** must be kept under control, as must the tendency for **changes** to proliferate.

Problems are bound to arise and must be solved sensibly and expeditiously. At C Hospital, the objective of the project, pay harmonisation, is potentially extremely contentious and it will be very important to resolve employee concerns quickly without imposing an ongoing insupportable financial burden on the hospital.

Completion

The final phase of the project is **completion and review**. This phase involves a number of important but often neglected activities.

Completion itself is often neglected. All activities must be properly and promptly finished, and **documentation** must be completed. This is particularly important on a payroll project where accuracy and timeliness of payment are of crucial importance.

At some point, the HR department must formally **accept** that the project is **complete** and **take responsibility** for any future action that is required in relation to the new pay system, such as the maintenance of the system. The HR department will want to ensure that the project being handed over **conforms** to the latest **requirements definition** and **project specification.**

Completion will involve the **disbandment** of the project team. It is important for future projects that before the team members return to their previous roles there is a **formal process** that gathers the **lessons learned** so that they are available to future project teams and help those projects to avoid any mistakes or difficulties encountered while developing the payment system.

Chapter 9B

9B.1 Critical path analysis is a technique used to identify the key tasks of a project and their interrelationship. The diagrams show the sequencing of a project and clearly identify critical activities which directly influence the outcome of the project, and non-critical activities which can allow for some flexibility.

9B.2

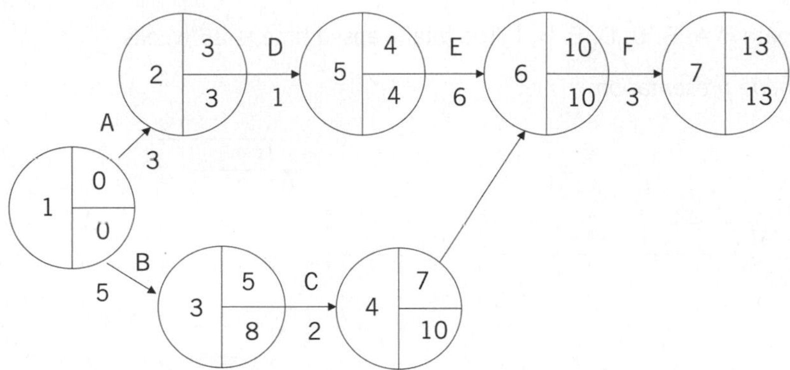

Critical path: ADEF

9B.3 To ensure that the client is satisfied, and to ensure that the project was managed effectively, and that information gathered will be used to improve future projects.

9B.4 The amount and timing of the requirement for a resource over the life of a project.

9B.5 A, B, C. Quality, timescale and budget

A project will be rated successful if it is completed at the specified level of quality, on time and within budget. Projects are seldom conflict-free or efficient in their use of all resources.

Critical path analysis

Critical path analysis (one of the following)

Activity-on-line presentation

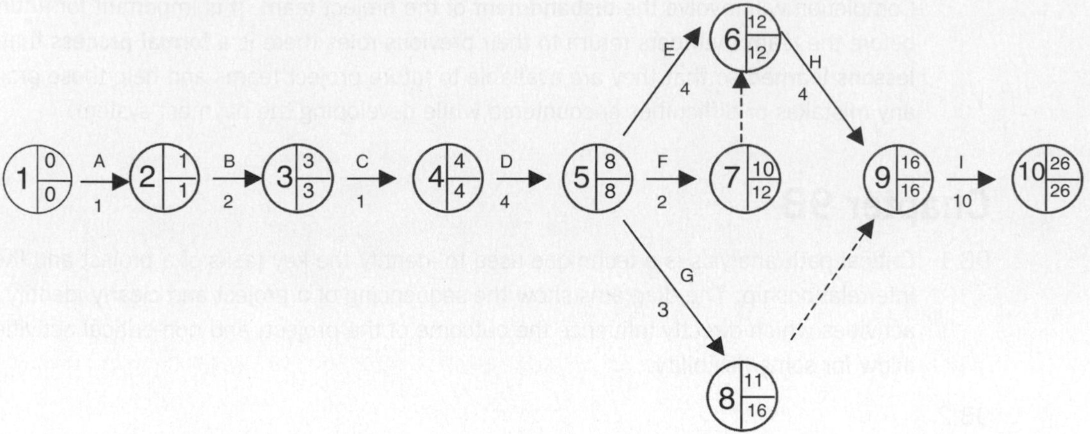

The critical path is A, B, C, D, E, H, I. The total elapsed time is 26 weeks.

Activity-on-node presentation

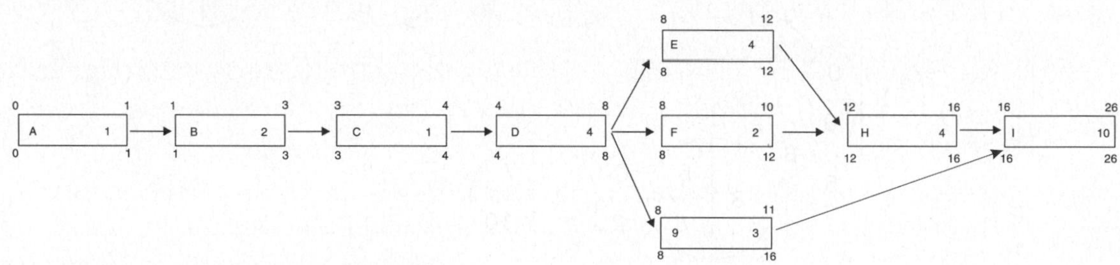

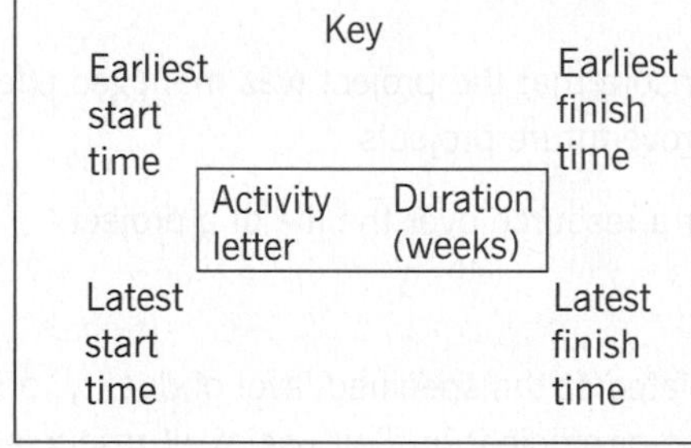

Chapter 10

10.1 Users, suppliers, team, steering committee and management

10.2 The team they are managing may come from diverse backgrounds and are from various levels of seniority around the business.

10.3 C. Tuckman. You should be able to identify the team-relevant theories of Belbin and Steiner as well.

10.4 A, E. Resolving conflict and teambuilding

They are the types of activity that are more prevalent in project work than managing an accounts section.

10.5 A, B, C. Ensure the project team has the resources required to perform the tasks assigned, help new team members integrate into the team and take action to keep the project on target for successful completion.

Part of the responsibilities to management, rather than to the project, are to keep management informed and to ensure resources are used efficiently.

MFS

REPORT

To: Managing Director MFS Ltd
From: Systems Accountant
Date: May 200X
Subject: Project management at MFS

The introduction of a new computer system has the potential to cause considerable disruption to an organisation.

Some problems are presently being experienced at MFS, particularly in connection with the transitional arrangements during the development of the new system. For example, the 'going live' extension from 18 months to 2 years suggests that personnel costs will be at least one-third over budget.

Project management techniques can help monitor and control projects. The principles are outlined below.

A **project** involves the management of a number of **disparate yet interdependent tasks**, within a **timetable** and a **budget** set in advance. A particular project is unique, in that by its nature, once done it is never repeated.

Efficient management of the resources and process of the project is vital if the project is to be completed successfully – that is, on time, within budget and to the required quality.

The consistent lateness of IT-related projects at MFS Ltd implies that the organisation would benefit from the application of appropriate project management techniques. Workable policies need to be developed as soon as possible to prevent further damage being done to the company, for example through regulatory breaches and a further reduction in employee morale.

A suggested approach to project management

Form the project board or steering committee. A steering committee comprising senior user department personnel, a member of the finance department and various systems professionals should be appointed to oversee the project.

Appoint a project manager. This person will manage and oversee the execution of the project, and is responsible for its successful completion. The project manager presents the timetable and budget to the steering committee for their approval and authorisation.

Plan the project. The **goals** of the project are identified, and the **tasks needed to achieve them** are outlined. These are then matched to the manpower resources available, so that a **project plan** can be outlined and agreed. Tools such as work-breakdown structure, critical path analysis and Gantt charts are useful aids. The schedule will indicate **when** each task has to be completed, and in **which order**. **Each stage** of the project is then planned in its own right. The stages of the project may be determined by the systems development methodology adopted.

Control the project. Actual outcomes are compared to the plan, and any discrepancies investigated and addressed as soon as they become apparent.

The monitoring process should take into account four criteria.

- **Time**, by reference to critical path analysis or Gantt charts
- **Resources**, by measuring available resources and percentage utilisation
- **Costs**, by reference to the MIS and budgets
- **Quality**, as appropriate

Regular progress meetings should be held by the project manager with members of the project team to monitor performance.

Specified **documentation** is produced at the end of each stage for review and approval, in accordance with quality control criteria established.

At the end of each stage, progress will be reported to the steering committee. **Users** should be consulted, as their approval is necessary to demonstrate that the project is meeting its objectives.

Complete the project. The resulting system must meet the technical criteria (quality) specified (eg response times). All relevant documentation must be completed to an adequate standard, project files must be complete and there should be a clear relationship evidenced between the work done in the various successive stages of the project.

Post-implementation audit. The project should be reviewed in terms of both the **technical quality** of the output and the **efficiency** with which project tasks and management were carried out.

Stakeholders' feedback should be gained to ensure all viewpoints are covered.

Lessons that can be learned from the project should be documented to prevent the same mistakes being made on similar projects in the future.

Z Company

(a) **Problems associated with project meetings and recommendations to resolve them**

Unnecessary meetings

The effectiveness of every hour the individual spends in a meeting has to be considered in terms of opportunity cost. **T needs to ensure that he gets value for money**. The first question about any proposed meeting should be whether or not it should be held at all. If the meeting will purely be a forum for disseminating information, a memo may be a more efficient means of communication.

Unsuitable participation in the meeting

Participants who have nothing to contribute, or to whom the meeting is irrelevant, are wasting time. Only those people with a genuine need to be at a meeting, and a genuine contribution to make, should be invited. This is an important consideration for project meetings, because of the need for stakeholder representation and communication.

Unclear objectives and remit

Unclear objectives will lead to irrelevancies being discussed. T should decide the objectives or desired outcomes of the meeting, and design the agenda (and conduct the discussion) accordingly. Project problem-solving meetings should have clear guidance on their decision-making authority.

Lack of planning and co-ordination

When involving a number of people, particularly when they do not work at the same location, **lack of planning can sabotage the meeting** (by preventing key stakeholders from attending), its tone (by

creating frustration) and its effectiveness (eg by failing to include vital items on the agenda). T must give plenty of notice of the meeting, and send a formal notification of the meeting with either an agenda or a request for any further items for the agenda. (This is important to ensure that all stakeholder concerns and inputs have an opportunity to be aired.)

Poorly constructed agenda

Lack of a detailed pre-planned agenda causes problems by not allowing participants to prepare themselves for discussion and (even more crucially) not providing a framework for the meeting. It will be much harder for T to keep the meeting 'on track' if there is no 'track'! In order to minimise this problem, T should ensure that the agenda:

(i) **Follows a logical order**, with the most important and time-consuming matters in the middle (to focus quality attention)

(ii) **Gives sufficient detail about the purpose of each item** to guide preparation and discussion

(iii) **Shows the start and finish times of the meeting**, and also roughly how much time will be allocated to each item, in order to facilitate timekeeping

Poor chairing/leadership of the meeting

Whoever is leading the project meeting must be aware of the role of chair (leader or facilitator), and should have appropriate skills. Poor leadership can cause problems such as: the meeting getting off-agenda; uncontrolled conflict and 'power plays' by different participants; lack of equitable contribution (so that some stakeholders fail to get heard or give their input); lack of protocols for conduct and processes such as debate and decision making; and failure to get to 'closure' (all discussion, no decision). These problems may have contributed to T's dissatisfaction with the earlier project meetings he attended.

A skilled and experienced chair or discussion facilitator should be appointed for the task. This may be T as project manager, or it may be a role that revolves among the project team over the period of the project. The leader should be supported by a secretary (or minutes taker) to record the discussion and decisions.

Lack of minutes and follow-up action

A lack of records of decisions can create uncertainty and conflict about what was agreed and whose responsibility it was to take action. Lack of defined responsibilities for action can lead to inaction! All meetings should be minuted. After the meeting, the person responsible for taking minutes needs to check with the chair that minutes and action points are a fair reflection of events. Action points should specify the action to be taken, by whom the action should be taken, and by when. There should be follow-up and progress check on those with responsibilities before the next meeting.

(b) **Project closure and review**

T is quite right to be concerned about failure to finish off a project properly. Because project management is episodic in nature, it is **difficult to improve**. The lack of continuous operation means that the skills and experience developed during a project are likely to fragment and atrophy after it is complete. The completion and review phase involves a number of important but often neglected activities that T should ensure are carried out at the conclusion of his new project.

(i) **Completion** itself is often neglected. All project deliverables must be, in fact, delivered and all activities properly and promptly finished; care must be taken that contractors do not either leave small things undone or, if paid by time, spin things out for as long as possible.

(ii) **Documentation** must be completed. This is important on any project, but it is vital if there are quality certification issues or it is necessary to provide the user with operating documentation. Indeed, these two types of documentation should be specified as deliverables at the outset. Contracts, letters, accounting records and so on must be filed properly.

(iii) **Project systems** must be closed down, but in a proper fashion. In particular, the project accounts and any special accounting systems must remain in operation and under control until all costs have been posted but must then be closed down to avoid improper posting.

(iv) **Handover** must take place where the project has been managed for a client under contract. At some point, the client must formally accept that the contract is complete and take responsibility for any future action that may be required, such as the operation and maintenance of a system.

(v) **Immediate review** is required to provide staff with immediate feedback on performance and to identify short-term needs such as staff training and remedial action for procedure failures.

The review process

A thorough review is the organisation's opportunity to make significant **improvements in how it manages its projects**. T should ensure that his review has clear **terms of reference** and covers all aspects of the project, possibly organised on a functional basis. This cannot be done on the cheap: appropriate quantities of management time and attention must be allocated to the review process and to the assimilation of its results and recommendations.

Post-completion audit

The post-completion audit is the final stage of the review process. **It is a formal review of the project that examines the lessons that may be learned and used for the benefit of future projects.** Did the end result of the project meet the client's expectations: was it delivered on time and on budget? Was the management of the project as successful as it might have been, or were there bottlenecks or problems?

The audit helps to identify problems that might occur on future projects with similar characteristics, as well as to provide feedback for improvement of the performance of the project team. In other words, any project is an opportunity to learn how to manage future projects more effectively. It should be clear that the audit has the potential to reduce the costs associated with future projects.

Longer-term review

Longer-term review is useful for the consideration of **lifetime costs**, which should be the eventual criterion for project success. It also allows individuals time to reflect on their experiences and to learn more thoroughly from them.

INDEX

Note. Key terms and their references are given in **bold**.

4D model, 358

Abdication, 172
Absorption, 363
ACAS, 192, 195
Accidents, 292
Accountability, 171
Accountability and audit, 308
Accounting for competitors, 105
Accounting rate of return, 348
Acquisitions and mergers, 138
Action-centred leadership, 184
Activities, 33
Activity on arrow presentation, 376
Activity on node, 378
Actual Cost of Work Performed (ACWP), 373
Adair, 184
Adaptability culture, 226
Adaptation, 320, 328
Adaptive strategy, 14
Advanced factors, 84
Advantages of a formal system of strategic planning, 10
After-sales service, 34
Age discrimination, 202
Alliances, 140, 334
Alternative courses of action, 111
Analysers, 225
Ansoff, 136
Anthony, 269
Anthony's classification of managerial activity, 224
Apollo, 223
Appraisal procedures, 288
Approaches to negotiation, 248
Arbitration, 420
Artefacts, 74, 215, 217
Ashridge Management College, 177
Ashridge studies, 177
Asset specificity, 37
Athena, 223
Atkinson, 190
Audit committee, 308
Authority, 169
Avoidance, 363
Avoidance strategies, 261

Balance of trade, 71
Balanced scorecard, 44
Balogun and Hope Hailey, 320, 321
Bargaining, 46
Bargaining power of customers, 125
Bargaining power of suppliers, 125
Barney, 30
Barriers to communication, 241, 247
Barriers to entry, 124
Baseline plan, 371
Basic factors, 84
Basic resources (threshold resources), 30
BCG matrix, 103
Beer and Nohria – Theory E and Theory O, 325
Behaviour, 215
Belbin, 424
Beliefs and values, 74, 217
Benchmarking, 141
Benefits of improving corporate governance, 306
Better control, 10
Big data, 118
Blake and Mouton, 180
Body language, 247
Boston classification, 103
Boston Consulting Group (BCG), 103
Bottom-up budgeting, 372
Boundaries, 35
Bounded rationality, 10, 37
Boyd, 175
Braithwaite and Drahos, 66
Brand competitors, 100
Breakthrough products, 131
BRICS economies, 88
Brunsson, 11
Budget, 344
Budget Report, 373
Budgeted Cost of Work Performed (BCWP), 373
Budgeted Cost of Work Scheduled (BCWS), 373
Budgeting Worksheet, 373
Budgets, 50
Buffers, 386
Bureaucracy, 187, 223
Bureaucratic authority, 259
Bureaucratic control, 272
Burns and Stalker, 186
Business ethics, 301, 304
Business partner, 275
Business plan, 285

CACI, 117
Cadbury report, 306
Calculative contract, 196
Capacity expansion, 63
Capital, 84
Carnegie Mellon Software Engineering Institute, 356, 400
Cash cows, 103
Causes of accidents, 292
Causes of conflict, 254
Centrality, 169
Chairperson, 431
Chandler, 20
Change, 13, 175
Change agent, 329, 331
Change control, 352, 403
Change management, 328
Charismatic leaders, 330
Charles Handy, 260

Checkpoint, 353
Chief executive, 330
Child care, 205
CIMA's Code of Ethics for professional accountants, 302
Clan control, 226, 272
Classical school, 158, 159
Club culture, 223
Cluster, 86
Coase, 37
Coca-Cola, 100
Coercive contract, 196
Coercive power, 168
Combined Code, 306
Commitment, 175, **197**
Communication, 111, 239, 412
Communication difficulties, 242
Comparative advantage, 83
Comparative analysis, 141
Compare and contrast project control systems, 398
Compensation, 199
Competition, 64, 252
Competitive advantage, 6, 130
Competitive Advantage Of Nations, 83
Competitive forces, 123
Competitive position, 100
Competitive products, 131
Competitive rivalry, 126
Competitive strategy, 130
Competitor analysis, 100, **101**
Competitor intelligence system, 102
Competitor profiles, 141
Competitor response profiles, 102
Competitors, 101
Completion and review, 361
Completion report, 397
Complexity and dynamism, 61
Compliance based approach, 301
Compliance with the Code, 308
Computer systems, 116
Conciliation Officer, 199
Configuration management, 351
Conflict, **251**, 252, 256
Conflict-handling styles, 256
Confrontation and negotiation, 259
Connected stakeholders, 78
Consistency culture, 226
Consolidated industry, 101
Consortia, 139
Constructive compromise, 247
Consultancies, 107
Consultancy firms, 116
Consultants, 259, 330
Consultation, 172
Consults, 185
Contextual features model, 321
Contingency approach, 224
Contingency plan, 363
Contingency theory, 176, 182
Contingency theory – Woodward, 189
Contingency time allowances, 385
Continuous organisation, 187
Continuum of leadership styles, 177
Control, 51
Control environment, 284
Control framework, 283
Control gates, 375
Control procedures, 284
Control processes, 273
Control strategies, 274
Control system, 274
Control system features, 271
Controlling project changes, 402
Co-operative behaviour, 259
Co-operative contract, 196
Core competences, 30
Core employees, 73
Core resources and competences, 30
Corporate appraisal, 9, **140**
Corporate culture, 295, 302
Corporate governance, 304
Corporate Governance Code, 309
COSO, 284
Cost advantages of existing producers, independent of economies, 125
Cost leadership, 130
Cost variance, 373
Cost-benefit analysis, 348
CPA, 383
Crafting strategy, 12
Creativity, 28
Crisis stabilisation, 331
Critical activities, 375
Critical chain project management (CCPM), 385, 386
Critical path, 377, 380, 381
Critical Path Analysis (CPA), 375, 376
Critical success factors (CSFs), **48**, 50, 129
Crystal glass industry, 87
CSF analysis, 49
CSR, 300
Cultural iceberg, 216
Cultural strength, 221
Cultural values, 222
Cultural web, 219, 325
Culture, **74**, **215**, 216, 217, 221, 242, 296, 323
Culture and excellence, 220
Culture and strategy, 225
Culture and structure, 222
Customer needs, 77
Customers, 82, 125, 172
Customs, 74
Cyert and March, 11, 45

Data Protection Act 1998, 117
Database application packages, 116
Database information, 116
Deal and Kennedy, 221, 226
Decisional role, 165
Decision-making process, 110
Defenders, 225

Delayering, 173, 335
Delegation, 172
Deliberate strategies, 12, 13
Delphi model, 77
Demand conditions, 85
Demography, 72
Denison, 225
Dependencies and interactions, 372
Dependency, 169
Detecting discontinuity, 13
Developing people, 164
Diamond, 84
Differentiation, 130
Dionysus, 223
Direct discrimination, 203
Direct Mail Services Standards Board (DMSSB), 117
Direction, 175
Directors, 307
Directors' remuneration, 307
Disability Discrimination Acts, 202
Disciplinary procedures, 192
Disciplinary situations, 192
Discontinuity, 13
Dismissal, 198
Disneyland Paris, 215
Disputes Review Board, 420
Disseminator, 165
Distinctive capabilities, 31
Distributive leadership, 428
Disturbance handler, 165
Diversity, 206
Divestment and rationalisation, 63
Divisional form of organisation, 38
Divisionalised organisation, 20
Documentation and reports, 390
Dogs, 104
Dorming, 427
Double loop control, 11
Drucker, 10, 163
Drucker, Peter, 7
Dummy activity, 377
Duties of a project manager, 411

Earliest event time, 377
Earliest start times, 381
Ecological feasibility, 348
Ecology, adaptation and individualisation, 28
Ecology model, 28
Econometrics, 114
Economic environment, 68
Economic factors and the management accountant, 71
Economic growth, 75
Economic policy, 69
Economist Intelligence Unit, 116
Effective control systems – the 6 As, 271
Electronic communication, 244
Electronic Data Interchange (EDI), 108
Email, 244
Emergent strategies, 12
Emergent strategy, 13
Emerging industries, 63
Employee relations, 261
Employees, 77
Employment Act 2002, 192
Employment contracts, 286
Employment Equality (Age) Regulations 2006, 202
Employment Equality (Religion or Belief) Regulations 2003, 202
Employment Relations Act 1996, 202
Employment Tribunal, 199
Empowerment, 173
Enforces consistency at all levels, 10
Entrepreneur, 165
Entry barriers, 63
Environment, 59
Environmental analysis and uncertainty, 113
Environmental data, 117
Environmental factors, 59
Environmental feasibility, 348
Environmental fit, 61
Environmental information and analysis, 113
Environmental interactions, 62
Environmental scanning, 107
Environmental uncertainty, 37
Equal opportunities, 201
Equal pay legislation, 202
Equality Act (2010), 202
Equitable pay, 197
Estimates, 373
Ethics, 299, 300
EU, 64
European Central Bank, 64
Eurostar, 125
Evolution, 320, 328
Evolutionary view, 252
Exchange rate, 72
Existential culture, 223
Exit barrier, 102
Expected time, 385
Expert power, 168
Experts, 223
Explanation, 172
Export consultants, 116
Export of natural commodities, 90
Export-led industrialisation, 91
External appraisal, 141
External information, 107
External sources, 116
External stakeholder, 78

Factor conditions, 84
Factor costs, 83
Fairness and equity, 196
Fayol, 158
Feasibility study, 347
Feedback, 13
Fiedler, 182
Field and Keller, 358
Figurehead, 164

Financial control, 274
Financial feasibility, 348
Financial resources, 169
Firm infrastructure, 34
Firm strategy, structure and rivalry, 85
Fiscal policy, 69
Five forces, 123
Five project management process area, 355, 357
Flexibility, 48, 173
Flexible firm model, 190
Float time, 382
Float times, 382
Focus, 130
Focus strategy, 132
Forcefield analysis, 323
Forecast, 114
Form competitors, 100
Formal approach, 7
Forming, 426
Formulating an effective equal opportunities policy, 204
Forward pass, 377
Founder, 220
Fragmented industry, 101
Free float, 382
Freewheeling opportunism, 17, 18
French and Bell, 218
French and Raven, 168
Friedman, 300
Functional authority, 170
Functional decomposition, 359
Functional flexibility, 190
Functions of management, 158
Future orientation, 115

Gantt chart, 374, 383, 388
Gap analysis, 359
Garden tools, 85
General environment, 60
Generic competitors, 100
Generic strategy, 127
Ghoshal and Bartlett, 28
Gido and Clements' project control process, 402
Global business regulation, 66
Globalisation, 66, 304
Goals, 40
Goal conflict, 46
Goal setting, 41
Goal structure, 46, 49
Government economic policy, 69
Government spending, 69
Greater investment, 70
Greenbury report, 306
Grievance, 195
Group, 422
Group functioning, 426
Guide to the Project Management Body of Knowledge, 354, 398

Hampel report, 306
Handy, 190, 222
Harris and Ogbonna, 336
Harrison, 222
Hawthorne studies, 161
Health and safety, 289, 290
Health and Safety (Consultation with Employees) Regulations 1996, 292
Health and Safety (Display Screen Equipment) Regulations 1992, 292
Health and safety and workstations, 292
Health and Safety at Work Act 1974, 289, 290
Health and safety legislation, 64
Health and safety policy, 295
Hersey and Blanchard, 183
Hierarchy, 187
Hierarchy of objectives, 40, 41, 49
Higgs report, 306
Highlight reports, 353
Hoffmann-LaRoche, 13
Hofstede, 215
Hofstede model, 228
Hooley, 39
Horizontal alignment, 47
Housing market, 70
How trade-offs are made, 46
Human relations, 160
Human resource management, 34
Human resource management strategies, 261
Human resource strategy, 285
Human resources, 84
Hybrid chief executive, 330
Hygiene factors, 161

IDEAL, 356, 400
Identifies risks, 10
Identifying projects, 347
Ignorance, 61
Impact of government, 63
Impact of information technologyon the competitive forces, 127
Imperfect information, 112
Implementation, 51, 111
Implementation of strategy, 9, 10
Import-substitution, 90
Improved products, 131
Improving communication, 243
Inbound logistics, 34
Incremental/adaptive strategy, 14
Incrementalism, 14
Independent float, 382
Indirect discrimination, 203
Individualized Corporation, 28
Industrial relations (IR), 260
Industrialisation strategies, 90
Industry, 123
Industry competitors, 100
Industry life cycle, 128
Industry structure, 101
Inflation, 70, 71
Inflation and interest rates, 70
Influence, 168, 246

Influences on organisational culture, 220
Influencing government, 64
Information bureaux, 107
Information culture, 115
Information for planning and control, 109
Information services, 108
Informational role, 164
Infrastructure, 84
Innovation, 128
Integration devices, 259
Integrity based approach, 301
Intended strategies, 12
Interest rates, 71
Intergroup training, 259
Internal appraisal, 141
Internal control, **283**, 308
Internal data sources, 107
Internal information, 107
Internal sources, 116
Internal stakeholders, 77
International environment, 229
International trade, 66
International trade and exchange rates, 71
Internet, 108
Interpersonal role, 164
INTRO, 356, 400
Investment centres, 271
Involvement culture, 226
Involvement of the private sector, 70
Iron Triangle, 401

Jargon, 242
Job losses, 335
Job rotation, 259
Johnson, Scholes and Whittington, 12
Johnson and Scholes, 5, 49, 61, 219, 273
Joins, 185
Joint ventures, 139

Kaplan and Norton, 44
Katz and Kahn, 174
Katzenbach and Smith, 423
Key Performance Indicators (KPIs), 48
Key tasks, 50
King report, 309
Knowing the business, 13
Knowledge, 84
Knowledge workers, 173
Kotler, 100
Kotler, P, 102
Kotter, 174
Kram, 297

Latest event time, 377
Latest start times, 382
Le Shuttle, 125
Leader, 164
Leadership, **174**, 220, **329**
Leadership style, 177, 185
Leadership styles and project management, 414
Leading indicators, 114
Learning, 12
Learning curve effect, 130
Learning organisation, 10
Legal framework, 62, 290
Legal impediment, 199
Legitimate (or position) power, 168
Legitimate power, 169
Levels of control, 269
Lewin, Lippitt and White, 179
Liaison, 164
Libraries, 108
Licensing agreement, 139
Likert, 179
Limitations and problems of team working, 423
Limited communication, 259
Lindblom, 14
Line and staff authority, 170
Line authority, 170
Linkages, 35
Logical incrementalism, 15
LoNGPEST, 60
Long-term and short-term objectives, 45

Mail Order Protection Scheme, 117
Mailing Preference Service, 117
Maintenance factors, 161
Management, **157**, 174
Management accounting, 18
Management by exception, 363, 414
Management by Objectives (MbO), 47, 163
Management information system, 116
Management of ethics, 301
Management of Health and Safety at Work Regulations 1992, 291
Management planning, 34
Management principles, 158
Management processes, 164
Management styles, 179
Management tasks, 163
Managerial grid, 180
Managerial role, 164
Managers, 77
Managing a business, 163
Managing conflict, 256
Managing diversity, 206
Managing managers, 163
Managing patterns, 13
Managing project risk, 362
Managing stability, 13
Managing stakeholder disputes, 419
Managing worker and work, 163
Manual handling and protective equipment, 292
March, 45
Market, 123
Market, bureaucratic and clan control, 271
Market control, 271
Market growth, 101
Market share, 102, **103**
Market size, 101
Marketing and sales, 34

Markets or hierarchies, 36
Maslow's hierarchy of needs, 162
Matrix management, 415
Maylor, 358, 361
Mayo, 167
McGregor, 181
McKinsey 7 S model, 218
Mechanistic, 186
Mechanistic organisations, 186
Media, 116
Mediation, 420
Mendelow matrix, 419
Mentoring, **297**
Meta-technology, 77
Methods of growth, 138
Microsoft Access, 116
Microsoft Project, 379, 380, 381, 388
Miles and Snow, 225, 227
Milestones, 375, 395
Mintzberg, 12, 14, 164, 167, 256, 299
Mintzberg 5 Ps, 6
Misconduct, 199
Mission, **38**, 40
Mission and objectives, 9
Mission culture, 226
Mission statement, **39**, 302
Monetary policy, 69
Monitor, 164
Motivators, **161**
Mourning/adjourning, 427

Negative discipline, 191
Negative power (Handy), 168
Negotiating, **247**
Negotiation, **247**, 248, 420
Negotiation process, 248
Negotiator, 165
Neo-human relations school, 161
Network analysis, **375**, 376
Network analysis or Critical Path Analysis (CPA), 375
Network diagram, 374, 388
Network organisations, 38
Networks, 334
Networks of influence, 334
New products, 64
New technology, 173
Non-capability, 199
Non-substitutability, 169
Non-verbal communication, 244, 247
Norming, 426

Objective, 5, 157
Objective, 164
Official functions, 187
Oftel, 70
Ofwat, 70
Ohmae, 11
Open system, 165
Operational control, **110**, 271
Operational management, 224
Operations, 34
Operations planning, 50
Opportunities and threats, 141
Opportunity costs, 83
Oral and face to face communication, 243
Organic growth, 138
Organic organisations, 186
Organisation, 157
Organisation culture, **217**
Organisational consistency, 21
Organisational iceberg, 218
Organisational learning, 28
Organisational 'memory', 115
Organisational objectives, 45
Organisational politics, 255, 256
Other control systems, 400
Other substantial reason, 199
Ouchi, 227, 230, 271
Ouchi: Theory Z, 227
Outbound logistics, 34
Output control, 272
Outsourcing, 30, 31, 38, **280**
Overseas Trade, 116

Packaged holidays, 75
Paradigm, 320, 332
Partnering, 420
PASSCASH, 220
Patent Office, 116
Payback period, 348
Perfect information, **112**
Performance agreement, 285
Performance and development plan, 285
Performance appraisal, **286**
Performance management, 284, **285**
Performance measurement, 271
Performing, 426
Peripheral employees, 73
Person culture, 223
Personal centralised control, 273
Personality, 426
Persuasion, **246**
PERT, 384
PEST, 60
PESTEL, 60
Peters, 220
Peters and Waterman, 220, 221
Pharmaceuticals industry, 64
Physical resources, 84
Planning, 8
Planning cycle, 10
Pluralist view, 252
PMBOK and PRINCE2, 398
Policy, **5**
Political and legal environment, 62
Political behaviour, 256
Political risk and political change, 65
Political risk checklist, 65
Politics, 334
Porter, 33, 83, 123, 130
Porter's diamond, 83

Positioning approach, 29, 32
Positioning-based strategy, 141
Positive (or constructive) discipline, 191
Positive discipline, 191
Positive discrimination, 203
Post-completion audit, **397**, 398
Post-completion audit report, 398
Power, **167**, 334
Power centres, 168
Power culture, 223
Power distribution, 255
Power skills of change agents, 330
Power structures, 334
Primary activities, 34
Primary objectives, 41
PRIME, 41
PRINCE2, 350
Priorities, 50
Priority setting, 46
Private sector, 157
Problems
    definition, 111
    recognition, 111
Problems with contracts, 37
Problems with hierarchies, 38
Process of appraisal, 288
Processing strategic intelligence, 115
Procurement, 34
Product breakdown, 353
Product innovation, 128
Product or process team, 424
Product safety and standardisation, 64
Production possibility curve, 75
Product-market mix, 136
Product-market strategy: direction of growth, 136
Profit, 41
Profit centres, 271
Progress report, **394**
Progressive discipline, 193
Project, **343**
Project authorisation, **390**
Project board, 351, **418**
Project brief, 358, **390**
Project budget, **372**
Project champion, **418**
Project change procedure, 402
Project changes, 402
Project charter, **390**
Project Evaluation and Review Technique (PERT), 384
Project failure, 403
Project initiation document, 352, 358, **390**
Project Initiation Meeting, 390
Project life cycle, 356
Project management, **344**
Project Management Institute, 354
Project management maturity model, 361
Project management plan, **390**
Project management software, 381, 388, 389
Project management tools, 345
Project manager, 400, **411**, 412, 418
Project manager responsibilities, 412
Project meetings, 398
Project objectives, 401
Project owner, **418**
Project planning, 411
Project processes, 352
Project requirement, 347
Project scope, 359
Project specification, 347
Project sponsor, **418**
Project stakeholders, **417**
Project success factors, 346
Project support team, **418**
Project team, 223, 418, 424, **432**
Project troubleshooting, 400
Project working, 343
Projects and continuous improvement, 405
Prospectors, 225
Protectionism, 71
Psychological contract, 196
Public sector, 157
Purchasing power parity, 72
Pure project organisation, 414
Purposeful persuasion, 247

Qualitative research, **108**
Quality, 344, 351
Quality control, 412
Quality manager, **418**
Quantifiable risk, 362
Quantitative research, **109**
Question marks, 104
Quinn, 15

Race Relations (Amendment) Act 2000, 202
Race Relations Act, 202
Rational model, **7**, 8
Rationalism, 14
Rationality, 187
Reactors, 225
Rearward pass, 377
Reconciling, 13
Reconstruction, 320, 328
Recruitment and selection, 204
Reduction, 363
Redundancy, 199, 200
Redundancy programmes, 335
Referent (or personal) power, 168
Regional policy, 63
Regression analysis, 114
Regulation strategies, 260
Related and supporting industries, 85
Relations with shareholders, 308
Relative market share, **103**
Remuneration committee, 307
Repetitive Strain Injury or RSI, 292
Reporting of Injuries, Diseases and Dangerous Occurrences Regulations (RIDDOR 1995), 295
Reports on corporate governance, 306
Resignation, 198

Resource allocator, 165
Resource based strategy, 29, 38, 141
Resource histogram, **386**
Resource planning, 50
Resource-based approach, 29, 32
Resources, 9, **343**
Responses to risk, 363
Responsibility, **171**
Retirement, 198
Reverse engineering, 359
Review and control, 51
Revolution, 320, 328
Reward (or resource) power, 168
Rewarding effective teams, 430
Riddor 1995, 295
Risk, **112**, 226, 349, 362
Risk and uncertainty in decision making, 112
Risk assessment, 362
Risk contingency plan, 363
Risk management, 349, 362
Risk manager, **418**
Risks with Big Data, 122
Rituals, 74, 215, 217
Rivalry, 127
Rivalry amongst current competitors in the industry, 126
Role culture, 223
Role of IT, 115
Role of the finance function, 274
Role of the manager, 157
Routines, 333
Rules, 187

Sarbanes-Oxley Act 2002, 308
Satisficing, 46
Scarcity of resources, 254
Scenario building, 9
Schedule variance, 373
Scope, 115
Secondary objectives, 42
Second-tier emerging nations, 89
Selective reporting, 242
Self discipline, 191
Sells, 185
Sensitivity analysis, 112
Sequential attention, 46
Services, **68**
Service Level Agreement (SLA), 281
Service Level Contract (SLC), 281
Sex discrimination, 202
Sex Discrimination and Equal Pay (Miscellaneous Amendments) Regulations 1996, 202
Shamrock organisation, 190
Shared objectives, 427
Shared servicing, 282
Shareholders, 308
Short-termism, 71
Sign-off, 374
Situation analysis, 319
Situational Leadership, 183
Six Sigma, 356, 398, 399, 400
Skills required of a project manager, 412
Slippage, 395, 401
Small businesses, 18
SMART, 40
Smith report, 306
Social and cultural environment, 72
Social facilitation, 423
Social feasibility, 348
Social responsibility, **299**
Socially constructed risk, 362
Socio-technical systems, 166
Sources, availability and quality of data for environmental analysis, 107
South African framework, 309
Specialisation, 187
Specialists, **418**
Spokesperson, 164
Stability, 13
Staff appraisal system, 286
Staff authority, **170**
Stage model of change, 322
Staged payments, 385
Stakeholders, 45, **77**, 330, 332, 419
Stakeholder analysis, 332
Stakeholder goals and objectives, 77
Stakeholder groups, 9, 332
Stakeholder mapping, 80, 421
Stakeholder power, 420
Stakeholder view, 299
Standard deviation, 385
Stars, 103
Start-ups, 18
Statutory disciplinary procedure, 193
STEEPLE, 60
Steering committee, 351
Steiner, 426
Sternberg, 301
Stewart, 188
Stock Exchange Combined Code, 307
Storming, 426
Strategic analysis, 9
Strategic business unit (SBU), **27**
Strategic change, 319
Strategic choice, 9
Strategic contingencies, 169
Strategic control, 270
Strategic decisions, 5
Strategic intelligence, **115**
Strategic intent, 38
Strategic issues of small businesses, 18
Strategic issues of start-ups, 18
Strategic leadership, 329
Strategic management, 224
Strategic objectives, 11
Strategic options evaluation, 9
Strategic options generation, 9
Strategic plan, **5**
Strategic planning, 7, **109**
Strategic planning committee, 11
Strategies for managing conflict, 259
Strategy, **5**, 336

Strategy and structure, 21
Strategy Safari, 16
Strategy selection, 9
Strengths and weaknesses analysis, 141
Strengths of team working, 423
Strong culture, 221
Structural separation, 259
Structure of information flows, 115
Style theories, 176
Styles of change management, 327
Subcontracting, 139
Subcultures, 74
Substitute products, 125
Substitutes, 127
Super-ordinate goals, 259
Suppliers, 82
Support activities, 34
Survival and success factors, 129
SWOT, 140, 349
Symbolic processes, 333
Symbols, 217, 333
Symptoms of conflict, 253
Systems integration, 281

Tactical control, 270
Tactical management, 224
Tactics, 5
Tannenbaum and Schmidt, 177
Target market segments, 332
Task culture, 223
Task environment, **60**
Task interdependence, 254
Task performance, 429
Taylor, 159, 167
Team, **423**
Team building, 427
Team development, 426
Team effectiveness, 429
Team functioning, 429
Team identity, 427
Team member satisfaction, 429
Team roles, 424
Team solidarity, 427
Team-based rewards, 430
Teambuilding, 345, 411
Team-building exercises, 428
Technical feasibility, 347
Technological developments, 13
Technological environment, 75
Technology development, 34
Tells, 185
Termination of contract, 198
The communication process, 241
The finance function and external stakeholders, 278
The finance function and other parts of the organisation, 278
The Health and Safety at Work Act 1974, 291
The Health and Safety Executive (HSE), 291
The Project Management Body of Knowledge (PMBOK), 354
The strategy clock, 134
The Workplace directive, 292
Theories of leadership, 176
Theory X, 185
Theory Y, 181, 185
Theory Z, 227
Thomas, 256, 262
Threat from substitute products, 125
Threat of new entrants, 124
Threshold competences, **30**
Time horizon, 61, 115
Time penalties, 385
Time series analysis, 114
Time/Cost/Quality Triangle, 401
Timescale, 344
Tjosvold and Deerner, 253
Tone of voice, 247
Top-down budgeting, 372
Total float, 382
Trade associations, 116
Trade deficit, 71
Trade journals, 116
Trade-off, 45
Trade-off between objectives, 44
Trait theory, 176
Transaction, **36**
Transaction costs, **36**
Transactional leaders, 174, 330
Transference, 363
Transformational leaders, 175
Triggers, 319
Trist and Bamforth, 166
Tuckman, 426
Turnaround, 331
Turnbull committee, 306
Turnbull Report, 283
Types of change, 320
Types of competitor, 100
Types of groups, 422
Types of power, 168
Types of risk, 362

UK Corporate Governance Code, 306
Uncertainty, **112**, 169, 255
Unfair dismissal, 199
Unique resources, **30**
Universality of management principles, 158
Unquantifiable risk, 362
Unsolicited mail, 117
US framework, 308
Users, **418**

Value, 33
Value chain, **33**
Value chain analysis, 21, 33
Value system, 35
Variances, 385
Vendors, **418**
Vertical alignment, 47
Vertical integration, 37, 38
Victimisation, **203**

Virtual organisations, 38
Vision, 40

Weber, 169, 187
What if? analyses, 389
Williamson, 37, 38
Win-win strategy, 259
Work Breakdown Structure (WBS), 352, 371
Work packages, 371
Working time, 295
Working Time Directive, 295
Working Time Regulations 1998, 295
Workplace (Health, Safety and Welfare) Regulations 1992, 292
World population, 73
Written communication, 243
Wrongful dismissal, 198

Yukl, 174

Zaleznik, 174
Zeus, 223

BPP
LEARNING MEDIA

BPP
LEARNING MEDIA

BPP
LEARNING MEDIA

Notes

Review Form – Paper E2 Project and Relationship Management (11/16)

Please help us to ensure that the CIMA learning materials we produce remain as accurate and user-friendly as possible. We cannot promise to answer every submission we receive, but we do promise that it will be read and taken into account when we update this Study Text.

Name: ______________________ **Address:** ______________________

____

____

How have you used this Study Text?
(Tick one box only)

- ☐ Home study (book only)
- ☐ On a course: college ______________________
- ☐ With 'correspondence' package
- ☐ Other ______________________

Why did you decide to purchase this Study Text? *(Tick one box only)*

- ☐ Have used BPP Texts in the past
- ☐ Recommendation by friend/colleague
- ☐ Recommendation by a lecturer at college
- ☐ Saw information on BPP website
- ☐ Saw advertising
- ☐ Other ______________________

During the past six months do you recall seeing/receiving any of the following?
(Tick as many boxes as are relevant)

- ☐ Our advertisement in *Financial Management*
- ☐ Our advertisement in *Pass*
- ☐ Our advertisement in *PQ*
- ☐ Our brochure with a letter through the post
- ☐ Our website www.bpp.com

Which (if any) aspects of our advertising do you find useful?
(Tick as many boxes as are relevant)

- ☐ Prices and publication dates of new editions
- ☐ Information on Text content
- ☐ Facility to order books off-the-page
- ☐ None of the above

Which BPP products have you used?

Text	☑	*Passcard*	☐
Kit	☐	*i-Pass*	☐

Your ratings, comments and suggestions would be appreciated on the following areas.

	Very useful	*Useful*	*Not useful*
Introductory section	☐	☐	☐
Chapter introductions	☐	☐	☐
Key terms	☐	☐	☐
Quality of explanations	☐	☐	☐
Case studies and other examples	☐	☐	☐
Exam skills and alerts	☐	☐	☐
Questions and answers in each chapter	☐	☐	☐
Chapter overview and summary diagrams	☐	☐	☐
Quick quizzes	☐	☐	☐
Question Bank	☐	☐	☐
Answer Bank	☐	☐	☐
Index	☐	☐	☐

Overall opinion of this Study Text *Excellent* ☐ *Good* ☐ *Adequate* ☐ *Poor* ☐

Do you intend to continue using BPP products? *Yes* ☐ *No* ☐

On the reverse of this page is space for you to write your comments about our Study Text. We welcome your feedback.

The BPP Learning Media author team can be emailed at: cimaqueries@bpp.com

Please return this form to: CIMA Product Manager, BPP Learning Media Ltd, FREEPOST, London, W12 8BR

TELL US WHAT YOU THINK

Please note any further comments and suggestions/errors below. For example, was the text accurate, readable, concise, user-friendly and comprehensive?